FIRST TEXTILES

THE BEGINNINGS OF TEXTILE MANUFACTURE IN EUROPE AND THE MEDITERRANEAN

Proceedings of the EAA Session Held in Istanbul (2014) and the 'First Textiles' Conference in Copenhagen (2015)

Edited by

MAŁGORZATA SIENNICKA, LORENZ RAHMSTORF

and

AGATA ULANOWSKA

OXBOW | books
Oxford & Philadelphia

First published in the United Kingdom in 2018. Reprinted as a paperback in 2021 by
OXBOW BOOKS
The Old Music Hall, 106–108 Cowley Road, Oxford, OX4 1JE

and in the United States by
OXBOW BOOKS
1950 Lawrence Road, Havertown, PA 19083

Paperback Edition: ISBN 978-1-78925-687-1
Digital Edition: ISBN 978-1-78570-799-5 (epub)

A CIP record for this book is available from the British Library

Library of Congress Control Number: 2018958402

Printed in the United Kingdom by Short Run Press, Exeter

Typeset in India by Versatile PreMedia Services. www.versatilepremedia.com

For a complete list of Oxbow titles, please contact:

UNITED KINGDOM
Oxbow Books
Telephone (01865) 241249
Email: oxbow@oxbowbooks.com
www.oxbowbooks.com

UNITED STATES OF AMERICA
Oxbow Books
Telephone (610) 853-9131, Fax (610) 853-9146
Email: queries@casemateacademic.com
www.casemateacademic.com/oxbow

Oxbow Books is part of the Casemate Group

Front cover: Flax (upper left corner) © Agata Ulanowska; textile from Niederwil-Egelsee (upper right corner) © Fabienne Médard; textile
from Feldmeilen (lower left corner) © Fabienne Médard; replicas of spindle whorls (small middle right) © Agata Ulanowska;
crescent-shaped loom weight from Tiryns (lower right corner) © Małgorzata Siennicka.

Contents

List of contributors

EVA ANDERSSON STRAND (evaandersson@hum.ku.dk) is Associate Professor of Textile Archaeology and director of the Centre for Textile Research, Saxo Institute, University of Copenhagen. Her publications range from Viking Age Scandinavia to the Bronze Aegean and Eastern Mediterranean and more particularly focus on the cultural, social and economic impact of textiles and textile production.

JOHANNA BANCK-BURGESS (johanna.banck-burgess@rps.bwl.de) is a textile archaeologist at the State Office for Cultural Heritage, Baden-Württemberg in Esslingen. Her research deals with textile manufacture in prehistoric Central Europe, with a special focus on the Neolithic and Iron Ages.

NECULAI BOLOHAN (neculaibolohan@yahoo.com) is Assistant Professor in the Faculty of History at the Alexandru Ioan Cuza University of Iași. His research focuses on South-East Europe during the Bronze Age, pottery analysis and forensic archaeology.

IGNACIO CLEMENTE-CONTE (ignacio@imf.csic.es) is researcher at the Spanish National Research Council (CSIC-IMF) in Barcelona. His research interests comprise use-wear analysis, bone and lithic tools and high-mountain archaeology.

CATARINA COSTEIRA (catarinacosteira@gmail.com) holds a PhD in Archaeology from the University of Lisbon and currently works at the School of Arts and Humanities, UNIARQ – Centre for Archaeology, University of Lisbon. Her research focuses on the Late Neolithic and Chalcolithic periods (4th /3rd millennia BC), prehistoric textiles and Chalcolithic pottery.

MIRIAM DE DIEGO (mdediego13@gmail.com) is a PhD candidate at the Department of Prehistory of the Universitat Autònoma de Barcelona (UAB). Her research interests include archaeology, ethnography, textile technology and use-wear analysis.

AXEL DIEDERICHSEN (axel.diederichsen@agr.gc.ca) is curator and research scientist in the Plant Gene Resources of Canada at the Saskatoon Research Centre, Agriculture and Agri-Food. His area of expertise is the characterisation, evaluation, maintenance, distribution and acquisition of plant germplasm of crop species and their wild relatives.

GIORGOS GAVALAS (georgios.gavalas@gmail.com) is archaeologist at the Ephorate for Antiquities of the Cyclades of the Hellenic Ministry of Culture and Sports. He has been a collaborator in numerous excavation projects on the Cycladic Islands and extensively published, amongst other subjects, about prehistoric Cycladic textile tools, marble figurines and vessels.

ANA GRABUNDŽIJA (ana.grabundzija@fu-berlin.de) investigated textile tools from pile-dwellings in the pre-Alpine area after completing her thesis on "Archaeological Evidence for Early Wool Processing in South East and Central Europe" at the TOPOI A-4 research group ("Textile Revolution"). She is currently evaluating the impact of particular environmental and socio-cultural factors on technological adaptations, advancements and their transfer.

KARINA THERESIA GRÖMER (karina.groemer@nhm-wien.ac.at) is a textile archaeologist at the Natural History Museum, Vienna (Department of Prehistory). She specialises in textile analysis, textile tools and reconstruction of prehistoric costume. Her current research focuses on the analysis of textiles from graves and salt mines, covering a time-span from 2000 BC until 1000 AD.

PETYA HRISTOVA (petya_hristova@sbcglobal.net) is an independent scholar residing in the San Francisco Bay Area. She received her PhD from the University of California, Los Angeles and has excavated classical and prehistoric sites in Bulgaria. She works on ancient economy, craft specialisation, and interactions between ancient Thrace, Greece and other cultures of the eastern Mediterranean.

SIMON JEPPSON (simon.jeppson@slu.se) is a doctoral student at the Department of Plant Breeding at the Swedish University of Agricultural Science in Alnarp.

SABINE KARG (Sabine.Karg@fu-berlin.de) currently leads a project in the Institute of Prehistoric Archaeology at the Freie Universität Berlin about flax (*Linum usitatissimum* L.), financed by the German Research Council (DFG).

CIPRIAN-CĂTĂLIN LAZANU (lazanucip@yahoo.com) works at the Muzeul Județean „Ștefan cel Mare" in Vaslui. His research focuses on Eastern Romania during the Bronze Age and further on bronze metallurgy.

Romina Laurito (romina.laurito@beniculturali.it) works at the Museo Nazionale Etrusco di Villa Giulia in Rome. Her expertise includes textile archaeology of the Near East and Etruria, as well as the study of seals and sealings.

Janet Levy (janetl@post.bgu.ac.il) is affiliated with the Ben-Gurion University of the Negev in Israel. Her doctoral thesis was devoted to fibre and textile technologies and their significance in the development of formative villages in the Ancient Near East. Her research interests include prehistoric costume, music, dance, magic and shamanism in Antiquity and traditional societies.

Ulla Mannering (ulla.mannering@natmus.dk) is a senior researcher at the National Museum of Denmark. Her primary area of research is prehistoric North European textile production and clothing, prehistoric plant fibre materials, experimental archaeology, clothing in iconographic sources, and Roman textiles. She is one of the initiators of the Danish National Research Foundation's Centre for Textile Research (CTR) at the University of Copenhagen.

Rui Mataloto (rmataloto@gmail.com) holds a MA in Prehistory and Archaeology from the University of Lisbon and currently works for the Redondo Municipality. In his research, he focuses on the Late Neolithic and Bell Beaker period, society and economy.

Fabienne Médard (Fabienne.medard@anatex.fr) has studied Fine Arts with special training as a conservator of art before specialising in archaeology and developing an interest in archaeological and ethnographic textiles. She holds a Ph.D. in prehistoric archaeology from the University of Paris X-Nanterre. She has directed projects focusing on Neolithic textile activities in western Europe, among others dedicated to the interactions between textile production and the environment.

Millán Mozota (millanm@imf.csic.es) is a technician in archaeological research at the Spanish National Research Council (CSIC-IMF, Barcelona). He is interested in use-wear analysis, bone tool technology and 3D scanning.

Antoni Palomo (antoni.palomo@gencat.cat) is curator at the Archaeological Museum of Catalonia in Barcelona. His research interests include the Neolithic period, lacustrine dwellings, underwater archaeology, prehistoric technology and experimental archaeology.

Raquel Piqué (Raquel.pique@uab.cat) is a Professor of Archaeology in the Department of Prehistory at Universitat Autònoma de Barcelona. She is interested in the use of plant resources in the first farming societies. She co-directs the research project on the Early Neolithic lake dwelling of La Draga (Banyoles, Spain).

Lorenz Rahmstorf (lorenz.rahmstorf@uni-goettingen.de) is a Professor in the Department of Pre- and Protohistory at the University of Göttingen. His main research interests are concerned with the 3rd and 2nd millennia BC of the Aegean, Europe and West Asia, weight metrology, early trade, textile production, transfer of innovations and urbanisation processes.

María Irene Ruiz de Haro (pomerania79@gmail.com) is affiliated with the University of Granada. Her research interests include textile archaeology, Phoenicians, and the protohistory of the Western Mediterranean.

Maria Saña (Maria.Saña@uab.cat) is a lecturer at the Universitat Autònoma de Barcelona in the Department of Prehistory. Her research interests include zooarchaeology and the first Neolithic societies in the Mediterranean.

Deniz Sari (deniz.sari@bilecik.edu.tr) completed her PhD entitled "The Cultural and Political Development of Western Anatolia in Early and Middle Bronze Ages" at both Istanbul University and Strasbourg University. She is currently an Assistant Professor at the Department of Archaeology of the University of Bilecik Seyh Edebali and director of the Research Centre for Experimental Archaeology in Bilecik. She is mainly interested in the Bronze Age material culture and social-cultural interactions of Anatolia, as well as in experimental archaeology.

Małgorzata Siennicka (msiennickaa@gmail.com) is an ERC Associate in the Archaeological Institute at the University of Göttingen and holds a PhD in Aegean archaeology from the University of Warsaw. Her research interests focus on the Neolithic and Bronze Age Aegean and Eastern Mediterranean, prehistoric cloth and textile production, craftsmanship, balance weights and metrology, and settlement archaeology.

Xavier Terradas (terradas@imf.csic.es) is a researcher at the Spanish National Research Council (CSIC-IMF, Barcelona). His work focuses on the study of technological innovations and technical skills in Prehistory, raw materials sourcing and lithic production of the first farming communities, mainly in the western Mediterranean basin.

Agata Ulanowska (a.ulanowska@uw.edu.pl) is an Assistant Professor at the Department of Aegean Archaeology of the Institute of Archaeology of the University of Warsaw. Her research interests focus on the Bronze Age Aegean, textile production and technology, experimental and experience archaeology, as well as on Aegean seals and sealing practices.

Sophia Vakirtzi (sophiavakirtzi@hotmail.com) is a fellow at ARTEX, the "Hellenic Centre for Research and Conservation of Archaeological Textiles". She holds a PhD from the University of Crete. She has extensive fieldwork experience in Greek prehistoric excavations, and has worked for the Athens Archaeological Society (Akrotiri Excavations) and for the Hellenic Ministry of Culture. Her research focuses on prehistoric textile technologies and prehistoric fibre economy in the Aegean.

Preface

It is a great pleasure to write a preface to this significant volume of work, spanning from the Iberian Peninsula to Scandinavia and to the Levant and Eastern Europe.

All contributions deal with the material culture of cloth making and thread manufacture. When studying material culture, what we see primarily in the form of things, are the results of actions. A loom weight was *crafted* from clay, was *shaped*, was *used* for weaving, was *broken* one day, and was eventually *discovered* by an archaeologist.

Thus, things are the results of actions, and the results of designs and plans. Yet, these things would only be achievable if there were also *hands* to twist the spindles, and *bodies* to bend and stretch when collecting fibres and weaving; *fingertips* that would judge the fineness of a thread, detect irregularities and knots; *eyes* to detect colours and hues; *noses* imbued with odours of lanolin and dust of flax and hemp. All these bodily functions work together to achieve the material culture presented here.

Likewise, we see in textile words that they are formed as results of actions: the word *textile* comes from the Latin *textum*, 'what has been woven', a verbal adjective turned into a noun. The word *wool*, according to new research by Birgit Annette Olsen, originates from a verb meaning 'to pluck' and hence designates what has been plucked off the sheep.

Moreover, to achieve the textiles and yarn through bodily actions, and to use textile tools, require repetition and skill, cognitive processes, perseverance and precision.

And while people were doing this, what did they name it? How did they coin textile tools, how did they choose to name thread and fabrics?

In textile research, including reconstructed vocabulary provided by the field of comparative linguistics can be useful, especially where the Indo-European language family is an important source of information for areas without textual records. The early Near Eastern textual sources provide additional knowledge of textile technologies, such as qualities, purposes, colours and dyes, value, and use that is not available in archaeological sources.

The title of the volume deals with perennially debated issues in archaeology and history: the ***first*** and the ***origin***. However, luckily, the volumes move far beyond this simplistic view and also explore the interwoven questions of why, and how. This is done both out of intellectual curiosity, but also because among the *firsts* are examples of such advanced technology and sophistication, that the scholars rightly question both how far this is indeed the first and earliest, or only a fortuitous find? Secondly, the stereotyped idea that culture, materiality and technology will start out as simple and coarse and then develop into complexity and sophistication also has to be questioned. The textile realm is an excellent case for doing so. Much of what we see in this volume is extremely early and extremely advanced.

The researches undertaken in this volume demonstrate that, while there may be some *firsts*, it is more the simultaneous multitude and plurality that prevail. Loom types emerge in different places simultaneously or diachronically, people seek answers to problems by implementing different – or similar – solutions in distant places.

The richness of techniques and usages is astonishing: Strings, bands, ribbons, pouches, ornamentation and practicality. Before cloth was properly woven, textile techniques were used for millennia to attach, accommodate, cover, shield, highlight, and carry. Clothing was only one, and a rather late, usage of this diverse technological field.

Another significant aspect of this volume is how string technology and cloth are *entangled* with other technologies, and it probably does not even make sense to speak of a distinct textile technology; skin, basketry, fur, fibres, and dyes draw on innovations from all directions and are closely *interwoven*. Deliberate imitations of fur in textiles, and textile techniques imitating strings and curls illustrate the playful and the connectivity.

This volume explores times and areas, which are currently hotly debated in archaeo-linguistics and archaeo-genetics, and much is at stake: to understand when the current Europeans entered Europe. Indeed, the realm of textiles, clothing, strings, skin and fur is a significant new contribution to this debate, which is often characterised by another focus on material culture in the shape of dynamic, (male?) symbols, such as axes, drinking vessels, horses and chariots. This volume, instead, offers the possibilities to think about *when* those humans came with their Indo-European words for wool, sheep, textiles, spinning and weaving.

Hence, where in the material culture, and where in Europe, and where in the textile archaeological artefacts do we see traces of the old European Neolithic, and where do we see traces of new people using Indo-European words and entering Europe in the Chalcolithic and Early Bronze Age? Linguists can often provide an outline of which words belong to the very early loan/substrate words of the Neolithic, and which words belong to the shared Indo-European fund. Can we map the early material culture of textiles in a similar way?

By detecting small irregularities in the established sound laws of otherwise widespread Indo-European words in Europe, linguists can suggest how Indo-European dialects also borrowed words from the Neolithic inhabitants of Europe. Some semantic fields are particularly prone to borrowing words from the locals, such as local flora and fauna, domestic plants, and agricultural terminology.

The Aegean is unique in this respect. It offers textile tools, contexts, a few textile remains, and textual evidence of both Mycenaean Greek and the earlier non-Indo-European Minoan substrate language. A true patchwork of terms: cloth terms with IE etymology (*pa-wo, pharos*), non-IE etymology, probably Minoan (*tu-na-no*) and Semitic loan words (*ki-to, khiton*). Textile tools are likewise termed according to IE vocabularies such as *elakate*, distaff (in Mycenaean found in the occupational designation *a-ra-ka-te-ja*, spinning women) and the loom, *histós* from *histamai,* (in Mycenaean Greek the occupational designations for weavers, *i-te-we* and *i-te-ja-o*), but spindle whorl, *spondylos,* attested in later Greek, has typical pre-Greek or Minoan elements. This was demonstrated by Betchen Barber in the 1990s, but we still have difficulties merging the linguistic and textile technological data and making sense of them.

The editors are to be congratulated for their great efforts in hosting two conferences and offering this rich patchwork of data to the scholarly community. We who were fortunate to participate in the Copenhagen conference in 2015 will also remember Małgorzata and Lorenz's baby girl, who came to the world shortly after: Rita, a wonderfully strong name and also quite appropriately the Mycenaean adjective for the first textile crop, flax/ linen, attested as *ri-ta* on the Knossos L(1) tablets, which record *ri-ta pa-we-a*, linen *pa-we-a* cloth.

Marie-Louise Nosch

1

Introduction

Małgorzata Siennicka, Lorenz Rahmstorf and Agata Ulanowska

'First Textiles' – a research project in the Centre for Textile Research, SAXO Institute at the University of Copenhagen (2013–2017)

This book is one of the results of the collaborative research project 'First Textiles. The Beginnings of Textile Manufacture in Europe and the Mediterranean', implemented in 2013–2017 at the University of Copenhagen.[1] The project was designed to elucidate the beginnings of textile manufacture, tools and techniques in the Epipalaeolithic, Neolithic and Early Bronze Age in Europe and the Mediterranean. Its aim was to bring together scholars who work on actual remains of prehistoric fabrics, undertake scientific analyses, deal with textile technologies and implements, study archaeobotanical and zooarchaeological material, and focus on ethnographic evidence and experimental approach to textile studies. We sought to discuss latest advances in the methodologies, technologies, material and scientific studies, as well as recent archaeological finds associated with the earliest textiles.

The main activities of the project consisted of the organisation of two international scientific meetings[2] and the subsequent publication of their proceedings, incorporated in the present volume.

'First Textiles' – research questions

The main research objective of the 'First Textiles' project was to present the recent studies and evidence for the beginnings of textile production and its social meanings in various parts of Europe and the Near East, mainly in the Epipalaeolithic, Neolithic and Early Bronze Age. A remarkable intensification of textile research, which has resulted in launching major research programmes and individual projects,[3] as well as publication of ground-breaking and very useful works,

including both theoretical and object-related studies of textiles, textile tools and techniques, can be observed in the recent years.[4] New discoveries and studies of preserved textiles, their representations, descriptions and imprints, a wide range of textile tools, as well as advanced scientific and experimental analyses of finds, have considerably improved our knowledge about the prehistoric manufacture of textiles.[5]

The central research topics of the *First Textiles* project were:

- The most ancient textiles: survey of the preserved examples of the earliest archaeological fibres, textiles, basketry, cordage; use of animal skins and furs for clothing; microscopic and scientific analyses of the remains and manufacture of fibres, textiles, basketry and cordage; analyses of pigmentation and dyeing techniques.
- Imprints of fibres, textiles, cordage, basketry and mats in various materials: methods and analyses.
- Raw materials: archaeobotanical and zoological studies; exploitation and use of plant and animal fibres, bast and tree-bast, skins and furs in the prehistory; domestication of flax; use of hairy and woolly wool; introduction and spread of sheep woolly wool; 'the textile revolution'.
- Scientific methods of analysing ancient textiles and the provenience of fibres: strontium isotope tracing; ancient DNA; protein analysis, *etc.*
- Development and changes of textile techniques: introduction and development of various techniques of twisting, splicing, spinning and plying of fibres, as well as twining, looping and weaving of textiles; other textile techniques, such as needlework or tablet weaving; decoration and dyeing of textiles throughout the prehistory.
- Studies of textile tools: functional and typological analyses of textile implements, *e.g.* spindle whorls,

distaffs, hooks, loom weights, various kinds of simple and advanced looms, tablets, frames, beaters, weaving swords, needles, *etc.*

- Experimental archaeology and ethnographical analogies: new methods and developments; the role of experimental archaeology in reconstructions of early textiles, tools and techniques.
- The social context of early textiles: the meaning of textiles and cloths in the society; use of textiles in habitation, religious and funerary contexts; textiles as manifestations of social status, culture, wealth and gender; distribution, exchange and trade of the raw materials and textiles; modes of textile production; work organisation and specialisation.

Studying prehistoric textiles – a brief overview of the available evidence and methods

The manufacture of textiles[6] and clothing was one of the most essential daily activities in prehistory. Textiles were objects of practical use, and at the same time had cultural, social and symbolic meaning, crucial for displaying the identity, gender, social rank and status or wealth of their users. This can be well demonstrated for literate societies of the Bronze Age. Written and iconographic evidence shows that textiles and their production must have been crucial both for society and the economy.[7] For a few regions, for example from the Late Bronze Age Aegean, our knowledge about the late prehistoric textiles and cloths is fairly good because of numerous archaeological,[8] textual[9] and iconographic data.[10] However, the evidence of textile products, clothing and techniques in the earliest stages of the prehistory is rather scarce.[11] Due to the gaps in the archaeological evidence, we are dealing with scattered pieces of information about the daily textile products and technologies, and their meaning for the society. As a result of frequently unfavourable preservation conditions, organic materials, such as furs, skins, wooden and bast products, animal and vegetal fibres, cordage and textiles, only seldom survive to our times, and then usually in a very damaged and fragmented condition. Nevertheless, single pieces of textile, which have been accidentally conserved – sometimes astonishingly well – by water, dry air or ice, carbonised, preserved by metal corrosion or mineralised, allow us to gain some important insights into the original prehistoric fibres and garments.[12]

In order to collect as much information as possible about preserved fibres, threads or pieces of textiles – and also of textile imprints and textile tools – various scientific and analytic methods can be applied.[13] Researchers usually start with a macroscopic examination of an item, *i.e.* with the naked eye and a magnifying glass, but more precise studies should be undertaken with microscopes, such as a reflected-light microscope, transmitted-light microscope or scanning electron microscope (SEM).[14] The latter is particularly

useful for identification of fibres (*e.g.* plant or animal raw materials, and specific species), as well as for determination of their condition and quality (*e.g.* their damage) and the manner in which the fibres were processed. A portable digital microscope is particularly convenient for field studies (*e.g.* Dino-Lite USB Microscope). Threads can be comprehensively analysed for their diameters and structure (single yarns, plied yarns, twist direction and angle), and pigmentation. Textiles are measured, described by the type of weave they were made of (*e.g.* tabby, twill) and density (*i.e.* the number of warp and weft threads per centimetre). In addition, X-ray and digital tomography can be applied to investigate *e.g.* structures of mineralised textiles, while chromatographic techniques, such as high-performance liquid chromatography (HPLC), are necessary in order to identify dyeing techniques of coloured fibres and threads.[15]

Besides archaeological textiles, another important category of material represents indirect evidence of unpreserved textiles: impressions of cord, fabric, basketry and mats, mainly on clay (*e.g.* on pottery and sealings), as well as on soil and bitumen, provide us with significant information regarding technical features of fibres, threads, textiles, their structure and various manufacturing technologies. At the same time they inform us about the use of textile products, *e.g.* in manufacture and decoration of pottery, in administrative practices, when impressions of textiles, cordage, basketry and wickerwork are preserved on reverse sides of clay sealings used for securing doors, storage jars, baskets or in funeral contexts.[16] The impressions of textiles, made both unintentionally and on purpose, usually show tabby (plain weave), often open and balanced. It has been suggested that the domination of tabby on the imprints does not necessarily imply its most frequent use in the prehistory. More probably, the imprints of textiles derive from simple and ordinary fabrics used in relation to ceramic production (*e.g.* as support for the pots produced) or to wrapping objects.[17] Similarly, the impressions on clay of basketry and mats give us important insights into the complexity of various textile techniques used in the prehistory.[18]

Another group of artefacts that are of extraordinary significance for the studies of prehistoric textiles and their production are textile tools, such as spindle whorls, loom weights, needles and other implements used for making of textiles and clothing.[19] These objects, which are frequently discovered at archaeological sites, were primarily made of stone and clay, as well as bone, metals and of wood (though this is much less frequently preserved).[20] Detailed studies of textile implements in their primary context can reveal the whole range of information regarding the final products made with their use, *i.e.* threads and textiles,[21] and thus they offer sometimes the only possible method to reconstruct prehistoric textiles and the techniques of their manufacture.[22] While the universal manner in which people used to spin with spindle whorls or weave on looms has not considerably changed throughout the time, various classes of objects may be characteristic only for particular periods or areas (*e.g.* cuboid loom weights in Bronze Age Crete), while the others were common in many, even distant cultures (*e.g.* conical spindle whorls or pyramidal loom weights which remained in use over millennia).[23] To give maximum insights into the textile techniques, the implements should preferably be studied in wider chronological, archaeological, archaeobotanical and zooarchaeological contexts according to their chronologies and find circumstances.[24]

Finally, in the attempt to enhance our understanding of ancient textiles, experimental archaeology has proved to be a valuable method successfully practised for many years now.[25] The scope of archaeological experiments is indeed wide[26] and includes, among other things, reconstructions of specific textile and dyeing techniques, *e.g.* tablet weaving or purple dyeing, as well as reconstructions of archaeological textiles and garments,[27] along with experiments exploring the function of textile tools, and defining those parameters of tools that have a direct impact on the final products, *i.e.* yarns and fabrics.[28] A potential specialisation of textile tools suggested by their particular expedience for specific textile techniques, such as the practicability of spools as weights in tablet weaving[29] or crescent-shaped weights in twill weaving,[30] has also been examined. Finally, non-discursive elements of textile knowledge, such as the skills of textile workers and their kinaesthetic knowledge, as well as manners of transmission of textile knowledge and skills, have also been studied using experimental methods.[31]

Focus on first textiles

One fundamental issue for early humans during the Pleistocene was a need for 'portable thermal protection' during the ice ages. I. Gilligan suggested by his 'Thermal Model' that 'trends visible in the archaeological record reflect the relevant environmental parameters that promoted the acquisition of thermally effective clothing'.[32] It is debated whether clothing was already used during the Lower Palaeolithic. Indirect evidence suggests the use of pelts for clothing.[33] Indicators are here the selective preservation of animal body parts or the use-wear and residue analyses (*e.g.* from the Schöningen site in Lower Saxony) that may suggest hide processing.[34] Single pelts were removed from the carcass and pierced ('simple clothing'), or several pelts were joined together ('complex clothing'), which required piercing tools, such as bone awls.[35] This stage does not include yet woven pieces. However, the production techniques for cordage and basketry are intertwined with the basic idea of joining fibres into a woven product. As recently summarised, the earliest evidence for tree-bast basketry and cordage in Europe and the Near East dates back to the Palaeolithic.[36] E. Barber and more recently K. Hardy, who reviewed the role of string for early humans, have considered

string and cord fundamental textile categories, involved in production of various types of nets (fishing, carrying, hair nets), and thus to be a basic structure for other items of clothing.[37] One of the earliest known pieces of evidence for cordage and textile production comes from Dolní Věstonice and Pavlov I,[38] dating to the Upper Palaeolithic (*c.* 29,000–24,000 BP, Gravettian). These are impressions on small fired and unfired pieces of clay of baskets, mats, cordage, netting and textiles, *e.g.* simple and diagonal twined pieces made of plant fibres.[39] Among numerous examples of plant fibres recently excavated in Dzudzuana Cave in Georgia and dating to *c.* 30,000 BP, some were interpreted as being twisted and plied, or even dyed;[40] however, certain doubts about the identification of the fibres and the methods of the identification,[41] as well as deliberate twisting and dyeing of the fibres[42] have been expressed. Other evidence for twisted and plied fibres of cordage comes from Ohalo II and dates to 19,000 BP,[43] while another one (imprint of a cord) from Lascaux dates to 17,000 BP.[44] Indirect indication for use of string dates to even 300,000 BP: two perforated objects (a bone point and a wolf incisor) were discovered in Repolusthöhle in Austria, while pierced shells which appear to have use-wear pattern come from the South African site of Blombos (75,000–80,000 BP).[45] Other suggestive evidence includes potential depictions of woven garments, such as the twisted cords hung from a belt in the rear view of the Gravettian figurine from Lespugne, France.[46] A bone needle with a well-preserved eye was recently discovered in the Denisova Cave in Siberia and is claimed to date to *c.* 50,000 BP.[47] Other examples came from layers dating to *c.* 40,000 years ago and later from Eurasia,[48] *e.g.* from the Mezmaiskaya Cave in Caucasus.[49] In all these cases, it is not possible to say whether threads made of twisted plants or rather of other materials, such as human or animal hair, sinew, gut, or hide, were used as strings.[50]

One of the oldest linen threads, which dates to *c.* 10,000 years ago, was found attached to a comb in the Murabba'at caves.[51] The first Neolithic fabrics are known only from their preserved impressions in clay and bitumen, but they seem to have been quite sophisticated and tightly woven, perhaps produced on heddle looms.[52] The examples from Jarmo in northern Iraq (7th millennium BC) show plain balanced weaves.[53] The oldest identified textile pieces of plant threads in the Near East – twined, not woven – were discovered at Nahal Hemar in Israel (*c.* 7000 BC, Pre-Pottery Neolithic B),[54] at Tell Halula in Syria (mineralised textile specimens dating to *c.* 7600–7300 BC, Pre-Pottery Neolithic B),[55] and at Çayönü in Turkey (pseudomorph dating to *c.* 7000 BC),[56] while at Çatalhöyük in Anatolia (*c.* 6500–6400 BC)[57] both twined textiles and finely woven examples of simple tabby, cords and threads of linen were preserved mainly in burials.[58]

The first remains of a horizontal ground loom – or as suggested by C. Breniquet[59] of a backstrap loom

– are evidenced in a Pre-Pottery Neolithic B (*c.* 7th–6th millennium BC) House 1b at El Kowm in Syria.[60] Also the Chalcolithic cave at Nahal Mishmar ('The Cave of the Treasure') in the Levant contained the wooden beams of a horizontal loom.[61] The oldest representation of a ground loom on a bowl from Badari from Egypt dates only to the 5th millennium BC.[62] Whereas the horizontal ground loom is considered to be one of the oldest types of looms,[63] the first appearance of warp-weighted loom could have been simultaneous or slightly later, as far as the present evidence indicates. A warp-weighted loom, from which clay or stone loom weights are virtually the only elements preserved in the archaeological material, seems to have been in use already in the Early Neolithic, and was particularly widespread during the Bronze Age.[64] Suggestions were made that some Upper Palaeolithic objects made of mammoth phalanges could have served as loom weights,[65] however, up to now the oldest unambiguous loom weights date back to at least late 7th–6th millennia BC (*e.g.* from Çatalhöyük, Greece, or Hungary).[66] The oldest known representations of a warp-weighted loom come from the iconography of the Minoan glyptic and are dated to about the 20th century BC,[67] and are also seen on the Great Rock of Naquane in Val Camonica (Italy) dated to the 14th century BC.[68] A simplified graphic form of the warp-weighted loom has also been recognised in the Linear A sign AB 54.[69]

The use of other kinds of simple twining and weaving devices, such as a simple frame, rigid heddle loom or backstrap loom, can only be suggested or indirectly demonstrated for early prehistory, since no actual remains of such implements have come to light until now.[70] It is questionable whether woven textiles played any substantial role before the end of the Neolithic period in the 3rd millennium BC in temperate Europe. There are potential loom weights from Central Europe, including the Carpathian basin, from the 6th and 5th millennia BC,[71] but their number is still low. Twined textiles were apparently much more often used.[72] The Ice Man ('Ötzi') was wearing mainly furs from domestic and wild animals as clothing in the late 4th millennium BC.[73]

Based on the available iconographic evidence from the Palaeolithic and Neolithic periods, it can be suggested that the first textile products, such as strings and twined textiles, were only sporadically used for clothing, and more frequently for other practical purposes, such as preparing cords, ropes, nets, textiles used in mortuary contexts, or personal adornment (which, on the other hand, could include elements of clothing, such as corded skirts, belts or headdress).[74] From the times when the first written and iconographic evidence is available, woven textiles and cloths seem to have been perceived as particularly prestigious and valuable. We know that woven clothing is first attested in the Uruk archaic texts and iconography as a symbol of power, and it was worn by priest-kings,

dignitaries, goddess and priestesses.[75] Before this date, it is difficult to indicate whether woven textiles were used for making cloth already at the time of the invention of weaving on the advanced looms, such as a ground loom and a warp-weighted loom. These weaving implements must have considerably improved and quickened the process of textile making, providing the possibility of manufacturing larger pieces of fabrics. Probably, woven cloths were considered extraordinary and reserved for the elites at the beginning,[76] but, with time, the use of woven textiles was intensified and became more frequent in various (social, symbolic or religious) contexts, such as in daily use as cloth and in the household, in burials and even as exchange goods and means of payment.[77] At the same time, large sheep flocks, raw wool and the manufacture and distribution of wool fabrics became strictly controlled and administrated by major institutions, and played an important role in the political economy.[78]

The types of fibres used for prehistoric textiles depended, among other things, on the available material, *i.e.* wild or domesticated animals and plants.[79] The scientific methods of analysing textiles and recognising the provenience of animal fibres (*e.g.* DNA analysis, strontium isotope tracing) have recently developed significantly, and in some cases we are able to get precise information about their origins.[80] It seems indisputable that the first fibres, which were used for making cords, mats, baskets and textiles, were prepared from plants, particularly tree-bast and bast plants like flax.[81] Vegetal raw material like flax or hemp has remained in use in textile production ever since, however, animal raw materials like leather, fur, hair and hairy wool must have also played a significant role in cloth making from the very beginning.[82] The introduction and dissemination of long-staple wool (the so-called woolly wool) in the East Mediterranean, south-east Europe and the Aegean (*c.* 6th–3rd millennia BC), truly revolutionised textile production, while in temperate Europe the woolly sheep only appeared by around 2000 BC.[83] Wool is processed differently than linen, as no chemical but only mechanical processes are required in order to produce fibres ready to spin, and this does not require specialised knowledge.[84] The woolly wool would have had several advantages over plant fibres like flax in specific uses, *e.g.* for cold climate clothing, as water-repellent clothing or as a fireproof material.[85] The woolly wool fibres are longer than those of the short-staple wool, and can be easily spun into longer yarns of a wide range of thickness; wool has better thermal insulation properties; has high plasticity when wet and may be shaped into a desired form by felting; woollen textiles are warm and comfortable due to the structure and high elasticity of wool fibres. Finally, wool can be easily dyed into a wide range of colours. This opened up new possibilities for people to use colours to emphasise their diversity in appearance, gender, ethnicity, social and economic status, *etc.*

The introduction of woolly wool significantly contributed to important innovations in the manufacture of textiles, such as changes in spinning technologies or intensification of dyeing techniques.[86]

Twisting and spinning of plant and animal fibres must have belonged to the daily activities of prehistoric people. Accurate fibre processing, including preparation of raw material, twisting, splicing and spinning, in order to attain yarns suitable for weaving and for other textile activities (such as cordage, looping, netting, twining or sewing) was certainly demanding, time-consuming and required certain advanced skills and experience. Twisting could have been achieved by various means, *e.g.* by using fingers, hand palms, by twisting a thread on the thigh or by using hooks.[87] Yet, by using a special tool, such as stick (spindle) with an attached flywheel (spindle whorl), the process becomes faster and the yarn can be twisted more tightly. While wooden and bone sticks (spindles) are seldom preserved in the archaeological material,[88] spindle whorls are often discovered at prehistoric sites in a wide range of materials (clay, stone, bone, rarely wood), of various types (conical, biconical, spherical, cylindrical, discoidal), and a variety of dimensions (from tiny 'beads' to very large and heavy tools) and with different surface treatments (slipped, polished, painted, incised). Their origins can be traced in the Near East even as early as in the Pre-Pottery Neolithic B phase when the first pierced discs occurred, perhaps used as primitive spinning tools.[89] Towards the end of the 7th and in the 6th millennium BC, pierced potsherds and properly fired clay whorls of various shapes were utilised more commonly in the Near East and the Aegean.[90] As has been demonstrated in a series of experimental tests, various parameters of spindle whorls, and particularly their weights and diameters, can be informative of types and qualities of the produced yarns.[91] In some cases, potential changes in use of fibres can also be suggested, *e.g.* a shift from plant towards animal fibre processing.[92] Bast fibres, especially flax, were spliced in order to achieve longer yarns.[93] Moreover, all kinds of yarns could have been plied and cabled, *i.e.* more threads were twisted together in order to attain stronger or thicker yarns, suitable for making, for example, thicker outdoor cloths, sacks, rugs, blankets and other coarse textiles.[94]

The production of woollen and linen textiles were obviously crucial industries in the prehistoric world.[95] The large-scale and multidisciplinary research project titled 'The Textile Revolution', recently completed at TOPOI in Berlin, was focused on investigating the innovation of wool production related to the spread of sheep husbandry in later Neolithic and Chalcolithic Europe and the Near East, by considering various pieces of evidence.[96] The huge data-set comprises evidence from numerous sites from the Near East and Central Europe dating to *c.* 7000–2000 BC, including archaeological (*e.g.* textile tools), archaeozoological, geoarchaeological, textual and pictorial data related to the early use of wool. It will certainly answer many questions regarding the introduction and spread of wool in the prehistory.[97] The international 'FLAX network' and a research project devoted to flax in the Neolithic have been recently launched by Dr. Sabine Karg in Berlin.[98]

'First Textiles' – proceedings of two conferences

This volume presents the results of two international conferences held in Istanbul (2014) and in Copenhagen (2015) organised by Dr. Małgorzata Siennicka (currently an ERC Research Associate in the Archaeological Institute, University of Göttingen; formerly an Associate Professor in the Centre for Textile Research – CTR, University of Copenhagen), together with Dr. Lorenz Rahmstorf (Head of the Institute of Prehistory and Early History at the University of Göttingen; previously an Associate Professor in SAXO Institute, University of Copenhagen) and Dr. Agata Ulanowska (currently an Assistant Professor in the Institute of Archaeology at the University of Warsaw; formerly a post-doctoral researcher in the Centre for Research on Ancient Technologies of the Institute of Archaeology and Ethnology, Polish Academy of Sciences in Łódź).

Textiles in a social context

'**Textile Production in Europe and the Mediterranean in the 4th and 3rd Millennia BCE (Istanbul, September 2014).**' The first meeting took place on 13 September 2014 during the European Association of Archaeologists (EAA) conference in Istanbul. The session aimed to explore the social context and cultural aspects of textile manufacture based on archaeological, ethnographical, textual, iconographic and experimental evidence. It comprised 18 oral and three poster presentations,[99] from which six papers are presented in this volume.

First Textiles

'**The Beginnings of Textile Manufacture in Europe and the Mediterranean (Copenhagen, May 2015).**' A two-day international conference took place on 7–8 May 2015 in the Danish National Research Foundation's Centre for Textile Research at the University of Copenhagen and in the National Museum of Denmark. The aim of the conference was to discuss recent achievements in the research field of the prehistoric textiles and techniques in Europe and the Near East from the Epipaleolithic (Natufian culture), Neolithic, Chalcolithic to the Bronze Age. From the 21 papers delivered at the conference,[100] 12 are published in this volume.

All contributions from the both conferences have been peer-reviewed and are presented here in the chrono-geographical order.[101]

The first paper of this volume, 'Early loom types in ancient societies', by **Eva Andersson Strand**, offers an introduction to various types of looms most probably employed in prehistory, of which the archaeological evidence is, however, often limited or absent. These comprise a horizontal loom, a vertical two-bar loom, a warp-weighted loom and also simpler weaving implements. After a brief introduction to the loom set-up and elementary technical issues, various loom types in prehistoric Europe and the Near East are presented. Finally, possible reasons for the variety of looms used at the same time are discussed.

Sabine Karg, Axel Diederichsen and **Simon Jeppson** summarise the results of a pilot study of flax domestication in Europe and using biometric measurements on recent and archaeological flax seeds. The scholars conclude that archaeological seeds of cultivated plants and their wild relatives could be better interpreted if the old plant remains are compared with material obtained from 'genebanks', which include a wide range of diverse material of crop plants and crop wild relatives. They postulate continuing similar comparisons with other seed material from other crops of agriculture in the old world.

In her paper 'From adorned nudity to a dignitary's wardrobe: symbolic raiment in the southern Levant 13,500 BC–3900 BC', **Janet Levy** outlines the evidence of various kinds of attire, such as headwear, girdles, belts and straps, which in Palaeolithic and Neolithic Eurasia seem to reflect symbolic use and meaning than rather having a purely everyday function. Evidence for clothing in the southern Levant is rare until the late 5th millennium, and the frequency of its iconography increases in the Near East and Egypt in the 4th millennium BC. The author discusses various kinds of textile items within their cultural context in order to identify their social and technological implications.

The earliest 'cloth culture' in Denmark is the subject of **Ulla Mannering**'s contribution. It offers a survey of the archaeological finds made of skin, non-woven textiles, and of a variety of tools dated mainly to the Mesolithic and Neolithic periods (*c.* 8000–1700 BC), *i.e.* before the remarkable transformation of textile production in the Early Bronze Age. The knowledge of making threads and textiles out of nettle and bast fibres, including looping and twining techniques, was widespread, along with the tradition of using skins for the production of clothes and other items. Nonetheless, these crafts often remain invisible in the archaeological record.

In their contribution titled 'Loom weights and weaving in the archaeological site of São Pedro (Redondo, Portugal)', **Catarina Costeira** and **Rui Mataloto** investigate a large assemblage (over 3700 artefacts) of weaving tools, namely perforated rectangular and oval clay plaques and crescent-shaped objects, dating to the 4th and 3rd millennia BC. The suggested weights were predominately light (up to 100 g) and thin (less than 2 cm), and as such they may have been used for twining, but also in tablet weaving and in a warp-weighted loom, allowing manufacture of a large variety of fabric types.

The joint paper of **Miriam de Diego, Raquel Piqué, Antoni Palomo, Xavier Terradas, Maria Saña, Ignacio Clemente-Conte** and **Millán Mozota** presents evidence of exceptionally well-preserved wooden and bone tools from the Early Neolithic (6th–5th millennia BC) waterlogged site of la Draga (Banyoles, Spain). A thorough archaeological study of the objects, combined with archaeobotanical and zooachaeological data, comparative studies of ethnographic material and, finally, the use-wear analyses of replicas of the uncovered tools used for experimental spinning and weaving, such as bone awls, wooden spindle-like objects and combs, allowed the researcher to demonstrate the oldest evidence of textile production that has yet been found in the Iberian Peninsula.

María Irene Ruiz de Haro systematically examines the use of spinning bowls between Egypt and the Iberian Peninsula from the Chalcolithic period to the Iron Age. The author discusses the typology, differences and functions of the vessels employed in the process of spinning flax fibres, and presents their chronological, geographical and typological development.

In the paper titled 'From the loom to the forge. Elements of power at the end of Neolithic in western Europe: a focus on textile activities', **Fabienne Médard** discusses technical and socio-economic changes in textile implements, mainly spindle whorls and loom weights, which are commonly found at many Neolithic sites in western Europe. She examines changes in the morphological and technical features of the tools, well detectable especially towards the end of the Neolithic. Finally, the social and economic role of textile craft and its economic importance within the community is addressed.

Johanna Banck-Burgess's paper outlines some ideas for the planned research on Neolithic and Early Bronze textile manufacture in the pile dwellings at Lake Constance and in Upper Swabia in south-west Germany. Excellently preserved textile assemblages, *e.g.* string and rope fragments, fishing nets, twined bast textiles and other finds, such as sewn bark containers, baskets and spindle whorls, are going to be comprehensively and interdisciplinarily analysed in the near future.

Experiments with replicas of the Late Neolithic crescent-shaped objects from Melk-Spielberg in Austria are presented by **Karina Grömer**. The author made tests with various copies of the crescent-shaped weights in band weaving on a warp-weighted loom and in twining techniques on a twining frame. The main aim of the experiments was to prove whether the weights could have been used in all the weaving techniques, and to compare the use-wear on the original weights with the copies, both fired and unfired.

Spindle whorls from the Eneolithic human burials in the Pannonian Plain are examined in a study by

Ana Grabundžija. The carefully recorded data was statistically analysed in regard to the technical parameters, such as diameter, height, perforation diameter, weight, weight/diameter and diameter/height ratio. The quality of production and decoration, and, finally, a broader 'cross-cultural' context of use of spindle whorls were investigated. The author argues that some developments in technologies of fibre processing, such as use of plant and animal fibres, or plying yarns, may have influenced symbolical meanings of the tools, which accordingly demonstrated social and economic changes of the societies.

Neculai Bolohan and **Ciprian-Cătălin Lazanu** present unique remains of mineralised plant textiles exposed in a grave mound of the Early Bronze Age in Popeni (eastern Romania). Fragments of mats and textiles, probably made of plant fibres in open tabby weave on a warp-weighted loom, formed a large shroud (4.90×2.90 m), which originally underlay wooden flooring and covered the burial.

'Social contexts of textile production in Bulgaria during the Late Chalcolithic: from multimedia work-areas to material, social and cultural transformations' is discussed in the paper of **Petya Hristova**. Various pieces of evidence for textile production, particularly textile tools are presented. It is suggested that textile manufacture was often undertaken in 'multimedia work-areas' or 'workshops' in the same contexts as other craft activities, such as pottery making, gold working or bone working.

Weaving with the copies of the loom weights from Early Bronze Age Tiryns in Greece is addressed in the first contribution of **Agata Ulanowska**. She attempts to identify the functionality of loom weights by means of archaeological experimentation performed by students of archaeology from the University of Warsaw. Three types of loom weights – cylindrical with three perforations, crescent-shaped and large cones, are tested on a warp-weighted loom and in band weaving, and their use-wear marks are examined.

In his contribution 'Textile tools and manufacture in the Early Bronze Age Cyclades: evidence from Amorgos and Keros', **Giorgos Gavalas** discusses recently published data on textile tools from the Cycladic islands in the Aegean, and the development of textile manufacture in various contexts during the 3rd millennium BC. The main focus lies on frequently preserved spinning implements, *i.e.* clay and stone spindle whorls and perforated sherds. Moreover, the evidence of metal and bone pins, needles and awls, as well as mat and textile imprints in clay and scarce remains of textiles are summarised. As no loom weights are preserved from the discussed sites, it is suggested that a vertical loom was not employed there.

Sophia Vakirtzi systematically analyses tool assemblages related to fibre crafts, mainly spindle whorls, and focuses on the social context of the yarn industry on the Aegean islands in the Early Bronze Age. Typological classification, metrological analysis and distribution of spindle whorls are carefully presented and discussed with the purpose of defining cultural, technological and economic aspects of the manufacture of yarns.

In her second paper, titled 'In search of "invisible" textile tools and techniques of band weaving in the Bronze Age Aegean', **Agata Ulanowska** devotes attention to the indirect evidence of specialised looms for band weaving, such as the loom with a rigid heddle, which were potentially known in Bronze Age Greece but are not preserved in the archaeological material. Their use may be presumed due to certain technological and procedural sequences of textile manufacturing, such as preparing a starting border for weaving on a warp-weighted loom or making bands and narrow fabrics, which can be recognised in the Late Bronze Age iconography.

The Early Bronze Age textile implements from the Eskişehir region in north-western Anatolia are introduced by **Deniz Sarı**. Spindle whorls, pierced discs, brushes, loom weights and other tools potentially used in textile production in three chosen settlements representing different socio-economic models (Küllüoba, Demircihöyük, and the citadel of Keçiçayırı) are examined.

Romina Laurito investigates continuity and change in textile making at Arslantepe (Turkey) during the 4th and 3rd millennia BC. She investigates various spinning, weaving and other textile implements, as well as imprints of textiles on clay sealings, and focuses on their social contexts and meanings. She demonstrates which elements regarding textile manufacture remained unchanged and which altered over two millennia in this important settlement in the Malatya plain.

Remarks and acknowledgements

The collaborative research project 'First Textiles. The Beginnings of Textile Manufacture in Europe and the Mediterranean' was launched in 2013 by Małgorzata Siennicka, at that time a Marie Skłodowska-Curie Fellow. The idea of the project was inspired by Marie-Louise Nosch, Director of the Danish National Research Foundation's Centre for Textile Research in the SAXO Institute, University of Copenhagen. She saw a serious need to review and systematise recent achievements in the research field of the most ancient textiles and textile techniques, and to set the agenda for further research. She kindly invited Małgorzata Siennicka to direct this project. Due to the much-appreciated encouragement, valuable advice and help of two leaders of CTR, Marie-Louise Nosch and Eva Andersson Strand, a project focusing on the beginnings of textile manufacture, tools and techniques, principally in the Epipalaeolithic, Neolithic and Early Bronze Age in Europe and the Mediterranean, was successfully carried out.

The Danish National Research Foundation's Centre for Textile Research provided generous funding for the organisation of the conference in Copenhagen (2015) and the publication of this volume, and supported the session in Istanbul (2014). We are deeply grateful for all this support. The first day of the conference in Copenhagen was hosted by CTR, while the second one was held in the National Museum of Denmark. We would like to express our gratitude to the directors of the two institutions, as well as our collaborators, especially Eva Andersson Strand and Ulla Mannering, for their outstanding support. Our especial thanks go to the student helpers, staff and colleagues at CTR, and particularly to Egzona Haxha, Camilla Søgaard Ebert and, above all, to Line Lerke, who kindly devoted her time and energy to help superbly in all stages of the conference organisation.

The International Research Network Ancient Textiles from the Orient to the Mediterranean (ATOM) was a scientific partner of the conference.

Małgorzata Siennicka would like to kindly thank the Research Executive Agency of the European Commission and the Marie Skłodowska-Curie Actions for funding her research on textile tools from Early Bronze Age Greece carried out at the University of Copenhagen.[102] The organisation of, and participation in, the conference in Istanbul was possible due to research funding of her Marie Skłodowska-Curie project and the kind support of the Marie Curie Alumni Association's Micro Travel Grant.

The University of Warsaw contributed to the research project 'First Textiles' and the publication of this volume in a twofold manner. It provided funds for Agata Ulanowska's organisation of, and participation in, the conference in Istanbul. In addition, the language proofreading of this volume was possible thanks to the generous support of the Vice-Rector of the University of Warsaw, Maciej Duszczyk, who kindly agreed to co-finance this edition with the University fund for supporting basic research, and to whom we are deeply indebted.

We would like to warmly thank Paul Barford for the language proofreading of this volume.

Finally, we sincerely thank all peer-reviewers and experts who kindly advised on the submitted papers and this publication (in alphabetical order): Eva Alarm, Carmen Alfaro Giner, Susan J. Allen, Bogdan Athanassov, Marta Bazzanella, Catherine Breniquet, Brendan Burke, Tomasz J. Chmielewski, Horia Ciugudean, Ulrike Claßen-Büttner, Lindy Crewe, Maria Cybulska, Ida Demant, Don Evely, Isaac Gilead, Elke Kaiser, Katrin Kania, Daniela Kern, Ourania Kouka, Raiko Krauß, Agnete Wisti Lassen, Emmanuelle Martial, António M. Monge Soares, Cherine Munkholt, Marie-Louise Nosch, Jane Peterson, Agathe Reingruber, Yorke Rowan, Ulf-Dietrich Schoop, Isabelle Sidéra, Irene Skals, Anna Smogorzewska, Iris Tzachili, Jennifer Webb, John Peter Wild and Zuzanna Wygnańska.

Joanne Elizabeth Cutler (1962–2018) (photo: M. Siennicka).

We would like to dedicate this publication to the memory of our dear and loving friend and colleague, Joanne Cutler, who sadly passed away on 24 January 2018 after a long illness. Jo was a lovely, warm person, and a talented and dedicated researcher. For many years she studied textile production in the prehistoric Aegean.[103] She participated in the Istanbul conference in 2014 and delivered a paper on technological and social aspects of textile production in Neolithic and Early Bronze Age Crete. Jo initially wanted to submit a contribution to this volume, but her numerous activities and fieldwork, and finally her illness, did not let her finish her paper on time. We miss her.

Notes

1   http://ctr.hum.ku.dk/research-programmes-and-projects/ previous-programmes-and-projects/first-textiles/, accessed 2 October 2018.

2   A session 'Textiles in a Social Context. Textile Production in Europe and the Mediterranean in the 4th and 3rd Millennia BCE' was organised on 13 September 2014 during the 20th Annual Meeting of the European Association of Archaeologists in Istanbul. A two-day conference, 'First Textiles', took place on 7–8 May 2015 in Copenhagen. For brief reports, see Siennicka 2015; Siennicka *et al.* 2015.

3   For example numerous research programmes and individual projects have been undertaken at the Centre for Textile Research at the University of Copenhagen, see http://ctr.hum. ku.dk/, accessed 2 October 2018.

4   It is not possible to list here all the recent publications regarding textiles and textile production. A selection of the studies of the beginnings of textile manufacture is mentioned in the notes of this chapter.

5   *Cf.* Andersson Strand 2012.

6   The term textile is here understood as 'any type of construction made of fibres' (after Andersson Strand 2012, 22 and Andersson Strand *et al.* 2012, 13). For terminology related to fibres, textiles, textile techniques, products of animal skin and cloths, see *e.g.* Broudy 1979; Burnham 1980; Emery 1980; Seiler-Baldinger 1994; Desrosiers 2010; Harris 2010; Michel and Nosch 2010; Gilligan 2016; Grömer 2016; Gaspa *et al.* 2017; Grömer *et al.* 2017.

7   *Cf.* Barber 1991; McCorriston 1997; Tzachili 1997; Burke 2010; Nosch and Laffineur 2012; Breniquet and Michel 2014a.

8   For example, Carington Smith 1992; Rahmstorf 2008; 2011.

9   For example, Killen 2007; Nosch 2012.

10 For example, Barber 1991, 311–357, 394–395; Crowley 2012; Jones 2015; Shaw and Chapin 2016.

11 For example, Good 2001; Gleba 2011.

12 On the preservation of textiles, see *e.g.* Gleba 2008, 37–38; Gleba and Mannering 2012a, 2–3; Grömer 2016, 20–33.

13 For an overview of sources and methods of analysing archaeological textiles, see *e.g.* Andersson Strand *et al.* 2010; Gleba 2011.

14 Rast-Eicher 2016.

15 Gleba and Mannering 2012a, 3–4, table 0.1; Hofmann-de Keijzer 2016, 144–147.

16 For textile imprints on pottery, see *e.g.* Crowfoot 1954; Adovasio 1975–1977; Grömer and Kern 2010; for textile imprints on clay sealings, see *e.g.* Müller and Pini 1997; Müller 2004; Laurito 2007; Frangipane *et al.* 2009; Andersson Strand *et al.* 2017; Laurito this volume; for textile imprints in funeral contexts, see *e.g.* Siennicka 2018; forthcoming a; Bolohan and Lazanou this volume.

17 Breniquet 2013, 3; Hristova this volume.

18 Crowfoot 1954; Carington Smith 1975, 110–115; Adovasio 1975–1977; Wendrich 1991; 2012; Adovasio 2010, 10.

19 For example, Mårtensson *et al.* 2009; Rahmstorf 2015; Grömer 2016, esp. 72–118.

20 For recent reviews of textile production in Bronze Age Europe, see Gleba and Mannering 2012b; Grömer 2016; for the Near East, see *e.g.* Breniquet *et al.* 2012; for the Aegean, see *e.g.* Burke 2010; Nosch and Laffineur 2012; Harlow *et al.* 2014.

21 Andersson Strand and Nosch 2015.

22 See Costeira and Mataloto; de Diego *et al.*; Ruiz de Haro; Médard; Banck-Burgess; Grabundžija; Gavalas; Vakirtzi; and Sarı in this volume.

23 For example, Barber 1991; *cf.* various contributions in Andersson Strand and Nosch 2015; Siennicka 2012; Siennicka forthcoming b.

24 For example, the TOPOI research group http://www.topoi.org/group/a-4/, accessed 2 October 2018.

25 For recent summaries of experimental archaeology on textile research, see *e.g.* Peacock 2001; Andersson Strand 2010; 2015, viii; Hopkins 2013; Olofsson 2015.

26 *Cf.* Peacock 2001; Olofsson 2015.

27 On a few recent reconstructions of textile techniques and archaeological fabrics, see *e.g.*: tablet-weaving – Ræder Knudsen 2012; 2014; Karisto and Grömer 2017; garments – Nørgaard 2008; Demant 2017; purple dyeing – Kanold 2017.

28 Mårtensson *et al.* 2009; Kania 2013a; 2013b; various contributions in Andersson Strand and Nosch 2015; especially Olofsson *et al.* 2015. See also contributions of de Diego *et al.*; Grömer; Ulanowska in this volume.

29 Ræder Knudsen 2012; 2014.

30 Lassen 2013; 2015.

31 *Cf.* Andersson Strand 2010; Bender Jørgensen 2012a; 2012b; Ulanowska 2016a; forthcoming a.

32 Gilligan 2010.

33 Hosfield 2017, 536.

34 Rots *et al.* 2015; Gilligan 2017, 543.

35 Gilligan 2010, fig. 3.

36 Stordeur 1989; Rast-Eicher 2005, 117–118; Breniquet 2008, 53–62; 2014, 54–55; for a recent summary of the oldest evidence of the production and use of cordage see also Piqué *et al.* 2018.

37 Barber 1991, 39–41; 1994, 42–70; Hardy 2008.

38 Adovasio *et al.* 1996.

39 Adovasio *et al.* 1996; Soffer *et al.* 2000.

40 Kvavadze *et al.* 2009.

41 Bergfjord *et al.* 2010 argue that, if solely basing on fibre identification techniques presented in the paper of Kvavadze *et al.* 2009, the fibres from the Dzududzuana Cave cannot be identified as flax, but only as bast fibres without recognisable species. *Cf.*, however, a technical comment of Kvavadze *et al.* 2010.

42 C. Breniquet has suggested (2013, 6–7) that it is not certain whether the plant fibres from the Dzudzuana Cave were deliberately dyed and twisted.

43 Nadel *et al.* 1994.

44 Leroi-Gourhan 1982.

45 Hardy 2008.

46 Barber 1991, 40, fig. 2.1; Gilligan 2010, 58.

47 http://siberiantimes.com/science/casestudy/news/n0711-worlds-oldest-needle-found-in-siberian-cave-that-stitches-together-human-history/, accessed 2 October 2018.

48 Gilligan 2010, 49–50; 2016, 3.

49 Golonova *et al.* 2010, 306, fig. 4.1–4, table 2.

50 *Cf.* Hardy 2008, 271.

51 Schick 1995; Shimony 1995.

52 *Cf.* Adovasio 1975–1977, 227.

53 Adovasio 1975–1977.

54 Schick 1988; 1989; Shamir 2015, 17.

55 Alfaro Giner 2012.

56 Vogelsang-Eastwood 1993; Good 1998, 657.

57 Ryder 1965; Fuller *et al.* 2014, 122.

58 Hodder 2013, 3–4, fig. 1.2; Tung 2013, 13–14, fig. 2.6. For a recent brief summary of textile, basketry and cordage finds from Çatalhöyük see Bender Jørgensen and Rast-Eicher 2017.

59 Breniquet 2013, 7.

60 Stordeur 2000, 49–50, fig. 14.1–3; Breniquet 2008, 143–144, fig. 34; 2013, 7.

61 Bar-Adon 1980, 178–182; Breniquet 2008, 140–143, fig. 33; 2010, 53; Shamir 2014, 147–148, figs. 7–1, 7–2; 2015, 18, fig. 7.

62 Brunton and Caton-Thompson 1928, 54, pl. 47 no. 70k; Vogelsang-Eastwood 1992, 28; 2000, 276–277, fig. 11.6.

63 *Cf.* Andersson Strand this volume with further references.

64 Hoffmann 1964; Barber 1991.

65 Soffer *et al.* 2000, 514.

66 Mellaart 1962, 56; Carington Smith 1975, 90–91; Barber 1991, 93–100; Pèrles 2001, 248–252; Rahmstorf 2015, 6.

67 Ulanowska 2016b; 2017, 60–61.

68 Bazzanella 2012, 210–211, fig. 8.15. For a possibly later date of the Val Camonica carvings *cf.* Grömer 2016, 110.

69 *Cf.* Ulanowska 2017, 60 with further references.

70 Völling 2008, 119–148; Andersson Strand this volume; Ulanowska this volume.

71 Rahmstorf 2015, 6 with further references.

72 Rast-Eichner and Dietrich 2015; Banck-Burgess 2016, 363.

73 O'Sullivan *et al.* 2016.

74 Barber 1994, 42–70; Soffer *et al.* 2000; Breniquet 2013, 8; Boyd 2018, 254–258; Médard this volume; Levy this volume.

75 Breniquet 2013, 8–10.

76 Breniquet 2013, 10.

77 Breniquet 2013, 10–20; *cf.* Burke 2010, 90.

78 McCorriston 1997; Breniquet 2013, 21–22; 2014, 58, 72–74; Breniquet and Michel 2014b, 6–9.

79 On culture-specific uses of raw materials, textiles and clothing, see Harris 2012 and Gleba 2017. On early craft use of plant and animal fibres, see papers in a recent volume by Andersson 2018.

80 For example, Andersson Strand *et al.* 2010; Brandt *et al.* 2011; Gleba and Mannering 2012a, 3–4; Frei 2014; 2015; Brandt 2015; Frei *et al.* 2017.

81 For example, Körber-Grohne and Feldtkeller 1998; Rast-Eicher 2005; Breniquet 2008, 85–90; Karg 2011; Karg *et al.* this volume; Médard this volume; Banck-Burgess this volume.

82 Breniquet 2008, 90–97; Völling 2008; Andersson Strand 2012, 28–30; Harris 2012; 2014; Grömer *et al.* 2017; Mannering this volume.

83 Nosch 2015; Bender Jørgensen and Rast-Eicher 2018, 27.

84 *Cf.* Ryder 1987; 1992; Breniquet 2008, 83–87; Andersson Strand 2012; 2014.

85 For the general properties of flax and wool, see Harris 2010; Popescu and Wortmann 2010; Ulanowska forthcoming b.

86 On natural dyeing techniques, see *e.g.* Cardon 2003; Hofmann-de Keijzer 2016, 141–144, 148–169.

87 For example, Crowfoot 1931; Barber 1991, 42–44; Tiedemann and Jakes 2006.

88 *Cf.* Langgut *et al.* 2016 on one of the earliest (Late Chalcolithic, *c.* 5th–4th millennium BC) wooden spinning implements, such as spindles and distaffs, found in the southern Levant.

89 Rooijakkers 2012, esp. 99–103.

90 Carington Smith 1975, 118–122; Barber 1991, 51, 54, 59–60; Gibbs 2008.

91 For example, Grömer 2005; Mårtensson *et al.* 2006; Chmielewski and Gardyński 2010; Verhecken 2010; Andersson Strand 2011, 5; Olofsson *et al.* 2015; for a combination of various parameters that influence the quality of spun yarn, *cf.* Kania 2013a; 2013b; Verhecken 2013.

92 *Cf.* Rooijakkers 2012; Grabundžija and Russo 2016; Becker *et al.* 2016, 113–114, 119; Grabundžija this volume.

93 Barber 1991, 44–51; Bender Jørgensen and Rast-Eicher 2016, 70–71; Gleba and Harris 2018.

94 Carington Smith 1992, 680.

95 Barber 1991; Breniquet and Michel 2014a.

96 http://www.topoi.org/group/a-4/, accessed 2 October 2018.

97 Becker *et al.* 2016.

98 Karg 2011; S. Karg's DFG project: 'Know-how in der Flachsproduktion – Spezialisierte Bauern des Jung– bis Endneolithikums (4300–2200 B.C.) im circum-alpinen Raum. Eine interdisziplinäre Studie zur Ausbreitungs- und Nutzungsgeschichte der Kulturpflanze Lein' (http://gepris.dfg.de/gepris/projekt/289510075, accessed 2 October 2018.); the international FLAX project: http://archaeometrie.berliner-antike-kolleg.org/flax, accessed 2 October 2018. See also Karg *et al.* this volume.

99 Siennicka *et al.* 2015.

100 Siennicka 2015; Siennicka *et al.* 2015.

101 Unfortunately, not all papers originally presented in Istanbul and in Copenhagen could be published in the present volume. The full list of the delivered papers and the abstracts can be found on the webpage of CTR: http://ctr.hum.ku.dk/research-programmes-and-projects/previous-programmes-and-projects/first-textiles/, accessed 2 October 2018.

102 'Greek textile tools. Continuity and changes in textile production in Early Bronze Age Greece' (PIEF-GA-2012–329910). Marie Curie Actions Intra-European Fellowship (2012–2017).

103 Joanne Elizabeth Cutler (1962–2018), https://www.arch.cam.ac.uk/joanne-elizabeth-cutler-1962–2018, accessed 2 October 2018.

Bibliography

Adovasio, J. M. 1975–1977 The textile and basketry impressions from Jarmo. *Paléorient* 3, 223–230.

Adovasio, J. M. 2010 *Basketry Technology. A Guide to Identification and Analysis. Updated Edition.* Walnut Creek, California.

Adovasio, J. M., Soffer, O. and Klíma, B. 1996 Upper Palaeolithic fibre technology: interlaced woven finds from Pavlov I, Czech Republic, c. 26,000 years ago. *Antiquity* 70, 526–534.

Alfaro Giner, C. 2012 Textiles from the Pre-Pottery Neolithic site of Tell Halula (Euphrates Valley, Syria). *Paléorient* 38.1–2. Dossier thématique/Thematic file, C. Breniquet, M. Tengberg, E. Andersson and M.-L. Nosch (eds.), Préhistoire des Textiles au Proche-Orient/Prehistory of Textiles in the Near East, 41–54.

Andersson, P. C. 2018 Early craft uses of plant and animal fiber. *Quaternary International* 468, Part B, 211–290.

Andersson Strand, E. 2010 The experimental textile archaeology. In E. Andersson Strand, M. Gleba, U. Mannering, C. Munkholt and M. Ringgaard (eds.), *North European Symposium for Archaeological Textiles X.* Ancient Textiles Series 5. Oxford and Oakville, 1–3.

Andersson Strand, E. 2011 Tools and textiles – production and organisation in Birka and Hedeby. In S. Sigmundsson (ed.), *Viking Settlements and Viking Society. Papers from the Proceedings of the Sixteenth Viking Congress, Reykjavík and Reykholt, 16th–23rd August 2009.* Reykjavík, 1–17.

Andersson Strand, E., 2012 The textile chaîne opératoire: using a multidisciplinary approach to textile archaeology with a focus on the ancient Near East. In *Paléorient* 38.1–2. Dossier thématique/Thematic file, C. Breniquet, M. Tengberg, E. Andersson and M.-L. Nosch (eds.), Préhistoire des Textiles au Proche-Orient/Prehistory of Textiles in the Near East, 21–40.

Andersson Strand, E. 2014 Sheep, wool and textile production. An interdisciplinary approach to the complexity of wool working. In C. Breniquet and C. Michel (eds.), *Wool Economy in the Ancient Near East and the Aegean. From the Beginnings of Sheep Husbandry to Institutional Textile Industry*. Ancient Textiles Series 17. Oxford and Philadelphia, 41–51.

Andersson Strand, E. 2015 Introduction. In E. Andersson Strand and M.-L. Nosch (eds.), *Tools, Textiles and Contexts. Investigating Textile Production in the Aegean and Eastern Mediterranean Bronze Age*. Ancient Textiles Series 21. Oxford and Philadephia, vii–xiii.

Andersson Strand, E., Frei, K. M., Gleba, M., Mannering, U., Nosch M.-L. and Skals, I. 2010 Old textiles – new possibilities. *European Journal of Archaeology* 13.2, 149–173.

Andersson Strand, E., Breniquet, C., Nosch, M.-L. and Tengberg, M. 2012 Introduction au dossier 'Préhisoire des textiles au Proche-Orient'/Introduction to the file 'Prehistory of textiles in the Near East.' *Paléorient* 38.1–2. Dossier thématique/Thematic file, C. Breniquet, M. Tengberg, E. Andersson and M.-L. Nosch (eds.), Préhistoire des Textiles au Proche-Orient/Prehistory of Textiles in the Near East, 13–20.

Andersson Strand, E. and Nosch, M.-L. (eds.) 2015 *Tools, Textiles and Contexts. Investigating Textile Production in the Aegean and Eastern Mediterranean Bronze Age*. Ancient Textiles Series 21. Oxford and Philadelphia.

Andersson Strand, E., Breniquet, C. and Michel, C. 2017 Textile imprints on bullae from Kültepe. In F. Kulakoğlu and G. Barjamovic (eds.), *Movement, Resources, Interactions. Proceedings of the 2nd Kültepe International Meeting, Kültepe, 26–30 July 2015*, Kültepe International Meetings 2. Turnhout, 87–104.

Banck-Burgess, J. 2016 *Unterschätzt. Die Textilien aus den Pfahlbauten. In 4000 Jahre Pfahlbauten*. Ostfildern, 358–364.

Bar-Adon, P. 1980 *The Cave of the Treasure*. Judean Desert Studies. Jerusalem.

Barber, E. J. W. 1991 *Prehistoric Textiles. The Development of Cloth in the Neolithic and Bronze Ages with Special Reference to the Aegean*. Princeton.

Barber, E. J. W. 1994 *Women's Work. The First 20,000 Years. Women, Cloth, and Society in Early Time*. New York and London.

Bazzanella, M. 2012 Italy: Neolithic and Bronze Age. In M. Gleba and U. Mannering (eds.), *Textiles and Textile Production in Europe: From Prehistory to AD 400*. Ancient Textile Series 11. Oxford and Oakville, 203–213.

Becker, C., Benecke, N., Grabundžija, A., Küchelmann, H.-Ch., Pollock, S., Schier, W., Schoch, Ch., Schrakamp, I., Schütt, B. and Schumacher, M. 2016 The Textile Revolution. Research into the origin and spread of wool production between the Near East and Central Europe. In G. Graßhoff and M. Meyer (eds.), *eTOPOI. Journal for Ancient Studies. Special Volume 6: Space and Knowledge. Topoi Research Group Articles*, 102–151 (http://journal.topoi.org/index.php/etopoi/article/view/253, accessed 5 January 2018).

Bender Jørgensen, L. 2012a Introduction to part II: technology as practice. In M. L. Stig Sørensen and K. Rebay-Salisbury (eds.), *Embodied Knowledge. Perspectives on Belief and Technology*. Oxford, 91–94.

Bender Jørgensen, L. 2012b Spinning faith. In M. L. Stig Sørensen and K. Rebay-Salisbury (eds.), *Embodied Knowledge. Perspectives on Belief and Technology*. Oxford, 128–136.

Bender Jorgensen, L. and Rast-Eicher, A. 2016 Innovations in European Bronze Age textiles. *Prähistorische Zeitschrift* 91.1, 68–102.

Bender Jørgensen, L. and Rast-Eicher, A. 2017 Cordage, basketry, textiles and hides. In Çatalhöyük 2017 Archive Report, 181–183 (http://catalhoyuk.com/sites/default/files/Archive_Report_2017.pdf, accessed 2 February 2018).

Bender Jørgensen, L. and Rast-Eicher, A. 2018 Fibres for Bronze Age textiles. In L. Bender Jørgensen, J. Sofaer and M. L. Stig Sørensen (eds.), *Creativity in the Bronze Age. Understanding Innovation in Pottery, Textile, and Metalwork Production*. Cambridge, 25–49.

Bergfjord, C., Karg, S., Rast-Eicher, A., Nosch, M.-L., Mannering, U., Allaby, R. G., Murphy, B. M. and Holst, B. 2010 Comment on '30,000-Year-Old Wild Flax Fibers'. *Science* 328, 1634-b (https://doi.org/10.1126/science.1186345, accessed 2 October 2018.).

Boyd, B. 2018 Ecologies of fiber-work: animal technologies and invisible craft practices in prehistoric southwest Asia. *Quaternary International* 468, 250–261 (DOI: https://doi.org/10.1016/j.quaint.2017.06.050, accessed 24 April 2018).

Brandt, L. Ø., 2015 Unravelling textile mysteries with DNA analysis. In M.-L. Nosch, Z. Feng and L. Varadarajan (eds.), *Global Textile Encounters*. Ancient Textiles Series 20. Oxford and Philadelphia, 81–85.

Brandt, L. Ø., Tranekjer, L. D., Mannering, U., Ringgaard, M., Frei, K. M., Willerslev, E., Gleba, M. and Gilbert, M. T. P. 2011 Characterising the potential of sheep wool for ancient DNA analyses. *Archaeological and Anthropological Sciences* 3, 209–221.

Breniquet C. 2008 *Essai sur le tissage en Mésopotamie des premières communautés sédentaires au milieu du IIIe millénaire avant J.-C.* Travaux de la Maison René-Ginouvès 5. Paris.

Breniquet, C. 2010 Weaving in Mesopotamia during the Bronze Age: archaeology, techniques, iconography. In C. Michel and M.-L. Nosch (eds.), *Textile Terminologies in the Ancient Near East and Mediterranean from the Third to the First Millennia BC*. Ancient Textiles Series 8. Oxford and Oakville, 52–67.

Breniquet, C. 2013 Functions and uses of textiles in the Ancient Near East. In M.-L. Nosch, H. Koefoed and E. Andersson Strand (eds.), *Textile Production and Consumption in the Ancient Near East. Archaeology, Epigraphy, Iconography*. Ancient Textiles Series 12. Oxford and Oakville, 1–25.

Breniquet, C. 2014 The archaeology of wool in early Mesopotamia. In C. Breniquet and C. Michel (eds.), *Wool Economy in the Ancient Near East and the Aegean. From the Beginnings of Sheep Husbandry to Institutional Textile Industry*. Ancient Textiles Series 17. Oxford and Philadelphia, 52–78.

Breniquet, C., Tengberg, M., Andersson, E. and Nosch, M.-L. (eds.) 2012 Préhistoire des Textiles au Proche-Orient/Prehistory of Textiles in the Near East. *Paléorient* 38.1–2. Dossier thématique/Thematic file.

Breniquet, C. and Michel, C. (eds.) 2014a *Wool Economy in the Ancient Near East and the Aegean. From the Beginnings of Sheep Husbandry to Institutional Textile Industry*. Ancient Textiles Series 17. Oxford and Philadelphia.

Breniquet, C. and Michel, C. 2014b Wool economy in the Ancient Near East and the Aegean. In C. Breniquet and C. Michel (eds.), *Wool Economy in the Ancient Near East and the Aegean. From the Beginnings of Sheep Husbandry to Institutional Textile Industry*. Ancient Textiles Series 17. Oxford and Philadelphia, 1–11.

Broudy, E. 1979 *The Book of Looms. A History of the Handloom from Ancient Times to the Present*. Hanover and London.

Brunton, G. and Caton-Thompson, G. 1928 *The Badarian Civilisation and Predynastic Remains Near Badari*. London.

Burke, B. 2010 *From Minos to Midas, Ancient Cloth Production in the Aegean and in Anatolia*. Ancient Textiles Series 7. Oxford and Oakville.

Burnham, D. K. 1980 *Warp and Weft. A Textile Terminology*. Ontario.

Cardon, D. 2003 *Le monde des teintures naturelles*, Paris.

Carington Smith, J. 1975 Spinning, weaving and textile manufacture in Prehistoric Greece – from the beginning of the Neolithic to the end of the Mycenaean Ages; with particular reference to the evidence found on archaeological excavations. Unpublished PhD thesis, University of Tasmania.

Carington Smith, J. 1992 Spinning and weaving equipment. In W. A. McDonald and N. C. Wilkie (eds.), *Excavations at Nichoria in Southwest Greece. Vol. II. The Bronze Age Occupation*. Minneapolis, 674–711.

Chmielewski, T. and Gardyński, L. 2010 New frames of archaeometrical description of spindle whorls: a case study of the Late Eneolithic spindle whorls from the 1C site in Gródek, district Hrubieszów, Poland. *Archaeometry* 52.5, 869–881.

Crowfoot, G. M. 1931 *Methods of Hand Spinning in Egypt and the Sudan*. Bankfield Museum Notes, Second Series 12. Halifax.

Crowfoot, G. M. 1954 Textiles, basketry, and mats. In Ch. Singer, E. J. Holmyard and A. R. Hall (eds.), *The History of Technology. Volume I. From Early Times to Fall of Ancient Empires*. Oxford, 413–455.

Crowley, J., 2012 Prestige clothing in the Bronze Age Aegean. In M.-L. Nosch and R. Laffineur (eds.), *KOSMOS. Jewellery, Adornment and Textiles in the Aegean Bronze Age. Proceedings of the 13th International Aegean Conference/13e Rencontre égéenne internationale, University of Copenhagen, Danish National Research Foundation's Centre for Textile Research, 21–26 April 2010*. Aegaeum 33. Leuven and Liège, 231–238.

Demant, I. 2017 Making a reconstruction of the Egtved clothing. *Archaeological Textiles Review* 59, 33–43.

Desrosiers, S. 2010 Textile terminologies and classifications: Some methodological and chronological aspects. In C. Michel and M.-L. Nosch (eds.), *Textile Terminologies in the Ancient Near East and Mediterranean from the Third to the First Millennia BC*. Ancient Textiles Series 8. Oxford and Oakville, 23–51.

Emery, I. 1980 *The Primary Structures of Fabrics. An Illustrated Classification*. Baltimore.

Frangipane, M., Andersson Strand, E., Laurito, R., Möller-Wiering, S., Nosch, M.-L., Rast-Eicher, A. and Wisti Lassen, A. 2009 Arslantepe, Malatya (Turkey): textiles, tools and imprints of fabrics from the 4th to the 2nd millennium BCE. *Paléorient* 35.1, 5–30.

Frei, K. M. 2014 Provenance of archaeological wool textiles: new case studies. *Open Journal of Archaeometry* 2, 5239 (https://doi.org/10.4081/arc.2014.5239, accessed January 2018).

Frei, K. M., 2015 The traceable origin of textiles. In M.-L. Nosch, Z. Feng and L. Varadarajan (eds.) *Global Textile Encounters*. Ancient Textiles Series 20. Oxford and Philadelphia, 86–92.

Frei, K. M., Mannering, U., Vanden Berghe, I. and Kristiansen, K. 2017 Bronze Age wool: provenance and dye investigations of Danish textiles. *Antiquity* 91.357, 640–654.

Fuller, D. Q., Bogaard, A., Charles, M. and Filipović, D. 2014 Macro- and micro- botanical remains from the 2013 and 2014 seasons. *Çatalhöyük 2014 Archive Report*, 118–129 (http://catalhoyuk.com/sites/default/files/media/pdf/Archive_Report_2014_0.pdf, accessed 2 February 2018).

Gaspa, S., Michel, C. and Nosch, M.-L. 2017 *Textile Terminologies from the Orient to the Mediterranean and Europe, 1000 BC to 1000 AD*. Zea E-Books 56 (http://digitalcommons.unl.edu/zeabook/56, accessed 15 March 2018).

Gibbs, K. T. 2008 Pierced clay disks and Late Neolithic textile production. In J. M. Córdoba, M. Molist, C. Pérez, I. Rubio and S. Martínez (eds.), *Proceedings of the 5th International Congress on the Archaeology of the Ancient Near East, Madrid, April 3–8 2006*. Madrid, 89–96.

Gilligan, I. 2010 The prehistoric development of clothing: archaeological implications of a thermal model. *Journal of Archaeological Method and Theory* 17, 15–80.

Gilligan, I. 2016 Clothing. In T. K. Shackelford and V. A. Weekes-Shackelford (eds.), *Encyclopedia of Evolutionary Psychological Science*, 1–8 (https://doi.org/10.1007/978–3–319–16999–6_3009–1, accessed 15 March 2018).

Gilligan, I. 2017 Clothing and hypothermia as limitations for midlatitude hominin settlement during the Pleistocene. A comment on Hosfield 2016. *Current Anthropology* 58, 534–535.

Gleba, M. 2008 *Textile Production in Pre-Roman Italy*. Ancient Textile Series 4. Oxford.

Gleba, M. 2011 Textiles studies: sources and methods. *Kubaba* 2, 2–26.

Gleba, M. 2017 Tracing textile cultures of Italy and Greece in the early first millennium BC. *Antiquity* 91.359, 1205–1222.

Gleba, M. and Harris, S., 2018 The first plant bast fibre technology: identifying splicing in archaeological textiles. *Archaeological and Anthropological Sciences* (https://doi.org/10.1007/s12520-018-0677-8, accessed 4 October 2018).

Gleba, M. and Mannering, U. 2012a Introduction: textile preservation, analysis and technology. In M. Gleba and U. Mannering (eds.), *Textiles and Textile Production in Europe: From Prehistory to AD 400*. Ancient Textile Series 11. Oxford and Oakville, 1–24.

Gleba, M. and Mannering, U. (eds.) 2012b *Textiles and Textile Production in Europe: From Prehistory to AD 400*. Ancient Textile Series 11. Oxford and Oakville.

Golovanova, L. V., Doronichev, V. B. and Cleghorn, N. E. 2010 The emergence of bone-working and ornamental art in the Caucasian Upper Palaeolithic. *Antiquity* 84, 299–320.

Good, I. 1998 Bronze Age cloth and clothing of the Tarim Basin: the Chärchän evidence. In V. Mair (ed.), *The Bronze Age and Early Iron Age People of Eastern Central Asia. Vol. 2: Genetics and Physical Anthropology, Metallurgy, Textiles, Geography and Climatology, History, and Mythology and Ethnology*. Journal of Indo-European Studies Monograph 26. Washington, 656–668.

Good, I. 2001 Archaeological textiles: a review of current research. *Annual Review of Anthropology* 30, 209–226.

Grabundžija, A. and Russo, E. 2016 Tools tell tales – climate trends changing threads in the prehistoric Pannonian Plain, *Documenta Praehistorica* 53, 301–326 (https://doi.org/10.4312/dp.43.15, accessed 2 October 2018).

Grömer, K. 2005 Efficiency and technique – experiments with original spindle whorls. In P. Bichler, K. Grömer, R. Hofmann-de Keijzer, A. Kern and H. Reschreite (eds.), *Hallstatt Textiles: Technical Analysis, Scientific Investigation and Experiment of Iron Age Textiles*. British Archaeological Reports International Series 1351. Oxford, 107–116.

Grömer, K., 2016 *The Art of Prehistoric Textile Making. The Development of Craft traditions and Clothing in Central Europe*. Veröffentlichungen der Prähistorischen Abteilung 5. Vienna.

Grömer, K. and Kern, D. 2010 Technical data and experiments on corded ware. *Journal of Archaeological Science* 37, 3136–3145.

Grömer, K., Russ-Popa, G. and Saliari, K. 2017 Products of animal skin from Antiquity to the Medieval Period. *Annalen des naturhistorischen Museums in Wien, Serie A*, 69–93.

Hardy, K. 2008 Prehistoric string theory. How twisted fibres helped to shape the world. *Antiquity* 82, 271–280.

Harlow, M., Michel, C. and Nosch, M.-L. 2014 *Prehistoric, Ancient Near Eastern and Aegean Textiles and Dress. An Interdisciplinary Anthology*. Ancient Textiles Series 18. Oxford and Philadelphia.

Harris, J. 2010 *5000 Years of Textiles*. London.

Harris, S. 2012 From the parochial to the universal: comparing cloth cultures in the Bronze Age. *European Journal of Archaeology* 15.1, 61–97.

Harris, S. 2014 Introduction. Leather in archaeology: between material properties, materiality and technological choices. In S. Harris and A. J. Veldmeijer (eds.), *Why Leather? The Material and Cultural Dimensions of Leather*. Leiden, 9–21.

Hodder, I. 2013 2013 Season review. In *Çatalhöyük 2013 Archive Report*, 1–7 (http://catalhoyuk.com/sites/default/files/media/pdf/Archive_Report_2013.pdf, accessed 2 February 2018).

Hoffmann, M. 1964 *The Warp-weighted Loom: Studies in the History and Technology of an Ancient Implement*. Studia Norvegica 14. Oslo.

Hofmann-de Keijzer, R. 2016 Dyeing. In K. Grömer, *Art of Prehistoric Textile Making. The Development of Craft Traditions and Clothing in Central Europe*. Veröffentlichungen der Prähistorischen Abteilung 5. Vienna, 140–169.

Hopkins, H. 2013 *Ancient Textiles, Modern Science. Re-creating Techniques through Experiment. Proceedings of the First and Second European Textile Forum 2009 and 2010*. Oxbow and Oakville.

Hosfield, R. 2017 A reply to Gilligan. *Current Anthropology* 58, 536.

Jones, B. 2015 *Ariadne's Threads: The Construction and Significance of Clothes in the Aegean Bronze Age*. Aegaeum 38. Leuven and Liège.

Kania, K. 2013a The spinning experiment – influences on yarn in spinning with a handspindle. In H. J. Hopkins (ed.), *Ancient Textiles – Modern Science. Re-creating Techniques through Experiment. Proceedings of the First and Second European Textile Forum 2009 and 2010*. Oxford and Oakville, 11–29.

Kania, K. 2013b Soft yarns, hard facts? Evaluating the results of a large-scale hand-spinning experiment. *Archaeological and Anthropological Sciences* 7.1, 1–18.

Kanold, I. B. 2017 Dyeing wool and sea silk with purple pigment from *Hexaplex trunculus*. In H. Landenius Enegren and F. Meo (eds.), *Treasures from the Sea. Sea Silk and the Shellfish Purple Dye in Antiquity*. Ancient Textiles Series 30. Oxford and Philadelphia, 67–72.

Karg, S. 2011 New research on the cultural history of the useful plant *Linum usitatissimum L.* (flax), a resource for food and textiles for 8,000 years. In S. Karg (ed.), *Special issue: FLAX – New Research on the Cultural History of the Useful Plant Linum usitatissimum L. Vegetation History and Archaeobotany* 20.6, 507–508 (https://doi.org/10.1007/s00334–011–0326-y, accessed 15 April 2018).

Karisto, M. and Grömer, K. 2017 Different solutions for a simple design: new experiments on tablet weave HallTex 152 from the salt mine Hallstatt. *Experimentelle Archäologie in Europa 16. Jahrbuch 2017. Festschrift für Mamoun Fansa zum 70. Geburstag*, 60–69.

Killen, J. T. 2007 Cloth production in Late Bronze Age Greece: the documentary evidence. In C. Gillis and M.-L. B. Nosch (eds.), *Ancient Textiles, Production, Craft and Society, Proceedings of the First International Conference on Ancient Textiles, Held at Lund Sweden and Copenhagen, Denmark, on March 19–23, 2003*. Ancient Textiles Series 1. Oxford, 50–58.

Körber-Grohne, U. and Feldtkeller, A. 1998 *Pflanzliche Rohmaterialien und Herstellungstechniken der Gewebe, Netze, Geflechte sowie anderer Produkte aus den neolithischen Siedlungen Hornstaad, Wangen, Allensbach und Sipplingen am Bodensee*. Siedlungsarchäologie im Alpenvorland V. Forschungen und Berichte zur Vor- und Frühgeschichte in Baden-Württemberg 68. Stuttgart, 131–242.

Kvavadze, E., Bar-Yosef, O., Belfer-Cohen, A., Boaretto, E., Jakeli, N., Matskevich, Z. and Meshveliani, T. 2009 30,000-year-old wild flax fibers. *Science* 325.5946, 1359 (https://doi.org/10.1126/science.1175404, accessed 2 October 2018).

Kvavadze, E., Bar-Yosef, O., Belfer-Cohen, A., Boaretto, E., Jakeli, N., Matskevich, Z. and Meshveliani, T. 2010 Response to comment on '30,000-Year-Old Wild Flax Fibers'. *Science* 328, 1634 (https://doi.org/10.1126/science.1187161, accessed 2 October 2018).

Langgut, D., Yahalom-Mack, N., Lev-Yadun, S., Kremer, E., Ullman, M. and Davidovich, U. 2016 The earliest Near Eastern wooden spinning implements. *Antiquity* 90.352, 973–990.

Lassen, A. W. 2013 Technology and palace economy in Middle Bronze Age Anatolia: the case of the crescent shaped loom weight. In M.-L. Nosch, H. Koefoed and E. Andersson Strand (eds.), *Textile Production and Consumption in the Ancient Near East. Archaeology, Epigraphy, Iconography*. Ancient Textiles Series 12. Oxford and Oakville, 78–92.

Lassen, A. W. 2015 Weaving with crescent shaped loom weights. An investigation of a special kind of loom weight. In E. Andersson Strand and M.-L. Nosch (eds.), *Tools, Textiles and Contexts. Investigating Textile Production in the Aegean and Eastern Mediterranean Bronze Age*. Ancient Textiles Series 21. Oxford and Philadelphia, 127–137.

Laurito, R. 2007 Ropes and textiles. In M. Frangipane (ed.), *Arslantepe. Cretulae. An Early Centralised Administrative System Before Writing*. Arslantepe V. Roma, 381–394.

Leroi-Gourhan, A. 1982 The archaeology of Lascaux cave. *Scientific American* 246.6, 104–113.

Mårtensson, L., Andersson, E., Nosch, M.-L. and Batzer, A. 2006 *Technical Report. Experimental Archaeology. Part 2:2 Whorl or Bead? 2006. Tools and Textiles – Texts and Contexts Research Programme. The Danish National Research Foundation's Centre for Textile Research (CTR), University of Copenhagen* (http:// ctr.hum.ku.dk/research-programmes-and-projects/previous-programmes-and-projects/tools/technical_report_2–2__ experimental_arcaheology.pdf, accessed 15 April 2018).

Mårtensson, L., Nosch, M.-L. and Andersson Strand, E. 2009 Shape of things: understanding a loom weight. *Oxford Journal of Archaeology* 28.4, 373–398.

McCorriston, J. 1997 The fiber revolution. Textile extensification, alienation, and social stratification in ancient Mesopotamia. *Current Anthropology* 38.4, 517–535.

Mellaart, J. 1962 Excavations at Çatal Hüyük: first preliminary report, 1961. *Anatolian Studies* 12, 41–65.

Michel, C. and Nosch, M.-L. (eds.) 2010 *Textile Terminologies in the Ancient Near East and Mediterranean from the Third to the First Millennia BC*. Ancient Textiles Series 8. Oxford and Oakville.

Müller, W. 2004 Bemerkungen zur den Tonplomben und Siegelabdrücken auf Gefässen und ‚Gewichten'. In I. Pini (ed.), *Kleinere griechische Sammlungen. Neufunde aus Griechenland und der westlichen Türkei. Ägina – Mykonos*. Corpus der minoischen und mykenischen Siegel V Suppl. 3.1. Mainz, 43–60.

Müller, W. and Pini, I. 1997 Die 'Schnüre' in den Plomben und die Gegenstandsabdrücke. In I. Pini (ed.), *Die Tonplomben aus dem Nestorpalast von Pylo*s. Mainz, 67–69.

Nadel, D., Danin, A., Werker, E., Schick, T., Kislev, M. E. and Stewart, K. 1994 19,000-year-old twisted fibers from Ohalo II. *Current Anthropology* 35.4, 451–458.

Nørgaard, A. 2008 A weaver's voice: making reconstructions of Danish Iron Age textiles. In M. Gleba, C. Munkholt and M.-L. Nosch (eds.), *Dressing the Past*. Ancient Textiles Series 3. Oxford, 43–58.

Nosch, M.-L. 2012 From texts to textiles in the Aegean Bronze Age. In M.-L. Nosch and R. Laffineur (eds.), *KOSMOS. Jewellery, Adornment and Textiles in the Aegean Bronze Age. Proceedings of the 13th International Aegean Conference/13e Rencontre égéenne internationale, University of Copenhagen, Danish National Research Foundation's Centre for Textile Research, 21–26 April 2010*. Aegaeum 33. Leuven and Liège, 43–53.

Nosch, M.-L. 2015 The Wool Age: traditions and innovations in textile production, consumption and administration in the Late Bronze Age Aegean. In J. Weilhartner and F. Ruppenstein (eds.) *Tradition and Innovation in the Mycenaean Palatial Polities. Proceedings of an International Symposium held at the Austrian Academy of Sciences, Institute for Oriental and European Archaeology, Aegean and Anatolia Department, Vienna, 1–2 March, 2013*. Österreichische Akademie der Wissenschaften. Philosophisch-historische Klasse Denkschriften 487. Band. Mykenische Studien 34. Vienna, 167–201.

Nosch, M.-L. and Laffineur, R. (eds.), *KOSMOS. Jewellery, Adornment and Textiles in the Aegean Bronze Age. Proceedings of the 13th International Aegean Conference/13e Rencontre égéenne internationale, University of Copenhagen, Danish National Research Foundation's Centre for Textile Research, 21–26 April 2010*. Aegaeum 33. Leuven and Liège.

Olofsson, L. 2015 An introduction to experimental archaeology and textile research. In E. Andersson Strand and M.-L. Nosch (eds.), *Tools, Textiles and Contexts. Investigating Textile Production in the Aegean and Eastern Mediterranean Bronze Age*. Ancient Textile Series 21. Oxford and Philadelphia, 25–38.

Olofsson, L., Andersson Strand, E. and Nosch, M.-L. 2015 Experimental testing of Bronze Age textile tools. In E. Andersson Strand and M.-L. Nosch (eds.), *Tools, Textiles and Contexts. Investigating Textile Production in the Aegean and Eastern Mediterranean Bronze Age*. Ancient Textile Series 21. Oxford and Philadelphia, 75–100.

O'Sullivan, N. J., Teasdale, M. D., Mattiangeli, V., Maixner, F., Pinhasi, R., Bradley, D. G. and Zink, A. 2016 A whole mitochondria analysis of the Tyrolean Iceman's leather provides insights into the animal sources of Copper Age clothing. *Scientific Reports* 6, 31279 (https://doi.org/10.1038/srep31279, accessed 2 October 2018).

Peacock, E. E. 2001 The contribution of experimental archaeology to the research of ancient textiles. In P. Walton Rogers, L. Bender Jørgensen and A. Rast-Eicher (eds.), *The Roman Textile Industry and its Influence. A Birthday Tribute to John Peter Wild*. Exeter, 181–192.

Pèrles, C. 2001 *The Early Neolithic in Greece. The First Farming Communities in Europe*. Cambridge (http://dx.doi.org/10.1017/CBO9780511612855, accessed 15 April 2018).

Piqué, R., Romero, S., Palomo, A., Tarrús, J., Terradas, X. and Bogdanovic, I. 2018 The production and use of cordage at the Early Neolithic site of La Draga (Banyoles, Spain). *Quaternary International* 468 (July), 262–270 (https://doi.org/10.1016/j.quaint.2016.05.024, accessed 23 April 2018).

Popescu, C. and Wortmann, F.-J. 2010 Wool – structure, mechanical properties and technical products based on animal fibres. In J. Müssig (ed.), *Industrial Applications of Natural Fibres. Structure, Properties and Technical Applications*. Chichester, 254–266.

Ræder Knudsen, L. 2012 Case study: the tablet woven borders of Verucchio. In M. Gleba and U. Mannering (eds.), *Textiles and Textile Production in Europe: From Prehistory to AD 400*. Ancient Textile Series 11. Oxford and Oakville, 254–263.

Ræder Knudsen, L. 2014 Tacit knowledge and interpretation of archaeological tablet-woven textiles. In S. Bergerbrant and S. H. Fossøy (eds.), *A Stitch in Time. Essays in Honour of Lise Bender Jørgensen*. Gothenburg, 91–110.

Rahmstorf, L. 2008 *Kleinfunde aus Tiryns. Terrakotta, Stein, Bein und Glas/Fayence vornehmlich aus der Spätbronzezeit*. Tiryns. Forschungen und Berichte 16. Wiesbaden.

Rahmstorf, L. 2011 Handmade pots and crumbling loomweights: 'Barbarian' elements in eastern Mediterranean in the last quarter of the 2nd millennium BC. In V. Karageorghis and O. Kouka (eds.), *On Cooking Pots, Drinking Cups, Loomweights and Ethnicity in Bronze Age Cyprus and Neighbouring Regions. An International Archaeological Symposium Held in Nicosia, November 6th–7th 2010*. Nicosia, 315–330.

Rahmstorf, L. 2015 An introduction to the investigation of archaeological textile tools. In E. Andersson Strand and M.-L.

Nosch (eds.), *Tools, Textiles and Contexts. Investigating Textile Production in the Aegean and Eastern Mediterranean Bronze Age.* Ancient Textiles Series 21. Oxford and Philadelphia, 1–23.

Rast-Eicher, A. 2005 Bast before wool: the first textiles. In P. Bichler, K. Grömer, R. Hofmann-de Keijzer, A. Kern and H. Reschreiter (eds.), *Hallstatt Textiles. Technical Analysis, Scientific Investigation and Experiment on Iron Age Textiles.* British Archaeological Report International Series 1351. Oxford, 117–132.

Rast-Eicher, A. 2016 *Fibres. Microscopy of Archaeological Textiles and Furs.* Archaeolingua 36. Budapest.

Rast-Eicher, A. and Dietrich, A. 2015 *Neolithische und bronzezeitliche Gewebe und Geflechte. Die Funde aus den Seeufersiedlungen im Kanton Zürich.* Monographien der Kantonsarchäologie Zürich 46. Zürich.

Rooijakkers, C. T. 2012 Spinning animal fibres at Late Neolithic Tell Sabi Abyad, Syria? In *Paléorient* 38.1–2. Dossier thématique/ Thematic file, C. Breniquet, M. Tengberg, E. Andersson and M.-L. Nosch (eds.), Préhistoire des Textiles au Proche-Orient/ Prehistory of Textiles in the Near East, 93–109.

Rots, V., Hardy, B. L., Serangeli, J. and Conard, N. J. 2015 Residue and microwear analyses of the stone artifacts from Schöningen. *Journal of Human Evolution* 89, 298–308.

Ryder, M. L. 1965 Report of textiles from Çatal Hüyük. *Anatolian Studies* 15, 175–176.

Ryder, M. L. 1987 The evolution of the fleece. *Scientific American* 256.1, 100–107.

Ryder, M. L. 1992 The interaction between biological and technological change during the development of different fleece types in sheep. *Anthropozoologica* 16, 131–140.

Schick, T. 1988 Nahal Hemar Cave. Cordage, basketry and fabrics. *'Atiquot. English Series* 18, 31–43.

Schick, T. 1989 Early Neolithic twined basketry and fabrics from the Nahal Hemar Cave, Israel. In *Tissage, corderie, vannerie. IXe Rencontres Internationales d'Archéologie et d'Histoire, Antibes, Octobre 1988.* Juan-les-Pins, 41–52.

Schick, T. 1995 A 10,000 year old comb from Wadi Murabba'at in the Judean Desert. *'Atiquot. English Series* 27, 199–202.

Seiler-Baldinger, A. 1994 *Textiles: A Classification of Techniques.* Washington, DC.

Shamir, O. 2014 Textiles, basketry and other organic artifacts of the Chalcolithic period in the Southern Levant. In M. Sebbane, O. Misch-Brandl and D. M. Master (eds.), *Masters of Fire Copper Age Art from Israel.* Princeton, 139–152.

Shamir, O. 2015 Textiles from the Chalcolithic period, Early and Middle Bronze Age in the southern Levant. *Archaeological Textiles Review* 57, 12–25.

Shaw, M. C. and Chapin, A. P. 2016 *Woven Threads. Patterned Textiles of the Aegean Bronze Age.* Ancient Textiles Series 22. Oxford and Philadelphia.

Shimony, C. 1995 Fiber identification. *'Atiquot. English Series* 27, 204.

Siennicka, M. 2012 Textile production in Early Helladic Tiryns. In M.-L. Nosch and R. Laffineur (eds.), *KOSMOS. Jewellery, Adornment and Textiles in the Aegean Bronze Age. Proceedings of the 13th International Aegean Conference/13e Rencontre égéenne internationale, University of Copenhagen, Danish National Research Foundation's Centre for Textile Research, 21–26 April 2010.* Aegaeum 33. Leuven and Liège, 65–76.

Siennicka, M. 2015 Textiles in a Social Context and First Textiles – two conferences on prehistoric textiles. *Archaeological Textiles Review* 57, 128–129.

Siennicka, M. 2018 Étude d'empreintes de textile. In A. Philippa-Touchais, N. Papadimitriou and G. Touchais (eds.), La Deiras. *Bulletin de Correspondance Héllenique* 139–140 (2015–2016), 837–838.

Siennicka, M. forthcoming a Two textile imprints from Tomb XXI at Deiras, Argos. In G. Touchais, A. Philippa-Touchais and N. Papadimitriou (eds.), *Publication of W. Vollgraff's excavations at Deiras, Argos.*

Siennicka, M. forthcoming b Craftspeople, craftsmanship and textile production in Early Bronze Age Greece. In K. Sarri and L. Quillien (eds.), *Textile Workers. Skills, Labour and Status of Textile Craftspeople Between Prehistoric Aegean and Ancient Near East. Proceedings of the Workshop Held at the 10th ICAANE, 25. April 2016, Vienna.* Oriental and European Archaeology. International Series.

Siennicka, M., Ulanowska, A. and Rahmstorf, L. 2015 Textiles in a social context. Textile production in Europe and the Mediterranean in the 4th and 3rd millennia BCE. *The European Archaeologist* 43 (Winter), 41–44 (https://www.e-a-a.org/EAA/Publications/TEA/Archive/EAA/Navigation_Publications/TEA_content/Archive.aspx#37, accessed 2 October 2018).

Soffer, O, Adovasio, J. M. and Hyland, D. C. 2000 The 'Venus' figurines. *Current Anthropology* 41.4, 511–525.

Stordeur, D. 1989 Vannerie et tissage au Proche-Orient néolithique: IXe–Ve millénaire. In *Tissage, corderie, vannerie. IXe Rencontres Internationales d'Archéologie et d'Histoire, Antibes, Octobre 1988.* Juan-les-Pins, 19–39.

Stordeur, D. (ed.) 2000 *El Kowm 2. Une île dans le désert. La fin de Néolithique précéramique dans la steppe syrienne.* Paris.

Tiedemann, E. J. and Jakes, K. A. 2006 An exploration of prehistoric spinning technology: spinning efficiency and technology transition. *Archaeometry* 48.2, 293–307.

Tung, B. 2013 Excavations in the North Area, 2013. In *Çatalhöyük 2013 Archive Report,* 8–44 (http://catalhoyuk.com/sites/default/files/media/pdf/Archive_Report_2013.pdf, accessed 2 February 2018).

Tzachili, I. 1997 Υφαντική και υφάντρες στο Προϊστορικό Αιγαίο. Ηράκλειο and Αθήνα.

Ulanowska, A. 2016a Towards methodological principles for experience textile archaeology. Experimental approach to the Aegean Bronze Age textile techniques in the Institute of Archaeology, University of Warsaw. *Prilozi Instituta za arheologiju u Zagrebu* 33, 317–339.

Ulanowska, A. 2016b Representations of textile tools in Aegean glyptic. Cuboid seal from the Tholos Tomb A in Aghia Triada. In P. Militello and K. Żebrowska (eds.), *Sympozjum Egejskie. Proceedings of the 2nd Students' Conference in Aegean Archaeology: Methods – Researches – Perspectives. Institute of Archaeology, University of Warsaw, Poland, April 25th, 2014.* Syndesmoi 4. Catania, 109–125.

Ulanowska, A. 2017 Textile technology and Minoan glyptic. Representations of loom weights on Middle Minoan prismatic seals. In K. Żebrowska, A. Ulanowska and K. Lewartowski (eds.), *Sympozjum Egejskie. Papers in Aegean Archaeology* 1. Warsaw, 57–66.

Ulanowska. A. forthcoming a Contemporary actors and Bronze Age textile techniques from Greece. Experience approach to textile work, its specialisation and apprenticeship. In K. Sarri and L. Quillien (eds.), *Textile Workers. Skills, Labour and Status of Textile Craftspeople Between Prehistoric Aegean and Ancient Near East. Proceedings of the Workshop Held at the 10th ICAANE, 25. April 2016, Vienna.* Oriental and European Archaeology. International Series.

Ulanowska, A. forthcoming b Different skills for different fibres? The use of flax and wool in textile technology of Bronze Age Greece in light of archaeological experiments. In W. Schier and S. Pollock (eds.), *The Competition of Fibres. Textile Production in Western Asia and Europe (5000–2000 BC).* Berlin Studies of the Ancient World.

Verhecken, A. 2010 The moment of inertia: a parameter for the functional classification of worldwide spindle-whorls from all periods. In E. Andersson Strand, M. Gleba, U. Mannering, C. Munkholt and M. Ringgaard (eds.), *North European Symposium for Archaeological Textiles X.* Ancient Textiles Series 5. Oxford and Oakville, 257–270.

Verhecken, A. 2013 Spinning with the hand spindle: an analysis of the mechanics and its implications on yarn quality. *Archaeological Textiles Review* 55, 97–101.

Vogelsang-Eastwood, G. 1992 *The Production of Linen in Pharaonic Egypt.* Leiden.

Vogelsang-Eastwood, G. M. 1993 One of the oldest textiles in the world? The Çayönü textile, *Archaeological Textiles Newsletter* 16 (June), 4–7.

Vogelsang-Eastwood, G. 2000 Textiles. In P. T. Nicholson and I. Shaw (eds.), *Ancient Egyptian Materials and Technology.* Cambridge, 268–298.

Völling, E. 2008 *Textiltechnik im Alten Orient. Rohstoffe und Herstellung.* Würzburg.

Wendrich, W. 1991 *Who is Afraid of Basketry. A Guide to Recording Basketry and Cordage for Archaeologists and Ethnologists.* Centre for Non-Western Studies Publication 6. Leiden.

Wendrich, W. 2012 (1st edition 1999) *The World According to Basketry. An Ethno-archaeological Interpretation of Basketry Production in Egypt.* Costen Digital Archaeology Series 2 (https://escholarship.org/uc/item/6n42w0rg#main, accessed 15 March 2018).

2016 World's oldest needle found in Siberian cave that stitches together human history, *The Siberian Times*, 23 August 2016 (http://siberiantimes.com/science/casestudy/news/n0711-worlds-oldest-needle-found-in-siberian-cave-that-stitches-together-human-history/, accessed 14 February 2018).

2

Early loom types in ancient societies

Eva Andersson Strand

Introduction

One general challenge for archaeology is that we can never expect to find all remains of the past and that an archaeological record never mirrors ancient everyday life accurately.[1] Houses and furnishing, tools and textiles (and the people themselves) have naturally disappeared. This premise is particularly valid for textile research, where the preservation of textiles and tools is extremely rare. Textile tools, such as looms, were, and are, preferably made of perishable materials, *e.g.* wood, and therefore rarely preserved. In the interpretation of textile production, it is crucial to be aware of and consider this fundamental premise in our reconstruction of the production in the past. Still, there are questions to be asked and discussed which can give new perspectives and approaches and an important understanding of the complexity of, as well as the social, cultural and economic impact of, textiles and textile craft in ancient societies. The aim of this paper is therefore to render looms visible even in areas and periods where the archaeological evidence is scarce or absent, and, furthermore, to initiate a discussion to reach a more differentiated view of looms and textile production. The first part of this paper focuses on basic knowledge of loom set-up and weaving, which (and how) various sources can be used when studying loom types and weaving. Next, the uses and suitability of different loom types, their possibilities and limitations will be compared and discussed. Finally, the question of why there has been, or rather is, a need for different types of loom will be raised in order to prompt discussion of some of the more general assumptions.

The focus is on the types of looms that were already being used in ancient societies and not the more advanced looms such as treadle looms or draw looms. The target area is Europe and the ancient Near East. Unfortunately, it is not possible to include a full discussion of looms and weaving from a global perspective (for example South America or South-East Asia) in this paper.

The study of looms

A commonly used definition of a loom today is 'a device used to weave cloth and tapestry. The basic purpose of any loom is to hold the warp threads under tension to facilitate the interweaving of the weft threads. The precise shape of the loom and its mechanics may vary, but the basic function is the same'.[2] Another more general definition is that of Eric Broudy, who writes in his publication *The Book of Looms*: 'for this book, however, the term "loom" is best defined more generally as any frame or contrivance for holding warp threads parallel to permit the interlacing of the weft at the right angles to form a web'.[3] The latter definition is broader and includes other textile techniques in addition to weaving. This is important in the following discussion and this text will therefore refer to Broudy's definition of a loom.

The idea of stretching the warp threads between two beams appears in different variations in many different cultures and time periods all over the world.[4] Due to the fact that looms do not survive in the archaeological record, it is yet not possible to estimate how far in time this tradition goes back. With this device, one can produce a large piece of dense cloth suitable for, for example, clothing. Additionally, the stretched warp threads, often divided into different sheds, make it easier to insert the weft. Altogether this makes a loom a very efficient tool on which one can produce many different types and qualities of fabrics.

Since the device can be made of only one or more wooden bars/parts, it is difficult to identify a loom in an archaeological context, especially for excavators who have no or little experience of this type of tool or weaving. It is therefore essential to study looms with the aid of different sources and from different types of evidence and perspectives, and it is also important to understand how a specific type of loom works.

Before weaving

It is important, before discussing different loom types, to understand the loom set-up and weaving process. Before weaving, the warp threads have to be prearranged in a more or less fixed set. The set-up is done in slightly different ways, depending on which loom type is being used, but the principles for the three loom types discussed in this paper are generally the same. The first step is to warp the warp threads. Depending on the length of the fabric and the desired density (number of threads per centimetre), the number of metres of yarn required has to be calculated. For example, the weaving of a fabric that is 2 m wide and 4 m long, with 20 threads per centimetre, requires approximately 16,000 m of warp yarn. Each warp thread has to be of the intended length of the fabric plus approximately 2–5% needed for thrums. In order to make the warping easier, one can warp

several threads together. One warping method, known from Middle Bronze Age Egypt as well as from ethnographic sources, is to wind the yarn between pegs fastened on a wall (Fig. 2.1 A).[5] Another method also known from the Bronze Age Mediterranean is to wind the warp yarn on supported uprights (Fig. 2.1 B).[6] The length between the first and the last peg/upright is the length of the warp threads, including thrums. A third warping method for the horizontal ground loom is to warp and heddle at the same time. This method is still today used by the Bedouins in, for example, Jordan. The process of warping the warp-weighted loom can be slightly different; in this case, the warp threads are woven into a band known as a starting border band. This method is well known from ethnographic studies in northern Scandinavia, which have documented the use of slightly different warping frames associated with this technique; for example, the warping frame with three uprights as used by the Sami (Fig. 2.1 C).[7]

The prepared warp is then stretched between two bars (horizontal and vertical two-bar looms) or, in the case of the warp-weighted loom, the starting border is tied to the starting border rod and the warp threads are fastened to loom weights (Fig. 2.2). It is important that the warp threads are

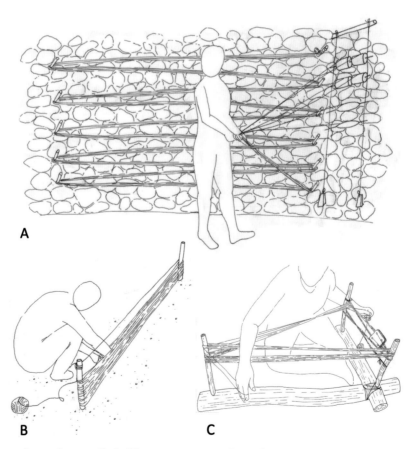

Fig. 2.1 A. Warping on pegs fastened to a wall; B. Warping on supported uprights; C. Warping on a warping frame (drawing: Annika Jeppsson; © Annika Jeppsson and CTR).

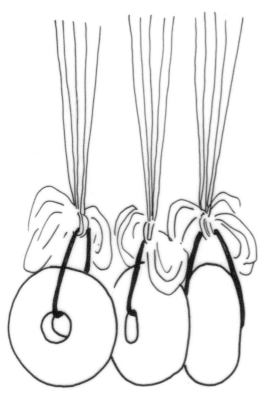

Fig. 2.2 The warp threads attached to the loom weight (drawing: Annika Jeppsson; © Annika Jeppsson and CTR).

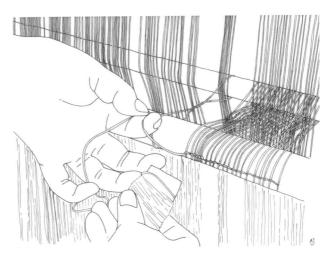

Fig. 2.3 Heddling the warp threads to heddle rods (drawing: Annika Jeppsson; © Annika Jeppsson and CTR).

held taut; if the threads are too loose it will not be possible to change the shed (the space through which the weft is passed) when weaving, and if they are too taut it is more difficult to pack the threads. Similarly, if the threads are very thin they might break. Another important factor is that the warp threads should hang straight down or slightly outwards. This is generally demonstrated on depictions of looms, independently of which type of loom is represented.[8]

In the process of weaving, the weft is inserted between the warp threads. The simplest but also most time-consuming way is to pick each warp thread individually and insert the weft thread underneath. This technique is especially used for weaves with non-continuous patterns such as tapestry weaving.

However, to make the weaving process faster, the warp threads can be divided into different layers so that sheds can be created. This is done by heddling the warp threads to heddle rods (Fig. 2.3). The heddles, usually made of string, are used to attach each individual warp thread to the heddle rods. When weaving tabby on a vertical two-bar loom or a horizontal ground loom, warp threads number 1, 3, 5, 7, 9, *etc.* are attached to a heddle rod. The heddle bar can then be used to lift all these alternate warp threads at the same time, thus creating a shed.

Once the set-up is completed, one can start to weave. In a tabby weave, the heddle rod is lifted and the weft thread is inserted between the two layers of warp threads.

In the next step, the first layer of threads goes back into its original position and the weft thread is again inserted between the two layers. The heddle rod is then lifted again, and so on. When weaving twill, which requires more than two sheds and more than one rod, the weaving depends on how many layers of threads need to be lifted at the same time; for example, in a 2/2 twill two of the four layers are always lifted at the same time. Before inserting a new weft thread, the first weft has to be packed with a tool such as a wooden beater. The weft can be kept on a shuttle, which could be a wooden stick or a bone pin on which the weft yarn is wound. A multifunctional weaving tool is the single ended or double ended pin-beater, a wooden or bone stick with one or two pointed ends. This can be used to separate the threads in the weave. A pin-beater is also useful when producing a weave with non-continuous patterns, to help lift the warp threads.[9] Another weaving tool sometimes found is a weaving comb, especially used for weaves with non-continuous patterns.

How can we gain a more differentiated understanding for the use of loom types?

When considering the evidence of looms or the lack of looms in different areas and time periods, it is important to take into account various types of evidence that we have in the various regions. In order to gain new insights and perspectives, we need to combine different methods and approaches.

Archaeological evidence

Tools: looms and/or parts of looms and other tools related to weaving such as pin-beaters, weaving beaters and weaving combs should always be recorded carefully.[10] Parts of warping devices should also be noticed.

Textiles can, in rare cases and if well preserved, indicate characteristics distinctive for a specific loom type, such as the woven starting border for a warp-weighted loom or warp locks indicating that the fabric has been woven on a two-bar loom.[11]

Contexts: features that are important to note include any postholes that held loom uprights, associated pits, rows or clusters of loom weights and furthermore, their positioning in a room. Additionally, walls or places suitable for warping should be taken into account.

Iconography: images of textile tools and textile production can be found on Egyptian friezes, Greek vases, Roman tombs, and drawings from later historical periods such as drawings of the 19th-century Icelandic loom.[12] Nevertheless, it is clear that the majority of these images were not primarily made to show the loom and how it was used. It is important to take this aspect into consideration, for example when discussing large-scale production for everyday use. Even if the looms are often depicted in detail and give the impression that the artist was painting/drawing from life, it is still important to be aware that the loom type featured does not necessarily represent the loom on which all everyday textiles were produced.

Often images of both the warp-weighted looms and the two-bar looms are a part of a story, tale or myth. Their primary objective is not to depict an exact construction of the loom, but rather to focus on the loom representation itself, as on a painting on a Greek drinking vessel showing Telemachus and Penelope at the loom. The ladies on the Carolingian (9th-century) Utrecht Psalter are perhaps not producing textiles for everyday use but rather textiles for the church, something that during this period had become a common task among high-status women.[13] Also, in the case of the paintings in Roman and Etruscan tombs, for example, were they made to show the tools or production processes in use or do they appear merely as an indication of the occupation of the deceased or episodes from their daily life?

Another aspect is the dating of the iconography. The date of an image can never be considered as a specific dating of or the origin of various loom types. The loom could have been frequently used also in other places long before it was reproduced.

Texts: ancient written sources can give some information. They pose, however, a challenge similar to that of the iconography; such texts were generally not written in order to describe the looms and how they function. They are usually part of a story or an administrative text.[14] One example is a 4000-year-old Ur III text (T.32 Rs I 6–14) translated by H. Waetzoldt, which gives a clear description of the production of a gauze textile 3.5×3.5 m made of hard twisted warp thread and heavier weft threads made of a mixed and combed fourth-class wool; however, the text does not tell us about the loom type or any tool used. Actually, many other ancient texts give information on the length and width or weight of the textiles. This, of course, is important for our understanding of the textiles produced but generally this tells us little of how they were made and from what materials.[15] A different and much later example is from early Scandinavian medieval law texts such Grágás and Bualøg. In these the prices are mentioned in relation to the size of the textile. The width is generally 2–3 aln (98–147 cm) and the length of a cloth could be up to 30 aln (15 m).[16] The loom used has been interpreted to be the warp-weighted loom, but the loom type is not explicitly mentioned.[17] To conclude, it is the textiles that are important in texts, their quality, size and price, not the type of tools used to produce them. Literary sources also present the problem of the adjustment of the terminology to suit literary aims; the reader needs to be knowledgeable both about weaving and about the texts, and they are therefore evidence that is difficult to use.[18]

Ethnographical studies: these are very important for our understanding of a loom's function, its possibilities and limitations. Marta Hoffmann's work on the documentation of the warp-weighted loom in northern Scandinavia, or other studies of traditional weaving on the two-bar loom in Syria and the Egyptian horizontal ground loom, and additionally weaving using the backstrap loom in Peru, are just some examples.[19] Other important studies are Broudy and his impressive work describing looms from all around the world, and Venice Lamb's work in which she has documented looms around the Mediterranean, in the Near East and Africa.[20] Their work clearly demonstrates the complexity of identifying a loom type, since so many have been in use.

However, it is important to include in the discussion the fabric produced and the use of ethnographic sources. The fabrics manufactured in northern Scandinavia were not textiles for clothing but coarse rugs and blankets; the textiles produced in Jordan and Turkey are also generally rugs and carpets. Today, very few textiles are made for clothing on those loom types. This has to be considered when applying ethnographic knowledge to an archaeological context.

Experimental archaeology and experiments are also used in order to get a better understanding of the loom's function. Previously, several tests were made in order to reconstruct specific fabrics.[21] In the 'Land of Legends, Centre for Historical-Archaeological Research and Communication' (Lejre, Denmark), different loom types such as the warp-weighted and the vertical two-bar looms have been tested since the 1980s, focusing on the looms' suitability for different weaves.[22] At the Danish National Research Foundation's Centre for Textile Research, several tests have been done in order to assess the function of a loom weight in the warp-weighted loom.[23] Furthermore, Karina Grömer, Martin Ciszuk, Lena Hammarlund and others have also conducted several important tests and compared different loom types.[24] Since testing of tools has become more frequently used as a method in textile research, the number of tests is rapidly growing (see *e.g.* this volume). Their results give an understanding of the limitations and possibilities of different looms as well as of the differences between various loom types. It is important, however, to conduct such experiments according to specific guidelines on experimental archaeology to allow for a critical evaluation. Furthermore, one must use as authentic materials as possible. It is also essential to relate the test to the archaeological material. For example, if one wants to test a set-up of a fabric on a warp-weighted loom from a *specific time period or region*, the loom weights used should be reconstructed on the basis of corresponding archaeological finds. Furthermore, the yarn used in the loom should be of the same material and same quality as the analyses of the contemporary textiles demonstrate. If not, the results can be directly misleading.[25]

Ancient loom types

It is an open question what types of looms have been used in ancient societies and why. Many scholars, for example Margarete Hald, Marta Hoffmann, John Peter Wild, Lise Bender Jørgensen, Elizabeth Barber, Martin Ciszuk, Lena Hammarlund, Karina Grömer and Ulla Mannering, have done important research on the development and use of different types of looms.[26] The loom types generally discussed are the two-bar looms (horizontal and the vertical) and the warp-weighted loom. Important questions that have been frequently addressed include the origin and meaning of a specific loom type, and where people started to use it, how and why it spread.[27] In order to answer these questions, the first step is to understand these loom types, their differences and similarities, and gain a basic knowledge of their function.

Two-bar looms

In all looms the warp threads are stretched, and to stretch the threads between two bars is fundamental and occurs with some variation in most looms such as backstrap and treadle looms. Additionally, a two-bar loom can be vertical, horizontal and also put at an angle.[28]

Horizontal ground loom

The horizontal ground loom (Fig. 2.4) is considered to be the oldest loom type, but the earliest depiction is dated only to the early 4th millennium BC and comes from Badari, Egypt.[29] The depiction shows four-corner pegs holding two beams at either end and warp running between them. Furthermore, a piece of woven cloth and three bars painted across the middle presumably show shed – heddle – and beater bars. There is also early pictorial evidence for the use of this type of loom in the eastern Mediterranean, for example, on an early cylinder seal from Susa, an early city in today's Iran also dated to the 4th millennium BC. In paintings from Egypt, two weavers are depicted, sitting on either side of the loom, changing the shed, inserting and beating the weft. The heddle rod is supported with heddle jacks.[30]

There are few remains of these looms, such as warp beams, rods and heddle jacks, preserved in Egypt and Palestine. The interest of the use of heddles and heddle bars as presented already on the dish from Badari, Egypt, has been pointed out by Barber.[31] If the interpretation is correct, this must have made the weaving easier and faster, since all the warp threads could be lifted at the same time. The width varies: the average is 1.2–1.5 m, but there are mentions of textiles that are up to 2.7 m wide. It is difficult to estimate the length of the fabric, as it has been suggested that 'The length of the cloth woven on a ground loom is limited only to the amount of thread spun'.[32] However, it is

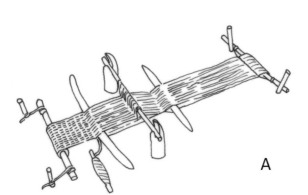

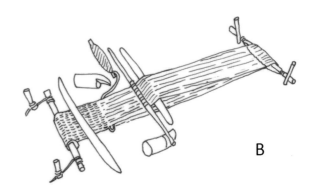

A   B

Fig. 2.4 Horizontal ground loom (drawing: Annika Jeppsson, after Broudy 1979; © Annika Jeppsson and CTR).

Fig. 2.5 Horizontal ground loom (courtesy the Beduin Bani Hamida project; photo: Cécile Michel; © Cécile Michel).

Fig. 2.6 Two-bar loom with a tubular warp, Land of Legend (photo: Ulla Mannering; © Ulla Mannering).

important to take into account that the length and the width are determined by the specific use of the textile produced.

The available evidence of archaeological textiles indicates that this loom type was mainly used for weaving tabby and basket weaves.[33] Further, according to the archaeological material, the ancient textiles produced were generally linen.[34] The quality does of course vary, but it is evident that, despite the seeming simplicity of this loom type, one can produce elaborate textiles with many threads per centimetre in both warp and weft.

Textiles manufactured on the horizontal two-beam loom have most frequently been found in Egypt.[35] The analyses demonstrated that they are generally tabbies, but some analyses show that there has also been a combination of different techniques as a linen sheet patterned with weft looping from Deir-el-Bahari dated to *c.* 2000 BC demonstrates.[36]

The horizontal ground loom is still in use today in, for example, Jordan to produce rugs and other quite coarse wool textiles with generally very coarse yarn. In the Bani Hamida Bedouin weaving project (Fig. 2.5), the width of the loom varies but a loom more than 1 m wide is unusual, while the warp is *c.* 10 m long, cut and used for 4 rugs.[37] The technique used is mainly plain weave, but weft twinning technique is

also applied to make bands as well as rugs. These weavers also use so-called half heddles, and the warping and heddling is done at the same time as they warp directly on the loom. If just weaving a tabby, this is very convenient and makes the setting-up process much easier and faster, especially when weaving very dense fabrics.

The vertical two-bar loom

There are several types of vertical two-bar looms. What they have in common is that the warp is held in tension between two beams that are fixed to the uprights and that the weft is packed from the bottom and up. The simplest vertical two-bar loom is just a wooden frame without any shed bars; more elaborate looms are, for example, the Egyptian and Roman vertical looms with advanced equipment for separate sheds.[38] The two-bar vertical loom can have tubular warp, and in this case the length of the warp is decided by the size of the loom (Fig. 2.6). However, the warp can also be fastened with a twined starting cord attached to a beam, the warp is then rolled on to the beam and in this case the warp may be longer (see below). When weaving on this loom the

Fig. 2.7 Two-bar loom with a continuous warp (courtesy of Dokumacı Fadime Koyuncu, Çavdar, Turkey 2015).

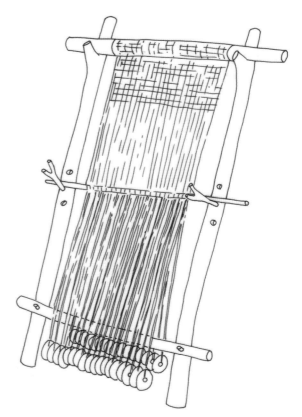

Fig. 2.8 Warp-weighted loom (drawing: Annika Jeppsson; © Annika Jeppsson and CTR).

weavers sit in front of it and the number of weavers varies, probably depending on the width of the loom.

It has been suggested that the two-bar loom originated in Syria or Mesopotamia, but the earliest visual representation occurs in Egypt during the last part of the 2nd millennium BC. It has also been proposed that this loom could have been developed in connection with the introduction of wool. Wool is quite easy to dye, and this could have inspired weaving with non-continuous patterns; the two-bar loom is considered to be the most convenient loom for this weaving technique.[39]

Today, the vertical two-bar loom is used all over the world, generally for carpet and non-continuous patterns/tapestry weaving. The use of the loom demonstrates that it can vary considerably in size, from small looms to very wide and high ones. One can buy a table tapestry loom 64 cm wide,[40] while artists in Atelje 61 in Petrovaradin in Serbia weave tapestries on looms with a width of 4 m.[41] In Turkey, Kelim rugs are sometimes still woven on bar looms on which the warp is fastened to a metal beam attached to the beam. The loom is 1.8 m high and the weaving width is 1.2 m (Fig. 2.7). The warp can be *c.* 10 m long, which is enough for 3–4 carpets.[42]

Warp-weighted loom

A warp-weighted loom is generally upright and can be placed leaning against a wall or a beam in the roof. When weaving, one stands in front of it and weaves from the top down. The weft is beaten upwards. The vertically hanging warp threads are kept taut by the attached loom weights

(Fig. 2.8). Loom weights can be made of either clay or stone, and vary in size and in shape, depending on the region and time period. In some areas, such as Scandinavia, the loom weights have been of the same type for more than 1000 years; in other areas, such as in the Middle and Late Bronze Age Aegean, there are many different types of loom weights. Since it is their mass and thickness that are the functional parameters of the weights, the shape of the loom weight (if it is round pyramidal, conical, *etc.*) could maybe also be related to various traditions and cultural influences.[43] For example, in the Roman period, the loom weights in England were mainly pyramidal or conical, but in the following Anglo-Saxon period, loom weights instead became doughnut-shaped, which is the same type used in Scandinavia, from where the Anglo-Saxons probably emigrated.[44] The number of weavers can vary, but if the loom is narrow one weaver is enough. However, if the loom is very wide, it is plausible that at least two weavers were working side by side.

The most direct proof for the warp-weighted loom is the discovery of sets of loom weights. On the basis of finds of loom weights it has been suggested by Elizabeth Barber that the warp-weighted loom was used in Central Europe, for example in Hungary, and perhaps Anatolia, already in 6th and maybe 7th millennium BC, *i.e.* in the early Neolithic period. Their use expanded into Greece and northern Italy, further to the west (*e.g.* Switzerland) and to Scandinavia and England in the Bronze Age.[45]

Except for the loom weights, there is very little archaeological evidence for the warp-weighted loom. Even if the loom weights are similar, the looms could vary between regions, for example Scandinavian Viking Age and Bronze Age Aegean. It is, of course, also clear that the fabrics produced on the looms would have been different and based on the different needs and desires of the communities.

Textiles that may be seen as evidence of the warp-weighted loom have woven starting borders, but there are also other possibilities. Even if there seems to be a connection between tablet weaving and the warp-weighted loom, it is irrelevant for the construction or technical possibilities of the loom. Furthermore, there are several other types of starting borders. According to Ciszuk and Hammarlund, 'all types of selvedges seem to have been used in connection with the warp-weighted loom but this use seems thus to be associated to the regional craft tradition rather than the type of loom'.[46] Finds of rows of loom weights have indicated that the loom could be very wide, reaching several metres – indicating that more than one weaver was working at the same time.[47] Nordic early medieval texts tell us that 2–3 alns (98–147 cm) were suitable for this loom.[48]

Pictorial evidence for the warp-weighted loom is quite late compared with the evidence for the ground loom. It is depicted in the Late Bronze Age on rock carvings in northern Italy from the 14th century BC and may be also represented in a Cretan Linear A sign.[49] Later, the warp-weighted loom is depicted on Greek vases, and later still on drawings from 18th-century AD Iceland. It is obvious that there are differences in depictions of warp-weighted looms from various time periods and areas, but it is also interesting to note the similarities. For example, the loom weights on any given loom are generally shown as being of the same size and hanging side by side.[50]

The warp-weighted loom can be used to produce many different types of textile and is especially well suited for producing twills. In order to attach the warp threads to a loom weight, a loop is tied through the loom-weight hole and the warp threads are attached to the loop. When using stone or clay weights without a hole, a loop is tied around the weight. To weave a tabby on a warp-weighted loom, alternate warp threads are placed in front of or behind a rod or shed bar on the loom. Two rows of loom weights are generally used. One row of loom weights hangs in front of the shed bar, while the others hang behind it. The first warp thread is fastened to a loom weight in the front layer, the second to a loom weight in the back layer, the third to the front layer and so on. Depending on the size of the loom weight, a certain number of threads are attached to each individual weight.[51]

Other warp-weighted looms

It should also be noted that there are also other types of warp-weighted looms from, according to images, a later period, for example in Egypt.[52] According to the images, the warp on different types of pit looms was often kept taut by very heavy loom weights, often just one or two. The warp threads were separated in different sheds on heddle rods and a similar system was used as in a treadle loom. Furthermore, the images generally show one weaver, which is a saving of labour compared to the other looms discussed in this article.[53]

Summary

All the loom types described above have their specific advantages and disadvantages. The working position when weaving on the two-bar looms is sitting, while one is standing when weaving on the warp-weighted loom. Generally, two or more weavers operated the horizontal two-bar ground loom, but when weaving on the vertical two-bar or warp-weighted loom there could be just one or more, depending on the width of the loom. These differences also affect the choice of the area used for weaving, in view of access to light and there being the necessary space in a room, and these things have to be considered when discussing the working place for a loom in its context.

The advantage of the horizontal ground loom is that the warp can be very long. 'The length of the cloth woven on a ground loom is limited only to the amount of thread spun.'[54] There is ethnographic evidence for fabrics that are *c.* 10 m long, but the warp could probably be much longer.[55] According to analyses of archaeological textiles, the width could be substantially more than 2.8 m, but the average width of cloth known from Bronze Age Egypt is 0.9–1.2 m.[56] The analyses of linen textiles from Egypt demonstrate that one can weave very dense tabbies (thread/cm), but archaeological evidence for twills and wool textiles are here more or less non-existent. On the other hand, weaving on this loom can be combined with other textile techniques, such as twining.[57]

The main advantage of the two-bar loom is that the fabric woven can be very wide and also quite long. However, the narrow shed on the two-beam loom where the warp is less flexible does not permit a long shot of weft.[58] Therefore, it is plausible that the number of weavers working on the same fabric was related to the width. An excellent example is the analysis of the early Iron Age bog textiles in Denmark that demonstrate that 2–4 weavers had been working simultaneously at the same loom.[59] Even if today this loom type is generally used for weaving rugs and tapestries, the Danish finds clearly demonstrate that it has been possible to weave coarser twills (10–12 threads per centimetre) on two-bar looms.

The advantage of the warp-weighted loom is that the warp can be long; up to 15 m, as mentioned above, and it can

Table 2.1 Different loom types. NB more modern types have been excluded (after Broudy 1979)

The warp-weighted loom	*The two-bar loom*	*Pueblo and Navajo looms*	*The backstrap and other primitive looms*	*The treadle loom*
The Greek loom	The horizontal loom	The Pueblo vertical loom	The backstrap loom	The pit treadle loom
The Scandinavian loom	• The Egyptian loom	The Navajo loom	The Peruvian loom	• The Indian loom
The Chilkat loom	• The modern ground loom		The Mesoamerican loom	The horizontal treadle loom
	• The American Southwest loom		The Atayal loom	The Chinese loom
	The vertical loom		The Ainu loom	The western loom
	• The Egyptian loom		The bent-stick loom	
	• The Roman loom		The Arawak loom	
	• The Palestinian loom		The Araucanian loom	
	• The Salish loom			
	• The Sub-Saharan African loom			
	• The loom in the Dark Ages			
	• The tapestry loom			

also be more than 1.2 m wide.[60] In contrast to the two-bar loom, the shed that can be open on a warp-weighted loom is exceptionally wide and allows the weft yarn dolly to be thrown or passed by hand over a long distance. Therefore, this loom is also very suitable for weaving dense fabrics and twills. This is because on a warp-weighted loom the warp threads are separated into layers that lie one behind the other, while on a vertical two-beam and a horizontal ground loom all the warp threads lie side by side in one layer.

Threads made of all types of fibres can be woven on any of these three loom types, but it is clear that, archaeologically and historically, the horizontal ground loom is related to linen while the warp-weighted loom is above all related to wool.

Other loom types

There are several other types of looms that could be included in this discussion. Broudy's publication *The Book of Looms* published in 1979 listed several different loom types (Table 2.1). The types are based on archaeological and ethnographical evidence and demonstrate the many variations of looms. What is striking is that there are not only several different types of advanced looms but also different types of more simple looms, which could also have been used in ancient societies.

Why are there so many different types of looms?

It is evident that, hypothetically, all types of textiles could be produced on all types of looms.

If loom weights are found, it is clear that the warp-weighted loom was used, but it should be stressed that their lack does not exclude other types of looms being in use. The evidence for looms is scarce or generally lacking in most areas, but Egypt is a fantastic exception, where the iconography demonstrates the use of different loom types. This clearly indicates that textile production/weaving must not be excluded from the archaeological record, even if archaeological, textual or iconographic evidence are lacking.

It is important to note that different loom types could and have been used simultaneously. Today, for example, the horizontal treadle loom and the vertical two-bar loom are both used in northern Europe. However, the vertical two-bar loom is here generally used for non-continuous patterns/tapestry weaving, while the treadle loom is commonly used for weaving tablecloths, towels, fabrics for clothing and sometimes rugs. It is clear that this is not anything new. In Egypt, for example, the horizontal ground loom was used simultaneously with the vertical two-beam loom, and in Roman late antiquity it was the warp-weighted loom that was used at the same time as the vertical two-bar loom. Interpretations further suggest that they were used to produce different types of fabrics.[61]

This therefore raises the question whether the type of loom utilised was only based on craft traditions or if some types were better adapted for a specific production. Another important question to ask is the nature of the textiles being produced.

Transmission of knowledge, new technology and looms

According to Broudy, the manner in which looms developed was to a large extent dependent on what fibre was used, especially for the warp; also the fibre together with the loom governed which types of weaving techniques were possible.[62] As mentioned above, it is possible to weave with all different types of fibres. However, it is not only the type of fibres that should be discussed but also the type of fabrics produced. The use of a particular loom would depend on, for example, whether one was producing thin fabric for clothing with a high quality and many threads per centimetre, or a coarse wool fabric used for outer garment or as a sailcloth. The question is also when people started to weave textiles in larger quantities and for clothing.

It is therefore important in this discussion to include a mention of textile techniques that could have been used before weaving. In regions with early well-preserved textiles, such as Peru, it is evident that non-woven fabrics, such as sprang, gauze and twining, were used, maybe before weaving fabrics.[63] The textiles from Peru dated from *c*. 3500 BC and onwards are truly unique in the world, and they clearly demonstrate how much information can be lacking when textiles are not preserved. They also show how different techniques can be combined. These textiles can be, and have been, produced on very simple looms like the backstrap loom or a simple frame. In the same way, mats and rugs can be twined on just two uprights. What is also interesting is that these tools are still in use in Peru. In ancient Europe and the Near East, there are very few non-woven textiles preserved from the earliest periods, and none complete, but there are some indications of twined textiles in the Early Bronze Age in North Caucasus.[64] Furthermore, twining is today a common technique still used by the Bedouins.[65] These techniques should therefore also be considered when discussing ancient textile production in Europe and the Near East.

Weaving was not a technique that was invented in just one day in ancient societies; weaving is most likely based on an earlier tradition of producing textiles, where different types of tools such as looms were used. The question is, can it actually be considered a completely new technique? Weaving tabbies and twills is in general a less complicated process than twining, gauze and sprang techniques. If using heddles, instead of twining every single thread, you can lift all warp threads at the same time and insert the weft thread in one go. Weaving tabbies and twills can be said to be a rationalisation of the processes through the introduction of a mechanism for the handling of the warp and thereby the weaving process is rendered faster. Additionally, it made possible the weaving of fabrics that were wider, longer and also denser than textiles made in the other techniques. Of course, there are also more complicated and time-consuming weaving techniques like non-continuous patterns, and what

is interesting is that this technique does not demand a mechanised handling of the warp. Maybe this was one of the first techniques using both a warp and a weft.

It is plausible that there were old tools used to produce textiles in other techniques when new fibres became utilised and/or when the need or demand for textiles increased. If a weaver was used to one tool it is possible that she or he would use the same type at least in the beginning, even if the technique differs. Broudy's definition of a loom being a 'device used to produce a textile' may be considered more correct, and the same is true for the idea that looms for weaving cloth developed from earlier traditions of textile production.

However, this does not answer the question why some loom types have become more commonly used, or at least considered to be so, in different regions. Even if some fibre types are better suited to use on some specific looms, it is clear that all fibre sorts can be woven on all types of looms. So why do we have several types of looms, why not just one and why have they changed? In Peru, the backstrap loom has been in use for 5000 years, in the Old World it is the two-beam vertical loom, horizontal and vertical looms which are still in use, while the warp-weighted loom has been replaced by the treadle loom.

Who and what decides which loom(s) to use? Could it be possible to master weaving on two different types of loom? Because of the lack of relevant material, it is impossible to answer the question concerning what came first in the Old World. In Peru, it is clear that two-beam looms were first used to produce non-woven textiles and only later for weaving. There has never been a tradition there for weaving twills, but only tabbies and tapestries. A new raw material or new technique does not necessarily require a new tool, in this case a loom. It is reasonable to believe that one tested first the new material and new technique with the old and familiar tool, and then improved the tools and methods in order to meet the new demand, such as a larger quantity produced. It is important to include this perspective in the discussion of the transmission of new techniques and tools.

The possible answer is that it is not only the fibre or the efficiency that dictates the type of loom used; the tradition and knowledge, and further technology and resources, but also the needs and desires of society are all important parameters. It is the totality of these interactions that is expressed during textile production and, furthermore, in the choice of tools.[66] Textile craft and textile craft production can, in a broad sense, be said to meet the social and psychological needs of human beings, and facilitate social coherence.[67] It has been argued that technologies (and therefore plausibly also the tools), are 'areas in which agents construct social identities and forge power relations also producing and using utilitarian objects for practical ends'.[68] Another important aspect is that weaving is in various cultures related to different rites. One example is the Berber women in Kabylia.[69] Here all processes, when transforming the 'clothing' of animals (wool) to human clothing are sacred and connected with different rituals, and are therefore in some way or another spiritual. The textile tools are sacred and, when the fabric is woven, the loom is considered to be dead.[70] All these aspects clearly demonstrate the complexity, but also the importance, of including them when discussing the use of different tool types such as looms and textiles and textile production. As discussed in the previous sections, in order to get the best yield and the most desired result, several decisions have to be made when producing a fabric. Historically, the access to fibres and yarn, different types of loom, the need for different types of textiles and, last but not least, craft traditions have influenced these choices.

Summary and further remarks

In this article, the basic knowledge on weaving and different loom types have been introduced together with a suggestion of the possibilities of finding evidence of different loom types in archaeological and historical contexts. The author has also discussed the similarities and differences between different loom types and argued for the possibility that different types of looms could have been used simultaneously.

The issue of which loom can be considered 'the first loom' depends on our definition of a loom and what is produced on it. It is clear that it will never be possible to answer this question and maybe it is not even interesting. What, however, is interesting is that the loom with shed bars and heddles has to be considered as the first human-built machine allowing a larger, quicker and more rationalised production of fabrics. What is important is the discussion and the understanding of the complexity of textile production, which includes several factors such as the needs, desires of the society and its exercise of choice, as well as access to technology and raw materials. In the field of the study of the ancient textile crafts, there are details and knowledge hidden in the archaeological textile material that are difficult to see, understand and interpret. The skills and the complexity of the textile crafts cannot be underestimated even if they are often invisible in archaeological contexts today. The findings of the ancient textiles from Peru clearly demonstrate that the absence of evidence is not necessarily evidence of absence. Additionally, the important discussion of textile production has to be related to the 'landscape of textile production' in time and space, and include resources, techniques, tools, society, organisation and people.

One should never stop asking the questions *why* and *how* and should continue to highlight the importance of textiles and textile production in ancient societies, even if the textile material (woven or non-woven) is scarce or lacking.

Notes

1   I kindly thank Jo Cutler, Magdalena Öhrman and Lena Bjerregaard for many constructive and interesting discussions and Magdalena also for proofreading. I further warmly thank the editors of this publication for the possibility to include my work and above all for their patience. This article is written with support from the Centre for Textile Research, Copenhagen University.
2   http://en.wikipedia.org/wiki/Loom, accessed 4 October 2018.
3   Broudy 1979, 14.
4   For example, Broudy 1979; Lamb 2005.
5   Kemp and Vogelsang-Eastwood 2001, 314.
6   Vogelsang-Eastwood 1992, 23.
7   For example, Hoffmann 1964, 65.
8   For example, Hoffmann 1964; Barber 1991, 81–115; Gleba 2008, 29–33; Andersson Strand 2012.
9   Andersson Strand 2015.
10   For example, Hoffmann 1964; Broudy 1979; Barber 1991; Kemp and Vogelsang-Eastwood 2001.
11   For example, Hoffmann 1964; Bender Jørgensen 1986; Ciszuk and Hammarlund 2008; Mannering *et al.* 2012.
12   For example, Hoffmann 1964; Broudy 1979; Barber 1991; Kemp and Vogelsang-Eastwood 2001; Shaw and Chapin 2016.
13   For example, Broudy 1979, 58; Fell 1984.
14   For example, Hoffmann 1964; Michel and Nosch 2010.
15   Watezoldt 1972; 2010; Firth and Nosch 2012; Andersson Strand and Cybulska 2013.
16   Hoffmann 1964.
17   Hoffmann 1964; Østergård 2003.
18   For example, Michel and Nosch 2010; Brøns 2017; Öhrman forthcoming a.
19   For example, Ling Roth 1918; Crowfoot 1921; Crowfoot and Crowfoot 1936–1937; Hoffmann 1964; Bjerregaard 1977; Hald 1980; Stærmose Nielsen 1999; Bjerregaard and Huss 2017.
20   Broudy 1979; Lamb 2005.
21   For example, Hald 1980.
22   For example, Batzer and Dokkedal 1992; Andersson 2000; Andersson Strand 2016.
23   Olofsson *et al.* 2015.
24   For example, Ciszuk 2000; 2004; Kemp and Vogelsang-Eastwood 2001; Ciszuk and Hammarlund 2008; Belanova-Štolcová and Grömer 2010.
25   For example, Olofsson *et al.* 2015.
26   For example, Hoffmann 1964; Wild 1970; Hald 1980; Bender Jørgensen 1986; Barber 1991; Ciszuk and Hammarlund 2008; Grömer 2010; Mannering *et al.* 2012.
27   For example, Barber 1991.
28   Broudy 1979.
29   Broudy 1979, 38; Barber 1991, 83.
30   Barber 1991, 84.
31   Barber 1991, 83.
32   Barber 1991, 84.
33   Vogelsang-Eastwood 1992, 28–29.
34   Barber 1991; Vogelsang-Eastwood 1992.
35   For example, Vogelsang-Eastwood 1992, 29.
36   Barber 1991, 150.
37   Oral information from a Bani Hamida weaver, 29 March 2014; see also http://www.traditionaltextilecraft.dk/355733317, accessed 4 October 2018.
38   Ciszuk 2000; Kemp and Vogelsang-Eastwood 2001.
39   Broudy 1979, 44; Barber 1991, 113.

40 For example, https://www.georgeweil.com/schacht-tapestry-loom-64cm, accessed 4 October 2018.
41 Mokdad 2014, 19.
42 Personal information from Dokumacı Fadime Koyuncu, Çavdar, Turkey 2015.
43 Cutler 2012.
44 Andersson Strand and Heller 2017.
45 Barber 1991.
46 Ciszuk and Hammarlund 2008.
47 For example, Belanová-Štolcová and Grömer 2010.
48 Hoffmann 1964; Østergård 2003.
49 del Freo *et al.* 2010.
50 For example, Hoffmann 1964; Barber 1991, 81–115; Gleba 2008, 29–33.
51 Olofsson *et al.* 2015.
52 For example, Broudy 1979.
53 It is beyond the topic and aim of this article to further discuss these loom types, but the author suggests that this loom type should be included in the more general discussion of the introduction and the development of the treadle loom.
54 Vogelsang-Eastwood 1992, 29.
55 Hilden 1999.
56 Barber 1991, 85.
57 Barber 1991; Kemp and Vogelsang-Eastwood 2001.
58 Wild 1970, 68.
59 Mannering 2011.
60 Hoffmann 1964; Grömer 2007; 2010.
61 For example, Broudy 1979; Barber 1991; Kemp and Vogelsang Eastwood 2001; Öhrman forthcoming b.
62 Broudy 1979, 14.
63 Bjerregaard and Huss 2017.
64 Shislina *et al.* 2003.
65 For example, Naouri 2013, 54.
66 Andersson Strand *et al.* 2010.
67 Costin 2007, 146.
68 Dobres 1999.
69 Makilam 2007.
70 Makilam 2007, 79, 91.

Bibliography

Andersson, E. 2000. Textilproduktion i Löddeköpinge endast för husbehov? In F. Svanberg and B. Söderberg (eds.), *Porten till Skåne, Löddeköpinge under järnålder och medeltid.* Riksantikvarieämbetet 32. Lund, 158–187.

Andersson Strand, E. 2012. The textile *chaîne opératoire*: using a multidisciplinary approach to textile archaeology with a focus on the Ancient Near East. *Paléorient* 38.1–2. Dossier thématique/Thematic file, C. Breniquet, M. Tengberg, E. Andersson and M.-L. Nosch (eds.), Préhistoire des Textiles au Proche-Orient/Prehistory of Textiles in the Near East, 21–40.

Andersson Strand, E. 2015. The basics of textile tools and textile technology – from fibre to fabric. In E. Andersson Strand and M-L. Nosch (eds.), *Tools, Textiles and Contexts. Investigating Textile Production in the Aegean and Eastern Mediterranean Bronze Age.* Ancient Textiles Series 21. Oxford and Philadelphia, 39–60.

Andersson Strand, E. 2016 Segelduk och segeldukssproduktion i arkeologisk kontext. In M. Ravn, L. Gebauer Thomsen, E. Andersson Strand and H. Lyngstrøm (eds.), *Vikingtidens sejl.* Arkeologiska skrifter. Copenhagen, 21–50.

Andersson Strand, E. and Cybulska, M. 2013 Visualising ancient textiles – how to make a textile visible on the basis of an interpretation of an Ur III text. In M.-L. Nosch, H. Koefoed and E. Andersson Strand (eds.), *Textile Production and Consumption in the Ancient Near East Archaeology, Epigraphy, Iconography.* Ancient Textiles Series 12. Oxford and Oakville, 113–127.

Andersson Strand, E., Frei, K., Gleba, M., Mannering, U., Nosch, M.-L. and Skals, I. 2010 Old textiles – new possibilities. *European Journal of Archaeology* 13.2, 149–173.

Barber, E. J. W. 1991 *Prehistoric Textiles: The Development of Cloth in the Neolithic and Bronze Ages with Special Reference to the Aegean.* Princeton.

Batzer, A. and Dokkedal, L. 1992 The warp-weighted loom: some new experimental notes. In L. Bender Jørgensen and E. Munksgaard (eds.), *Archaeological Textiles in Northern Europe: Report from the 4th NESAT Symposium.* Copenhagen, 231–234.

Belanová-Štolcová, T. and Grömer, K. 2010 Loom-weights, spindles and textiles–Textile production in Central Europe from the Bronze Age to the Iron Age. In E. Andersson Strand, M. Gleba, U. Mannering, C. Munkholt and M. Ringgaard (eds.), *North European Symposium for Archaeological Textiles X.* Ancient Textiles Series 5. Oxford and Oakville, 9–20.

Bender Jørgensen, L. 1986 *Forhistoriske tekstiler i Skandinavien.* Nordiske Fortidsminder serie B 9. Copenhagen.

Bjerregaard, L. 1977 *Techniques of Guatemalan Weaving.* New York.

Bjerregaard, L. and Huss, T. 2017 *Pre-Columbian Textiles in the Ethnological Museum in Berlin.* Zea E-Books 52 (http://digitalcommons.unl.edu/zeabook/52/, accessed April 2017).

Brøns, C. 2016 *Gods and Garments: Textiles in Greek Sanctuaries in the 7th to the 1st Centuries BC.* Ancient Textiles Series 28. Oxford and Philadelphia.

Broudy, E. 1979 *The Book of Looms: A History of the Handloom from Ancient Times to the Present.* Hanover and London.

Ciszuk, M. 2000 Taquetés from Mons Claudianus – analyses and reconstruction. In D. Cardon and M. Feugère (eds.), *Archéologie des textiles des origines au Ve siècle, Actes du colloque de Lattes, oct. 1999.* Monographies Instrumentum 14. Montagnac, 265–282.

Ciszuk, M. 2004 Taqueté and damask from Mons Claudianus: a discussion of Roman looms for patterned textiles. In C. Alfaro, J. P. Wild and B. Costa (eds.), *Purpureae vestes: Actas del I Symposium Internacional sobre Textiles y Tintes del Mediterráneo en época romana.* Valencia, 107–113.

Ciszuk, M. and Hammerlund, L. 2008 Roman looms – a study of craftsmanship and technology in the Mons Claudianus Textile Project. In C. Alfaro, J. P. Wild and B. Costa (eds.), *Purpureae Vestes. Textiles y tintes del Mediterráneo Antiguo.* Valencia, 119–134.

Costin, C. L. 2007 Thinking about production: phenomenological classification and lexical semantics. *Archaeological Papers of the American Anthropological Association* 17.1, 143–162.

Crowfoot, G. M. 1936–1937 Of the warp-weighted loom. *Annual of the British School at Athens* 37, 36–47.

Crowfoot, G. M and Crowfoot, J. W. 1921 *Spinning and Weaving in the Sudan*. Sudan Notes and Records 4.1, 20–38. Published as eBook by JSTOR (https://www.jstor.org/stable/41715716? seq=1#page_scan_tab_contents, accessed May 2017).

Cutler, J. 2012. Ariadne's Thread: the adoption of Cretan weaving technology in the wider southern Aegean. In M.-L. Nosch and R. Laffineur (eds.), *KOSMOS. Jewellery, Adornment and Textiles in the Aegean Bronze Age. Proceedings of the 13th International Aegean Conference/13e Rencontre égéenne internationale, University of Copenhagen, Danish National Research Foundation's Centre for Textile Research, 21–26 April 2010.* Aegaeum 33. Leuven and Liège, 145–154.

Del Freo, M., Nosch, M.-L. and Rougemont, F. 2010. The terminology of textiles in the Linear B tablets, including some considerations on Linear A logograms and abbreviations. In C. Michel and M.-L. Nosch (eds.), *Textile Terminologies in the Ancient Near East and Mediterranean from the Third to the First Millennia BC*. Ancient Textiles Series 8. Oxford and Oakville, 338–373.

Dobres, M.-A. 1999 *The Social Dynamics of Technology: Practice, Politics, and World Views*. Washington, DC.

Fell, C. 1984 *Women in Anglo-Saxon England*. Oxford.

Firth, R. and Nosch, M.-L. 2012 Spinning and weaving wool in Ur III administrative texts. *Journal of Cuneiform Studies* 64, 53–70.

Gleba, M. 2008 *Textile Production in Pre-Roman Italy*. Ancient Textiles Series 4. Oxford.

Grömer, K. 2007. Bronzezeitliche Gewebefunde aus Hallstatt und die Entwicklung der Texiltechnologie zur Eisenzeit. In A. Rast-Eicher and R. Windler (eds.), *NESAT IX. Archäologische Textilfunde – Archaeological Textiles. Braunwald, 18.–20. Mai 2005*. Ennenda, 53–59.

Grömer, K. 2010 *Prähistorische Textilkunst in Mitteleuropa, Geschichte des Handwerkes und Kleidung vor den Römern*. Wien.

Hald, M. 1980 *Ancient Danish Textiles from Bogs and Burials*. Copenhagen.

Hilden, J. M. 1999. *Beduin Weaving Looms* (http://www.beduinweaving.com/webarchive/loom/loom01.htm, accessed April 2017).

Hoffmann, M. 1964. *The Warp-weighted Loom. Studies in the History and Technology of an Ancient Implement*. Studia Norvegica 14. Oslo.

Kemp, B. J. and Vogelsang-Eastwood, G. 2001 *The Ancient Textile Industry at Armana*. London.

Lamb, V. 2005 *Looms Past and Present, Around the Mediterranean and Elsewhere*. King's Lynn, Norfolk.

Ling Roth, H. 1918 *Ancient Egyptian and Greek Looms*. Published as an eBook (2008) by Project Gutenberg (https://www.gutenberg.org/files/25731/25731-h/25731-h.htm, accessed May 2017).

Makilam, 2007 *Symbols and Magic in the Arts of Kabyle Women*. New York.

Mannering, U. 2011 Early Iron Age craftsmanship from a costume perspective. In L. Boye, P. Ethelberg, L. Heidemann Lutz, P. Kruse and A. B. Sørensen (eds.), *Arkæologi I Slesvig.*

Archäologie in Schleswig. 61st International Sachsen symposium publication 2010 Haderslev, Danmark. Neumünster, 85–94.

Mannering, U., Gleba, M. and Bloch Hansen, M. 2012 Denmark. In M. Gleba and U. Mannering (eds.), *Textiles and Textile Production in Europe From Prehistory to AD 400*. Ancient Textiles Series 11. Oxford and Oakville, 91–118.

Michel, C. and Nosch, M.-L. (eds.) 2010 *Textile Terminologies in the Ancient Near East and Mediterranean from the Third to the First Millennium BC*. Ancient Textiles Series 8. Oxford and Oakville.

Mokdad, U. 2014. Gobeliner fra Serbien – nu med dansk islæt. *RAPPORTER fra tekstilernes verden* 3.

Naouri, K. 2013 *Hands and Hearts, Weavings from Jordan*. Amman.

Öhrman, M. forthcoming a The soundscape of textile work in the Roman world: old sources/new methods. In K. Cooper and A. Surtees (eds.), *New Approaches to Ancient Material Culture*. Leiden.

Öhrman, M. forthcoming b Roman looms in Potamius of Lisbon's Epistula de Substantia. In M. S. Busana, M. Gleba and F. Meo (eds.) *Textiles and Dyes in the Mediterranean. Economy and Society. Proceedings of VI PURPUREAE VESTES International Symposium (Padua, 17–20 October 2016)*, Zaragoza.

Olofsson, L., Andersson Strand, E. and Nosch, M.-L. 2015 Experimental testing of Bronze Age textile tools. In E. Andersson Strand and M-L. Nosch (eds.) *Tools, Textiles and Contexts. Investigating Textile Production in the Aegean and Eastern Mediterranean Bronze Age*. Ancient Textiles Series 21. Oxford and Philadelphia, 75–100.

Østergård, E. 2003 *Woven Into the Earth. Textiles from Norse Greenland*. Aarhus.

Shaw, M. C. and Chapin, A. P. 2015 *Woven Threads: Patterned Textiles of the Aegean Bronze Age*. Ancient Textiles Series 22. Oxford and Philadelphia.

Shislina, N., Orfinskaya, O. and Golikov, V. 2003 Bronze Age textiles from the North Caucasus: new evidence of fourth millennium BC fibres and fabrics. *Oxford Journal of Archaeology* 22.4, 331–344.

Stærmose Nielsen, K.-H. 1999. *Kirkes Væv. Opstadvævens historia og nutidige brug*. Forsøg med Fortiden 6. Lejre.

Vogelsang-Eastwood, G. 1992 *The Production of Linen in Pharaonic Egypt*. Leiden.

Waetzoldt, H. 1972. *Untersuchungen zur Neusumerischen Textilindustrie*. Studi Economici e Technologici 1. Roma.

Waetzoldt, H. 2010. The colours and variety of fabrics from Mesopotamia during the Ur III Period (2050 BC). In C. Michel and M.-L. Nosch (eds.), *Textile Terminologies in the Ancient Near East and Mediterranean from the Third to the First Millennia BC*. Ancient Textiles Series 8. Oxford and Oakville, 201–208.

Wild, J. P. 1970. *Textile Manufacture in the Northern Roman Provinces*. Cambridge.

Zhao, F., Wang, Y., Luo, Q., Long, B., Zhang, B., Xia, Y., Xie, T., Wu, S. and Xiao, L. 2017 The earliest evidence of pattern looms: Han Dynasty tomb models from Chengdu, China. *Antiquity* 91.356, 360–374.

Discussing flax domestication in Europe using biometric measurements on recent and archaeological flax seeds – a pilot study

Sabine Karg, Axel Diederichsen and Simon Jeppson

Introduction

Flax (*Linum usitatissimum* L.) has a dual use: the seeds contain oil for multiple uses and very fine fibres can be produced from the stems.[1] Several plant characteristics distinguish a special plant type for each of the two usage groups, and it has been known for a long time that fibre flax has in general much smaller seeds than linseed flax. Studies on archaeological flax seeds dated to several time periods between the 4th millennium BC and the 1st millennium AD from Germany, Italy and southern Scandinavia have indicated that the replacement of larger-seeded flax by smaller-seeded fibre flax is evident from archaeological seed material. It is therefore assumed that already in prehistoric times two distinct usage groups of the flax plant existed, *i.e.* linseed and fibre flax.[2]

Archaeological records of flax types are frequent, as linseed and linen production constituted an integral part of most early agricultural societies.[3] The oldest flax records derive from the area of the Fertile Crescent and date to the 9th millennium BC.[4] In Europe, the archaeological evidence for cultivated flax can be traced back to the 6th millennium BC.[5] Recent excavations in sites that are located in the Circum-Alpine region suggest that flax cultivation and textile production was probably performed by specialised craftsmen from the 4th millennium BC onwards.[6]

Biometrical studies on archaeological flax seeds from Europe indicate a distinct change in seed size during the 4th/3rd millennium BC,[7] as smaller seeds replaced the larger seeds that occur in deposits of an earlier date. This shows that small-seeded flax types were either introduced from the Near East or were developed in Europe. The latter would indicate that the European Neolithic societies had profound knowledge in developing and improving crop plants. Future studies will investigate the question whether flax textiles and textile tools became more abundant during this time period, and whether the linseed type for seed oil use of flax became less popular because other oil sources (crops or animal fat) were available.

Using diverse genebank material, W. Kulpa and S. Danert demonstrated that the seed size is one of the characteristics distinguishing linseed and fibre flax.[8] As archaeological remains are often seeds, the Danish palaeoethnobotanist Hans Helbæk, in his reflective article on the evolution and history of *Linum* from 1959, also indicated the diagnostic evidence of seed size.[9]

Systematic seed measurements by archaeobotanists on flax have so far only been reported for uncharred seeds deriving from Neolithic lake-dwelling sites in southern Germany,[10] and on charred material dated to the Roman Iron Age period from Italy and from southern Scandinavia.[11]

By utilising observations made on living and diverse flax material from the collection at Plant Gene Resources of Canada for elucidating the history of agricultural practises and flax domestication, we continue a tradition of crop plant research that was very active in the late 19th and first half of the 20th centuries. N. I. Vavilov particularly pointed to the fact that the diversity in living plant material of crops has the same relevance for historical research as the commonly used archaeological findings and documents.[12]

The evolution and domestication of flax, its dispersal from its geographical origin, the discovery and the development of its multiple uses are still not fully understood.[13] It remains a challenge to establish where the different flax types were developed and which usages were dominating at different locations. The goal of our investigations is to determine the usage groups of flax in the archaeological material. This will improve the understanding of the pace of knowledge transfer concerning flax cultivation for oil and/or for fibre use.

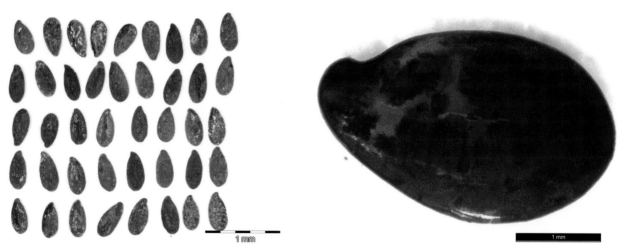

Fig. 3.1 a. Archaeological flax seeds from Egypt, Schweinfurth collection at Berlin/Dahlem, ID=S. Schw. Nr. 166; b. Archaeological flax seed from Switzerland, IPNA collection Basel, ID=Zürich Kanal Sanierung Seefeld 1064 layer 9.

Often, archaeological findings are restricted to seeds only. To support identification of the usage group, we use recent seed material to establish a solid basis for the comparison of seed dimensions measured in archaeological seed findings with different usage groups of cultivated flax and with *L. bienne*, the wild progenitor of the cultivated species.

We use fresh seed material of diverse flax types from a genebank collection, including old landraces from all over the world, to gain more definite insights into which seed sizes are associated with each usage group of flax. We want to use this information to estimate the thousand seed weight (TSW) of the archaeological seed material which allows only measuring the seed width and length. The objective is to improve our ability to determine into which usage group the archaeological findings belong.

Materials and methods

The fresh seed material of diverse flax was selected from the Canadian national genebank, Plant Gene Resources of Canada (PGRC), which preserves a collection of about 3500 accessions of cultivated flax and the related wild species of the genus *Linum*.[14] For this study, seeds of 50 accessions of cultivated flax (*L. usitatissimum*) and ten accessions of the wild progenitor (*L. bienne* Mill.) were chosen. The wild material originated from seeds collected in Turkey and was selected to be diverse in seed size based on an earlier study.[15] The seed material of the cultivated flax was selected to cover the entire range of flax diversity and, besides all usage groups, the whole range of 1000 seed weights observed in flax was included.[16] The cultivated flax material included 12 distinct fibre types (*L. usitatissimum* convar. *elongatum*), ten distinct linseed types (*L. usitatissimum* convar. *mediterraneum*), 19 intermediate types (*L. usitatissimum* convar. *usitatissimum*) and nine dehiscent flax types (*L. usitatissimum* convar. *dehiscens*).

All seeds originated from seed increases conducted in the field at Saskatoon, Province Saskatchewan, Canada, by PGRC between 1998 and 2005 for cultivated flax and from greenhouse increase for *L. bienne* conducted in 2008. The number of seeds sampled from each accession was counted and the 1000 seed weight (TSW) was determined by weighing an amount of 150 to 490 air-dried seeds (average 269 seeds).

A subsample of the same seeds from each accession was used for automated measurements of seed length and seed width using scanned images of the seeds. The images for analysis were made with a scanner at 600 dpi resolution (Epson Perfection V370 Photo Scanner, using the back-lit region for 35 mm negative scanning). The image analysis was conducted using open-source software (ImageJ 1.49). The number of seeds scanned ranged from 38 to 198 per accession, with an average of 91 seeds. Pearson correlations between the seed dimensions' width and length with the TSW were calculated using the computer program Microsoft Excel. Non-linear regressions were also considered. The obtained regression functions between seed widths and seed lengths with TSW were used to estimate a TSW for the archaeological seed samples.

For the archaeological flax, measurements of length and width of seeds from three different excavation sites in Egypt, and four settlements in Switzerland, were conducted. The flax finds from Egypt belong to the Schweinfurth collection that is stored in the archive of the Botanical Museum in Berlin-Dahlem[17] and date between the 2nd millennium BC and the 1st millennium AD. The flax finds are preserved in dry conditions (Fig. 3.1 a). The seeds were measured at the Botanical Museum in Berlin-Dahlem with an Olympus SZX16 with DP72 stereo microscope by using an image analysis program. The ID, number of seeds, measurements and datings are listed in Table 3.1.

The flax seeds from the Neolithic pile-dwelling sites in Switzerland are kept in the archive of the Institute of

Table 3.1 Measurements of seed length, seed width and estimation of thousand seed weight (TSW) in archaeological flax seeds from Egypt

Site name	Sample ID	Preservation	Dating (BC)	Dynasty after Germer (1988)	n	Length (mm)			Width (mm)			Estimated TSW (g) based on seed length		
						Max.	Min.	Mean	Max.	Min.	Mean	Max.	Min.	Mean
Gurna	S.Schw. Nr. 166	dry	1189–1069	20th	100	5.67	4.39	4.87	2.5	1.95	2.25	11.65	5.89	7.76
Meir	S.Schw. Nr. 168	dry	1994–1781	12th	1	4.56	4.56	4.56	2.09	2.09	2.09	6.51	6.51	6.51
Abusir el Meleq	S.Schw. Nr. 169	dry	3rd mill.	pre-dynastic	4	3.9	3.88	3.89	1.74	1.67	1.69	4.29	4.23	4.26

Table 3.2 Measurements of seed length, seed width and estimation of thousand seed weight (TSW) in archaeological flax seeds from Switzerland

Site name	Sample ID	Layer	Preservation	Dating (BC)	n	Length (mm)			Width (mm)			On seed length		
						Max.	Min.	Mean	Max.	Min.	Mean	Max.	Min.	Mean
Zürich Kanal Sanierung Seefeld	1064	9	wet	c. 3900	11	3.71	3.25	3.46	2.19	1.89	2.03	3.76	2.64	3.12
Zürich Kanal Sanierung Seefeld	1457	9	wet	c. 3900	11	3.89	3.28	3.48	2.21	1.79	1.99	4.26	2.71	3.17
Zürich Opernhaus	1996-1B	13	wet	3175–3157	11	3.2	2.65	2.93	1.89	1.44	1.7	2.53	1.53	2.00
Zürich Opernhaus	5593-1B	14	wet	3090	11	3.09	2.77	2.92	1.93	1.47	1.72	2.31	1.72	1.98
Zürich Kanal Sanierung Seefeld	1139	C	wet	c. 2700	11	3.73	2.83	3.14	1.98	1.62	1.82	3.81	1.82	2.41
Zürich Kanal Sanierung Seefeld		C	wet	c. 2700	10	3.42	2.58	2.92	2.02	1.61	1.77	3.02	1.43	1.98
Bieler See, Sutz V			wet	c. 2700	10	3.43	2.91	3.26	2.04	1.76	1.87	3.05	1.97	2.66

Integrative Prehistory and Archaeological Science (IPNA) at Basel University. The material was waterlogged, which means that the seeds had been preserved in wet conditions (Fig. 3.1 b). The seeds from four different settlements were measured at the IPNA with a Leica Z16 APO microscope and using an image analysis program. For the ID, number, measurements and dating of the Swiss flax seeds see Table 3.2.

Results

TSW and seed dimensions of fresh seed material

The ranges of variation for TSW and seed length of wild progenitor and cultivated flax did not overlap (Table 3.3).

The TSW in *L. bienne* ranged from 0.87 to 1.92 g, while in the cultivated seeds it ranged from 3.23 to 12.23 g. Seed length in *L. bienne* ranged from 2.08 to 2.90 mm and in cultivated flax from 3.51 to 5.81 mm. In seed width, the variation did not show a distinct gap between wild and cultivated flax, as the mean value of the broadest seeds in *L. bienne* was 1.77 mm, while the narrowest seed in cultivated flax was 1.78 mm. The findings demonstrate that seeds of wild *L. bienne* from Turkey are much smaller than those of cultivated flax and that there is a distinct gap in particular in seed length and TSW. Among the four groups of cultivated flax, the mean values of all three measurements, *i.e.* TSW, seed width and seed length, increased in the order: fibre flax (*L. usitatissimum* convar. *elongatum*), dehiscent flax (convar. *dehiscens*), intermediate flax (convar. *usitatissimum*) to large-seeded flax (convar. *mediterraneum*). However, based on all three seed characteristics, only the convar. *mediterraneum* can be distinguished from the other three groups by having the largest and heaviest seeds. Figure 3.2 also shows that the wild progenitor *L. bienne* is distinctly covering the lower range of values for all three seed characters, while the large-seeded flax *L. usitatissimum* convar. *mediterraneum* covers the upper end of the variation.

Seed length and width in the archaeological seed material

The Egyptian collection had only one sample with a total of 100 seeds. From two additional samples it was possible to measure one and four seeds, respectively (Tab. 3.1). Seed length of the 100 seeds that date to around 1200 BC ranged between 4.39 and 5.67 mm. The seed width varied between 1.95 and 2.5 mm. The measurements of the single seed from sample S. Schw. Nr. 168 dates to 1800 BC, and fits into the mean of the 100 seeds from sample S. Schw. Nr. 166, whereas the four seeds from the 3rd millennium BC (sample S. Schw. Nr. 169) are definitely smaller.

The Swiss material originated from four archaeological settlements that date between 3900 and 2700 BC. Table 3.2 shows that the seed length ranged between 2.58 and 3.89 mm. The seed width varied between 1.44 and 2.21 mm.

Relationship between seed dimensions and TSW in fresh seed material

The linear regressions of seed length and seed width with TSW were both tight (r>9.6), demonstrating the larger seeds are heavier and indicating that seed length and seed width are good indicators of the TSW (Fig. 3.3). The regressions based on a power function were even tighter, and from Figure 3.3 it can be seen that, in particular, in the lower end of the seed width and the seed length the power function was largely in accordance with the observed values on recent seed material.

Estimations of TSW in the archaeological seed material

For estimating TSW of the archaeological seed remains, we used the values of the seed length and the power function, as the seed dimensions of the archaeological findings were in the lower end of the ranges or even below the minimum values found in recent cultivated flax, in which the power function provided better estimates. In the Schweinfurth material from Egypt, the overall estimated TSW based on measured seed length ranged from 4.26 g in the oldest finding (S. Schw. Nr. 169) to 7.76 g in the sample dating to the 20th dynasty (S. Schw. Nr. 166). However, one outlier seed in the latter sample had an estimated TSW of 11.65 g.

In the Swiss material, the estimated TSW ranged from 1.98 g to 3.17 g based on seed length measurements. Such TSW would be smaller than any TSW found in fresh seeds in diverse genebank material of cultivated flax (Table 3.3). The decline in seed size and, accordingly, in estimated TSW from the older samples to the younger samples is evident.

Agrobotanical assessments of the archaeological seed material

In the Schweinfurth material from Egypt, the seed length and seed width measurements were mostly in the range of measurements found in recent cultivated flax, albeit at the lower end of the distribution range. Some seeds were smaller than in all recent flax seeds. One single seed (in sample S. Schw. Nr. 166) had a seed length measurement (5.67 mm) that indicated that it fell into the large-seeded usage group, convar. *mediterraneum*. None of the seed width measurements indicated such a large-seeded flax type. Based on these findings, and given the overlap of ranges of variation in the usage groups of cultivated flax, we cannot conclude whether it was an intermediate or a fibre flax that gave rise to this seed material. Compared to recent material, the seeds are definitely small and more typical for the fibre flax (convar. *elongatum*).

The Neolithic material from Switzerland had small seeds and the dimensions were below the range of the measurements we found in recent flax material, but above the range of what we found in the wild progenitor. Based on this, we suggest that this flax was not cultivated for seed use, but that it was a fibre flax. The seed dimensions fall partly in the range of variation of the wild progenitor *L. bienne*. In order to confirm the results of the presented pilot study, a follow-up study is going to investigate flax seeds from more than 60 archaeological sites from all over Europe.

Discussion

It is not surprising to see a tight relationship between seed length and TSW and seed width and TSW, respectively. The flax seed is flat, and the seed width is more difficult to assess when measuring seed material restricted to traditional measurement methods. Using a computer-scanned image for analysis allows for great precision and assessing a large number of seeds. Therefore, we are confident that the regression functions we established are useful to estimate a TSW for a flax seed for which only the length or width measurements are available. In archaeological material, the DNA is often disintegrated and certain physical measurements are the only way to compare the old seeds with fresh seeds. We used uncharred seeds from the archaeological findings only, as the charred seeds will have changed in length and width. However, we

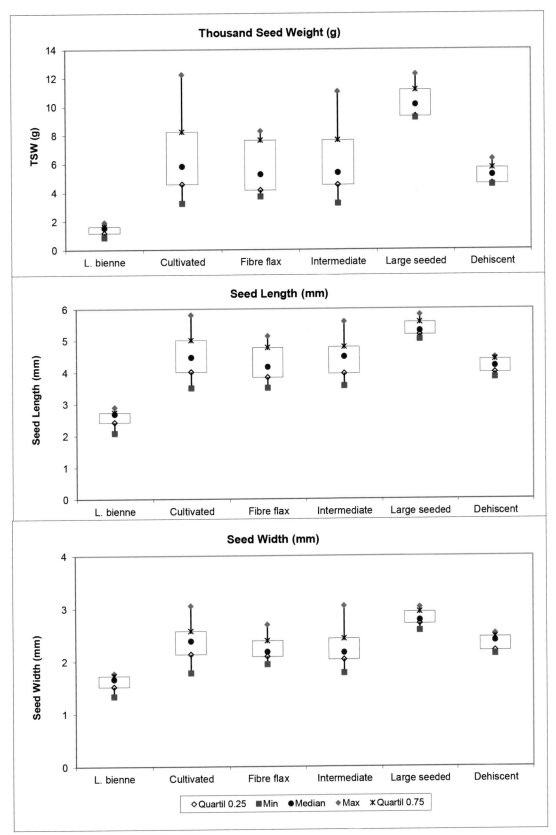

Fig. 3.2 Box-plot diagrams illustrating the ranges of variation for thousand seed weight (TSW), seed length and seed width in recent seeds of L. bienne, *cultivated flax and four subgroups of cultivated flax.*

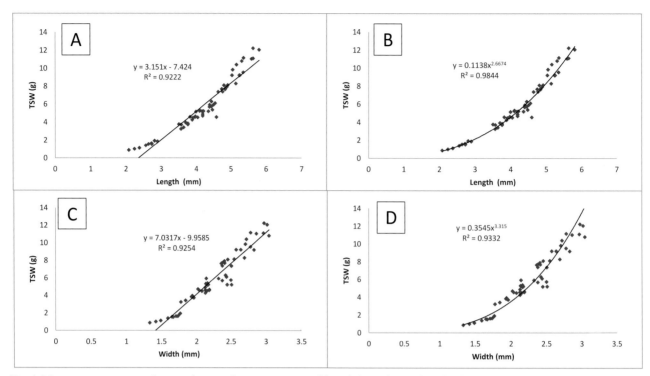

Fig. 3.3 Linear regressions and power function for associating seed length (A and B) and seed width (C and D) with thousand seed weight based on assessing seeds of 10 accessions of the wild progenitor (L. bienne) and 50 accessions of cultivated flax.

Table 3.3 Variation of thousand seed weight, seed length and seed width in recent seeds of L. bienne, *cultivated flax and four subgroups of cultivated flax*

		L. bienne	*Cultivated*	*Fibre flax*	*Intermediate*	*Large seeded*	*Dehiscent*
	n	*10*	*50*	*12*	*19*	*10*	*9*
Thousand seed weight	Mean (g)	1.44	6.70	5.84	6.03	10.39	5.15
	SD (g)	0.35	2.56	1.77	2.30	1.18	0.64
	Var %	24.44	38.21	30.30	38.20	11.37	12.49
	Min. (g)	0.87	3.23	3.71	3.23	9.19	4.51
	Max. (g)	1.92	12.23	8.28	11.03	12.23	6.29
Seed length	Mean (mm)	2.58	4.53	4.28	4.41	5.35	4.18
	SD (mm)	0.26	0.62	0.55	0.56	0.26	0.24
	Var %	10.21	13.78	12.97	12.77	4.91	5.71
	Min. (mm)	2.08	3.51	3.51	3.57	5.04	3.82
	Max. (mm)	2.90	5.81	5.14	5.59	5.81	4.45
Seed width	Mean (mm)	1.61	2.37	2.24	2.25	2.80	2.33
	SD (mm)	0.15	0.33	0.24	0.33	0.15	0.16
	Var %	9.35	13.94	10.65	14.71	5.32	6.77
	Min. (mm)	1.34	1.78	1.94	1.78	2.58	2.13
	Max. (mm)	1.77	3.05	2.69	3.05	3.02	2.51

cannot fully exclude that the seed length and width may also have changed in this material, and probably these values have been reduced, as the seeds have shrunk over the long period since harvesting at the ancient locations in Egypt and in Switzerland. Therefore, we may err by underestimating the size of the archaeological seeds in the fresh state. However, even by adding 25% to the seed dimensions, we would still estimate that the seeds were smaller than in the large-seeded flax (*L. usitatissimum* convar. *mediterraneum*) grown exclusively for seed use and typical for flax landraces grown up to recently in India and Northern Africa.

The investigations underline that archaeological seed findings of cultivated plants and their wild relatives can be much better interpreted by comparing the old seed material, or other plant remains for that matter, with material that can be obtained from genebanks preserving a wide range of diverse material of crop plants and crop wild relatives. We propose conducting similar comparisons with other seed material from other crops of agriculture in the old world. Specific to flax, we also suggest assessing the micromorphology of the diverse flax material available from genebanks to determine whether seed coat features or other seed characters could also assist in better associating archaeological seed material with specific subgroups of cultivated flax, because in most cases seed size alone was not conclusive in our study.

Controlled charring of fresh seeds from diverse genebank material may also allow a better comparison of archaeological seed with recent material.

Conclusions

It could be shown that detailed knowledge of seed character diversity from systematically characterising genebank material improved identification and interpretation of archaeological seed findings. We suggest expanding such investigations in flax by using more seed characteristics. A similar approach in other crops would greatly enhance our understanding of the dispersion and domestication of crop plants.

Notes

1   Sabine Karg thanks the Centre for Textile Research and the SAXO Institute at University of Copenhagen, Denmark for a travel grant awarded in 2014. This research also received support from the SYNTHESYS Project, http://www.snthesys.info/, which is financed by European Community Research Infrastructure Action under the FP7 'Capacities' Program (grant no. DE-TAF-3837), as well as from the German Research Council (grant no. KA 4329/1–1).
2   Karg 2011.
3   Zohary *et al.* 2012.
4   Helbæk 1959.
5   Kreuz 2007.
6   Maier and Schlichtherle 2011.
7   Herbig 2009; Herbig and Maier 2011.
8   Kulpa and Danert 1962.
9   Helbæk 1959.
10   Herbig and Maier 2011.
11   Bosi *et al.* 2011; Larsson 2013.
12   Vavilov 1926.
13   Fu and Allaby 2010.
14   Diederichsen and Fu 2008.
15   Uysal *et al.* 2012.
16   Diederichsen *et al.* 2013.
17   Germer 1988.

Bibliography

Bosi, G., Rinaldi, R. and Mazzanti, M. B. 2011 Flax and weld: archaeobotanical records from *Mutina* (Emilia Romagna, northern Italy), dated to the Imperial Age, first half 1st century A.D. *Vegetation History and Archaeobotany* 20.6, 543–548.

Diederichsen, A. and Fu, Y. B. 2008 Flax genetic diversity as the raw material for future success. *Proceedings of the International Conference on Flax and Other Bast Plants, Saskatoon, Canada, July 21–23, 2008*, 270–280.

Diederichsen, A., Kusters, P. M., Kessler, D., Bainas, Z. and Gugel, R. K. 2013 Assembling a core collection from the flax world collection maintained by Plant Gene Resources of Canada. *Genetic Resources and Crop Evolution* 60, 1479–1485.

Fu, Y. B. and Allaby, R. G. 2010 Phylogenetic network of *Linum* species as revealed by non-coding chloroplast DNA sequences. *Genetic Resources and Crop Evolution* 57, 667–677.

Germer, R. 1988 *Katalog der altägyptischen Pflanzenreste der Berliner Museen.* Ägyptologische Abhandlungen 47. Wiesbaden.

Helbæk, H. 1959 Notes on the evolution and history of Linum. *Kuml* 1959, 103–129.

Herbig, C. 2009 *Archäobotanische Untersuchungen in neolithischen Feuchtbodensiedlungen am westlichen Bodensee und in Oberschwaben.* Frankfurter Archäologische Schriften 10. Bonn.

Herbig, C. and Maier, U. 2011 Flax for oil or fibre? Morphometric analysis of flax seeds and new aspects of flax cultivation in Late Neolithic wetland settlements in southwest Germany. *Vegetation History and Archaeobotany* 20.6, 527–533.

Karg, S. (ed.) 2011 FLAX – new research on the cultural history of the useful plant Linum usitatissimum L. *Vegetation History and Archaeobotany* 20.6.

Kreuz, A. 2007 Archaeobotanical perspectives on the beginning of agriculture north of the Alps. In S. Colledge and J. Conolly (eds.), *The Origins and Spread of Domestic Plants in Southeast Asia and Europe.* London, 259–294.

Kulpa, W. and Danert, S. 1962 Zur Systematik von *Linum usitatissimum* L. *Kulturpflanze.* Beiheft 3, 341–388.

Larsson, M. 2013 Cultivation and processing of *Linum usitatissimum* and *Camelina sativa* in southern Scandinavia during the Roman Iron Age. *Vegetation History and Archaeobotany* 22, 509–520.

Maier, U. and Schlichtherle, H. 2011 Flax cultivation and textile production in Neolithic wetland settlements on Lake Constance and in Upper Swabia (south-west Germany). *Vegetation History and Archaeobotany* 20.6, 567–578.

Uysal, H., Kurt, K., Fu, Y. B., Diederichsen, A. and Kusters, P. 2012 Variation in morphological and phenotypic characters of pale flax (*Linum bienne* Mill.) from Turkey. *Genetic Resources and Crop Evolution* 59, 19–30.

Vavilov, N. I. 1926 Studies on the origin of cultivated plants. *Bulletin of Applied Botany and Plant Breeding* 26, 1–248.

Zohary, D., Hopf, M. and Weiss, E. 2012 *Domestication of Plants in the Old World*. Oxford.

4

From adorned nudity to a dignitary's wardrobe: symbolic raiment in the southern Levant 13,500 BC–3900 BC

Janet Levy

Introduction

Clothing, body covering, strictly utilitarian, portable insulation, is what permitted man's survival in parts of the world with harsh climatic conditions where fire and shelter were insufficient protection against sustained cold.[1] Clothing is the medium that facilitated man's expansion out of Africa. Middle Palaeolithic clothing or its representations have not survived, but there are proxies. Former palaeoclimates are known, as are man's physiological threshold to sustained exposure to cold. Sites located in cold environments with substantial archaeological thickness attest to the use of clothing, as do toolkits with a predominance of scrapers, blades and piercing tools for processing hides, manufacturing consistent with manufacturing simple clothing. Changes in the toolkit with the advent of eyed needles and bone awls correspond to cold peaks in the palaeoclimate and the need for more complex, multiple layers of fitted clothing with ethnographic correlates.[2]

However, utilitarian clothing, pragmatic solutions to climatic conditions, so essential to man's very existence, was obviously not considered sufficiently significant to appear in representations. An isolated example of an ivory figurine wearing a fitted trouser suit and hood, similar to Inuit clothing, with markings indicating fur, was recovered from the Siberian Upper Palaeolithic site of Buret.[3] On the other hand, items of attire of symbolic content, reflecting the extraordinary and not the quotidian, appear across Eurasia, on a wide range of Venus figurines, also from the Upper Palaeolithic, obese, naked females fashioned in ivory, stone and fired clay. Items of headwear predominate, followed in frequency by girdles, belts and straps.[4] A similar but later repertoire of symbolic clothing, actual artefacts and representations, is observed in the Epipalaeolithic and Neolithic periods in the southern Levant, although items of clothing are worn with equal frequency by both males and females, and also children (Fig. 4.1). Evidence for clothing in the southern Levant, real

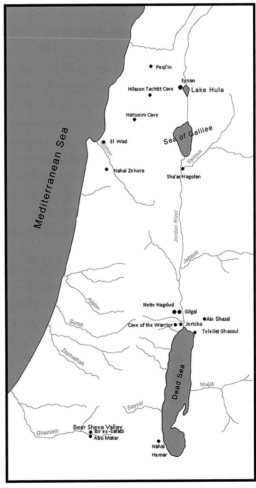

Fig. 4.1 Map of sites referenced in text.

or inferred, is very rare prior to the late 5th millennium, to the best of my knowledge. All that has been excavated or acquired, or that has been discussed in the literature, has been included in this article. Graphic representations appear with increasing frequency in both Mesopotamia and the Nile Valley from the 4th millennium onwards.[5] My intention is to discuss these artefacts, embedded in their cultural milieu, in chronological sequence, and to tease out their social and technological implications.

Man has a tendency to create representations of the supernatural in an anthropomorphic mode. The representations may be real, exaggerated, idealised or stylised. Mythology, verbal tradition, attributes to the supernatural entities emotions and practices from his familiar world. Ethnography attests to the replication of body treatment, painting, tattooing, scarification and the wearing of certain clothing types on figurines, ceramics, wood carvings and rock art.[6] Drabsch argues that ancient representations reflect the culture that created them – behavioural modes and artefact repertoire.[7] This approach will be used throughout this article, assuming that representations of clothing are not flights of fantasy, but based in a degree of reality issuing from the real world of the representation maker.

Natufian (13,500–9600 BC)

The first explicitly identifiable item of headwear appears among the Natufian hunter-gatherers, the earliest sedentary people of South-west Asia, located primarily in the Galilee-Carmel area. The Natufian culture is characterised by intensive gathering and processing of wild cereals, gazelle hunting, domesticated dogs, stone architecture, on-site concentrations of burials and intensive investment in artistic endeavours – realistic, zoomorphic and anthropomorphic in bone and stone.[8]

El Wad, a cave site in the Carmel range, contains about 100 burials – only five are accompanied by traces of personal ornament, each a single individual from a group burial. Two are identified as adult males and a third a child.[9] The child is decorated with beads of gazelle phalanges, a raw material available from the kitchen midden, and the others with tusk shells (*dentalium*), the *fossile directeur* of the culture, collected from the seashore, currently *c.* 15 km distant, but then somewhat further away. Several headdresses, cemented to the skulls by calcareous concretions, have retained their original configurations.

The most complex headdress features two tripartite fan-like arrangements spreading across the skull from the temples to the crown – shells of equal length were aligned and symmetry was retained throughout (Fig. 4.2). To have retained this configuration in position, the shells must have been sewn onto a cap. A second headdress features a circlet, seven rows deep, paralleling the contour of the head, and a third has rows of pendant fringes suspended from a circlet with *tibio tarsus* (partridge leg joint) end beads.[10]

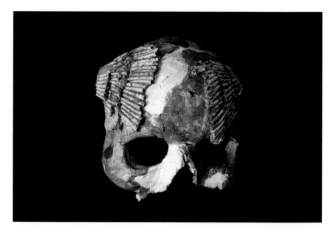

Fig. 4.2 Natufian headwear, tusk shell (dentalium) *from El Wad (courtesy of President and Fellows of Harvard College, Peabody Museum of Archaeology and Ethnology, PM#61–23–60/N10296.0; digital file # 98790058).*

Tusk shells are hollow, but one of the two apertures is less than 1 mm and must have been abraded before stringing.[11] Sewing needles have not been found, but awls are well attested.[12] Raw materials for sewing thread of vegetal origin or sinew were at hand, particularly sinew, since the gazelle was a major component of the diet. Sinew cordage, resembling in appearance and dimensions nylon fishing line used by today's amateur anglers, would have been the optimal choice for the task.

The spacing of the gazelle bone beads from the headwear of the child led the excavators to suggest they had been attached to a hairnet. Hairnets as items of headwear are attested as representations in Upper Palaeolithic Eurasia and in the southern Levant in the PPNA, PPNB and the Chalcolithic as representations and artefact types.[13] Netting techniques are not new to the region. Indirect evidence for its use in fishing, twisted vegetal cordage and *in situ* notched net sinkers are attested at the submerged site of Ohallo II, on the shores of the Lake of Galilee dated to 23–25 ka cal. BP.[14]

At Eynan in Upper Galilee, there is a single occurrence of a burial, probably female, with a pair of gazelle horns positioned at the top of the skull.[15] The tight association suggests they were tied to the head at the time of burial. Horns as items of headwear, particularly with masks, are an attribute of shamans characterised by ecstatic behaviour as observed on the wall of the cave of Les Trois Frères, France, with a date similar to that of Eynan.[16] In the Nahal Hilazon Tachtit Cave there was also found a female shaman burial: an elderly woman congenitally disabled, interred with exotic grave goods and extensive evidence of funerary feasting.[17]

The Hayonim Cave, also in western Galilee, attests to an on-site concentration of burials with four individuals buried with ornaments, both male and female, and all young adults. The most intensively decorated was a single, primary burial, a male with *c.* 400 *dentalium* beads in the region of the neck and a fox-tooth girdle.[18] It has been suggested that the girdle and neck adornments were not only decorative items but also functioned as sets of dance accoutrements, intentionally manufactured in that mode, strung musical rattles, which made body movements audible and maintained rhythm when dancing in ritual situations.[19]

Pre-Pottery Neolithic A (PPNA, 9700–8500 BC)

The first sub-division of the Levantine Neolithic is characterised by villages located primarily in the Jordan Valley with domestic round structures in mud brick, and public buildings, *e.g.* the Tower of Jericho, in grouted field stone. The economy is based on the cultivation of morphologically wild cereals, hunting with aerodynamic arrowheads and exploitation of migratory and waterfowl.[20] Fibre technology is not inferred but apparent: two-ply vegetal cordage associated with hafting polished axes, twined basketry waterproofed with bitumen, three-strand braiding and matting in weft wrapping technique.[21]

Two tiny, stylised, clay figurines, one complete and the other the head only, were recovered from the site of Netiv Hagdud, from a discard context between two houses, indicating their use, probably by females, in domestic ritual. The head is flat and on its surface appears a central incision on the short axis crossed by five equidistant parallel lines extending to the perimeter of the head. The configuration would appear to be indicative of headwear, a marker of a social role, affiliation or reproductive status.[22] The geometric, organised appearance of the configuration suggests either a soft, openwork construction in cordage, as twining, a technique attested at the site, or a more rigid basketwork-like structure.

At Gilgal, 1 km distant from Netiv Hagdud, a deliberately hidden cache of a schematic female figurine of limestone covered by two polished axes was discovered. The figurine features a transverse incision in the region of the hips, deep long clefts on both faces and 12 vertical incisions.[23] The artefact is in the same vein as a series of figurines from the Upper Palaeolithic of Eurasia, the most well known of which is the Venus of Lespugue. There, the pendant cords of the more elaborately carved figurine feature transverse-oblique incisions, indicative of twisted cordage. This artefact type is not restricted to the Upper Palaeolithic, but also found in Neolithic and Bronze Age contexts and as an actual late 2nd millennium woollen artefact from Egtved, Denmark. It has survived in its derived form, amongst rural Balkan communities in nuptial rites, as a garment worn over traditional bridal wear.[24] The swaying fringes are an attention-focusing mechanism with inherent erotic properties. Thus, it would appear that the girdle, a garment of *longue durée* and wide geographic dispersion, is a medium for messaging capability and/or availability for socially sanctioned reproduction.

Pre-Pottery Neolithic B and C (PPNB, PPNC, 8500–6500 BC)

The major PPNB sites, located along the Jordan Valley, evidence an economy based on cultivating domestic cereals, pulses and flax, hunting in the early phase, combined with raising sheep and goats in the later phase and an ideology focused on selected adult skull removal and their elaboration.[25] Fibre technology is attested by coiled basketry, coiled and twined matting, innovative containers of coiled and spiralled cordage with bitumen adhesive and thigh-spun linen yarn and fabrics manufactured in a range of non-loom techniques.[26]

The earliest known actual item of clothing, mesh headwear (a tapered cone, extending minimally beyond the contour of the head, manufactured from Z-spun S-plied domestic flax), was recovered as two major fragments from the lowest stratum of a small, Judean desert cave site, Nahal Hemar. The site is considered by some scholars to be a ritual depot for artefacts of ideological value that were damaged or were no longer relevant, and by other scholars a sacred locale where structured, magical rites were conducted by costumed shamans.[27] The artefact, believed to have been a shaman's headdress, found in association with cultic regalia, typical of shaman-type behaviour,[28] consists of three structural elements, a headband, the body of the artefact and a solid, knotted, conical appendage at the apex (Fig. 4.3 a).

The headband is manufactured by a compacted interlinking technique with the two overlapping ends sewn together, the body of the headdress of *c.* 100 symmetrically disposed meshes, with concentrations of square knots at the intersections, diminishing in size towards the apex, and an appendage, a rigid, spirally arranged cone which extends a couple of centimetres beyond the contour of the headdress composed of a dense agglomeration of knotted looping. Scattered meshes, some embellished with modified marine shells, but with slight differences in yarn diameter and knot types, attest to at least three additional items of headwear.[29] A number of selected adult, male skulls, the skulls of the ancestors, also cached at the site, were coated with a layer of collagen-based glue over which were superimposed rolled cords, also of collagen, repeating the diagonal mesh motif as observed on the headwear (Fig. 4.3 b). The outer face of a head fragment of a plaster statue also features the mesh motif.[30] The three pieces of complementary evidence strongly suggest that netted headgear was worn in ceremonies by inspired cultic specialists and probably by dignitaries, too.

Two caches, *c.* 40 items, of flat, fragile, lime plaster statues, some two-thirds human body size and others busts, were recovered from Ain Ghazal. Most are generic anthropoids: two feature breasts and one features a pudenda. Facial features are finely painted, but the bodies are completely plain, apart from two that feature red vertical

Fig. 4.3 a. Shaman's linen headwear Nahal Hemar, from Bar-Yosef and Alon 1988 (courtesy of the IAA); b. Decorated skull with mesh motifs in collagen, Nahal Hemar, from Bar-Yosef and Alon 1988 (courtesy of the IAA).

lines: one from the shoulders to mid- chest and the other on the thighs – probably indicating clothing. All the statues feature a rough recessed area above the forehead. The excavator and analysts argue that the statues viewed in a static, frontal mode during public ceremonies were dressed in gender-specific clothing and also headwear – thus explaining the incongruity between highly elaborately modelled faces and plain bodies and the androgynous aspect of the statues.[31] One may speculate, drawing analogies from Nahal Hemar, that clothing was manufactured from plied yarn, thigh spun from cultivated flax worked up into small items of clothing manufactured in labour-intensive twining, weft wrapping, looping or knotting techniques.

Pottery Neolithic (PN, 6400–4500 BC)

The Yarmukian (6400–5800 BC), the first significant pottery-producing culture in the region, located in northern and central southern Levant, features a village economy based on cereals and pulses and a full complement of barnyard animals, and also the first unequivocal evidence for spindle whorls.[32] The sites, primarily small with semi-subterranean pit architecture, also feature very large enclosed courtyard dwellings, 500–700 m² designed for extended families. Sha'ar Hagolan, the most intensively excavated site, is characterised by a large repertoire of detailed, fired clay figurines featuring elements of attire. They are highly standardised, assembled from multiple pre-prepared parts and found mostly in discard contexts.[33]

The figurines, primarily female, with a very authoritative mien, mostly seated, feature small breasts and massive thighs, buttocks and bellies, but lack genitalia. The dominant features are large, long, backward-sloping heads positioned on bodies lacking necks, and diagonally slanted, 'coffee bean' eyes (Fig. 4.4 a). There are four mainstream interpretations of the 'head' and an alternative reading: a mask, skull modification, a beehive type coiffure or an item of headwear. Skull modification, a marker of social inclusion or exclusion, is attested osteologically across south-west Asia from the PPNB onwards, with residual south-west Asian evidence of the practice amongst the Yoruk of early 20th-century Turkey.[34] A coiffure seems unlikely since the hair seems to be gathered into a bun at the nape of the neck. A mask is also unlikely: a mask is a medium that enables shamans to cross to other worlds and communicate with the supernatural.[35] It would appear conceptually incongruous for a figurine, a representation of some aspect of the supernatural, to be portrayed with a mask. A high rigid hat, later a widespread marker of royalty and deities, is a valid possibility, but the representations are completely smooth and lack indications of raw material or technique of manufacture. Female figurines with backward-sloping heads/hats and diagonal eyes are not unique to the Yarmukian, but appear somewhat later in the Mesopotamian sphere.[36]

In sharp contrast to these views, A. Gopher and E. Orrelle, and Orrelle[37] argue that the head constitutes a juxtaposing and fusion of primary, male and female sexual attributes: the hat a rampant phallus, the engorged cheeks testicles and the coffee bean eyes and the pouting lips vulvae. It is further argued that the figurines constitute repositories of encoded information, expressing tension between males and females.

Most of the figurines feature a garment of two identical, but not joined, pieces, passing either between the breasts or between the breast and the arm, over the shoulder and down the back and forward to the edges of the belly, leaving the navel exposed. A second garment appears on some: a scarf-

Fig. 4.4 a. Head of clay figurine, Sha'ar Hagolan, from Garfinkel 1999 (courtesy of Yossi Garfinkel); b. Clay figurine, Sha'ar Hagolan, from Garfinkel 1999 (courtesy of Yossi Garfinkel).

like item that encircles the base of the head and descends as two parallel strips down the back. An unusual figurine (Fig. 4.4 b), a female standing as opposed to seated, with comparatively large pendant breasts, features a scarf with a series of parallel incisions on its lower edge, its short axis.[38]

These parallel incisions are yarn fringes. Normally, yarn fringes would appear on the long axis at the end of the scarf. This phenomenon could occur in a narrow fabric manufactured in the warp twining technique using a simple flat, narrow raised surface with paired bilaterally notched pebbles attached to the ends of the warp threads, which are alternatively thrown backwards and forwards enclosing the weft thread. The technique was suggested as that used in the manufacture of the fabrics attested as impressions on lime plaster from the PPNB site of Tell Halula on the Euphrates.[39] The technique is also attested ethnographically in Iran, amongst the Nanays of Siberia and amongst the Ainu.[40] The faunal profile of the site of Sha'ar Hagolan does not produce evidence of fish, although it is a riverine site and the material was dry and wet sieved.[41] A considerable number of bilaterally notched pebbles, traditionally identified as net sinkers, were, however, recovered from the site.[42] I propose that some of these notched pebbles may have been used in fabric production in the warp twining technique.

The Wadi Raba (5800–5100 BC), the second major culture of the PN, extending within the Mediterranean region from Upper Galilee to the Soreq Valley, is characterised by small villages practising mixed farming, including the exploitation of the indigenous olive.[43] Ideological changes are evidenced in underfloor burial of infants in ceramic jars and a dearth of anthropomorphic representations.[44]

A chalk figurine, 4 cm high, a surface find from close to the intensively excavated Wadi Raba site of Nahal Zehora, attests to a fully clothed mature, bearded male. Incised grooves indicate the folds of a cloak enveloping the individual from the neck to the soles of the feet. The head is exposed with an oval bun above the nape of the neck, as appears on Yarmukian figurines. One side of the cloak is decorated with a large six-rayed star, possibly an attribute marking a cultic role.[45]

Despite the small dimensions of the figurine, it is possible to suggest the raw materials and techniques of production of the cloak. Were it a fabric or textile, neither of which have been recovered from Wadi Raba cultural levels, it would be very difficult, if not impossible, to create a star from a side or end position at the loom. Early textiles feature elaborations at the accessible extreme edges or ends.[46] It is probably made from the skins of either sheep or goat, thin and well dressed, since it falls in three folds at the neck. The skins would have been devoid of hair in order that the large and obviously important star would have been clearly visible. It is possible that the motif was etched in using a heated bone awl or hammered in with a chisel headed bone tool. Both awls with calcined tips and sets of chisel-headed bone tools are attested from the local Natufian and Proto Neolithic in the Zagros, and a tooled leather belt appears on a monumental, anthropoid statue at PPNA Göbekli Tepe, Anatolia.[47] However, that would have been rather an aggressive technique for thin leather. More probable is surface painting with ochre or sewn appliqué work in leather of a contrasting colour. Use of ochre in processing leather is known in the region from the Natufian.[48] Sewing needles have not been recovered from Wadi Raba sites. In fact, needles are only attested on the rarest of occasions in all periods in the southern Levant. However, the use of both awls and thorns, and finger-manipulated thread, was attested in the Nile Valley in the early 20th century.[49]

Chalcolithic (*c.* 4500–3800/3700 BC)

The predominant culture of the Chalcolithic period, the Ghassulian dated 4500–3800/3700 BC centred primarily in the northern Negev, at the desert interface, throughout the Judean desert, the Jordan Valley and in the coastal plain, features villages with an economy based on mixed farming including cultivation of fruit trees. Despite its predominantly rural aspect, the Ghassulian had an extremely highly developed technology with none comparable from the Euphrates to the Nile. Technological innovations are attested in the production of large frescos, the use of the potter's wheel, the manufacture of a copper artefact repertoire of unparalleled magnitude and virtuosity, in open casting and the lost wax technique, vegetable tanning of hides and linen textile production, including textiles of unprecedented dimensions, using the horizontal ground loom with heddle technology and the earliest evidence for dyed yarn of one colour only.[50]

Two types of headwear are attested, one conforming to the contours of the head and the second extending beyond it. Two sculpted ceramic heads,[51] modelled protomes of ossuaries from the burial cave of Peqi'in, Upper Galilee, exhibit two-dimensional, schematic headwear representations painted in red. One features S-twisted cords that descend from the crown and spread across the head, and a second is a grid, possibly spaced twining, also of S-twisted cords that cover the head from the forehead to the nape of the neck. Both heads have little round ears and one has a beard, features exclusive to male representations.

Two ivory heads, recovered from the Beer Sheva Valley sites of Bir es-Safadi, feature headwear that extends vertically beyond the contours of the head.[52] One, a head with the bottom broken off, is surmounted by a tall, narrow-based structure springing from the crown of the head. A second, much damaged head, recovered from a cache of ivory artefacts and basalt bowls, features a narrow-based, pyramidal structure equal in height to the head itself. All four sides are covered with incised diagonal meshes of equal size. The construction, organised and by necessity rigid, may be a representation of an artefact manufactured in a basketwork technique. Both these highly stylised, unstable structures appear to be representations of ceremonial headwear the nature of which would require that they were attached to the head by a set of straps, although such pragmatic aspects are frequently ignored in symbolically charged artefacts.

The excavation, by various expeditions from the 1920s until 1995, of the site at Teleilat Ghassul has produced a considerable number of frescos, covering whole walls. They came from all chronological phases and were found across the site. All had been seriously damaged by seismic activity and most were too fragmentary to discern motifs or scenes. The surviving evidence consists of few preserved fragments, poor photographs and some interpretative watercolour paintings made at the time of the discoveries. Only nine of the most coherent frescos were published.[53] 'The Notables' measuring 4.5×0.5 m, with an estimated original height of 1.5 m, reflects a ritual event, featuring a line of people, feet and legs only, standing or seated before a multi-rayed star. The first two individuals are seated with their feet on footstools. The first clearly features footwear with uppers.[54]

In 1977, the 'The Procession' fresco (Fig. 4.5 a) was excavated and successful conservation undertaken. It features three horned and masked individuals moving in the same direction, wearing mid-calf length gowns, including one with a straight hem indicative of a textile woven on a loom. Two of the individuals wear gowns of a single colour, and the third, the tallest, wears a gown with vertical bands of multi-coloured zigzags.[55] Multi-coloured linen garments are not recorded in the southern Levant or in Egypt. Linen, the only textile raw material of the period, is very difficult to dye.[56] The zigzag motif would require the use of multiple heddles or tapestry weaving on an upright loom and/or contrasting colour for effective display. Neither the requisite weaving nor dyeing technologies to achieve such results were present at this early stage of textile production. The earliest representation of brightly coloured, patterned clothing, undoubtedly wool, appears 2000 years later – worn by a Semitic trading-craftsmen clan entering Egypt.[57]

Drabsch's seminal study of the frescos sheds new light and perspectives on the nature of ritual practices at the site.[58] She argues that the reconstruction of 'The Procession' is both compressed and erroneous. There are not three but eight ranked figures of a robed, priestly class, also including naked acolytes, all masked, bearing aloft cultic equipment, progressing towards a shrine/temple. The reconstruction, primarily concerned with aspects of the cult, does not significantly change the above observations

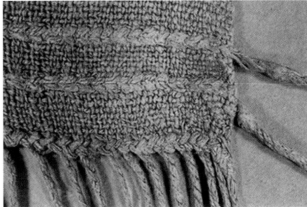

Fig. 4.5 a. Fresco, 'The Procession', Teleilat Ghassul (after Cameron 1981, frontispiece drawn by Natanel Levy); b. Detail of linen shroud, the Cave of the Warrior (after Schick 1998, pl. 3.7; photos: Clara Amit; courtesy of Orit Shamir and IAA); c. Detail of linen sash, the Cave of the Warrior (after Schick 1998, pl. 3.9; photo: Clara Amit; courtesy of Orit Shamir and IAA).

on the zigzag patterning and the technological aspects of textile production, apart from the suggested use of gloves.[59] Gloves require specialist tailoring in their manufacture. Such precision and skill was not observed on Ghassulian textiles.

The star fresco from the site has also been reassessed, with several motifs reassembled as three gowned, masked figures, one with horns, also in a processional mode.[60] Zigzag motifs appear on the robes both vertically and horizontally. The reconstruction of 'The Procession' is structured, formal and hierarchical, inconsistent with shamanistic activity. Drabsch proposes evolving/transitional shaman-priests.[61]

Shamanistic behaviour with the participants entering altered states of consciousness induced by hallucinogens and/or intensive, rhythmic music or dancing is characterised by ceremonies in which individuals wear horns and masks. Multi-cultural research attests to a series of reoccurring visual phenomena experienced by the participants – shimmering, incandescent, moving zigzags, parallel lines and grids accompanied by varied and saturated colours. I suggest

that the fresco, created after the ceremony by a shaman or participant fresco specialists, subconsciously employing the principle of integration, decoded the entoptic zigzag against a stored, referential, mental database and effected a fit, imposing the zigzag pattern on gowns. This specific combination has ethnographic analogies in rock art.[62]

Only 12 km east of Teleilat Ghassul, the Cave of the Warrior revealed an undisturbed, adult male burial, dated to 3800 BC with a spectacular mortuary assemblage. The deceased was laid out on a twill reed mat wearing a mid-calf-length wrap around kilt and a sash, and enveloped in a folded and sewn, bag-like shroud. He was surrounded by burial goods, including two sandals, all generously sprinkled with ochre during the mortuary rites. The shroud, rectangular and archaeologically intact, measuring 7×2 m, features two manually inserted decorative bands in various weft thread combinations at each end, warp tassels and a weft fringe. Unique to this assemblage is the use of *c.* 150 m of dyed black yarn as contrasting narrow warp stripes close to each edge and in the decorative bands (Fig. 4.5 b).[63] The dyed yarn is not dyed in the conventional sense of the word; the colouring agent has been smeared on the surface and mechanically pressed into the individual plied yarns before weaving. The textile was woven from yarn lengths, two weft widths long. They were looped around the outer warps in a quasi-knot and formed a loose fringe, in contrast to weaving with a continuous length of yarn and forming selvedges on each side. The technique, very time-consuming, was employed to avert loss of width during the weaving of such a long textile. The manufacture of a textile of such dimensions, without loss of width, lacking weaving errors and with even yarn density maintained throughout, attests to considerable textile skills.

The kilt, 1.4×0.9 m, is morphologically similar to the shroud but lacks the dyed warp stripes. The sash, 2×0.2 m, completes the textile outfit. Both ends feature two bands in low relief of countered weft twining followed by a looped and knotted finishing border and long twisted tassels (Fig. 4.5 c).[64] Wrap-around kilts and sashes are observable standard Egyptian male attire from the early Kingdom (3000 BC) onwards.[65]

On the mat next to the burial lay two cowhide leather sandals tanned with concentrated vegetable tannin and splotched with red ochre, from the mortuary ritual, also a preservative. They feature an outer and inner sole held together by a series of slits and grooves and secured to the foot by straps. There is no differentiation between left and right foot. An elaboration is observed in protective counters at the heel and also toecaps. The sandals were worn together but are not a pair. One had worn out and been replaced by a single new sandal, sufficiently different to suggest that it had not been made by the same hand as the other.[66]

Thus, there is an observable, close conceptual correlation, over a distance of 12 km, between the graphic representations at Teleilat Ghassul of ritual specialists and the excavated artefacts of the wardrobe of the well-dressed dignitary from the Cave of the Warrior.

Discussion

Clothing is a medium of display, perceived by the viewer emotively and cognitively. Clothes of large dimensions, eye-catching through their vibrant colours and glitter, excite the emotions, while the raw material, its rarity or danger in its acquisition and the skill or time in the manufacture of the artefact is evaluated cognitively. Until the Ghassulian, evidence for clothing or its representations is limited to sporadic occurrences recorded from mortuary contexts, from *loci* of ritual or depictions on artefacts associated with ritual. They are invariably of small dimensions – the slow techniques of yarn production and fabric manufacture imposed these limitations. Communal ceremonies, mortuary rites, life-cycle events, ceremonies tied to seasonality and

subsequently agriculture and celestial events with costumes, extraordinary clothing including masks, feasting, music and dancing, all evidenced in the archaeological record, were a major mechanism for dissipating intra-communal tension and enhancing social cohesion.[67]

The Ghassulian evidences both a continuation of existing sartorial traditions and innovations in attire. Until the Yarmukian, headwear, the predominant item of attire in all periods, conforms to the contours of the head. This is suitable for small communities where individuals and roles are known. The Ghassulian evidences both head-hugging headwear, configurations of cordage and netting and highly visible constructions that tower above the head. A trajectory traced over the millennia attests to sporadic manifestations of attire. The Judean desert cave sites attest to hundreds of textiles, the raw materials of raiment, from fragments measuring 1–2 cm to those measuring 7×2 m, in association with domestic repertoires and mortuary contexts.[68]

The widespread adoption of drop spinning and the accrued skills are what facilitated the take-off of the Ghassulian textile industry.[69] Two-ply thigh-spun yarn is produced while seated, at the rate of 10 mph.[70] Single-ply yarn is spun in the drop-spinning technique in either a stationary or mobile mode at the rate of 62 mph, and plied at 95 mph, equating to two-ply yarn spun at the rate of 23 mph.[71] Drop spinning is characterised by increased efficiency, permitting multi-tasking, increased speed of production and by improved yarn quality able to withstand sustained tension and friction, a prerequisite for mechanised weaving with heddle technology.[72] The convergence of the two complementary technologies, drop spinning and mechanised weaving on a horizontal ground loom, both characterised by rapid efficient production, enabled the metamorphoses of the industry. While prior to this juncture, fabric manufacture had involved hand-produced, labour-intensive, small fabrics, the shift to mechanised interlacing capable of producing textiles of dimensions large enough to cover the whole body, hitherto impossible with the slow techniques of yarn and fabric manufacture, engendered a new concept of self. The adorned nudity that had characterised the imagery of previous millennia became *passé*, and full body garments became *de rigueur*.

Conclusions

Both across Eurasia and in the southern Levant, headwear appears more frequently than any other item of clothing in all cultural phases of prehistory. This headwear does not serve pragmatic purposes. It is an item of costume. Costume, dancing and music are aspects of human behaviour observed from the Upper Palaeolithic. Individually, but particularly as a cluster, they are a very effective mechanism for enhancing social cohesion and diffusing tensions and the potential for intra-societal conflict.[73]

Hairnets are the commonest type of headwear with the widest geographic and chronological dispersion.[74] They appear in the Eurasian Upper Palaeolithic[75] and throughout the local Neolithic and Chalcolithic, continuing into the Hellenistic, Roman and Byzantine periods as impressions, representations and artefact types.[76] In the southern Levant, the earliest items of symbolic wear were created from faunal products; the at-hand bone debris of kitchen middens and from collected, conveniently shaped or naturally perforated, minimally modified seashells, assembled into aesthetic bone, shell and tooth configurations, as exemplified in the Natufian El Wad and Hayonim caves.

Later symbolic wear was manufactured from vegetal raw materials which had passed through two manufacturing stages: first it had been processed into cordage or yarn and subsequently worked in twining, knotting and interlinking techniques into flexible fabric or fibre constructs, as witnessed at Netiv Hagdud, Gilgal or Nahal Hemar. Early manufactured items of apparel were invariably of small dimensions, such as the hip girdle from Gilgal. The labour-intensive techniques of yarn and fabric manufacture imposed these limitations.

Changes in headwear traditions from those hugging the contours of the head of the Natufian, the PPNA and the PPNB, to those extending beyond the contour of the skull, from the Yarmukian, are directly related to demographic growth. Fourth millennium Egypt, with royal crowns, of half human body height, epitomises the trend.[77]

The appearance of leather footwear in the 4th millennium is a factor of preservation related to the use of vegetal tanning agents. It may be the accidental result of colouring the sandals or intentional innovative vegetal tanning. Nevertheless, footwear was an attribute of the well-off. Sandals appear on the Narmer Palette (3000 BC) on the extended arm of a warrior-servitor as an attribute of royal power.[78]

The dimensions of the shroud from the Cave of the Warrior, far in excess of pragmatic needs, and its elaborate warp tassels are examples of conspicuous consumption.[79] The warp tassels were manufactured from the warp thread ends of the textile that for technical reasons could not be woven, but in a more frugal situation the threads would have been individually cut off and re-spun into usable yarn. The fact that in this case they were not may herald the advent of social hierarchy. Significant changes in clothing conventions, as observed in the Ghassulian, correlate with major technological changes in yarn and textile manufacture.

The transition in the Ghassulian to a textile economy was only partial – despite the recovery of an extensive repertoire of linen remains, nothing beyond the thickness of a modern standard linen tablecloth has been found.[80] Therefore, the use of the skins of the herded animals continued in use as cold weather and nightwear. The transition only became complete with widespread access to insulating wool in the 4th–3rd millennia, although the use of wool in the southern Levant is not attested earlier than the Middle Bronze Age (2000 BC).[81]

In spite of the limitations of linen clothing to warm weather and daytime wear, the evidence from the Ghassulian saw the beginning of a considerable change in human sartorial behaviour. From the Ghassulian onwards, clothing of woven cloth covering the whole body became the cultural norm for all those in positions of authority throughout southwest Asia. Technological limitations and also high labour and resource costs in linen manufacture initially limited it to the select few, but ultimately, and particularly with the genesis and wide availability of wool, it became the cultural norm for all strata of society.

Notes

1   I would like to express my gratitude to the organisers of the First Textile Conference for inviting me to participate in this prestigious conference, to my advisor Professor Isaac Gilead for his ever-astute comments, to Patrice Kazminski for his cyber-graphic wizardry and to my good friend and colleague Yehuda Mansell.
2   Gilligan 2010, 15–22.
3   Delporte 1979, 203, no. 1.
4   Soffer *et al.* 2000, 514–522.
5   Vogelsang-Eastwood 1993; Breniquet and Michel 2014.
6   Groucher 2010, 213–215.
7   Drabsch 2015, 164, 166.
8   Bar-Yosef 2002, 103, 114, 126.
9   Belfer-Cohen 1995, 11.
10 Garrod and Bate 1937, 18, pls. VII.1, 2, VI.2.
11 Kurzawska *et al.* 2013, 611.
12 Stordeur 1988, figs. 5, 12; Campana 1989, 37, 55, 72.
13 Delporte 1979, fig. 12; Schick 1988, fig. 12; Shalem *et al.* 2013, pl. IX, figs. 4.40.i, 4.40.2.
14 Nadal *et al.* 1994, 451; Nadal and Zaidner 2002, 52, fig. 3; Weinstein-Evron *et al.* 2015, 1.
15 Perrot and Ladiray 1988, 59, fig. 32.
16 Clottes and Lewis-Williams 1996, 46, 54, fig. 45.
17 Grosman *et al.* 2008, 17665; Munro and Grosman 2010, 15365.
18 Belfer-Cohen 1988, 302–304; Braun 2002, fig. II.1.
19 Shaham 2012, 197–200.
20 Bar-Yosef and Gopher 1997b, 247–260.
21 Crowfoot 1982, 548–549, figs. 221–222; Schick 1997, 197–199, figs. 6.5.1–6.5.2; 2010, 245–247, figs. 15.2–15.3.
22 Bar-Yosef and Gopher 1997a, 177–178, figs. 6.1.1–6.1.2.
23 Hershman and Belfer-Cohen 2010, 187–188, fig. 11.2.
24 Barber 1991, 181, fig. 6.9, 255–258, figs. 11.3–11.6.
25 Banning 1998, 204–205, 214–216, 228.
26 Schick 1988, 31–43.
27 Bar-Yosef and Alon 1988, 28; Goren *et al.* 1993, 130; Garfinkel 1994, 170–172.
28 Bar-Yosef and Alon 1988, 19–20, 25–27.
29 Schick 1988, 35–36.
30 Bar-Yosef and Alon 1988, 20.
31 Schmandt-Besserat 1998, 1, 5, 9, fig. 2.3.

32   Garfinkel 1999, 29; 2004, 107, 200.
33   Miller 2001, 225; Garfinkel *et al.* 2012, 105–106, 117, 122.
34   Lorentz 2010, 126–133, 140.
35   Eliade 1972, 93, 179.
36   Woolley 1955, pl. 20.
37   Gopher and Orrelle, 1996, 273; Orrelle 2014, 74.
38   Miller, 2001, 195; Garfinkel 2004, 164–165.
39   Alfaro Giner 2012, 47.
40   Wulff 1966, 221, fig. 309; Kent and Nelson 1976, 152.
41   Hesse 2001, 248.
42   Garfinkel 1999, 37.
43   Gopher 2010, 1571; Namder *et al.* 2014, 4.
44   Gopher 2010, 1492; Orrelle and Gopher 2000, 300.
45   Noy 1999, 106, 109.
46   Schick 1998, 11, fig. 3.15.
47   Campana 1989, 54, 132; Schmidt 2010, 245.
48   Dubreuil and Grosman 2009, 949.
49   Crowfoot 1921, 27.
50   Gilead 1988; Schick 1998, 20; Rowan and Golden 2009.
51   Shalem *et al.* 2013, 129, figs. 4.40.1–4.40.2, pl. IX.
52   Perrot 1959, 9, pl. III C; 1964, pl. LII.2.
53   Mallon *et al.* 1934; Cameron 1981.
54   Mallon *et al.* 1934, pl. 66.
55   Cameron 1981, frontispiece.
56   Barber 1991, 15.
57   Newberry 1893, pl. XXVII.
58   Drabsch 2015.
59   Drabsch 2015, 158.
60   Drabsch 2015, 105–106, fig. 127.
61   Drabsch 2015, 21.
62   Lewis-Williams and Dowson 1988, 203, 212, fig. 4.
63   Koren 1998, 100.
64   Schick 1998a, 6–22.
65   Vogelsang-Eastwood 1993, 86.
66   Schick 1998b, 34–38; Ashkenazi 2008, 76–78.
67   Ronen 1979, 59; Bar-Yosef and Alon 1988, 23–27; Schick 1988, 35–36; Garfinkel 2003; Munro and Grosman 2010; Shaham 2012.
68   Schick 1998, 6–22; 2002, 223–229.
69   Levy and Gilead 2012, 131–134; 2013, 30–39.
70   MacKenzie 1991, 76, 82.
71   Bird 1968, 14; Tiedemann and Jakes 2006, 293.
72   Levy and Gilead 2012, 128, 135.
73   Garfinkel 2003; Shaham 2012.
74   Schick 1988, 39.
75   Soffer *et al.* 2000, 518.
76   Sheffer and Webber 2004, 226–230 with numerous references therein.
77   Pritchard 1969, 92, 93.
78   Pritchard 1969, 92, 93.
79   Veblen 1953 (1899).
80   Cindorf *et al.* 1980, 229–234.
81   Shamir 2005, 23.

Bibliography

Alfaro Giner, C. 2012 Textiles from the Pre-Pottery Neolithic site of Tell Halula (Euphrates Valley, Syria). *Paléorient* 38.1–2.

Dossier thématique/Thematic file, C. Breniquet, M. Tengberg, E. Andersson and M.-L. Nosch (eds.), Préhistoire des Textiles au Proche-Orient/Prehistory of Textiles in the Near East, 41–54.

Ashkenazi, H. 2008 The archaeology of the individual: reconstructing the life of deceased from the Cave of the Warrior. Unpublished MA thesis. University of Tel Aviv.

Banning, E. 1998. The Neolithic period: triumphs of architecture, agriculture and art. *Near Eastern Archaeology* 61.4, 188–237.

Barber, E. 1991. *Prehistoric Textiles. The Development of Cloth in the Neolithic and Bronze Ages with Special Reference to the Aegean.* Princeton.

Bar-Yosef, O. 2002 Natufian: a complex society of foragers. In B. Fitzhugh and J. Hebu (eds.), *Beyond Foraging and Collecting.* New York, 91–149.

Bar-Yosef, O. and Alon, D. 1988 Nahal Hemar Cave, the excavations. *'Atiqot* 18, 1–30.

Bar-Yosef, O. and Gopher, A. 1997a Miscellaneous finds: the human figurines from Netiv Hagdud. In O. Bar-Yosef and A. Gopher (eds.), *An Early Neolithic Village in the Jordan Valley.* American School of Prehistoric Research Bulletin 43. Princeton 177–180.

Bar-Yosef, O. and Gopher, A. 1997b Discussion. In O. Bar-Yosef and A. Gopher (eds.) *An Early Neolithic Village in the Jordan Valley.* American School of Prehistoric Research. Bulletin 43, 247–266.

Belfer-Cohen, A. 1988 The Natufian graveyard in Hayonim Cave. *Paléorient* 14.2, 297–308.

Belfer-Cohen, A. 1995 Rethinking social stratification in the Natufian culture: the evidence from the burials. In S. Campbell and A. Green (eds.), *The Archaeology of Death in the Ancient Near East.* Oxford, 9–16.

Bird, J. 1968 Handspun yarn production rates in the Cuzco region of Peru. *Textile Museum Journal* 2.3, 9–16.

Braun, J. 2002 *Music in Ancient Israel/Palestine.* Grand Rapids and Michigan.

Breniquet, C. and Michel, C. (eds.) 2014 *Wool Economy in the Ancient Near East and the Aegean: from the Beginnings of Sheep Husbandry to Institutional Textile Industry.* Ancient Textile Series 17. Oxford and Philadelphia.

Cameron, D. 1981 *The Ghassulian Wall Paintings.* London.

Campana, D. 1989 *Natufian and Proto-Neolithic Bone Tools.* British Archaeological Reports International Series 494. Oxford.

Cindorf, E., Horowitz, S. and Blum, R. 1980 Appendix C: textile remains from the caves of Nahal Mishmar. In P. Bar-Adon (ed.), *The Cave of the Treasure.* Jerusalem, 229–234.

Clottes, J. and Lewis-Williams D. 1996 *The Shamans of Prehistory.* New York.

Crowfoot, G. 1921 Spinning and weaving in the Sudan. *Sudan Notes and Records* 4.1, 20–39.

Crowfoot, E. 1982 Textiles, matting and basketry. In K. Kenyon and T. Holland (eds.), *Excavations at Jericho IV.* London, 546–550.

Delporte, H. 1979 *L'image de la femme dans l'art Préhistorique.* Paris.

Drabsch, B. 2015 *The Mysterious Wall Paintings of Teleilat Ghassul, Jordan.* Sydney.

Dubreuil, L. and Grosman, L. 2009 Ochre and hide-working at a Natufian burial place. *Antiquity* 83, 935–954.

Eliade, M. 1972 *Shamanism: Archaic Techniques of Ecstasy*. Trans. W. R Trask. Princeton.

Garfinkel, Y. 1994 Ritual burial of cultic objects: the earliest evidence. *Cambridge Archaeological Journal* 4.2, 150–188.

Garfinkel, Y. 1999 *The Yarmukians*. Jerusalem.

Garfinkel, Y. 2003 *Dancing at the Dawn of Agriculture*. Austin.

Garfinkel, Y. 2004 *The Goddess of Sha'ar Hagolan*. Jerusalem.

Garfinkel, Y., Ben-Shlomo, D. and Marom, N. 2012 Sha'ar Hagolan: a major Pottery Neolithic settlement and artistic center in the Jordan Valley. *Eurasian Prehistory* 8.1–2, 97–143.

Garrod, D. and Bate, D. 1937 *The Stone Age of Mount Carmel*. Oxford.

Gilead, I. 1988 The Chalcolithic period in the Levant. *Journal of World Prehistory* 2.4, 397–443.

Gilligan, I. 2010 The prehistoric development of clothing: archaeological implications of a thermal model. *Journal of Archaeological Method and Theory* 17, 15–80.

Gopher, A. 2010 The Pottery Neolithic in the southern Levant – a second Neolithic revolution. In A. Gopher (ed.), *Village Communities of the Pottery Neolithic Period in the Menashe Hills, Israel*. Monograph Series 29. Tel Aviv, 1525–1611.

Gopher, A. and Orrelle, E. 1996 An alternative interpretation for the material imagery of the Yarmukian, a Neolithic culture of the sixth millennium BC in the southern Levant. *Cambridge Archaeological Journal* 6.2, 255–279.

Goren, Y., Segal, I. and Bar-Yosef, O. 1993 Plaster artifacts and the interpretation of Nahal Hemar Cave. *Journal of Israel Prehistoric Society* 35, 120–131.

Grosman, L., Munro, N. and Belfer-Cohen, A. 2008. A 12,000-year-old Shaman burial from the southern Levant (Israel). *Proceedings of National Academy of Science* 105.46, 17655–17659.

Groucher, K. 2010 Figuring out identity: the body and identity in Ubaid. In R. Carter and G. Philip (eds.), *Beyond the Ubaid*. Studies in Ancient Oriental Civilization 63. Chicago, 113–123.

Hershman, D. and Belfer-Cohen, A. 2010 'It's magic!': artistic and symbolic material manifestations from the Gilgal sites. In O. Bar-Yosef, N. Goring-Morris and A. Gopher (eds.), *Gilgal*. Jerusalem, 185–216.

Hesse, B. 2001 Between the revolutions: animal use at Sha'ar Hagolan during the Yarmukian. In Y. Garfinkel and M. Miller (eds.), *Sha'ar Hagolan 1*. Oxford, 247–255.

Kent, K. and Nelson, S. 1976 Net sinkers or weft weights? *Current Anthropology* 17.1, 152.

Koren, Z. 1998 Color analysis of the textiles. In T. Schick (ed.), *The Cave of the Warrior*. IAA Reports 5. Jerusalem, 99–106.

Kurzawska, A., Bar-Yosef Mayer, D. and Mienis, H. 2013 Scaphoped shells in the Natufian culture. In O. Bar-Yosef and F. Valla (eds.), *Natufian Foragers in the Levant: Terminal Pleistocene Social Changes in Western Asia*. Ann Arbor, 611–621.

Levy, J. and Gilead, I. 2012 Spinning in the 5th millennium in the southern Levant: aspects of the textile economy. *Paléorient* 38.1–2. Dossier thématique/Thematic file, C. Breniquet, M. Tengberg, E. Andersson and M.-L. Nosch (eds.), Préhistoire des Textiles au Proche-Orient/Prehistory of Textiles in the Near East, 127–139.

Levy, J. and Gilead, I. 2013 The emergence of the Ghassulian textile industry in the southern Levant Chalcolithic period (c. 4500–3900 BCE). In M.-L. Nosch, H. Koefoed and E. Andersson Strand (eds.), *Textile Production and Consumption in the Ancient Near East*. Ancient Textile Series 12. Oxford, 26–44.

Lewis-Williams, J. and Dowson, T. 1988 The signs of all times. *Current Anthropology* 29.2, 201–245.

Lorentz, K. 2010 Ubaid head-shaping: negotiations of identity through physical appearance. In R. Carter and G. Philip (eds.), *Beyond the Ubaid*. Studies in Ancient Oriental Civilization 63. Chicago, 125–148.

MacKenzie, M. 1991. *Androgynous Objects String Bags and Gender in Central New Guinea*. Reading.

Mallon, A., Koeppel, R. and Neuville, R. 1934 *Teleilath Ghassul I*. Rome.

Miller, M. 2001 The function of the anthropomorphic figurines: a preliminary analysis. In Y. Garfinkel and M. Miller (eds.), *Sha'ar Hagolan 1*. Oxford, 221–233.

Munro, N. and Grosman, L. 2010 Early evidence (ca. 12,000 BP) for feasting at a burial cave in Israel. *Proceedings of the National Academy of Science* 107.35, 15362–15366.

Nadel, D., Danin, A., Werker, E., Schick, T., Kislev, M. and Stewart, K. 1994. 19,000 Years-Old Twisted Fibres from Ohallo II. *Current Anthropology* 35.4, 451–458.

Nadel, D. and Zaidner, Y. 2002 Upper Pleistocene and Mid Pleistocene net sinkers from the Sea of Galilee. *Journal of the Israel Prehistoric Society* 32, 49–71.

Namder, D., Amrani, A., Getzov, N. and Milevski, I. 2014 Olive oil storage during the fifth and sixth millennium BC at Ein Zippori, northern Israel. *Israel Journal of Plant Sciences*, 62.1–2, 1–10.

Newberry, P. 1893 *Beni Hasan I*. London.

Noy, T. 1999 *The Human Figure in Prehistoric Art in the Land of Israel*. Jerusalem.

Orrelle, E. 2014. *Material Images of Humans from the Natufian to Pottery Neolithic Periods in the Levant*. British Archaeological Reports International Series 2595. Oxford.

Orrelle, E. and Gopher, A. 2000. The Pottery Neolithic period. In I. Kuijt (ed.), *Life in Neolithic Farming Communities*. New York, 295–322.

Perrot, J. 1959 Statuettes en ivoire et autre objects en ivoire et en os provenant des gisements préhistoriques de la région de Béersheba. *Syria* XXXVI, 8–19.

Perrot, J. 1964. Les ivoires de la 7e campagne de fouilles à Safadi près de Beershéva. *Eretz Israel* 7, 92–93.

Perrot, J. and Ladiray, D. 1988 *Les hommes de Mallaha (Eynan) Israel*. Paris.

Pritchard, J. 1969 *The Ancient Near East in Pictures Related to the Old Testament*. Princeton.

Ronen, A. 1979 *Introducing Prehistory*. London.

Rowan, Y. and Golden, J. 2009 The Chalcolithic period of the southern Levant: a synthetic review. *Journal of World Prehistory* 22, 1–92.

Schick, T. 1988 Cordage, basketry and fabrics. *'Atiqot* 18, 31–43.

Schick, T. 1997 Miscellaneous finds: a note on the perishable finds from Netiv Hagdud. In O. Bar-Yosef and A. Gopher (eds.), *An Early Neolithic Village in the Jordan Valley*. American School of Prehistoric Research Bulletin 43, 197–200.

Schick, T. 1998a The textiles. In T. Schick (ed.) *The Cave of the Warrior*. IAA Reports 5. Jerusalem, 6–22.

Schick, T. 1998b The sandals. In T. Schick (ed.) *The Cave of the Warrior.* IAA Reports 5, Jerusalem, 34–38.

Schick, T. 2002 The early basketry and textiles from caves in the Northern Judean Desert. *'Atiqot* 41, 223–239.

Schick, T. 2010 Basketry finds from Gilgal I. In O. Bar-Yosef, N. Goring-Morris and A. Gopher (eds.), *Gilgal.* Jerusalem, 245–249.

Schmandt-Besserat, D. 1998 Ain Ghazal 'monumental' figures. *Bulletin of the American Schools of Oriental Research* 310, 1–19.

Schmidt, K. 2010 Göbekli Tepe – the Stone Age sanctuaries. New results of ongoing excavations with a special focus on sculptures and high reliefs. *Documenta Prehistorica* XXXVII, 239–256.

Shaham, D. 2012 The articulation of music and visual arts during the Natufian culture in the Levant. In E. Anati, L. Oosterbeek and F. Mailland (eds.), *The Intellectual and Spiritual Expressions of Non-Literate People.* British Archaeological Reports International Series 2360. Oxford, 197–213.

Shalem, D., Gal, Z. and Smithline, H. 2013 *Peqi'in.* Kinneret Academic College.

Shamir, O. 2005. Textiles in the land of Israel from the Roman period till the early Islamic period in the light of the archaeological finds. Unpublished PhD thesis, University of Jerusalem.

Sheffer, A. and Webber, M. 2004. Traces of a hairnet. In P. Figueras (ed.), *Horvat Karkur `Ilit.* Beer Sheva, 226–231.

Soffer, O., Adovasio, M. and Hyland, D. 2000 The 'Venus' figurines. *Current Anthropology* 41.4, 511–537.

Stordeur, Y. 1988 *Outils et armes en os de gisement natoufien de Mallaha (Eynan) Israel.* Paris.

Tiedemann, E. and Jakes, K. 2006. An exploration of prehistoric spinning technology. *Archaeometry* 48.2, 293–307.

Veblen, T. 1953 (1899) *The Theory of the Leisure Class.* New York.

Vogelsang-Eastwood, G. 1993 *Pharaonic Egyptian Clothing.* Leiden.

Weinstein-Evron, M., Langgut, D., Chaim, S., Tsatskin, A. and Nadal, D. 2015 Late Pleistocene palynological sequence from Ohallo II, Sea of Galilee Israel. *Transactions of the Royal Society of South Africa* (https://doi.org/10.1080/003591 9X.2015.1053554, accessed 29 April 2018).

Woolley, L. 1955 *Ur Excavations IV: The Early Periods.* Oxford.

Wulff, H. 1966 *Traditional Crafts of Persia.* Cambridge, Massachusetts.

The earliest cloth culture in Denmark

Ulla Mannering

Introduction

This article presents an overview of Danish archaeological finds of skin objects, non-loom textiles and tools dated to the Stone Age, *i.e.* the period before the boom in Scandinavian loom textile production in the Early Bronze Age that may account for the characteristics and preconditions for this early production, here termed the cloth culture.[1] The Danish Stone Age covers the late Palaeolithic (*c.* 12,500–9000 BC), the Mesolithic (9000–4000 BC) and the Neolithic (4000–1700 BC). The first two periods are characterised in the region by small-scale societies that depended on hunting and fishing conditioned by the ever-near coastline, while the Neolithic was the period when agriculture and animal husbandry was introduced.[2] From these periods, a limited but still informative number of finds occur, which provide information on the techniques and tools used for this production. Each in their way, the finds contribute with important knowledge to our overall understanding of the earliest cloth culture in Denmark.

Throughout the years, several researchers have been studying and publishing different parts of the large Danish prehistoric textile and skin collections,[3] but compared to the well-preserved Bronze and Early Iron Age collections of textile and skin materials, the evidence for the earliest cloth culture in the Stone Age is scattered and difficult to access.[4] As part of the work of the Danish National Research Foundation's Centre for Textile Research (DNRF64) in Copenhagen, a team consisting of archaeologists, conservators, hand weavers and researchers from the natural sciences have been exploring some of these Danish collections (2005–2016). The primary focus was placed on the textile and skin garments recovered from the Danish peat bogs; a collection primarily dated to the Early Iron Age (500 BC–AD 400). Also explored, however, was the material from the Bronze Age (1700–500 BC), as well as the evidence for the earliest cloth culture in Denmark, particularly in connection with the large temporary exhibition on 'Fur. An Issue of Life and Death' shown at the National Museum of Denmark in winter 2014/2015. Furthermore, two recent Danish PhD projects have focused on the introduction of agriculture in Scandinavia,[5] and the development of prehistoric sheep and wool in Scandinavia[6] that each, in their own way, provide important information on the earliest production of skin and textile materials.

The earliest skin and fur technology

The earliest Scandinavian depiction of human figures has been found on an auroch bone from Ryemarksgård in western Zealand dated to *c.* 8000 BC, *i.e.* the early Mesolithic.[7] Although the incised drawing is not particularly detailed concerning the clothing, it is accepted that the figures are clad in some kind of skin garment, and it is generally assumed that the primary clothing materials used by the Scandinavian hunter/gatherer population in this period were animal skins and hides.

There can be no doubt that skins and furs were crucial for the survival in the northern hemisphere, and fur-bearing animals provided not only food, but also warm, windproof and waterproof clothing. There are many stone and bone tools in Scandinavian museum collections that could have been used for fur and skin preparation, such as scrapers for cleaning the hides and awls for preparing holes for stretching and sewing (Fig. 5.1).[8] Further, club arrows show that sometimes it was desirable to kill an animal without perforating the skin. This kind of hunting equipment was probably used to hunt birds and smaller fur animals, as exemplified by the skulls found at the settlement of Agernæs

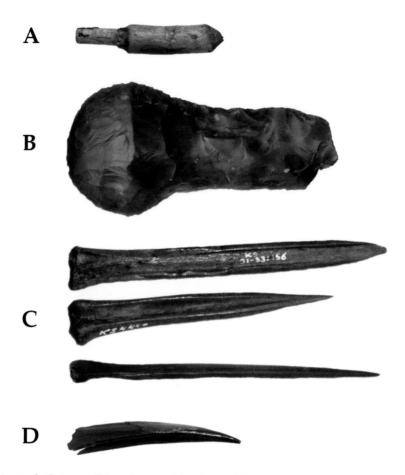

Fig. 5.1 Different Stone Age tools that may all have been used for skin and fur preparation: A. The upper part of a club-headed wooden arrow from the settlement Holmegård IV in southern Zealand. This type of arrow was used in order not to penetrate the skin. The arrow is dated to c. 6500 BC. It is c. 5 cm long; B. A large flint spoon-shaped scraper found near Skotterup in northern Zealand. The scraper is dated to c. 2000 BC, and is c. 10 cm long; C. The three bone awls could have been used to make holes in skins before they were sewn together. The awls were found in Kongemosen in western Zealand and are dated to c. 6000 BC. They are c. 10–12 cm long; D. The spine of a spurdog shark found at Præstelyngen in western Zealand. This was most likely used as a needle. The tool is dated to c. 4000 BC. It is c. 4 cm long (all photos: National Museum of Denmark).

on Funen, dated to *c.* 4200 BC.[9] At this settlement, bones from more than 60 individual animals, mainly pine marten, but also wolf, wild cat and lynx, were found. Cut marks on the forehead of the skulls show that the animals were skinned, and thus hunted for their fur. The same pattern is observed at the Ringkloster seasonal hunting settlement in eastern Jutland dated to the period *c.* 5400–3550 BC.[10] Another special feature recorded at the Agernæs settlement is the remains of at least 10 domesticated dogs with similar cut marks, indicating that, apart from being very useful hunting companions, dog fur was such an important raw material that it was not wasted when the dogs could not be used for other purposes.[11] This phenomenon is also known from Arctic clothing where dog skins are used, especially for the trimming of hoods.[12]

More information on skin clothing can be extracted from graves such as the Mesolithic double grave from Dragsholm in north-western Zealand, dated to *c.* 5000 BC. In this grave, two females were buried wrapped in skins or dressed in skin clothes elaborately decorated with no less than 144 animal tooth pendants, mainly from red deer. Red ochre was also found in the grave, indicating that the skins could have been coloured with this pigment. Other examples of graves from northern Zealand with similar decorations using large numbers of animal teeth and shells come from Bøgebakken grave 8 and the graves from Gøngehusvej.[13] In particular, double grave 7, dated to *c.* 5000 BC, the skeleton of a middle-aged woman, *c.* 40 years old, and a three-year-old child, have provided valuable information about the clothing.[14] Parts of the grave were covered by a layer of red ochre, *i.e.* around the child, the head and legs of the woman, but not on her torso, which makes it less likely that the ochre in this case derives from the colouring of the clothing. On each side of the woman's pelvis and on the right shoulder lay three small toe bones of a roe deer.[15] The skin was probably used as some kind of clothing or covering, or was used as a sling for carrying the child.[16] Two flat bone knives, which could have been used for skin preparation, were placed by the woman's chest, and at her head were found the beak of a grebe together with a long bone pin. Skin from sea birds is especially suited for lining winter garments and headgear, and it is most probable that the beak derives from a cap made of bird skin, which was fastened to the woman's hair with the pin.[17]

Despite the fact that these finds only give indirect evidence about the clothing placed in the graves, they are the first clear evidence of a clothing culture dependent on skin and fur as raw materials. The elaborate decorations made of animal teeth and shells would have given the clothing both colour contrasts and sound effects during movement,[18] and necklaces and pendants in amber show that status, aesthetic taste and identity were expressed through the clothing.[19]

The earliest Danish skin find

The earliest find of a Stone Age object of skin found in Denmark is the fragment from Tværmose in western Jutland, which is ^{14}C-dated to *c.* 3000 BC (3090–2950 BC).[20] The piece is made of calf skin, measures 16×3.5 cm (Fig. 5.2)

Fig. 5.2 A calf skin from the bog Tværmose in western Jutland. The piece measures 16×3.5 cm and has regular holes from sewing on one side. Remains of the sewing thread are also preserved. This material is not identified. The function of this object is not known and could be a clothing object or a container for the 70 perforated and stringed hazel-nuts and the three small amber beads (photo: National Museum of Denmark).

and has remnants of fine sewing along one edge. Based on this detail there can be no doubt that it represents a crafted item, but whether it was a clothing item or a container for the approximately 70 perforated and stringed wild hazelnuts and three small irregular amber discs found with it is not known. Both suggestions are feasible. As the piece is made of calf skin, the find further demonstrates that the technology of the use of animal skins, initially based on the hunting of wild animals, was brought into the Neolithic animal husbandry production tradition. This tradition, primarily based on livestock such as cattle, sheep and goats, was maintained in the subsequent periods.

Although no complete finds of Stone Age skin clothing have been found in Scandinavia, it is not unlikely that the earliest Scandinavian clothing tradition may have been comparable to the known Arctic clothing tradition using body-tight or close-fitting clothing items like parkas and trousers.[21] On the other hand, it is important to emphasise that there is no proof for trousers being part of the Scandinavian clothing tradition, either in the Bronze Age or until the Roman Iron Age in the first centuries AD, when textile trousers appear for the first time in the North German bog finds.[22]

Spinning technology

Another important and basic technology that can be traced back to the Mesolithic is the spinning technology used to make cords and ropes, which is a technology as old as mankind and closely linked to the life of the Stone Age hunters. In Denmark, several cords dated to the Mesolithic have been found. They are all made of various plant materials. The cords are often linked to fishing gear, like nets, fishing lines, leisters and traps.[23] A fragmented but still well-preserved fishing or carrying net was found in 1876 in the bog of Christiansholm, near Copenhagen on Zealand.[24] There are also reports of a fishing net found in the 1950s in Åmosen in western Zealand, together with net sinkers and cords made of lime bast, but the net was unfortunately too degraded to be preserved.[25] During the more recent underwater excavation of the settlement at Møllegabet in the waters south of Funen, fishing gear, plant fibre cords and floor layers with nettle stems and seeds were found, which indicate a varied use of the available plant fibre resources.[26] The fact that the mature parts of nettles, *e.g.* seeds and wooden stem parts, were found inside the settlement area suggests that the nettles were used for some kind of fibre production and possibly also a kind of textile production, and not for food production.

Among the more unusual finds is the cord found around the neck of a young, presumably female, bog skeleton found in Sigersdal Mose in northern Zealand ^{14}C-dated to *c.* 3500 BC.[27] The cords are now preserved as fragments in lengths varying from 2.5 to 23 cm, but presumably they

Table 5.1 Stone Age textiles belonging to the collections of the National Museum of Denmark. The analyses are made by Irene Skals. See also Fig. 5.4

Site	Mus.No.	Size/cm	Description	Thread construction		
		CORDS		*Density/cm*	*Ply/Twist*	*Diameter/mm*
Sigersdal mose	A44102	Length 2.5–23	12 cord frags of 2 types. In 1 frag., the 2 types are tied together in a knot		Z3s Z2s	Z:3.5 (s:1.3) Z:3 (s:1.5)
Tulstrup mose	A 40120	Length 6 & 7	Quite heavily degraded parts of a cord		S4z	S:7 (z:3)
Tulstrup mose	A40122	Length 8	2 plaited cords of 5 single threads		No	8
Tulstrup mose	A40123	Length 8; in total *c.* 30	4 cords, 1 ending in a knot		S3z	S:6–7 (z:2–3)
		SEWING			*Twist*	*Diameter/mm*
Bolkilde mose	A54657	Many frags & loose threads	Needle-binding		Z	1
		TWINING		*Passive* *Active*	*Passive* *Active*	*Passive* *Active*
Tulstrup mose	A40121	10–15×5	Open twining where the distance between the passive threads is 8 mm and the active threads 3 mm	1 2 pairs	No No	2–3 2
Tulstrup mose	A40122	7.5×4.5	Dense twining in a tabby pattern. The passive threads cannot be determined	3 2	No No	2–3 2–3
Tulstrup mose	A40124	19.5×7–10	Fan-like open twining. The structure is expanded by adding extra passive threads. 2 active threads are crossed at 1 of the edges. At the other edge is seen an area, 5×2 cm, with a tabby-like twining	1 4–5 pairs	No No	5 4–5

all belong to the same cord made of plant fibres, although the specific species used has not been identified (Table 5.1). Most of the pieces are plied of three threads or elements, while some only consist of two elements. It is uncertain if the latter are merely less well preserved or represent a different type of cord. The cords measure 3.0–3.5 mm in diameter and are thus very thin; probably too thin to have served as a hanging/strangling cord, as the placement around the neck may otherwise imply.

Tools related to the spinning technology such as spindle whorls have not been identified in a Danish Stone Age context, probably because spinning was performed with tools other than the weighted spindle. This could, for instance, have been a spinning hook, and it is likely that the quite thick wool yarns used in Early Bronze Age weaving were produced using a spinning tool like this. I further suggest that a wooden tool (Fig. 5.3) found

during underwater excavations at Tudse Hage on western Zealand that the excavators until now have not linked to any particular specialised function[28] is a spinning hook. The angled shape of the stick makes it definitely suitable for spinning yarns, and supports this new interpretation. Hopefully, the identification of this tool will increase the recognition of other related textile tools in other Mesolithic or Neolithic contexts in the future.

The earliest Danish plant fibre textiles

The first evidence of non-loom produced textile structures appear in Denmark in the late Mesolithic. The most well-preserved examples come from the site of Tybrind Vig on western Funen, which are ^{14}C-dated to *c.* 4200 BC.[29] From here several pieces made in the needle-binding technique have been recorded.[30] The preserved pieces are all slightly

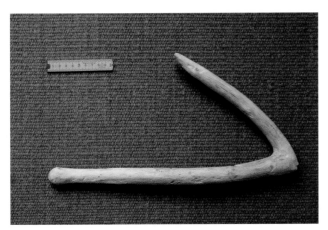

Fig. 5.3 The V-shaped tool from the Tudse Hage submarine settlement in western Zealand in Denmark. The tool, made of hazel, is 38 cm long, and would function ideally as a spinning hook. The settlement is dated to 5000–4000 BC (National Museum of Denmark, photo: Per Lotz).

different, but generally produced using long threads made of willow bast, poplar bast or various grasses. It is not known what these pieces were used for, nor if they were part of larger pieces used for clothing or domestic purposes, although the latter is probably the most likely. A similar piece made in the needle-binding technique was found in 1946 together with two male bog skeletons from Bolkilde on Als in southern Jutland, dated to *c.* 3400 BC.[31] Today the piece is very fragmented, the largest measuring 5×6 cm in a Z-twisted thread (Table 5.1). The fact that the piece was found together with human remains may suggest that its function was related to clothing. Underneath the neck of one of the skeletons was also found a plaited cord, which unfortunately is not preserved today. The needle-binding piece from Bolkilde is made of lime bast.

Other quite coarse textile structures, more akin to basketry, have been found in the Tulstrup Mose bog in northern Zealand.[32] These pieces are made of plaited or twisted threads and cords, sometimes worked into more solid structures using the twining technique (Table 5.1). In these cases, too, the fibres have been identified as lime bast.

One of the Tulstrup pieces consists of four entangled cords, each approximately 8 cm long, one of which ends in a knot (A40123, Fig. 5.4 C). Today, the threads are almost black and preserved in an oily substance that makes further analysis difficult. Another piece consist of two plaited cords, each 8 cm long, linked to a dense tabby structure made of 2–3 mm wide lime bast threads (A40122, Fig. 5.4 B). The latter may be compared to the structure of weaving, but should most likely be seen as made in a kind of basketry or matting technique. The third item is a typical twined piece (A40121, Fig. 5.4 A), made in open twining with one passive and two active (pairs) threads/cm. The passive threads are slightly thicker than the active ones and measure *c.* 3 mm in diameter. The last item from Tulstrup is a very interesting piece of open twining with

a fan-like shape created by inserting extra passive threads (A40124, Fig. 5.4 D). At the lower fragmented edge, two active threads are crossed, but why this is done is uncertain. Along the upper fragmented edge, a smaller area with a much denser tabby structure is seen. Whether this is part of the basic structure or belongs to another underlying piece cannot be determined due to the present fragile condition.

It is uncertain whether the twined pieces from Tulstrup Mose should be seen as structures that were used for clothing or whether they had other utilitarian purposes. The piece with the inserted extra passive threads has similarities with a twined piece from the pole-built settlement complex from Wetzikon-Robenhausen in Switzerland dated to 4000–3300 BC, which also belongs to the collections of the National Museum of Denmark.[33] One of these pieces that have the same insertion of extra threads may be interpreted as remains of a hat or cloak, but whether the same interpretation can be applied to this piece is uncertain.

Some of the structures mentioned above have surfaces that resemble tabby weaving, but it is not until the beginning of the Early Bronze Age that the weaving technology is securely documented in Scandinavia. Doughnut-shaped clay loom weights have been found in limited numbers in settlement contexts dated to the Neolithic, indicating the presence of the warp-weighted loom or a similar weight-controlled loom type, but due to the scattered finds these are not recognised as representing evidence of systematic and regular textile production. Examples of the doughnut-shaped loom weights are, for instance known from the settlement Lindebjerg on Funen, dated to *c.* 2000 BC.[34] A more complex find of loom weights was recovered in Nørre Holsted in southern Jutland. More than 17 doughnut-shaped loom weights were found in a pit together with bell beaker pottery, which dates the find to *c.* 2300 BC, *i.e.* the late Neolithic.[35] Recently, two similar large finds of doughnut-shaped loom weights from Neolithic contexts have been excavated in Sønder Nærå and Sankt Klemens on Funen. In Sønder Nærå, a pit inside a house contained more than seven loom weights weighing 600–800 g, dated to 2000–1700 BC, *i.e.* the very end of the Neolithic.[36] In the latter case, 13 loom weights were found in a large oval pit, but without any obvious connections to a settlement.[37]

Although the context and dating of the Nørre Holsted loom weights are not quite certain and still debated, the finds demonstrate that weaving was known and undertaken in the Neolithic, and that the hitherto scattered and not very prominent finds of loom weights are signs of a possibly growing weaving technology in Scandinavia. Further, as it is difficult to differentiate between Neolithic doughnut-shaped loom weights and the much later loom weights from the Viking Age (AD 800–1050), it cannot be excluded that many loom weights found in uncertain contexts have wrongly been ascribed to the Viking Age merely by comparison. In Scandinavia doughnut-shaped loom weights were produced without much variation for

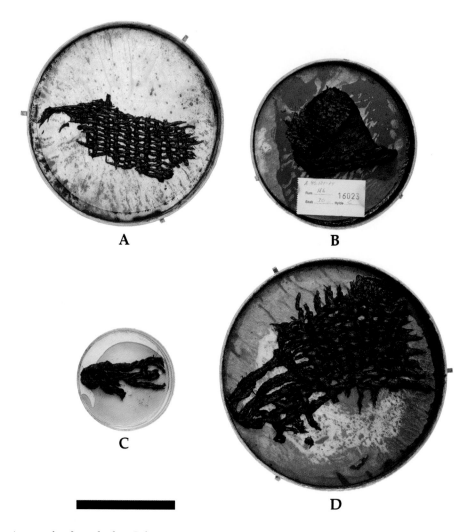

Fig. 5.4 The Stone Age textiles from the bog Tulstrup Mose in northern Zealand as they are preserved today: A. NM A40121; B. NM A40122; C. NM A40123; D. NM A40124. Among the finds are plied and plaited cords as well as several types of twined textiles. The material is lime bast. These finds are dated by the accompanying pottery to c. 3700 BC. *The black bar scale is 10 cm long (photo: National Museum of Denmark).*

more than 3000 years, and a re-evaluation of these finds may add new information to our understanding of the earliest textile production in Denmark.

Altogether, the first non-loom produced textiles preserved in Denmark testify to a technology based on plant fibres. It is not until the Early Bronze Age, c. 1700 BC, that wool fibres start to appear in the Scandinavian archaeological record used in true woven textiles, although the Style I flint dagger found in Weipenkathen in northern Germany dated to c. 2400–2000 BC can be seen as the first sign of the important role that this material was about to attain.[38]

Conclusion

The various finds presented in this overview can all be related to the earliest skin and textile production and are each in their way pieces of a larger picture of Stone Age visual appearance and everyday life. Compared to the dramatic transformation in textile production that can be documented via the Early Bronze Age textiles, where a fully developed wool technology materialises from its earliest appearance, the present knowledge of the Stone Age cloth culture offers a fascinating insight into a long and well-established tradition of the use of animal skin, spinning and sewing that did not need the weaving technology to cover the basic need for warm and practical clothing.

Further, it is evident that the textile craft in the Early Bronze Age was strongly influenced by the much older skin craft, and that the skin and the textile crafts had many common features and technological similarities.[39] The overlap between the two crafts can, for instance, be seen in the textiles imitating fur, such as the piled male hat and the shaggy male cloak found in the male oak coffin grave from Trindhøj in southern Jutland.[40] Although there are no skin clothing items preserved from the Early Bronze Age in Denmark, except shoes and belts, the textile clothing clearly demonstrates the technological link in patterns and techniques used, which eventually disappear in the

Early Iron Age. In the succeeding Iron Age period, on the contrary, textile and skin technologies were eventually completely separated and have to be seen and understood as two different crafts with different standards and traditions. However, this did not mean that skins and furs were no longer used for clothing. Skin clothing remained important in the Late Iron Age clothing tradition as well.

The earliest Scandinavian cloth culture was built on a tradition of using skins and local wild plant materials like nettle, different bast materials and grasses for the production of clothes and other utensils. The knowledge of processing and making threads of nettle and bast fibres was widespread and highly developed, and the know-how was definitely transferred into the Early Bronze Age textile technology, although this production is not very visible in the archaeological record. Likewise, spinning and sewing techniques were deeply integrated in the cloth culture, and also visible in the tool production from the very beginning. The non-loom textile techniques used were either based on different looping techniques, like needle-binding, or the basketry technique, like twining. Although loom weights are known from the Neolithic, it is not until the Early Bronze Age that weaving can be documented in Scandinavia. However, even based on the well-preserved Early Bronze Age textiles, identifying which type of loom these textiles were produced on is not straightforward. Danish Early Iron Age textiles indicate that the two-beam loom with a tubular warp without the use of warp tension was the preferred tool for weaving in Scandinavia, at least until the Common Era. Therefore, the lack of loom weights in an archaeological context cannot, just as in the case of spindle whorls, be taken as proof that weaving did not take place at all. It is definitely possible that in the Stone Age, as in later periods, the production of textiles could have been made using tools that did not leave clear traces in the archaeological record.

Although the finds presented here are fragmented and scattered, they still make it possible to compile a detailed and diverse picture of the earliest skin and textile production, and a clothing technology that also includes information on aesthetic appearances and colours. Altogether, the finds give a detailed and tangible understanding of the early Scandinavian cloth culture, which can be used in more general discussions of the organisation and development of prehistoric societies and their cloth cultures.

Notes

1   Harris 2008; 2012.
2   Jensen 2013.
3   Broholm and Hald 1940; Hald 1980; Bender Jørgensen 1986.
4   Bender Jørgensen 1990; Mannering *et al.* 2012; Mannering and Skals 2013.
5   Sørensen 2014.
6   Brandt 2015.
7   Brøndsted 1940; Jensen 2013, 58.

8   Noe-Nygaard 1971.
9   Richer and Noe-Nygaard 2003; Richter 2005.
10 Andersen 1998; Rowley-Conwy 1998.
11 Richter and Noe-Nygaard 2003, 21; Vang Petersen 2013.
12 Hatt 1914; Schmidt 2014.
13 Albrethsen and Brinch Petersen1976; Brinch Petersen *et al.* 1979, 42–47.
14 Brinch Petersen 1990; Brinch Petersen *et al.* 1993.
15 Jensen 2013, 118–119.
16 Vang Petersen 2015, 219.
17 Brinch Petersen *et al.* 1993, 67.
18 Brinch Petersen 1973; 1974; 2015, 147–152; Price *et al.* 2007.
19 Ebbesen 1995; Vang Petersen 2013, 159.
20 Ebbesen 2009, 47–48.
21 Schmidt 2014.
22 Schlabow 1976; Plicht *et al.* 2004.
23 Skaarup 1983; Skaarup and Grøn 2004, 111.
24 Müller 1897, 133; Kock 1998, 280–281.
25 Rønne 1989, 23.
26 Skaarup and Grøn 2004, 132–133, 141.
27 Bennike *et al.* 1987, 86, 105–106.
28 Lotz 2012.
29 Andersen 2013.
30 Bender Jørgensen 1990; Andersen 2013.
31 Bennike *et al.* 1986.
32 Becker 1947, 10–14; Bender Jørgensen 1990, 7.
33 Mannering and Skals 2013.
34 Jæger and Laursen 1983.
35 Rindel 1993.
36 Borre Lundø and Hansen 2015, 23–24.
37 Borre Lundø and Hansen 2015, 24–26.
38 Cassau 1935; Barber 1991, 184; Sørensen 2014, 28.
39 Broholm and Hald 1940, 18–19.
40 Broholm and Hald 1940, 27–39.

Bibliography

Albrethsen, S. E. and Brinch Petersen, E. 1976 Excavations of a Mesolithic cemetery at Vedbæk, Denmark. *Acta Archaeologica* 47, 1–28.

Andersen, S. H. 1998 Ringkloster. Ertebølle trappers and wild boar hunters in eastern Jutland. *Journal of Danish Archaeology* 12 (1994–1995), 13–60.

Andersen, S. H. 2013 *Tybrind Vig – Submerged Mesolithic Settlements in Denmark.* Jutland Archaeological Society Publications. Aarhus.

Barber, E. 1991 *Prehistoric Textiles: The Development of Cloth in the Neolithic and Bronze Ages with Special Reference to the Aegean.* Princeton.

Becker, J. C. 1947 Mosefundne lerkar fra yngre Stenalder. *Aarbøger for Nordisk Oldkyndighed og Historie* 1947, 1–318.

Bender Jørgensen, L. 1986 *Forhistoriske tekstiler i Skandinavien. Prehistoric Scandinavian Textiles.* Nordiske Fortidsminder Serie B Vol. 9. Copenhagen.

Bender Jørgensen, L. 1990 Stone-Age textiles in North Europe. In P. Walton and J. P. Wild (eds.), *Textiles in Northern Archaeology. NESAT III. Textile Symposium.* York and London, 1–10.

Bennike, P., Ebbesen, K. and Bender Jørgensen, L. 1986 Early Neolithic skeletons from Bolkilde bog, Denmark. *Antiquity* 60, 199–209.

Bennike, P., Ebbesen, K. and Bender Jørgensen, B. 1987 The bog find from Sigersdal. *Journal of Danish Archaeology* 5 (1986), 85–115.

Borre Lundø, M. and Hansen, J. 2015 Vævning i senneolitikum. *Fynboer og Arkæologi* 2, 22–27.

Brandt, L. Ø. 2015 Species identification of skins and development of sheep wool. An interdisciplinary study combining textile research, archaeology, and biomolecular methods. Unpublished PhD thesis. University of Copenhagen.

Brinch Petersen, E. 1973 Dobbeltgraven fra Dragsholm. *Nationalmuseets Arbejdsmark*, 187–188.

Brinch Petersen, E. 1974 Gravene ved Dragsholm. Fra jæger til bønder for 6000 år siden. *Nationalmuseets Arbejdsmark*, 112–120.

Brinch Petersen, E. 1990 Nye grave fra Jægerstenalderen. Strøby Egede og Vedbæk. *Nationalmuseets Arbejdsmark*, 19–33.

Brinch Petersen, E. 2015 *Diversity of Mesolithic Vedbæk*. Acta Archaeologica Supplementa XVI, Acta Archaeologica 86, Vol. I.

Brinch Petersen, E., Alexandersen, V., Petersen, P. V. and Christensen, C. 1979 Vedbækprojektet. Ny og gammel forskning. *Søllerødbogen* 1979, 21–97.

Brinch Petersen, E., Alexandersen, V. and Meiklejohn, C. 1993 Vedbæk, grave midt i byen. *Nationalmuseets Arbejdsmark*, 61–69.

Broholm, H. C. and Hald, M. 1940 *Costumes of the Bronze Age in Denmark: Contributions to the Archaeology and Textile-History of the Bronze Age*. Copenhagen.

Brøndsted, J. 1940 Human figures on a Danish Mesolithic Urus bone. *Acta Archaeologica* 11, 207–212.

Cassau, A. 1935. Ein Feuersteindolch mit Holzgriff und Lederscheide aus Wiepenkathen, Kreis Stade. *Mannus* 27, 199–207.

Ebbesen, K. 1995 Spätneolithische Schmuckmode. *Acta Archaeologica* 66, 219–279.

Ebbesen, K. 2009 En skinddragt fra Møgelmose i Jelling – Nye dateringer af oldtidens skinddragter. *Aarbøger for Nordisk Oldkyndighed og Historie* 2006, 37–51.

Hald, M. 1980 *Ancient Danish Textiles from Bogs and Burials*. Copenhagen.

Harris, S. 2008 Textiles, cloth, and skins: the problem of terminology and relationship. *Textile* 6.3, 222–237.

Harris, S. 2012 From the parochial to the universal: comparing cloth cultures in the Bronze Age. *European Journal of Archaeology* 15.1, 61–97.

Hatt, G. 1914 *Arktiske skinddragter I Eurasien og Amerika. Et etnografisk studie*. Copenhagen.

Jæger, A. and Laursen, J. 1983 Lindebjerg and Røjle Mose. Two Early Bronze Age settlements on Fyn. *Journal of Danish Archaeology* 2, 102–117.

Jensen, J. 2013 *The Prehistory of Denmark. From the Stone Age to the Vikings*. Gyldendal.

Kock, E. 1998 *Neolithic Bog Pots from Zealand, Møn, Lolland and Falster*. Nordiske Fortidsminder Serie B Vol. 16. Copenhagen.

Lotz, P. 2012 Stenalderredskaber af træ fra Tudse Hage del 3. *Fund and Fortid* 1, 8–11.

Mannering, U., Gleba, M. and Bloch Hansen, M. 2012 Denmark. In M. Gleba and U. Mannering (eds.), *Textiles and Textile Production in Europe from Prehistory to AD 400*. Ancient Textiles Series 11. Oxford and Oakville, 91–118.

Mannering, U. and Skals, I. 2013 Stenaldertekstilerne i Nationalmuseets Komparative Samling. *Nationalmuseets Arbejdsmark*, 80–95.

Müller, S. 1897 *Vor Oldtid. Danmarks Forhistoriske Archæologi*. Copenhagen.

Noe-Nygaard, N. 1971 Spur Dog spines from prehistory and early historic Denmark. An unexpected raw material for precision tools. *Bulletin of the Geological Society of Denmark* 21, 18–33.

Plicht, J. v. d., Sanden, W. A. B. v. d., Aerts, A. T. and Streurman, H. J. 2004 Dating bog bodies by means of ^{14}C-AMS. *Journal of Archaeological Science* 31, 471–491.

Price, T. D., Stanley, S. A., Bennike, P., Heinemeier, J., Noe-Nygaard, N., Brinch Petersen, E., Vang Petersen, P. and Richards, M. P. 2007 New information on the Stone Age graves at Dragsholm, Denmark. *Acta Archaeologica* 78.2, 193–219.

Richter, J. and Noe-Nygaard, N. 2003 A Late Mesolithic hunting station at Agernæs, Fyn, Denmark. Differentiation and specialization in the late Ertebøll-Culture, heralding in the introduction of agriculture? *Acta Archaeologica* 74, 1–64.

Richter, J. 2005 Selective hunting of pine marten, *Martes martes*, in Late Mesolithic Denmark. *Journal of Archaeological Science* 32.8, 1223–1231.

Rindel, P. O. 1993 Bønder fra stenalder til middelalder ved Nørre Holsted – nye arkæologiske undersøgelser på den kommende motorvej mellem Vejen og Holsted. *Mark og Montre* 1993, 19–27.

Rønne, P. 1989 Sænkesten. *Skalk* 6, 21–24.

Rowley-Conwy, P. 1998 Meat, furs and skins: Mesolithic animal bones from Ringkloster, a seasonal hunting camp in Jutland. *Journal of Danish Archaeology* 12 (1994–1995), 87–98.

Schlabow, K. 1976 *Textilfunde der Eisenzeit in Norddeutschland*. Neumünster.

Schmidt, A. L. 2014 Skin clothing from the North – new insights into the collection of the National Museum. In H. Gulløv (ed.), *Northern Worlds – Landscapes, Interactions and Dynamics. Research at the National Museum of Denmark. Proceedings of the Northern Worlds Conference Copenhagen 28–30 November 2012*. Studies in Archaeology and History 22, 273–292.

Skaarup, J. 1983 Submarine stenalderbopladser i Det sydfynske øhav. Fortidsminder og Bygningsbevaring. *Antikvariske Studier* 6, 137–161.

Skaarup, J. and Grøn, O. 2004 *Møllegabet II. A Submerged Mesolithic Settlement in Southern Denmark*. British Archaeological Reports International Series 1328. Oxford.

Sørensen, L. 2014 *From Hunter to Farmer in Northern Europe. Migration and Adaptation during the Neolithic and Bronze Age*. Acta Archaeologica Supplementa XV, Acta Archaeologica 85, Vol. II.

Vang Petersen, P. 2013 Mesolithic dogs. In O. Grimm and U. Schmölcke (eds.), *Hunting in Northern Europe until 1500 AD. Old Traditions and Regional Developments, Continental Sources and Continental Influences*. Neumünster, 147–162.

Vang Petersen, P. 2015 Papooser og amuletter – jægerstenalderens børneværn. *Nationalmuseets Arbejdsmark*, 282–295.

Loom weights and weaving at the archaeological site of São Pedro (Redondo, Portugal)

Catarina Costeira and Rui Mataloto

Introduction[1]

Ceramic plaques and crescent-shaped ceramic artefacts are fairly common in Late Neolithic and Chalcolithic sites (late 4th and early 3rd millennia BC), especially in settlements in the westernmost area of Iberia (in what is now Portugal),[2] though they do not seem to be common finds from funerary contexts.[3] The plaques are four-cornered, square, rectangular, oval or trapeze-shaped ceramic artefacts, which usually have several perforations. Crescents are semi-circular objects of varying sections that usually have two perforations.

Despite the frequent occurrence of these artefacts, their function has remained an enigmatic issue to several generations of Portuguese archaeologists, who did not always associate them with weaving,[4] and often treated them somewhat dismissively. By the late 20th century, however, the technical use of these so-called loom weights had become firmly established, several quantitative and provenance analyses were undertaken[5] and a number of studies, which aimed at standardising terminologies and the criteria for their analysis, were carried out.[6] In the 2000s and 2010s, loom weights were the subject of many academic studies that approached their typology and context in a more complex manner, often including relevant reflections on the weaving techniques of which they formed part.[7] The experimental approach of prehistoric weaving in this region has, however, not been applied.

Raw materials

Research on the fibres themselves is still at a very early stage and is severely conditioned by the scarcity of remains found and the frequently insular characteristics of Portuguese archaeology.[8]

In the area of what is Portugal now, there is a great variety in the shape and size of the loom weights dating to the end of 4th and 3rd millennia BC. This diversity seems to be related, in many cases, to the different areas where the objects were found. In northern and central Portugal, only plaques are found: these are usually square, oval or rectangular-shaped, have two or four perforations and are size-wise and, especially, weight-wise very robust.[9] In the southern areas of Portugal, both plaque and crescent-shaped weights are found, and both types are usually lighter and more delicate.[10] These differences in the shape and size may be related to the use of various types of fibres and even different types of looms, and could be a sign of the existence of diverse weaving traditions and styles in western Iberia.

In the Iberian Peninsula, cloth remains dating to the period between the 4th and the 2nd millennium BC are quite rare, and usually are associated with Bronze Age burial sites in the south-east, where a dry climate provides better conditions for their survival.[11] A wide range of vegetal fibres was used, and, even though flax seems to be the most common, other kinds of fibres were probably used for weaving. As some south-eastern Iberian burials show, flax was used to a great extent. Some complete sets of linen clothing have actually been found, as in the case of the burial at Cueva Sagrada, dating to a period similar to the one addressed in this paper,[12] and burial 121 at Castellón Alto, dating to the 2nd millennium BC.[13]

In Portugal, the admittedly scarce evidence seems to point in the same direction. Linen textile dating to the mid-3rd millennium BC has been found in Algarve and, as in the burial at Cueva Sagrada,[14] it featured some red lines produced by a dye based on Common madder (*Rubia tinctorum* L.).[15] This plant was an introduction to the Mediterranean basin, and was mentioned in the writings of Pliny the Elder as a plant that was used for a long time to produce textile dye.[16] Archaeozoological studies have lent some additional strength to the argument that plant fibres were used more commonly. In São Pedro, even though loom weights are quite common, the animal bones uncovered show that deer was prevalent and wool-bearing species relatively scarce (*Ovis/Capra* 9%).[17]

We therefore believe that southern Portugal and, in fact, the entirety of the Iberian south, would have followed the Mediterranean and Middle Eastern trends in the preferred use of plant-based fibres (especially flax) for weaving, and that the shift towards the preferential use of wool occurs at a later period.[18]

Wool use, albeit rare, can also be attested in the southern regions of the Peninsula during the 2nd millennium BC, as demonstrated by the woollen cap found in burial 121 of Castellon Alto.[19] Therefore, although both vegetable and animal fibres were used during the 3rd and 2nd millennia BC, we would argue that vegetable fibres and flax in particular were more frequently used in the production of clothing.

The São Pedro archaeological site

São Pedro is located in the Redondo municipality of the Évora district in the inland region of the Alentejo in southern Portugal (Fig. 6.1). The archaeological site discussed here is located on the top of a hill, overlooking the eastern Redondo plains and the southern foothills of the Serra d'Ossa, a territory that seems to have been occupied extensively during the Late Neolithic and Chalcolithic.

Between 2004 and 2009, the site was subjected to a thorough salvage operation, due to its impending destruction by the construction of a road. The excavation encompassed an area of around 2000 m², approximately two-thirds of the total area of the site. During the last decade, São Pedro has been the subject of many studies concerning its phasing,[20] specific archaeological contexts, like the bell-beaker phase,[21] artefact studies[22] and archaeozoological analyses.[23]

The archaeological record suggests that São Pedro was occupied between the late 4th millennium and most of the 3rd millennium BC. This time frame has been divided into five main phases (Fig. 6.2), which feature distinct spatial organisations, different types of architecture and different types of artefacts. Phase 1 appears to be an open settlement, characterised by structures built mostly of perishable materials, and dated some time between the late 4th and early 3rd millennia BC. This open settlement is followed

Fig. 6.1 Overview of the São Pedro site identifying the sectors and location in Iberian Peninsula (cartographic archive of Rui Mataloto).

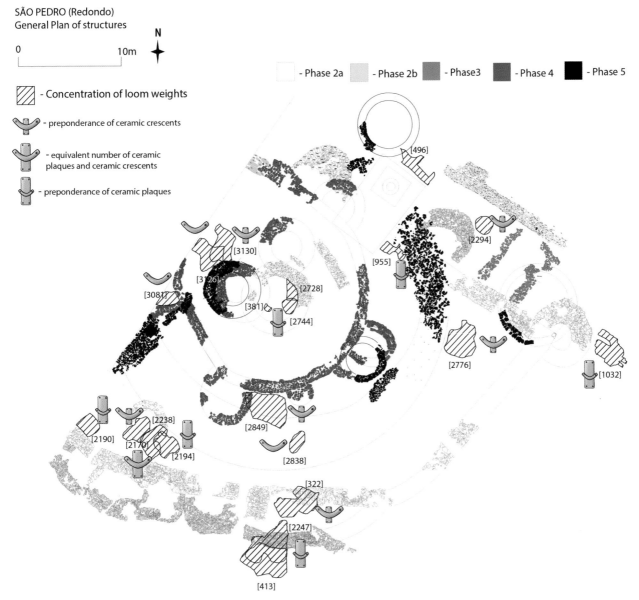

SÃO PEDRO (Redondo)
General Plan of structures

N

0   10m

⬛ - Concentration of loom weights

- preponderance of ceramic crescents

- equivalent number of ceramic plaques and ceramic crescents

- preponderance of ceramic plaques

- Phase 2a   - Phase 2b   - Phase3   - Phase 4   - Phase 5

[496]
[3130]
[3126]
[308]
[381]
[2728]
[2744]
[955]
[2294]
[2776]
[1032]
[2190]
[2238]
[2170]
[2194]
[2849]
[2838]
[322]
[2247]
[413]

Fig. 6.2 General plan of São Pedro site with main structures and loom weight concentrations.

by the first major construction phase 2, characterised by the appearance of the first line of walls, a polygonal structure with four large turrets on the outside. In addition to the enclosing walls, this phase also features two large circular stone buildings, possibly towers, located in the central area of the site, and several other smaller structures made of perishable materials.

Around the mid-3rd millennium BC, following the abandonment and destruction of most of the previous structures, a light and dispersed reoccupation of the site seems to have taken place (phase 3). This stage, however, does not seem to be related to any significant buildings.

Phase 4 features the construction of a new circular wall, roughly 20 m in diameter, with several round turrets on the

outside. Even though two towers were again built inside the fortification, most of the stone arrangements and structures made of perishable materials were located on the outside of the fortification.

Another apparently undefended phase follows the abandonment of the previous structures, featuring a number of stone foundations for huts, scattered throughout the excavated area. The artefacts belonging to this stage include a small number of bell-beakers and other elements characteristic of the late 3rd millennium BC.[24] The end of this occupation is marked by a large pavement in stone, which surrounds the ruin of the old settlement. This structure, composed of one or two lines of stones, may have been intended to highlight the area, possibly in an effort to

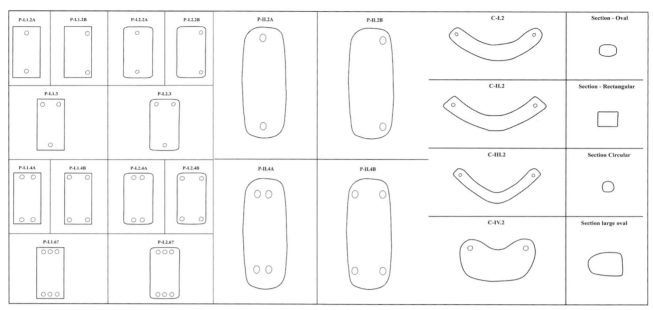

Fig. 6.3 Typological organisation of loom weights (after Costeira 2010): P-I- Rectangular plaques; P-II- Oval plaques; C-I- Oval section crescent; C-II- Rectangular section crescent; C-III- Circular section crescent; C-IV- Large oval section crescent.

reinforce group cohesion and identity towards the end of the 3rd millennium BC.

The dynamic construction activity and the succession of stages in which large structures were abandoned or dismantled affects the stratigraphic formation process in São Pedro and means that there is a scarcity of primary contexts.

The loom weights

We have analysed the entire assemblage of loom weights discovered in various phases of São Pedro, adding therefore a broader scope to the discussion in previous publications.[25] This analysis includes some new elements, in part due to the revision of the classification of the potsherds that is currently taking place. The technological and typological assessment of the discussed artefacts follows the criteria previously established by Costeira (2010), and subsequently modified by Costeira and Mataloto (2013). These criteria have already been tested in the study of evidence from other archaeological sites.[26]

The 3709 loom weights analysed are, for the most part, poorly preserved fragments that make up 98% of the assemblage. Two different types of plaques (rectangular and oval) were defined based on the general shape, and several sub-varieties were proposed based on the shape of their edges (straight or rounded), corners (straight or rounded), number of perforations (two, three, four and six) and their location (centred or uncentred). Different types of crescent-shaped weights were defined solely on the basis of the shape of their section (oval, rectangular and circular), as all entirely preserved examples have a centred perforation in each extremity (Figs. 6.3 and 6.4).

Most of the plaque weights belong to the rectangular type, which accounts for 92% of this group. Oval-shaped plaques make up only 4% of the sample, whereas the remaining fragments could not be classified. Rectangular plaques have, for the most part, rounded corners and edges (79%), whereas straight-edged and straight-cornered plaques are fewer in number (21%).

Plaques can feature two perforations (one on each side), three perforations (two on one side and one on the other), four perforations (two on each extremity) and six perforations (three per side). The frequency of plaques with four perforations (53%) is slightly larger than the number of plaques with two (47%), and the remaining varieties are very scarce. There is only one example of a plaque having three perforations and two fragments which have three perforations on the preserved side. Plaques with two and six perforations are not only rare among the weights found in São Pedro, but seem to be quite uncommon on other Chalcolithic sites, even if a number of similar items has been discovered in other sites of the south-east Peninsula, such as Los Millares and Terrera Ventura.[27] The correct assessment of the number of asymmetrical types is difficult, given the scarcity of intact pieces that could mean that these types were more common than it would seem.

In most of the plaques with two perforations, the holes are centred, whereas in the case of tools with four perforations, the holes are usually closer to the sides (Fig. 6.3).

The crescent-shaped weights found in São Pedro fall under into four distinct groups, distinguished by their section, which correspond well to other Chalcolithic sites of the southern Iberian Peninsula. Quantity-wise, oval-sectioned crescents are the most prevalent type, accounting for 65% of all crescents. Circular-sectioned crescents are the second most common group (23%) and rectangular-sectioned crescents are the least common (11%). The crescent SPD [0] 2558 (Fig. 6.4) has a number of features – such as a relatively straight and robust shape and a very wide oval section – which set it apart from other crescents found at this site. However, since similar artefacts have been found at nearby sites, such as Monte da Ribeira,[28] Perdigões[29] and Mercador,[30] this particular form was identified as a specific type. It is also worth mentioning that similar loom weights have been found throughout the Iberian Peninsula, both inland[31] and on the Mediterranean coast,[32] as well as in some areas of Central Europe.[33]

An analysis of the size, thickness, weight and distance between the perforations of the loom weights is a fundamental step towards understanding the actual function of these tools. However, the large number of fragmented weights affects the quality of the data obtained (total weight, for instance, could only be measured directly in the case of 95 artefacts). Generally speaking, most crescents and plaques are usually no more than 2 cm thick and weigh less than 100 g. This shows that the loom weights in this assemblage are fairly thin and light (Fig. 6.4), especially in comparison to those found in other Chalcolithic sites of the Iberian Peninsula[34] and Europe.

The diameter of the perforations in the plaque weights varies between 0.1 cm and 0.7 cm; however, most of them fall under the 0.3 to 0.5 cm range. In the case of the crescents, the diameters of the perforations vary slightly more, ranging from 0.2 to 1.0 cm; however, diameters between 0.3 to 0.5 cm are again more common. Even though complete examples are quite rare, there is a possibility of a relationship between the larger perforations and four-holed oval and rectangular plaques, and the heavier oval-sectioned crescents.

The distance between perforations on opposite sides is similar in both types of weights: in plaques the distance ranges from 4.1 to 10.9 cm and in crescents from 5.7 to 9.1 cm.

For the most part, the weights analysed are well fired and made from a compact and relatively homogeneous granitic fabric that includes some medium to small temper. Surfaces seem to be predominantly smoothed, while decorations very scarce. It is found on four plaques and three crescents.

Provenance of the loom weights

In São Pedro, loom weights were found throughout the excavation area, spanning the several phases of the occupation, in fairly heterogeneous deposits but, for the most part, poorly preserved and in small numbers. This suggests that loom weights were present in the stratigraphy mostly as the result of being discarded.

However, in sectors B, D and F, several stratigraphic units have been uncovered, *e.g.* the filling of pits, in which

large numbers of loom weights (10 to 50) were preserved (Fig. 6.2). In the interpretation of these sets of weights, we must take into account the diversity of types and the fragmentation of tools. This being said, we do not consider the 138 weights found in pit [1032] in sector D (Fig. 6.2) as remains of a loom *in situ*, due to the high degree of fragmentation of the weights themselves. In our opinion, it seems more likely that these artefacts were discarded alongside other materials from the domestic sphere and weaving may have taken place in the nearby dwellings. The loom weights found in sectors B and F are similarly preserved and therefore their interpretation involves similar problems.

On the other hand, we find it relevant that the large concentrations of loom weights usually comprise one dominant type.

In sector D, inside pit [2336] a group of 50 crescents was uncovered, mostly oval-sectioned, of which 14 were almost complete and deposited on the west side of the pit. In this particular case, the discarding of an entire set of weights seems quite plausible.

In addition to the pits, some other features, such as the hut/tower [345], have provided a large number of loom weights. However, once more the presence of several types, the great variety of deposits in which they were found and the general poor state of their preservation do not suggest the presence of looms in these contexts (Fig. 6.2).

The location of the weights in the different areas of the site of São Pedro and, especially, the distribution of the larger sets might support the hypothesis that weaving areas existed in the living spaces. Regarding the phasing of the stratigraphic units in which large numbers of loom weights were found, these belong for the most part to the early phases (1 and 2) of the site.

The large concentrations seem to be located in apparently peripheral areas, or in relation to the walls – on their inner sides in the south-western area of the site (in concentrations from [2170], [2190], [2194], [2238]) or on the outside of the fortifications in the north-east (filling of [1032]) (Fig. 6.2). However, we cannot be sure that the concentrations date to the same phases. These concentrations may be related to the areas in which weaving took place in a more intense way. Nevertheless, this does not mean that weaving on smaller scale was not a general occupation on the site.

The available data show that both types of loom weights appear in every single phase of the site, even though an increased number of crescents are documented in the later stages.

A brief consideration of the function of crescents and plaques

The study of Iberian loom weights usually focuses on their morphological and technological aspects, usually forgoing traseological analyses and experimental approaches based on the reconstruction of the looms themselves. This

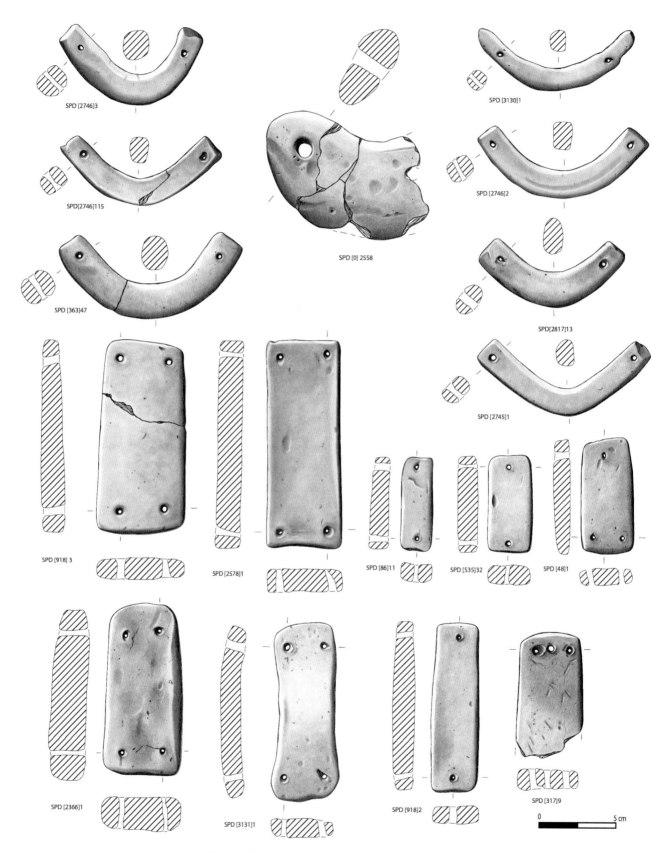

SPD [2746]3

SPD[2746]115

SPD [363]47

SPD [0] 2558

SPD [3130]1

SPD [2746]2

SPD[2817]13

SPD [2745]1

SPD [918] 3

SPD [2578]1

SPD [86]11

SPD [535]32

SPD [48]1

SPD [2366]1

SPD [3131]1

SPD [918]2

SPD [317]9

0   5 cm

Fig. 6.4 Plaques and crescents from the São Pedro site.

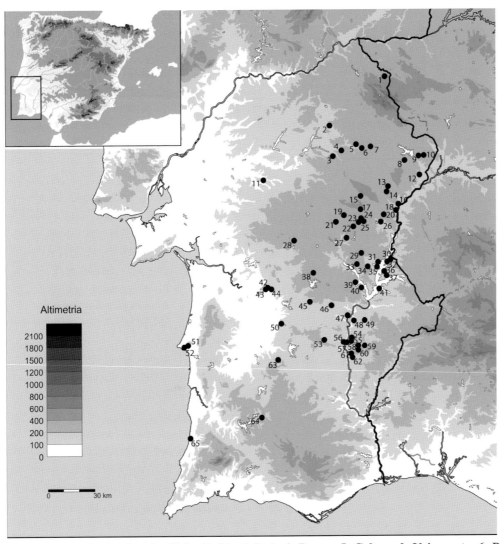

1-Castelo de Vidais; 2- Alter do Chão; 3- São João 1; 4- Braga; 5- Cabeço de Vaiamonte; 6- Pombal
7-Santo António 3; 8- Cabeço do Torrão; 9- Santa Vitória; 10- Cabeço do Cubo; 11- Castelo de Pavia
12-Paraíso; 13- Aboboreira; 14- Famão; 15 - Salgada; 16- Malhada das Mimosas; 17-Argolia
18-Perdigoa; 19-Colmeeiro; 20-Cubo; 21-Currais 1; 22-Cabido; 23-São Pedro; 24- Monte da Ribeira
25- Caladinho; 26- São Gens; 27- Grou 1; 28- Castelo do Giraldo; 29- Perdigões; 30- Mercador
31- Porto das Carretas; 32- Castelo do Azalinho; 33- Torre do Esporão; 34- Areias 15; 35- Barrisqueira 2
36- Moinho de Valadres; 37-Monte do Tosco; 38- Murteiras; 39- Senhora da Giesteira; 40- Outeiro
41- Cerros Verdes 3; 42-Castelo Torrão; 43-Monte da Tumba; 44-Cabeço da Mina; 45-Cabeço da Azurria
46-Alto da Mangaancha; 47- Sala 1; 48- Magoita; 49-Parreirinha 4; 50- Porto Torrão; 51- Monte Novo 1
52-Vale Pincel 2; 53- Alto do Outeiro; 54- Casa Branca 7; 55-Santa Margarida; 56- Três Moinhos
57-Foz do Enxoé; 58- Alto de Brinches 3; 59-Torre Velha 3; 60- Atalaia do Peixoto; 61- Cerro dos Castelos
de São Brás; 62- São Brás; 63-Castelo de Aljustrel; 64- Cortadouro; 65-Montes de Baixo

Fig. 6.5 Settlements in Alentejo (southern Portugal) with loom weights (after Costeira and Mataloto 2013).

limits our approach to the weaving techniques to a purely theoretical basis.

The quantity, morphological similarities, the presence of perforations with similar diameters (0.3–0.7 cm) and their symmetrical positions are probably the best arguments for suggesting that the plaques were used in weaving.

The shape of the rectangular plaques, the diverse number of perforations, the variety of the positions of perforations and relatively small size and weight of the tools may suggest their employment in tablet weaving, as has already been argued by several authors, such as Carmen Alfaro,[35] Cardito Rollán,[36] Rui Boaventura[37] and Sergio Gomes.[38]

The interpretation of this type of plaque as weaving tablets may explain their various forms. The different number and location of the perforations would influence the numbers of rotations of the plaques and the size of the fabrics produced. Tablets are generally very hard to trace in the archaeological record, due to the use of perishable materials and the diversity of plaque types. The fact that the remains are often scattered makes it difficult to identify the minimum number of plaques used in tablet weaving. Wear marks would, for the most part, appear on the perforations, but they are difficult to interpret due to the multiple uses of the plaques, which result in multidirectional traces.

The heavier rectangular and oval-shaped plaques could have been used as weights on a vertical loom. If so, it is suggested that the diversity of shapes and sizes of the plaques and the different types of looms involved would allow the production of a large variety of fabrics.

The dimensions of the several types of crescents (*e.g.* width, thickness, length and distance between the perforations) are similar to those of the plaques, especially if we compare the types of tools with only two perforations. These similarities, already observed by other authors,[39] seem to support the hypothesis that both types of tools were used in the same type of process. Even though this hypothesis has not yet been experimentally tested, it has been suggested that the shape of the crescents might allow various manipulation of threads, *e.g.* twining. The larger crescents could have been used as weights in vertical looms; this hypothesis is supported by experimental work carried out in other parts of Europe.[40]

Final considerations

The intensification of archaeological excavations carried out in the Iberian south-west (namely in the Alentejo region) in the last two decades has greatly increased the number of excavated sites datable to the 4th and 3rd millennia BC. Many of these sites have provided large amounts of ceramic loom weights that represent both types, crescents and plaques (Fig. 6.5), or comprise only one type, which may be related to the region.[41] The large amount of recently available data requires a proportionally larger focus on the study of weaving in this period, even if direct evidence of this activity (fibres and fabrics) remains very scarce and restricted to a couple of linen fabrics found at funerary sites[42] and imprints on pottery and clay[43] preserved in settlements. The scarcity of archaeological textiles is directly related to the climate and geology of the area, which do not facilitate the preservation of organic matter.

Therefore, the study of ceramic loom weights becomes an essential component of the understanding of the looms themselves and the types of cloth that may have been produced by using them.

In the future, we consider it essential to extend the morphological and metrical study of the artefacts carried out at the site of São Pedro also to other sites. Moreover, the reconstruction of looms and experimental weaving with replicas of crescents and plaques should be performed, in order to verify the functionality of these tools. Additionally, it is crucial to understand whether the light weight of these artefacts could limit their use as loom weights. The reconstruction of the spinning process, based on an analysis of the spindle whorls found in São Pedro, is also a question we hope to investigate in the future.

With this paper, we aim to fill in some gaps in the patterns of distribution of the prehistoric loom weights in Western Europe.

Notes

1 The paper was written during a PhD scholarship from Fundação para a Ciência e Tecnologia (FCT) SFRH/BD/76693/2011, Uniarq/FL-UL, the Municipality of Redondo. The authors thank Richard Peace for the text translation to English.
2 Costeira 2010; Pereira 2010; 2012; Costeira and Mataloto, 2013; Gonçalves *et al.* 2013.
3 Rocha 2005, 147–148; Andrade 2009.
4 Correia 1921; Vasconcelos 1929; Paço 1940.
5 Silva and Soares 1987; Gonçalves 1989.
6 Diniz 1994; Valera 1997.
7 Gomes 2003; 2013; Costeira 2010; Pereira 2010.
8 Paço 1954; Soares and Ribeiro 2003; Móran 2014, 250.
9 Valera 1997; 2007; Gomes 2003; Pereira 2010; Arnaud 2013.
10 Costeira 2010; Gomes 2013.
11 Alfaro 1984; Jover Maestre and López Padilla 2013.
12 Ayala 1987; Rivera and Obón 1987; Alfaro 1992; 2005.
13 Molina *et al.* 2003.
14 Jover Maestre and López Padilla 2013, 153.
15 Soares and Ribeiro 2003.
16 Pliny the Elder N. H. 19.17.
17 Davis and Mataloto 2012.
18 McCorriston 1997, 518.
19 Contreras *et al.* 2000, 89; Rodríguez-Ariza *et al.* 2004, 14; Jover Maestre and López Padilla 2013, 150.
20 Mataloto *et al.* 2007; 2009; Mataloto 2010.
21 Mataloto *et al.* 2015.
22 Costeira 2010; 2012; Costeira and Mataloto 2013; Costeira *et al.* 2013.
23 Davis and Mataloto 2012.
24 Mataloto *et al.* 2015.
25 Costeira and Mataloto 2013.
26 Mataloto *et al.* 2012; Costeira 2013.
27 Cardito Rollán 1996, 138–139, fig. 11.
28 Calado 2001, 164, fig. 28.
29 Valera 1998, 102.
30 Gomes 2013, 110.
31 López-Plaza 1979; Martín de la Cruz 1986.
32 Barber 1991.
33 Grömer 2010, 106.
34 Valera 1997; Gomes 2003; Pereira 2010; 2012.
35 Alfaro 1984.
36 Cardito Rollán 1996, 142–143.

37   Boaventura 2001, 51–53.
38   Gomes 2013, 116.
39   Boaventura 2001, 52; Gomes 2013, 117–118.
40   Grömer 2010, 106; Grömer this volume; Ulanowska this volume.
41   Costeira and Mataloto 2013.
42   Soares and Ribeiro 2003; Valera 2014, 43–44.
43   Calado 2001, 105.

Bibliography

Alfaro, C. 1992 Two copper age tunics from Lorca, Murcia (Spain). In L. Bender-Jørgensen and E. Munksgaard (eds.), *Archaeological Textiles in Northern Europe. Report from the 4th NESAT Symposium 1–5 May 1990 in Copenhagen.* Copenhagen, 20–30.

Alfaro Giner, C. 1984 *Tejido y cestería en la Península Ibérica: Historia de su técnica e industrias desde la Prehistoria hasta la Romanización.* Biblioteca Prehistorica Hispana 21. Madrid.

Alfaro Giner, C. 2005 Informe sobre los restos textiles y de cestaria procedentes de Cueva Sagrada (Lorca, Murcia). In J. J. Eiroa García (ed.), *El cerro de la Virgen de la Salud (Lorca).* Colección Documentos: Serie Arqueología 5. Murcia, 227–246.

Andrade, M. 2009 Megalitismo e comunidades megalíticas na área da Ribeira Grande (Alto Alentejo) – definição e caracterização do fenómeno de 'megalitização' da paisagem na área austral do Norte alentejano. Unpublished MA thesis, Universidade de Lisboa.

Arnaud, J. 2013 Reflexões em torno das placas de cerâmica com gravuras de Vila Nova de S. Pedro (Azambuja). In J. Arnaud, A. Martins and C. Neves (eds.), *A Arqueologia em Portugal – 150 anos.* Lisboa, 447–455.

Ayala, M. M. 1987 Enterramientos calcolíticos de la sierra de la Tercia, Lorca, Murcia. Estudio preliminar. *Anales de Prehistoria y Arqueología* 3, 9–24.

Barber, E. J. W. 1991 *Prehistoric Textiles: The Development of Cloth in the Neolithic and Bronze Ages with Special Reference to the Aegean.* Princeton.

Boaventura, R. 2001 *O sítio calcolítico do Pombal (Monforte): Uma recuperação possível de velhos e novos dados.* Trabalhos de Arqueologia 20. Lisboa.

Calado, M. 2001 *Da Serra d'Ossa ao Guadiana: um estudo de pré-história regional.* Lisboa: Instituto Português de Arqueologia. Trabalhos de Arqueologia 19.

Cardito Róllan, L. M. 1996 Las manufacturas textiles en la prehistoria: Las placas de telar en el Calcolítico Peninsular. *Zephyrus* 49, 125–145.

Contreras, F., Rodrigez, O., Cámara, J. and Moreno, A. 2000 *Hace 4000 años. Vida y muerte en dos poblados de la Alta Andalucía. Catálogo de exposición.* Jaén.

Correia, V. 1921 *El Neolitico de Pavia (Alentejo, Portugal).* Memoria/Junta para ampliación de estudios e investigaciones cientificas, Comisión de investigaciones paleontológicas y prehistóricas 27. Madrid.

Costeira, C. 2010 Os componentes de tear do povoado de S. Pedro (Redondo, Alentejo Central), 3° milénio a.n.e. Unpublished MA thesis, Universidade de Lisboa.

Costeira, C. 2012 Placas e crescentes – Análise de um conjunto de componentes de tear do sítio arqueológico de S. Pedro (Redondo, 3° milénio a.n.e.). *Arqueologia e História* 62–63, 23–37.

Costeira, C. 2013 Os componentes de tear do sítio arqueológico Alto de Brinches 3 (Serpa, Baixo Alentejo). In J. Jiménez Ávila, M. Bustamente and M. García Cabezas (eds.), *Actas del VI Encuentro de Arqueologia del Suroeste Peninsular.* Villafranca de los Barros, 595–624.

Costeira, C. and Mataloto, R. 2013 Os componentes de tear do povoado de S. Pedro (Redondo, Alentejo Central). In J. Jiménez Ávila, M. Bustamente and M. García Cabezas (eds.), *Actas del VI Encuentro de Arqueologia del Suroeste Peninsular.* Villafranca de los Barros, 625–667.

Costeira, C., Mataloto, R. and Roque, C. 2013 Uma primeira abordagem à cerâmica decorada do 4°./3°. Milénio a.n.e. dos povoados de S. Pedro. (Redondo). In J. Arnaud, A. Martins and C. Neves (eds.), *A Arqueologia em Portugal – 150 anos.* Lisboa, 397–406.

Davis, S. and Mataloto, R. 2012 Animal remains from Chalcolithic São Pedro (Redondo, Alentejo): evidence for a crisis in the Mesolithic. *Revista Portuguesa de Arqueologia* 5.15, 47–85.

Diniz, M. 1994 Pesos de tear e tecelagem no calcolítico em Portugal. *Trabalhos de Antropologia e etnologia* 34.3–4, 133–149.

Gomes, S. 2003 Contributos para o estudo dos pesos de tear de castelo Velho de Freixo Numão (Vila Nova de Foz Côa): exercícios de interpretação do registo arqueológico. Unpublished MA thesis, Universidade do Porto.

Gomes, S. 2013 Tecelagem e Pesca: os pesos. In A. C. Valera (ed.), *As Comunidades agro pastoris na margem esquerda do Guadiana (2ª metade do IV aos finais do II milénio AC).* Évora, 109–126.

Gonçalves, V. S. 1989 *Megalitismo e metalurgia no Alto Algarve Oriental: Uma aproximação integrada.* Lisboa.

Gonçalves, V. S., Sousa, A. C. and Costeira, C. 2013 Walls, gates and towers. Fortified settlements in the south and centre of Portugal: some notes about violence and walls in the 3rd millennium BCE. *Cuadernos de Prehistoria y Arqueología de la Universidad de Granada* 23, 35–97.

Grömer, K. 2010 *Prähistorische Textilkunst in Mitteleuropa – Geschichte des Handwerkes und Kleidung vor den Römern.* Wien.

Jover Maestre, F. J. and López Padilla, J. A. 2013 La producción textil durante la Edad del Bronce en el cuadrante suroriental de la península Ibérica: materias primas, productos, instrumentos y procesos de trabajo. *Zephyrus* 71, 149–171.

Lopez Plaza, S. 1979 Aportaciones al conocimiento de los poblados eneolíticos de la Meseta Norte española: La cerámica. *Setúbal Arqueológica* 5, 76–102.

Martin De La Cruz, J. C. 1986 *Papa Uvas II. Aljaraque, Huelva. Campañas de 1981 a 1983. Excavaciones Arqueológicas de España.* Madrid.

Mataloto, R. 2010 O 4.°/3.° milénio a. C. no povoado de São Pedro (Redondo, Alentejo Central): fortificação e povoamento na planície centro alentejana. In V. S. Gonçalves and A. C. Sousa (eds.), *Transformação e mudança no Centro e Sul de Portugal no 3.° milénio a.n.e. Actas do Colóquio Internacional.* Cascais, 263–296.

Mataloto, R., Estrela, S. and Alves, C. 2007 As fortificações calcolíticas de São Pedro (Redondo, Alentejo Central, Portugal). In E. Cerrillo and J. Valadés (eds.), *Los primeros campesinos de La Raya: Aportaciones recientes al conocimiento del neolitico y calcolítico en Extremadura y Alentejo*. Actas de las Jornadas de Arqueología del Museu de Cáceres 1. Cáceres, 113–141.

Mataloto, R., Estrela, S. and Alves, C. 2009 Die kupferzeitlichen Befestigungen von São Pedro (Redondo), Alentejo, Portugal. *Madrider Mitteilungen* 50, 3–39.

Mataloto, R., Costeira, C., Davis, S., Clemente, R. and Santos, I. 2012 Os povoados de fossos do Paraíso: uma ocupação do IV/III milénios a. C. na região de Elvas. Balanço das intervenções 2009–2010. In M. Deus (ed.), *Actas do V Encontro de Arqueologia do Sudoeste Peninsular*. Almodôvar, 39–72.

Mataloto, R., Costeira, C. and Roque, C. 2015 Torres, cabanas e memória – A fase V e a cerâmica campaniforme do povoado de São Pedro (Redondo, Alentejo Central). *Revista Portuguesa de Arqueologia* 18, 81–100.

McCorriston, J. 1997 The fiber revolution: textile extensification, alienation and social stratification in Ancient Mesopotamia. *Current Anthropology* 38.4, 517–535.

Molina, F., Rodríguez-Ariza, M.ª O., Jiménez Brobeil, S. and Botella, M. 2003 La sepultura 121 del yacimiento argárico de El Castellón Alto (Galera, Granada). *Trabajos de Prehistoria* 60.1, 153–158.

Morán, E. 2014 Alcalar, organização do território e processo de formação de um estado prístino V–III milenio a.n.e. Unpublished PhD thesis, Universidade de Sevilha.

Paço, A. 1940 *Placas de Barro de Vila Nova de S. Pedro*. Congresso do Mundo Português, Memórias e comunicações apresentadas ao congresso de Pré e Proto-História vol. I. Lisboa, 236–249.

Paço, A. 1954 *Sementes Pré-Históricas do Castro de Vila Nova de S. Pedro*. Série 2, 5. Lisboa.

Pereira, M. 2010 Pesos de tear e elementos de tear na Pré-história recente portuguesa: contributos para pensar o processo arqueológico. Unpublished MA thesis, Universidade do Porto.

Pereira, M. 2012 Rethinking past practices: two contributions to the study of loom elements. *Journal of Iberian Archaeology* 15 (http://adecap.blogspot.pt/p/journal-of-iberian-archaeology-vol-15.html, accessed 4 October 2015).

Pliny the Elder, *The Natural History*, ed. J. Bostock and H. T. Riley (http://www.perseus.tufts.edu/hopper/text? doc=Plin.+Nat.+toc, accessed 5 October 2015).

Rivera, D. and Obón, C. 1987 Apéndice 11: Informe sobre los restos vegetales procedentes del enterramiento calcolítico de la Cueva Sagrada (Comarca de Lorca, Murcia). *Anales de Prehistoria y Arqueología* 3, 31–37.

Rocha, L. 2005 Origens do megalitismo funerário no Alentejo central: a contribuição de Manuel Heleno. Unpublished PhD thesis, Universidade de Lisboa.

Silva, C. T. and Soares, J. 1976–1977 Contribuição para o conhecimento dos Povoados calcolíticos do Baixo Alentejo e Algarve. *Setúbal Arqueológica* 2–3,179–272.

Silva, C. T. and Soares, J. 1987 O povoado fortificado do Monte da Tumba I – Escavações arqueológicas de 1982–86 (resultados preliminares). *Setúbal Arqueológica* 8, 29–79.

Soares, M. and Ribeiro, M 2003 *Identificação, análise e datação de um tecido pintado proveniente de um monumento megalítico da necrópole de Belle France (Monchique, Algarve, Portugal)*. V Congreso Ibérico de Arqueometría. Libro de Resúmenes de Actas. Cádiz, 155–156.

Valera, A. 1997 *O castro de Santiago (Fornos de Algodres – Guarda). Aspectos da calcolitização da bacia do Alto Mondego*. Textos Monográficos 1. Lisboa.

Valera, A. 1998 Análise da componente cerâmica do povoado dos Perdigões. In M. Lago. C. Duarte, A. Valera, J. Albergaria, F. Almeida and A. F. Carvalho (eds.), O povoado dos Perdigões (Reguengos de Monsaraz): dados preliminares dos trabalhos arqueológicos realizados em 1997. *Revista Portuguesa de Arqueologia* 1.1, 80–104.

Valera, A. 2007 *Dinâmicas locais de identidade: estruturação de um espaço de tradição no 3º milénio a. C. (Fornos de Algodres, Guarda)*. Fornos de Algodres.

Valera, A. 2014 *Bela Vista 5 – Um recinto do final do 3º milénio a.n.e. (Vidigueira, Beja)*. Era monográfica 2. Lisboa.

Vasconcelos, J. L.1929 *Antiguidades do Alentejo*. O Arqueólogo Português Série I.28, 158–200.

Evidence of textile technology in the Early Neolithic site of La Draga (Banyoles, Spain). Some hypotheses

*Miriam de Diego, Raquel Piqué, Antoni Palomo, Xavier Terradas,
Maria Saña, Ignacio Clemente-Conte and Millán Mozota*

Introduction

Evidence of early prehistoric textiles in archaeological sites is scarce due to the extremely low level of preservation of organic materials.[1] The oldest textile fragments recovered were made mainly from vegetable fibres. Later on, wool might also have played an important role. Both vegetable and animal fibres are characterised by fragility and low resistance to decomposition in soil; wool, due to its physical features, as Carmen Alfaro noted in her work, is even more infrequently preserved.[2]

Several studies indicate that plant fibres have been used for textile production in Europe since the Neolithic. Evidence from Central Europe (the Circum-Alpine lake dwellings) supports this assumption.[3] In this area, both linen and textile implements, such as loom weights and spindle whorls, date even to 3400 BC. In the Iberian Peninsula, fragments of woven linen fabrics have been found, for example, in Later Neolithic burials in the Cacín river basin (Alhmana, Granada),[4] at the Chalcolithic site of Cueva Sagrada (Lorca, Murcia)[5] and Los Millares (Almería) dated 2700 BC,[6] and at the Bronze Age site of Castellon Alto.[7] Wool also appears in Bronze Age contexts.[8]

Despite the fragility and bad preservation conditions of the fabrics, the tools employed in textile production, usually made of pottery, stone, bone or antler, are well preserved in the archaeological material. However, not all textile implements are present in the archaeological record. As ethnography and the archaeology demonstrate,[9] wood has also been used to produce tools, however, such objects are rarely preserved. Moreover, due to the lack of functional analyses and the possibility that multifunctional tools may have been used, it is not always easy to identify the primary function of the objects. Needles, bows, awls, spindles and shuttles are part of an incipient textile technology developed during the Neolithic period. The lacustrine sites of the Circum-Alpine lakes have provided abundant evidence of Neolithic textile tools. For example, at the site of Horgen[10] (Late Neolithic, around 3080–3030 BC), combs made of bone and antler, involved in the separation of linen fibres, have been documented.[11] Similar instruments, such as awls, spatulas, spindles and spindle whorls, have also been found in the lake dwellings of southern Germany, such as at Lake Constance.[12]

In the Iberian Peninsula, several Neolithic sites have also produced tools potentially related to textile production. One of the best-known sites is Cueva de los Murciélagos, Granada, dated to 5200–4600 BC.[13] Together with basketry and textile fragments made from esparto grass, bone spatulas, awls and a possible warping instrument made of wood were identified there. In the Early Neolithic site of Sarsa Cave, Valencia, various implements made of bone, such as spatulas and awls, were recovered.[14] In Gavàmines, dated to the 4th millennium cal. BC, a crescent-shaped loom weight (Lagozza type) was found[15] and has been considered as one of the earliest pieces of evidence of the use of the warp-weighted loom in Catalonia. In the Iberian Peninsula, the first evidence of spindle whorls, mostly made of ceramic and stone, are dated to the Late Neolithic.[16]

Other instruments, such as tauteners and warping instruments, also associated with weaving in modern communities,[17] have been identified in the Iberian Peninsula and discussed in detail.[18] They were discovered in several Late Neolithic caves in Almería, as well as in Cueva del Toro, Cueva de Hundidero-Gato, Cueva del Nerja (Málaga) and Cueva de la Murcielaguina in Córdoba.[19] Finally, tablet weaving (also called card weaving) is documented in the Iberian Peninsula since the 4th millennium BC.[20]

Our lack of knowledge about the origins and development of textile technology in prehistoric societies is certainly due to the fact that fabrics and some tools involved in textile processes made of wood (*e.g.* spindles, combs, wooden looms and frames) are usually not preserved in the archaeological record, especially not in the prehistoric layers, and use-wear studies on inorganic implements often cannot inform us about the exact functions of the tools. The process of textile production begins with management of natural resources, gathering, producing yarns and threads made of animal or vegetal fibres, twining, looping and/or weaving, and ends with the finished product – a textile. All the sequences of this important technology very probably occupied a large part of the economic and domestic activities in prehistoric households. Nevertheless, research has usually been focused only on one of the phases of textile production, such as spinning or weaving, and on some of the tools involved, like spindle whorls or loom weights. This is obviously the consequence of the preservation of the material of which these tools were made. Tools made of ceramic and stone, such as loom weights and spindle whorls, are more frequently found in the archaeological record than others made of perishable materials.

This paper is focused on the study of wooden and bone tools discovered at the site of La Draga (Banyoles, Catalonia), a waterlogged site of the Early Neolithic period (5300–4900 cal. BC). A large number of bone and wood artefacts exceptionally preserved in anaerobic conditions have been discovered in the stratification units associated with the early phase of the site. Among them were found wooden objects, such as spindle-like objects or shuttles and combs, as well as bone needles, awls and other bone tools. All these instruments are similar to those used by ancient and modern societies in the processes of spinning and weaving. Due to these similarities, their use in textile processes has been suggested.[21] Textile fragments have not been found on the site so far.

The main question of our research is to determine whether the artefacts from La Draga were used for textile production, and explore whether other archaeobiological evidence supports the idea of textile production in the early Neolithic of the Iberian Peninsula (6th millennium cal. BC). The aim is to provide new data on the origins and development of textile technology in the region, as well as on the textile processes and tools involved. An analysis of the use-wear on the objects could determine the use of these tools in textile production, and if this could be shown this would be the oldest evidence of textile production in the Iberian Peninsula known so far.

The site of La Draga

La Draga is a lake dwelling located in the north-eastern part of the Iberian Peninsula (Fig. 7.1), on the eastern shore of l'Estany de Banyoles (Lake Banyoles), a small lake lying at 170 m above sea level, 50 km from the Mediterranean coast and 40 km south of the Pyrenees.

The site lies on the eastern shore of Lake Banyoles, and some sectors are now partially covered by water.[22] Due to some parts of the site not being under the water table while others are, the preservation of the archaeological material is unequal. Four sectors have been excavated since 1991:

– Sector A is on dry land and the archaeological level is above groundwater, it corresponds to the highest part of the site at the greatest distance from the lake. In this sector only the lower tips of the posts stuck deeper into the water table are preserved.
– Sectors B and D are also located on dry land but closer to the shoreline. The archaeological level is covered here by the water table. Organic material is well preserved in this area.
– Finally, sector C is nowadays submerged under the current water level of the lake. In this sector organic material is also well preserved.

The excavations have shown that the site was occupied by the first farmers attested in the region in the Early Neolithic. Two episodes of occupation have been recognised up to now. The oldest structures (5324–4977 cal. BC) were made of wood, used as the main raw material, while the stratigraphically later phase (5210–4796 cal. BC) is represented by paved surfaces of travertine slabs. The layers of the later phase are above the water table and for this reason the organic material is not preserved. According to the archaeological record and chronology, La Draga belongs to the impressed Cardial-ware culture in the western Mediterranean.[23]

The archaeozoological studies have proved the importance of livestock for the subsistence of the community.[24] *Bos taurus*, *Capra hircus*, *Ovis aries* and *Sus domesticus* were bred and kept both for meat and possibly for other products. Cereal-based agriculture was fully consolidated[25] with naked wheat (*Triticum aestivum/durum/turgidum*) as the most significant crop (99% of all the grains and the main crop at the site). Other cereal crops are barley and naked barley (*Hordeum vulgare* and *Hordeum vulgare* var. *Nudum*), hulled wheat as emmer (*Triticum dicoccum*) and einkorn wheat (*Triticum monococcum*). Legumes (*Vicia faba*, *Pisum sativun*) and possibly poppies (*Papaver somniferum*) were also cultivated. The exploitation of wild resources played a minor role in the subsistence of the village.[26]

The site of La Draga has provided an exceptional assemblage of vegetal fibres and objects made of wood.[27] Among them are kitchen implements (bowls, ladles and scoops, stirrers, spatulas), woodworking tools (adze handles), agricultural tools (sickles and digging sticks), weapons (bows and arrows), baskets for carrying or storage, ropes

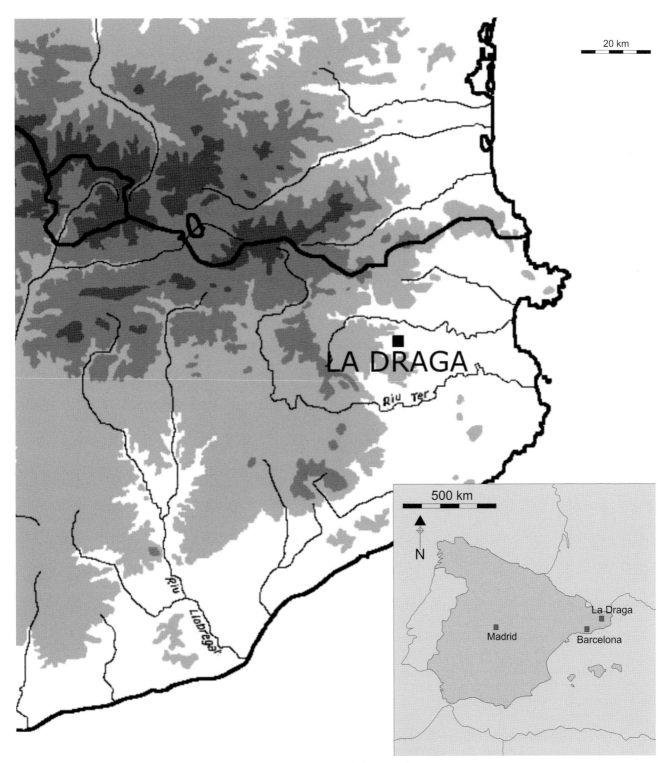

Fig. 7.1 Location of the Neolithic site of La Draga.

and other objects of unknown function were found. A set of objects that could have been used for weaving (Fig. 7.2), among them two combs and eight double-pointed objects or spindles, all made of boxwood, should also be mentioned. Finally, an impressive collection of bone objects (awls, needles and perforated bones) has been recovered.[28]

Methodology

The study of the Neolithic textile technology in Catalonia and the Iberian Peninsula is a challenge, because of the poor preservation of fabrics and lack of research tradition in this field. For this reason, our knowledge of early textile production regarding the types of fibres used and the

Fig. 7.2 Wooden and bone tools from La Draga. 1. comb made of boxwood, 2. spindle-like object made of boxwood, 3–5. bone awls made of a ruminant metapodial, 6. bone awl made of the tibia of a ruminant.

instruments involved is scant. Some experimental studies and functional analyses of Neolithic bone artefacts have been done,[29] but this work was not focused on textile technology. As a consequence, there is a lack of identification criteria for instruments potentially linked to textile production. However, use-wear analyses have been proved to be the most suitable methodology for determination of the functions of the implements.[30]

The research carried out on wooden and bone tools from La Draga is focused on their morphology and comparative studies of ethnographic material, as well as on experimenting in order to obtain a reference collection of traces for use-wear analysis.

First of all, a morphological description of the artefacts was carried out, aiming to identify tools and their possible functions. The archaeological finds were classified according to the ethnographically described activities in which they could have been used. Some implements used by

modern Quechua and Aymara weavers from Bolivia[31] have morphological similarities to the tools recovered at La Draga.

A series of experiments were then carried out with the aim of reproducing these tools and using them in order to verify their functionality (Fig. 7.3). The authors replicated activities with them according to the use of similar tools in traditional textile practises of modern Quechua and Aymara weavers from the Bolivian Altiplano.

The tools involved in production processes have well-developed traces of wear from use, such as polish, striations and possible fragmentation. Accordingly, the analysis of use-wear allows us to figure out how the tools were used, verifying their function through the identification of the type of material they were used on as well as the tool kinematics.[32] Based on this premise, some of the tools from La Draga were reproduced and used to verify the hypothesis that they were related to textile production. Nevertheless, there is little information from the use-wear analysis of tools

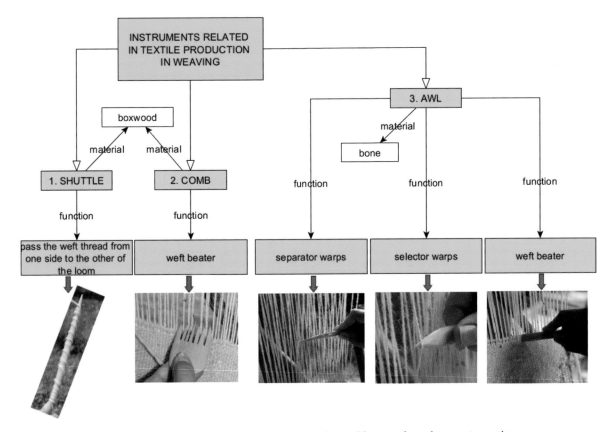

Fig. 7.3 Testing potential functions of reconstructed wooden and bone tools in the experimental programme.

made of organic materials, such as wood or bone, and these studies are still at a preliminary stage, and more research is needed in order to provide a good reference collection for the study of archaeological tools.

We used replicas of the bone awls, wooden spindle-like objects and combs for spinning and weaving. The experiments had a twofold aim. The first was to reproduce the activities they had been used in and verify the effectiveness of the tools, and the second was to obtain a collection of use-wear traces produced by different actions related to textile activities. The fibre used in this first experimental approach was wool, and a horizontal loom was built to weave with wool threads. The replicated movements followed the patterns of those used by modern weavers as a model. The use-wear developed on the surfaces of the experimental tools was analysed in order to observe and register its characteristics and details. Finally, the archaeological tools were compared with the use-wear produced on the surface of the experimental tools. The use-wear analysis on archaeological and experimental awls, spindles-like needles and combs has been conducted under microscope with magnification of 50×, 100× and 200×, as has been previously done on different materials and described by R. Christidou (1999)[33] and A. Legrand (2007).[34] Exceptionally, 500× magnification was used to observe more detailed features.

Material analysed and the results

We reproduced some of discovered bone and wooden artefacts, *e.g.* combs, awls and spindle-like objects, and used them as similar tools are used in traditional textile craft today. After that, we analysed use-wear under microscope. The first results are presented below.

The combs

Three archaeological combs made of boxwood (*Buxus sempervirens*), one of them carbonised, have been documented at the site (Figs 7.2 and Table 7.1).[35] There were also several fragments of comb teeth recovered. The better-preserved comb (54×70×5 mm) still preserves six of eight teeth, conical in shape with a circular section, a length of between 35 and 40 mm and 5 mm in diameter. Of the second one only the handle is preserved, together with one tooth, measuring 58 mm (length), 22 mm (width) and 7 mm (thickness). Both combs have a perforation in the proximal part, probably for suspension. Furthermore, a rectangular piece of comb, which still preserves one tooth, and 14 conical teeth have been recovered. This comb has similar morphological features to the other examples.

In none of the items was it possible to observe traces of manufacture, because the surfaces of the combs had been

Table 7.1 Analysed archaeological material from La Draga

Shape	No. items	Material	Measurements (mm)			
			Length	*Width*	*Thickness*	*Diameter*
Comb	3	Boxwood (*Buxus sempervirens*)	70	54	5	
			58 (frag.)	22	7	
			41 (frag.)	22	6	
Comb teeth	6		40>35			5
	1		15 (frag.)			
	5		<48			4
	1		48			5
	1		24	5	2	
Spindle-like objects	9	Boxwood (*Buxus sempervirens*)	310			6
			159 (frag.)			10
			242			8
			366			10
			265			13
			155			7
			285 (frag.)			9
			130 (frag.)			7
			100 (frag.)			7
Awls	15	metapodial bone	69<77	8.5<12	4<5.5	

entirely polished at the end of the manufacture process. Notwithstanding, the distal areas of the teeth are rounded and worn because of use.

Although made of bone, which makes it difficult to compare it directly with wood, it is interesting to mention that the combs from Los Castillejos de Montefrio[36] show deep parallel and transverse striations on the proximal portion of each of the teeth. The use of these combs has been related to combing human hair as a result of hygienic and aesthetic needs. These sorts of traces are not present in the combs of La Draga, which suggests that these combs were used for another purpose.[37]

Ethnographic evidence shows that combs can be used for combing vegetal or animal fibres in order to clean them and untangle them before spinning. During weaving, combs can also be used as weft beaters to obtain a denser and more compacted fabric.

We reproduced a comb and used this replica for combing wool, and as a weft beater during the weaving of wool threads on a vertical loom (Fig. 7.3). The tool proved its effectiveness for both activities.

On the replicated comb, use-wear is seen on the top and along the teeth, as we observed on the archaeological item. Nevertheless, we have not yet been able to carry out a use-wear analysis due to the fact that many more hours of work are needed to obtain conclusive results. Moreover, it has

not been possible to observe microscopic use-wear on the archaeological combs, not only because of the restoration of the artefacts but also because of their condition (one is carbonised).

Spindle-like objects

Nine long spindle-like objects made of boxwood (*Buxus sempervirens*) have been recovered, some of them fragmented. It is suggested that they had been used as spindles for spinning and/or shuttles for weaving. In addition, according to their morphology and size, the small objects might be ideal for looping or knotting.

These artefacts have circular sections and the maximum diameters are located in the centre of their length. Their sizes oscillate between 242 and 310 mm in length, and 6 to 10 mm in diameter (Fig. 7.2 and Table 7.1). One small example, measuring 155 mm in length and 7 mm in diameter, has also been documented. The surfaces of these tools were entirely polished during the process of manufacture, thus it is not possible to perceive technological use-wear. Regarding the variability in size, it can be hypothesised that the thicker items – being more resistant – were used as spindles (to withstand the force of tension) during spinning. Spindle whorls have not been found at the site so far, but spinning can also be performed without whorls. In this case, the fibre is pulled and twisted while it

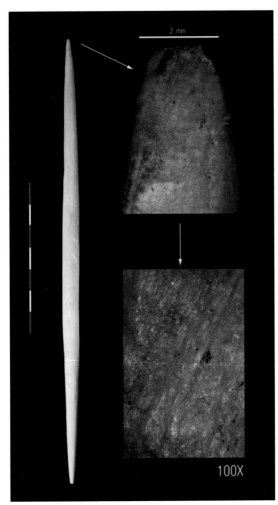

Fig. 7.4 Use-wear on the replica of a long spindle-like object.

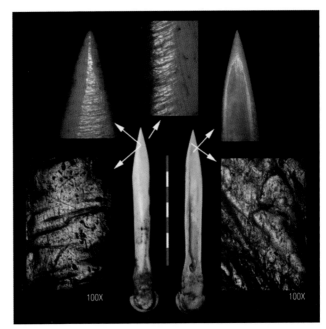

Fig. 7.5 The replicas of two awls and the use-wear.

Bone awls

Fifteen bone awls made of caprine metapodials and three of ruminant metapodials have been found at La Draga (Fig. 7.2 and Table 7.1). Their sizes range between 69 mm and 77 mm in length, 8.5 mm to 12 mm in width, and 4 mm to 5.5 mm in thickness.[38] There were more such items discovered in the 2014 excavation campaign, which are being currently analysed.

Awls could be used during the process of weaving as weft beaters to increase the density of textile, and also to select and separate warp threads.

The replicas of two awls were used for six hours replicating the weaving process (Figs. 7.3 and 7.5). One awl was used as a weft beater and also as a thread selector and separator. The second one was only used as a weft beater in order to see more clearly the use-wear caused by the specific movement and use: one side of the distal area was worn due to the contact with the material worked.

The experimental use of awls involving wool threads caused striations of various sizes and orientations, and some irregular depressions (Fig. 7.5). In general, we observe a polished and rounded surface with use-wear and thick, short and transverse striations. Use-wear resulting from working with wool threads involves slightly rounded elevated flat surfaces, and general polishing of both high and deeper areas, bone fractures resulting from the pressure during work, a greater wear on the distal area and a rounded shape. However, more hours of work are required to achieve conclusive results.

Three archaeological awls[39] have been analysed so far, while the other analyses are still ongoing. We have observed

is wound tightly around the spindle, retaining the torsion and tension of the thread drawn. Another possibility is that the spindle whorls were made of perishable materials, thus they have not been preserved. Moreover, longer and thinner objects could have been used as shuttles, with the weft threads wrapped around them; in this manner they passed between the warp threads from one side of the loom to another, and make the fabric. The fact that the shuttle is thinner eases the work.

We used a long spindle-like object as a spindle for two hours and turned the spindle with one hand while the yarn was tightly twisted with the other hand. Thicker spindles are preferable, since they are more resistant to the force and pressure during the stretch. Another two-hour experiment revealed that the longest tool with the smallest diameter was the most suitable to be used as a shuttle in the warp-weighted loom. Use-wear analysis on this experimental tool demonstrates parallel striations as a result of friction, and an incipient polishing (Fig. 7.4). Use-wear analysis on the archaeological items has not yet been carried out.

mainly the distal areas, where use-wear is more evident. In general, the tips are polished and in some cases they are broken.

Two archaeological awls have rounded distal areas, are polished and show linear striations. The polishing is concentrated on the most prominent areas of their surface, indicating little pressure was applied to the used material, so depressions are more visible and defined, leaving deeper areas less polished and with more pronounced striations. Also, they show longitudinal striations and short, perpendicular striations in several directions.

The comparison with our experimental material used with wool has provided negative results, but the reference collection on bone use-wear of the Laboratory of Archaeology and Anthropology (Institució Milà i Fontanals CSIC, Spain) has allowed the identification of the raw material used: the fact that the surface looks very shiny with few depressions and striations, and deep dark areas are not polished, suggests that these two awls were used with plant fibres.

The third awl[40] has a high polish, shows abrasion and very small superficial striations, indicating work with hide.

Discussion

The results obtained from the study of the combs, needles or spindle-like objects, and awls from La Draga offer rather indirect evidence of textile production. Morphological studies and experiments confirm the effectiveness of the combs found at La Draga for combing before spinning, as well as weft beaters during weaving. Since we have not analysed use-wear on the archaeological and reproduced items, we are not at this time able to determine whether they were used with vegetal or animal fibres.

Morphological analysis of the awls, the parallels in ethnography and archaeology, and experiments with the reproduced tools confirm the effectiveness of awls used in weaving as weft beaters, also as selectors and separators of the threads. However, the use-wear analysis on the archaeological awls indicates the use of vegetable fibres as well as skin, which in any case can be expected.

Finally, the results of analyses of the long needle-like objects show the probability that they have been used as spindles and/or shuttles, not only due to similar features as archaeological and ethnographical items, but also because of the results of the experiments that confirmed their effectiveness for spinning and weaving. These needle-like objects have shapes and measurements similar to the archaeological shuttles, *e.g.* from Nasca,[41] which were made of wood, are at least 28 mm long, 10–15 mm thick, and their central parts are thicker. However, the use-wear analysis of the archaeological spindles has not been possible until now.

According to the morphology and characteristics of these tools, as well as the experimental studies of their effectiveness, we could demonstrate their potential relation with textile production. Unfortunately, the use-wear analyses are not conclusive for several reasons. First of all, the fragility and the restoration of the artefacts make the observation under the microscope and the corresponding interpretation difficult. Secondly, more experiments are needed in order to obtain a good reference collection of use-wear. In this sense, it is necessary to intensify the experimental work. For the moment, our experiments have focused on animal fibres, but it is necessary to include vegetal fibres, such as nettle and flax, which we have already started to do.

The tools analysed, combs, awls and needle-like objects, were employed in the processes of combing, spinning and weaving. However, there are more tools recorded at the site that represent other activities related to textile production. A possible tautener, an instrument for winding threads after spinning, and also for warping before weaving, should be mentioned here. This tautener resembles items found in the Andes.[42] The probable tauteners made of a scapula are characterised by a denticulate edge. These tools are used to maintain the torsion and tension of the thread after spinning. Also, there are probably warpers made of bone and knuckle bones. In addition, there are fragments (medial and proximal areas) of three bone eyed needles at La Draga, although the eyes are broken.

All these instruments allow attesting the manufacture of some kind of products made of fibres. The large number of instruments that could be involved in various textile processes confirms the importance of this activity for the inhabitants of La Draga.

Regarding the type of the fibres that were used, the data obtained from the use-wear analysis of the instruments are scarce for the moment. The analysed awls suggest the use of vegetal fibres. Also, the analysis of mussel shells[43] (*Mytilus galloprovincialis*) under the microscope has demonstrated that they were used for processing vegetal fibres. As mentioned before, fabrics have not been discovered at the site until now. However, several ropes have been documented.[44] They confirm knowledge of techniques of acquisition and processing of vegetal fibres by the inhabitants from La Draga.

The study of seed and fruit remains from the site[45] has not provided evidence of cultivation of flax (*Linum usitatissimum* L.). However, several remains of nettle (*Urtica dioica*) have been identified. The analyses of rope fibres have allowed identification of two types of bast fibres for their manufacturing; one of them is from the inner bark of trees, and another is some kind of herbaceous bast.[46] The anatomical features of the herbaceous bast do not allow the determination of whether it comes from flax or nettle. The fact that flax has not been identified at the site suggests the possibility of the use of *Urtica dioica* for production of some of the ropes. Nettle has also been used traditionally for textile production.[47] More experiments with vegetal fibres are needed in order to increase our knowledge of their use by the inhabitants of La Draga, and more generally to document technical practices in the Cardial-ware culture in the western Mediterranean.

Animal fibres have not been recovered on the site until now. However, the characterisation of the demographic patterns of the flocks and the physical characteristics of the animals have provided some comparative data of husbandry strategies. Several authors, based on ethnographic examples, suggest the possibility of identifying specialised production strategies, such as the exploitation of wool, by studying slaughtering profiles.[48] According to Stein,[49] for example, the systematic exploitation of animal fibres used for textiles was based on allocating greater economic value to adult individuals and maintaining them for a longer period than if they were kept only for food. The slaughtering patterns at La Draga show that a significant proportion of all the domesticated animals – cattle, pig, goat and sheep – were killed at their meat optimum.[50] Consequently, meat was probably the main product obtained from domestic animals. Nevertheless, some sheep were kept until a relatively advanced age. This could mean that products other than meat, such as wool, were obtained from this species as well. On the other hand, goats and sheep present different dynamics regarding the obtained mortality profiles: there was a high percentage of goats slaughtered in infancy and a higher percentage of sheep killed in adult stages. This suggests a probable exploitation of sheep fibres. Consequently, the archaeozoological data from La Draga prove that husbandry strategies most probably included exploitation of domestic animal fibres on a small scale.

Conclusions and perspectives

The aim of this research has been to consider the existence of an incipient textile production at the Early Neolithic site of La Draga. Given that until now no remains of textiles have been found, we have proposed a preliminary study based on indirect evidence, mainly on tools potentially involved in textile production process. This approach was suggested by the good preservation of wooden and bone implements on the site. La Draga provides a unique opportunity to obtain new data about the origins and development of textile technology in the Iberian Peninsula, as well as the processes and the tools involved.

According to their morphology and sizes, the combs, long spindle-like objects and awls from La Dragas show similarities with ethnographic textile tools. The experimental work confirms the effectiveness of these tools in combing, spinning and weaving. The use-wear analyses of the experimental and archaeological tools are still in progress, but for the moment it is possible to confirm that awls were used for processing vegetal fibres. Other data from the site, such as the use of bast fibres for the production of ropes and the use of mussel shell tools for processing the fibres, also supports

the hypothesis about the knowledge of techniques of vegetal fibres processing. However, the hypothesis of production of animal fibres cannot be entirely excluded, since the slaughtering patterns may suggest this kind of exploitation.

Notes

1   The research was funded by the projects HAR2009–13494-C02–01, HAR2012–38838-C02–01, HAR2009–13494-C02–02, HAR2012–38838-C02–02 and 2014/100822. The archaeological excavations have been funded by Departament de Cultura (Generalitat de Catalunya). Ignacio Clemente-Conte, Millan Mozota, Antoni Palomo, Raquel Piqué and Xavier Terradas are members of the research Group AGREST (SGR 2014 1169), Maria Saña is member of the research Group GRAMPO (2014 SGR 1248) funded by AGAUR. We thank Ajuntament de Banyoles, the Centre d'Arqueologia Subaquàtica and the Museu Nacional d'Arqueologia de Catalunya for the support for the work in La Draga, and to the students, researchers and professionals who have participated in the excavation since the 1990s. We also thank Igor Bogdanovic for his contribution to this work.
2   Alfaro 1984, 21.
3   For example, Barber 1991; Jacomet 2004, 162–177; Médard 2006; 2008, 23–28; Ruiz de Haro 2012, 133–145.
4   Capel et al. 1981, 123–166.
5   Rivera Núñez and Obón de Castro 1987, 31–37; Alfaro 2005, 229–246.
6   Alfaro 1984, 121.
7   Molina et al. 2003, 153–158.
8   Alfaro 1984; Molina et al. 2003, 153–158; Rodríguez-Ariza et al. 2004, 13–15; Jover and López 2013, 149–171.
9   For example, Kemp and Vogelsang-Eastwood 2000, 274–276; Médard 2000, 23–34; Burke 2010, 162.
10 Barber 1991; Akeret and Jacomet 1997, 235–239.
11 Sidéra 1993; 2000, 118–156.
12 Maier and Schlichtherle 2011, 567–578; cf. Banck-Burgess this volume.
13 Carrasco and Pachón 2009, 227–287.
14 García Borja et al. 2011.
15 Borrell and Bosch 2012, 318–319.
16 Martínez Rodríguez et al. 1989, 59–65; Martínez and Alcázar Godoy 1992, 10–19.
17 See the morphology and functionality of some items in Rivera Casanova 2012, 151–152; Arnold and Espejo 2013, 76, 83–86; Arnold et al. 2013, 60–61, 65–66.
18 Meneses Fernández 1993, 317–323; Cardito 1996, 125–145; Carrasco et al. 2009, 5–69; Ruiz de Haro 2012, 133–145.
19 Cardito 1996, 125–145.
20 Cardito 1996, 125–145.
21 Bosch et al. 2006.
22 Bosch et al. 2000; 2006; 2011; Palomo et al. 2014, 58–73.
23 Palomo et al. 2014, 70.
24 Saña 2011, 177–212.
25 Antolin and Buxó 2011, 147–174.
26 Saña 2011, 177–212; Antolin and Buxó 2011, 147–174.
27 Bosch et al. 2006; Palomo et al. 2013, 383–396; Pique et al. 2018; Terradas et al. 2017.

28 Bosch *et al.* 2000; 2006; 2011; Legrand 2011, 111–123.

29 Gibaja and Mozota 2015, 65–77; Mozota *et al.*2017.

30 Sidéra 1993; 2001, 221–229; Maigrot 2003; Legrand 2007; Legrand and Sidéra 2007, 291–304; van Gijn 2007, 81–92.

31 Arnold and Espejo 2010; Arnold and Espejo 2013; Arnold *et al.* 2013.

32 For example Gibaja 2007, 49–74; Lemoine 1997; Legrand 2007.

33 Christidou 1999.

34 Legrand 2007.

35 Bosch *et al.* 2006.

36 See the use-wear analysis of wooden combs by M. Altamirano (2014, 361–371).

37 *Cf.* also the spectacular use-wear analyses of bone combs by M. Altamirano (2014, 361–371).

38 Legrand 2011, 114.

39 ID: 890/11, 893/45 and 890/14.

40 ID: 890/14.

41 See Arnold *et al.* 2013, 91.

42 Rivera Casanova 2012, 143–162.

43 Clemente and Cuenca 2011, 137–145.

44 Bosch *et al.* 2006.

45 Antolín and Buxó 2011, 147–174.

46 Piqué *et al.* 2018.

47 Bergfjord *et al.* 2012.

48 Stein 1987, 101–111.

49 Stein 1987, 101–111.

50 Saña 2011, 177–212.

Bibliography

Akeret, O. and Jacomet, S. 1997 Analysis of plant macrofossils in goat/sheep faeces from the Neolithic lake shore settlement of Horgen Scheller – an indication of prehistoric transhumance? *Vegetation History and Archaeobotany* 6, 235–239.

Alfaro, C. 1984 *Tejido y cestería en la Península Ibérica. Historia de su técnica e indústrias desde la Prehistoria hasta la romanización.* Madrid.

Alfaro, C. 2005 Informe sobre los restos textiles, de cestería y de cuero procedentes de Cueva Sagrada I (Lorca, Murcia). In J. J. Eiroa, *El cerro de la Virgen de la Salud (Lorca): excavaciones arqueológicas, estudio de materiales e interpretación histórica.* Murcia, 229–246.

Alfaro, C. 2012 Textiles from the Pre-Pottery Neolithic site of Tell Halula (Euphrates Valley, Syria). *Paléorient* 38.1–2. Dossier thématique/Thematic file, C. Breniquet, M. Tengberg, E. Andersson and M.-L. Nosch (eds.) Préhistoire des Textiles au Proche-Orient/Prehistory of Textiles in the Near East, 41–54.

Altamirano, M., 2014 *Los peines óseos de Los Castillejos en las Peñas de los Gitanos (Montefrío, Granada).* Actas del II Congreso de Prehistoria de Andalucía, 361–371.

Antolín, F. and Buxó, R. 2011 L'explotació de les plantes al jaciment de la Draga: contribució a la història de l'agricultura i de l'alimentació vegetal del neolític a Catalunya. In J. Bosch, J. Chinchilla and J. Tarrús (eds.), *El poblat lacustre del neolític antic de La Draga: Excavacions de 2000–2005.* Monografies del CASC 2. Girona, 147–174.

Arnold, D. and Espejo, E. 2010 *Ciencia de las mujeres.* La Paz.

Arnold, D. and Espejo, E. 2013 *El textil tridimensional: la naturaleza del tejido como objeto y como sujeto.* La Paz.

Arnold, D., Espejo, E. and Maidana, J. L. 2013 *Tejiendo la vida. La colección textil del Museo Nacional de Etnografía y Folklore, según la cadena de producción.* La Paz.

Barber, E. J. W. 1991 *Prehistoric Textiles: The Development of Cloth in the Neolithic and Bronze Ages with Special Reference to the Aegean.* Princeton.

Bergfjord, C., Mannering, U., Frei, K. M., Gleba, M., Scharff, A. B., Skals, I., Heinemeier, J., Nosch, M.-L. and Holst, B. 2012 Nettle as a distinct Bronze Age textile plant. *Scientific Reports* 2.664, 1–4 (DOI:10.1038/srep00664, accessed 27 March 2017).

Borrell, F. and Bosch, J. 2012 Las minas de variscita de Gavà (Barcelona) y las redes de circulación en el Neolítico. *Rubricatum: revista del Museu de Gavà* 5, 315–322.

Bosch, A., Chinchilla, J. and Tarrús, J. (eds.), 2000 *El poblat lacustre neolític de la Draga. Excavacions de 1990–1998.* Monografies del CASC 2. Girona.

Bosch, A., Chinchilla, J. and Tarrús, J. (eds.) 2006 *Els objectes de fusta del poblat neolític de la Draga. Excavacions de 1995–2005.* Monografies del CASC 6. Girona.

Bosch, A., Chinchilla, J. and Tarrús, J. (eds.) 2011 *El poblat lacustre del Neolític antic de la Draga. Excavacions 2000–2005.* Monografies del CASC 9. Girona.

Burke, B. 2010 *From Minos to Midas. Ancient Cloth Production in the Aegean and in Anatolia.* Ancient Textiles Series 7. Oxford and Oakville.

Capel, J., Carrasco, J. and Navarrete, M. S. 1981 Nuevas sepulturas prehistóricas en la cuenca del río Cacín (Alhama de Granada). *Cuadernos de Prehistoria de la Universidad de Granada* 6, 123–166.

Cardito, L. M. 1996 Las manufactura textiles en la Prehistoria: las placas de telar en el Calcolítico peninsular. *Zephyrus: Revista de prehistoria y arqueología* 49, 125–145.

Carrasco, J. and Pachón, J. A. 2009 Algunas cuestiones sobre el registro arqueológico de la cueva de los murciélagos de Albuñol (Granada) en el contexto neolítico andaluz y sus posibles relaciones con las representaciones esquemáticas. *Cuadernos de Prehistoria y arqueología de la Universidad de Granada* 19, 227–287.

Carrasco, J., Pachón, J. A. and Gámiz, J. 2009 Los separadores de hileras de collar en la prehistoria peninsular. Un estudio crítico. *Antiquitas* 21, 5–69.

Christidou, R., 1999 Outils en os néolithiques du Nord de la Grèce. Étude technologique. Unpublished PhD thesis, Université Paris X-Nanterre.

Clemente, I., Cuenca D. 2011 Instrumentos de trabajo de concha. In A. Bosch, J. Chinchilla, and J. Tarrús (eds.), *El poblat lacustre del Neolític antic de la Draga. Excavacions 2000–2005.* Monografies del CASC 9. Girona, 137–145.

García Borja, P., Salazar-García, D. C., Pérez Fernández, A., Pardo Gordó, S. and Casanova Vañó, V. 2011 El Neolítico antiguo cardial y la Cova de la Sarsa (Bocairent, València). Nuevas perspectivas a partir de su registro funerario. *Munibe (Antropologia-Arkeologia)* 62, 175–195.

Gibaja, J. F. 2007 Estudios de traceología y funcionalidad. *Praxis Archaeologica* 2, 49–74.

Gibaja, J. F. and Mozota, M. 2015 'For a few awls more.' Bone tools in northeastern Iberia Neolithic burials (4th–5th millennia cal BC). A morpho-technical and functional approach. *Journal of Archaeological Science: Reports* 4, 65–77.

Jacomet, S. 2004 Archaeobotany. A vital tool in the investigations of lake-dwellings. In F. Menotti (ed.), *Living on the Lake in Prehistoric Europe, 150 Years of Lake-dwelling Research.* London, 162–177.

Jover, F. J. and López, J. A. 2013 La producción textil durante la Edad del Bronce en el cuadrante suroriental de la Península Ibérica: materias primas, productos, instrumentos y procesos de trabajo. *Zephyrus* 71, 149–171.

Kemp, B. J. and Vogelsang-Eastwood, G. 2001 *The Ancient Textile Industry at Amarna.* London.

Legrand, A. 2007 *Fabrication et utilisation de l'outillage en matières osseuses du Néolithique de Chypre: Khirokitia et Cap Andreas-Kastros.* British Archaeological Reports International Series 1678. Oxford.

Legrand, A. 2011 L'industrie osseuse de La Draga. In A. Bosch, J. Chinchilla and J. Tarrús (eds.), *El poblat lacustre del neolític antic de La Draga. Les campanyes dels anys 2000–2005.* Monografies del CASC 9. Girona, 111–123.

Legrand, A. and Sidéra, I. 2007 Methods, means, and results when studying European bone industries. In C. Gate and R. Walker (eds.), *Bones as Tools: Current Methods and Interpretations in Worked Bone Studies.* British Archaeological Reports International Series 1622. Oxford, 291–304.

Lemoine, G., 1997 *Use Wear on Bone and Antler Tools from the Mackenzie Inuit.* British Archaeological Reports International Series 679. Oxford.

Maier, U. and Schlichtherle, H. 2011 Flax cultivation and textile production in Neolithic wetland settlements on Lake Constance and in Upper Swabia (south-west Germany). *Vegetation History and Archaeobotany* 20.6, 567–578.

Maigrot, Y. 2003 Etude technologique et fonctionnelle de l'outillage en matières dures animales. La station 4 de Chalain (Néolithique final, Jura, France). Unpublished PhD thesis, Université de Paris I.

Martínez Rodríguez, F. and Alcázar Godoy, J. 1992 Enterramientos prehistóricos en Alcalá del Valle (Cádiz). *Revista de Arqueología* 133, 10–19.

Martínez Rodríguez, F., Pereda Acién, C. and Alcázar Godoy, J. 1989 Primeros datos sobre una necrópolis prehistórica de excepcional interés: El Cerro de la Casería de Tomillos (Alcalá del Valles, Cádiz). *Anuarios Arqueológicos de Andalucía* 3, 59–65.

Médard, F. 2000 La préhistoire du fil en Europe occidentale: méthodes et perspectives. In D. Cardon and M. Feugere, *Archéologie des textiles des origines au Ve siècle. Actes du colloque de Lattes (October 1999).* Montagnac, 23–34.

Médard, F., 2006 *Les activités de filage au Néolithique sur le Plateau suisse. Analyse technique, économique et sociale.* CRA-monographies 28. Paris.

Médard, F., 2008 L'acquisition des matières textiles d'origine végétale en préhistoire. In V. Zech-Matterne, M. Derreumaux and S. Preiss (eds.), *Archéologie des textiles et teintures végétales. Actes de la table ronde Archéobotanique 2006, Compiègne, 28–30 juin 2006.* Les nouvelles de l'archéologie 114. Paris, 23–28.

Meneses Fernández, M. A. 1993 Reconstrucción técnica, experimentación y estudio comparativo de los 'tensadores textiles' de hueso del Neolítico y Calcolítico en Andalucía

(España). In P. C. Anderson, S. Beyries, M. Otte and H. Plisson (eds.), *Traces et fonction: les gestes retrouvés. Actes du Colloque International de Liège, 8–9–10 décembre 1990.* Etudes et recherches archéologiques de l'Université de Liège 50. Liège, 317–323.

Molina, F., Rodríguez-Ariza, M. O., Jiménez Brobeil, S. and Botella, M. 2003 La sepultura 121 del yacimiento argárico de El Castellón Alto (Galera, Granada). *Trabajos de Prehistoria* 60.1, 153–158.

Mozota, M., Palomo, A., Clemente, I. and Gibaja, J. F. 2017 Experimental program: Neolithic awls and spatulas. In R. Alonso, D. Canales and J. Baena (eds.), *Playing with the Time. Experimental Archaeology and the Study of the Past.* Burgos, 61–66.

Palomo, A., Piqué, R., Terradas, X., López, O., Clemente, I. and Gibaja, J. F. 2013 Woodworking technology in the Early Neolithic site of La Draga (Banyoles, Spain). In P. C. Anderson, C. Cheval and A. Durand (eds.), *Regards croisés sur les outils liés au travail des végétaux.* Antibes, 383–396.

Palomo, A., Piqué, R., Terradas, X., Bosch, A., Buxó, R., Chinchilla, J., Saña, M. and Tarrús, J. 2014 Prehistoric occupation of Banyoles lakeshore: results of recent excavations at La Draga site, Girona, Spain. *Journal of Wetland Archaeology* 14, 58–73.

Piqué, R., Romero, S., Palomo, A., Tarrús, J., Terradas, X. and Bogdanovic, I. 2018 The production and use of cordage at the Early Neolithic site of La Draga (Banyoles, Spain). *Quaternary International* 468 (July), 262–270 (https://doi.org/10.1016/j.quaint.2016.05.024, accessed 23 April 2018).

Rivera Casanova, C. 2012 Tecnología Textil durante el período Formativo en los valles Central y Alto de Cochabamba. *Arqueoantropológicas* 2, 143–162.

Rivera Núñez, D., Obón de Castro, C. 1987 Informe sobre los restos vegetales procedentes del enterramiento calcolítico de la Cueva Sagrada (comarca de Lorca, Murcia). *Anales de Prehistoria y Arqueología* 3, 31–37.

Rodríguez-Ariza, M. O., Molina, F., Botella, M. C., Jiménez Brobeil, S. A. and Alemán, I. 2004 Les restes parcialment momificades de la sepultura 121 del jaciment argàric de Castellón Alto (Galera, Granada). *Cota zero* 19, 13–15.

Ruiz de Haro, I. 2012 Textil: la producción del tejido en la Prehistoria y la Protohistoria. *Arqueología y Territorio* 9, 133–145.

Saña, M. 2011 La gestió dels recursos animals. In A. Bosch, J. Chinchilla and J. Tarrús (eds.), *El poblat lacustre del Neolític antic de la Draga. Excavacions 2000–2005.* Monografies del CASC 9. Girona, 177–212.

Sidéra, I. 1993 Les assemblages osseux en bassins parisien et rhénan du VIe au IVe millénaire B. C. Histoire, techno-économie et culture. Unpublished PhD thesis, Université Paris-1.

Sidéra, I. 2000 Les Matières dures animales. L'outillage en os et en ivoire. In D. Ramseyer (ed.), *Muntelier/Fischergässli. Un habitat néolithique au bord du lac de Morat 895 à 3820 avant J.C.,* Cahiers d'Archéologie fribourgeoise 15. Fribourg, 118–156.

Sidéra, I. 2001 Domestic and funerary bone, antler and tooth objects in the Neolithic of Western Europe: a comparison. In A. M. Choyke and L. Bartosiewicz (eds.), *Crafting Bone: Skeletal Technologies through Time and Space. Proceedings of* the 2nd meeting of the Worked Bone Research Group (ICAZ), 31 August–5 September 1999. Oxford, 221–229.

Stein, G. J. 1987 Regional economic integration in early state societies: third millennium BC pastoral production at Gritille, southeast Turkey. *Paléorient* 13.2, 101–111.

Terradas, X., Piqué, R., Palomo, A., Antolín, F., López, O., Revelles, J. and Buxó, R. 2017 Farming practices in the Early Neolithic according to agricultural tools: evidence from La Draga site (northeastern Iberia). In O. García-Puchol and D. C. Salazar-García (eds.), *Times of Neolithic Transition along the Western Mediterranean*. Fundamental Issues in Archaeology.

Berlin, 199–220 (https://doi.org/10.1007/978–3–319–52939–4_8, accessed 26 April 2018).

van Gijn, A. 2007 The use of bone and antler tools: two examples from the late Mesolithic in the Dutch coastal zone. In C. Gates St-Pierre and R. B. Walker (eds.), *Bones as Tools: Current Methods and Interpretations in Worked Bone Studies*. British Archaeological Reports International Series 1622. Oxford, 81–92.

Vogelsang-Eastwood, G. 2000 Textiles. In P. T. Nicholson and I. Shaw (eds.), *Ancient Egyptian Materials and Technology*. Cambridge, 271–274.

From east to west: the use of spinning bowls from the Chalcolithic period to the Iron Age

María Irene Ruiz de Haro

Introduction

This paper aims to review the archaeological evidence for a type of bowl with internal handles, seeking a functional definition of it as a tool, in order to answer a series of questions regarding its use.[1] Below, I present arguments in favour of including this bowl type among the tools used for textile production and discuss its chronological, geographical and typological development. The focus of the study is the bowl's place in the process of spinning flax fibres, where and why innovation or adoption of its use as a textile tool occurred and its manner of application to the flax fibre.

Discussion of the definition, function, uses, chronology and geography of spinning bowls

Bowls with internal handles: their shapes, types and uses

The object of this study is a type of vessel made of clay or stone (ceramic types being the most common), of a shape that can be classified within the ceramic typology as a bowl with a handmade or wheel-thrown body and handmade internal handle or handles.

Despite variations in body shape, a characteristic shared by all these vessels is the presence of internal handles that vary in number from one to four. The handles may be located in the centre of the bottom or elsewhere on the inside, and extend vertically to just below the rim of the bowl. These internal handles, which are the defining trait of this object category, usually have a number of grooves worn on the inside of the loop.

Information on the use of bowls with internal handles can be gained, on the one hand, from actual finds of such vessels in archaeological contexts and, on the other hand,

from iconographic evidence of ancient Egyptian wall paintings and funerary models.[2] The latter provide us with important information about the function of such bowls as tools used in the process of textile production, specifically in the production of linen yarn. Based on this evidence, several textile researchers have suggested that the objects under consideration are spinning bowls.[3] While all these scholars agree that these objects were used during the processing of flax fibre, they differ in their interpretations of details of their usage. Depending on typological characteristics, the bowls could have been used during spinning, for adding twist to the yarn or for moistening flax fibre.[4] The presence of grooves on the inner surfaces of the loops caused by the friction of fibres pulled across their surface indicates that they were employed to give tension to the yarn and to guide it. The bowl shape indicates its function as a container for flax fibre or yarn, and possibly for water added to activate the adhesive properties of flax.[5] I will, therefore, retain the use of the term 'spinning bowl', as used by other scholars.[6]

The spinning bowl was a textile tool employed in flax processing. Its function was to moisten hanks or a ball of yarn after it had been processed using the spliced drafting technique. In addition to guiding yarn to the spindle through grooves located on the inside of its handles, it determined the number of fibres and the thickness of the yarn. It was a sort of distaff, but its function was additionally to supply hand-fed fibre. A final, quantitatively and qualitatively superior, thread was achieved through the use of two spinning techniques (spliced and continuous drafting).

Functional analysis of the spinning bowls based on ancient Egyptian iconography

Several seminal works have examined in detail the wall paintings depicting textile production workshops in which spinning bowls are represented: this paper mainly follows the research of Grace M. Crowfoot, T. Dothan, Barry J. Kemp, Gillian Vogelsang-Eastwood and Susan Allen.[7] Lastly, there is an interesting study by Hero Granger-Taylor on the textile material from Lahum and the evidence for linen yarn preparation and spinning bowls in the production process.[8]

Tomb scenes and models from ancient Egypt indicate knowledge of the spinning bowl and of various operations carried out using this object (fibre wetting and stretching). It appears that it could have been used in a variety of methods, with or without additional accessories. Moreover, the function of the spinning bowl can be elucidated thanks to several specimens found during excavations of settlements, as well as remains of textiles produced using the spliced drafting technique.

A survey of the archaeological material can help determine certain characteristics of spinning bowls related to their function. The bowl shape of this tool is a decisive and invariable trait in all the periods in which this yarn pre-processing tool is documented, and therefore its design is standardised. The general characteristics of the spinning bowl are purely functional, for it is used in the pre-processing of flax fibres before passing them on to the spindle. It is utilised as a container for previously prepared, *i.e.* deseeded, retted, beaten and combed linen strands. The minor variations in the form of this tool throughout history did not affect its use as humidifier and softener for linen strands.

Another functional characteristic of spinning bowls is that many of them have the inner part of the bowl carefully polished, even burnished, which indicates that this area was actively used during the work.

The function of the inner handles and their variations are key to understanding this textile production tool. The position of the handles is usually in the centre of the bowl's internal surface, and their number ranges from one to four. In some cases the handles are attached to the walls of the bowl, or one point of attachment is on the bottom and the other on the wall of the bowl. These two latter cases, as well as the horizontal or vertical position of the handles, may indicate the use of different spinning techniques.

Variation in the position and number of handles tells us about the different production modes in which the spinning bowl was used. The function of the handles was to arrange, stretch and tighten flax fibres as they passed through.

The number of handles may depend on the spinning process, particularly the number of spindles and thread thickness used. It also indicates the number of spinners working with each of the spinning bowls —which, in turn, depended on their knowhow— since the spinning bowl allows the release of the hands from a distaff, allowing the pulling of yarn of a calibrated thickness through the

grooves in the handles to the spindle. Therefore, the number of handles also suggests the number of people involved in the preparation of linen skeins.

The most important feature of the inner handles is that their grooves bear marks or notches previously made in them. Nevertheless, a more thorough study of those traces is needed in order to learn more about the way the handles were used. Studies based on graphic documentation would benefit from research on micro wear and micro traces.

The splicing technique is another key issue in the study of flax processing using this tool. This technique has been only documented in textile remains found in Egypt,[9] southern Levant and eastern Switzerland.[10] It is also depicted on the walls of ancient Egyptian tombs, where we can see the preparation of flax fibres following three technical steps: first, the removal of leaves and roots, retting, beating and combing flax; second, the splicing of the cut thread's ends, forming balls of spliced flax; and, finally, introducing those balls into the spinning bowl to wet and stretch them for spinning with the continuous drafting technique.

The procedural stages of spinning with spinning bowls

The process of spinning using a spinning bowl can be divided into three stages. The first is splicing and twisting, or 'thigh-spinning'.[11] The spinner uses friction between the hand and the leg, or uses other accessories, as in Ancient Egypt, where polished stones were used to help create a triangular wedge from the spliced fibres,[12] or as in Classical Greece, where spinning was performed using the *epinetron*, a tool helping in the yarn splicing technique.[13]

At the start of the second stage, balls of spliced yarn were placed in the spinning bowl, which acted as a tool for conducting the wet yarn through the grooves of the handles.

The relevant aspect in this case is the function of internal loops and grooves, because these are key to achieving productive efficiency, as well as qualitative and quantitative improvement. The width of the grooves could also determine the desired fineness of the thread and facilitate obtaining linen thread of a certain thickness.

The third stage consists of making the thread in the technique of continuous drafting with the use of a spindle and whorl. The spindle is a tool that maximises the efficiency of hand movements in creating thread, and the spinning bowl gives the spinner more freedom to operate several spindles at once,[14] since operating the spindle by the spinner only requires rhythmic movement to get the spliced yarn wound into balls and to control the continued rotation of the spindle with a whorl running the final yarn.

Examination of the spinning techniques reveals an uneven process of innovation. For example, in Egypt we see the use of a technique of making thread in which the primitive method of spliced spinning and the new continuous

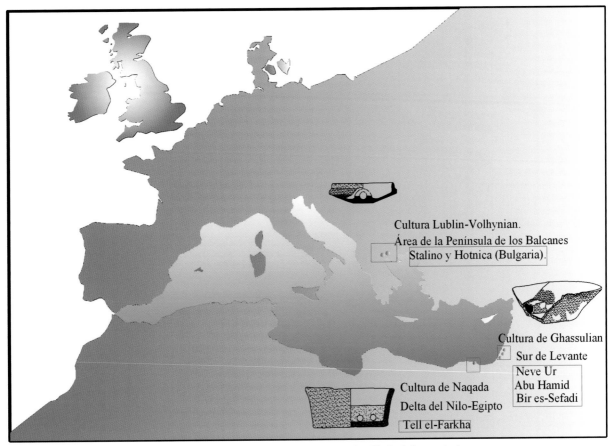

Fig. 8.1 Beginnings of spinning bowls in the Chalcolithic period.

drafting technique coexist already at the start of the Neolithic period.[15] In this case, we are not dealing with a transition from one spinning technique to another, but with the creation of a new technique that combines tradition and innovation, and this innovation occurs at the stage of the spinning technique in which the spinning bowl is used.

The diachronic evolution of spinning bowls

The spinning bowls documented in the Chalcolithic period, in the areas of southern Levant, the Balkans and Egypt, all have in common their bowl shape and the fact that they are all made of clay (Fig. 8.1).[16] These bowls vary in form by region, from conical bowls with low walls found in the area of the Balkans to bowls with straight, higher walls in southern Levant and Egypt. Conical bowls from the southern areas of the Levant and Bulgaria commonly have one handle. However, the handle's position and section differs depending on the geographic area in which the bowl type is found. In the case of Bulgaria, the handle is placed in the centre of the bottom and it has a rounded section,[17] whereas in the southern Levant it is placed on the wall and has a flattened section.[18] Egyptian bowls are a different case: two loop handles, each with one end attached to the side of the bowl,

meet in the middle, dividing the vessel into two halves. In one example from Tell el-Farkha, these loops are converted to a vertical partition.[19] The bowls may also have vertical partitions with two openings (merged loops), giving a total of four holes.[20] This variation in form among spinning bowls may indicate functional differences and the use of different techniques in Bulgaria and in the southern Levant on the one hand, and in Egypt on the other.

In the Bronze Age, changes occurred in the typology of the spinning bowl, suggesting progress in its technical development as a textile production tool. It was made mostly in clay, although some of them were also made of stone. We lack archaeological evidence from Bulgaria in this period,[21] but in the southern Levant and Egypt spinning bowls were still in use.[22] In the Aegean region, the situation is similar, for the spinning bowl was used in Crete and later in other areas of mainland Greece,[23] as well as in more distant regions such as north-western Iberia, in the Late Bronze Age.[24] The spinning bowls acquired a more homogeneous form in all the areas here discussed; the majority have a bowl shape with high walls and two inner handles. In this period, the use of this spinning tool spread and was widely employed across the eastern Mediterranean (Fig. 8.2).

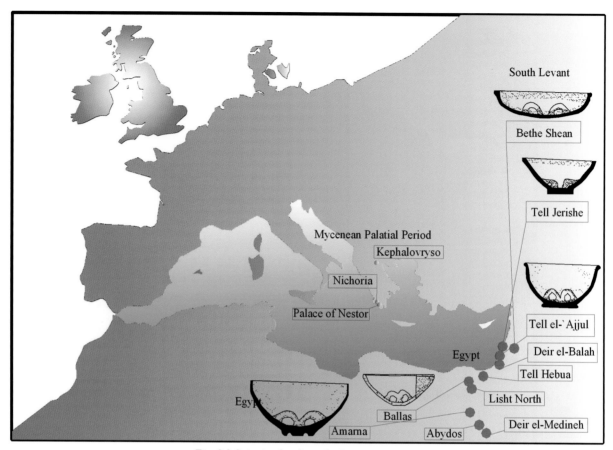

Fig. 8.2 Spinning bowls in the Late Bronze Age.

In the Iron Age, the evidence for the use of spinning bowls in the Aegean disappears,[25] whereas in the other aforementioned areas it continues to be used until Roman times in both the Iberian Peninsula and Egypt.[26] During the Iron Age, variation in forms once again increased, both in the shape of the bowls and in the position of the handles (attached to the centre of the bottom or to the walls, or both), which suggests further progress in the technical aspects of the use of this tool.

The beginnings of the use of the spinning bowl in the Chalcolithic period: southern Levant, the Balkans and Egypt

The appearance of the spinning bowl in the Chalcolithic period reflects the tradition and evolution of the cultivation of flax and the development of fibre-processing techniques, including the different techniques used for making yarn, which occurred during the Neolithic period. It is at this point that we may place the technological breakthrough that involves the use of the spinning bowl and a marked increase in the documented numbers of spindle whorls. This coincides with the beginning of other archaeologically verifiable developments, such as an increase in regional trade and attestations of craft workshops.[27]

The different techniques used to produce thread can be divided into three main types. The first is the spliced drafting technique,[28] the second is a variation of the first, the innovation consisting in spinning with a spindle but without a whorl. Whorls are not attested archaeologically until the Early Neolithic,[29] although we cannot exclude that other objects and techniques were used but did not leave traces in the material record. The third is a spinning technique using a spindle with a whorl placed in different positions on the spindle shaft.[30]

The birth of this innovation took place in the southern Levant, as this is where the oldest examples of spinning bowls have been documented to date.[31] Its use then spread slowly, possibly through trade networks in Anatolia, into the Balkans. From the southern Levant it also spread to Egypt, where its use was to continue for millennia. It is also possible that the innovation occurred there independently.[32]

Spinning bowls in the southern Levant

The Chalcolithic period in the southern Levant was characterised by the existence of a stratified society led by tribal chiefs. The populations living in villages relied on agro-pastoral activities for subsistence and were involved in craft production. Chronologically, this period falls between 4500 and 3700–3500 BC.[33]

The first spinning bowls are recorded in the Ghassulian culture, including one found in Neve Ur, two in Abu Hamid in the Jordan Valley and four in Bires-Safadi located within the cultural impact zone of Beersheba.[34]

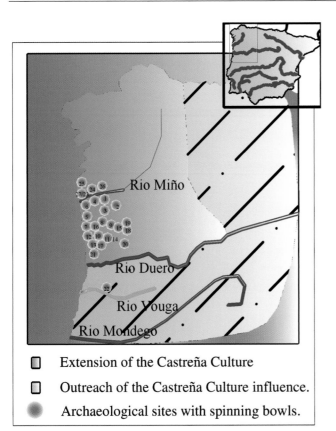

Fig. 8.3 Distribution of the Castreña culture and spinning bowls: *Distrito de Viana do Castelo in Portugal:* 1. Castro de Cossourado (Paredes de Coura), 2. Castro de Cristelo (San Sebastiao), 3. Castro de Romarigáes (Alto da Cidade), 4. Castro de Coto da Pena (Caminha), 5. Castro de Santa Lucia (Monte de Santa Lucia), 6. Castro de Lovelhe (Vilanova de Cerveira); *Distrito de Braga in Portugal:* 7. Castro Máximo (San Vicente), 8. Castro de Lanhoso (Póvoado do Lanhoso), 9. Castro de San Juliâo (Vila Verde), 10. Castro do Pego (Cunha), 11. Castro do Briteiros (Guimarâes), 12. Castro de Penices (Gondifelos), 13. Castro das Erminadas (Jesufrei), 14. Castro de Sabroso (Guimarâes), 15. Castro de Santo Ovideo (Fafe), 16. Castro de Lago (Amares), 17. Castro de Frijáo (Cunha); *Distrito de Vila Real in Portugal:* 18. Castro de Castroeiro (Modin de Basto), 19. Castro del Muro da Pastoira (Redondelo); *Distrito de Viseu in Portugal:* 20. Castro de Senhora da Guia (Baioês); *Distrito de Porto in Portugal:* 21. Castro de Monte Mozinho (Penafiel), 22. Castro de Monte Padrâo (Monte do Córdova); *Southern area of Galicia (Spain):* 23. Castro de Torroso (Mos, Pontevedra), 24. Castro de A Cidade de Carneiro (Fozara, Pontevedra), 25. Castro de Vigo (Vigo, Pontevedra), 26. Castro de Troña (Puenteareas, Pontevedra), 27. Castro de Santa Trega (A Guarda, Pontevedra).

four inner handles have been recorded, as well as numerous fragments of other examples. All are of the same type: a bowl with a flat base and straight walls, and two to four internal handles.[38]

The economic importance of the textile craft becomes particularly noticeable during this period, and is focused on the production of linen fabrics. The site of Bires-Safadi may serve as a good example of a place where intensification of the textile craft occurred.[35]

The introduction of the spinning bowl and *Linum usitatissimum* L.: a working hypothesis

The introduction of the spinning bowl is documented in the Chalcolithic period in the eastern Mediterranean area, and its function is exclusively related to the flax fibre. The domestication of this textile fibre begins with the domestication of *Linum angustiflium* and transition to *Linum usitatissimum* L. in about the 9th millennium BC in the Near East (and in about the 6th millennium BC in Central Europe).[39] Linen thread is known to have been used in the Negev region as early as 10,000 years ago.[40] Therefore, we can include this textile tool in the context of innovations taking place during the Chalcolithic period, aimed at achieving a linen thread of better quality or a faster way to spin as much as possible in the shortest time possible.

With the Neolithic, new raw materials became available for the production of fabrics, leaving behind or in the background the 'bast culture in fabrics', as hitherto the fibre used was tree-bast. The launch of the production of linen fabrics in the Neolithic period did not bring significant changes in the process of transforming plants into textile fibres suitable for being spun, but major innovations did occur in the spinning and weaving technology.[41] The introduction of the spinning bowl in the Chalcolithic might have been linked to the domestication of a new type of flax and the continuation of innovation in thread production, as well as to the importance of use and demand for linen textiles.

Spinning bowls in the Balkans

The specimens documented in the Balkans are associated with the cultural phase of the Carpathian-Balkan Neolithic (*c.* 4100–3650 BC), and in the Chalcolithic with the Lublin-Volhynian culture, which includes the Balkan Peninsula.[36]

The finds of spinning bowls are known from two sites. One was found inside a house in Slatino (Chardako, Bulgaria), a settlement dated to the Early Chalcolithic. Another bowl from a domestic context comes from Tell Hotnica (District Velico, Ternovo, Bulgaria) and is dated to the Later Chalcolithic. Although the finds represent different typological forms and come from chronologically distant periods, they both have a bowl shape and a single centrally located inner handle.[37]

Spinning bowls in Egypt

Egyptian examples come from slightly later contexts, ranging from the Chalcolithic to the Protodynastic period (Naqada IIIA–IIIB, 3600–3300 BCE). They have been found at Tell el-Farkha, a settlement located in the eastern Nile Delta and inhabited from the early Naqada period to the Early Dynastic period. Two complete spinning bowls with

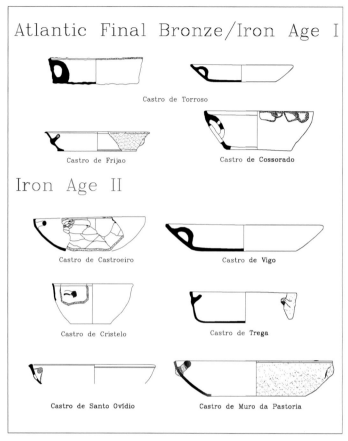

Fig. 8.4 Typology of spinning bowls of the Iberian Peninsula.

Analysis of the geographical distribution of spinning bowls during the Bronze and Iron Age

During the Bronze Age (*c.* 3500–1100 BC), a new quantitative and qualitative change in textile production is worthy of note. In the Early Bronze Age we observe advances in spinning and weaving technology, among other fields related to the consumption, distribution and trade in textiles. Textile production played an important role in the economy of emerging kingdoms, resulting in the creation of production centres that focused on the temple or palace.[42]

Cultural variability in the use of different techniques and technologies of spinning and weaving during the Bronze Age meant that in some areas the spinning bowl was used only residually, while in others its use continued for millennia, as in the case of Egypt. This may certainly be connected to the economic importance of linen fabrics in particular cultures and areas, which should be taken into account when analysing the spinning bowls' geographical and chronological distribution.[43]

In the case of the southern Levant, continuity in the use of the spinning bowl could be related to the linen textile tradition that did not disappear even with the introduction

of new fibres such as wool. It could also be tied to the relations between the Levant and Egypt, where linen was continuously used during this period.

The evidence for the spinning bowl in the Iberian Peninsula is a separate case, for it is only documented in the Castreña culture from the Late Bronze Age to the Roman period. It seems that the use of the spinning bowl was here an autonomous innovation, although probably connected to the introduction of *Linum usitatissimum* L. as a textile fibre.

Nevertheless, the increased use of wool as a fibre by the Early Bronze Age or even earlier certainly affected the development of spinning and weaving techniques (Fig. 8.2).[44]

Spinning bowls in the Iron Age

The common occurrence of the spinning bowl during the Bronze Age in Greece and Crete was followed by its subsequent decline in the Iron Age (1200–539 BC).[45] This may be explained by the increasing dominance of wool as a textile fibre in the Aegean area, which led to a decline in the use of the spinning bowls.[46] The spinning technology may have also led to the change in flax processing from splicing to spinning, resulting in the termination of spinning bowl use in Crete and Greece by the Early Iron Age. However, its use continued in the Levant at least until the 7th century BC, while in Egypt it continued until the Roman period.[47]

The spinning bowl in the Iberian Peninsula

While the development of the spinning bowl reviewed up to this point has been noted by numerous scholars, an area that has not been considered in detail is the western Mediterranean. My research on textile production during the Phoenician colonisation of the Iberian Peninsula has identified numerous examples of what I believe to be spinning bowls. All of them date from the Late Bronze Age to Iron Age, and come from a number of important archaeological sites, which form a cultural and geographical entity (Fig. 8.5).

From cooking pots with inner handles to spinning bowls in the Castreña culture of the north-western Iberian Peninsula

During the period in question, the area of the Iberian Peninsula was occupied by the Castreña culture, which is dated from 1200–700 BC up to the 3rd century BC (Fig. 8.3). From the Late Bronze Age to the Iron Age, there is continuity in settlement patterns and ceramic typology accompanied by an increased occurrence of fortified towns.[48]

Exogenous influences in this period are marked by trade, which brings to the Castreña culture a number of features, such as new aesthetic forms of dress with clearly oriental influence. This is clearly related to this culture's integration into Atlantic-Mediterranean trade routes.[49]

The assemblage of Castreña ceramics from north-west Portugal and Galicia (Spain) includes vessel forms interpreted as cooking pots[50] made of the common ceramic household ware.[51] It has been argued that this type of vessel, which has horizontal or vertical internal handles, would have been suspended above a fireplace, serving as a specialised type of kitchen equipment[52] whose appearance was due to changes in culinary practice.[53]

However, its use as a cooking pot is not likely, as pointed out by António Baptista Lopes. In his doctoral thesis, Lopes argued that these vessels, appearing in the deposits of the Castreña culture from the Late Bronze Age, could not have functioned as suspended cooking pots if they had only two internal loops, as is the case of the vast majority of specimens. A further argument against their use as cooking pots is their open shape and low walls.[54]

These bowls, however, are typologically very similar to the southern Levantine examples of spinning bowls discussed above. Thus, the question arises regarding their origin in the Iberian Peninsula.

Typology and morphological observations of ceramic spinning bowls documented in the north-west of the Iberian Peninsula

The notion that the bowls with internal handles belong to the sphere of textile technology is based on several observations (Fig. 8.5).

The first is their typological similarity to bowls documented in the eastern Mediterranean, where their use as textile tools has been demonstrated. It should, however, be emphasised that, while a wide typological variety exists among the spinning bowls from the Iberian Peninsula, in most cases, the internal handles are positioned horizontally on the wall of the bowl.

The second observation is that spinning bowls found in well-documented contexts primarily appear in settlement areas where craft activities including textile production are evidenced.[55]

Bowls found in southern Galicia (Spain), in the first phase, Iron Age I (8th–5th centuries BC), have the internal handles affixed by piercing the wall of the bowl rather than by attaching with slip, and this technique continues into Iron Age II. The bowls were made by hand using the coiling technique, although in the last phase of Iron Age II some specimens were made on the wheel.[56] The handles of the spinning bowls of the Iberian Peninsula bear marks (grooves) on the inside of the handles, a characteristic they share with all bowls used as textile tools.[57] The smoothing of the inner zone of these bowls is shown in many examples. The internal smoothing is not found in other ceramics in the Castreño cultural group (Fig. 8.4).[58]

The origin of the spinning bowl in the Iberian Peninsula: an imported or local technological innovation for spinning flax?

One reason to assume that our object of study is a foreign form and a technological import from the Phoenicians is that it first appears in northern Portugal. Its occurrence coincides with the economic and cultural contact of this region's population with the Phoenicians who settled along the coast of Portugal and established links with the area of southern Galicia.[59] The problem with this hypothesis is that there is no evidence for spinning bowls in the areas of Phoenician settlement in the Iberian Peninsula.

The working hypothesis focuses, therefore, on indigenous innovation in spinning flax, and suggests that the same technological element was invented by various cultures independently while seeking a solution to the same problem, in this case flax processing. But this hypothesis may only be supported by the absence of the spinning bowls in Phoenician colonies.

The changes adopted in flax processing may have occurred during the Late Bronze Age and Iron Age I due to commercial contacts with the Phoenicians. These

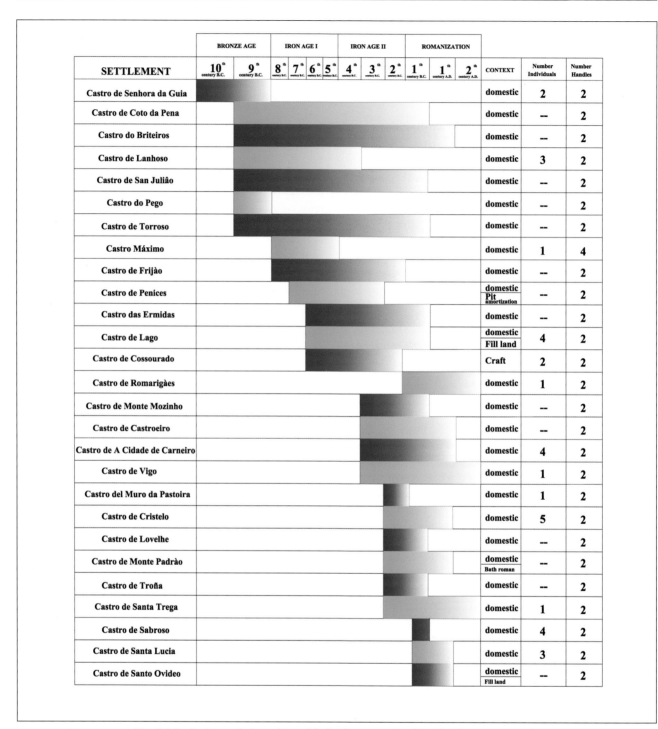

Fig. 8.5 Beginning and chronology of finds of spinning bowls in the Iberian Peninsula.

relations resulted in major socio-economic, religious and aesthetic changes, including the new aesthetic trends in clothing and ornament recorded in the archaeological evidence. It is possible, for example, that the adoption of the fibula as a fastener of clothing during the Late Bronze Age was accompanied by new forms of dress.[60] Imported luxury fabrics with new decorative patterns,[61] designed and produced in high-quality flax and wool, were obtained through the Phoenician trade circuits and subsequently also imitated by people of the peninsular north-west.

Conclusion

I have argued that the spinning bowl developed within the procedural sequence of spinning flax to thread. It was used as a container for a liquid used to wet flax fibres, while its handles stretched the linen strands before they passed on to the spindle.

To understand the creation and use of the spinning bowl in conjunction with two spinning techniques (spliced and continuous drafting), we must identify the variables of technological change.

We must study not only the *chaîne opératoire* but, as archaeologists, we need to broaden our understanding of the bowls' contexts. Spinning practices are sensitive to fluctuations in demand for textiles which influence the production process by improving qualitative and quantitative efficiency.

The typological analysis of the spinning bowl shows an increase of formal variation during the Chalcolithic period and at the end of the Iron Age (Roman period), whereas the forms were more standardised during the Bronze and Iron Ages, suggesting fluctuations in the degree of specialisation in the production of flax yarn.

It is reasonable to assume that the presence of the spinning bowl in the Iberian Peninsula was a consequence of indigenous innovation or indirect influence, since this object is not documented in the Phoenician colonial area of Iberia.

Nevertheless, it is necessary to continue studying the formal and functional aspects of the spinning bowl in order to understand its use in the process of flax spinning.

Notes

1 I would like to express many thanks to Dr. Margarita Gleba and the PROCON project, and Dr. Pedro Aguayo de Hoyos, my esteemed doctoral supervisor, whose help has been essential during the conducting of this research.
2 Allen 1997, appendix 1 and 2.
3 Barber 1991, 72.
4 Dothan 1963, 97–112; Barber 1991, 192; Allen 1997, 19; Hageman 2006, 16.
5 Allen 1997, 25–28.
6 Barber 1991, 72; Kempt and Vogelsang-Eastwood 2001, 295; Hageman 2006, 15.
7 Crowfoot 1931; Dothan 1963; Allen 1997, 20–25; Kemp and Vogelsang-Eastwood 2001.
8 Granger-Taylor 1998, 104–105.
9 Granger-Taylor 1998, 103–107.
10 Shamir 2015, 17; Shamir and Rosen 2015, 129–139.
11 Tiedemann and Jakes 2006, 295.
12 Granger-Taylor 1998, 104; Tiedemann and Jakes 2006, 293–294.
13 Barber 1991, 77–78.
14 Barber 1991, 42, 46; Kemp and Vogelsang-Eastwood 2001, 74–75.
15 Barber 1991, 44, 47–48; Mączyńska 2012, 66–67.
16 Chmielewski 2009; Mączyńska 2012; Levy and Gilead 2013.
17 Chmielewski 2009, 223–224.
18 Levy and Gilead 2012, 133.
19 Mączyńska 2012, 70.
20 Kemp and Vogelsang-Eastwood 2001, 293.
21 Chmielewski 2009, 224

22 Dothan 1963, 101–103.
23 Barber 1991, 73–74.
24 Rey 1986–1987, 186–187.
25 Barber 1991, 76–77.
26 Martins 1987, 57; Barber 1991, 77; Allen 1997, 25–26, 36–38.
27 Crowfoot 1931, 7–11; Barber 1991, 54–62; Joffe *et al.* 2001, 10; Chmielewski 2009, 227.
28 Tiedemann and Jakes 2006, 293–294.
29 Barber 1991, 51–68.
30 Barber 1991, 39–42.
31 Rowan and Golden 2009, 7; Levy and Gilead 2012, 127, 133, 134; Shamir 2014, 140–147.
32 Ciałowicz 2012.
33 Joffe *et al.* 2001, 10.
34 Rowan and Golden 2009, 7; Levy and Gilead 2012, 127, 133, 134; Shamir 2014, 140–147.
35 Levy and Gilead 2013, 26–33.
36 Chmielewski 2009, 223.
37 Chmielewski 2009, 224–226.
38 Ciałowicz 2012, 171; Mączyńska 2012, 65–73; Sobas 2012, 186–196.
39 Rast-Eicher 2005, 120.
40 Rast-Eicher 2005, 120.
41 Rast-Eicher 2005, 117–124.
42 Wild 2003, 46–47.
43 Wild 2003, 33.
44 Wild 2003, 43.
45 Chmielewski 2009, 224.
46 Wild 2003, 33.
47 Dothan 1963, 112; Allen 1992, 36–38.
48 Rocha de Araújo 2009, 27–28.
49 Ruiz-Gálvez 1998, 282–287.
50 Rey 1990–1991, 141–163; Matos da Silva 2006, 495–496.
51 Martins 1987, 54.
52 Ayán 2001, 41–52.
53 González Ruibal 2006–2007, 295.
54 Baptista 2003, 151–152.
55 Senna-Martinez 1994, 219; Baptista 2003, 73–180; Matos 2006, 572–579.
56 Rey Castiñeira 1986–1987, 184–182; Rey Castiñeira 1990–1991, 142, 147–148.
57 Hidalgo Cuñarro and Costas Goberna 1979, 181.
58 Soeiro *et al.* 1981, 344; Soeiro 1985–1986, 28; Matos da Silva 2006. While many examples of spinning bowls show evidence of polishing or burnishing on the interior, this surface treatment is not found on other ceramics in the Castreño culture.
59 Ruiz-Gálvez 1998.
60 Ruiz-Gálvez 1998.
61 Cortegoso 2000, 127–135; Vilaça 2008, 390.

Bibliography

Allen, S. 1997 Spinning bowls: representation and reality. In J. Philipps (ed.), *Ancient Egypt, the Aegean, and the Near East. Studies in Honour of Martha Rhoads Bell*. San Antonio, 17–38.

Ayán Vila, X. M. 2001 Arqueotectura 2: la vivienda castreña. Propuesta de reconstrucciónen el castro de Elviña. *Laboratorio de Arquoloxía e Formas Cultuais*, Universidade de Santiago de Compostela. *Tapa* 23, 1–122.

Baptista Lopes, A. 2003 Proto-história e Romanizaçào do Baixo Minho. Unpublished PhD thesis, University of Porto.

Barber, E. J. W. 1991 *Prehistoric Textiles: The Development of Cloth in the Neolithic and Bronze Ages with Special Reference to the Aegean*. Princeton.

Chmielewski, T. J. 2009 Let's twist again ... or on the Eneolithic methods of yarn production. *Studii de Preistorie* 6, 223–236.

Ciałowicz, K. M. 2012 Protodynastic and Early Dynastic settlement on the Western Kom. In M. Chłodnicki, K. M. Ciałowicz and A. Mączyńska (eds.), *Tell El-Farkha I. Excavations 1998–2011*. Poznań, 163–180.

Cortegoso Comesaña, M. 2000 Tipología de las fíbulas de loscastros gallegos, a través de los ejemplares publicados. *Gallaecia* 19, 125–141.

Crowfoot, G. M. 1931 *Methods of Hand Spinning in Egypt and Sudan*. Bankfield Museum Notes 2.12. Halifax.

Dothan, T. 1963 Spinning-bowls. *Israel Exploration Journal* 13.2, 97–112.

González Ruibal, A. 2006–2007 *Galaicos. Poder y comunidaden el Noroeste de la Península Ibérica (1200 a. C.–50 d. C.)* Vol. II. A. Coruña.

Granger-Taylor, H. 1998 Evidence for linen yarn preparation in Ancient Egypt. The hanks of fibre strips on the ball of prepared rove from Lahum in the Petrie Museum of Egyptian Archaeology. In S. Quieke (ed.), *Lahum Studies*. London, 103–107.

Hageman, R. K. 2006 A continuous thread: flax spinning in Ancient Egypt. *The Ostracon. The Journal of the Egyptian Study Society* 17.1, 14–16.

Hidalgo Cuñarro, J. M. and Costas Goberna, F. J. 1979 El Castro Acidade de Caneriro, Fozara (Ponteareas). *El Museo de Pontevedra* 33, 151–215.

Joffe, A. H., Dessel, J. P. and Hallote, R. S. 2001 The Gilat woman. Female iconography, Chalcolitic cult and the end of South Levantine Prehistory. *Near Eastern Archaeology* 64.1–2, 7–23.

Kemp, B. J. and Vogelsang-Eastwood, G. 2001 *The Ancient Textile Industry at Amarna*. London.

Levy, J. and Gilead, L. 2012 Spinning in the 5th millennium in the southern Levant: aspects of the textile economy. *Paléorient* 38.1–2. Dossier thématique/Thematic file, C. Breniquet, M. Tengberg, E. Andersson and M.-L. Nosch (eds.), Préhistoire des Textiles au Proche-Orient/Prehistory of Textiles in the Near East, 127–139.

Levy, J. and Gilead, L. 2013 The emergence of the Ghassulian textile industry in the southern Levant Chalcolithic Period (*c.* 4500–3900 BCE). In M.-L. Nosch, H. Koefoed and E. Andersson Strand (eds.), *Textile Production and Consumption in the Ancient Near East. Archaeology, Epigraphy, Iconography*. Ancient Textiles Series 12. Oxford, 26–44.

Mączyńska, A. 2012 Were spinning bowls used in Predynastic Period? Finds from Tell el Farkha. In J. Kabaciński, M. Chłodnicki and M. Kobusiewicz (eds.), *Prehistory of Northeastern Africa. New Ideas and Discoveries*. Studies in African Archaeology 11. Poznań, 65–75.

Martins, M. 1987 A cerâmica proto-histórica do Vale do Cávado: tentativa de sistematizaçao. *Cuadernos de Arqueología* Série II, 4, 35–77.

Matos Da Silva, M. F. 2006 O povoamento proto-histórico e a romanizaçào da Bacia superior do Rio Coura: estudo, musealizaçao e divulgaçao. Unpublished PhD thesis, University of Granada.

Rast-Eicher, A. 2005 Bast before wool: the first textiles. In Bichler, K. Grömer, R. Hofmann-de Keijzer, A. Kern and H. Reschreite (eds.), *Hallstatt Textiles: Technical Analysis, Scientific Investigation and Experiment of Iron Age Textiles*. British Archaeological Reports International Series 1351. Oxford, 117–132.

Rey Castiñeira, P. 1986–1987 Algunas consideraciones sobre cerámica castreña. *Zephyrus* 39–40, 184–192.

Rey Castiñeira, P. 1990–1991 Cerámica indígena de los castors costeros de la Galicia occidental: Rias Bajas. Valoración dentro del contexto general de la cultura Castreña. *Castrelos* 3–4, 141–163.

Rocha de Araújo Pinho, J. M. 2009 *O Iº Milénio A. C. e o estabelecimiento rural romanonavertente fluvial do Ave. Dinâmicas de estabelecimento sob o ponto de vista geo-espacial*. Lisboa.

Rowan, Y. M. and Golden, J. 2009 The Chalcolithic period of the southern Levant: a synthetic review. *Journal of World Prehistory* 22, 1–92.

Ruiz-Gálvez Priego, M. L. 1998 *La Europa Atlánticaen la Edad del Bronce. Unviaje a las raíces de la Europa occidental*. Barcelona.

Senna-Martinez, J. C. 1994 Entre Atlântico e Mediterrâneo: algunas reflexôes sobre o Grupo Baiôes/Santa Luzia e o desenvolvimento do Bronze Final Peninsular. *Trabalhos de Arqueológia da EAM* 2, 215–232.

Shamir, O. 2014 Textiles, basketry and other organic artifacts of the Chalcolithic period in the southern Levant. In M. Sebbane, O. Misch-Brandl and D. M. Master (eds.), *Masters of Fire: Copper Age Art from Israel*. Princeton, 139–152.

Shamir, O. 2015 Textiles from the Chalcolithic period, Early and Middle Bronze Age in the southern Levant. *Archaeological Textiles Review* 57, 12–25.

Shamir, O. and Rosen, S. A. 2015 Early Bronze Age textiles from the Ramon I Rock Shelter in the Central Negev. *Israel Exploration Journal* 65.2, 129–139.

Sobas, M. 2012 Pottery from the western Kom. In M. Chłodnicki, K. M. Ciałowicz and A. Mączyńska (eds.), *Tell El-Farkha I. Excavations 1998–2011*. Poznań, 181–187.

Soerio, T. 1985–1986 Muro da Pastoria, Chaves. Campanha de Escavaçao de 1982–83. *Revista Portugalia* 6/7, 21–28.

Soerio, T., Centeno, R. M. S. and Coelho F. Da Silva, A. 1981 Sondagem arqueologica do Castro de Sabroso. *Revista de Guimarães* 91, 340–350.

Tiedemann, E. J. and Jakes, K. A. 2006 An exploration of prehistoric spinning technology: spinning efficiency and technology transition. *Archaeometry* 48.2, 293–307.

Vilaça, R. 2008 Redlexôes em torno da presença mediterránea no centro do territorio portugués, na charneira do Bronze para o Ferro. In S. Celestino, N. Rafel and X. L. Armada (eds.), *Contacto cultural entre el Mediterráneo y el Atlántico (siglos XII–VIII ane) La precolonización a debate*. Madrid, 371–400.

Wild, J. P. 2003 Anatolia, Mesopotamia and the Levant in the Bronze Age, *c.* 3500–1100 BC. In D. Jenkins (ed.), *The Cambridge History of Western Textiles*. Cambridge, 43–48.

From the loom to the forge. Elements of power at the end of Neolithic in western Europe: a focus on textile activities

Fabienne Médard

Between 5500 and 2000 before our era, during the Neolithic Period, human communities progressively started to form and hierarchies started appearing. If the absence of writing makes gaining knowledge of such societies difficult, the material evidence defines the contours. (*Signes de richesse* 2015)

The recent exhibition 'Signes de richesse. Inégalités au Néolithique' presented at the Musée National de Préhistoire des Eyzies-de-Tayac[1]

sheds light on the symbolical dimension of the exchange of objects and shows the way in which they respond to the sociological considerations resulting from the new statuses of groups or individuals ... The circulation of raw materials and of technologies does in fact hold a key place at the heart of the community and should not be reduced to its trading value.[2]

After many years of research devoted to the analysis of Neolithic tools and textile remains, this article continues the same reflection. Following the analysis of remains found on the Neolithic sites in the Swiss Plateau[3] and the later analysis of other remains from related geographical areas (eastern France, Belgium, northern Italy, southern Germany), the homogeneity of the Neolithic tools and of the textile production revealed itself. This in turn allows the expansion of the synthesis to other areas of western Europe. Attention may be switched to the significance of technical changes brought upon textile activities more than on the circulation of materials and on production itself.

Research problems and methodology

Research into the characterisation and interpretation of the development of textile production in the Late Neolithic period and early Bronze Age is part of the broader history of technology. It offers an approach to human phenomena that comes from the specific view of prehistoric archaeology where, deprived of written testimony and with little iconography, research has to be confined to the boundaries of material culture, and it is this that provides the facts that allow synthesis.[4] Technological analysis is the foundation of this approach.[5] To understand the choice of technique used is to understand one of the founding elements of culture, seen from the perspective of the objects that man places between him and his environment. Mauss emphasised the '... cases of invention, of positioning of principles are rare';[6] the technical act is significant. Based on this idea, documenting textile activity is paramount to understanding if this was a field of innovation or whether on the contrary, it was frozen in tradition and production habits. Documenting textile activity is a means by which we can examine the organisation of societies, their environment, their economy, science, culture and history.

Engaging many disciplines, the subject of textile production is thus centred on four main axes: technological, socio-economic, cultural and historical developments. The first objective of research in the area is to highlight ruptures, changes, stagnation or technical innovations in the field of textile production. The second is to describe and understand these developments in their respective socio-economic contexts. The third objective is to interpret the results obtained on the synchronic and diachronic planes.

Data

In the field of textiles, archaeological research is mainly based on three categories of remains: spindle whorls, loom weights and textile remains. Other artefacts exist, and there are also architectural elements most likely related to this craft; however, these will only offer additional or anecdotal information. Also taken into account are other objects whose shapes are less obvious, but would be tempting to associate either rightly or wrongly with the textile craft. From the acquisition of raw materials to the creation of the products, there is actually scope in textile production for the use of the most diverse tools. Among them are instruments potentially used to collect and process fibres: barking spuds, microdenticular lithic tools, a variety of pointed tools, combs, beaters, *etc.*, or weaving instruments such as weaving swords.[7] Research also shows that the tools of Neolithic textile craft making are relatively rarely found.[8] It must therefore be acknowledged that the exact use of many tools remains unknown and that the interpretation of their function is often speculative.

While not present on all Neolithic sites, textile remnants abound in archaeological deposits located in wetlands. Proof of great diversity, they are testament to skilful and inventive techniques in the fields of spinning (threads and ropes), weaving (twining and woven) and netting. The craftsmen skilfully combined various forms of technical processes, sometimes using weaving, basketry, braiding, embroidery, *etc.*, within the same piece.[9] These remains can be fundamental in defining the raw materials used in production, technical choices made, knowledge required and sometimes the use to which the products were put. They cannot, however, yet be dated on the basis of technical criteria alone. They have no inherent chronological significance. Their characteristics and differences can in no way be interpreted as signs of change or evolution. To be meaningful, the technical characteristics of textiles require to be appreciated in the *longue durée*.[10] The few millennia that define the Neolithic are not enough.

Consequently, because they are available in great numbers on the sites and because their use is proven in the field of textile production, the spindle whorls and loom weights are the only tools that allow for an in-depth study of the developments in technology. Made of clay or stone, they are usually well preserved, and enough of them have been found to provide a statistically significant sample on which to base interpretations of trends in the long term.

Changes and technical evolution

Within the first line of research statement at the beginning, both categories of remains deliver accurate results when utilised for typological and technological analysis.

Significant typological modifications

Typological analysis is a prerequisite for the study of the evidence for textile production. Observations of the characteristics of the array of tools collected during the course of archaeological fieldwork concentrate on the examination of their raw material, the traces of shaping, decorations and firing of such items; they are also based on morphological assessment of the tools, their shapes and their dimensions. This method of research requires the establishment of strict standards set according to criteria eliminating all subjectivity. This allows an objective comparison of elements from different geographic and chronological and cultural contexts.

Spindle whorls are undoubtedly the category of textile tools most available for study. Detailed analysis of their craftsmanship shows that they were considered ordinary implements with strictly utilitarian use. The modelling and the careless manner by which the perforation was made suggest they were made quickly and their imperfections were left unchanged. The clay used was often coarse. If the object bears some form of decoration, this ornament is frequently of poor quality, and only the effect of mechanical movement rather than an attempt to increase the aesthetic value, and seems even less likely to have had any symbolic significance. It is likely that, as remarkable as it was, the activity of spinning was not perceived to be an exceptional art.[11] There is a considerable diversity in the typology of spindle whorls, six main types exist: discoidal with rounded edges, and those with flat edges, conical, bi-conical, hemispherical and conical with rounded tops. Their interpretative value is reduced due to their uneven representation in the chronology. Evidently, the discoidal spindle whorl makes up the overwhelming majority of the examples produced and used throughout the Neolithic (Fig. 9.1 A). They account for nearly 90% of the spindle whorls found,[12] and this suggests a stability that allows us to assume that if the craftsmen at the time did not seek to diversify their tools, they were satisfactory enough to attain their production targets, making their production relatively uniform over the whole period. As we will see, this stability is nevertheless replaced by greater diversity of form in the Late Neolithic period (Fig. 9.1 A–C).

Just like the spindle whorls, the loom weights give no clue that any value had been assigned to them. Until the beginning of the Late Neolithic, loom weights were characterised by the use of coarse clay, an uneven modelling technique and low temperature firing. Fragile, brittle and susceptible to decay in the short- to medium-term, they were

Fig. 9.1 (opposite) A. Breakdown of the various types of Neolithic spindle whorls; B. Terracotta spindle whorls. Arbon-Bleiche site 3, Thurgau (Switzerland), Late Neolithic (Benguerel et al. 2010, fig. 2); C. Stone spindle whorls. Delley-Portalban site II, Fribourg (Switzerland), Middle Neolithic (photo: Service archéologique cantonal, Fribourg); D. Breakdown of the types of Neolithic loom weights (Médard 2010a); E. Assortment of piriform loom weights. Arbon-Bleiche site 3, Thurgau (Switzerland), Middle Neolithic (photo: Amt für Archäologie, Thurgau); F. Variety of oblong loom weights. Delley-Portalban site II, Fribourg (Switzerland), Late Neolithic (photo: Service archéologique cantonal, Fribourg).

A

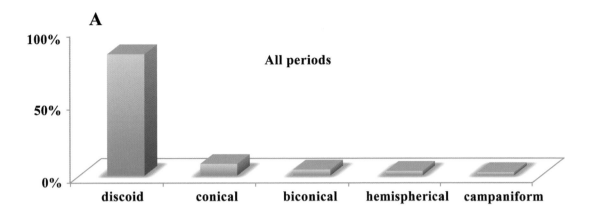

All periods

100%

50%

0%

discoid   conical   biconical   hemispherical   campaniform

B

C

D

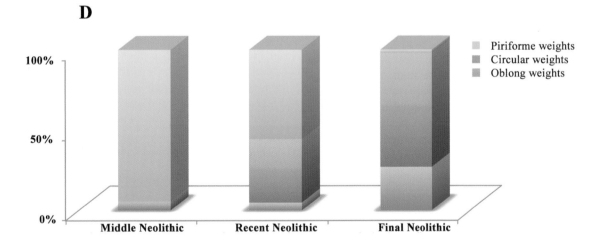

Piriforme weights
Circular weights
Oblong weights

100%

50%

0%

Middle Neolithic   Recent Neolithic   Final Neolithic

E

F

replaceable at low cost. Yet cluster analysis highlights the obvious signs of change between the Middle Neolithic and Final Neolithic (Fig. 9.1 D–F). Changes in design appear and the examples that are mainly piriform-shaped during the mid-Neolithic are gradually replaced by circular pieces that constitute the large majority of the weights during the Final Neolithic (Fig. 9.1 D). This change, along with a decrease in the weight and an improvement in the firing of the ceramics, accompanies a significant increase in the number recovered from archaeological contexts of the Late Neolithic.[13]

Changing technical properties

The typological approach considers the tool solely as an object; the technological approach seeks to clarify its functionality. Essential for defining and understanding textile production, the technological approach is integral to the typological analysis that uses these results. Therefore, it is based on the same corpus of artefacts.

The spindle whorls and loom weights are primarily technical objects, the mechanical properties of which are determined by their dimensions (height, width, diameter, thickness) and mass. The whorl, working as a flywheel, turns the spindle axis in a rotational movement. This rotation is influenced by the speed and amplitude parameters that are subjected to the weight and measurements of the object. For this reason, the dimensions, including mass, are tantamount as they directly affect the mechanical skills of the whorl.[14] It is the same for the loom weights: used on vertical looms, they act as ballast for keeping warp yarns taut. Their mass is likely to give an indication of the strength of the thread as well as of the mounting the warp yarns (distribution of the threads, number of threads on each loom weight, thread count of the cloth, *etc.*). The morphology of the loom weights is crucial: diameters, lengths, widths and thicknesses affect the space occupied by the alignment of the weights at the bottom of the loom. The set-up of the weaving loom rests on the right balance between the tension of the warp thread and the space occupied by the weights at the bottom of the loom.[15]

The technological characterisation of spindle whorls is based on the calculation of the moment of inertia and the rotational speed. The first affects the ability of the whorl to turn without being restarted. The greater the moment of inertia, the longer the whorl turns; the lower it is, the shorter the rotation. The moment of inertia varies according to the shape of the object, its mass and its radius. The speed of rotation indicates the number of turns of the spindle whorl under the effect of a single given impulse for a set time. It is influenced by changes in diameter: the shorter the diameter of the spindle whorl, the faster the rotation.[16] These two parameters are the most appropriate expression of technical properties sought by the Neolithic spinners in their work.

These parameters help demonstrate that the Neolithic spindle whorls were used to spin threads of less than 1 mm diameter, distinguishing them from strings and rope. The latter were systematically made of a different material. This was bast fibre, requiring different manufacturing techniques (Fig. 9.2 A–F).[17] Analysis of textile remains has also shown that threads measuring less than 1 mm in diameter were exclusively made from flax fibres and they were exclusively dedicated to the production of woven fabrics, as opposed to fabrics made of string and bast ropes (Fig. 9.2 G–H).[18] The whorls were therefore used to spin fine flax fibres reserved for textiles made on the loom. Thus, one can assume that most of the Neolithic loom weights ensured a tension suitable for weaving this type of thread, and that the same loom weights had dimensions in line with the desired product.

In summary, all the data collected on the basis of the technological analysis of loom weights and spindle whorls indicate that they were used for spinning flax threads of a diameter under 1 mm, that the threads produced were in turn intended exclusively for weaving on looms and that the finished works were characterised by an average of 10 threads per cm both in warp and weft (Fig. 9.2 D).[19]

Confirmed changes in textile production in the Late Neolithic

The synthesis of typological and technological results renders visible developments, changes and notable modifications in the tools, as well as identifying particularities. This development also partly refers to the results of textile analysis, including what is known about raw materials, threads, thread count and weaving systems. These features establish the necessary link between the tool and the finished product.[20]

On the diachronic level, the Neolithic spindle whorls indicate significant morphological changes happening at

Fig. 9.2 (opposite) A. Skein of yarn. Mozartstrasse site, Zürich (Switzerland), Middle Neolithic (Bleuer and Hardmeyer 1993, pl. 271.1); B. Web of string. Sutz-Lattrigen site VII Innen, Bern (Switzerland), Neolithic (photo: F. Médard); C. Corded weave. Meilen, Meilen-Vorderfeld site, Zürich (Switzerland), Middle Neolithic (photo: F. Médard); D. Evidence of three categories of diameters corresponding to thread, string and rope (Médard 2006a); E. Linen – field, plant, skein (drawing: https://www.old-bookillustrations.com/illustrations/flax/, photos: F. Médard); F. Bast, lime-bast during extraction (experimentation and photo: F. Médard). Bark (drawings: http://www.ville-geneve.ch/themes/en-vironnement-urbain-espaces-verts/arbres/decouvrir-arbres/tilleul/tilleul-petites-feuilles/) and tree (drawings: http://www.ville-gen-eve.ch/themes/environnement-urbain-espaces-verts/arbres/decou-vrir-arbres/tilleul/tilleul-grandes-feuilles/); G. Peruvian woman walking and spinning (photo: D. Ramseyer); H. rope-making from the bark of a baobab. Dogon Country (Mali) (photo: F. Médard); I. illustrations of weaving and twining systems (drawings: F. Médard).

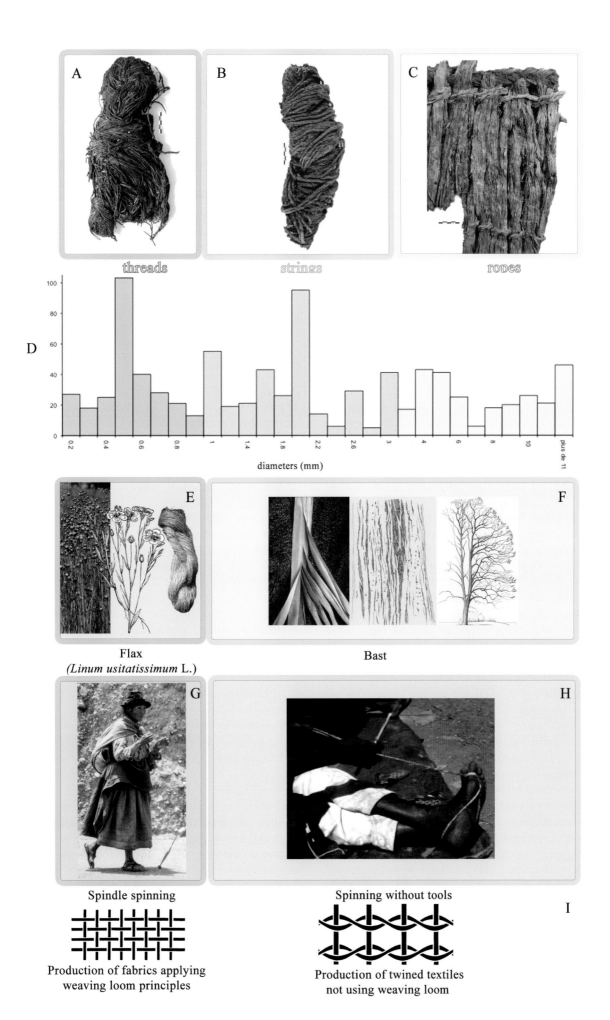

threads

strings

ropes

D

diameters (mm)

Flax
(*Linum usitatissimum* L.)

Bast

Spindle spinning

Production of fabrics applying
weaving loom principles

Spinning without tools

Production of twined textiles
not using weaving loom

I

the end of the period, refuting the common conception that this secular, ordinary object cannot reveal a morphological evolution. The analysis reveals the diversification and evolution of the types of spindle whorls in the Late Neolithic (Fig. 9.3). These changes in the technical properties of spindle whorls are characterised by the gradual increase of the masses and thickness visible in part of the samples, and these reflect a change in the production: spindle whorls were now turning more and longer.

Conversely, among the Late Neolithic whorls, a new category appears characterised by faster speeds and motions of shorter duration. These changes are not without impact on the quality of the thread made: experiment shows that increased moments of inertia and lower speeds mean an increase in the diameter of the thread, while the opposite will generate finer thread. The emergence of a new category of spindle whorls in the Neolithic thus indicates changes related to the diversification of production targets, which also reflects the evolution of the weights (Fig. 9.3).[21]

From the Middle to Late Neolithic, loom weights also changed in their morphology, becoming more homogeneous and exhibiting a better finish, as well as now being almost systematically fired. They became thinner, and thus their number on the loom increased. Their individual mass was almost halved, the largest decline occurring between the Late and Final Neolithic.[22]

The end of the Neolithic period is marked by significant changes in textile tools, as seen in the simultaneous weight reduction in some of the spindle whorls and in all of the loom weights. This convergence of elements can only be explained as being a result of changes related to the production of the thread, and that of the finished products. Assuming continuing production habits of the Middle Neolithic to the Late Neolithic, the changes observed in the loom weights would have allowed an increase in the number of weights at the bottom of the loom, an increase in the number of warp threads per linear centimetre of cloth and a finer distribution of tension exerted on each thread. These fine adjustments are perfectly consistent with the thinner threads being used by this time. The conditions were therefore met for weaving finer and denser structures. However, the changes that occurred in the Late Neolithic may also indicate a more profound change in production practices influenced by new needs.[23]

Here, attention should be turned to the rising importance of a new category of thread created by the widespread exploitation of a new fibre: wool (Fig. 9.3). The choice of raw material was decisive in many ways: it affected manufacturing techniques, the choice of tools and, ultimately, the quality of the products.[24] The decrease in mass of the loom weights and spindle whorls may well reflect the new use of wool. Due to its shorter fibres, wool yarn has a far lower tensile strength compared to plant fibres (flax), which,

because they have longer fibres, need more weight while being spun.[25]

Socio-economic changes

The second line of research consists of determining the place of activities connected with textile production within the community, and to assess their economic importance. In this context, determining changes in the *longue durée* is of paramount importance, and it defines the essence of the observed changes.

If the analysis of textile tools allows for a reasoned reflection (see above), the socio-economic approach is based primarily on a multidisciplinary approach. The understanding of the production contexts involves a use of diverse sources of information. As such, the analysis of textile remains as well as characterisation of the material are essential. Documenting the acquisition, treatment and processing of the raw material, the identification and origin of the fibres allows a broader reflection on the management of the environment: from the exploitation of the natural resources to agricultural and pastoral activities. The archaeobotanical and archaeozoological data[26] in conjunction with recent research in palaeogenetics[27] allow discussions on the origin of the textile materials, understanding their selection, identifying their destination, estimating their value and volume, as well as linking these developments to those of the textile production.

Similarly, spatial analysis of tools found on archaeological sites refines the understanding of textile activities and their organisation within the village communities. The spindle whorls and loom weights mainly provide information about places where spinning and weaving took place. Either grouped or sparse, they show either localised activity, or activity performed without constraints on its location. Spatial distribution of the tools in domestic areas, waste pits and storage areas is likely to indicate the degree of specialisation of the textile activities, their level of importance in the village, but also and more broadly the evolution of trends over time.[28] Intensification, stagnation and regression of activities connected with textile production and utilisation are likely to be documented in this same way.

Uneven technical skills

Neolithic textile production includes all products made of fibre that incorporate techniques of roping, basketry, spinning, weaving and netting.[29] From the point of view of a socio-economic approach to the past, the most significant process was weaving, and that contained two product categories: fabrics produced by twining and weaving.[30] Although they coexisted throughout the Neolithic, they belong to two completely separate spheres (Fig. 9.4 C–D). The first and fundamental difference between them lies

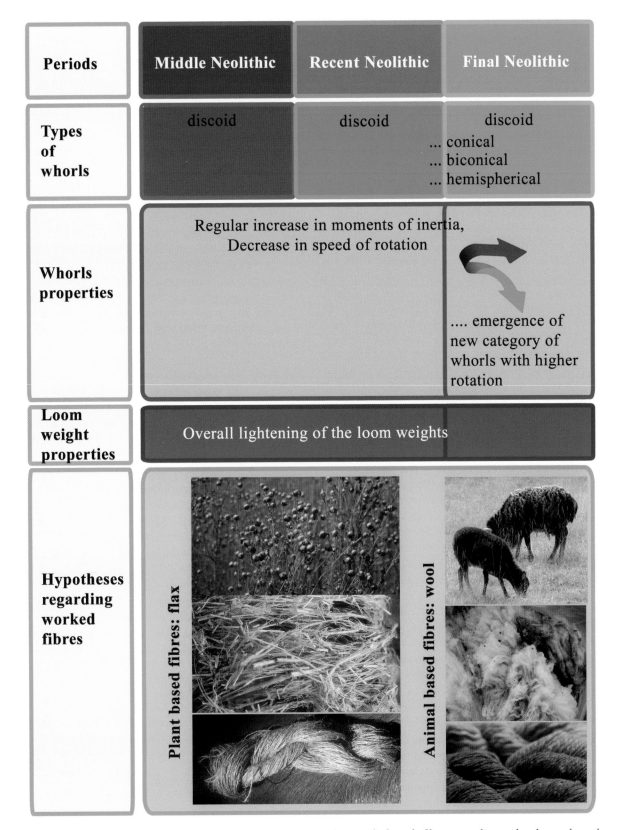

Fig. 9.3 Evolution of textile tools during the Neolithic. Hypothesis regarding worked textile fibres according to the observed trends.

in the manufacturing techniques: the corded weave has a minimalist technical implementation, while using the weaving loom requires a high level of preparation (Fig. 9.4 E–F). The loom operates in a semi-automatic fashion with the fitting of one (or more) heddle bar for separating the layers of warp threads in one quick motion. This ingenious device significantly reduces production times, but requires a long and sophisticated preparation process.[31] Requiring high levels of abstraction, the handling of such a device calls for complex mathematical reasoning and the ability to anticipate the final outcome, relating to both the thread warping as well as the interlacing. As we shall see, this mental projection and expertise were not available to all.

Dedicated textile fibres

One other noteworthy aspect lies in the field of the textile fibres. Analyses show that most of the fabrics were woven from flax threads, unlike twined textiles, which were made from strings of bast (Fig. 9.4 A–B).[32] However, obtaining flax fibres requires considerable work and consumes more time and effort than the process employed to obtain bast. Flax production involves agricultural activities conditional on the adoption of the sedentary lifestyle of the Neolithic populations.[33] The acquisition of bast is not related to agriculture; it comes from the natural environment and probably was a technique that had been inherited from populations of the Palaeolithic period. On this level, the two materials are in opposition, an opposition accentuated by clearly different uses in the Neolithic.[34] The use of flax for the manufacture of woven fabrics is therefore a deliberate intention, and not due to the lack of alternative materials.

Moreover, finds of archaeological textiles add to the evidence of the importance of bast fibres: whatever the nature of the settlement, the remains of material produced by twining are significantly higher in number than those of plain-woven fabrics. Judging by the number of times this is found to be the case, woven products made by twining occupied a prominent place in Neolithic textile production. It is assumed that there will be a lower proportion of linen pieces compared to those made from bast. This difference raises questions about the place or position of the two types of products, a subject that should be explored.[35]

In this environment, flax stands out as a product both less accessible and also available in limited quantities. Probably appreciated for its ability to be spun, its silky feel and flexibility, it appears mainly as an uncommon material reserved for a very few, if not exceptional products. These observations are followed up by the technical analysis of plain-woven fabrics. Borders and ornaments show that the Neolithic weavers were uninterested in the speed and ease of execution, repetition or standardisation. The remains found exemplify this: the samples are very often works in progress as strands, knots, yarn and braids were added, making each of the pieces unique. These unique additions undoubtedly

slowed the production.[36] It is clear that the possibilities and the technical abilities of the loom were only partially exploited. Its use is placed halfway between the technique of weaving and that of the high-warp tapestry. This should be interpreted as a sign of immaturity: the under-utilisation of the loom is not due to lack of knowledge of the technique, but due to social, economic and spiritual constraints as well as specific needs.[37]

Dedicated spaces

It can be suggested that the spatial distribution of spindle whorls in the settlements reflects at least partially the areas used for spinning activities. However, the systematic dispersion of spindle whorls in residential areas indicates that in the Neolithic such activity had no spatial constraints. As evidenced by the ethnological sources, spinning does not oblige the craftsman to practice his or her craft in a dedicated workspace.[38] These observations allow us to describe spinning as a domestically common and pervasive activity in the Neolithic. No changes are perceptible at this level, regardless of the cultural group.

The spatial distribution of the loom weights on archaeological sites is the most reliable evidence by which we can detect spaces dedicated to textile activities. The finds can signify areas where loom weights were discarded, stored and, in the best case, the location where the looms were actually operating.[39] When the ground is undisturbed and the site plans sufficiently precise, the loom weights appear in the proximity of the outer walls of buildings as well as the interior partitions of buildings. Until the Late Neolithic, in the villages where the organisation of buildings can be reconstructed, loom-weight concentrations are associated with only very few housing units. The consistent sparseness of their presence suggests that weaving was not a commonplace activity practised by everyone, nor was it conducted in all the houses. In some instances, the building that contains a loom is slightly away from the village, unique both in terms of its location and the activity it houses (*e.g.* Chalain 19 site, 32nd–31st century).[40] It was not until the Final Neolithic period that loom-weight groupings become

Fig. 9.4 (opposite) A. Spool of thread. Kleiner-Hafner site, Zürich (Switzerland), Middle Neolithic (Les Lacustres, 2004); B. Clump of bast. Port Stüdeli site, Bern (Switzerland), Middle Neolithic (photo: F. Médard); C. Linen cloths made on a loom. Sites: Meilen, Meilen-Vorderfeld, Zürich (Switzerland), Middle Neolithic; Port Stüdeli, Bern (Switzerland), Middle Neolithic (photos: F. Médard); D. Corded weave. Auvernier Port site, Neuchâtel (Switzerland), Middle Neolithic (photo: F. Médard). Net. Meilen-Vorderfeld site, Zürich (Switzerland), Middle Neolithic (photo: F. Médard); E. Stone spindle whorls. Delley-Portalban II site, Fribourg (Switzerland), Neolithic (photo: Service Archéologique Cantonal, Fribourg). Reconstructed loom and loom weights, Neolithic (reconstruction and photos: F. Médard); F. Amerindian woman of the Gran Chaco (Paraguay), twining technique (photo: V. Regher).

more prevalent on sites, indicating the increase in the number of spaces dedicated to weaving. This phenomenon occurs in a context where the population increases, together with the number and size of villages. Evidently, the weaving activity was undergoing major developments that involved at the same time a loss of the confidentiality of the techniques of the craft. According to the words of Andrew Sherratt, this 'democratisation' of weaving accompanied the 'Secondary Products Revolution', together with the introduction of the wheel and of the plough, the consumption of dairy products and the domestication of long-haired sheep.[41] This 'Revolution', perceptible in many domains, brought qualitative and quantitative changes in textile production. Implicitly, it is possible that at this time the perception of weaving activities slid towards the sphere of banal everyday activities.

Weaving as an instrument of power: from elitism to democratisation

The third line of research is to interpret the results from a chronological-cultural perspective. At the heart of the development are the changing importance of textile activities within societies, social organisations and demographic factors.

Before the Late Neolithic

Of the views exposed thus far, we will maintain the idea that, before the Final Neolithic period, spindle whorls were used in relatively standardised production involving threads which themselves were poorly diversified and essentially dedicated to the production of cloth. The art of weaving is, in fact, the work of a few specialised craftsmen, a craft potentially belonging to a privileged group, protective of their know-how. Fabric production is thus limited in quantity, giving the finished pieces the value of rarity, to which must be added the value of the raw materials carefully selected for this purpose. Reserved for the production of woven fabrics, flax fibre is also supposed to have been a rare material (or made rare), and intended for small pieces. It seems that wool (the remains of which have disappeared due to adverse preservation conditions) was not considered an alternative at this time. Research in this area indeed indicates that the fleece of Neolithic ovicaprids did not have the required qualities, nor did it provide appropriate quantities of wool, to meet the requirements of a textile production operation.[42]

Another reflection of the rarity of the selected textile material, flax, is the narrowness of the fabrics. Most measure probably far less than 50 cm wide. These estimates, based on spatial analysis of loom weights and preserved textile remnants, support the hypothesis that Neolithic craftspeople would not have known the manufacturing of fabrics in large

widths, a phenomenon known only from the Bronze Age onwards.[43] Both the quality of the finishing of the work as well as the dimensions indicate that the textiles were designed as fully-fledged pieces, not with future assemblies in mind. The selvedges are remarkably regular.[44] They border the four sides of the textile piece and demonstrate a quest for aesthetic value more than the need to strengthen and provide parallel edges to the fabric structure (Fig. 9.5 A). During this period, the fabrics made on looms were not intended for clothing. They were not meant to be cut or sewn, and are too narrow to drape a body, as was the case in later periods (*e.g.* costumes from the Bronze Age and Antiquity).[45] They could have been designed as ornamental clothing accessories, scarves, belts or bands, used for bartering or as ostentatious signs of wealth reserved for the elite.[46]

It seems that garments were still essentially attained by assembling animal skins and by using fur. As organic materials of animal origin are not preserved in lake settlements, no pieces of clothing of this period had been found before the discovery of the 'Ice Man'. Fully dressed in skins, this discovery gave scholars enough elements for examination and gave them cause to rethink previous notions of the nature of Neolithic costume (Fig. 9.5 B).[47]

Thus, textiles appear to have been rare and precious goods. The appearance of some of them at the time of their unearthing confirms this: folded or tied up in a bundle preventing the folds from coming undone, they seem to have been thought as objects needing special attention before being 'stored'. The care given to the packaging reinforces the idea that they were not objects of common use (Fig. 9.5 A).[48]

Late Neolithic

Starting in the Late Neolithic, spindle whorls and loom weights become more substantial, more numerous and more diverse. They suggest there was an increase in spinning and weaving activities linked to the new demands in yarn and

Fig. 9.5 (opposite) A: Long band of linen cloth. Niederwil-Egelsee site, Thurgau (Switzerland), Middle Neolithic (Hundt 1991, fig. 224). Menhir-statue of Mas-Capelier 1, Aveyron (France), Neolithic (Philippon 2002, 27). Roll of cloth. Twann-Bahnhof site, Bern (Switzerland), middle Neolithic (photo: Archäologischer Dienst, Bern). Roll of cloth. Muntelier-Platzbunden site, Fribourg (Switzerland), late Neolithic (Ramseyer and Michel, 1990, pl. X.1); B: Skins being treated (contemporary Morocco). Illustration of a deer. Reconstruction of Iceman costume (Ötztal, Italy), Late Neolithic. Contemporary Orogen woman's fur clothing (Inner Mongolia) (http://www.harbinice.com/photo-p3328-v284-elun-chun-beautiful-girl.html); C: Image of crowd, pencil (artist: Michel Houssin). Sheep and wool from ancient breed, Soay type (photo: F. Médard). Reconstruction of a vertical loom with loom weights and heddle rod, of the late Neolithic–beginning of Bronze Age (reconstruction M.-P. Puybaret, France; photo: F. Médard).

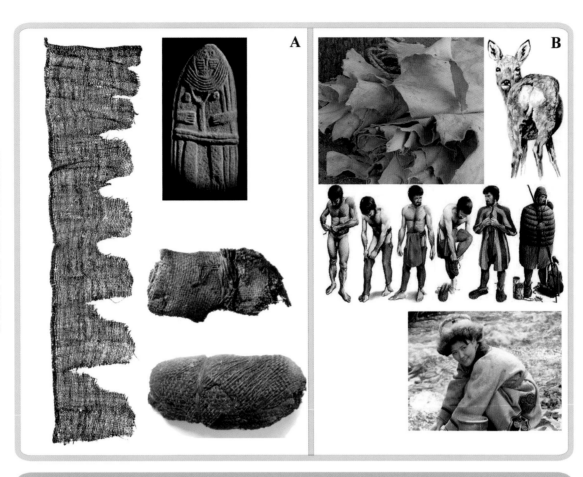

Increase in
population

cloth, as well as an increase in this demand. Meanwhile, archaeozoological data indicates the increasing importance of domesticated animals, the increase in size of ovicaprids and changes in the age structure of herds due to their use for secondary products.[49] The increase in livestock and repeated selected breeding to improve certain elements including the quality of fleeces, favoured the introduction of wool in textile production of that period. Andrew Sherratt believed that this change was initiated during the middle of the 3rd millennium. Complementary to plant-based fibre in the first instance, wool would have supplanted the other fibres from the 2nd millennium onwards.[50] The fact that materials of animal origin were not preserved in lake settlements would explain why textile remains, so abundant there from the Neolithic deposits, become almost non-existent from those of the Bronze Age.

Genetic improvements in ovicaprids, the modified livestock management that resulted and the evolution of the textile tools suggest that the emergence of wool and the democratisation of its weaving would lead to its expansion in a period of significant population growth. Under such conditions, the products of hunting and the skins of domesticated animals were no longer sufficient to ensure the necessary amount of material to dress a population that had become too large. Wool became an important alternative to animal hides. It required the killing of far fewer animals and thus was less expensive in natural resources; it was available from a renewable source and therefore offered clear economic benefits (Fig. 9.5 C).

Weaving belongs (like oxen hitching, the cart, the travois or metallurgy) in the long list of the major innovations of the Neolithic. Like most decisive innovations, it experienced a phase of valorisation of the specific know-how implemented, the singularity of products made and the power of those who possessed them. At this time in its history, it proved to be an instrument that fostered the emergence of social inequalities. 'The first powerful beings probably became so with the growing awareness of the power of practical knowledge ...'[51] It would not be surprising that the new features that emerged in the Final Neolithic were accompanied by a transfer of elements of power relegating weaving to the rank of common craft while slowly being replaced by metallurgy, which gained importance in the same period. This form of power based on the exclusivity of practical knowledge was now in the hands of metal smiths whose work was based on the mastery of fire, and in part served the art of war.

Notes

1   France, Dordogne; June–November 2015.
2   *Signes de richesse* 2015.
3   Médard 2000; 2006a; 2010a.
4   Leroi-Gourhan 1968.
5   Leroi-Gourhan 1949.

6   Mauss 1935; see Granal 1951.
7   Martial *et al.* 2011; 2013; Martial and Médard 2007.
8   Rast-Eicher and Thijsse 2001; Médard 2006a; 2010a; 2010b.
9   Vogt 1937; Médard 2010a; 2012; Rast-Eicher and Dietrich 2015.
10 Braudel 1958, 729. Archaeology often needs 'vast chronological spaces' to produce meaning.
11 Médard 2006a, 127–128.
12 Médard 2006a, 157.
13 Médard 2010a, 56.
14 Médard 2006a, 105–106.
15 Médard 2000, 94–95; 2010, 149; Grömer 2010, 118.
16 Médard 2006a, 105–106.
17 Médard 2006a, 118.
18 Seiler-Baldinger and Médard 2014; Altorfer and Médard 2000; Médard 2006a, 86–97.
19 Médard 2010a.
20 Médard 2006a, 114–118.
21 Médard 2006a, 114–118, 157.
22 Médard 2000, 44–56; 2010a, 46–47; Rast-Eicher 1997, 323–324.
23 Médard 2010a, 56.
24 Seiler-Baldinger and Médard 2014.
25 Rast-Eicher 1997, 325–326.
26 Schibler *et al.* 1997; Sherratt 1997.
27 Frei *et al.* 2009; Andersson Strand *et al.* 2010; Brandt *et al.* 2011.
28 Médard 2006a, 121–130; 2010a, 50–55; Bostyn *et al.* 2014, 701–709.
29 Médard 2008, 23.
30 Médard 2012, 370.
31 Seiler-Baldinger and Médard 2014, 25.
32 Médard 2010a, 145–146.
33 Martial and Médard 2007.
34 Médard 2008.
35 Pétrequin 2010, 16.
36 Médard 2010a; 2012.
37 Martial and Médard forthcoming.
38 Médard 2006a; 2006b.
39 Hoffmann 1964, 313; Grömer 2010, 115.
40 Médard 2010a, 150; Petrequin and Petrequin 2005.
41 Sherratt 1981; Petrequin and Petrequin 2005.
42 Rougeot 1982; 1988; Ryder 1983; 1992.
43 Winiger 1995, 143, 184.
44 Médard 2012, 370.
45 See for example Broholm and Hald 1940; Roche-Bernard and Ferdière 1993; Croom 2002; Grömer 2016, *etc.*
46 Médard 2010a, 149.
47 Höpfel *et al.* 1992; Spindler *et al.* 1995.
48 Médard 2006a, 147; 2010a, 139.
49 Schibler *et al.* 1997, 329–361; Sherrat 1997, 183.
50 Sherrat 1997, 203–205.
51 Pétrequin and Pétrequin 2005; Barbe and Callens 2008.

Bibliography

Altorfer, K. and Médard, F. 2000 Nouvelles découvertes textiles sur le site de Wetzikon-Robenhausen (Zürich, Suisse). Sondages 1999. In D. Cardon and M. Feugère (eds.), *Archéologie des textiles. Des origines au Vème siècle, Actes du colloque de Lattes (octobre 1999), Coll. Instrumentum*. Montagnac, 35–75.

Andersson Strand, E., Frei, K., Gleba, M., Mannering, U., Nosch, M.-L. and Skals, I. 2010 Old textiles – new possibilities. *European Journal of Archaeology* 13.2, 1–25.

Barbe, P. and Callens, S. 2008 L'origine des inégalités. Religion et innovation à l'Âge du cuivre. *Innovations* 27.1, 11–25.

Benguerel, S., Brem, H., Geisser, H., Hasenfratz, A., Leuzinger, U., Müller, Ch. and Rast-Eicher, A. 2010 *Gesponnen, Geflochten, Gewoben. Archäologische Textilien zwischen Bodensee und Zürichsee, Ausstellung des Museum für Archäologie, Frauenfeld, Thurgau (4 Juli–17 Oktober 2010)*. Frauenfeld.

Bleuer, E. and Hardmeyer, B. 1993 *Zürich 'Mozartstrasse'. Neolithische und bronzezeitliche Ufersiedlungen 3. Die Neolithische Keramik*. Berichte der Zürcher Denkmalpflege Monographien 18. Zürich.

Bostyn, F., Beugnier, V., Martial, E., Médard, F., Monchablon, C. and Praud, I. 2014 Habitat et économie au Néolithique final. L'exemple du site de Raillencourt-Sainte-Olle (Nord) entre activités domestiques et productions artisanales. *Bulletin de la Société Préhistorique Française* 111.4. Paris, 679–726.

Brandt, L., Tranekjer, L. Ø., Mannering, U., Ringgaard, M. G., Frei, K. M., Gleba, M. and Gilbert, M. T. P. 2011 Characterising the potential of sheep wool for ancient DNA analyses. *Archaeological and Anthropological Sciences* 3, 209–221.

Braudel, F. 1958 Histoire et sciences sociales: la longue durée. *Annales. Economies, Sociétés, Civilisations* 4, 725–753.

Broholm, H.-C. and Hald, M. 1940 *Costumes of the Bronze Age in Denmark*. Copenhagen.

Croom, A. T. 2002 *Roman Clothing and Fashion*. Gloucestershire.

Frei, K. M., Frei, R., Mannering, U., Gleba, M., Nosch, M.-L. and Lyngstrøm, H. 2009 Provenance of textiles – a pilot study evaluating the Sr isotope system in wool. *Archaeometry* 51.2, 252–276.

Granal, G. 1951 La technologie comparée en ethnologie. *Revue de géographie de Lyon*, 26.4.

Grömer, K. 2010 *Prähistorische Textilkunst in Mitteleuropa. Geschichte des Handwerkes und der Kleidung vor den Römern*. Veröffentlichungen der Prähistorischen Abteilung 4. Wien.

Grömer, K. 2016 *The Art of Prehistoric Textile Making. The Development of Craft Traditions and Clothing in Central Europe*. Veröffentlichungen der Prähistorischen Abteilung 5. Vienna.

Hoffmann, M. 1964 *The Warp-Weighted Loom. Studies in the History and Technology of an Ancient Implement*. Studia Norvegica 14. Oslo.

Höpfel, F., Platzer, W. and Spindler, K. (eds.) 1992 *Der Mann im Eis, 1. Bericht über das Internationale Symposium 1992 in Innsbruck*. Innsbruck.

Hundt, H.-J. 1991. Die Textilien. In H.-T. Waterbolk and W. van Zeist, *Niederwil, eine Siedlung des Pfyner Kultur* Band I–IV. Academia Helvetica 1. Bern 1991.

Leroi-Gourhan, A. 1949 Notes sur les rapports de la technologie et de la sociologie. *L'année sociologique* 2 (3e série), 766–772.

Leroi-Gourhan, A. 1968 L'expérience ethnologique. In *Ethnologie générale. Encyclopédie de la Pléiade*. Paris, 1816–1825.

Les Lacustres, 150 objetsracontent 150 histoires 2004 *Exhibition catalogue 27 février–13 juin 2004, Musée National Suisse*. Zürich.

Martial, E. Cayol, N., Hamon, C., Maigrot, Y., Médard, F. and Monchablon, C. 2011 Production etfonction des outillages au Néolithique final dans la vallée de la Deûle (Nord-Pas-de-Calais, France). In F. Bostyn, E. Martial and I. Praud (eds.), *Le Néolithique dans le nord de la France dans son context européen: habitat et économie aux 4ème et 3ème millénaires avant notre ère. Actes du 29ème colloque interrégional sur le Néolithique, Villeneuve d'Ascq, 2–3 octobre 2009*. Revue archéologique de Picardie 28. Amiens, 365–390.

Martial, E. and Médard, F. 2007 Acquisition ettraitement des matières textiles d'origine végétale en Préhistoire. L'exemple du lin. In V. Beugnier and P. Crombé (eds.), *Plant Processing from a Prehistoric and Ethnographic Perspective/Préhistoire et ethnographie du travail des plantes. Proceedings of a Workshop at Ghent University (Belgium) November 28, 2006*. British Archaeological Report, International Series 1718. Oxford, 67–82.

Martial, E. and Médard, F. forthcoming The operating sequence for textiles during the late Neolithic in northern France. A basis of reflection for the Bronze Age. In Y. Lorin and R. Peake (eds.), *Textiles. L'archéologie du textile à l'âge du Bronze et au premier âge du Fer*. Actes du colloque de l'APRAB.

Martial, E., Médard, F., Cayol, N., Hamon, C., Maigrot, Y. and Monchablon, C. 2013 Chaîne opératoire textile au Néolithique final dans le nord de la France: méthodologie et premiers résultats de l'approche pluridisciplinaire. In P. Anderson, C. Cheval and A. Durand (eds.), *Regards croisés sur les outilsliés au travail des végétaux. XXXIIIème Rencontres internationals d'archéologie et d'histoire d'Antibes, Antibes-Juan-les-Pins, 23–24–25 octobre 2012*. Antibes, 341–354.

Mauss, M. 1935 Les techniques du corps. *Journal de psychologie normale et pathologique* 32, 271–293.

Médard, F. 2000 *L'artisanat textile au Néolithique. L'exemple de Delley-Portalban II (Suisse) 3272–2462 avant J.-C*. Collection Préhistoires 4. Montagnac.

Médard, F. 2006a *Les activités de filage au Néolithique sur le Plateau suisse. Analyse technique, économique et sociale*. Collection CRA monographies 28. Paris.

Médard, F. 2006b La fusaïole: au delà des idéesreçues … In L. Astruc, F. Bon, V. Léa, P.-Y. Milcent and S. Philibert (eds.), *Normes techniques et pratiques sociales. De la simplicité des outillages pré- et protohistoriques, XXVIème rencontres internationals d'archéologie et d'histoire d'Antibes, Antibes–Juan-les-Pins, 20–22 octobre 2005*. Antibes, 275–280.

Médard, F. 2008 L'acquisition des matières textiles d'origine végétale en préhistoire. L'apport des données expérimentales et ethnologiques. *Archéologie des textiles et teintures végétales. Actes de la table ronde Archéobotanique 2006, Compiègne, 28–30 juin 2006. Les Nouvelles de l'Archéologie* 114, 23–28.

Médard, F. 2010a *L'art du tissage au Néolithique. IVème–IIIème millénaire avant J.-C. en Suisse*. Collection CRA monographies 30. Paris.

Médard, F. 2010b Les pesons – Die Webgewichte; Les textiles – Die Textilien. In U. Eberli, (ed.), *Die horgenzeitliche Siedlung Pfäffikon-Burg* 3. Monographien der Kantonsarchäologie Zürich 40.1–40.2. Zürich, 220–227.

Médard, F. 2012 Switzerland: Neolithic period. In M. Gleba and U. Mannering (eds.), *Textiles and Textile Production in Europe*.

From Prehistory to AD 400. Ancient Textiles Series 11. Oxford and Oakville, 366–377.

Pétrequin, P. 2010 Introduction. In F. Médard, *L'art du tissage au Néolithique. IVème–IIIème millénaire avant J.-C. en Suisse.* Collection CRA monographies 30. Paris, 11–20.

Pétrequin, P. and Pétrequin, A.-M. 2005 Premiers attelages de boeufs à Chalain (Jura, France) au XXXIe siècle avant J.-C. *Revue de Paléobiologie. Volume special* 10, 197–207.

Philippon, A. (ed.) 2002 *Statues-menhirs. Des énigmes de pierre venues du fond des ages.* Rodez.

Ramseyer, D. and Michel, R. 1990 *Muntelier/Platzbünden. Gisement Horgen, 1. Rapport de fouille et céramique.* Archéologie fribourgeoise 6. Editions Universitaires. Fribourg (Suisse).

Rast-Eicher, A. 1997 Die Textilien. In J. Schibler, H. Hüster-Plogmann, S. Jacomet, C. Brombacher, E. Gross-Klee and A. Rast-Eicher (eds.), *Ökonomie und Ökologie neolithischer und bronzezeitlicher Ufersiedlungen am Zürichsee. Ergebnisse der Ausgrabungen Mozartstrasse, Kanalisationssanierung Seefeld, AKAD/Pressehaus und Mythenschloss in Zürich.* Monographien der Kantonsarchäologie 20. Zürich, 300–328.

Rast-Eicher, A. and Dietrich, A. 2015 *Neolithische und Bronzezeitliche Gewebe und Geflechte. Die Funde aus den Seeufersiedlungen im Kanton Zürich.* Monographien der Kantonsarchäologie Zürich 46. Zürich.

Rast-Eicher, A. and Thijsse, A. 2001 Anbau und Verarbeitung von Lein: Experiment und archäologisches Material. *Zeitschrift für Schweizerische Archäologie und Kunstgeschichte* 8.1, 47–56.

Roche-Bernard, G. and Ferdière, A. 1993 *Costumes et textiles en Gaule romaine.* Paris.

Rougeot, J. 1982 Connaissance de la laine. La 'naissance de la laine' ou l'évolution des caractères de la toison du mouton. *La navette. Revue d'art etd'information sur le tissage, la tapisserie, le filage et la teinture végétale* 17, 8–13.

Rougeot, J. 1988 La laine. *L'INRA et le développement agricole* 35, 8–10.

Ryder, M. L. 1983 A re-assessment of Bronze Age wool. *Journal of Archaeological Science* 10.4, 327–331.

Ryder, M. L. 1992 The interaction between biological and technological change during the development of different fleece types in sheep. *Anthropozoologica* 16, 131–140.

Seiler-Baldinger, A. and Médard, F. 2014 Les textiles cordés: armures et techniques. *Bulletin de liaison du CIETA* 84–85, 21–37.

Sherratt, A. 1981 Plough and pastoralism: aspects of the secondary products revolution. In I. Hodder, G. Isaac and N. Hammond (eds.), *Pattern of the Past. Studies in Honour of David Clarke.* Cambridge, 261–305.

Sherratt, A. 1997 *Economy and Society in Prehistoric Europe. Changing Perspectives.* Edinburgh.

Signes de richesse 2015 *Inégalités au Néolithique, Catalogue d'exposition, Musée National de Préhistoire des Eyzies-de-Tayac (France, Dordogne), 27 juin–15 novembre 2015.* Paris.

Spindler, K., Rastbichler-Zisernig, E., Wilfing, H., Nedden, D. and Nothdurfter, H. 1995 *Der Mann im Eis. Neue Funde und Ergebnisse.* Wien and New York.

Vogt, E. 1937 *Geflechte und Gewebe der Steinzeit.* Monographien zur Ur-und Frühgeschichte der Schweiz. Antiqua 1. Basel.

Winiger, J. 1995 Die Bekleidung des Eismannes und die Anfänge der Weberei nördlich der Alpen. In K. Spindler, E. Rastbichler-Zissernig, H. Wilfing, D. zur Nedden and H. Nothdurfter (eds.), *Der Mann im Eis. Neue Funde und Ergebnisse* Band 2. Wien and New York, 119–187.

Textile manufacture in the prehistoric pile dwellings of south-west Germany: planned investigation

Johanna Banck-Burgess

Introduction – geographic and culture-historical classification

The settlement remains on Lake Constance and in Upper Swabia, attributed to the so-called pile-dwellers of the Circum-Alpine region, have been termed 'cultural heritage sites of the first order'.[1] Evidence of settlements, covering a period of more than 4000 years, can be traced back to the beginning of the Later Neolithic, in the second half of the 5th millennium BC, extending into the Iron Age. It is, however, the finds and features from the wetland settlements of the Late and Final Neolithic as well as the Early Bronze Age that provide a detailed image of settlement structures and activities, living conditions, the environmental context as well as the available craft techniques and diet. Amongst these discoveries are textile assemblages that represent an outstanding group of finds that will undergo comprehensive interdisciplinary analysis over the next 10 years. This paper offers an outline of initial ideas for the planned investigation.

UNESCO World Heritage

Research in the wetland settlements on the lakes to the north and south of the Alps and in Upper Swabia[2] has a tradition going back to the middle of the 19th century.

The preservation conditions are sensational. The specific environment within these sites has conserved objects made out of organic materials, such as textiles, deer antler, bone, wood or botanic macro remains, giving a completely new insight into the everyday life of the so-called pile-dwellers.[3] While researchers were, for a long time, assuming the existence of a typical pile dwelling – often depicted in rather romantic ways – it has now been established that various types of construction existed, which, depending on the location, ranged from ground-level to raised constructions.[4]

To a large extent, prehistoric lakeshore settlements owe their preservation to the sterile layers of lacustrine marl that accumulated above damp occupation layers, forming a protective layer after the settlements were no longer actively occupied. This 'detritus' was thus hermetically sealed and preserved up to the present day. In most cases, these settlements are conveniently located close to the shore and can be investigated during the winter months when the water levels are much lower, whereas those settlements located further into the water can only be examined by underwater archaeologists.

In Upper Swabia, after the silting up of lakes, peat and mud has ensured the preservation of settlement remains, on occasion including infrastructure like pathways and tracks.[5] Owing to the exceptional preservation conditions for organic materials, the exploration of pile dwellings is characterised by a high degree of interdisciplinary research that, apart from the archaeological sciences, involves palaeobotany, dendrochronology, entomology, anthropology and sedimentology.[6]

In 2011, the enormous significance of these ancient monuments, comprising some 900 known pile-dwelling sites in Switzerland, eastern France, northern Italy, Slovenia, Austria and south-west Germany, has led UNESCO to protect 18 sites. Current excavations are largely restricted to settlement areas at risk, and the major focus and efforts are aimed at protecting and preserving this cultural heritage.

History of research – current state of research
Cultural geography: sites

This contribution will focus on textiles from pile-dwelling settlements in Baden-Württemberg (south-west Germany), specifically Upper Swabia and the area around Lake

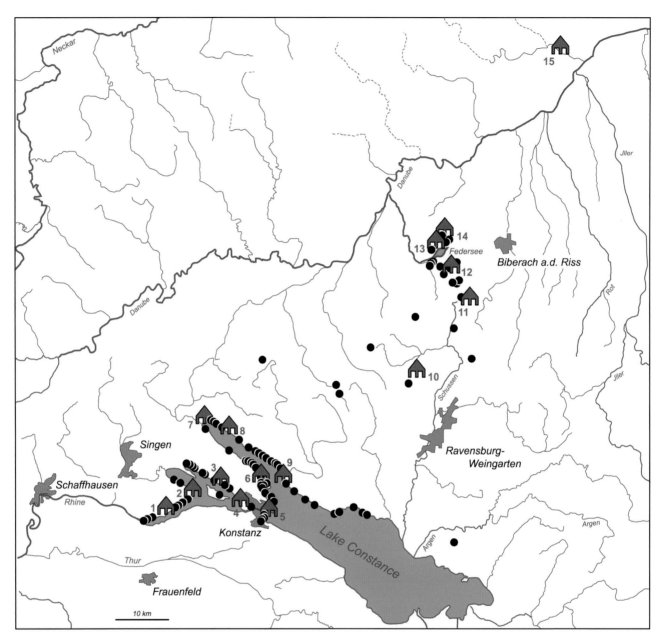

Fig. 10.1 UNESCO World Heritage. Nominated prehistoric pile dwellings in Baden-Württemberg (© Landesamt für Denkmalpflege Baden-Württemberg).

🏠 *UNESCO World Heritage nominated prehistoric pile dwellings in Baden-Württemberg: 1 Wangen-Hinterhorn, 2 Hornstaad-Hörnle, 3 Allensbach-Strandbad, 4 Wollmatingen-Langenrain, 5 Konstanz-Hinterhausen, 6 Litzelstetten-Krähenhorn, 7 Bodman-Schachen/Löchle, 8 Sipplingen-Osthafen, 9 Unteruhldingen-Stollenwiesen, 10 Wolpertswende-Schreckensee, 11 Olzreute-Enzisholz, 12 Bad Buchau-Siedlung Forschner, 13 Alleshausen-Grundwiesen, 14 Alleshausen/Seekirch-Ödenahlen, 15 Blaustein-Ehrenstein.*

• associated prehistoric pile dwellings in Baden-Württemberg

Constance, most of which have been excavated by the State Office for Cultural Heritage Baden-Württemberg (Fig. 10.1).

Located just north of the Alps, Lake Constance is one of the largest lakes in Europe, covering an area of 536 square kilometres (63 km long, 14 km wide). The lake borders Germany, Switzerland and Austria. Although there are numerous old as well as stray finds found in sondages, the textiles available for study consist above all of extensive assemblages from well-documented excavations carried out in the course of the past 30 years. The number of items of equipment related to textile manufacture is significantly smaller than that of textile finds. While this equipment has so far only rarely formed the focus of scholarly attention,[7] various researchers have dealt extensively with individual textile assemblages. In the latter context, mention must be made of Annemarie Feldtkeller who, in 1998 in cooperation with the botanist Udelgard Körber-Grohne, published more than 100 finds from the Late Neolithic settlement of Hornstaad am Untersee (district of Constance). Setting a benchmark to the present day, the publication provides a comprehensive description of the manufacturing techniques and materials of the finds.[8] In 2014, Aenne Schwoebel largely completed the recording of the extensive textile assemblage from settlement phase Hornstaad-Hörnle IA, comprising more than 1000 textile fragments.[9] This phase covered a short time span of only 15 years; on the basis of dendrochronological analysis, it can be dated to between 3917 and 3902 BC.[10]

The 160 textile fragments from the pile dwelling at Ludwigshafen-Seehalde in the district of Constance were also found in a Late Neolithic occupation layer, which is related to the so-called 'Ludwigshafen cult house'.[11] These finds were examined by Feldtkeller, but have not yet been published. A particularly exciting textile assemblage comes from Sipplingen-Osthafen, where the 16 to 17 occupation layers cover a period of some 1000 years (3919 to 2855 BC). Among the 250 textile finds there are noticeable clusters in layers relating to the early Pfyn culture (around 3850 BC), as well as during the middle and later Horgener culture in the centuries around 3000 BC.[12] Exceptional stray finds or historic discoveries from the area around Lake Constance are additionally known from Allensbach, Wangen-Hinterhorn[13] or Bodmann-Schachen.[14]

Apart from stray finds, notable textile assemblages from Upper Swabia have been found at the pile-dwelling settlements of Degersee[15] and Seekirch-Achwiesen.[16] The small textile assemblage from Degersee, comprising some 26 individual objects, is among the oldest finds from Neolithic wetland settlements in the pre-Alpine region (3999–3979 cal. BC).[17] While the Degersee textiles derive from Late Neolithic occupation layers, the finds from Achwiesen can be attributed to the latest Neolithic cultural group (Goldberg III, dated to *c.* 2800–2400 BC). Exceptional stray finds from elsewhere in Upper Swabia come from Aichbühl, Bad-Buchenau-Torwiesen and Olzreute-Ensisholz.

As opposed to the situation with regard to the studies of textiles from the pile dwellings of Switzerland and eastern France, which have been published mainly by Emil Vogt,[18] and in the last 20 years by Antoinette Rast-Eicher and Fabienne Médard,[19] there is as yet no comprehensive review of textiles from similar contexts in south-west Germany. Nevertheless, the finds analysed so far, as well as unpublished textile assemblages, have a great potential for further research into the manufacture of textiles in this region during this period, that is, made by the earliest known farmers and subsequent cultural groups for a period of more than 2000 years.

Finds assemblages: recording and research potential

Without making specific reference to individual assemblages or stray finds, it is still possible to highlight the spectrum of manufacturing techniques and functions that can be characterised as typical for the Circum-Alpine region from the Late Neolithic to the Early Bronze Age. This includes string and rope fragments (Figs. 10.3–10.4), sewn bark containers (Fig. 10.2), various mesh fabrics mainly attributed to fishing nets, coil-built basket remains and

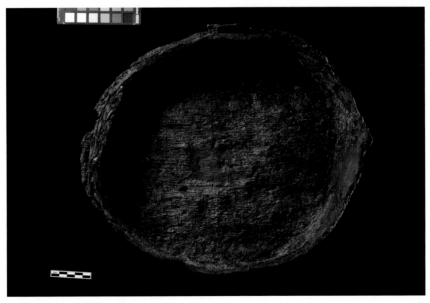

Fig. 10.2 Bark container. Exceptionally robust, watertight and light receptacles, sewn bark containers were of immeasurable value for the everyday life of the pile-dwellers. The vessels were made from inverted bark of coppiced shoots of lime (Hornstaad-Hörnle IA: Ho 1987–43–40–6) (© YAM/Landesamt für Denkmalpflege Baden-Württemberg).

Fig. 10.3 Textile elements such as strips of bast, simple twine or strings were, apart from birch tar, the most important materials for fixing or mounting tools (bone chisel; Olzreuter Ried/Federsee area: OL 10 2009–48 Q 213/239–1/2) (© YAM/Landesamt für Denkmalpflege Baden-Württemberg).

countless variations of twined textiles used for textiles of a range of functions (Figs. 10.5–10.6). Their uses range from sieves to containers, as well as items of clothing. Apart from this, fabrics as well as unique production and processing techniques are represented in the material, demonstrating the wide range of available production techniques and the applications of textiles.

Individual aspects regarding the current state of research will be considered below under future research aims. At this stage it will suffice to pick out three factors in particular

that demonstrate why the textiles from south-west German pile-dwelling settlements present an outstanding resource for archaeological textile research.

a. On the basis of extensive textile assemblages, it is possible to document the development of textile manufacture from the Late Neolithic to the Early Bronze Age; this covers a period of more than 2000 years. This period also includes the transition to metal-using cultures.

b. The existence of extensive textile assemblages – comprising considerably more than 1000 individual items – in individual occupation layers at sites like Hornstaad-Hörnle IA, means that this assemblage can be used to study textile manufacture and use within a settlement environment covering a precisely dated period of only a few years. The distribution of the textiles can indicate whether there are similar distribution patterns in all houses and whether there were special production centres, houses associated with specialised fishing activities or special places for the treatment of bast fibres. In this instance, textile archaeology can call upon a detailed set of excavation records, generated by a sequence of investigations covering a period of almost 15 years, the analysis of which is still ongoing, carried out in an interdisciplinary framework including archaeology, earth sciences (sedimentology) as well as biological sciences (palaeobotany, archaeozoology, dendrochronology).[20]

c. Other sites, like Sipplingen-Osthafen, have yielded stratified textile finds representing occupation layers dating to the Late and Latest Neolithic periods.[21] It is thus possible to follow the development of textile production at a particular site for a period of nearly 1000 years.

Future research aims

Overarching thematic foci

The proposals outlined below will form part of a research project that is currently being planned and which is going to be established at the State Office for Cultural Heritage in Esslingen from 2017/2018.

These themes will have as their focus the changes and continuities in textile production from the Late Neolithic to Early Bronze Age. Research will examine the question of whether the textile finds allow the identification of changes in production techniques characteristic for distinct cultural groups or certain periods. It will look at which aspects of textile production remain unchanged from the Late Neolithic to the Early Bronze Age. The focus of this research will be on new discoveries, that is, finds from the well-documented research excavations carried out in the past 30 years. Research will concentrate on assemblages from narrowly defined occupation layers such as Hornstaad-Hörnle IA, from Lake Constance or from Lake Degersee (Upper Swabia), as well as from sites with stratification that

Fig. 10.4 Rope had a significant role, particularly with regard to house construction. Important factors included fixation and strengths of knots, as well as deflection of forces (Hornstaad-Hörnle IA: Ho 1973–38–9000–900–4) (© YAM/Landesamt für Denkmalpflege Baden-Württemberg).

yields evidence of occupation over longer periods of time. The latter include Sipplingen and Ludwigshafen-Seehalde, both settlement areas on Lake Constance with occupation layers of the main archaeological groups from the Late Neolithic to the Early Bronze Age.

The second area of focus will examine textiles as an indication of cultural development. All the finds exhibit an impressive variety of production techniques and demonstrate the manifold uses of textiles and their inherent properties. They may also reveal how important and irreplaceable

textiles were in any sphere of everyday life. Apart from textiles for domestic uses and garments, this applies in particular to technical textiles. The study of the textiles can thus contribute towards the description of everyday culture, confirming or establishing a new perspective on the cultural achievements of these early cultures – in this instance, the first farmers in the pre-Alpine region.

The third area of research is related to the second, and addressed the thesis 'Textile functionality – a precondition for sedentism'. It is assumed that almost all known

Fig. 10.5 No conclusive explanation has so far been found for the function of bonnet-shaped non-woven fabrics, often interpreted as children's caps (Hornstaad-Hörnle IA: Ho 1973–38–9000–241) (© YAM/Landesamt für Denkmalpflege Baden-Württemberg).

techniques that can be traced in this region from the Late Neolithic to the Early Bronze Age, that is, over a period of more than 2000 years, had been in existence right from the beginning of the Late Neolithic. The Late Neolithic textiles from Hornstaad-Hörnle IA, Ludwigshafen-Seehalde and Sipplingen-Osthafen represent settlement communities that are among the earliest arable farmers at Lake Constance. They display a level of knowledge of textile production that is indicative of a long tradition and extensive experience.

In this context, it ought to be examined to what extent the former level of textile products contributed to the possibility for the transition from a hunter-gatherer existence to sedentism, because the level of textile production was already relatively advanced. The properties of textile products facilitated applications, particularly in the field

of technology, which were irreplaceable because of their materials and production techniques and which could not be replicated through the use of wood, bone, horn, clay, stone or fur. The properties of the latter materials limit their possible uses. In contrast, and presupposing adequate production techniques, textile fibres, tree-bast and bark offer an almost unlimited array of functionality.

Research focus

The cultural-historical significance of textiles made from tree-bast fibres

Textile producers had possessed a consolidated knowledge of the use of tree-bast fibres for textile production since the beginning of settlement. It is questionable whether

Fig. 10.6 Twining is the most frequently employed production technique for Late Neolithic textiles from pile-dwellings at Lake Constance. Their use for various objects and purposes is as varied as their appearance (Hornstaad-Hörnle IA: Ho 1985–53–46) (© YAM/Landesamt für Denkmalpflege Baden-Württemberg).

resulted in product replacement. This replacement would have coincided with a reduction in the knowledge of the use of tree-bast fibres, thus leading to a loss within the area of functional textiles that had a significant influence upon the everyday life of Late and Latest Neolithic culture groups. With this premise in mind, the analysis of the tree-basts will be carried out to address the following research questions. Which tree-bast fibres were utilised and which processing methods employed? What possible applications can be inferred in conjunction with the various production techniques? Is it possible to recognise differences, from the Late Neolithic to the Early Bronze Age, in the range of the tree-bast fibres used and the methods employed in their processing, which might indicate a reduction in the significance of tree-bast fibre over the course of the Latest Neolithic?

For the production of both textile fibres as well as bark containers, coppiced shoots could have been used. They occur when the primary growth axis of the tree, its main stem or trunk, is cut down. There is no evidence in the pollen diagrams for targeted cultivation/utilisation of coppiced lime trees as the trees do not blossom in this condition. It could even be supposed that a so-called lime decline was closely linked with the use of coppicing, at least periodically. Several deciduous trees have this regenerative capability – amongst others, lime. As far as determinations of textiles from pile-dwelling settlements are concerned, the material is predominantly bast from lime trees.

Spindle whorls and linen

The previously known distribution of finds of botanical macro remains of flax and of archaeological small finds such as spindle whorls may not necessarily reflect the situation in existence during the Late Neolithic and the Early Bronze Age.

A change in textile production during the Latest Neolithic phase has been linked to the surge in the number of spindle whorls and increased evidence for various intermediate and end products resulting from the processing of flax. In south-west Germany, this is also supported by evidence of the cultivation of the new fibre, flax with smaller seeds. The smaller seeds are interpreted as an indicator of the decreasing significance of flax as an oil plant and an emphasis on the production of fibres.[22] In the south-west German-Swiss region, the occurrence of spindle whorls is mainly associated with the Latest Neolithic Horgen culture. Spindle whorls of the Urnfield period, which is a later phase of the Bronze Age, have a different shape compared to Neolithic whorls. They are particularly characterised by concave bases or being extremely small.

In this context the circumstances of discovery, or rather the preservation conditions, of the listed botanical macro remains of flax seed and of textile products made of flax should be investigated with regard to their comparability. The

there was only little demand for the use of flax fibres in the production of fabrics. Flax fibres were merely employed in the production of fine filet nets used in fishing, which by the Late Neolithic used highly specialised catching techniques. The project's aim is to examine whether the increasing use of flax as a textile fibre eventually resulted in a slow loss of well-founded knowledge of the use of tree-bast fibres. The use of flax as a fibre for the production of woven textiles could have caused these textile techniques (or rather the range or variations of techniques within given textile production) to be discontinued. The period under consideration saw the arrival of the first farmers and ended with the beginning of metal-using cultures, and any changes detected in textile production could have happened in parallel to the cultural phases. These changes at the time of the establishment of weaving did not necessarily lead to an advanced development of textile production, but instead

Late Neolithic phase of Lake Constance has predominantly yielded textiles from domestic assemblages in the immediate vicinity of houses. There are no finds from outside these working areas, which derive from processing stages that were carried out on the fringes of, or beyond, the house/settlement area due in part to the risk of fire. These processing stages include, in particular, those that occur during the processing of flax fibres, like breaking or heckling of flax stems. Secondly, by using the finds of fabrics and nets from Late and Latest Neolithic culture groups as well as those from the Early Bronze Age, it is intended to study possible changes in the quality of flax fibres, which might be indicative of advances in their processing. A third area of research should look into the occurrence of spindle whorls. The fine threads of Late Neolithic finds of fabrics and nets provide conclusive evidence for the existence of a degree of virtuosity in spinning, which could not have been achieved without suitable spinning equipment. Despite the fact that whorls may have been made out of materials that did not survive, the assemblages from the lakeside settlements include objects that might have been used as spindle whorls. Objects from Hornstaad-Hörnle, examined by Marion Heumüller and included in the category of items of personal adornment, might serve as examples in this regard.[23] These objects include discoid beads, stone discs and rounded sherds. The apparent scarcity of spindle whorls from Late Neolithic contexts might possibly be explained by the circumstance that almost exclusively researchers have been looking only for spindle whorls that conform to accepted notions of what they should look like, namely spindle whorls made of clay. A critical appraisal should, therefore, be carried out of those finds and their contexts which would provide a more detailed understanding spinning activities and the use of flax fibres.

Different topics

The individual strands of enquiry pursued in this research project can barely be separated from one another. Thus, the use of flax fibres can only be studied in close conjunction with the examination of the fine fishing nets or woven textiles. One line of enquiry will focus upon the proposition that the use of flax fibres was introduced to southern Germany in the context of fishing, and its use in weaving was only a subsequent development. In this context it is also relevant to establish whether weaving was an innovation or the continuation of an established technique. The production techniques of twined textiles suggest that weaving developed via twine-weave warp fabrics.[24] This was an obvious evolution, indicative of continuity in the area of textile technology, which occurred locally and probably simultaneously at several sites within the Pre-Alpine region. There would have been access to flax fibres, which were already being used in the production of fine nets.

The examination of the functionality of containers made from ceramics, basketry and bark will also be a topic

of research. There has been much discussion about the phenomenon of the ceramics of the Horgen culture. This rough, coarse pottery is notably distinct from the pottery of later culture groups. Our current understanding, influenced by aesthetic premises, automatically associates this with a loss of craft skills. The contemporary textiles show the opposite. The textile finds from Horgen-period contexts like Sipplingen-Osthafen or Wangen display a relatively high level of skilled textile manufacture technique, well versed in the production of intricate fabrics.

The Horgen culture, for example, will be examined to see to what extent functional shortcomings in the array of available pottery may have been compensated through the use of receptacles made of organic materials, for instance basketry or bark containers. A lack of ceramic forms, particularly regarding size and weight, could be indicative of the use of receptacles made of organic materials. In the situation that there were only a small number of hanging vessels within the spectrum of ceramic forms, this might similarly be an indication for the use of baskets or other receptacles for this purpose. The research will include an analysis of sewn bark vessels. Only a limited range of materials would have been available for vessels. Fired pottery was frequently too heavy and, moreover, prone to breaking. Equally, baskets with closed walls were rather heavy, and the rough woven structure of the inner wall could blemish the surface of delicate fruits like berries. Precious fruit juice would drip away or would be absorbed. Thus, gathering berries or honey required a sturdy but lightweight receptacle with smooth internal walls. Bark vessels from wetland settlements have so far received little attention. Frequently, they have been loosely subsumed under the term birch vessels, in reference to birch vessels from Russia and other north-east European countries. This happened predominantly with regard to birch boxes, which in their present form rather meet the demand for folkloristic souvenirs. The versatility of such vessels is demonstrated in Russian Novgorod, where birch bark vessels continue to be produced for use today. Among their many uses, their function similar to that of thermos flasks, keeping hot drinks or food warm for more than 12 hours, would have been of great advantage. It was tempting to deduce a similar function for bark vessels from wetland settlements, but this was not feasible. From a glance at the differences within the climatic zones it quickly becomes obvious that neither the quantity nor quality of birch in the region of the present study would have been suitable for the production of birch-bark vessels for everyday use. Attempts by experimental archaeologists at producing vessels from the bark of indigenous birch beyond the Nordic climatic zone usually failed or were extremely difficult. Whether the bark of other trees could have been used for this purpose remains largely unknown. Some light is shed on this by the current use of the vessels known as the 'Omel' in the region of Belsen in Swabia. Following a long-established tradition, small buckets made from lime-tree bark for gathering cherries are produced there to this day.[25] Due to the local soil conditions, cherry trees have been cultivated there for generations. The production of sewn bark containers from coppiced shoots of lime follows a sequence of simple but exactly defined stages. No experimental archaeology trials have yet been carried out to determine the applications of receptacles made from lime-tree bark, whether they would, for instance, have been suitable as watertight, heat-storing containers. The project aims to demonstrate the significance of these bark vessels for Neolithic and Early Bronze Age cultural groups.

Beside the preserved organic remains, the investigations will also consider animal fibres, fur and leather. The soil conditions in these wetland settlements are not conducive to the preservation of textiles made from animal fibres or any remains of fur or leather. It should be considered therefore whether there is evidence, in the form of implements, or through archaeozoological analysis, for the processing of wool. Which applications can be assumed for fur and leather? Finally, there will be investigations concerning the textile production tools made of wood, bone or stone. This part of the research could focus upon a compilation of a catalogue of implements associated with textile production that will allow researchers to assess the relevance of their informative value on questions relating to textile production.

Conclusion/Summary

The textiles from the south-west German pile-dwelling settlements of the Late and Latest Neolithic as well as the Early Bronze Age offer an exceptional resource for the analysis of textile production of these periods. Within the scope of this research project, which is still at the planning stage, the following thematic topics and queries will be investigated.

On the one hand, the research will consider textile production in regard to its functionality as well as its significance within a given occupation layer, and at the same time consider the chronological sequence from the Late Neolithic to Early Bronze Age as a way to identify characteristics specific of a cultural phase. The available finds should be examined from the point of view of determining the degree to which the production and use of textiles, and technical textiles in particular, which had already been fully developed by the earliest farmers, contributed to the development of sedentism.

Apart from thematic topics considering basic research, other individual topics or research questions will cover the complexity and significance of textile production within the context of Neolithic and Early Bronze Age cultures. Is there, over the course of the Latest Neolithic, a shift in production that favoured the manufacture of fabrics, but coincided with a loss of knowledge about the use of tree-basts and, consequently, their possible applications? The focus of investigations in this context will be analyses of

the selection, processing techniques and properties of tree-basts, as well as preservation conditions of macro remains of flax and the quality of the flax fibre within the context of its use in nets and fabrics. The research will also investigate to what extent flax fibres were first used for the manufacture of gillnets for fishing before being introduced as a resource used in textile weaving. In this context it is also intended to examine the premise that weaving was a local invention that, in terms of production technique, evolved out of the warp fabrics of twined textiles.

It is likely that a close interrelationship existed between textile receptacles and pottery; where this was necessary, it seems that vessel forms, sizes and weight classes uncommon in the ceramic inventory were provided by using sewn bark containers and baskets. This premise will be investigated, as will be the significance of fur and leather. The analysis of implements related to textile production will be another research area that will contribute towards a more comprehensive picture about the prehistoric textile production of the earliest pile-dwelling farmers.

Notes

1   This paper was translated by Jörn Schuster, ARCHÆOLOGICALsmallFINDS, Templecombe.
2   Ruttkay 2004; Schlichtherle 1986; 1997; Schlichtherle and Suter 2009; Vaquer and Briois 2006. See also various contributions in *4000 Jahre Pfahlbauten. State Exhibition Baden-Württemberg Catalogue 2016.*
3   Numerous references and discussions of individual assemblages of material can be found in *4000 Jahre Pfahlbauten. State Exhibition Baden-Württemberg Catalogue 2016.*
4   Pétrequin 2016.
5   Schlichtherle *et al.* 2004.
6   For example, Hornstaad-Hörnle IA, see Dieckmann *et al.* 2006. For the pile-dwelling settlements at Lake Degersee, see Mainberger *et al.* 2015.
7   Feldtkeller 2003. On this topic, see also the publications by Médard 2000a; 2000b; 2006; 2010; Médard and Moser 2006; Rast-Eicher and Dietrich 2015.
8   Körber-Grohne and Feldtkeller 1998.
9   Schwoebel unpublished catalogue.
10   Billamboz 2006.
11   Köninger 2002.
12   The finds assemblage is being analysed at the time of writing.
13   Schlichtherle 1988.
14   Köninger 2006.
15   Banck-Burgess 2015.
16   Feldtkeller 2004.
17   Maier *et al.* 2010.
18   Vogt 1937; 1948.
19   See *e.g.* Rast-Eicher 1995; 1997; Médard 2000a; 2000b; 2006; 2010; Médard and Moser 2006. See also Vogt 1937; 1948; Altorfer *et al.* 2000–2001; Leuzinger and Rast-Eicher 2011; Rast-Eicher and Dietrich 2015. For material-specific analyses, see Schoch 2015.
20   For example, Maier 2001; Dieckmann *et al.* 2006; Matuschik 2011.
21   Billamboz *et al.* 2010.

22   Herbig and Maier 2011; Maier and Schlichtherle 2011; Karg 2015.
23   Heumüller 2009.
24   Médard and Moser 2006; Rast-Eicher and Dietrich 2015, 112.
25   Fischer 1988.

Bibliography

4000 Jahre Pfahlbauten. State Exhibition Baden-Württemberg Catalogue 2016. Archäologisches Landesmuseum Baden-Württemberg und Landesamt für Denkmalpflege im Regierungspräsidium Stuttgart (eds.) Ostfilder.

Altorfer, K., Huber, R. and Médard, F. 2000–2001 Taucher, Thesen und Textilien. Neue Untersuchungen zum jungneolithischen Textilhandwerk in den Feuchtbodensiedlungen von Wetzikon-Robenhausen (Kanton Zürich). *Plattform. Zeitschrift des Vereins für Pfahlbau und Heimatkunde e. V.* 9/10, 78–93.

Banck-Burgess, J. 2015 Textilien vom Degersee. In *Pfahlbausiedlungen am Degersee – Archäologische und naturwissenschaftliche Untersuchungen*, Materialhefte zur Archäologie in Baden-Württemberg 102. Berichte zu Ufer- und Moorsiedlungen Südwestdeutschlands VI. Stuttgart, 265–280.

Banck-Burgess, J. 2016a Unterschätzt. Die Textilien aus den Pfahlbauten. In *4000 Jahre Pfahlbauten. State Exhibition Baden-Württemberg Catalogue 2016*, 358–364.

Banck-Burgess, J. 2016b Mehr als nur Leder. Kleidung in den Pfahlbausiedlungen. In *4000 Jahre Pfahlbauten. State Exhibition Baden-Württemberg Catalogue 2016*, 152–155.

Banck-Burgess, J. 2016c Unverzichtbar im Alltag. Textilhandwerk bei den neolithischen Pfahlbauern. *Denkmalpflege in Baden-Württemberg. Nachrichtenblatt der Landesdenkmalpflege* 1.45, 24–27.

Bazzanella, M. and Rast-Eicher, A. 2003 Storia della ricerche. In M. Bazzanella, A. Mayr, L. Moser and A. Rast-Eicher (eds.), *Textiles: intrecci e tessuti dalla preistoria europea. Catalogo della mostra tenutasi a Riva del Garda - La Rocca, dal 24 maggio al 19 ottobre 2003.* Trento, 23–29.

Bazzanella, M., Mayr, A., Moser, L. and Rast-Eicher, A. (eds.) 2003 *Textiles: intrecci e tessuti dalla preistoria europea. Catalogo della mostra tenutasi a Riva del Garda - La Rocca, dal 24 maggio al 19 ottobre 2003.* Trento.

Billamboz, A. 2006 Dendroarchäologische Untersuchungen in den neolithischen Ufersiedlungen von Hornstaad-Hörnle. In B. Dieckmann, A. Harwath and J. Hoffstadt, *Hornstaad-Hörnle I. A. Die Befunde einer jungneolithischen Pfahlbausiedlung am westlichen Bodensee.* Siedlungsarchäologie im Alpenvorland IX. Forschungen und Berichte zur Vor- und Frühgeschichte in Baden-Württemberg 98. Stuttgart, 297–414.

Billamboz, A., Maier, U., Matuschik, I., Müller, A., Out, W., Steppan, Kh. and Vogt, R. 2010 Die jung- und endneolithische Seeufersiedlung von Sipplingen 'Osthafen' am Bodensee: Besiedlungs- und Wirtschaftsdynamik im eng begrenzten Naturraum des Sipplinger Dreiecks. In I. Matuschik, Chr. Strahm, B. Eberschweiler, G. Fingerlin, A. Hafner, M. Kinsky, M. Mainberger and G. Schöbel (eds.), *Vernetzungen, Aspekte siedlungsarchäologischer Forschungen. Festschrift für Helmut Schlichtherle zum 60'ten Geburtstag.* Freiburg im Breisgau, 253–286.

Dieckmann, B., Harwath, A. and Hoffstadt, J. 2006 *Hornstaad-Hörnle I. A. Die Befunde einer jungneolithischen Pfahlbausiedlung am westlichen Bodensee.* Siedlungsarchäologie im Alpenvorland IX. Forschungen und Berichte zur Vor- und Frühgeschichte in Baden-Württemberg 98. Stuttgart.

Feldtkeller, A. 2003 Nierenförmige Webgewichte – wie funktionieren sie? *Archaeological Textiles Newsletter* 37, 16–20.

Feldtkeller, A. 2004 Die Textilien von Seekirch-Achwiesen. In Schlichtherle, H., Köninger, J., Feldtkeller, A. and Maier, U. (eds.), *Ökonomischer und ökologischer Wandel am vorgeschichtlichen Federsee. Archäologische und naturwissenschaftliche Untersuchungen.* Hemmenhofener Skripte 5. Freiburg im Breisgau, 187–231.

Feldtkeller, A. and Schlichtherle, H. 1998 Flechten, Knüpfen und Weben in Pfahlbausiedlungen der Jungsteinzeit. *Archäologie in Deutschland* 1.1998, 22–27.

Fischer, T. 1988 Die Omel. Ein traditionsreiches Kirschenerntegefäß. In A. Borsdorf (ed.), *1888–1988 Einhundert Jahre Liederkranz 1888 Belsen e. V. Festbuch zum Jubiläumsjahr.* Belsen, 47–50.

Haffner, A., Pétrequin, P. and Schlichtherle, H. 2016 Ufer- und Moorsiedlungen. Chronologie, kulturelle Vielfalt und Siedlungsformen. In *4000 Jahre Pfahlbauten. State Exhibition Baden-Württemberg Catalogue 2016*, 59–64.

Herbig, C. and Maier, U. 2011 Flax for oil or fibre? Morphometric analysis of flax seeds and new aspects of flax cultivation in Late Neolithic wetland settlements in southwest Germany. *Vegetation History and Archaeobotany* 20.6, 527–533.

Heumüller, M. 2009 *Der Schmuck der jungneolithische Seeufersiedlung Hornstaad-Hörnle IA im Rahmen des mitteleuropäischen Mittel- und Jungneolithikums.* Siedlungsarchäologie im Alpenvorland X. Forschungen und Berichte zur Vor- und Frühgeschichte in Baden-Württemberg 112. Stuttgart.

Karg, S. 2015 Überlegungen zur Kultur- und Anbaugeschichte des Leins. In A. Rast-Eicher and A. Dietrich, *Neolithische und bronzezeitliche Gewebe und Geflechte. Die Funde aus den Seeufersiedlungen im Kanton Zürich.* Monographien der Kantonsarchäologie Zürich 46. Zürich and Egg, 27–33.

Köninger, J. 2002 Zum Fortgang der Tauchsondagen in den Ufersiedlungen von Ludwigshafen-Seehalde/Bodensee. *Nachrichtenblatt Arbeitskreis Unterwasserarchäologie* 9, 66–70.

Köninger, J. 2006 *Die frühbronzezeitliche Ufersiedlung von Bodman-Schachen I – Befunde und Funde aus den Tauchsondagen 1982–1984 und 1986.* Siedlungsarchäologie im Alpenvorland VIII. Forschungen und Berichte zur Vor- und Frühgeschichte in Baden-Württemberg 85. Stuttgart.

Körber-Grohne, U. and Feldtkeller, A. 1998 Pflanzliche Rohmaterialien und Herstellungstechniken der Gewebe, Netze, Geflechte sowie anderer Produkte aus den neolithischen Siedlungen Hornstaad, Wangen, Allensbach und Sipplingen am Bodensee. In D. Planck (ed.), *Siedlungsarchäologie im Alpenvorland V.* Forschungen und Berichte zur Vor- und Frühgeschichte in Baden-Württemberg 68. Stuttgart, 131–242.

Leuzinger, U. and Rast-Eicher, A. 2011 Flax processing in the Neolithic and Bronze Age pile-dwelling settlements of eastern Switzerland. *Vegetation History and Archaeobotany* 20.6, 535–542.

Maier, U. 2001 *Archäobotanische Untersuchungen in Hornstaad-Hörnle IA.* Siedlungsarchäologie im Alpenvorland 6. Stuttgart.

Maier, U., Mainberger, M., Merkt, J., Kleinmann, A., Vogt, R., Späth, S. and Baum, T. 2010 Das DFG-Projekt 'Degersee': Fortgang der Arbeiten und neue Entdeckungen. *Archäologische Ausgrabungen in Baden-Württemberg* 2009. Stuttgart, 69–74.

Maier, U. and Schlichtherle, H. 2011 Flax cultivation and textile production in Neolithic wetland settlement on Lake Constance and the Upper Swabia (south-west Germany). *Vegetation History and Archaeobotany* 20.6, 567–578.

Mainberger, M., Merkt, J. and Kleinmann, A. (eds.) 2015 *Pfahlbausiedlungen am Degersee – Archäologische und naturwissenschaftliche Untersuchungen*. Materialhefte zur Archäologie in Baden-Württemberg 102. Berichte zu Ufer- und Moorsiedlungen Südwestdeutschlands VI. Darmstadt.

Marguet, A. and Rey, P. J. 2007 Le Néolithique dans les lacs alpins français. Un catalogue réactualisé. In M. Besse (ed.), *Sociétés néolithiques. Des faits archéologiques aux fonctionnements socio-économiques*. Cahiers d'archéologie romande 108, 379–406.

Matuschik, I. 2011 *Die Keramikfunde von Hornstaad-Hörnle I–VI. Besiedlungsgeschichte der Fundstelle und Keramikentwicklung im beginnenden 4. Jahrtausend v. Chr. im Bodenseeraum.* Siedlungsarchäologie im Alpenvorland XII. Forschungen und Berichte zur Vor- und Frühgeschichte in Baden-Württemberg 122. Stuttgart.

Médard, F. 2000a Découverte d'un 'métier à tisser' – Néolithique en Suisse. *L'Archéologie nouvelle* 6, 47–50.

Médard, F. 2000b *L'artisanat textile au Néolithique. L'example de Delley-Portalban II (Suisse) 3272–2462 avant J.-C.* Préhistoires 4. Montagnac.

Médard, F. 2006 *Les activités du filage au Néolithique sur le Plateau Suisse. Analyse technique, économique et sociale.* Collection CRA monographies 28. Paris.

Médard, F. 2010 *L'art du tissage au Néolithique. IVe–IIIe millénaires avant J.-C. en Suisse.* Monographies du CRA 30. Paris.

Médard, F. and Moser, F. 2006 Observations sur la fabrication expérimentale d'étoffes cordées, Pardubice (CZ). *Journal of (Re)construction and Experiment in Archaeology* 3, 16–22.

Pétrequin, P. 2016 Warum Pfahlbauten? In *4000 Jahre Pfahlbauten. State Exhibition Baden-Württemberg Catalogue 2016*, 65–67.

Rast-Eicher, A. 1995 Baumbaste – Fasermaterial für Geflechte und Gewebe. *Tugium* 11, 57–59.

Rast-Eicher, A. 1997 Die Textilien. In J. Schiebler, H. Hüster-Plogmann, St Jacomet, Ch. Brombacher, E. Gross-Klee and A. Rast Eicher (eds.), *Ökonomie und Ökologie neolithischer und bronzezeitlicher Ufersiedlungen am Zürichsee. Ergebnisse der Ausgrabungen Mozartstrasse, Kanalisationssanierung Seefeld, AKAD/Pressehaus und Mythenschloss in Zürich.* Monographien der Kantonsarchäologie Zürich 20. Zürich and Egg, 300–328.

Rast-Eicher, A. and Dietrich, A. 2015 *Neolithische und bronzezeitliche Gewebe und Geflechte. Die Funde aus den Seeufersiedlungen im Kanton Zürich.* Monographien der Kantonsarchäologie Zürich 46. Zürich and Egg.

Ruttkay, E. 2004 Prehistoric lacustrine villages on the Austrian lakes: past and recent research developments. In F. Menotti (ed.), *Living on the Lake in Prehistoric Europe. 150 Years of Lake-Dwelling Research.* London and New York, 50–68.

Schlichtherle, H. 1988 Die Pfahlbauten von Wangen. Von der Ausgrabung Kaspar Löhles zur modernen Forschung. In H. Berner, *Öhningen 1988 – Beiträge zur Geschichte von Öhningen, Schienen und Wangen.* Singen, 21–46.

Schlichtherle, H. (ed.) 1997 *Pfahlbauten rund um die Alpen.* Sonderheft Archäologie in Deutschland. Stuttgart.

Schlichtherle, H. and Wahlster, B. 1986 *Archäologie in Seen und Mooren. Den Pfahlbauten auf der Spur.* Stuttgart.

Schlichtherle, H., Köninger, J., Feldtkeller, A. and Maier, U. (eds.) 2004 *Ökonomischer und ökologischer Wandel am vorgeschichtlichen Federsee. Archäologische und naturwissenschaftliche Untersuchungen.* Hemmenhofener Skripte 5. Freiburg im Breisgau.

Schlichtherle, H. and Suter, P. (eds.) 2009 *Pfahlbauten. Palafitte. Pile Dwellings. Kolisca.* UNESCO-Welterbe-Kandidatur Prähistorische Pfahlbauten rund um die Alpen. Bern.

Schlichtherle, H., Bleicher, N., Dufraisse, A., Kieselbach, P., Maier, U., Schmidt, E., Stephan, E. and Vogt, R. 2010 Bad Buchau-Torwiesen II: Baustrukturen und Siedlungsabfälle als Indizien der Sozialstruktur und Wirtschaftsweise einer endneolithischen Siedlung am Federsee. In E. Classen, T. Doppler and B. Ramminger (eds.), *Familie-Verwandtschaft-Sozialstrukturen: Sozialarchäologische Forschungen zu neolitischen Befunden.* Fokus Jungsteinzeit. Berichte AG Neolithikum 1. Kerpen-Loog, 157–178.

Schoch, H. 2015 Materialien zur Herstellung von Geweben und Geflechten. In A. Rast-Eicher and A. Dietrich, *Neolithische und bronzezeitliche Gewebe und Geflechte. Die Funde aus den Seeufersiedlungen im Kanton Zürich*, Monographien der Kantonsarchäologie Zürich 46. Zürich and Egg, 23–27.

Vaquer, J. and Briois, F. (eds.) 2006 *La fin de l'Âge de Pierre en Europe du Sud. Matériaux et productions lithiques taillées remarquables dans le Néolithique et le Chalcolithique du sud de l'Europe. Actes de la table ronde de l'EHESS. Carcassonne, 5–6 septembre 2003.* Édition des Archives d'Écologie Préhistorique. Toulouse, 25–42.

Vogt, E. 1937 *Geflechte und Gewebe der Steinzeit.* Monographien zur Ur- und Frühgeschichte der Schweiz 1. Basel.

Vogt, E. 1948 Vanneries et tissus à l'âge de la pierre et du bronze en Europe. *Tirage à part des Cahiers Ciba* 15, février, 506–540.

Late Neolithic weaving tools from Melk-Spielberg in Austria: experiments with crescent-shaped weights

Karina Grömer

Archaeological background

At Melk-Spielberg in Austria, a Late Neolithic fortified settlement was discovered.[1] A pit of the Baalberge Group (southern Funnel Beaker culture) contained three loom weights of a very distinct shape, differing from the well-known egg- or cylinder-shaped loom weights of the Late Neolithic in Central Europe. Those crescent-shaped weights were the basis for a series of experiments intended to examine their functionality.

Central Europe in the Late Neolithic period

The Neolithic in Central Europe covers the period from *c.* 5600 to 2300 BC.[2] A warm and humid climate had generally been predominant since the beginning of the Neolithic, but from *c.* 3800 BC, the Late Neolithic onwards, the climate began to change to a slightly cooler transitional period. This seems to be a significant turning point, not only according to climate, but also technologically and socio-economically.

In the millennia before the Late Neolithic period, cultures were purely agriculturally focused; social and economic changes then occurred. Different social groups are archaeologically identifiable in the cemeteries, *e.g.* specific tools and weapons suggest that warriors and craftsmen emerged as new social groups. This period saw the beginnings of copper metallurgy, for that time being mainly used for jewellery, later tools were also made of this metal, and gold was also employed. In this era, the new sought-after raw material meant an economic and cultural boom in regions with copper and gold deposits, especially the Carpathian region. The Alpine areas, too, were now settled. The four-wheeled cart made its first appearance in Central Europe, evidenced by finds of wooden wheels from Switzerland and Slovenia and zoological evidence for domestic horses.[3]

Human mobility increased through the use of wagons and horses; for millennia, it had only been possible to travel on foot or by water. The wheel and carts were also important for the development of agriculture, enlarging the areas that could be worked. The principle of the rotating axis was already familiar from the use of spindles in the Neolithic.

In contrast to the extensive and relatively homogeneous Early Neolithic Linear Pottery culture, the Late Neolithic in Europe saw a breakdown into many different and successive regional cultural groups that maintained contacts to neighbouring areas. For textile research, the cultures of the lakes around the Alps are of particular interest, since organic materials and, therefore, textiles have been preserved in the wetlands. These include the Pfyn (3900–3500 BC) and Horgen (3500–2800 BC) cultures that occurred in what is now Switzerland during the Late Neolithic; the Funnel Beaker culture (Baalberge group; 3800–3400 BC), and the Cham and Jevišovice cultures (3400–2800 BC) in what is today Austria.[4] There are more cultural groups in the area, but those are the main ones we are referring to here. Of particular interest also is the Iceman Ötzi,[5] a mummy found in 1991 near an old mountain pass in the Ötztal Alps with clothing and equipment, which has survived *c.* 5300 years in the ice of the glacier.

Textiles and tools in the 4th and 3rd millennia BC

As far as we know, the textile technology of the first Stone Age farmers in Central Europe was based on bast fibres, such as lime-bast, flax, *etc.* According to sparse finds, only in the Late Neolithic are we able to trace the first wool textiles. At the end of the 4th millennium BC, a larger sheep emerged in Central Europe, and in the 3rd millennium BC the slaughtering pattern altered and more animals survived to an older age, which can be interpreted as change from use of these animals for milk and meat to their exploitation as a source of wool. The 3rd millennium BC was the time when wool emerged as raw material for textiles in Europe in general.[6]

Basic spinning and weaving techniques had already been developed, but in Central Europe textile products made in basketry techniques, matting, cordage and twining techniques were more common than spun and loom-woven items. This can be recognised from the lakeside settlements during the 4th and 3rd millennium BC, which present excellent conditions for the preservation of organic finds. Late Neolithic lake dwellings from Switzerland, south Germany, northern Italy and Austria have yielded large woven fabrics, bands and twined fabrics.[7] At least from the beginning of the Bronze Age onwards, woven textiles begin to dominate the textile and 'cloth culture'.[8]

Textile tools recorded for the period (*c.* 3500–3000 BC) show great variation (Fig. 11.1). There is, for example, differentiation in size and weights of spindle whorls in the Central European Jevišovice culture (in eastern Austria, Czech Republic) and Chamer culture (in western Austria and southern Germany), where very large and heavy items predominated,[9] while in the Swiss lakeside dwellings smaller examples were found. We also know of spools, loom weights or bone artefacts from recently excavated sites Krems-Hundssteig, Melk-Spielberg, Melk-Wachtberg and Meidling-Kleiner Anzingerberg,[10] Austria.

The evidence of the oldest find of a warp-weighted loom *in situ* in Austria is important for our understanding of the development in textile crafts in this area. The find from Krems-Hundssteig consists of 35 egg-shaped loom weights found lying in a line of 1.2 m length in a house within the fortified settlement (¹⁴C date *c.* 3150 BC).[11]

Crescent-shaped loom weights

In this contribution, we focus on determining the possible functions of the crescent-shaped weights, exemplified by the three examples from the site Melk-Spielberg (Baalberge Group of the Funnel Beaker culture).[12] They are 16–18 cm long and 6 cm thick. The weight of the complete items was about 450 g. The distance between the holes of the weights was about 12 cm. The original finds seem to be unfired or lightly fired (Fig. 11.1).

Examples of crescent-shaped weights have also been found in the area around the Alps, in Hungary, northern Italy, Austria, Czech Republic and southern Germany, and in western Iberia, all in Late Neolithic contexts.[13] Unfortunately, they are usually found as single items within settlements, thrown away in settlement pits like broken pots and other settlement waste. At the site Lagozza di Besnate in northern Italy,[14] several crescent-shaped weights were found in settlement pits, always together with spindle whorls. This type of loom weight is common in the Lagozza

culture (*c.* 3800–3600 BC), and it is thought that this is the origin of the spread of crescent-shaped weights to Central Europe (together with early copper technology).[15] One of the most interesting contexts of these weights is known from Melchendorf in Germany:[16] two crescent-shaped weights, 20 cm long, were found in a pit, together with the body of a 40-year-old man. The finds are contemporary with the items from Melk-Spielberg and have a similar shape, length and weight. The loom weights served as grave goods, but it is not known if the two weights form a functional tool-set or if they were meant as a part of a bigger group of objects.

From Spain, in the settlement El Malagón (Prov. Granada), in a context dating to the end of the Late Neolithic/beginning of the Copper Age (*c.* 3000 BC),[17] a larger number of crescent-shaped weights were excavated within a house (hut F). More than 30 items were deposited densely packed together – maybe indicating the former use on a loom. The Spanish weights are slender and 26 cm long, and their form, shape and weight differ from those from Central Europe. The crescent-shaped loom weights from Late Neolithic and Chalcolithic contexts in southern Portugal are discussed in this volume by C. Costeira and R. Mataloto.

Further to the east, in Sardinia, Bulgaria, Albania, Greece and Turkey,[18] crescent-shaped loom weights are well known in the Early and Middle Bronze Age contexts, of the mid- and end of the 3rd millennium BC and early 2nd millennium. At the site Demircihüyük in Turkey,[19] a total of 74 crescent-shaped weights were excavated from various archaeological contexts. Most of the weights were found in the settlement layers dated to *c.* 2000 to 1800 BC, but they were also found in a grave of a child – maybe as a grave gift. The shape, size and weights differ a bit, but all are smaller than those known from Central Europe. The weights are between 100 and 250 g (averaging about 150 g), the distance between the holes is about 7 and 13 cm. Some of the crescent weights from Anatolia have decoration like seal impressions or other types of marks.[20]

Methodology

The exact function of these unfired or lightly fired artefacts is reconstructed in different ways. For our experiments, we presume that the objects were used as weights and we applied different experimental variants: the crescent-shaped weights were used for band weaving, on a warp-weighted loom and in twining techniques. For the design of the experiments, analogies from ethnographic sources were also employed. We tested the possible uses of tools, even if the evidence for a specific technique comes from a region and period far beyond.

Variants of experiments

Three different loom set-ups were tested in use with these crescent-shaped weights. The first was a simple band loom

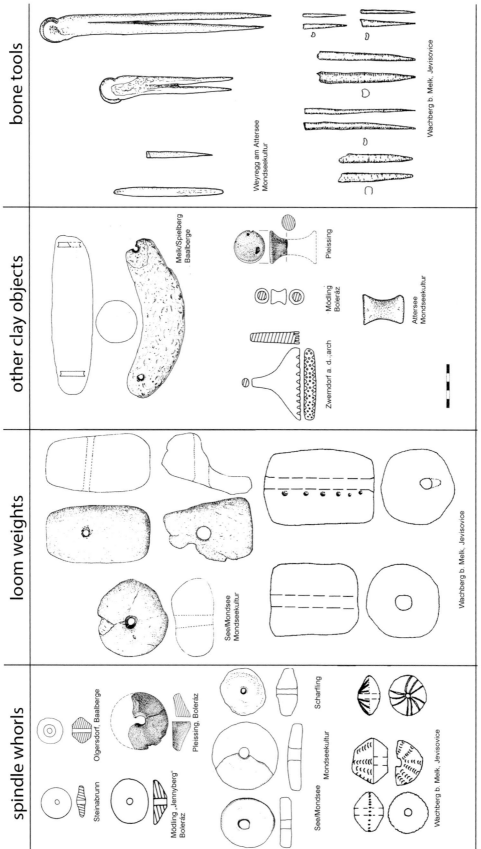

Fig. 11.1 Textile tools from Austria of the 4th millennium BC (drawing: K. Grömer; after Grömer 2006, Fig. 5).

with two weights. The next was a warp-weighted loom with over 10 weights, and the last was a twining frame with crescent weights tightening vertical active elements ('warp twining').

The original finds from Melk-Spielberg seem to have been unfired or lightly fired. For the experiments, weights of clay and some of clay mixed with sand were produced. It was also tested whether the preparation of the weights (fired or unfired) had any effect on the use-wear.

Reconstructed tools

The crescent weights were prepared in the same shape and mass as the original artefacts from Melk-Spielberg. The reconstructed objects were crescent-shaped, 16–18 cm long and 5–6 cm thick. Their weight was 400–500 g. The distance between the holes of the weights was about 11–12 cm. They were made by Ludwig Albustin in the open-air museum Asparn an der Zaya in Austria, and used in all the variants of experiments.

Additionally, for some of the twining experiments at Lejre in Denmark (with flax and lime-bast) smaller crescent-shaped weights were used as well. They were produced in the Lejre pottery workshop, as reconstructions of finds from Turkey (*c.* 2000–1200 BC), for experiments carried out by Agnete Wisti Lassen.[21] They are smaller, 250 g in weight, 12 cm long, 2.5 cm thick. The distance between the holes is 9 cm.

Documentation

Each part of the experiments was documented by photography (a snapshot of the materials used, the hand movements during preparation and beginning, the weaving, *etc.*). A form was used for the written documentation, and this recorded data concerning duration, participation, information about equipment used, individual production steps and procedure, a graphic record of the use-wear on the loom weights, observations and results.

The main aim of the experiments was to compare the use-wear on the original weights with the traces resulting from the different experiments. Therefore, different weaving and twining activities were tested for several hours, until the first traces of use (*e.g.* resulting from weights rubbing or clapping on each other) appeared. Usually that happened first on the unfired weights. The use-wear was documented on a sheet. To see the rubbing effect of the threads inserted in the holes more easily, blue pigment was added to the threads. It highlighted the movements of the threads within the holes. By obtaining a picture of use-wear marks resulting from a specific use of crescent weights in different experiments, it is possible that the function of the artefacts might be clearer.

Crescent-shaped weights and the band-loom

There is some archaeological evidence for the use and production of wider bands in the Late Neolithic. Woven bands with 7–15 cm width were found (for example) at the lake dwellings of Zürich-Utoquai, Feldmeilen 'Vorderfeld' or Muntelier 'Platzbünden' (second half of the 4th millennium BC).[22] Those fabrics are usually tabbies made with plied yarn and about 8–12 threads per cm.

Experimental set-up (Fig. 11.2)

The experiment was inspired by the work and publication of Annemarie Feldtkeller.[23] The aim was to test the function of the weights for band-weaving. Few materials and equipment were used for the experiment: two reconstructed weights from Melk, linen yarn, one wooden stick for heddling. The woven fabric was, in accordance to the original finds, tabby (slightly ribbed variety with 12 warp and 6 weft threads per cm) and 9 cm wide.

The individual steps of the procedure were warping, attaching the two warp-layers (back and front row of the tabby warp) on separated crescent weights, preparing the heddles, crocheting of the space-keeper, tightening the warp with the weights again – and weaving.

Observations (handling and produced fabric)

The whole band-loom set up with two crescent-shaped weights can be used very easily for weaving. The shed for the weft thread can be opened very well, the two layers of the threads (back and front layer of the warp for tabby) are separated clearly.

The fabric was a 9 cm wide band, but a problem with the spacing of warp threads was observed. The warp threads for each layer were divided into two groups that were fastened to the two holes of the crescent weights. The tension on the threads differed a little bit according to their position. The weave, therefore, did not appear well balanced. The band shows a 'gap' in the centre and denser parts on the edges. Maybe this effect could be corrected with more practice using these tools.

The special function of the weights in a band loom is that they provide the two warp layers separated from each other. Band weaving with such a tool is very practicable. It is possible to weave bands such as were found in the Late Neolithic Swiss lake dwellings.

Crescent-shaped weights and the warp-weighted loom

In the Mediterranean region, objects of this special shape are found more often and they are significantly lighter and smaller than the Central European ones. They usually are interpreted as weights for a warp-weighted loom. In several experiments, replicas of those weights have been used on a simple loom with one shaft to produce tabby.[24] There were also attempts to employ two rows of crescent-shaped weights for twill weaving on a more complex loom with four shafts.[25]

However, in Central Europe, the crescent-shaped weights have usually been found as single items, far less than the

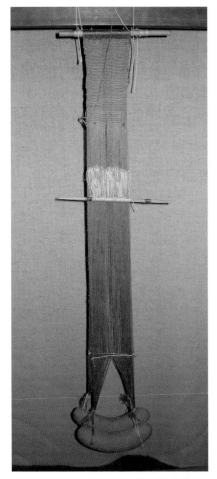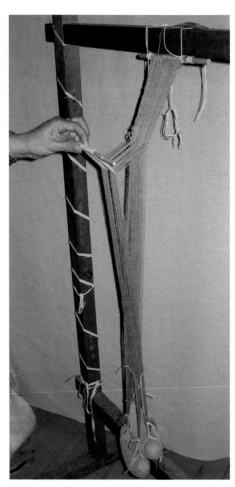

Fig. 11.2 Crescent-shaped loom weights used on a band loom (photos: K. Grömer).

numbers required for a loom set-up for twill or tabby. From the 4th and 3rd millennium BC, in Central Europe several larger fabrics woven on a warp-weighted loom have been preserved. All of them are tabbies, sometimes with starting borders, such as the one found at Wangen or Allensbach,[26] all dating to the Late Neolithic, between 3600–3000 BC. Of interest are woven textiles of the Funnel Beaker culture in Central Europe, such as from Rmíz in the Czech Republic (3600–3200 BC).[27] It is a flax tabby with 13 threads per cm. From the Jevišovice culture, we know a tabby fabric from Náměšt na Hané (Czech Republic).[28]

Experimental set-up (Fig. 11.3)

There is no archaeological evidence in the Late Neolithic in Central Europe of a woven twill textile. One of the earliest depictions of a warp-weighted loom is known from Val Camonica in Italy,[29] dated to the Bronze Age. There, a single shaft can be identified together with the loom weights. Therefore it was decided to use the crescent weights on a simple loom with one shaft.

The equipment for this experiment were 11 loom weights (reconstructions from Melk, alternating one fired and one unfired weight), linen yarn for the warp and weft (0.7 mm plied yarn), a long weaving sword and a loom with one

heddle rod and one shed rod. For warping, a ground warping frame was used, for weaving the repp starting border – a rigid heddle.

The individual steps of the procedure are warping and making a repp starting border, setting up the loom. For tensioning the warp threads with the crescent weights, the loom weights were arranged in one row – always one hole of the weight for the front warp layer, the other hole on the back warp layer. The next step was knitting the heddles, crocheting of the space-keeper, tensioning the warp with the weights – and weaving.

For the weaving experiment, 11 crescent weights were used. Considering the results of experiments done by the Lejre team and the CTR,[30] we estimated that 25 g tension per thread would be optimal. Since the crescents weigh 500 g, we arranged 20 threads (10 for the front and 10 for the back warp layer) to be attached to each weight. In that way a tabby fabric of 24 cm width was produced with a thread count 12 threads per cm in the warp and 8 threads per cm in the weft.

Observations (handling and produced fabric)

The crescents functioned very well when used as loom weights. A nice, well-balanced fabric can be woven with

tabby: natural shed

tabby: counter shed

Fig. 11.3 Crescent-shaped loom weights used on a warp-weighted loom (photos: K. Grömer).

them. The heddle rod can be moved very easily for opening and closing the shed for the weft.

For this experiment a shed rod was used, so the warp bundles and the weights were fixed at their place. On the Early Bronze Age depiction of a loom at Val Camonica, the bottom line could be a hint of the use of such a shed rod.

During weaving, the crescent loom weights are in a 'swinging' movement, the ends of the crescent weights tilt up and down. Without a shed rod, the loom weights also move sideward and strongly back and forth. With this movement, weaving is not easy and it is not possible to get a clear shed.

The experiments demonstrated clearly that it is possible to use these weights on a warp-weighted loom, especially in combination with a shed rod. The fabric produced with the loom is comparable with original finds.

Crescent-shaped weights for twining

Twining is an established Neolithic technique, employed to produce various two- and three-dimensional objects. The basic principle is to twine (wind) a flexible, active element around a passive flexible or stiff element to create a fabric. As we learn from archaeological and ethnographic sources,[31] various materials can be used, flexible taw material such as bast fibre, lime-bast, grass, willow, *etc.*, or even stiff material like straw, twigs, *etc.* The techniques to create those objects are also various. The simplest is to manipulate the materials just by hand, maybe by the help of a stick or pin beater. For more complex or huge items, such as large mats, there is ethnographic evidence for the use of a frame, *e.g.* from Korea.[32] For a twining frame, there are two possibilities of handling: the vertical elements can be fixed, and the horizontal elements can be used for twining weft, or the other way round for warp twining. The latter is of interest for our experiments, and we used the crescent-shaped weights as active moving vertical elements for twining.

In Late Neolithic Central Europe, various twining techniques were used to produce two- and three-dimensional objects. The most important finds belonged to the Iceman Ötzi, *e.g.* the knife sheath and the mat.[33] Sometimes the twined objects are as fine as woven textiles, but some are coarser. Some of the flat twinings (*Kettenstoffe*), such as the ones from Wetzikon-Robenhausen or Hornstaad,[34] as well as narrow twined 'bands' like from Wangen, are of interest here, since they could have been produced on a twining frame.[35]

Experimental set-up

The equipment for the twining-experiments was 8–12 weights, reproductions from Melk, fired and unfired, for Test 1, and Anatolian weights from the Lejre pottery workshop for Tests 2 and 3, a weaving sword and a simple frame to put the vertical elements on. Three series of experiments

were made: one twining with flax for the warp twines and bast for the 'weft', and two experiments with twisted lime-bast for the warp twines (Fig. 11.4). One of these was done with low twisted lime bast-stripes for the 'weft', the other with plied lime-bast.

First, the vertical active elements were fixed on the loom and the weights: one thread ran from one hole of the crescent weight, over the beam of the loom and back to the other hole of the weight. It was found to be absolutely necessary that all weights were in a row next to each other. For twining, the weights had to be turned (Fig. 11.4.3) and the 'weft' was passed through the shed.

Observations (handling and produced fabric)

Test 1: twining with flax and lime-bast. The functionality of the weights (handling while turning) was tested in this experiment. It was observed that the horizontal elements had to be very thick to get a dense fabric. The weight on the twined vertically tensioned threads pulls them so strongly downwards that a space appeared between the horizontal rows of thread.

On this first experiment, the rows of the active elements were placed at a distance of 1.2–1.5 cm from each other, as we know from the fabric from Hornstaad. For a large twined fabric (*e.g.* made with 20–30 weights – one for each twined row) this distance is acceptable.

Test 2: twining with lime-bast and wide twisted bast (inspired by the fabric of Hornstaad) (Fig. 11.4.1–2). The second experiment was testing a set up with twisted (not plied or twined) lime-bast as known from Hornstaad. In this experiment we used eight loom weights, placed at a distance of 1.2–1.5 cm. Twining with that set-up was very easy, it was possible to reach a similar product to the Hornstaad twining, but the weft-density was not that satisfying.

Test 3: twining with lime-bast and plied lime-bast threads (inspired by the fabric of Wangen). For the next experiment we used eight crescent weights, but placed very dense to get a warp-faced band (Fig. 11.4.4). We aimed to reproduce a band made with single lime-bast as the active element and plied lime-bast as the passive element. Such a band was found in Wangen.[36] From this piece it is clear that it was 'warp-twined', because both side borders survived.

The band from Wangen could be reproduced very easily and quickly, with the density of the active and passive parts equal to the original finds.

Results

In general, the functionality of the crescent weights for 'warp-twining' is very good – the vertical threads are the active elements and the horizontal threads are the passive ones. The active threads can be moved very easily and quickly. After they are turned, they are fixed in their position, held in place in a row. They do not turn back. The threads in the holes of the weights create a nice shed because of the

Fig. 11.4 Crescent-shaped loom weights used for twining (photos: K. Grömer).

distance of the holes. The passive elements can be easily threaded through the shed.

The experiments demonstrate that it is possible to carry out 'warp-twining' on such a frame with the help of crescent-shaped weights. The use-wear also fits this activity very well. But, on the other hand, some technical details on the fabrics (density, twist of threads) show that the twined fabrics of the Late Neolithic in Central Europe presumably were also produced without any tool, just by hand.

Use-wear

During work and after finishing each experiment, the use-wear on the crescent-shaped loom weights (Fig. 11.5)

was documented in detail. Using the weights on the band-weaving implement, some specific types of abrasion were documented: there are linear traces of a pulling movement from the upturned holes (in the direction of the weave). Another type of use-wear reflects rubbing on the larger sides of the tools resulting from the movement during opening and closing the shed.

While using the crescents as loom weights, the traces are different to those appearing with the use for a band loom. There is minor rubbing on the larger parts of the weights, in areas where the weights touch each other. But there is characteristic use-wear on the holes of the crescent weights. The typical traces are V-shaped, caused by the movement of

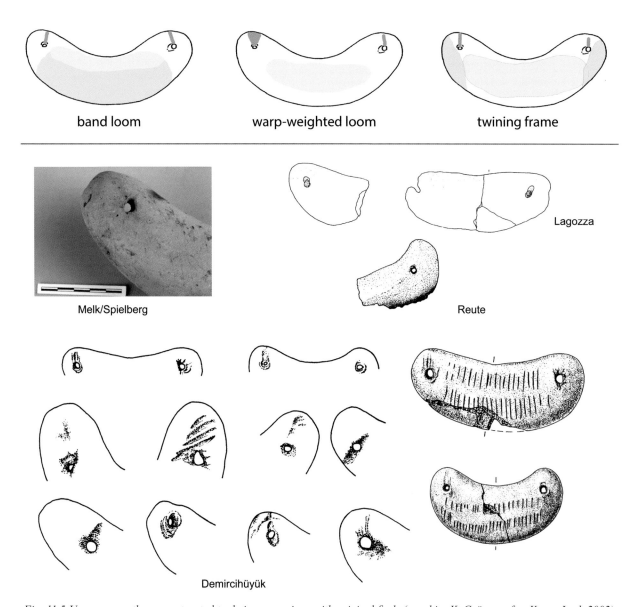

Fig. 11.5 Use-wear on the reconstructed tools in comparison with original finds (graphic: K. Grömer, after Krenn-Leeb 2002).

the weights tilting up and down. Sometimes linear vestiges of a pulling movement from the holes upwards were also recognised on the original finds.

For twining, use-wear is seen in clear linear traces of a pulling movement from the holes in direction to the fabric. Beside that, abrasion on the larger sides and on the edges of the tools appears, because the tools were always hitting each other while turning the weights.

The observations made during the different activities can be compared with original finds from Melk-Spielberg,[37] but also from Lagozza[38] or Demircihüyük.[39] The originals show linear use-wear on the holes, the typical V-shaped traces of use as loom weights cannot be recognised according to the publications. Therefore, the best interpretation is the use of crescents for band weaving and twining. The work

on the warp-weighted loom causes slightly different use-wear, because of the 'swinging' movement of the weights. Use-wear on the large sides of the weights is usually not recorded on the original finds. Interestingly, abrasion of the edges is documented on the Lagozza tools. This is typical for the use on a twining frame.

Conclusion

As indicated by the three variants of our experiments, crescent-shaped weights known from the Late Neolithic cultures around the Alps (*c.* 3800–2800 BC) can be used for different textile techniques such as band weaving, weaving a large textile on a loom or twining on a frame. Using these tools, it is possible to construct fabrics similar to ones found on Late Neolithic sites, especially bands and large fabrics in tabby, as well as the structures of twined textiles.

The first experiment was to test crescent-shaped weights on a band-loom, based on the experiments and publication of Annemarie Feldtkeller. It is possible to weave bands like the ones found in the Late Neolithic Swiss lake dwellings, and the use-wear on the crescent weights is comparable to the original weights.

The second experiment dealt with the warp-weighted loom and crescent loom weights, following the common interpretation of that type of tools in the Mediterranean region. The experiments showed clearly that it is possible to use those weights on a warp-weighted loom, especially in combination with a shed rod. The use-wear on the weights is somehow different to the original finds because of the swinging movement of the weights.

Lastly, the crescent loom weights were tested whether they could have functioned in twining. In the Central European Neolithic, various twining techniques were used to produce two- and three-dimensional objects. Some of the flat twinings could have been produced on a twining frame. The experiments show that it is possible to do 'warp-twining' on such a loom with the help of crescent-shaped weights. The use-wear (linear traces from the holes and rubbings on the edges), seen on the experimentally used weights, are comparable to those of the original finds. Some technical details on the fabrics (density, twist of threads) show, however, that the twined fabrics of the Late Neolithic in Central Europe presumably were produced without any tool, just by hand.

Following these experiments, some educated guesses can be made about the function of the crescent-shaped weights. Whatever it was, they must have been involved in the manufacture of some specific kind of textile, as loom weights of that shape are not at all common in the Late Neolithic in Central Europe. From the dates that are available so far, it seems as if one of the origins of those tools might be South-East Europe, for example the earliest dates for finds occur in places like Sălcuţa in Romania, Kamik in Albania or Šuplevec in Serbia, sites dating to the later 5th and early 4th millennia BC. Then the tools spread to the Lagozza culture in northern Italy (3800–3600 BC). The slightly later Melk-Spielberg examples are probably to be understood as products of a specific weaving or twining technique stemming from these areas. In western Europe (Spain, El Malagon *c.* 3000 BC, Portugal, São Pedro) and in Anatolia (early 3rd millennium BC) crescent loom weights also appear. We do not know that the function of the loom weights was the same during that long period and in all regions, or if the textile types, produced by the use of those tools, changed.

Notes

1   Krenn-Leeb 2002. The experiments were part of a research project on the textile technology of the Late Neolithic Jevišovice culture (*c.* 3000 BC) in Austria (cooperation with Alexandra

Krenn-Leeb, University Vienna). The experiments were carried out in August 2007 with a grant HAF 03/07 offered by the Lejre Archaeological-Experimental Centre (now Sagnlandet Lejre – Lands of Legends) in Denmark. Further experiments were also done within the framework of the lecture 'Experimental Archaeology' by the University Vienna in the open-air museum Asparn an der Zaya, Austria, in July 2008. We have to thank for help the following persons (alphabetical order): Ludwig and Vera Albustin, Anne Batzer, Ida Demant and Anne Reichert.

2   For a general overview, see Cunliffe 1998; Kristiansen 2000.
3   Discussion in Becker *et al.* 2016, 104–105.
4   In detail about the cultural groups, Urban 2000, 106–138.
5   Spindler 1995; Egg and Goedecker-Ciolek 2009.
6   Bender Jørgensen and Rast-Eicher 2015.
7   Rast-Eicher 1995; 2005; Bazzanella *et al.* 2003; Grömer 2006, figs. 9, 11, 16; Médard 2010; Rast-Eicher and Dietrich 2015.
8   Harris 2012.
9   Grömer 2006, fig. 5.
10 Pieler 2001, 504; Grömer 2005, figs. 1.1–7; Krenn-Leeb 2010.
11 Pieler 2001, 503–506, fig. 59.
12 Krenn-Leeb 2002, 302, figs. 21–26, pl. 5.
13 For collection of comparative finds, see Krenn-Leeb 2002, 302–306; Costeira and Mataloto in this volume.
14 Cornaggia Castiglioni 1964; Borrello 1984, 39, table 54; Odone 1997, 128.
15 Krenn-Leeb 2002, 310.
16 Bahn 1989.
17 Arribas *et al.* 1978, fig. 13, tables X, XV.
18 Borrello 1984, 39; Krenn-Leeb 2002, 307–308; Lassen 2013, fig. 5.4; Melis 2014.
19 Kull 1988, 200–201, fig. 190, see also catalogue.
20 See also Alp 1968; Weingarten 1990; Lassen 2013, 80.
21 Lassen 2013, 81–84; 2015. The smaller size and weight of reconstructions of Anatolian weights did not have a significant effect on the intended test of their usability with lime-bast. The basic mechanisms of turning the weights did not differ much in comparison to the Melk-Spielberg weights reconstructions.
22 Wininger 1995, fig. 51; Médard 2010, 202.
23 Feldtkeller 2003, 16–19, fig. 15.
24 Cornaggia Castiglioni 1964. See also later experiments: Bazzanella *et al.* 2003, fig. p. 105.
25 Lassen 2013, fig. 5.6; Ulanowska this volume.
26 Feldtkeller and Schlichtherle 1987, 79.
27 Baldia 2004, 69–70.
28 Smíd 1990, 67–69.
29 See Anati 1994, 158–159.
30 *Cf.* Lassen 2015, 132.
31 Seiler-Baldinger 1994; Rast-Eicher 1995; 2015; Médard 2010.
32 Hirschberg and Janata 1986, fig. 70.
33 Egg and Goedecker-Ciolek 2009, 88 (knife sheet) and 124 (mat or cloak).
34 Schlichtherle 1990.
35 Reinhard 1992, 51–53; Wininger 1995, 178, fig. 32; Médard 2010, 167, 180.
36 Courtesy of Annemarie Feldtkeller, who provided us with photos and graphics of this band.
37 Krenn-Leeb 2002, fig. 25.
38 Borrello 1984, pl. 54.
39 Kull 1988, 201–202, fig. 195.

Bibliography

Alp, S. 1968 *Zylinder- und Stempelsiegel aus Karahöyük bei Konya*. Türk Tarih Kurumu Yayinlari V.26. Ankara.

Anati, E. 1994 *Valcamonica Rock Art. A New History for Europe*. Studi Camuni XIII. English edition. Capo di Ponte.

Arribas, A., Molina, F., de la Torre, F., Nájera, T. and Sáez, L. 1978 El poblado de la edad del Cobre de 'El Malagon' (Cullar – Baza, Granada). Campana de 1975. *Cuadernos de Prehistoria de la Universidad de Granada* 3, 67–101.

Bahn, B. W. 1989 Eine Grube der Baalberger Kultur mit kultischem Befund von Melchendorf, Kr. Erfurt-Stadt. In F. Schlette and D. Kaufmann (eds.), *Religion und Kult in ur- und frühgeschichtlicher Zeit*. Berlin, 165–170.

Baldia, C. 2004 The oldest woven textile of the Funnel Beaker culture (4000–2900 cal BC) in North and Central Europe. In I. Jadin and A. Hauzeur (eds.), *La Néolithique au Proche Orient et en Europe. The Neolithic in the Near East and Europe*. British Archaeological Reports International Series 1303, 67–70.

Bazzanella, M., Mayr, A., Moser, L. and Rast-Eicher, A. 2003 *Textiles, intrecci e tessuti dalla preistoria europea. Museo Civico di Riva del Garda – La Rocca, 24 maggio –19 ottobre*. Trente.

Becker, C., Benecke, N., Grabundzija, A., Küchelmann, H.-C., Pollock, S., Schier, W., Schoch, C., Schrakamp, I., Schütt, B. and Schumacher, M. 2016 The textile revolution. Research into the origin and spread of wool production between the Near East and Central Europe. In G. Graßhoff and M. Meyer (eds.), *eTOPOI. Journal for Ancient Studies. Special Volume 6: Space and Knowledge. Topoi Research Group Articles*, 102–151 (http://journal.topoi.org/index.php/etopoi/article/view/253, accessed 5 January 2018).

Bender Jørgensen, L. and Rast-Eicher, A. 2015 Searching for the earliest wools in Europe. In K. Grömer and F. Pritchard (eds.), *Aspects of the Design, Production and Use of Textiles and Clothing from the Bronze Age to the Early Modern Era. NESAT XII. The North European Symposium for Archaeological Textiles, 21st–24th May 2014 in Hallstatt, Austria*. Archeolingua 33. Budapest, 67–72.

Borrello, M. A. 1984 *The Lagozza Culture (3rd millennium B.C.) in Northern and Central Italy*. Studi Archaeologici 3. Bergamo.

Cornaggia Castiglioni, O. C. 1964 I 'reniformi' della Lagozza. In Società archeologica comense (eds.), *Comum – Miscellanea di scritti in onore di Federico Frigerio*. Como, 129–171.

Cunliffe, B. (eds.) 1998 *Prehistoric Europe. An Illustrated History*. Oxford.

Egg, M. and Goedecker-Ciolek, R. 2009 Ausrüstung und Kleidung. In M. Egg and K. Spindler (eds.), *Kleidung und Ausrüstung der kupferzeitlichen Gletschermumie aus den Ötztaler Alpen*. Monographien des Römisch-Germanischen Zentralmuseums 77. Mainz, 57–164.

Feldtkeller, A. 2003 Nierenförmige Webgewichte – wie funktionieren sie? *Archaeological Textiles Newsletter* 37. Autumn, 16–19.

Feldtkeller, A. and Schlichtherle, H. 1987 Jungsteinzeitliche Kleidungsstücke aus Ufersiedlungen des Bodensees. *Archäologische Nachrichten aus Baden* 38/39, 79–80.

Grömer, K. 2005 Efficiency and technique – experiments with original spindle whorls. In P. Bichler, K. Grömer, R. Hofmann-de Keijzer, A. Kern and H. Reschreiter (eds.). *'Hallstatt Textiles.' Technical Analysis, Scientific Investigation and Experiments on Iron Age Textiles*. British Archaeological Reports International Series 1351, 107–116.

Grömer, K. 2006 Vom Spinnen und Weben, Flechten und Zwirnen. Hinweise zur neolithischen Textiltechnik an österreichischen Fundstellen. In A. Krenn-Leeb, K. Grömer and P. Stadler (eds.), *Festschrift für Elisabeth Ruttkay*. Archäologie Österreichs 17.2, 177–192.

Harris, S. 2012 From the parochial to the universal: comparing cloth cultures in the Bronze Age. *European Journal of Archaeology* 15.1, 61–97.

Hirschberg, W. and Janata, A. 1986 *Technologie und Ergologie in der Völkerkunde*. Mannheim.

Krenn-Leeb, A. 2002 Eine trichterbecherzeitliche Grube mit nierenförmigen Webgewichten von Spielberg bei Melk, Niederösterreich. *Preistoria Alpina* 37, 287–331.

Krenn-Leeb, A. 2010 Humanökologie der Kupferzeit – Interaktionen und Wirkungszusammenhänge zwischen Mensch, Gesellschaft und Umwelt am Beispiel der Jevišovice-Kultur. *Archäologische Forschungen in Niederösterreich* 4, 28–47.

Kristiansen, K. 2000 *Europe before History*. Cambridge.

Kull, B. 1988 *Demircihüyük. Die Ergebnisse der Ausgrabungen 1975–1978. V. Die mittelbronzezeitliche Siedlung*. Mainz.

Lassen, A. W. 2013 Technology and palace economy in Middle Bronze Age Anatolia: the case of the crescent shaped loom weight. In M.-L. Nosch, H. Koefoed and E. Andersson Strand (eds.), *Textile Production and Consumption in the Ancient Near East*. Ancient Textiles Series 12. Oxford and Oakville, 78–92.

Lassen, A. W. 2015 Weaving with crescent shaped loom weights. An investigation of a special kind of loom weight. In E. Andersson Strand and M.-L. Nosch (eds.), *Tools, Textiles and Contexts. Investigating Textile Production in the Aegean and Eastern Mediterranean Bronze Age*. Ancient Textiles Series 21. Oxford and Philadelphia, 127–137.

Médard, F. 2010, *L'art du tissage au Néolithique. IVe–IIIe millénaires avant J.-C. en Suisse*. Paris.

Melis, M. G. 2014 *Lo strumentario tessile della Preistoria. I pesi da telaio della Sardegna*. Sassari.

Odone, S. 1997 La Lagozza di Besnate (VA): new data from the Cornaggia Castiglioni excavations. *Prehistoria Alpina* 33, 127–132.

Pieler, F. 2001 Die archäologischen Untersuchungen der spätneolithischen Anlage von Krems-Hundssteig. In B. Wewerka, *Bericht zu den Ausgrabungen des Vereines ASINOE im Projektjahr 2001*. Fundberichte aus Österreich 40, 503–510.

Rast-Eicher, A. 1995 Gewebe und Geflechte. In W. E. Stöckli, U. Niffeler and E. Gross-Klee (eds.), *Die Schweiz vom Paläolithikum bis zum frühen Mittelalter*. SPM II, Neolithikum. Basel, 169–172.

Rast-Eicher, A. 2005 Bast before wool: the first textiles. In P. Bichler, K. Grömer, R. Hofmann-de Keijzer, A. Kern and H. Reschreiter (eds.), *'Hallstatt Textiles.' Technical Analysis, Scientific Investigation and Experiments on Iron Age Textiles*. British Archaeological Reports International Series 1351, 117–131.

Rast-Eicher, A. and Dietrich, A. 2015 *Neolithische und bronzezeitliche Gewebe und Geflechte. Die Funde aus den*

128   *Karina Grömer*

Seeufersiedlungen im Kanton Zürich. Monographien der
   Kantonsarchäologie Zürich 46. Zürich.
Reinhard, J. 1992 Stoffe mit Zwirnbindung und Steinwebstühle.
   Helvetica Archaeologica 23, 51–54.
Seiler-Baldinger, A. 1994 *Textiles. A Classification of Techniques.*
   Bathurst.
Schlichtherle, H. 1990 *Die Sondage 1973–1978 in den
   Ufersiedlungen Hornstaad-Hörnle I.* Siedlungsarchäologie im
   Alpenvorland I. Zürich.
Smíd, M. 1990 Ein Beitrag zur Erkenntnis der Äneolithischen
   Hügelgräberfgelder in Mittelmähren. In J. Poulík and V. Nekuda
   (eds.), *Praveke a Slovanské osídlení Moravy.* Brno, 67–72.

Spindler, K. 1995 *The Man in the Ice: The Preserved Body of a
   Neolithic Man Reveals the Secrets of the Stone Age.* London.
Urban, O. H. 2000 *Der lange Weg zur Geschichte. Die Urgeschichte
   Österreichs.* Wien.
Weingarten, J. 1990 The sealing structure of Karahöyük and some
   administrative links with Phaistos on Crete. *Oriens Antiquus*
   29, 63–95.
Wininger, J. 1995 Die Bekleidung des Eismannes und die
   Anfänge der Weberei nördlich der Alpen. In K. Spindler,
   E. Rastbichler-Zissernig, H. Wilfing, D. zur Nedden and H.
   Nothdurfter (eds.), *Der Mann im Eis. The Man in the Ice,* vol.
   2. Vienna, 119–188.

12

Two sides of a whorl. Unspinning the meanings and functionality of Eneolithic textile tools

Ana Grabundžija

Introduction

This analysis of the spindle whorls from human burials from Middle and Late Eneolithic sites in the Pannonian Plain focuses on exploring the relationship between the presumed technological function and the tool's symbolical significance.[1] This is based on a large sample of data on textile tools collected and processed within the TOPOI 'The Textile Revolution' research project designed to investigate the evidence for the early use of wool in prehistoric South-East and Central Europe. The two undividable aspects of the object's character, namely its functional and symbolical traits, were taken into consideration to determine its place within the framework of the production tradition to which it could be contextually, chronologically and, finally, technologically connected.

During the three-year project, 1152 spindle whorls were recorded in the textile tool database. Initially, the study included tools from 34 archaeological sites, but the analysis was performed on a restricted sample of these.[2] The final sample included 928 spindle whorls from 26 sites, of which 901 whorls provided necessary measurements for the basic functional analysis (Fig. 12.1). Only 10 spindle whorls (roughly 1%) from the entire sample were documented as a part of the material accompanying human burials.[3]

The project's recording protocol stipulated taking four main measurements (whorl diameter, perforation diameter, height and weight) and calculating weight/diameter and diameter/height ratios. This yielded a solid database for the analysis and reconstruction of spatio-temporal trends in the yarn production represented by the studied sample.

All spindle whorls in the database were documented in order to provide three separate categories of information: contextual, morphological and illustrative data. Unfortunately, not all specimens presented an equal amount of information. Hence, for the purpose of the functional analysis, a minimum criterion was determined requiring a reliable chronological assignment, typological determination and the measurements noted above.

Although tool samples from some of the studied sites had previously been published, spindle whorl details were not reported according to the above-mentioned protocol. Missing weight values were one of the main reasons for their additional recording, so they could fully meet the purpose of the functional analysis in this study.

The research was focused on the Eneolithic period, and it reviewed several production traditions dating from the Late Neolithic to the Early Bronze Age. Vinča culture whorls comprised the earliest sample, the Somogyvár-Vinkovci examples represented the latest tools studied in the project. Whorls from nine 'cultural groups' were investigated.

It was found that their representation in the final 26 site-cluster differs. This is due to two main reasons: first, the frequency of the spindle whorl occurrences increased during the Late Eneolithic period and, secondly, the sites chosen for the study were not equal in size and typology. Nonetheless, whorls for the majority of the cultures were documented on two or more sites, thus enabling basic site-to-site comparisons, with the exception of the Proto-Boleráz group.[4]

The included sites were chosen primarily on the basis of data availability and quality, and not only because they fitted in the time-range covered by the research project. Most of the sites had been investigated relatively recently in rescue excavations yielding a number of items from reliable contexts, in most cases absolutely dated. The exceptions were Ljubljansko Barje-Ig and Dobanovci, which had been were excavated during the 1880s and the 1960s.[5]

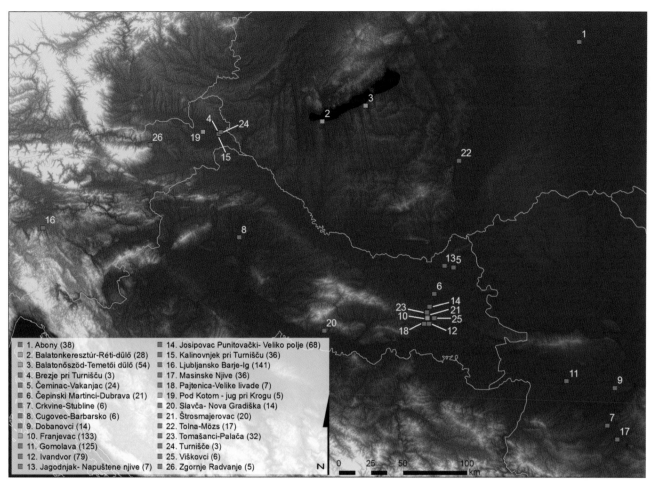

Fig. 12.1 Map showing the geographical distribution of the investigated sites with sample sizes given in brackets. Sites with human burials containing spindle whorls are marked in blue.

Context for the function of whorls

One of the main objectives of this research was to elucidate the period of major changes in textile technologies and to observe any trends or discontinuities that might be connected to the introduction of new fibre material(s) in the given region.

The morphological traits of the sampled spindle whorls were given special attention during the sampling and post-recording process, since, in the respective field of research,[6] it was precisely these characteristics that were proven responsible for the functionality of the tools. Both the whorl's shape and size determine its moment of inertia, a parameter crucial for the spinning process. While its weight has more influence on tension, the strength that pulls the fibres during the spinning process, its height and diameter have a greater influence on the rotation in terms of speed. Perforation diameter and position are another two traits that affect the whorl's rotation to a significant degree, but also are later responsible for its stability while it rotates.[7] The perforation is to some extent indicative of the spindle on which the whorl was used, therefore its dimensions and properties have to be considered, since they too influenced

the spinning.[8] It is the weight of a whorl that is generally considered as having a central role in its use in fibre processing; this is because it determines the functionality of the whorl in connection with both the raw material and the properties of the spun thread.[9]

There was a variety of raw materials used in textile production in the course of prehistory, both of animal and plant origin. Within these two groups, two materials are given special attention: flax fibre[10] and sheep wool.[11] Both species, plant and animal, went through an evolution that had great influence on the practice of the fibre production and processing, and which had, most likely, significantly shaped and changed textile technology. Possibly, both species were domesticated for nutritional purposes, while their later breeds were extensively used as a resource of raw material in the production of textiles; these two distinct types of fibres thus became a secondary product.[12] This modified exploitation of both of them could have led to intensification of, and changes in the structure of, textile production.

The fact that the fibre flax plant would have provided longer fibres in comparison to the shorter length of wool

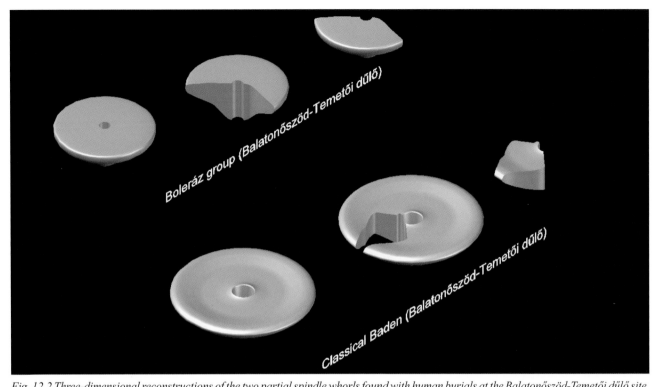

Fig. 12.2 Three-dimensional reconstructions of the two partial spindle whorls found with human burials at the Balatonőszöd-Temetői dűlő site.

of the early woolly breeds explains the main reason why this distinction resonated further in the dichotomy between spindle whorl types, or more precisely between their size and weight categories.

Plant fibres are, in comparison to wool, more often considered to have been spun with heavier weights.[13] Very heavy whorls, respectively 100 g and above, are most commonly thought to be connected with the full-length flax or long-staple wool of later specialised breeds, since only this amount of tension is adequate for very long fibres. Generally, heavier and coarser fibres necessitate heavy spindle whorls, while lighter and shorter fibres call for light ones. Spinning medium to heavy wool is connected with the use of whorls of medium weight, around 30 g.[14]

Experts assume that lighter weights were most likely chosen to produce thinner and lighter threads, while heavier weights were used for thicker and heavier yarns.[15] It was proven that the height and the diameter also have some effect on the resulting thread properties, due to their influence on the rotation. Consequently, the higher the rotation, the more tightly the yarn is spun.[16]

The mentioned standards ought to be taken with caution, since the actual spinning process is influenced by many factors combined. Besides the weight, size and shape of a whorl, additional traits such as the accumulated thread on the spindle,[17] the whorl's position on it,[18] the spinning technique used[19] and, finally, the spinner's skill and preference[20] have to be considered as well.

The segment of this paper addressing the functionality analysis reports on 385 completely preserved whorls, 165 half-preserved whorls, 228 partially preserved whorls and 123 whorls that had small fragments (less than 10%) missing. All 10 spindle whorls from the investigated human burial contexts were eligible for the analysis, since they complied with the four-measurement standard.

The weight values of the spindle whorls in the analysed sample were documented in four different reliability categories, depending on their state of preservation. The weights of complete whorls were documented in the complete weights category, the weights of almost complete examples with small fragments missing were documented in the estimated weights category (estimated weight ≈ weight if not complete), the weights of whorls of which only half was preserved were documented in the calculated weight category (calculated weight = weight if not complete doubled) and, finally, the weights of partially preserved samples were documented in the reconstructed weight category (reconstructed weight = density × volume).

Three-dimensional models were created for all partially preserved spindle whorls. Knowing the weight of the fragment and its volume, taken from the geometry of the virtual model, the density parameter for the material of which the whorl was made could be calculated. Finally, from the material's density parameter and the volume parameter, again taken from the geometry of the three-dimensional whorl model, calculation of the reconstructed weight was possible (Fig. 12.2).

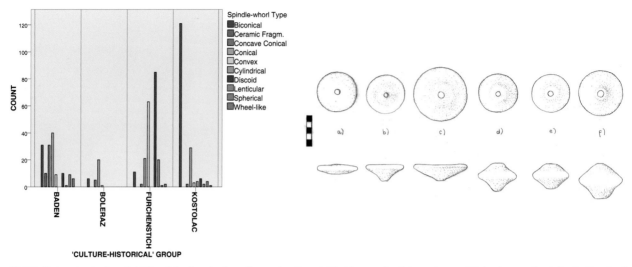

Fig. 12.3 Left: typological variability of the four 'cultural' samples that yielded human burial specimens. Right: human burial spindle whorl models according to their find context: a. discoidal spindle whorl found in a child burial at Pod Kotom-jug pri Krogu; b. conical spindle whorl from the Boleráz human burial at the Balatonőszöd-Temetői dűlő site; c. conical spindle whorl from the Classical Baden human burial at Balatonőszöd-Temetői dűlő site; d. biconical spindle whorl found in a female grave at Balatonkeresztúr-Réti-dűlő site; e. biconical spindle whorl found in a female burial at Đakovo-Franjevac; f. biconical spindle whorl found in a male burial at Đakovo-Franjevac.

Context for the meaning of whorls

Finds of spindle whorls in human burials, which are the main focus of this paper, are an exceptionally rare incidence in the context of the Eneolithic period.[21] The presence of these whorls in these special-deposit contexts accentuates their symbolical character. It also marks the early phase of the practice of placing spindles or their whorls in graves that becomes more frequent in the later prehistoric periods.[22]

This paper suggests that the beginning of their increased occurrences in graves might be understood primarily through the context of textile technology and its changing production structures. Consequently, they ought to be explained as reflecting altering social conditions and complexity related to those changes.

Five spindle whorls from the Pod Kotom-jug pri Krogu site were all attributed to the late phase of the Furchenstich cultural complex. Only one specimen of a discoidal type (almost completely preserved with several small fragments missing and having an estimated weight of 33 g) was found in a human burial context (Fig. 12.3 a). It was the only grave good object found in a cremation urn, together with the remains of a child who was under three years of age. Considering the fact that the site was a cemetery of urned cremations, all spindle whorls found around the burials can probably be reliably associated with graves. The rest of the sample includes one more spindle whorl of a discoidal type (again almost completely preserved with small fragments missing, having an estimated weight of 22.4 g), two completely preserved decorated lenticular specimens (weighing 37.7 g and 21 g), and finally one

lenticular spindle whorl (of which half is preserved, also decorated, with a calculated weight of 15.4 g).[23]

The Pod Kotom-jug pri Krogu cemetery is one of the oldest prehistoric cremation cemeteries in the region; it was completely excavated and consisted of 176 cremation burials in urns, the tops of which were in most cases damaged by ploughing.[24] The deceased were all cremated on a pyre and the anthropological analysis attested that the population (more than 50% of the analysed remains belonged to children and the remainder belonged to men and women in equal ratio, with an average age of 30) buried in the cemetery suffered from malnutrition.[25] The remains of the deceased were placed in urns with pierced bottoms and buried in pits with the occasional addition of grave goods: besides the discoidal spindle whorl from a child burial, some urns contained cremated animal bones, smaller stone artefacts were discovered in two cases, while a ladle with a solid handle and a thin copper plate were found in single cases.[26] The deliberate piercing of the urns and the sherds discovered in the vicinity of the graves (small beakers, spindle whorls and ladles) can be considered as a part of the ritual, for which analogies are known from the Boleráz cemetery at Pilismarót-Basaharc.[27] In addition to the Pilismarót-Basaharc site, some similarities can also be observed with the Neszmély and Szerencz cemeteries of the Balaton-Lasinja II–III phase.[28]

Two partially preserved spindle whorls were found in the human burials at the Balatonőszöd-Temetőidülő site, one conical, with a reconstructed weight of 48 g, attributed to the Boleráz group (Baden IIA) (Fig. 12.3 b), and the other, also of the conical type, attributed to the Baden culture

(Baden IIB/III) (Fig. 12.3 c), with a reconstructed weight of 128.7 g.[29] A specimen attributed to the Boleráz group was found in a pit together with a side-fragment of a mature person's skull of undetermined age and sex, thrown into the pit along with fragmented ceramic and animal bones of cattle, sheep and dog.[30] The other, Classical Baden, spindle whorl was found in a pit connected to the burial feature (both structures were a part of a larger pit complex) in which remains of a newborn baby and a child between 1½ and 2½ years of age were found together with a stone axe, fragmented ceramics and animal bones.[31]

At the Balatonőszod-Temetőidülő settlement, an unusually large number of the unearthed features and objects belonged to the sacral sphere, including the intramural burials and sacrificial pits. Human and/or animal skeletons were found in 75 features that were interpreted as intramural burials or blood sacrifices: large communal sacrifices (features that contained more than one animal skeleton or skeletal part often found together with human skeletons and other grave goods), features with human skeletons (blood sacrifices or intramural burials, sometimes with an animal beside the human skeleton) and features with animal skeletons (blood sacrifices or animal burials: cattle, small ruminants, pig and dog).[32] Grave goods, besides the animal skeletons and bones, included ceramic vessels and sherds, ladles, ochre lumps, spindle whorls, bone tools and both flaked and polished stone tools.[33]

A complete biconical spindle whorl weighing 71.2 g from the Balatonkeresztúr-Réti-dűlő site, attributed to the Baden culture (Baden IIB/III), was found in a grave burial with the skeleton of a 40–50-year-old female, together with *Dentalium* beads, a polished stone tool, a small piece of copper, animal bones and ceramic fragments (Fig. 12.3 d).[34] Only this, the richest of the nine graves from the Balatonkeresztúr-Réti-dűlő settlement that could be connected with the Late Eneolithic (Boleráz, Early Classical Baden and Late Classical Baden) occupation, yielded a spindle whorl. Interestingly, based on the distribution of finds at this site, evidence of textile production and leather working was attested in all three phases, but not in all households, and no household had evidence of both, which may reflect a certain division of labour.[35]

Two completely preserved biconical spindle whorls, both attributed to the Kostolac culture, were found with human burials at the Đakovo-Franjevac site. The lighter one, weighing 75.5 g, was found with the skull of a woman between 35 and 50 years of age, buried in a pit together with two stone tools, a fragment of a copper dagger and ceramic fragments (Fig. 12.3 e).[36] The heavier one, weighing twice as much (150 g), was found with a 20–35-year-old man, buried in a pit together with two pigs and ceramic fragments (Fig. 12.3 f).[37]

The female burial at Đakovo-Franjevac was a part of a larger sunken structure containing several dug features of uneven depth and dimensions. In one of them the cranial vault of a child aged between 5 and 10 years of age was found. The male burial pit was located adjacent to this large pit structure.

Only three more human burials were recovered at the site: one skull belonging to an adult male was found together with the skulls of two children (aged 0 to 5, and 5 to 10) in a single smaller pit that yielded only ceramic fragments.[38] Thus, the burial contexts in which the two spindle whorls were found appear to stand out due to the richer grave goods and animal sacrifices.

Interestingly, out of the 142 recorded features at Đakovo-Franjevac yielding Kostolac pottery, two particularly large structures (20×17 m), held the majority (62%) of the recovered spindle whorls. Out of the 121 spindle whorls excavated at the settlement and attributed to the Kostolac culture, 63 (more than 50% of the entire Đakovo-Franjevac sample and 37% of the entire Kostolac sample recorded in the database) were found in the southern, of the two large pit structures, in which the graves of a woman and child were discovered. Some of the more important finds in the same context as the 63 spindle whorls include eight polished stone tools, five grindstones, three small spools, two small ceramic axes, a small decorated ceramic tile and bone tools, namely *spatulae* and an awl.[39] Such a concentration of finds might indicate not just intensified and organised but also rather specialised spinning practice on the site.

No pattern could be observed in the relationship between the presence of spindle whorls in graves and the age and sex of the deceased. Women, men and very young children were buried with spindle whorls, suggesting that their presence was dictated by different and more complex symbolical factors. There was little clear evidence that there was a relationship between the appearance of spindle whorls as grave goods and a particular social status. Only at two sites (Balatonkeresztúr-Réti-dűlő and Đakovo-Franjevac) did certain burials yield a greater number of grave goods and luxury items that might suggest a substantially 'richer' context, while the recorded grave goods from the three other sites did not provide comparable information.

It is interesting to observe that there is an apparent correlation on all four investigated sites between animal burials and sacrifice and the use of spindle whorls as grave goods. This offers a plausible explanation for the connection between the particular textile tool category and the Late Eneolithic fertility cults, usually associated with animal burials, which 'in essence acted out the sacrifice of the god of nature and cereals, ensuring the fertility and the rebirth of nature, important to prehistoric communities, because their livelihood depended on cereals and domestic animals'.[40]

Data analysis

Six quantitative traits of the sampled spindle whorls, based on the four measured values (diameter, height, diameter of the perforation and weight) and the two measurement ratios (diameter/height and weight/diameter ratio) were statistically tested on several levels of comparison. The main goal of this analysis was to investigate whether the differences in their distribution among 'site', 'culture' and 'period' categories were statistically significant.

None of the considered variables presented a normal (Gaussian) distribution.[41] Values showed a high tendency to cluster, both in the cases of the main measurements and the tested ratios. This occurred on all levels of sampling, from the small site samples to the complete sample of 901 spindle whorls. This was the main reason why the non-parametric tests were considered as a starting point for the comparison between the groups, besides the fact that the sample sizes differed in the number of specimens (especially in the case of the human burial spindle whorl samples).

The *Kruskal-Wallis* test was chosen for the comparison of more than two groups (sites, cultures and periods), while the *Mann-Whitney* test was chosen for the comparison of two groups (human burial spindle whorl samples to their 'culturally' corresponding assemblages and the site-to-site comparison when less than three sites were represented for a single 'cultural group').[42]

Despite the fact that there was no normal distribution of the inspected metric variables, two parametric methods were applied: One-Way ANOVA with LSD and Bonferroni Post Hoc Multiple Comparisons tests (for the comparison of more than two groups) or Independent- Samples T Test (for the comparison of two groups) were thus subsequently performed in each case.[43] In all tests the significance level was set at 0.05. These methods were applied in order to compare the mean values of the investigated metric variables among the samples and to see how each group relates to another.

'Site' variable was included to compare tool samples from different localities attributed to the same cultural-historically defined groups.

Although both Kruskal-Wallis and One-Way ANOVA tests suggested that the spindle whorl assemblages from different sites were significantly different, the LSD and Bonferroni Post Hoc Multiple Comparisons tests and Independent Samples T Test, where applied (in the case of Kostolac and Boleráz groups, which were both represented by only two sites), revealed some significant correlations. In all these cases at least three out of six tested variables were correspondent between at least two sites per 'culture', except in the case of the Proto-Boleráz group, which was represented by only one assemblage and thus not tested at this level.

The 'culture' variable was included to compare tool samples from clusters of sites, all attributed to the same cultural-historically defined groups ('cultures').

Both non-parametric Kruskal-Wallis and One-Way ANOVA tests showed that there was no significant resemblance between the assemblages of different 'cultures'. Nonetheless, the outcome of the LSD and Bonferroni Post Hoc Multiple Comparisons tests again displayed some interesting correlations. One could argue that the resemblance tends to be more significant, judging by the number of the corresponding variables, among groups that are chronologically 'closer' to each other. For example, the Boleráz group and Classical Baden show significant resemblance in all of the tested variables. Among the investigated 'cultures' they represent an example of a similar or even shared textile tradition. The Lasinja set sample seems to be more similar to the Boleráz group sample than it is to Classical Baden one. An almost identical correlation is evident between Furchenstich and Proto-Boleráz assemblages, which are again closely related in chronological terms. They show significant resemblances in the distribution among each other of five out of six tested variables. Both of these assemblages show similarities to the above-mentioned Lasinja sample, although the distribution of their perforation diameter, height and diameter/height ratio values was significantly different (Figs. 12.4 and 12.5).

It is interesting to mention that the Kostolac sample shows the lowest similarity to any other Middle or Late Eneolithic assemblage and is only comparable to the Early Bronze Age samples, respectively Vučedol and Somogyvár-Vinkovci assemblages. It could also be argued that this is the main reason why, on a 'period' level of comparison, Middle and Late Eneolithic samples look so different. Even though the Lasinja 'culture' assemblage contributed to the possible 'continuity', while being comparable to the two Late Eneolithic as well as to two Middle Eneolithic samples, spindle whorls assigned to the Kostolac 'culture' assemblage greatly contributed to their level of 'discontinuity' (Figs. 12.4 and 12.5).

The 'period' variable was included to compare tool samples (spindle whorl assemblages) from different cultural-historically defined groups chronologically divided into four period classes: Late Neolithic, Middle Eneolithic, Late Eneolithic and Early Bronze Age.[44]

Again, both the Kruskal-Wallis and One-Way ANOVA tests suggested that the samples divided into different classes were significantly different, although the LSD and Bonferroni Post Hoc Multiple Comparisons tests once more revealed patterns that were not specified a priori. Late Eneolithic and Early Bronze Age assemblages showed significant resemblance in comparisons of the three tested values: perforation diameter, weight and weight/diameter ratio, while Late Neolithic and Middle Eneolithic samples showed a corresponding resemblance in the case of the two tested values: perforation diameter and weight values. Interestingly, when compared, Middle and Late Eneolithic samples showed no significant correspondence in the distribution of any of the investigated variables (Figs. 12.4 and 12.5).

In order to test whether there are some significant differences between spindle whorl samples from human burials and the spindle whorl assemblages with which

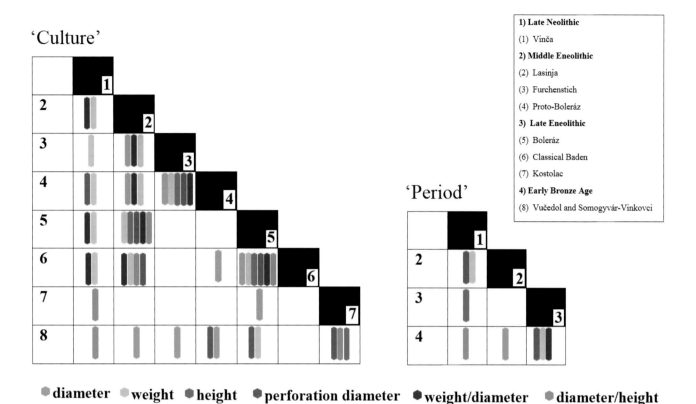

'Culture'

'Period'

1) **Late Neolithic**
(1) Vinča
2) **Middle Eneolithic**
(2) Lasinja
(3) Furchenstich
(4) Proto-Boleráz
3) **Late Eneolithic**
(5) Boleráz
(6) Classical Baden
(7) Kostolac
4) **Early Bronze Age**
(8) Vučedol and Somogyvár-Vinkovci

● **diameter** ● **weight** ● **height** ● **perforation diameter** ● **weight/diameter** ● **diameter/height**

Fig. 12.4 Grid-charts of the 'culture' and 'period' correspondence analysis, showing group-to-group resemblances in the distribution of metric values of spindle whorls. Metric variables are given in different colours.

they are 'culturally' associated, the 'human burial context' category was finally included in the 'culture' level of comparison. Both the Kruskal-Wallis and Independent Samples T Test confirmed their correlation in the case of all six metric traits that were tested.

To further investigate the 'cultural' dependence of the human burial spindle whorl samples, their qualitative traits, production quality, preservation status as well as their type and characteristics of decoration were tested, again with another non-parametric method. The Pearson Chi-Square test was used for their comparison with the assemblages to which they are 'culturally' related. The significance level was once again set at 0.05.

Only in the case of Classical Baden was there no significant difference found between the two respective pairs of samples, while in the examples of the Kostolac and Boleráz groups the quality of the production of the spindle whorls from burials was revealed to be significantly better than the average ('excellent', as opposed to 'good'). Regarding the decoration, only the Furchenstich sample proved to be independent, since the decorated spindle whorls from the cemetery may be considered uncommon (the complete Furchenstich assemblage holds less than 9% of the decorated spindle whorls). Also, the Furchenstich sample alone showed a significant difference regarding typology, where three lenticular and two discoid spindle whorls from

the burial contexts were not completely in accordance with the standards of the 'cultural' assemblage (the dominant type being discoidal, 41.5% followed by the convex type – 30.7%) (Fig. 12.6). In all other cases, burial spindle whorls were shown to be typologically 'culture'-dependent.

The same method was used again in order to investigate the correlations between the qualitative traits among different 'cultural' assemblages and, finally, between four different 'period' classes, based on their sample variances.

For all of the qualitative traits that were inspected, the hypothesis that they are 'culture' independent was rejected. Nonetheless, it is interesting to mention that, similar to the metric variables, qualitative traits tended to be 'shared' more often between the samples that are in a chronological sense more related. Even though typologically all samples show a tendency to be defined by the 'culture', some types are more frequently shared among different samples than others.

In terms of preservation status, it is evident that Furchenstich, Lasinja and Proto-Boleráz assemblages contain the most partially preserved spindle whorls, while the Classical Baden, Kostolac, Vučedol and Somogyvár-Vinkovci assemblages contain more complete ones, as does the Late Neolithic sample. This could be associated with both the types and sizes of the tools: the thin planate types tend to be more fragile than the sturdier spherical ones or bulging types of more prominent height.

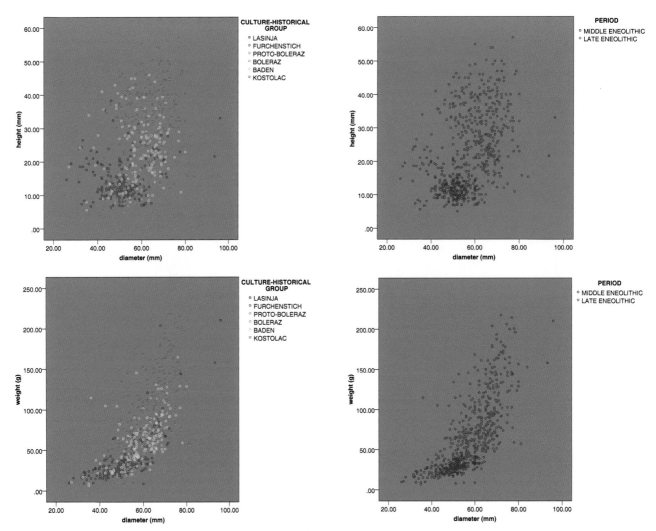

Fig. 12.5 The relationship between diameter and height and diameter and weight variables for the Eneolithic spindle whorls with respect to their 'cultural' affiliation (left) and 'periodical' placement (right).

As far as the quality of production is concerned, in the Proto-Boleráz, Late Vučedol and Somogyvár-Vinkovci samples, there are higher quantities of spindle whorls categorised as 'excellent', while in other assemblages the most frequent category comprises whorls of 'good' quality. Furthermore, it should be mentioned that a large portion of the Late Vučedol and Somogyvár-Vinkovci sample comes from the old excavations at Ljubljansko Barje-Ig, and it is quite probable that only the better-preserved tools were more frequently kept.

Decorated spindle whorls were under-represented in all contexts (less than ten percent), except in the context of Late Vučedol and Somogyvár-Vinkovci sample (33.33%). This might be, similar to preservation status, attributed to the biased sampling, although it should be mentioned that the Vučedol assemblage coming from the Gomolava and Slavča-Nova Gradiška sites also showed a slightly higher frequency of decorated whorls (15.8%), in comparison to other 'culture' assemblages.

Reflecting on the 'period' level of comparison, types and other qualitative traits again proved to be correlated. Spherical whorls are the dominant type in the Late Neolithic, while in the Middle Eneolithic convex and discoidal types are most frequently represented. In the Late Eneolithic, conical and biconical types became the most frequent, while the Early Bronze Age sample shows the absolute dominance of the biconical forms. This probably influenced the variance of the variable of preservation status, as explained above, since in all 'periods' the most represented category consists of the completely preserved spindle whorls, except in the Middle Eneolithic where partially preserved tools are the most common category in the sample.

Finally, the values of the production quality variable revealed that the most of the Late Neolithic spindle whorls are most frequently of 'good' production, which is followed by tools of 'medium', 'excellent' and (least frequently) 'poor' production. In the Middle Eneolithic, the ratio is similar, although 'medium' and 'excellent' categories are equally

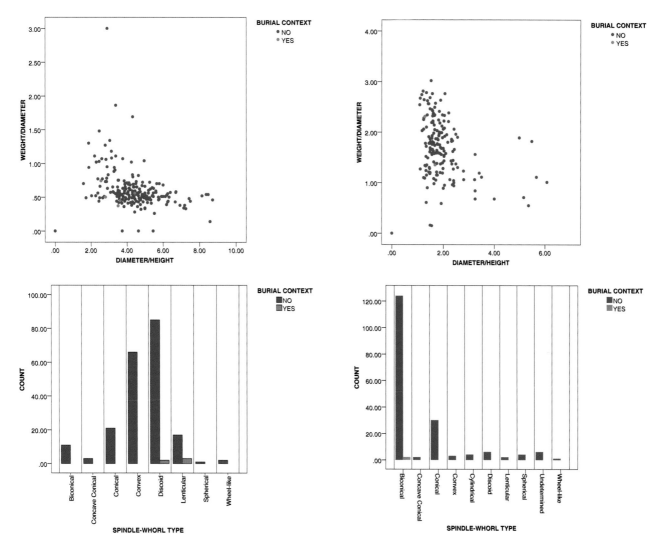

Fig. 12.6 Relationship between diameter/height and weight/diameter ratios for the Middle Eneolithic Furchenstich assemblage (left) and the Late Eneolithic Kostolac assemblage (right), together with the distribution of spindle whorl types (below). Samples from human burial contexts are designated in red colour.

represented in the sample. In the Late Eneolithic well-produced tools continue to be the most frequently represented, but followed by 'excellent', then 'medium' and, finally, least frequent were poorly produced spindle whorls. Finally, in the Early Bronze Age the 'excellent' production category is dominant, followed by the 'good', 'medium' and 'poor' production categories, in the respective order of representation.

Discussion of the results

Although assigning supposed symbolical meanings to textile tools seems to appear only occasionally in the course of the Eneolithic, at least judging by the burial ritual records, examples of spindle whorls from different cultural-historically defined contexts were used in this manner. The 'cross-cultural' comparison that was a part of the analysis showed that the practice of placing spindles or their whorls

in graves was not restricted to any one cultural group in this period and revealed the archetypal nature of the symbolical aspects assigned to these objects.

The analysed sample, however, demonstrated a recognisable 'culture'-dependent and consequently 'period'-related standardisation of the spindle whorls, in a typological, morphological and thus probably functional sense.

The 'site' groups considered in this study showed occasional correlation in the distribution of the investigated function-related spindle whorl properties. However, these instances should be more thoroughly investigated.

Furthermore, the same assemblages, when clustered in culture-historically defined groups, displayed a significant difference when tested with the same method, proving that the distribution of function-related variables among different samples is not coincidental and suggesting thereby that the tested variables are 'culture' dependent. In addition, those correlations that were detected between the particular assemblages of tools, at this level of comparison, could be interpreted as not at all random, since their 'connection' is explainable through the context of chronology.

Finally, this led to the observation of 'clustering' of the tested values according to the respective prehistoric 'period' classes, which enabled a consideration of the technological changes in the textile productions on a broader time scale.

The depositional character of the studied finds was added as an independent variable, in order to examine if the observed standardisation of the investigated tool type could reflect some sort of a specialisation of the spinning process among and within the investigated textile production structures.

The sampling method was intended to reveal trends in the textile technology in a broad chronological context of South-East and Central Europe. The aim was to observe the changes on an 'inter-cultural' and cross-regional scale. This is the main reason why the results of the described analysis are limited to answering specific questions in regard to the 'inner-cultural' conditions of the reviewed textile production structures and their dynamics.

The term 'production structure' was preferred in the portraying of the textile technologies. It was chosen mainly to avoid their definition as organised production, since this would imply several factors connected to social organisation, which were not the subject of the present research. Indeed, many factors, besides the social organisation (which may have been equally determined and altered under cultural and environmental influence), could have had an impact on the observed standardisation of tools, influencing a certain level of specialisation in the technological sense. Limited availability of the raw materials, their selection, the final conditioning of the product and the prevalence of specific techniques are just some of the possible explanations that were briefly addressed.

The data were also analysed with the intention to test if the examined special deposit character of the spindle whorls that were found in human burial contexts could be connected to the technological standard of these objects in the 'culture' as a whole (and consequently at the 'period' level). This relationship was examined statistically and it was found that, in terms of the pattern of occurrence of the quantitative characteristics studied (diameter, height, perforation diameter, weight, weight/diameter and diameter/height ratio), there was no statistically significant difference observed between the spindle whorls from human burials and the complete tool assemblages to which they are contextually related.

Research on spindle whorl functionality and its reliance on morphological traits has been a major focus of textile archaeology for decades.[45] So far, many methods have been applied in order to provide more insight into the nature of their dependence, with experimental research being the most valuable ones.[46] Two main interpretations have been

proposed for the reason for the great variance of metric traits evident in these tools. On one hand, it is suggested that it is related to the difference in fibres,[47] and on the other hand on the difference in techniques[48] that were used, while both, not excluding each other, predict that the most probable result of this diversity would be reflected in the quality and appearance of the final products (that is, the threads and consequently textiles).

An interesting peak in the sizes and weights recorded in the Late Eneolithic Kostolac sample could be ascribed to either the introduction of a new technique of fibre production, a particular raw material preference, a specific final product demand and standard, or be due to all of these factors combined. As shown by the 'later' Vučedol and Somogyvár-Vinkovci sample, this trend continues in the 3rd millennium BC as well, and it could be labelled as a peculiarity of the Late Eneolithic to Early Bronze Age transition.

It is more than probable that these changes in the proportions of tools influenced the character of the end product. In any case, this alteration in spindle whorl morphology is illustrative of greater adaptations at all levels of the production structure, ranging quite probably from the raw material procurement to the making, and finally the use, of the textiles. Investigating their reasons and origins is thus relevant not only for a better understanding of the textile production technology of the particular 'cultural groups', but also, as proven in the analysis, of the entire 'periods'. Even though these changes, possibly to be considered as innovations, appear to be 'culture-related', they also reveal patterns of 'inter-cultural' transmission on the chronological scale.

As mentioned above, animal sacrifices were found on all four sites that yielded human burial spindle whorls. The custom of animal burials can be traced from the Neolithic to the Bronze Age, although, in the context of the investigated region, most of the known occurrences date to the Late Eneolithic.[49] Furthermore, the presence of the particular animal species in the examined burial rituals may be indicative of their importance in the formation of the basic conditions of existence, or even suggestive of subsistence strategies and economic factors (cattle and pig are the main represented animals in the investigated Boleráz,[50] Baden[51] and Kostolac,[52] while sheep and goat are the most common in the Furchenstich[53] burial contexts).[54]

The zooarchaeological analysis of the faunal remains from the Pod Kotom-jug pri Krogu cemetery revealed sheep/goat as the most commonly found animal (66.7%) in the burials (reflecting the fact that children were buried with sheep or goat, women also, in addition to cattle, while men were buried with sheep, goat, cattle and red deer).[55] Extrapolated to the context of textile production and particularly to its fibre procurement/production level, this may help propose an explanation for the observed trends. If we assume such an early use of sheep wool for textiles, this could explain the dominance of the smaller size and lower weight values of spindle whorls in the Middle Eneolithic sample. On the other hand, the extremely high weight values, typical for the Late Eneolithic (particularly Kostolac) and Early Bronze Age assemblages, may be connected with the spinning of substantially longer (presumably plant) fibres and plying[56] of heavier, thick yarns or ropes.[57] Considering the fact that animal traction has been confirmed for the period,[58] harnessing of animals, increased agriculture, mobility and transport may all have promoted the trend reflected in the massiveness of the Late Eneolithic tools.

Discerning textile production structures and the many factors that influenced their change could provide us with more insight into the concepts of tradition and innovation, since they might offer a wider perspective of the social and environmental contexts that are crucial in order to address the dynamics of the technological developments.

Conclusions

The form of symbolism within the textile production system proposed in this paper is argued through a number of chronologically and 'culturally' defined examples of the Eneolithic textile production traditions recorded in the Pannonian Plain region. Spindle whorls, the most commonly recorded textile tools used in the transformation of fibre to thread and thread to cord, were documented and statistically compared on several levels of analysis, in order to demonstrate the inner homogeneity of separate 'cultural groups' and differences between them. The denotative and representative character of these objects, revealed by the results of the analysis, was directly connected to the textile technology, respectively fibre selection/production and processing.

With regard to their occurrences in the human burials investigated in this study, it is proposed that the specific developments in the fibre production and processing acted as a generator, or at least as an amplifier for the denotation of symbolical meanings to aspects of the technological process. These aspects, represented by the objects ritually placed in the burials, might be suggestive of their role and their attributes in the wider context of social and economic realities.

It appears not to be a coincidence, but a symptomatic occurrence that the spindle whorls deposited in burial contexts were morphologically and presumably functionally characteristic of the typical range of spindle whorls in use in the community's textile traditions. It is difficult to discern whether these morphological and thus functional traits should be connected to the prevailing raw material(s), dominant spinning technique(s) or possibly both. In both cases, which are likely to be connected to each other, it may be expected that they reflect to a certain degree the character of the final product. Unfortunately, because of the lack of actual evidence in the archaeological record, it is difficult to discuss the nature of this presumed connection.

Since the nature of the examples from the 'special deposits' was shown to be dependent on the characteristics of the assemblages of the archaeological culture they relate to, it is considered valid to describe them as reflective of the main technological preferences of their time of use. Consequently, they may be considered as an important source of information for the investigation of changes in the technology. The examples used in the burial ritual represent the main 'standards' observed in contemporary textile production and could be interpreted, among other things, as symbolical of their meanings. This dependence, therefore, did not erase the line between the object's meaning(s) and its functions(s), although it intertwined them in the resumed framework of the technological change.

In an effort to dispute this dichotomy, another one rose in the course of the analysis: a division between the Middle and Late Eneolithic spinning traditions. Substantial differences observed between these temporally separated textile productions propose numerous questions that have yet to be addressed. The addition of the assemblages from the Early Eneolithic period in a future analysis could result in a better understanding of the technological nature of this division.

Notes

1   I wish to thank everyone who provided me with the data for this research, in particular Jacqueline Balen, Alenka Tomaž, Szilvia Fábián and Tünde Horváth, who generously gave logistic help and comments during the process of recording of the human burial spindle whorl sample. My special gratitude goes to the *TOPOI Excellence Cluster* for making this research possible. Additionally, I would also like to acknowledge the *TOPOI A4 – TEXTILE REVOLUTION* research group, whose members invested full effort in guiding my research.

2   Site sample standard was set at minimum three recorded spindle whorls with complete metric and chronological data.

3   Further details on the described finds, their burial contexts and sites are published by the authors in the referenced site publications.

4   Classical Baden – 11 sites (147 tools), Boleráz group – two sites (32 tools), Furchenstich complex – 10 sites (205 tools), Lasinja – six sites (47 tools), Proto-Boleráz – one site (37 tools), Vinča – three sites (65 tools), Vučedol – two sites (38 tools), Somogyvár-Vinkovci – four sites (17 tools), Late Vučedol/Somogyvár-Vinkovci – one site (141 tools).

5   Slavča-Nova Gradiška and Gomolava are the only systematically excavated sites included in the study.

6   Grömer 2005; Chmielewski and Gardyński 2010.

7   Crewe 1998, 12.

8   Gleba 2008, 3.

9   Andersson 2003, 25.

10   Herbig Maier 2011; Karg 2011; Médard 2012; Harris 2014.

11 Ryder 1981; Halstead 2011; Andersson Strand 2014; Nosch 2014.
12 Sherratt 1981.
13 Barber 1991, 25.
14 Gleba 2008, 103–106.
15 Ryder 1983; Costin 1993.
16 Andersson 2003, 25; Kimbrough 2006.
17 Barber 1994, 37.
18 Barber 1991, 66; Breniquet 2008, 110–112.
19 Mazăre 2014, 21.
20 Kania 2015.
21 Nonetheless, it should be mentioned that, according to the current state of research, there is a great disproportion in the number of unearthed graves between both the periods and the individual regions (Bánffy *et al.* 2003; Lichter 2003), which may be reflected in the sample.
22 Škobrne 1999, 25; Blečić 2004: 61–62; Čondić 2010, 38–43; Karavanić 2011.
23 Šavel 2009, 59–138.
24 Šavel 2004, 42.
25 Šlaus 2000.
26 Šavel 2004, 42–44.
27 Torma 1973.
28 Bánffy 1991.
29 One object associated with a human sacrifice burial at the Balatonőszöd-Temetői dűlő site, which was originally published as a possible spindle whorl, was disregarded as a tool for spinning due to its irregular unsymmetrical shape and the asymmetrical position of its skewed perforation (Horváth 2013, 262–264). Consequently, this find was not included in the final sample and was left out of all of the analyses.
30 Horváth 2013, 360–361.
31 Archaeozoological finds included 2½- to 3-year-old cattle head and limb remains (time of death: October/April), 12–20-month-old sheep's head, vertebra and limb (time of death: March/November) and a 4- to 6-month-old pig's limb (time of death, August/October). Horváth 2013, 273–274.
32 Horváth 2010, 2.
33 Horváth 2010, 18.
34 Fábián 2014, 158.
35 Fábián 2014, 7.
36 Balen 2011, 37.
37 Balen 2011, 51.
38 Balen 2011, 58.
39 Balen 2011, 36–37, 135.
40 György 2013, 627.
41 Normal distribution and hypothesis testing are further discussed in VanPool and Leonard 2011, 86–96.
42 For more information about non-parametric tests for comparing groups, see VanPool and Leonard 2011, 262–284.
43 Analysis of variance is further explained in VanPool and Leonard 2011, 153–177.
44 Despite its integration with the Boleráz group (Stadler *et al.* 2001, 543) the Proto-Boleráz sample recorded from the Abony site was placed within the Middle Eneolithic assemblage together with Lasinja and Furchenstich spindle whorls. This was mainly due to its transitional character (Horváth 2001, 83), typological fusion with Lasinja and Furchenstich

(Horváth 2009, 105), its stylistic affiliation with 'stab and drag' or 'furchenstich' decoration complex (Kalicz 2001) and absolute dates that cluster between 3700 and 3500 BC (Horváth 2009, 104). The Vučedol sample recorded from the Gomolava and Slavča-Nova Gradiška sites was placed within the Early Bronze Age assemblage, together with the Somogyvár-Vinkovci spindle whorls. This is mainly because the big sample recorded from the Ljubljansko Barje-Ig site, which is only relatively dated (Korošec and Korošec 1969) to the 3rd millennium BC, did not permit finer classification according to the particular cultural-historically defined phases.
45 Ryder 1968; Barber 1991.
46 Médard 2006; Andersson Strand 2010.
47 Barber 1991, 52; Kimbrough 2006.
48 Mazăre 2014, 21.
49 György 2013, 628.
50 Horváth 2012, 119–125.
51 Horváth 2012, 119–125; Fábián 2014, 8.
52 Balen 2011, 165.
53 Šavel 2009, 137.
54 Although small ruminants did not have the same individual role as cattle in the animal burials at the Balatonőszöd-Temetői dűlő site, sheep were the most represented (they are the characteristic animal of mass sacrifices and the proportion of pregnant ewes and foetuses/new-born lambs is very high) (Horváth 2012, 119, 125–128). Despite the general dominance of cattle in sacrificial pits in the period, at Balatonkeresztúr pigs seem to dominate and the animal husbandry practices of the inhabitants of the settlement are characterised by the significant presence of the drought-tolerant small ruminants like sheep and goat (Fábián 2014, 8–9).
55 Šavel 2009, 137.
56 Hochberg 1979, 21; Barber 1991, 52.
57 Vakirtzi 2014, 53.
58 Fabiš 2005; Johannsen 2005; Isaakidou 2006.

Bibliography

Andersson, E. 2003 *Tools for textile production – from Birka and Hedeby*. Birka Studies 8. Stockholm

Andersson Strand, E. 2010 Experimental textile archaeology. In E. Andersson Strand, M. Gleba, U. Mannering, C. Munkholt and M. Ringgaard (eds.), *North European Symposium for Archaeological Textiles X*. Ancient Textiles Series 5. Oxford and Oakville, 1–3.

Andersson Strand, E. 2014 Sheep, wool and textile production. An interdisciplinary approach to the complexity of wool working. In C. Breniquet and C. Michel (eds.), *Wool Economy in the Ancient Near East and the Aegean. From the Beginnings of Sheep Husbandry to Institutional Textile Industry*. Ancient Textiles Series 17. Oxford and Philadelphia, 41–51.

Balen, J. 2011 *Đakovo – Franjevac. Late Eneolithic Settlement*. Musei Archaeologici Zagrabiensis Catalogiet Monographiae VII. Zagreb.

Bánffy, E. 1991 Cult and archaeological context in Middle and South-East Europe in the Neolithic and Chalcolithic. *Antaeus* 19–20, 183–249.

Bánffy, E., Bondár, M. and Virág, Z. 2003 Copper Age religion and beliefs. In V. Zsolt (ed.), *Hungarian Archaeology at the Turn of the Millennium. Copper Age*. Budapest, 132–137.

Barber, E. J. W. 1991 *Prehistoric Textiles. The Development of Cloth in the Neolithic and Bronze Ages with Special Reference to the Aegean*. Princeton.

Barber, E. W. 1994 *Women's Work: The First 20,000 Years – Women, Cloth and Society in Early Times*. New York.

Blečić, M. 2004 Grobnik u željezno doba. *Vjesnik Arheološkog muzeja u Zagrebu* 37, 47–117.

Breniquet, C. 2008 *Essai sur le tissage en Mésopotamie, des premières communautés sédentaires au milieu du IIIe millénaire avant J.-C.* Travaux de la Maison René-Ginouvès 5. Paris.

Chmielewski, T. and Gardyński, L. 2010 New frames of archaeometrical description of spindle whorls: a case study of the Late Eneolithic spindle whorls from the 1C site in Gródek, District of Hrubieszów, Poland. *Archaeometry* 52.5, 869–881.

Čondić, N. 2010 Liburnski grobovi na Zadarskom poluotoku. *Diadora* 24, 27–55.

Costin, C. L. 1993 Textiles, women and political economy in Late Prehispanic Peru. In B. Isaac (ed.), *Research in Economic Anthropology*. Greenwich, 29–59.

Crewe, L. 1998 *Spindle Whorls – A Study of Form, Function and Decoration in Prehistoric Bronze Age Cyprus*. Studies in Mediterranaen Archaeology Pocket-book 149. Jonsered.

Fábián, S. 2014 A badeni kultúra településtörténete a dél-balatoni régióban az újabb kutatási eredmények alapján. Unpublished PhD thesis, University of Budapest.

Fabiš, M. 2005 Pathological alteration of cattle skeletons, evidence for the draught exploitation of animals? In J. Davies, M. Fabiš, I. Mainland, V. Richards and R. Thomas (eds.), *Diet and Health in Past Animal Populations: Current Research and Future Directions*. Oxford, 58–62.

Gleba, M. 2008 *Textile Production in Pre-Roman Italy*. Ancient Textile Series 4. Oxford.

Grömer, K. 2005 Efficiency and technique – experiments with original spindle whorl. In P. Bichler, K. Grömer, R. Hofmann-de Keijzer, A. Kern and H. Reschreiter (eds.), *'Hallstatt Textiles.' Technical Analysis Investigation and Experiment on Iron Age Textiles*. British Archaeological Reports International Series 1351. Oxford, 81–90.

György, L. 2013 Late Copper Age animal burials in the Carpathian Basin. In A. Anders and G. Kulcsár (eds.), *Moments in Time. Papers Presented to Pál Raczky on his 60th Birthday*. Ősrégészeti tanulmányok/Prehistoric Studies I. Budapest, 627–642.

Halstead, P. and Isaakidou, V. 2011 Revolutionary secondary products: the development and significance of milking, animal-traction and wool-gathering in later prehistoric Europe and the Near East. In T. Wilkinson, A. Sherratt, S. and J. Bennet (eds.), *Interweaving Worlds: Systemic Interactions in Eurasia, 7th to 1st Millennia BC*. Oxford, 61–76.

Harris, S. 2014 Flax fibre: innovation and change in the Early Neolithic. A technological and material perspective. *Textile Society of America Symposium Proceedings*, Paper 913 (https://digitalcommons.unl.edu/tsaconf/913/, accessed 2 May 2018).

Herbig, C. and Maier, U. 2011 Flax for oil or fibre? Morphometric analysis of flax seeds and new aspects of flax cultivation in Late Neolithic wetland settlements in southwest Germany. *Vegetation History and Archaeobotany* 20.6, 527–533.

Hochberg, B. 1979 *Spin, Span, Spun: Fact and Folklore for Spinners*. Santa Cruz, California.

Horváth, L. A. 2001 *Interpretationsmöglichkeiten der urzeitlichen Kultgruben (Archäologische und religionsgeschichtliche Analyse Aufgrund einer kupferzeitlichen Kultstätte) – Az őskori kultuszgödrök értelmezésének lehetőségei (Egy rézkori kultuszhely régészeti és vallástörténeti elemzése)*. MFMÉ–Studia Archaeologica 7. Szeged, 43–89.

Horváth, T. 2009 The intercultural connections of the Baden 'culture'. In G. Ilon (ed.), *ΜΩΜΟΣ VI. Őskoros kutatók VI. Összejövetele*. Szombathely, 101–149.

Horváth, T. 2010 Transcendent phenomena in the Late Copper Age Boleráz/Baden settlement uncovered at Balatonőszöd-Temetői dűlő: human and animal 'depositions'. *Journal of Neolithic Archaeology* (http://dx.doi.org/10.12766/jna.2010.54, accessed 2 May 2018).

Horváth, T. 2012 Animal deposits in the Late Copper Age settlement of Balatonőszöd-Temetői dűlő, Hungary. In A. Pluskowski (ed.), *The Ritual Killing and Burial of Animals. European Perspectives*. Oxford, 115–137.

Horváth, T. 2013 *A Balatonőszöd–Temetői dűlő (M7/S10) lelőhely őskori településrészei. Digitális kiadás*. Budapest.

Isaakidou, V. 2006 Ploughing with cows: Knossos and the 'secondary products revolution'. In D. Serjeantson and V. Field (eds.), *Animals in the Neolithic of Britain and Europe*. Oxford, 95–112.

Johannsen, N. 2005 Palaeopathology and Neolithic cattle traction: methodological issues and archaeological perspectives. In J. Davies, M. Fabis, I. Mainland, M. Richards and R. Thomas (eds.), *Diet and Health in Past Animal Populations: Current Research and Future Directions*. Oxford, 39–51.

Kalicz, N. 2001 Die Protoboleráz-Phase an der Grenze von zwei Epochen. In P. Roman and S. Diamandi (eds.), *Cernavodă III. – Boleráz – Ein vorgeschichtliches Phänomen zwischen dem Oberrhein und der unteren Donau. Symposium Mangalia/ Neptun, 18–24. Oktober 1999*. Studia Danubiana, Ser. Symp. 2. Bucureşti, 385–435.

Kania, K. 2015. Soft yarns, hard facts? Evaluating the results of a large scale hand-spinning experiment. *Journal of Archaeological and Anthropological Sciences* 7, 113–130.

Karavanić, S. 2011 Temple rings and the structure of grave goods found in the Velika Gorica graveyard. *Prilozi Instituta za arheologiju u Zagrebu* 27, 83–94.

Karg, S. 2011 New research on the cultural history of the useful plant *Linum usitatissimum* L. (flax), a resource for food and textiles for 8,000 years, *Vegetation History and Archaeobotany* 20.6, 507–508 (https://doi.org/10.1007/s00334–011–0326-y, accessed 15 April 2018).

Kimbrough, C. K. 2006 Spindle whorls, ethnoarchaeology and the study of textile production in third millennium BCE northern Mesopotamia: a methodological approach. Unpublished PhD thesis, New York University.

Korošec, P. and Korošec, J. 1969 *Najdbe s koliščarskih naselbin pri Igu na Ljubljanskem barju/Fundgut der Pfahlbausiedlungen bei Ig am Laibacher Moor*. Arheološki katalogi Slovenije 3. Ljubljana.

Lichter, C. 2003 Continuity and change in burial customs – examples from the Carpathian Basin. In L. Nikolova (ed.),

Early Symbolical Systems for Communication in Southeast Europe. British Archaeologocal Reports International Series 1139. London, 135–152.

Mazăre, P. 2014 Investigating Neolithic and Copper Age textile production in Transylvania (Romania). Applied methods and results. In M. Harlow, C. Michel and M.-L. Nosch (eds.), *Prehistoric, Ancient Near Eastern and Aegean Textiles and Dress. An interdisciplinary anthology*. Ancient Textiles Series 18. Oxford and Philadelphia, 1–42.

Médard, F. 2006 *Les activités de filage sur les sites néolithiques du plateau suisse. Système technique de production du fil dans son contexte économique et social*. Monographies du CRA 28. Paris.

Médard, F. 2012 Switzerland: Neolithic period. In M. Gleba and U. Mannering (eds.), *Textiles and Textile Production in Europe: From Prehistory to AD 400*. Ancient Textiles Series 11. Oxford and Oakville, 367–377.

Nosch, M.-L. 2014 The Aegean Wool Economies of the Bronze Age. *Textile Society of America Symposium Proceedings*, Paper 900 (http://digitalcommons.unl.edu/tsaconf/900/. accessed 30 October 2018).

Parsons, J. R. and Parsons, M. H. 1990 *Maguey Utilization in Central Highland Mexico: An Archaeological Ethnography*. Anthropological Papers of the Museum of Anthropology. University of Michigan 82. Ann Arbor.

Ryder, M. L. 1968 The origin of spinning. *Textile History* 1, 73–82.

Ryder, M. L. 1981 Fleece changes in sheep. In M. Jones and G. Dimbleby (eds.), *The Environment of Man: The Iron Age to the Anglo-Saxon Period*. British Archaeological Report British Series 87. Oxford, 215–229.

Ryder, M. L. 1983 *Sheep and Men*. London.

Šavel, I., 2004 Eneolithic cremation cemetery. In D. Prešern (ed.), Zemlja pod vašimi nogami. Arheologija na avtocestah Slovenije. Vodič po najdiščih./The Earth Beneath Your Feet. *Archeology on the Motorways in Slovenia. Guide to Sites*. Ljubljana, 41–46.

Šavel, I. 2009 *Pod Kotom-jug pri Krogu I/II. Arheologija na avtocestah Slovenije*. Ljubljana.

Sherratt, A. G. 1981 Plough and pastoralism: aspects of the Secondary Products Revolution. In I. Hodder, G. Isaac and N. Hammond (eds.), *Pattern of the Past. Studies in Honour of David Clarke*. Cambridge, 261–306.

Škobrne, Ž. 1999 *Budinjak: Kneževski tumul*. Zagreb.

Šlaus, M. 2000 *Results of the Anthropological Analysis of Cremated Human Skeletal Remains from the Krog Site in Slovenia. Technical report*, Zagreb.

Stadler, P., Draxler, S., Friesinger, H., Kutschera, W., Priller, A., Rom, W., Steirer, P. and Wild, E. M. 2001 Absolute chronology for early civilizations in Austria and Central Europe using ^{14}C dating with accelerator mass spectrometry with special results for the absolute chronology of the Baden culture. In P. Roman and S. Diamandi (eds.), *Cernavodă III. – Boleráz – Ein vorgeschichtliches Phänomen zwischen dem Oberrhein und der unteren Donau. Symposium Mangalia/Neptun, 18–24. Oktober 1999*. Studia Danubiana, Ser. Symp. 2. Bucureşti, 541–562.

Torma, I. 1973 Die Boleráz Gruppe in Ungarn. *Symposium über die Entstehung und Chronologie der Badener Kultur*. Bratislava, 483–512.

Vakirtzi, S., Koukouli-Chrysanthaki, C. and Papadopoulos, S. 2014 Spindle whorls from two prehistoric sites on Thassos. In M. Harlow, C. Michel and M.-L. Nosch (eds.), *Prehistoric, Ancient Near Eastern and Aegean Textiles and Dress. An Interdisciplinary Anthology*. Ancient Textiles Series 18. Oxford and Philadelphia, 43–57.

VanPool, T. L. and Leonard, R. D. 2011 *Quantitative Analysis in Archaeology*. Chichester, West Sussex.

Plant textiles in a grave mound of the Early Bronze Age in eastern Romania

Neculai Bolohan and Ciprian-Cătălin Lazanu

Introduction

There are many investigated prehistoric sites in eastern Romania on which archaeological traces of textile production have been identified as a household craft alongside other well-known crafts of pottery or metallurgy. Despite the finds of textile production equipment, such as spindle whorls, loom weights and textile impressions, there so far have not been any traces of the textiles themselves discovered in archaeological excavations.[1] Among the most striking finds attesting the practice of spinning and weaving in the prehistoric period is an example from a nearly forgotten old excavation at Sucidava-Celei on the Danube in Romania; however, it has not yet been fully re-evaluated.[2] In recent years, the first steps forward were taken on the way of an overdue assessment of the issue of textile manufacture, taking into account the artefacts (spindle whorls, loom weights, textile imprints on pots) related to the processing of natural fibres and yarns.[3]

Due to local development works, an archaeological investigation project was started in eastern Romania, north of Popeni village, Găgeşti commune, Vaslui County (46°22′9.01″N and 27°58′48.73″E, GPS).[4] The site is located at the western extension of the Early Bronze Age Yamnaya burial barrow groups that are still visible in today's landscape. During the excavations, the western half of a tumulus was discovered and partially explored; this mound had not previously been mentioned by the archaeological monographs dedicated to the area under study.

Study area

The study area is situated in south-eastern Europe, east of the Carpathians, and is a part of the Elan basin. This area constitutes part of the Bârlad Plateau, a subdivision of the Moldova Plateau. The main geographical features are represented by: (1) the lower terraces of the Middle Elan River, and (2) the hilly areas and the adjacent slopes to the east and to the west of the river as we may see in Fig. 13.1.

The mound of Popeni is located at the southern extension of the Pogoceni hill, on the interfluve between the Elan River and the Culubăţ/Pogăcean creek. The valley is bordered on the west by Popeni Hill (169 m) and east by Rupturii Hill (193.7 m), which slopes gently down to the Elan valley.[5] A series of interfluvial peaks, oriented north-west–south-east, bound the Elan valley.

Natural environment

The main hydrographic unit is represented by the Elan River, a right-side tributary of the Prut River. It forms a relatively wide valley at the confluence, and has an oscillating current flow of 20 l/s in the upper basin and 72.5 l/s in the lower area. The typology of soils in the Elan valley consists of mollisols (chernozem, cambic chernozem), hydromorphic soils in the lower areas of the meadow, halomorphic soils and undeveloped soils, erodosoils or regosols.[6]

The natural vegetation of the middle Elan basin is characterised by a steppe and forest steppe vegetation with grasslands in which there appear cereal crops species, dicotyledonous species, shrubs and bushes. In the nearby meadow, there is a considerable amount of common reed. It is very likely that flax was cultivated here in the Bronze Age, given that this plant prefers cambic chernozem soils, well represented in the area under study. A good argument for the use of flax in this period is given by the palaeobotanical remains of the dwelling number 1 from Sucidava-Celei which, besides the textiles, includes *Linum usitatissimum* L. and *Camelina sativa* L. seeds.[7] The same

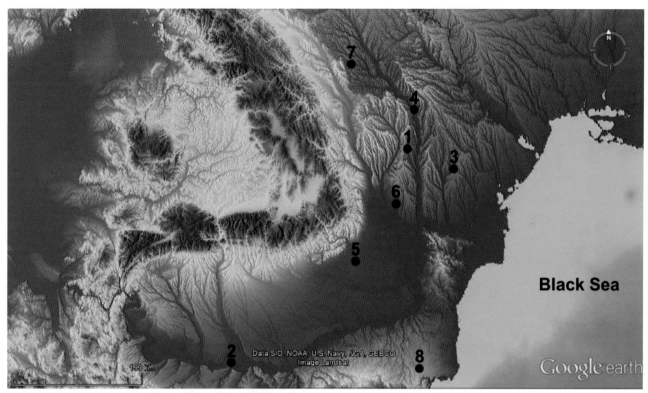

Fig. 13.1 A map of the area discussed in this paper and the archaeological sites mentioned in the text (by Ciprian Lazanu): 1. Popeni; 2. Sucidava-Celei; 3. Bălăbani; 4. Sărăţeni; 5. Smeeni-Movila Mare; 6. Lieşti-Movila Arbănaşu; 7. Prăjeni-Nelipeşti; 8. Plačidol-Goljamata Mogila, Google Earth/Maps-For-Free Relief http://ge-map-overlays.appspot.com/world-maps/maps-for-free-relief, accessed 4 August 2015).

can be expected for the use of nettle fibres, as already demonstrated for other areas.[8] Therefore, the specific environment of the middle Elan basin offers the possibility for processing natural fibres (rushes, nettle) or cultivating plants for fibre (flax).

The steppe and forest steppe fauna is relatively poor and is dominated by a series of specific rodents. Besides these, there are hare, birds and reptiles present.[9]

The conditions described above suggest that the life of the Early Bronze Age communities was in close relation with the type of environment. This triggered an intense exploitation of local sources and the diversification of domestic crafts such as textile manufacturing, which had a good start in the local Neolithic and Chalcolithic.[10]

Previous archaeological research

Research carried out in the vicinity of the mound includes two archaeological foci: a group of specific ash lenses dated to the Late Bronze Age and a settlement dated to the 2nd–3rd century AD. These two sites are separated by the River Elan.[11] Following the field research, in March 2013 a necropolis dated to the 2nd–3rd century AD was identified.[12] Paradoxically, although the area had been visited by archaeologists and monographs have been dedicated to the area of Popeni, the mound was not mentioned previously.

The current archaeological research

Only the western half of the tumulus T1 is preserved, the other half was destroyed by roadworks during construction of the DN (National Road) 244 B. The eastern slope of the preserved mound was therefore created by the workers at the end of the 1960s and is now a stable slope preserved by vegetation. The tumulus has a height of 2.80 m above the current level in the northern extremity; the N–S diameter is approximately 59 m and the E–W diameter is approximately 46 m.

The archaeological research of the tumulus T1 included excavation of the section S I which was dug mechanically and manually. This trench was oriented E–W, with a length of 42 m and a width of 2.70–2.80 m and with Point 0 (P0)[13] in the south-east corner.

The following stratigraphy has been registered: 1. arable layer observable down to −0.30 m with no archaeological content; 2. a transitional loose light brown layer with a thickness of approximately 0.50 m with no archaeological content; 3. a compact light brown layer, with a thickness in the centre of T1 of 1.70 m and archaeological content represented by three sherds and very small bone fragments extracted from a rodent burrow; 4. the funerary context that was initially identified in a form of a mineralised textile impression from −1.80 m; 5. the sterile geological layer starts at −2.45 m.

Fig. 13.2 Different stages of the archaeological excavation: a. general view on top of the wooden structure and the mats; b. the eastern side of the wooden structure; c. detail of the funerary pit; d. the skeleton within the funerary pit (a–d Neculai Bolohan photo archive).

The funerary context

The preserved half of the tumulus covers a funerary structure that survived in the form of a mineralised textile structure at the bottom (−2.25 m) of the northern profile (Fig. 13.2 a). By gradual digging we noticed that the textile structure stretches eastward and is situated slightly obliquely (ENE) from the central axis of S I. In the first stage of the excavation, the textile structure had an approximate size of 2.25×1.47 m and it was oriented along the long axis direction (WNW). The traces of textile fabric were 'fixed' by nine fragments of wood placed along the long axis (ENE) of the funerary contexts and representing fragments of the ends of seven beams or thick planks arranged side by side, from north to south (Fig. 13.2 b). In the middle of the described context there were no traces of fabric or wood fragments (Fig. 13.2 a). This suggests a burial, which had been covered with a textile 'structure', covered by the wooden flooring. Over time, due to the action of chemical and physical factors,[14] the wooden structure had decayed and had fallen into the funeral pit, entailing the destruction of the fabric in the central area of the pit (Figs. 13.2 a and c).

By gradually scraping the earth we uncovered a mineralised textile surface of 4.90 m along the E–W axis and 2.90 m along the N–S axis (Fig. 13.2 a; Fig. 13.3). It

consists of a succession of fabrics and mats covered with a wooden structure consisting of very thick beams. The excavation continued from −2.25 m above the wooden beams. At this point a layer of earth followed, brown with yellow sterile spots, with a thickness of 0.47 m. After this level the rectangular outline of the burial pit appeared with a yellow border and dark brown fill with a yellow spotted content. The pit has the following dimensions: 2 m on the E–W axis and 1.15 m on the N–S axis (Fig. 13.2 c).

At the bottom of the funeral pit, a human skeleton was discovered in a position crouched to the left. The left hand was flexed with the palm at the skull level; the right hand was placed in the pelvic area and the legs were strongly bent to the left side (Fig. 13.2 d). The skeleton's orientation was WNW. The osteological remains were in an extremely poor state of preservation. In the area of the right foot metatarsals and phalanges, a lump of yellow ochre was recovered and another lump of ochre was found in the area 0.30 m in front of the skull, in the north-west corner of the pit.[15] The bottom of the pit was at −3.25 m against the southern profile. There were no traces of archaeological material, although the earth filling was sieved and washed. The human osteological remains, extremely loose and crumbly were removed and conserved.

Popeni 2013
T1/M1

Fig. 13.3 General plan of the funerary context (drawings: Neculai Bolohan and Ciprian Lazanu; graphic design: Tudor Mandache and Sebastian Drob).

The funerary shroud

A textile shroud of 4.90×2.90 m was situated on top of the Early Bronze Age burial (Fig. 13.2 a). The material consisted of a succession of textiles and mats, with different surfaces (Fig. 13.4 a–b), covering the grave structure, and have been categorised as pieces of mineralised mats and pseudomorphic replaced textile mineral.[16] This was the first time an archaeological textile consisting of three-dimensional reliefs and negative impressions had been recovered from a Yamnaya (pit-grave) in eastern Romania.

The mats

After finishing the salvage excavation, we attempted to analyse the mats from the grave.[17] In the funerary context, there were unearthed two different types of mats:

1. Semi-decayed mats recovered from the top of the grave. It was very difficult to determine the type of the fibre/s or of the weaving pattern. It was possible to identify some of the vegetal fibre features, even though in some specific areas the morphology was very heterogeneous. The results might be supplemented through the analysis of phytoliths and pollen.
2. Heavily mineralised fragments of mats discovered on top of the skull and beneath the upper body at the bottom of the burial pit.[18] The textile in the area is preserved as a black-reddish layer with a thickness of 1–2 mm, which overlies the soil surface. With some exceptions in the area of the skull, no separate fibres were distinguishable; consequently, no observations concerning the morphology were possible.

The objectives of the macroscopic analysis were:

a. The first step was to determine the structural characteristics of the threads. The visual examination allowed the identification of very well-separated threads (Fig. 13.5 a) and the presence of some threads primarily spun in the Z twist direction. The angle of twisting is very hard to calculate, but one can say that in some places it might be, when looking at the torsion angle, very close to 0° (Fig. 13.5 b 3). The diameter of the threads is between 1–1.50 mm, meaning a coarse textile.[19]
b. The thickness of the textile is estimated according to the diameter of the warp and weft threads diameters. In the case under study, there are no major differences between them. The diameter ranges from 1 to 1.50 mm.
c. The density of the mats is assessed by counting the number of threads per cm. Thus, for the warp there are 2 threads per cm and for the weft there are 4–5 threads per cm (Figs. 13.5 b 1–2).
d. The structure of the mats is represented by the manner of combination of the warp threads and weft threads. So far, all the mats seem to be manufactured in an open tabby weave.[20] This kind of fabric, open tabby weave (Fig. 13.5 c–d), might be used for manufacturing veils.[21]
e. According to the visual analysis, a warp-weighted loom can be presumed to have been used for making the mats. These mats have different lengths (1.20–1.60 m), but a constant 0.80 m width (Fig. 13.4 a). In some cases the black colour of the starting border and of selvedges might be visible (Fig. 13.5 a).

As already stated, the techniques of weaving employed are inferable on the basis of the preserved mineralised

Fig. 13.4 Image of the south-eastern mat: a. general view and the dimension; b. detail (a–b Neculai Bolohan photo archive).

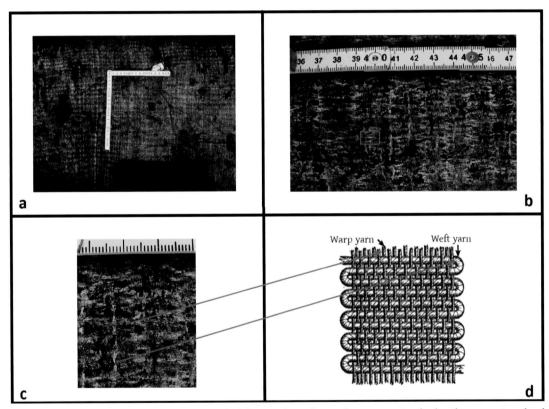

Fig. 13.5 Representation of the tabby weave: a. detail of the mat from the southern extremity; b. details concerning the density and the thickness of the threads; c. detail of interlacing of the threads; d. schematic representation of the structural elements (a–c Neculai Bolohan photo archive; d. after Marian 2009, fig. 52).

textiles and textile imprints on pots. The fibres were of lower quality and were mainly not spun. Simple looms of a horizontal or vertical type were initially used and, at a later stage, additional devices, including planks, heddles and reeds, were used in the weaving process to make narrow textile bands.[22]

Raw material

The archaeozoological remains on the site prove the extensive use of animals, which provided various resources for subsistence (milk, meat, bones, horns, wool). There are a limited number of artefacts that may be associated with the practice of domestic crafts, such as spinning or weaving but, until now, there has been no reliable evidence showing the use of wool yarn on the site under investigation. The use of animal skin for clothing cannot be excluded,[23] since it is already known that the subsistence of Yamnaya was based on herding.

'Europe was based not only on cultivated textile plants but also on the targeted exploitation of wild plants.'[24] Indeed, the evidence from the site indicates that vegetal fibres were the major raw material used for making the mats from the grave. At this state of the research, the only possibility to identify the plant fibres used for producing the mats is through analogies with the modern landscape and the presence of some phytoliths. On one hand, the possibility of using flax or nettle fibre may be presumed if we refer to the thickness of the threads and to their density. Furthermore, the typology of soils in the Elan river basin may support this supposition. On the other hand, the presence of phytoliths derived from aquatic plants (bulrush, reed) among the debris of the mats may indicate their use in the manufacture of the threads.[25] In addition, the remains of some specific tools (metal, flint or bone sickles) might be associated with collecting and processing these kinds of plants in the Early Bronze Age.

Some ecological and ethnographical remarks

The ecological conditions of modern eastern Romania are very likely similar to these of the Bronze Age steppe cultures. The communities were trying to adapt their needs and daily life to the environment. The tumulus is situated at the confluence of two small streams whose marshy shores offer a favourable place for aquatic plants such as reed, rushes, bulrush and sedges. These kinds of plants, especially the reed, are still relied upon today for household uses.

Ethnographic and historical comparisons indicate that mats were used and are still used in the construction of light summer houses, fences for sheepfolds, in the manufacture of mud-bricks and pottery, and as matting or for the covering of carts.

For the case under study, the preliminary results indicate that the community used the mats as a veil or shroud and as a funeral cloth for an important individual. This is the first case documented in the area under reconsideration.

Conclusions

During the archaeological excavation, we were able to combine the field experience with a new type of discovery. For the first time in Romania, such an investigation was conducted and reported in which an archaeological textile was observed properly and scientifically analysed. Very similar burials have been uncovered in the proximity of the Popeni tumulus (Fig. 13.1), with 'vegetal mats' similar to what was found there. These include those found in

the bottom of the pits in Tumulus 2: Grave 2; Tumulus 3: Grave 2; Tumulus 4: Graves 1, 3, 7, 10 at Bălăbani II, Taraclia County, Republic of Moldova;[26] the abundant 'vegetal beddings' and 'a funerary blanket' from tumuli 1–6 at Sărăţeni, Hânceşti County, Republic of Moldova;[27] the 'vegetal beddings' from Tumulus 1: Graves 5, 8, 11–21, 24, 26, 29 from Smeeni-Movila Mare, Buzău County;[28] Tumulus 78: Grave 1 at Lieşti-Movila Arbănaşu, Lieşti commune, Galaţi County;[29] Tumulus 1: Grave 1 at Prăjeni-Nelipeşti, Prăjeni commune, Botoşani County[30] or at a larger distance the 'vegetal fibres' in Tumulus 1: Grave 1, the mats from Tumulus 3: Grave 1, Tumulus 4: Grave 1, Tumulus 5: Grave 1 from Plačidol-Goljamata Mogila, Dobrič, Bulgaria.[31] Nevertheless, the core of these kinds of funerary customs is represented by some Yamnaya or Yamnaya-Katacombnaya burials like those from the Ingul basin.[32]

Our points of reference in this endeavour were represented by the knowledge and practice in the taphonomical investigations, and at the same time we attempted to understand the manner in which the ancient communities had interacted with the environment. The partial results of this contribution point to the necessity of the multidisciplinary approach that will lead to the amplification and diversification of the archaeological discourse. On the other hand, the uncovered textile shows the flexibility of the Yamnaya communities, which had managed to exploit local natural resources. Thus, we have a further example showing that there are other factors for the recognition of an individual status than the mere quantity or the splendour of artefacts,[33] but rather are exhibited by the large social effort put into creating this complex and perhaps the need to implement and diversify household technology. The inequality of the deceased, indicating the existence of some elites, might be seen in the monumentality of the mound and in the quantity and complexity of the mats as grave goods.

Notes

1   The financial support for Neculai Bolohan for this study was provided by the PCCA 1153/2011 No. 227/01.10.2012 Genetic Evolution: New Evidences for the Study of Interconnected Structures. *A Biomolecular Journey around the Carpathians from Ancient to Medieval Times* (GENESIS).

     We wish to express our thanks to Paula Mazăre who saw the discovery *in situ* and has given us valuable information and suggested some literature concerning the way to study prehistoric textiles. Unfortunately, for personal reasons, she was unable to participate until the end of the first scientific analysis of this discovery. Sergey Agulnikov provided a lot of data about similar discoveries researched in Republic of Moldova. The discussions with him were fruitful and we thank him. Many thanks to the students of the Alexandru Ioan Cuza University of Iaşi and the residents of Găgeşti commune, Vaslui County, Romania, who participated in this excavation. Margarita Gleba found the time to examine part of my photographic archive and to provide additional data concerning the study of prehistoric textiles and I warmly thank her. The graphic design of Fig. 13.3 belongs to Tudor Mandache and Sebastian Drob, and I thank them. Special thanks to Małgorzata Siennicka, Agata Ulanowska, Lorenz Rahmstorf, the organisers of the session 'Textiles in a Social Context. Textile Production in Europe and the Mediterranean in the 4th and 3rd Millennia BCE' at the European Association of Archaeologists, 20th Annual Meeting, 10–14 September 2014 in Istanbul, who have created a special spirit, offered support and patience.

    Neculai Bolohan was responsible for writing the text, the interpretation of all the data and the translation of the text. Ciprian-Cătălin Lazanu was responsible for preparing the database with similar discoveries from the area under consideration and for preparing the general map of the discoveries mentioned in the text. A special thanks to Georg Nightingale, who had the patience to improve the English version of the text.

2 'The archaeological excavations of the year 1977 carried out in the prehistoric tell, near the south-east tower of the Roman-Byzantine fortified town Sucidava-Celei revealed the relics of ten burnt dwellings near the surface. Under the adobe debris of dwelling number 1 [Fig. 13.3] there has been discovered, besides numerous material vestiges, a bed for sleeping, made out of twigs burnt to charcoal [Figs. 13.3, 13.4]. The bed (1,15 m x 0,75 m) was covered with a sack-like textile that was folded in three on the side facing the wall of the dwelling – this being proof that it served as head of the bed (1,25 m x 0,35 m). From the analysis of the textile thread as well as from the fact that I had found flax seeds in the dwelling, I concluded that the carbonised cover was made of flax. lt had been made by means of a "simple technique" of the so-called texture, of two shedding harnesses' (Fig. 13.5). The warp was made of two threads and the weft was made of simple threads, both the former and latter having a diameter of 2 mm thickness. Combining the spun threads with the simple ones, the strength of the textile and its thickness were increased, thereby making it warmer. The prehistoric textile of Sucidava-Celei 'is over 4000 years old (2275 BC according to 14C analysis), is the oldest discovery of such kind in this part of the Europe.' Nica 1981, 125.

3 Zaharia and Cădariu 1979; Săvescu 2004; Mazăre 2008; 2010; 2011a; 2011b; 2014; Marian 2009.

4 The financial support of the archaeological research was provided through the project Development and drilling works for the exploration well at Popeni, 2013 for the beneficiary CHEVRON Exploration and Production Romania SRL, Bucharest by Muzeul Judeţean 'Ştefan cel Mare' from Vaslui.

5 Băcăuanu *et al.* 1980, 322; Roşu 1980, 415–416.

6 Condorachi 2005, 265, 269.

7 Cârciumaru 1996, 142, 178–180, pl. XVI: 1, 4–5. For the very beginning of the presence of flax seed in the Carpathian basin, see Mazăre 2014, n. 47.

8 Bergfjord *et al.* 2012.

9 Băcăuanu *et al.* 1980, 322; Roşu 1980, 415–416.

10 Marian 2009; Mazăre 2010.

11 Udrescu 1973–1974, 23, no. 104, figs. 1 and 12; Coman 1980, 144, fig. 3; Rotaru 2009, 181–186.

12 Field survey by Ciprian Lazanu.

13 P0 represents the topographic datum point of the excavation.

14 A grave robbery cannot be excluded.

15 The first results of anthropological and DNA analyses have already been reported. N. Bolohan, L. D. Gorgan and M. Ciorpac, Analyses of a funerary context and the evaluation of DNA recovery from EBA human bones by different isolation methods, *T04S003, The Bioarchaeology of Ritual and Religion, EAA 20th Annual Meeting, Istanbul*, 12 September 2014, Session Organisers: A. Livarda, R. Madgwick and S. Riera Mora. http://www.eaa2014istanbul.org/, accessed 23 March 2017.

16 Unrub 2007, 167–168, nn. 1–3.

17 For the specific textile terminology we have used Marian 2009; Mazăre 2010; 2014; Lervad *et al.* 2011.

18 A similar discovery has been reported from the graves 1 and 2 in the tumulus at Rahman, in Dobrudja province of Romania: Ailincăi *et al.* 2014, 76, 78, 79–80.

19 Harris 2012, 85.

20 Some archaeological findings show that there is a local Cucuteni culture precedent of using the plain weave technique: Mazăre 2014, fig. 1: 22.

21 Andersson Strand 2010, 17.

22 Shishlina *et al.* 2000, 112.

23 Harris 2012, 83.

24 Bergfjord *et al.* 2012, 1.

25 Shishlina *et al.* 2000, 112.

26 Sava 1996, 192–194, figs. 14, 2; 4; 7; fig. 8; fig. 18, 2; 5. Aside these graves dated to Yamnaya culture (EBA), in the same area two mats were uncovered stemming out from the bottom of the graves 2 and 5 from the Tumulus 6, dated to the Multibelted Pottery culture (Middle Bronze Age). Sava 1996, 196, figs. 20, 7; 22, 3.

27 Leviţchi *et al.* 1996, 21–59, 84–88.

28 Motzoi-Chicideanu 2011, 149.

29 Brudiu 2003, 38–54, 101, fig. 8, 1.

30 Ursulescu and Şadurschi 1986, 15–20.

31 Panajotov 1989, 113–115, 118–119. The list of some kind of textile-mats discovered in funerary context within the area north and north-west of the Black Sea is much more extensive. See Häusler 1976; Panajotov 1989; Motzoi-Chicideanu 2011 with bibliography.

32 Shishlina *et al.* 2000, fig. 5.

33 See, for example, the 'clusters of textile fragments' and 'the rich furnishings' of the royal Tomb (T1) of Period VI B from Arslantepe, Malatya (Turkey). Frangipane *et al.* 2009, 17–18, fig. 15.

Bibliography

Ailincăi, S.-C., Mihail, F., Carozza, L., Constantinescu, M., Soficaru, A. and Micu, C. 2014 Une découverte funéraire du début de l'Âge de Bronze en Dobroudja (Sud-est de Roumanie). Le tumulus de Rahman (com. Casimcea, dep. Tulcea)/ Ranobrončanodobni grobni nalaz iz Dobrudže (jugoistočna Rumunjska). Tumul iz Rahmana (opć. Casimcea, okrug Tulcea. *Prilozi Instituta za arheologiju u Zagrebu* 31, 73–89.

Andersson Strand, E. 2010 The basics of textile tools and textile technology: from fibre to fabric. In C. Michel and M.-L.

Nosch (eds.), *Textile Terminologies in the Ancient Near East and Mediterranean from the Third to the First Millennia BC*. Ancient Textiles Series 8. Oxford and Oakville, 10–23.

Băcăuanu, V., Barbu, N., Pantazică, M., Ungureanu, A. and Chiriac, D. 1980 *Podișul Moldovei. Natură, om, economie*. București.

Bergfjord, C., Mannering, U., Frei, K. M., Gleba, M., Scharff, A. B., Skals, I., Heinemeier, J., Nosch, M.-L. and Holst, B. 2012 Nettle as a distinct Bronze Age textile plant. *Scientific Reports* 2, 664, 1–4 (DOI:10.1038/srep00664, accessed 27 March 2017).

Brudiu, M. 2003 *Lumea de sub tumulii din sudul Moldovei. De la indo-europeni la turanicii târzii – mărturii arheologice*. București.

Cârciumaru, M. 1996 *Paleoetnobotanica. Studii în Preistoria și Protoistoria României*. Agricultura preistorică și protoistorică a României. Iași.

Coman, G. 1980 *Statornicie, continuitate. Repertoriul arheologic al județului Vaslui*. București.

Condorachi, D. 2005 Soils from Fălciu hills. GIS analysis and representation. *Soil Forming Factors and Processes from the Temperate Zone* 4.1, 263–272 (http://factori.soilscience.ro/index.php/fspdzt/article/view/330/254, accessed 2 August 2015).

Frangipane, M., Andersson Strand, E., Laurito, R., Möller-Wiering, S., Nosch, M.-L., Rast-Eicher, A. and Wisti Lassen, A. 2009 Arslantepe, Malatya (Turkey): textiles, tools and imprints of fabrics from the 4th to the 2nd millennium BCE. *Paléorient* 35.1, 5–29.

Harris, S. 2012 From the parochial to the universal: comparing cloth cultures in the Bronze Age. *European Journal of Archaeology* 15.1, 61–97.

Häusler, A. 1976 *Die Gräber der älteren Ockergrabkultur zwischen Dnepr und Karpaten*. Berlin.

Lervad, S., Nosch, M.-L. and Dury, P. 2011 Verbal and non-verbal configurations of textiles: a diachronic study. In *Toth 2011. Actes de la Cinquième conference TOTh, Annecy, 26–27 mai 2011*, 201–220.

Levițchi, O., Manzura, I. and Demcenko, T. 1996 *Necropola tumulară de la Sărăţeni*. Bibliotheca Thracologica 17. București.

Marian, C. 2009 *Meșteșuguri textile în cultura Cucuteni*. Iași.

Mazăre, P. 2008 Impresiuni de țesături pe fragmente ceramice descoperite în situl preistoric de la Limba (jud. Alba). *Apulum. Acta Musei Apulensis* 45, 315–330.

Mazăre, P. 2010 Metodologia de investigare a textilelor arheologice preistorice. *Terra Sebus* 2, 9–45 (https://www.cclbsebes.ro/docs/Sebus_2_2010/01_Paula_Mazare.pdf, accessed 30 October 2018).

Mazăre, P. 2011a O tehnică preistorică de confecționare a textilelelor: tehnica șnurată. *Terra Sebus* 3, 63–89 (https://www.cclbsebes.ro/docs/Sebus_3_2011/03_PMazare.pdf, accessed 29 October 2018).

Mazăre, P. 2011b Textiles and pottery: insights into Neolithic and Copper Age pottery manufacturing techniques from Romania. *Archaeological Textiles Newsletter* 53, 28–34.

Mazăre, P. 2014 Investigating Neolithic and Copper Age textile production in Transylvania (Romania). Applied methods and results. In M. Harlow, C. Michel and M.-L. Nosch (eds.), *Prehistoric, Ancient, Near Eastern and Aegean Textile and Dress. An Interdisciplinary Anthology*. Ancient Textiles Series 18. Oxford and Philadelphia, 1–43.

Motzoi-Chicideanu, I. 2011 *Obiceiuri funerare în epoca bronzului la Dunărea mijlocie și inferioară*, I–II. București.

Nica, M. 1981 Date despre descoperirea celei mai vechi țesături de pe teritoriul României, efectuată la Sucidava-Celei, din perioada de trecere de la neolitic la epoca bronzului (2750–2150 î.e.n). *Studii și comunicări de istorie a civilizației populare din România, Muzeul Brukenthal* 1, 121–125.

Panajotov, I. 1989 Ямната култура в българските земи. *Разкопки и Изследвания* XXI. София.

Roșu, A.1980 *Geografia fiziă a României*. București.

Rotaru, M. 2009 *Antichitățile Elanului*, II. Bârlad.

Sava, E. 1996 Necropola tumulară Bălăbani – II. *Arheologia Moldovei* 19, 191–220.

Săvescu, I. 2004 Războiul de țesut cu greutăți. *Carpica* 33, 65–77.

Shishlina, N. I., Golikov, V. P. and Orfinskaya, O. V. 2000 Bronze Age textiles of the Caspian Sea maritime steppes. In J. Davis-Kimball, E. M. Murphy, L. Koryakova and L. T. Yablonksy (eds.), *Kurgans, Ritual Sites, and Settlements. Eurasian Bronze and Iron Age*. British Archaeological Reports. International Series 890. Oxford, 109–118.

Udrescu, T. 1973–1974 Descoperiri arheologice în jumătatea sudică a Moldovei cu privire la cultura Noua. *Carpica* 6, 17–43.

Unruh, J. 2007 Ancient textile evidence in soil structures at the Agora excavations in Athens, Greece. In C. Gillis and M.-L. B. Nosch (eds.), *Ancient Textiles. Production, Craft and Society. Proceedings of the First International Conference on Ancient Textiles, Held at Lund, Sweden, and Copenhagen, Denmark, on March 19–23, 2003*. Ancient Textiles Series 1. Oxford, 167–173.

Ursulescu, N. and Șadurschi P.1986 Săpăturile din 1985 din necropola tumulară de la Prăjeni (județul Botoșani). *Hierasus* 6, 15–20.

Zaharia, F. and Cădariu, S. 1979 Urme de textile pe ceramica neolitică descoperită în județul Caraș-Severin. *Banatica* 5, 27–34.

Social contexts of textile production in Bulgaria during the Late Chalcolithic: from multimedia work-areas to material, social and cultural transformations

Petya Hristova

Introduction

The evidence of early textiles from the area of the Varna culture in the eastern area of the Kodzhadermen – Gumelnitsa – Karanovo (KGK) VI complex (Fig. 14.1) fills in the lower end of the chronological scope of this volume. It exhibits a highly elaborate uses of textiles, both household and ceremonial, in habitation and funerary contexts, running in parallel to a wide distribution of shared forms of esteem associated with expression of status and gender and backed by levels of work organisation and specialisation.[1] Yet, various degrees of completeness and insufficient contextual information still limit our understanding of the processes in the region during the Late Neolithic and Chalcolithic periods.[2] Based on a literature survey, this paper is not exhaustive, and focuses on archaeological contexts suggestive of multimedia work areas.[3]

One of the most recognisable characteristics of the Late Neolithic/Chalcolithic in the Balkans, together with the preceding and following chronological periods, is the distinctive graphite-decorated pottery. While the most characteristic among a number of traits, this material does not indicate that there was a uniform culture throughout the region. As in the case of other periods in the prehistory of South-East Europe, the Chalcolithic is better thought of as 'a mosaic of … unexpected and complex variability'.[4]

Known from the eponymous site of the Varna cemetery, the Varna culture encompasses the coastal areas along the west Black Sea coast, between the Danube and the Stara Planina.[5] To the north-east it connects geographically with the east Danube River plain, to the north-west with the Middle Danube region, to the west and south with the Stara Planina along the Kamchiya River. The relief of the plateau-like plain is carved by numerous rivers, hence a patchwork of a multitude of level surfaces surrounded by steep ravines and seasonal streams. Most of the excavated settlement sites are located in the catchment area of the Kamchiya River which empties into the Black Sea, about 25 km south from the city of Varna. Some of the sites are now submerged, as is the case of the Golyamo Delchevo tell, a settlement with a cemetery, excavated in its entirety in the 1970s in the area of the present-day Tsonevo Reservoir. According to established chronological frameworks, the late Chalcolithic stretches for about 250 years between 4550 and 4300 BC cal.[6] The chronology is in need of modification, as the impact of the earlier dates, that is *c*. 4560 and 4450 BC, obtained through the first AMS radiocarbon dating from contexts of the Varna cemetery and published 11 years ago[7] has yet to be recognised. The issue is a complex one, it is still under discussion, and requires further research, more AMS radiocarbon dates from significant contexts and a whole number of sites, before establishing a revised chronology.[8]

Early forms of specialist production

Learning about the context and organisation of the production of craft goods is indispensable to understanding daily life, social and political relations.[9] Costin's broad programme of studying specialist production emphasises the presence of a full range of multiple variables in addition to technological aspects, such as issues of labour organisation, consumption and distribution.[10] Indeed, specialist production is as much a political, social and economic process as it is technological. While Costin's broad programme seeks to understand specialisation within the society as a whole, it is grounded in a simpler definition of specialist production: 'Whenever there are fewer producers than consumers of a particular good, we recognise specialist production'.[11] As Perlès and

Fig. 14.1 Map of the sites mentioned in the text (based on the map of the Early Chalcolithic and also Late Neolithic – the term preferred in the Greek periodisation – sites and cultures in the region: Demoule 2004, 269, Il. 4.19).

Vitelli note in their review of specialist production in the Greek Neolithic,

> it is important to recognise that 'specialists' have always existed. If we are to understand the dynamics of prehistoric societies from the Palaeolithic to the Bronze Age, what matters is precisely to document how specialisation evolved, the contexts in which it was practiced, the goods that were produced by specialists, how they were distributed, what promoted specialisation, and how the presence of specialists of any kind affected the organisation of society ... we have to specify, in each context and for each category of goods, the characteristics of the specialisation involved.[12]

On the basis of her thorough study of stone production, flint artefacts in particular, Manolakakis observes that at least two widespread forms of specialist production existed diachronically throughout the KGK VI in the areas now Bulgaria, southern Romania and northern Greece. Specialists working within the confines of domestic household production, satisfying the needs of the village community, performed their activities in parallel with specialists whose production demonstrates regional networks based on a balance of preferential activities among closely related KGK sites. The non-domestic production of long blades (also super blades) from brown-yellow flint realised in villages in the north-east only, on the other hand, suggests a complex division of non-itinerant labour and is defined as a specialised production performed by highly skilled specialists who might have worked at a professional level.[13]

The conspicuous and sumptuous aspects of the Varna cemetery have often been mentioned. Various genres of objects widely distributed throughout the region, such as pottery, implements, sceptres and figurines, are represented in Varna. The use of costly materials and highly skilled craftwork is impressively quantifiable.[14] The extraordinary wealth originates from a limited number of graves (65 in comparison to the total number of 320 excavated burials).[15] An array of objects exhibits craftwork in multiple media. Numerous objects are found embellished with gold either in the form of plating, appliqués and overlays made from sheet and foil, a blend of gold and graphite pottery decoration, or with jewellery in the form of gold wire rings.[16]

There are a number of artefacts that are still little understood; these include two pots with familiar decorative patterns carried out in a mixture of graphite and gold instead of the usual graphite only.[17] The vessels, a large plate and a small lidded bowl, form part of the assemblage found in symbolic grave 4.[18] Another vessel with gold (and graphite?) surface decoration dated to the same period is found at Krivodol, north-west Bulgaria,[19] and that is at the westernmost extension of the KGK complex in Bulgaria.[20] The objects must have been made in a multimedia work context by craftspeople with specialist knowledge about applying a kind of gold and graphite mixture, similarly

to painting the clay surface with graphite only and the subsequent firing. Examinations of the 'paint' demonstrate a homogeneous gold and graphite layer rather than post-firing treatment.[21] This brings to mind the skilled knowledge of the craftspeople in firing pottery using brightly coloured ores to achieve intended surface effects.[22] The gold, on the other hand, had not been obtained through mining. Previous studies in the 1990s, as well as the recent ones, both conclude that the Varna gold objects indicate placer gold exploitation from stream sediments.[23] The gold and graphite decoration repeats familiar graphite geometric patterns.[24] In a similar manner as with textiles, as we will see below, pottery also indicates various levels of domestic and specialist production.[25] Combining gold and graphite to achieve a certain surface effect is essentially different from the later evidence for possibly skeuomorphic silvering.[26] Both choices, to use gold-graphite decoration or silvering, however, express the important role of adornment, its symbolic, cultural and social aspects, intertwined with the origins of technological innovation.[27] Enmeshed materials and inter-media works created by specialists mark the period as one of the entanglement of tradition and novelty. It is difficult at present to contemplate the use of gold and graphite as a demonstration of a compelling new technological invention or a combination of tradition and experiment in search for new materials and decorative effects, a feature characteristic for the entire period and the Varna culture in particular. A recent study of all known 3130 gold objects from the Varna cemetery demonstrates the wide range of techniques used, with a certain overlap between the techniques of copper and gold working, a well-developed set of skills, reflecting an established technological tradition rather than various skill levels.[28] The graphite-gold decorated pots, however, demonstrate the use of gold in a way similar to using graphite and other colouring substances. In a nearby necropolis at Devnya, a context defined as a 'symbolic grave' produced an assemblage of fine pottery and included vessels of various sizes. One of the pots was found containing a large amount of manganese ore, pyrolusite, in the form of dust, others yield traces from making pseudo-firnis ceramics characteristic for the micro-region of the Ezerovo type Varna Lake settlements.[29] Pseudo-firnis fine pottery is known from the later horizons at Golyamo Delchevo, and a figurine also found there shows traces of surface treatment with pyrolusite.[30]

Whether the decorative effect is achieved through the use of gold plating as an inseparable component of composite objects or as a blend of elements to adhere to clay surfaces, this kind of materiality suggests work contexts that not only combined workers mixing together various materials but also incorporating essentially different skills that require various levels and characteristics of specialist work. Unique and exquisite, these examples share recognisably common features with the usual repertoire of object categories from the period. In addition, while nowhere else across the spatial extent of Kodzhadermen – Gumelnitsa – Karanovo VI complex has gold plating of the Varna kind been found, gold shaped as rings of thin wire are known both from the coast and the inland, from funerary contexts at a number of cemeteries at Varna, Durankulak and Golyamo Delchevo, as well as at Hotnitsa. Similar shapes made from copper are known from funerary contexts. They are found *in situ* attached as earrings (?) to a certain type of figurine with long ears with multiple perforations.[31]

The goldwork from the Varna cemetery indicates specialist production, but it is difficult at present to think about a more detailed understanding of its main aspects, whether specialist activities were performed at centralised or specialised workshops and what other structural characteristics can be perceived.[32] The authors suggest that the materiality of the Varna goldwork reflects an industry embedded in the long tradition of copper metallurgy in the region.[33]

Besides the use of gold as an indicator of combinations of skills to produce composite objects, another group of objects also suggests the existence of a multimedia work environment and skilled work. The industries and distribution networks of lithics have been well studied, whether it concerns obsidian in the Mediterranean zone south of the region or flint in the north Balkan region.[34] Transitions in the use of different materials to reproduce the same objects or even interactions between different crafts with the same end have also attracted scholarly attention. Numerous examples demonstrate that stone as well as bone implements were reproduced in metal, mostly copper, for both mundane and ceremonial purposes. Probable textile-related implements made of copper as well as of bone and interpreted as tools for making fishing nets are known from the prehistoric settlement in the locality of Redutite near the village of Telish, north-central Bulgaria.[35] Pseudomorphs are known from various sites, including the Varna I and Devnya cemeteries, but, while they provide valuable information about textiles and their uses, they do not demonstrate craft interaction for making a composite object.[36] The technological aspects of these transitions and interactions are still not well understood, but their study would contribute to our understanding of the period throughout the region. It is important to reiterate that experiment and novelty were embedded in staple industries, the production of textiles among others and the better understanding of a single example is inseparable from the understanding of the whole.

The study of textiles in Bulgarian archaeology

Almost every site report from the Bulgarian Chalcolithic mentions the presence of textile tools and implements such as loom weights and spindle whorls,[37] sometimes in statistically meaningful numbers,[38] and yet studies of textile production are practically absent from intra-site analyses and

studies of prehistoric economy and technology.[39] Textiles are only mentioned in the big picture provided by seminal works and topical studies.[40] As Margarita Gleba points out, the main difficulty arises from issues of preservation and accidental survival, but also issues of archaeological description, contextual information and data reuse.[41]

In addition to loom weights of fired clay, the extant examples of unfired clay weights used on Bulgarian sites[42] are a rare survival; others would most likely have disintegrated without entering the archaeological record. On the other hand, the great bulk of the material remains outside scholarly circulation because it is only partially published, or deposited unpublished in museum storage. Sometimes presented together with tools and implements from an occupation phase or horizon, sometimes only mentioned, the objects are not illustrated or described. As a rule, mass and full sets of measurements are rarely provided.

There are numerous examples of textiles preserved as imprints on clay vessels or house walls. Various patterns of pottery decoration might be viewed as textile representations. Fragments of cordage as well as threads of unidentified material are also known.[43] Mineralised remains of textiles used to wrap metal objects from both settlement and mortuary contexts are known, from Golyamo Delchevo and possibly Varna.[44] Petkov suggests that both loom weights and imprints of mats demonstrate the use of warp-weighted looms for making mats in addition to the use of small horizontal looms for making belts.[45] Unlike today, matting was done using straw from cereals as well as wetland plants.[46] The imprints of circular or round mats and textiles were likely made using techniques from basketry, hooked rugs and cordage. The bulk of the data consists, however, of tools and implements for textile making.[47]

Evidence of specialist textile production

Towards the end of the Neolithic and during the Chalcolithic, despite the numerous textile finds,[48] archaeological evidence of activities associated with textile production is scarce or ambivalent, which might lead us to assume that textile making was largely a domestic craft. Imprints,[49] the range of typical loom weights and the evidence of 'houses' as designated places for textile making within clusters of habitats ('villages', 'homesteads') during relatively lengthy periods of times, all suggest a level of production beyond satisfying the needs of a small community. Even a brief survey of evidence for craft activities suggests a discernible distinction between domestic crafts and specialist production, especially when objects as contexts of behaviour are also associated with spatial features. While the current state of the evidence of textiles points predominantly at a level of intra-communal specialisation, that is, the inhabitants in certain areas maintained the performance of their craft during lengthy periods of time to satisfy the needs of the

Fig. 14.2 The loom from the Golyamo Delchevo tell, in situ, *and side by side with a tentative identification of the individual loom weights (based on Todorova* et al. *1975, 26, fig. 11.1 and the author's study at Varna Museum in October 2015).*

local community only, in some cases the entire village participated at times in the making of textiles.[50]

Based on arrangement of loom weights in pairs in a regular chessboard pattern near walls or between stones, warp-weighted looms are identified in House 4, Horizon IV, Golyamo Delchevo,[51] in Ovcharovo[52] and in Sadievo.[53] Unlike Golyamo Delchevo, where various craft activities took place, textiles, pottery and antler work were the main crafts in Ovcharovo. A loom is mentioned briefly and variously either from House 5, Horizon X,[54] or House 6, Horizon VIII,[55] and will not be discussed in this paper. The excavators reported a number of various types of loom weights, round, oval, conical and pyramidal, 52 in total deposited in an area of 1.20 m² against the north wall of the house. The excavator suggests that a warp-weighted loom was installed to produce a fabric 1.20 m wide. Other textile finds are not reported.

The evidence of textiles from fully excavated sites such as Golyamo Delchevo tell demonstrates a wide production range – cordage, mesh fabric, mats and textiles.[56] The mats preserved as imprints from Horizons IV and VII are similar

and were most likely produced by plaiting with active systems in two directions, a primary textile technique with two or more sets of elements for which no implements other than simple poles, sticks or needles would be used, altogether difficult to identify in the archaeological record.[57] Weaving should also be considered.[58] Twill plaiting is also known from Sitagroi in northern Greece.[59]

Evidence for a diachronic dimension of making textiles in one and the same area of the habitat has been considered as an indicator of specialist activity.[60] At Golyamo Delchevo 12 round loom weights from Horizon IV, House 4, were found in a chess-like pattern (Fig. 14.2). On both ends of the row, two conical weights probably mark the width of a small warp-weighted loom. The fabric made on the loom would be 58 cm wide. The round weights with circular holes in the middle have ovoid cross-sections and show traces of wear (torus or discoid) on one side of the hole and no chipping along their outer edges. The weights are badly fired, and this probably occurred during the fire that burnt the whole settlement and ends the phase. They would have been used in only a sun-dried condition.[61] On the west of House 4

156 *Petya Hristova*

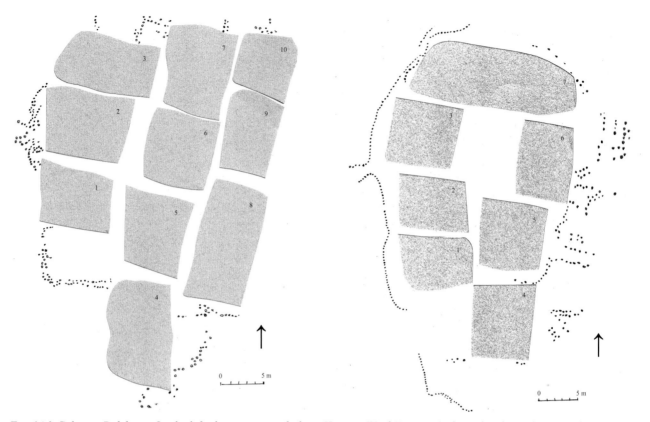

Fig. 14.3 Golyamo Delchevo. On the left: the occupational phase Horizon IV of House 4 (indicated with number 4 on the plan) where a loom in situ *was found. On the right: House 4 (indicated with number 4 on the plan) during the later occupational phase Horizon X where individual loom weights were found (Todorova* et al. *1975, 25 Horizon IV; 41 Horizon X). The loom and the loom weights are not represented.*

and south of the settlement entrance is situated a built well already in place during Horizon III.[62] Single finds that might be interpreted as loom weights and spindle whorls are found throughout its fill. It is notable that, during Horizon X, again there were a number of loom weights found in House 4 in front of a semicircular clay bench. The other finds from the assemblage are mentioned as evidence of tool making. The excavator views the finds and the features as evidence of a multimedia working area.[63] One and the same 'house' repeatedly used in the course of time for making textiles affirms the spatial aspect and diachronic dimension of likely specialist production (Fig. 14.3). The loom and the proximity of the well, rebuilt intermittently with care across several horizons, attest to an area where activities that use large volumes of water were performed, including stages such as preparing the fibres, finishing and dyeing.[64]

Changes at Golyamo Delchevo reflect dynamic processes and are indicative of the ebb and flow of fortunes, as well as the significance of the settlement in its local and regional contexts. A major renovation took place during Horizon VIII, when the north area was built as a working area for various activities. This coincides with evidence for more intense contacts with the coast in addition to contacts with the south.[65] Although bone pointed tools (needles) or

elaborate bone objects are known from a number of sites, the assemblage from Golyamo Delchevo demonstrates a close resemblance with the material from Sitagroi in northern Greece.[66] Industrial activities, with the use of various materials brought in from areas near and far, peak during Horizon X in House 4; the north area heavily used with industrial accumulations of charcoal (as a result of metalworking?).[67] In a world defined by house societies,[68] the 'house', its many structures and surrounding areas might not have always been related to households involved in a single mode of practice and might represent entangled relationships between units of kinship, production and consumption.[69]

Textiles and textile production in contexts of craft interaction

Textile making usually forms part of a multimedia work environment, whether as the means to an end or the finished product itself. Textiles were embellished with gold appliqués and beads made from sheet and foil gold, as in the Varna cemetery (Varna I). A number of gold strips rolled up in a spiral shape and further stretched, possibly from a chain, are found in the symbolic grave 4 (Varna I). In addition, a single bead of this kind was found in grave 1 there.[70] No further evidence is available to indicate the material with which the gold strip had been intertwined, but the shiny metal might have decorated cords from organic strings. Numerous concave round overlays from a number of graves in the Varna cemetery, as well as from funerary contexts elsewhere, had probably decorated ceremonial attire and personal clothing, as well as other textiles.[71]

The gold band in the shape of a few spiral coils from grave 25 in the necropolis of the Golyamo Delchevo tell might have been wound around a fibre core, a string or piece of cord. The archaeological context of the object, found under the cranial remains, indicates that it might have been used to decorate a ceremonial garment, possibly some form of headgear.[72] Similar gold 'spiral beads' are known from other funerary contexts at Golyamo Delchevo and Durankulak.[73]

The gold overlays and plating of Varna and elsewhere, Type D of the large group of so-called 'ring idols' (d = 3.8–2.0 cm), recall the existence of the spindle whorl in precious metal from Alaça Höyük (d = c. 5.2 cm).[74] A recent study of the goldwork from Varna concludes that 'standardised forms of gold implements were used in very similar ways in a wider region' and consequently that indicates 'a socially or religiously motivated standardisation'.[75] If the gold embellished textile implements or symbolic forms of such tools, this would have been in accord with the tendency to hold in high esteem everyday means of sustenance as well as of specialist crafts already well attested in Varna with regard to stone and copper tools.

The evidence is far from conclusive. Identifications of small finds generally classified as jewellery and often parts of multi-component entities is difficult. Gold rings from thin wire were found *in situ* near an assemblage of loom weights in Horizon IV at Madrets Tell.[76] Textile-based garments decorated with sheet gold bands are known from later periods. Narrow gold bands interwoven together to make small objects resembling miniature mats are known from 3rd millennium Ebla.[77] Sophie Desrosiers raises the interesting question whether the woven gold pieces were made by a weaver, or whether the textile technique was imitated by a jeweller.[78] A possible term for a textile made with silver and gold thread for particularly precious clothing is attested in a tablet from the Ebla archive (24th century) as well as gifts of textiles.[79] In addition to evidence of gold textiles from Late Bronze Age Mycenae's Circle A,[80] Circle B, graves Beta, Iota and Omicron, also provide evidence of sheet gold elements of possible ceremonial garments.[81] Dress and other textile decorative accessories for ceremonial purposes were made from thin gold foil during the Mycenaean period in Greece and the Aegean.[82]

The spatial aspect of the situating of work spaces for interrelated crafts often overlaps with the location of sites of household production. Moreover, with respect to assemblages *in situ*, differentiating between specialist work and unequal accumulation has always been a problem in tell settlements.[83] Recent studies, however, demonstrate the presence of flint-mining work stations and flint workshops for semi-processed commodities at sites with brief occupation, such as Kamenovo in north-east Bulgaria.[84] In addition to working flint at the skill level of professionals, there is evidence for antler working (and also ceramics?) as domestic production.[85] During the late phases of the flat settlement at Selevac, multiple activities take place inside the walls, such as food processing, food storage, pottery making, textile production, stone-tool processing and perhaps copper working.[86] During the occupation of Horizon X, destroyed by fire, at the large tell settlement at Ovcharovo, the find of 100 ceramic vessels in House 1 is interpreted as evidence of feasting or items for exchange, while the loom *in situ* from House 5 is associated with a textile workshop.[87] Possible multimedia work areas similar to the situation at Ovcharovo are known at sites in Romania such as Hîrşova and Căscioarele.[88] An assemblage from a settlement context destroyed by fire at Krivodol suggests craft activities in multiple media on a small scale.[89] A multimedia work area for textile and bone working is attested at Ruse Tell.[90] Copper working is attested at Mandalo[91] in addition to pottery making.[92]

Multimedia work areas or 'workshops' for textile and pottery making, textile and gold working, textile and bone working appear more often towards the middle of the Late Chalcolithic (Golyamo Delchevo), and this tendency was more pronounced towards its end and the beginning of Early Bronze Age at sites such as Krivodol in north-west Bulgaria, Mandalo[93] and Sitagroi[94] in north Greece. Mixing materials and techniques in a search for a particular visual effect imbued familiar shapes with transformative agency and eventually coincided with efforts not only to maintain but also expand existing social networks. While pursuing innovations within regional symbolic repertoires of prestige, specialists created conduits of technological advances in other media. Both skilled and unskilled work took place in such environments, and it is intriguing to speculate whether a certain trend towards a 'de-specialisation'[95] might have occurred in parallel to a wider distribution of objects made by specialists. Analyses of old excavation records, working with previously excavated data and new excavations would bring a more nuanced and better understanding of the long-term processes in the KGK cultural complex.

Notes

1   I am grateful to the organisers of the EAA conference session in Istanbul in September 2014 and editors of this volume, and especially to Małgorzata Siennicka for making the paper presentation possible and for providing invaluable editorial assistance. I am greatly indebted to Sarah Morris who guided my research, for her support and attention to the long-term

dimension of the Bulgarian and the Greek archaeological records. Many individuals at the Cotsen Institute of Archaeology have provided ideas that have been valuable in the research and the writing of this paper. I am thankful to Elizabeth Arkush, Lothar von Falkenhausen, Richard Lesure, Katina Lillios, John Marston, John Papadopoulos, Christine Thompson and David Scott. Ernestine Elster and Elizabeth Barber discussed the importance of textiles for a better understanding of Bulgarian prehistory and the prehistories of the neighbouring regions while I was pursuing my doctoral studies at UCLA. Sarah Morris and Elizabeth Carter directed the seminar and imparted a need to look beyond the regional specifics into the greater Aegean and eastern Mediterranean throughout later prehistory and the Late Bronze Age. Heather Miller led the seminar and advised my initial explorations of prehistoric technologies and cross-craft interaction. I am in debt to Marilyn Beaudry-Corbett and Colleen Delaney-Rivera for thoroughly discussing ceramic analysis and where pottery may lead us, considering working scales and social aspects. I thank Douglas Bailey and Peter Biehl for their helpful advice and encouragement during postdoctoral stages of my research. Thanks are also due to the two anonymous reviewers for reading an earlier version of the paper and their comments. I am so very grateful to Vanya Petrova, with whom I discussed various topics in the study of textiles in Bulgarian archaeology, and to Agata Ulanowska for her editorial help and thoughtful comments. All remaining inconsistencies or omissions are my responsibility.

2   A number of sites in northern Greece demonstrate affinities and shared materiality with well-known sites further north. While Late Neolithic is the term used in the study of the periods immediately preceding the Bronze Age in Greece, the term Chalcolithic is utilised in the Bulgarian literature. The problem of synchronicities has not yet been sufficiently studied; a certain overlap seems apparent, and both terms are used in this paper.

3   For the concept of multimedia workshop and a multimedia approach to the study of craft production on the basis of evidence from Late Bronze Age Mycenaean Greece, see Younger 1978; Dabney and Wright 1990; Laffineur 1995.

4   Tringham 2000, esp. 53, discussing the process of Neolithisation in Greece and further north throughout the region proposes the concept of a mosaic.

5   For the archaeological concept of the Varna culture and its historiography, see Dzhanfezova 2013, 35–36.

6   Manolakakis 2002.

7   Chapman *et al.* 2006.

8   For a thorough consideration of the issue, see Dzhanfezova 2013. On the need of multiple dates from significant archaeological contexts, see Levine and Stanish 2014. In a recent paper on the goldwork from Varna, the earlier dating is adopted, Leusch *et al.* 2015, esp. 354.

9   Costin 2004, 189.

10 Costin 2004, 190–191.

11 Costin 1991, 43.

12 Perlès and Vitelli 1999, 96.

13 Manolakakis 2005.

14 In advance of its publication in full, Tanya Dzhanfezova summarises the finds from the Varna cemetery during its two main periods of excavation between 1972 and 1991 as

follows: 'more than 3,000 gold artefacts (the total weight of which exceeds six kilograms), more than 160 metal artifacts, 230 flint tools, 650 vessels, 1,100 *Spondylus* and 12,200 *Dentalium* shell adornments and numerous other small finds' (2013, 33, with references to Ivanov 1988 and Slavchev 2009).

15 Leusch *et al.* 2015, 353–355.

16 The term 'gilding' is to be avoided as it usually denotes essentially different techniques, only available during later periods. Leusch *et al.* 2015, 359, mention 'gilding' in a broader sense. The authors agree with Chapman's observation that 'the implementation of gold within KGK-VI societies was driven by the polychromic aesthetics connected specifically with the material culture of the Copper Age in that region', Leusch *et al.* 2015, 364, referring to Chapman 2007. About the long-term dimension of such a general characteristic, and especially with regard to decorated tools, see Bailey 2000, 112–113, 184–185, 218–221.

17 A recent study of graphite deposits in Bulgaria demonstrates long-distance connections between sources of procurement and pottery making in settlement contexts, Leshtakov 2004. See also Yiouni 2001; Vandova 2004.

18 About the pots, see Todorova and Vajsov 2001, 97–98, cat. nos 619–620, pl. 57. The entire assemblage is also represented in Todorova and Vajsov 2001.

19 Mikov 1948; Raduncheva 1992.

20 This is a small vessel, considering the fragment representing the mouth and one of the handles, and the type is eventually comparable to the bowl from Varna's grave 4 (Varna I). It was found during excavations in the 1940s, about 30 years before the discovery of the Varna cemetery, Mikov 1948. While mentioned and illustrated with a museum photograph in a number of exhibition catalogs and articles (*e.g.* Éluère and Raub 1991; Raduncheva 1992; Bailey 2000), Todorova and Vajsov (2001) do not include it alongside Varna's gold-and-graphite vessels in their study of prehistoric jewellery from Bulgaria.

21 Éluère and Raub 1991; Raduncheva 1992.

22 Sherratt 1976, 572.

23 Leusch *et al.* 2015, 359.

24 Todorova and Vajsov 2001, 98, pl. 57.

25 Evans 1978.

26 See Sherratt 2007 for evidence for possibly skeuomorphic silvering from Poros in Crete, Mandalo in Macedonia and west Black Sea in Bulgaria. According to chemical analyses by Leusch *et al.* 2015, 357–358, the gold objects from Varna with high silver content do not indicate silver working, rather differential treatment, based on colour, of variations of gold including silver-rich natural gold.

27 Neither gold nor graphite are among the local resources in the Varna area, Leshtakov 2004; Bailey 2000, 221. Leusch *et al.* 2015, 359–362 argue convincingly for the presence of traceable exchange networks on a regional level as demonstrated by several commodities: flint, copper, *Spondylus* shell, as well as gold. For the role of adornment and the symbolic, social and cultural aspects, of the complex of techniques, materials and tools, see Nakou 1995; Chapman 2007; Sherratt 2007; see also Hansen 2011.

28 Dimitrov 2013. See also Leusch *et al.* 2015, 368–371, who argue that the gold metallurgy, although already in a

mature state in Varna, is embedded in the long technological development of copper metallurgy; the latter is well attested throughout the region. It is interesting to contemplate the question whether the goldwork from the five 'wealthy' burials is a result of gathering a number of objects with extended life-histories prior to their deposition, or the bulk of it is produced ad hoc and specifically for the purposes of these apparently ritual depositions, or both.

29 Todorova-Simeonova and Nacheva 1971.
30 Todorova 1975, 90–91, 189, table 75.1–8, Horizon XII, about the pottery; 39, 165–166, tables 51.9 and 52.10, Horizon VIII about the figurine.
31 Todorova and Vajsov 2001.
32 Leusch *et al.* 2015, 365–368.
33 Leusch *et al.* 2015, 368–371.
34 Manolakakis 2005.
35 Bone implements of this kind are well distributed on both sides of Danube, but at present only at Telish the shape traditionally known in bone is cast in copper, Gergov 1987, 48–50, fig. 6. A fragment of a bone tool with a piece of copper embedded in its surface is known from Horizon XII, Golyamo Delchevo Tell, Todorova 1975, 189, table 75.9.
36 For a review, see Petrova 2011, 220–231.
37 Todorova 1978, 70.
38 *Petkov 1965.* The arrangement of 37 loom weights against the wall of House 9 in Early Neolithic Rakitovo interpreted as a loom appears more likely to be an assemblage for another purposes, storage for example, rather than being traces of the loom itself. A. Chohadzhiev (2004, 232 and fig. 2) analysed the photograph from the excavation of House 9 in Rakitovo and the objects do not appear to have been arranged in pairs.
39 Similarly to other regions, see Gleba 2007. At the same time, identification should be well justified as not every object of similar shape represents a textile-related implement.
40 For example, Todorova 1986, 159–160; see also Evans 1978, 123.
41 Gleba 2007, 71; see also Wild 2007.
42 Todorova 1975.
43 Petkov 1965, 45.
44 Mostly wrapped around needles, see Todorova and Vajsov 2001, 48, no. 101, pl. 8.101 Golyamo Delchevo; possibly 49, no. 104, pl. 8.104 Varna, gr. 36; see also Gleba and Mannering 2012, 2. On the axe with traces from its textile wrapping from grave 40, Varna I, see Petrova 2006.
45 Petkov 1965, 45–46.
46 Petkov 1965, 49–51.
47 For a recent and thorough study of textiles in Bulgarian archaeology with a focus on the Bronze and Early Iron Age, see Petrova 2011.
48 Mazăre 2014 for Transylvania; Petkov 1965; Chohadzhiev 2004; and Petrova 2011 for Bulgaria.
49 Evaluating pattern distribution remains difficult as comparative research and regional data syntheses are yet to come. Demoule 2004 suggests caution with respect to the pottery.
50 For intra-communal specialisation, see Petrova 2011, 244–246. Petrova takes into account the preliminary results from recent excavations at Sadievo to suggest a possibility for accumulation of surplus at certain times.

51 Todorova 1978, 71; 1975, 26–27, fig. 11.1; 87; 1986, 159–160.
52 Todorova 1978, 71; 1983, 38–39; 1986, 159–160.
53 Petrova 2011, 189–190.
54 Todorova 1983, 39.
55 Todorova 1983, 89.
56 Todorova 1975, 151, table 37.8–9 illustrating pottery from Horizon IV, 161, table 47.26 illustrating pottery from Horizon VII.
57 For the classification and the technique, see Desrosiers 2010, 34–38, fig. 3.16.
58 Petkov 1965.
59 Elster 2003, pls. 6.15–16: mat impressions, twill plaiting; see also pl. 6.19 – cloth impression.
60 Making textiles in a particular area repeatedly and during a lengthy period of time, similarly to the situation in Golyamo Delchevo Tell, is attested in the settlement mound Radovan, Calaras County, southern Romania, see Petrova 2011, 245. Douglas Bailey applies a diachronic perspective to the Ovcharovo tell (1996).
61 Todorova 1975, 27 and fig. 11.1.
62 Todorova 1975, 27 and fig. 12.1.
63 Todorova 1975, 40, 86–87.
64 Gleba and Mannering 2012, 4–20, esp. 20.
65 Todorova 1975, 39. Pyrolusite from the area of Varna Lakes used for pottery and figurine decoration appears for the first time. Previously copper and graphite attest contacts with the south.
66 Todorova and Vajsov 2001, pl. 10.149–151, pl. 11.156–158; Elster 2003, 48–49 and fig. 2.18 c–e. A find reported as a 'zoomorphic vessel' in the shape of a 'dog' is part of the inventory of Horizon X (41; see also Todorova 1975, 176–177, tables 62–63, no. 13). This find appears to closely resemble the shaft-hole stone axe realistically shaped as a 'feline animal' reported from Sitagroi, Renfrew 1986, 186, fig. 8.4b, from the Main Area, PN/C; pl. XXV. Discussing the feline representation from Golyamo Delchevo, Ivanov and Vassilev mention that it might be associated with the role of cats, both wild and domesticated, on the basis of the faunal remains. Single bones from a domesticated cat adult (*Felis silvestris*) and a lion (*Panthera leo* L.) form part of the faunal record (1975, 248, 284–285).
67 In addition, wooden planking has never been used in the north area. The rest of the buildings at the same time yield traces of wooden planking beneath the floors and possibly were primarily designated for living, Todorova 1975, 40–41, 44–45 and fig. 26, 80–81, 82.
68 Borić 2008.
69 Hodder 2013, esp. 351. For the difficulty of distinguishing specialist from household production activities, see Allison 1999. See also LaMotta and Schiffer 1999.
70 Todorova and Vajsov 2001, 55, cat. no. 185, pl. 14 about grave 4 and p. 87, cat. no. 510, pl. 42 about the find in grave 1.
71 For a systematic overview, see Todorova and Vajsov 2001.
72 Todorova and Vajsov 2001, 38, pl. 2.30–31 'Zylinderförmige Perlen in Spiraltechnik'. For examples, see Völling 2008, 13, fig. 1; Desrosiers 2010, 29–31, fig. 3.9.
73 Todorova and Vajsov 2001, pl. 2.30–32.
74 Todorova and Vajsov 2001, pl. 23.312–317 for the Bulgarian material; Barber 1991, 61, fig. 2.24, 26 for Alaça Höyük. For

more Bronze Age examples of textile implements made from costly materials, see Petrova 2011, 55–57.

75   Leusch *et al.* 2015, 367–368.
76   *Petrova 2011, 187–188.*
77   Desrosiers 2010, 29 and fig. 3.5; 33 and figs. 3.1c, 3.9, 3.10; Gleba and Mannering 2012, 17.
78   Desrosiers 2010, 29.
79   Biga 2010, 149, 159.
80   Biga 2010, 159. For the use of metal thread, see also Gleba 2008.
81   Hristova 2010.
82   Konstantinidi-Syvridi 2014 reviewing dress accessories made from gold foil cut-outs.
83   Halstead 1993; Gaydarska *et al.* 2004.
84   Evans 1978, 121 reviews the use of caves to shelter craft activities in multiple media; Manolakakis 2011.
85   Manolakakis 2011.
86   Bailey 2000, 163.
87   Todorova 1983, 38–52.
88   Evans 1978.
89   Mikov 1948.
90   Georgiev and Angelov 1952.
91   Liritzis 1996, 224–225.
92   Valamoti 2002.
93   Andreou *et al.* 2001, 294 and n. 256; Nikolaidou *et al.* 2003
94   Elster 1997.
95   Perlès and Vitelli discussing craft specialisation in the Neolithic of Greece indicate the possibility of a certain trend towards de-specialisation during the Late Neolithic (1999).

Bibliography

Allison, P. M. 1999 Introduction. In P. M. Allison (ed.), *The Archaeology of Household Activities*. London and New York, 1–18.

Andreou, S., Fotiadis, M. and Kotsakis, K. 2001 [1996] The Neolithic and Bronze Age of northern Greece. In T. Cullen (ed.), *Aegean Prehistory: A Review*. Boston, 259–328.

Bailey, D. W. 1996 The life, times and works of House 59, Tell Ovcharovo, Bulgaria. In T. Darvill and J. Thomas (eds.), *Neolithic Houses in Northwest Europe and Beyond*. Oxford, 143–56.

Bailey, D. W. 2000 *Balkan Prehistory*. London and New York.

Barber, E. J. W. 1991 *Prehistoric Textiles: The Development of Cloth in the Neolithic and Bronze Ages with Special Reference to the Aegean*. Princeton.

Biga, M. G. 2010 Textiles and the administrative texts of the royal archives of Ebla (Syria, 24th century BC) with particular emphasis on coloured textiles. In C. Michel and M.-L. Nosch (eds.), *Textile Terminologies in the Ancient Near East and Mediterranean from the Third to the First Millennia BC*. Ancient Textiles Series 8. Oxford and Oakville, 146–172.

Borić, D., 2008 First households and house societies in European Prehistory. In A. Jones (ed.), *Prehistoric Europe: Theory and Practice*. Oxford, 109–142.

Chapman, J. 2007 The elaboration of an aesthetic of brilliance and colour in the Climax Copper Age. In F. Lang, C. Reinholdt and J. Weilhartnet (eds.), *Stephanos Aristeios: Archäologische Forschungen zwischen Nil uns Istros. Festschrift für Stefan Hiller zum 65. Geburtstag*. Vienna, 65–74.

Chapman, J., Higham, T., Slavchev, V., Gaydarska, B. and Honch, N. 2006 The social context of the emergence, development and abandonment of the Varna cemetery, Bulgaria. *European Journal of Archaeology* 9.2–3, 159–183.

Chohadzhiev, A. 2004 Weights and/or spools: distribution and interpretation of the Neolithic 'cocoon-like loom weights'. In V. Nikolov, K. Băčvarov and P. Kalchev (eds.), *Prehistoric Thrace*. Sofia, 231–238.

Costin, C. L. 1991 Craft specialization: issues in defining, documenting, and explaining the organization of production. In M. B. Schiffer (ed.), *Archaeological Method and Theory*. Tucson, 1–56.

Costin, C. L. 2004 Craft economies of ancient Andean states. In G. M. Feinman and L. M. Nicholas (eds.), *Archaeological Perspectives on Political Economies*. Salt Lake City, 189–221.

Dabney, M. and Wright, J. 1990 Mortuary customs, palatial society and state formation in the Aegean area: a comparative study. In R. Hägg and G. C. Nordquist (eds.), *Celebrations of Death and Divinity in the Bronze Age Argolid: Proceedings of the Sixth International Symposium at the Swedish Institute at Athens, 11–13 June, 1988*. Stockholm, 45–53.

Demoule, J.-P. 2004 Les récipients en céramique du Néolithique Récent (Chalcolithique): description, évolution et contexte régional. In C. Commenge-Pellerin (ed.), *Dikili Tash: Village préhistorique de Macédoine orientale* I. *Fouilles de Jean Deshayes (1961–1975)* 2. Bulletin de Correspondance Hellénique Supplément 37. Paris and Athènes, 63–270.

Desrosiers, S. 2010 Textile terminologies and classifications: some methodological and chronological aspects. In C. Michel and M.-L. Nosch (eds.), *Textile Terminologies in the Ancient Near East and Mediterranean from the Third to the First Millennia BC*. Ancient Textiles Series 8. Oxford and Oakville, 23–51.

Dimitrov, K. 2013 Technological development of the gold working techniques in Varna. In H. Angelova and M. Özdogan (eds.), *Where Are the Sites? Research, Protection and Management of Cultural Heritage*. Ahtopol, 55–80.

Dzhanfezova, T. 2013 Are the 'new' AMS Varna dates older? *Bulgarian e-Journal of Archaeology* 3, 31–66 (http://be-ja.org, accessed 15 January 2014).

Elster, E. 1997 Construction and use of the Early Bronze Age Burnt House at Sitagroi: craft and technology. In R. Laffineur and P. Betancourt (eds.), *TEXNH, Craftsmen, Craftswomen and Craftsmanship in the Aegean Bronze Age, Proceedings of the 6th International Aegean Conference*. Aegaeum 16. Philadelphia, 19–35.

Elster, E. 2003 Bone tools and other artifacts. In E. Elster and C. Renfrew (eds.), *Prehistoric Sitagroi: Excavations in Northeast Greece, 1968–1970, Vol. 2. The Final Report*. Los Angeles, 31–79.

Éluère, C. and Raub, C. J. 1991 Investigations on the gold coating technology of the Great Dish from Varna. In J.-P. Mohen and C. Éluère (eds.), *Découverte du métal*. Paris, 13–29.

Evans, R. 1978 Early craft specialization: an example from the Balkan Chalcolithic. In C. L. Redman (ed.), *Social Archaeology: Beyond Subsistence and Dating*. New York, 113–129.

Gaydarska, B., Chapman, J. C., Angelova, I., Gurova, M. and Yanev, S. 2004 Breaking, making and trading: the Omurtag Eneolithic spondylus hoard. *Archaeologia Bulgarica* 8.2, 11–33.

Georgiev, G. and N. Angelov 1957 Разкопки на селищната могила до Русе през 1950–1953. *Известия на Археологическия Институт* 21, 41–127.

Gergov, V. 1987 Медни находки от праисторическото селище в м. Редутите при с. Телиш, Плевенски окръг. *Археология* 4, 44–61.

Gleba, M. 2007 Textile production in proto-historic Italy: from specialists to workshops. In C. Gillis and M.-L. Nosch (eds.), *Ancient Textiles: Production, Craft and Society. Proceedings of the First International Conference on Ancient Textiles Held at Lund, Sweden, and Copenhagen, Denmark on March 19–23, 2003.* Ancient Textiles Series 1. Oxford, 71–76.

Gleba, M. 2008 *Auratae Vestes*: gold textiles in the Ancient Mediterranean. In C. Alfaro and L. Karali (eds.), *Purpureae Vestes II, Vestidos, Textiles y Tintes: Estudios sober la produccion de bienes de consumo en la antiguidad.* Valencia, 63–80.

Gleba, M. and Mannering, U. 2012 Introduction: textile preservation, analysis and technology. In M. Gleba and U. Mannering (eds.), *Textiles and Textile Production in Europe from Prehistory to AD 400.* Ancient Textiles Series 11. Oxford and Oakville, 1–24.

Halstead, P. 1993 Spondylus shell ornaments from the Late Neolithic Dimini, Greece: specialized manufacture or unequal accumulation? *Antiquity* 67, 603–609.

Hansen, S. 2011 Metal in South-Eastern and Central Europe between 4500 and 2900 BCE. In Ü. Yalçin (ed.), *Anatolian Metal* V. Bochum, 137–149.

Hodder, I. 2013 From diffusion to structural transformation: The changing roles of the Neolithic house in the Middle East, Turkey and Europe. In D. Hofmann and J. Smyth (eds.), *Tracking the Neolithic House in Europe: Sedentism, Architecture and Practice.* New York, 349–362.

Hristova, P. 2010 Masks and people: reconstructing the Early Mycenaean funerary ritual through archaeological images and context. Unpublished PhD thesis, University of California, Los Angeles.

Ivanov, I. 1988 Die Ausgrabungen des Gräberfeldes von Varna. In A. Fol and J. Lichardus (eds.), *Macht, Herrschaft und Gold, Das Gräberfeld von Varna (Bulgarien) und die Anfänge einer neuen europäischen Zivilisation.* Saarbrücken, 49–66.

Konstantinidi-Syvridi, E. 2014 Buttons, pins, clips and belts … 'Inconspicuous' dress accessories from the burial context of the Mycenaean period (16th–12th cent. BC). In M. Harlow, C. Michel and M.-L. Nosch (eds.), *Prehistoric, Ancient Near Eastern and Aegean Textiles and Dress. An Interdisciplinary Anthology.* Ancient Textiles Series 18. Oxford and Philadelphia, 143–157.

Laffineur, R. 1995 Craftsmen and craftsmanship in Mycenaean Greece: for a multimedia approach. In R. Laffineur and W.-D. Niemeier (eds.), *Politeia. Society and State in the Aegean Bronze Age. Proceedings of the 5th International Aegean Conference, University of Heidelberg, Archäologisches Institut, 10–13 April 1994.* Aegaeum 12. Liège, 189–199.

LaMotta, V. and Schiffer, M. 1999 Formation processes of house floor assemblages. In P. M. Allison (ed.), *The Archaeology of Household Activities.* London and New York, 19–29.

Leshtakov, P. 2004 Graphite deposits and some aspects of graphite use and distribution in Bulgarian Chalcolithic. In V. Nikolov, K. Băčvarov and P. Kalchev (eds.), *Prehistoric Thrace.* Sofia, 483–496.

Leusch, V., Armbruster, B., Pernicka, E. and Slavčev, V. 2015 On the invention of gold metallurgy: the gold objects from the Varna I Cemetery (Bulgaria) – technological consequence and inventive creativity. *Cambridge Archaeological Journal* 25.1, 353–376.

Levine, A. and Stanish, C. 2014 The importance of multiple ^{14}C dates from significant archaeological contexts. *Journal of Archaeological Method and Theory* 21, 824–836.

Liritzis, V. 1996 *The Role and Development of Metallurgy in the Late Neolithic and Early Bronze Age of Greece.* Uppsala.

Manolakakis, L. 2002 Функцията на големите пластини от Варненския некропол. *Археология* 43.3, 5–17.

Manolakakis, L. 2005 *Les industries lithiques énéolithiques de Bulgarie.* Rahden in Westfalen.

Manolakakis, L. 2011 A flint deposit, a tell and a shaft: a lithic production complex at Ravno 3-Kamenovo? In V. Nikolov, K. Bacvarov and M. Gurova (eds.), *Festschrift for Marion Lichardus-Itten.* Sofia, 225–244.

Mazăre, P. 2014 Investigating Neolithic and Copper Age textile production in Transylvania (Romania). In M. Harlow, C. Michel and M.-L. Nosch (eds.), *Prehistoric, Ancient Near Eastern and Aegean Textiles and Dress. An Interdisciplinary Anthology.* Ancient Textiles Series 18. Oxford and Philadelphia, 1–23.

Mikov, V. 1948 Предисторическото селище до Криводол, Врачанско. *Разкопки и проучвания* 1, 26–62.

Nakou, G. 1995 The cutting edge: a new look at Early Aegean metallurgy. *Journal of Mediterranean Archaeology* 8.2, 1–32.

Nikolaidou, M., Merousis, N., Papanthimou, A. and Papasteriou, A. 2003 From metron to context in Neolithic/Early Bronze Age Mandalon, northwestern Greece: the example of ceramics. In K. P. Foster (ed.), *METRON. Measuring the Aegean Bronze Age.* Aegaeum 24, 317–326.

Perlès, C. and Vitelli, K. D. 1999 Craft specialization in the Neolithic of Greece. In P. Halstead (ed.), *Neolithic Society in Greece.* Sheffield, 96–107.

Petkov, N. 1965 Праисторически плетки и тъкани от Софийското поле и близките му околности. *Археология* 7.1, 45–57.

Petrova, V. 2006 Textile remains from prehistoric graves from the territory of Bulgaria. *Bulletin of the Regional Museum of History Haskovo* 3, 30–34.

Petrova, V. 2011 Предачество и тъкачество в Севернобалканската област през бронзовата и ранножелязната епоха (III – първата половина на I хилядолетие пр. Хр). Unpublished PhD thesis, St Kliment Ohridski Sofia University.

Raduncheva, A. 1992 Към въпроса за рисуваните със злато енеолитни съдове. *Известия на Националния Археологически Музей* 8, 83–88.

Renfrew, C. 1986 Varna and the emergence of wealth in prehistoric Europe. In A. Appadurai (ed.), *The Social Life of Things: Commodities in Cultural Perspective.* Cambridge, 141–168.

Sherratt, A. 1976 Resources, technology and trade: an essay in early European metallurgy. In G. de G. Sieveking, I. H. Longworth and K. E. Wilson (eds.), *Problems in Economic and Social Archaeology.* London, 557–581.

Sherratt, S. 2007 The archaeology of metal use in the Early Bronze Age Aegean – a review. In M. Day and R. C. P. Doonan (eds.), *Metallurgy in the Early Bronze Age Aegean*. Oxford, 245–63.

Slavchev, V. 2009 The Varna Eneolithic cemetery in the context of the Late Copper Age in the East Balkans. In D. Anthony and J. Chi (eds.)c *The Lost World of Old Europe: The Danube Valley 5000–3500 BC*. Princeton, 105–123.

Todorova, H. 1975 Археологичрско проучване на селищната могила и некропола при Голямо Делчево, Варненско. In H. Todorova, S. Ivanov, V. Vassilev, M. Hopf, H. Quitta and G. Kohl (eds.), *Селищната могила при Голямо Делчево*. Sofia, 5–243.

Todorova, H. 1978 *The Eneolithic Period in Bulgaria in the Fifth Millennium B. C.* Oxford.

Todorova, H. 1983 Археологическо проучване на праисторически обекти в района на с. Овчарово, Търговищко, през 1971–1974 г. In H. Todorova, V. Vassilev, Z. Janusevic, M. Kovacheva and P. Valev, *Овчарово*. Sofia, 6–105.

Todorova, H. 1986 *Каменно-медната епоха в България*. Sofia.

Todorova, H. and Vajsov, I. 2001 *Die kupferzeitliche Schmuck Bulgariens*. Stuttgart.

Todorova-Simeonova, H. and Nacheva, V. 1971 Псевдофирнисова керамика от енеолитното наколно селище при с. Езерово, Варненски окръг. *Археология* 2, 66–75.

Tringham, R. 2000 Southeastern Europe in the transition to agriculture in Europe: bridge, buffer, or mosaic. In T. Douglas Price (ed.), *Europe's First Farmers*. Cambridge, 19–56.

Tringham, R. 2003 (Re)-Digging the site at the end of the 20th century: large scale archaeological fieldwork in a new millennium. In J. K. Papadopoulos and R. M. Leventhal (eds.), *Theory and Practice in Mediterranean Archaeology: Old World and New World Perspectives*. Los Angeles, 89–108.

Valamoti, S.-M. 2002 Investigating the prehistoric bread of northern Greece. *Civilisations* 49, 49–66.

Vandova, V. 2004 Late Neolithic clay vessels with graphitized surface from the Struma Valley. In V. Nikolov, K. Băčvarov and P. Kalchev (eds.), *Prehistoric Thrace, Proceedings of the International Symposium in Stara Zagora, 30 September–4 October 2003*. Sofia and Stara Zagora, 122–132.

Völling, E. 2008 *Textiltechnik im alten Orient, Rohstoffe und Herstellung*. Würzburg.

Yiouni, P. 2004 Surface treatment of Neolithic vessels from Macedonia and Thrace. *The Annual of the British School at Athens* 96, 1–25.

Younger, J. 1978 The Mycenae-Vapheio Lion group. *American Journal of Archaeology* 85, 285–299.

Wild, J. P. 2007 Methodological introduction. In C. Gillis and M.-L. Nosch (eds.), *Ancient Textiles: Production, Craft and Society. Proceedings of the First International Conference on Ancient Textiles Held at Lund, Sweden, and Copenhagen, Denmark on March 19–23, 2003*. Ancient Textiles Series 1. Oxford, 1–6.

Experimenting with loom weights. More observations on the functionality of Early Bronze Age textile tools from Greece

Agata Ulanowska

Introduction

Numerous finds of textile tools from Bronze Age Greece make up an important and broadly explored source of knowledge about textile technology and textile production.[1] The functionality of spindle whorls and loom weights, which are the best represented tools in the archaeological evidence, has been recently investigated under the Tools and Textiles – Texts and Contexts (TTTC) Programme of the Danish National Research Foundation's Centre for Textile Research in Copenhagen (CTR). As a result of this experimental approach, the main functional parameters of spindle whorls and loom weights were determined and a variety of yarns and fabrics produced using the specific tools have been suggested.[2] Further archaeological experiments imply that some of the examined tools, such as spools and crescent-shaped loom weights, may have been used as specialised implements employed in specific textile techniques[3] or as multifunctional devices to be applied in many techniques and for different purposes.[4]

This paper, by discussing the unique selection of Early Helladic (EH) loom weights from Tiryns,[5] refers to the problem of how to recognise the specific function of loom weights by means of archaeological experimentation. The bases for this discussion are the results of weaving trials performed by students of archaeology at the University of Warsaw during regular teaching courses, and by participants of international experience textile workshops organised by the author. For the purpose of these activities, several sets of clay copies of textile tools from Bronze Age Greece were modelled by students, including the implements from Tiryns, *i.e.* crescent-shaped, cylindrical and large conical weights. The presented observations and the suggested evaluation of a potential specialisation or multifunctionality of these tools have mostly resulted from an 'experience' approach

to textile production and weaving techniques in the Bronze Age Aegean cultures.

Early Helladic loom weights from Tiryns and their archaeological context

Recently, textile production in Early Helladic Tiryns (*c.* 2800–2000 BC) has been comprehensively examined by Małgorzata Siennicka. Amongst the finds interpreted as possible loom weights were three categories of implements that are not common in the panoply of textile tools from prehistoric Greece: cylindrical weights with three lengthwise perforations, large cones and crescent-shaped weights. According to M. Siennicka, the first two categories of implements have no close analogies in Greece or the neighbouring areas because of their unusual features, such as the said three perforations, the large diameter of the base of the cones and the overall heavy weight of both types of devices, whereas the crescent-shaped weights, although well known from Bronze Age Anatolia and other areas and periods, were very rarely found in the Bronze Age Aegean.[6] Therefore, all of these implements seemed to be particularly interesting for further experimenting in order to evaluate their suggested usefulness in weaving and the possible functional meaning of their specific features.

Three cylinders, two cones and two crescent-shaped implements were found in rooms R 142 and R 143 of a building R 142–144 where, according to M. Siennicka, the manufacturing of textiles may have taken place. They were dated to late EH II and EH II/III transitional phases (Horizons 8 and 9 respectively).[7] Although these tools were unearthed in areas near to each other, it is impossible to ascertain whether they may have been used together and if they may actually be linked to one chronological phase.[8]

Other crescent-shaped weights came from different and mixed contexts mostly dating to the later EH III phase.[9]

Experiential approach to textile techniques

The experiential use of reconstructed tools from EH Tiryns took place as part of hands-on experience activities included in the syllabus of academic courses about textile production in Bronze Age Greece conducted each year since 2011 in the Institute of Archaeology, University of Warsaw. The copies were also employed as textile tools by the participants of two hands-on experience workshops organised by the author in Warsaw in 2014 and 2015 for textile scholars and PhD students.

Personal hands-on experience in selected textile techniques is an inherent part of these courses and workshops, and it is primarily applied as a pedagogical tool introducing the basics of textile technology and terminology to students and participants. The main aim of this experiential approach is to get the actors acquainted with an initial body of knowledge of textile crafts, in addition to traditional academic lectures and readings, and it may be defined as 'experience textile archaeology'.[10]

As a result, the actors become more aware of the technological complexity of manufacturing of textiles and its labour-intensive character, and more responsive to understanding the functional relationship between the parameters of archaeologically preserved tools and the usually perished fabrics that were produced using them. Students participating in experience tests are also better prepared to perceive the socio-cultural dimensions of textile production, such as its high economic value, high level of social involvement and cooperation, and its symbolic significance.

All experiential activities are scheduled according to the *chaîne opératoire* in textile production, paying special attention to weaving. They comprise the following activities: modelling clay copies of archaeological tools, constructing simple looms and heddling devices, weaving on band looms such as rigid heddles and tablets, weaving on warp-weighted looms, basic interlinking in sprang and finishing. Spinning using the drop-spindle technique is demonstrated rather than practised. The activities are scheduled within a 60-hour timespan of a single course (there are 15 meetings altogether), plus 60 hours of students' homework.

Academic value of experience archaeology and methodological tenets of experiential tests

Experience textile archaeology, also defined as 'exploratory experimental archaeology'[11] or 'experiential activities',[12] is acknowledged as an important or even indispensable practical introduction to textile studies and as a tool of personal scholarly development. However, the experiential approach rarely produces an academic outcome, because hands-on activities in general are not designed to test previously formulated hypotheses based on archaeological evidence, and they are less formally organised and less controlled than scientific archaeological experiments. Nevertheless, according to Heather M.-L. Miller, exploratory experimental archaeology may contribute to the main objectives of experimental archaeology through testing the feasibility of reconstructions of use techniques.[13]

In the case of our experiments, nearly all participants are inexperienced or little experienced in the textile craft, the tests are not strictly controlled and there are several discrepancies between them and the strict rules postulated for the archaeological experiments. For example, although in weaving on warp-weighted looms and spinning we exclusively employ copies of textile tools from archaeological sites of Bronze Age Greece, the looms we use were produced to be the most simple but convenient tools for our needs. Their design has no direct references to any specific implements recorded in ethnographic, historical or iconographic evidence. In weaving tests, mechanically spun and inexpensive yarns are used, such as z-spun, S3-plied wool and acryl yarns of *c.* 1–1.5 mm diameter and a spin angle between 25–30°, and z-spun, S3-plied flax threads (*cf.* Table 15.2). The participants were aware of the differences between hand and mechanically spun yarns and of the rather high quality of Aegean Bronze Age textiles. However, our main objective was to understand the technology and mechanics of weaving rather than reconstruct the quality of archaeological textiles or an exact manner of performance in a given textile production technique.

Although our tests are basically of a tutorial character and experiments designed to answer previously formulated questions are undertaken only occasionally,[14] still the general methodological tenets of their performance have been worked out recently.[15] These tenets were inspired by the principles adopted in the experimental approach to textile studies undertaken as part of the Tools and Textiles – Texts and Contexts research programme of the Danish National Research Foundation's Centre for Textile Research,[16] and they may be described by following rules:

- all activities are scheduled according to the *chaîne opératoire* sequences and their temporal organisation, as Do It Yourself tasks;
- looms and weaving techniques are selected based on the current knowledge of the Aegean Bronze Age textile implements and weaves;
- all loom weights, spools and spindle whorls used in experience activities are copies of Bronze Age implements from archaeological sites in Greece;
- students/actors are always informed of gaps in archaeological evidence, either for operational sequences

of weaving, the construction of looms or certain categories of textile tools;

- students/actors are always informed that the manner in which they proceed is suggested by traditional craft and ethnographic analogies and that there may be more than one manner of execution for each of the tested activities;
- whenever there is a greater number of manners of execution or procedural choices, at least two of them are demonstrated and tested;
- the documentation system covers descriptions and photographs of all operational sequences combined with a card system for documenting pieces of experientially woven textiles and their weaving as the work of an individual;[17]
- students/actors are not skilled craftspeople and their observations on weaving can only be further analysed bearing in mind this important qualification.[18]

Nevertheless, since the range of hands-on activities is repetitive, documented and performed by numerous actors over a longer period of time,[19] it may be suggested that some of the observed regularities possess a value comparable to the scientific testing of textile tools. Obviously, experientially suggested functionality and possible specialisation or multifunctional use of the tested tools cannot be taken as proof that these implements were used in a similar manner in the past.

Modelling tools experience

All the original artefacts were made of poor quality clay and had smoothed surfaces, but each of the said types was modelled out of slightly different material. The traces of intensive burning that followed the damage of the cylinders with three perforations may suggest that these tools were originally unfired or very poorly fired. Only the crescent-shaped weights formed a homogeneous group of more carefully modelled and intentionally fired implements, despite their different loci of discovery and uncertain dating.[20]

Being unable to reconstruct the composition of the original clays, in our modelling experience we used high quality and ready-to-use clay that was available in a ceramic shop.[21] All copies were formed by students of archaeology who reshaped altogether three sets of EH loom weights from Tiryns using the best preserved artefact of each type as template. Most of the tools were fired for 4–6 hours in temperature of *c.* 950°C (bisque firing) in an electric ceramic kiln, but some of them were left unfired, only dried, in order to compare the possible appearance of wear marks on fired and unfired implements.

Since the weight of the loom weights was the parameter we intended to reconstruct with the utmost accuracy, in the preliminary tests the weight loss of the wet clay during drying shrinkage and then in firing was estimated.

However, since the tools were formed by hand by many actors, individual implements which belong to one set differ slightly in dimensions and weight, and there were also some differences in weight between the fired and unfired tools. All of these, as well as the differences between the parameters of the original and reconstructed implements, are shown in Table 15.1.

Experience of weaving on the warp-weighted loom

Weaving on the warp-weighted loom is practised with the actors in the manner I have been taught by Anna Grossman, archaeologist, spinner and weaver from the Biskupin Archaeological Museum in Poland, modified or adjusted according to scholarly descriptions of this technique,[22] practical solutions resulting from our experience and consultations with other colleagues. The actors are encouraged to work in groups of two to three participants and they commence work by weaving the starting border and then setting up the loom. According to the syllabus,[23] each student is obliged to participate in weaving a fabric on the warp-weighed loom, but the timespan of a single course rarely allows the participants to weave more than one small-sized textile with this specific tool (*cf.* Table 15.2).

The actors are always informed about the experimentally acknowledged correlations between the tension and the structure of a fabric (*e.g.* number of threads per cm) and the suggested optimal set-ups of the loom.[24] But, since the main aim of our weaving trials is to understand the general mechanics of the warp-weighted loom, the actors are free to choose their own set-ups and then they are expected to evaluate the results of their work.

Since all the original implements from Tiryns that were copied by us were acknowledged as possible loom weights, I decided to use them primarily for this specific function. There were no clear use-wear marks observed on the tools, except some traces of wear around the holes or perforations,[25] to indicate how exactly these tools may have been attached to the warp or, in fact, used. In our tests, warp threads were attached indirectly to these loom weights by adding a loop of thread by means of which every weight was suspended (Fig. 15.1).

The resulting textiles woven on the warp-weighted looms are predominantly coarse, strongly weft-faced tabbies of uneven quality (Table 15.2). In many cases, the tensioning of warp threads is quite high because the actors apparently prefer to start their weaving experience with heavily tensioned, sparsely distributed warp threads and strongly beaten weft; only after some time do they find it easier to weave more balanced fabrics with a lesser tension applied. Four set-ups illustrating basic parameters, such as the tension per thread, number of warp threads attached to a single weight and the structure of fabrics woven

Table 15.1 The comparison between the dimensions and weight of original and reconstructed implements (photos of original artefacts and their measurements by courtesy of Małgorzata Siennicka; photos of clay copies by Agata Ulanowska and Katarzyna Żebrowska)

	CYLINDERS WITH THREE PERFORATIONS		LARGE CONES		CRESCENT-SHAPED WEIGHTS	
	original artefact	copies: 14	original artefact	copies: 8	original artefact	copies: 23
length/height in cm	10	8.3–9.9	>10.5	10–11.5	16, 16.5	14–17
diameter/ thickness in cm	>7	6.5–7	11	9.5–11	4, 4.9	3.5–4.5
weight in g	600–650	562–578 fired 648–662 unfired	800	808–821 fired	459, 592	466–486 fired 497–514 unfired

using cylindrical, crescent-shaped and conical weights respectively, are presented in Table 15.2.

Cylinders with three perforations

Cylinders with three perforations were the first loom weights to be used in our tests and, until the spring semester of the academic year 2014/2015, nine textiles were woven with these tools by nine groups of 20 actors altogether. The cylindrical weights are highly valued by the actors using them, as being functional and easy to operate.

Their exceptional shape, with three lengthwise perforations but without any clear wear marks, made me face a problem of how to attach the warp threads to them, before any weaving tests started. My first assumption was that all three perforations were pierced for a functional purpose, therefore three additional fixing threads were drawn through all holes (Fig. 15.1). In seven weaving trials, the weights were positioned vertically side by side, but sometimes they hung without touching each other. This manner of tensioning has been evaluated by all the weavers as highly effective, since the applied tension was even and stable during the work and there was practically no need to correct it during the weaving process. However, it cannot fully explain why three perforations were pierced rather than two or just one hole, which, based on archaeological evidence, seems to have been a more common practice.[26]

Since the CTR experiments demonstrated that the heavy and thick loom weights are optimal for weaving open- or weft-faced fabrics made of thick yarn,[27] the cylinders with three perforations may have been the proper tools for this purpose. The weft-faced textiles woven in our trials generally correspond well to this correlation (Table 15.2). However, the quality of these experimentally produced fabrics, especially the number of warp threads per cm, should also be analysed with relation to the low skill level of the weavers who were not able to produce starting borders with more warp threads per cm.

In 2015, two different manners of setting up the cylindrical weights were tested. In both, cylinders were placed horizontally and, at first, only one of the perforations was used in order to draw just one loop to attach the loom weight to a bunch of warp threads. This set-up appeared to cause serious functional problems: it was difficult to place weights side by side and to provide an even tension for the warp. As a result, repetitive corrections to setting up the loom weights were required already during the phase of suspending the tools and then in weaving, making the entire work nearly impossible to perform. Moreover, the even greater thickness of tools used in this manner resulted in a more sparse distribution of warp (1.5–2 threads per cm), even with regard to the general low number of warp threads per cm in experiential fabrics.

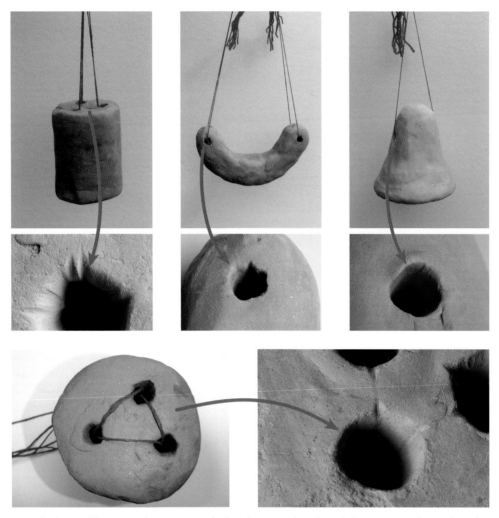

Fig. 15.1 The manner in which tested loom weights were attached to the warp threads and the use-wear observed on the reconstructed tools (photos: Miron Bogacki, Maciej Dąbski and Agata Ulanowska).

In the second attempt, the cylinders were attached in a similar manner to the spools, *i.e.* the threads were wound directly around the cylinders regardless of any perforations, and the cylinders were positioned side by side. This set up provided a stable and even tensioning during weaving, and was evaluated as comfortable and functional.

Crescent-shaped loom weights

The crescent-shaped loom weights were used for making tabby (two textiles, five actors) and twill weaves (four textiles, 10 actors). Both techniques have been previously suggested and tested, especially with regard to the tools from Late Neolithic Italy and Austria, and Middle Bronze Age Anatolia,[28] therefore, our experimenting was purely repetitive in character, except for the fact that weaving with crescent-shaped loom weights of different weight has been tried.

For tabby weaves, the crescent-shaped weights were hung up in one row, tensioning simultaneously warp threads divided into two layers. The students who used them reported that weaving went smoothly and easily, although they experienced some difficulties in distributing warp threads evenly. In my opinion, this problem resulted from the actors' lack of experience causing an uneven distribution of warp, rather than from any specific features of crescents or the tested set-up.[29] However, in the opinion of most students, crescent-shaped weights are more difficult to set up in comparison with other tested tools, such as cylindrical, discoid and spherical weights, which students clearly preferred for their weaving trials.

Weaving twill on the warp-weighted loom was a particularly interesting challenge for us, as, according to our knowledge, we would be the first to do it in Poland as part of an archaeological experiment. In 2015, twill weaves were at first tested by Anna Grossman and me with some help from our students – and then twill weaving was included in the programme of experience activities undertaken during the experience archaeology workshop in Warsaw and the regular

Table 15.2 Model loom set-ups and parameters of examples of tutorial fabrics woven using cylindrical, crescent-shaped and conical loom weights

Model loom set-ups and parameters of examples of fabrics woven with tools from Early Helladic Tiryns	Cylinders with three perforations	Crescent-shaped weights (tabby)	Crescent-shaped weights (2/1 twill)	Large cones
Number of threads per loom weight	15	8–14	8	12–15
Tension in g per thread	38	60–34	30	68–54
Diameter of warp thread in mm	1.5	1	1	1 (flax)
Diameter of weft thread in mm	1.5	1.5	1	1.5
Warp threads per cm	4	2–3	4	3
Weft threads per cm	8–7	5	9	15–16
Width of fabric in cm	60–57	36–29	26.5	27
Length of fabric in cm	15	23	9	11

University course. All woven textiles are narrow, uneven, tutorial fabrics with few warp threads per cm (*cf.* Table 15.2).

We have tested two set-ups for 2/1 twill in which crescents were combined with other loom weights, such as spools and, in the next trial, spherical weights, regardless of the archaeological evidence from EH Tiryns or elsewhere. The warp threads were already divided into three parts while weaving a starting border and two warp layers were attached to one row of crescents, whereas another type of weights was used to tension the front layer of warp threads. In the set-up for 3/1 and 2/2 twill, two rows of crescent-shaped weights were used and warp threads were divided into four layers. The front row served layers 1 + 2, the second one layers 3 + 4 respectively (Fig. 15.2).

Although the crescent-shaped weights from Tiryns are heavier than the copies of Anatolian tools used in the experiments performed by Agnete Wisti Lassen in Lejre,[30] they were operated equally easily and smoothly. The set-up with two rows of weights and three heddle bars was evaluated as being particularly functional because, besides the main advantages already listed by Lassen,[31] it provided a stable tension and facilitated clear opening of sheds, even when the initial positioning of weights, placed side by side in the overlapping rows, tangled in the process of weaving. Therefore, our initial experience with crescent-shaped weights fully confirms A. W. Lassen's opinion about the highly specialised use of these tools and their particular expediency in twill weaves.

Large cones

The peculiar form of the best-preserved EH cone from Tiryns, with a flat base and a diameter nearly equal to its height, does not have any direct analogies in the EBA Peloponnese, and only resembles pyramidal or conical loom weights from north Greece and Anatolia.[32]

They were employed as loom weights by five actors who wove two fabrics using them. In our evaluation of the overall feasibility of using conical weights for weaving, this unusual form seems to be responsible for a series of difficulties experienced, although yet again the lack of experience of the weavers should be taken into consideration (Fig. 15.3).

It was very difficult for us to position the weights side by side in a manner which would correlate the total thickness of weights with the width of the fabric,[33] but the low number of warp threads per cm (*cf.* Table 15.2) could also affect these problems. Being unable to provide the optimal set-up, we tried to avoid the effect of warp narrowing while weaving by attaching the spacing cord to the side posts of the loom that kept the warp threads distributed parallel. Still, the experimenters were hardly able to maintain an even tension of all the warp threads attached to a single cone while weaving, despite several attempts to improve the methods used for fixing it. Even in the best-evaluated set-up (*cf.* Table 15.2), in which the additional weight was attached and warp threads were wound around small sticks and then suspended by cones, the tension misaligned after several shed changes.

An argument supporting the view that the specific form of these cones may have caused the above-mentioned difficulties during work could possibly be provided by an interesting analogy coming, however, from a much later period. Joanna Słomska, in her publication of textile tools from an early medieval settlement in Tumiany-Rybaczówka in Poland, discusses two conical weights similar in shape and, in one case, weight.[34] Both implements bear traces of an intentional break on just one side of their flat oval bases. J. Słomska interprets this break as a production fault that may have appeared when the tools had dried off and the flat bases were cut with a string. However, it is also tempting to connect this damage with the technical problems that these tools may have caused in weaving, and intentional reduction of their diameter by breaking the edge to make them more suitable for hanging side by side.

Fig. 15.2 Two set-ups of crescent-shaped loom weights for 3/1, 2/2 and 2/1 twill weaves.

Tension per thread: 40–41g   Tension per thread: 54–68g

Fig. 15.3 Difficulties experienced in weaving using large conical weights. The arrows point to the following problems: left. Set-up with warp threads narrowing down; middle. Uneven tensioning of warp threads attached to one tool; right. Increasing the tension by adding an additional tool.

Other uses of Early Helladic tools from Tiryns

All the discussed types of tools were also used by us as weights in band weaving. The exact number of bands woven with gravity-tensioning, *i.e.* a vertical set-up of a band loom with warp threads tensioned by a weight, has not been registered. However, it may be estimated that at least three to five bands were woven in this manner during each academic course, as well as two to three starting borders. From these, four narrow bands woven on rigid heddles were registered on documentation cards and transferred to the Excel database.[35]

The crescent-shaped weights, specifically the implements from Late Neolithic Austria, have already been acknowledged by A. Feldtkeller as suitable tools for band weaving.[36] In Karina Grömer's reconstruction of this technique, the paired tools formed a kind of a device for band weaving in which the natural shed was provided by the thickness of both weights, whereas the counter-shed opened thanks to the heddles knitted to warp threads attached to the second crescent. At the same time, both crescents provided the necessary tension of warp. According to K. Grömer, weaving a broader band may cause technical problems resulting from the uneven spacing of warp threads.[37] Our tests were again repetitive but, nevertheless, worth undertaking mainly because of their pedagogical outcome, clearly demonstrating a broader range of possible methods of band making. In three trials undertaken by four actors, we wove three narrow bands, *e.g.* 4 cm in width. Band weaving on paired crescent-shaped weights was evaluated as smooth and easy even for the inexperienced actors and, since our bands were narrow, we did not observe the said problems with tension.

We made one attempt to use vertically suspended cylindrical weights in a similar manner, but without satisfying results. The cylinders were unstable and twisted around during the work, and their convex surfaces did not facilitate attempts to steady them; therefore weaving was troublesome and difficult, although still possible.

The cylinders with three perforations and large cones were also used as weights in our experimental weaving on rigid heddles. In this technique, the warp was set-up vertically between a fixed point and the suspended weight. The gravity-tensioned warp allows constant tension to be maintained, as in case of the tablet-weaving technique,[38] and makes it easier to keep the borders of a band even throughout the work. This set-up was not planned as part of the experienced activities, but it was suggested by one of the students who had tried it at home using bottles of water as weights. In consecutive trials undertaken in the classroom, cylindrical and conical weights were used randomly as handy tools of a weight appropriate for the task. In comparison with horizontal set-ups usually recorded in traditional rigid heddle-weaving techniques (between two

fixed points or between a fixed point and a weaver), the vertical tensioning has been evaluated as optimal by most students, but operation of the rigid heddle was described as more difficult.

Use-wear marks on the copies of Early Helladic tools from Tiryns

The use-wear marks appeared quite clearly on some of the unfired implements, being obviously less visible on the well-fired tools. The overall degree of wear has been affected by the fact that not all of the tools were used with equal frequency; moreover, cylinders and crescents were replicated as the first sets of tools, having been in use since autumn 2011, whereas the cones were modelled as late as February 2015.

The use-wear that can be seen on the edges of the tools mainly results from dropping the tools, as they accidentally slipped off warp threads or out of the hands of the actors. In the case of unfired tools, several times this led to their breaking up completely. However, abrasion marks that appeared around the holes of the cylinders and cones reflect the manner in which the tools were attached to the warp rather than any specific technique of use, whereas the use-wear marks radiating from the holes of the crescents seem also to result from the swinging movement of these tools during weaving (Fig. 15.1). Similar abrasion marks visible on the photographs of the best-preserved crescent-shaped weights form Tiryns may suggest that the EH crescents were used in a similar manner, but the use-wear marks around the perforations of the copies of cylindrical weights and cones, and the worn-out holes of the actual Bronze Age implements, do not bear any close resemblance.

Multifunctional or specialised? Final remarks

According to our experiential approach to the textile tools from Early Helladic Tiryns, all of them appeared to be useful or adaptable implements for multifunctional use: tensioning of warp threads in weaving on a warp-weighted loom and in band-weaving techniques, however, with noticeable differences regarding their suitability as loom weights.

The quite satisfactory results of weaving using the cylinders with three perforations and crescent-shaped weights contrast with our negative opinion about the large cones; however, the final evaluation of their usefulness as loom weights requires further experimenting, as well as analysis of use-wear marks on archaeological artefacts.

The suggested specialised use of crescent-shaped weights in the twill weaves and in band making has also been confirmed by us as possible, demonstrating that the same set of tools may be useful in various textile techniques. Therefore, it is possible to suggest that the widely discussed unusual shape of crescent-shaped weights may have served more than one specialist need.

This result stimulates a more general discussion of the actual input of archaeological experiments in defining possible specialisation of textile tools, with the important reservation that our tests had a purely experiential character. Nevertheless, the observed practicability of the tested techniques of use and even subjective feelings about the high expediency of crescents in twill weaving and band making,[39] as well as the resemblance between the use-wear marks on the copies and on the original crescent-shaped weights, should not be disregarded as a potential analogy to the techniques of use of these objects in past societies.

Could some textile tools have been both specialised and multifunctional implements at the same time? Let me suggest a positive answer that once again derives from our weaving experience. The multifunctional use of certain textile tools seems to be very natural when textiles have been produced in one place with a certain, however limited, range of available equipment. In such a working environment, any tool of a form and parameters usable in more textile techniques may have been sought and welcome.

Notes

1   I wish to warmly thank Dr. Małgorzata Siennicka and Prof. Lorenz Rahmstorf for inviting me to participate in the conference 'First Textiles. The Beginning of Textile Manufacture in Europe and the Mediterranean' in Copenhagen. I express my special thanks to Małgorzata Siennicka who also invited me to take part in her 'First Textiles' research project and who generously shared with me her expertise and knowledge of textile tools from Early Helladic Tiryns. I wrote this paper during my FUGA internship grant at the Centre for Research on Ancient Technologies of the Institute of Archaeology and Ethnology, Polish Academy of Sciences, awarded by the National Science Centre in Poland (DEC-2015/16/S/HS3/00085), and I wish to thank Prof. Jerzy Maik for his willingness to hold discussions and consultations about the functionality of textile tools. Finally, I would like to thank my colleagues from the Institute of Archaeology, University of Warsaw: Professors Kazimierz Lewartowski and Wojciech Nowakowski for their support of my experience approach to textile studies, especially for all hands-on activities undertaken with the students of this Institute. I warmly thank Andrzej Flis for improving my English.
2   Andersson and Nosch 2003; 2015; Mårtensson *et al.* 2005–2006; 2006a; 2006b; 2007a; 2007b; 2009; Andersson Strand 2010a; 2012.
3   Ræder Knudsen 2002, 228–229; 2012, 259–260; Gleba 2008, 140–143; Lassen 2013; 2015.
4   Mårtensson *et al.* 2007b; Siennicka and Ulanowska 2016; Grömer this volume.
5   Siennicka 2012; *cf.* Rahmstorf *et al.* 2015, 272–273.
6   Siennicka 2012, 69–71; Rahmstorf *et al.* 2015, 272–273.
7   Siennicka 2012, 67: the cylinders with three perforations were found in a concentration north of the hearth in Room 143,

whereas the large cones and crescent-shaped weights were unearthed in a corridor-like Room 144.
8   Siennicka 2012, 67, n. 16, 69.
9   Siennicka 2012, 70.
10   Andersson Strand 2010, 1–2; 2014, 41–42, *cf.* Ulanowska 2016a; 2016b, 45–48 for further discussion about the 'hands-on experience approach' as a part of experimental archaeology.
11   Miller 2007, 34–35.
12   Outram 2008, 3–4.
13   Miller 2007, 35.
14   Ulanowska 2012; 2014; Siennicka and Ulanowska 2016.
15   Ulanowska 2016a.
16   Mårtensson *et al.* 2005–2006, 3; 2009, 379; Andersson Strand 2010, 2.
17   For the card system of documentation of a woven textile and the work of an individual, see Ulanowska 2014, 153–157, figs. 1–2; 2016a; 2016b, 47, 51–52, fig. 1.
18   Ulanowska 2016a.
19   My observations of hands-on weaving experience are based on the work of 73 actors altogether, performed between the winter semester 2011 and summer semester 2015, but the number of actors using the copies of EH loom weights from Tiryns is visibly smaller: these specific numbers are given in the section discussing the weaving experience with specific tools.
20   Siennicka 2012, 69–71.
21   The commercial name of the clays we use is 'Masa ceramiczna – glina LPB' and 'Glina Dudziak'.
22   Hoffmann 1974; Mårtensson *et al.* 2005–2006; 2007a; 2009; Olofsson *et al.* 2015, 87–98.
23   For the detailed programme of the course and its specific learning outcomes, see Ulanowska 2016a; 2016c, fig. 1.
24   Mårtensson *et al.* 2007a; 2009; Olofsson *et al.* 2015, 88–92, 95–97.
25   Personal communication, Małgorzata Siennicka.
26   Siennicka 2012, 68, nn. 24 and 25; *cf.* Tzachili 2002–2003 who argues that numerous incised and very coarse cylindrical objects with one lengthwise perforation from Akrotiri served as tokens applied in a counting system rather than loom weights.
27   *Cf.* Mårtensson *et al.* 2007a; 2007b; 2009; Olofsson *et al.* 2015, 95–97.
28   *Cf.* Cornaggia Castiglioni 1964; Baioni *et al.* 2003; Lassen 2013; 2015; Grömer this volume.
29   A. W. Lassen made a similar suggestion with regard to Baioni's (Baioni *et al.* 2003) experimenting with tabby weaves and crescent-shaped loom weights (Lassen 2015, 128–129).
30   Lassen 2013, 83, 90, fig. 5.23; 2015, 131–132, fig. 4.4.12: the weight of MBA Anatolian crescents clustered between 100–300 g; whereas the copies used for archaeological experiment in Lejre, based on specific finds from Karahöyük Konya and Demircihöyük, weighed between 245–255 g.
31   Lassen 2013, 83–84; 2015, 136–137.
32   Siennicka 2012, 70, n. 33.
33   *Cf.* Mårtensson *et al.* 2007a, 15–16, figs. 8, 10, 15; 2009, 387–398, figs. 13, 15, 18; Olofsson *et al.* 2015, 91–92, figs. 4.1.19–20.

34 I would like to thank Jerzy Maik and Joanna Słomska for
    sharing this information with me; the dimensions and weight
    of the conical weights from Tumiany-Rybaczówka: cat. no.
    10/73: height 10.1 cm, diameter *c.* 8.5 cm, weight 514 g; cat.
    no. 34/73: height 10 cm, diameter *c.* 9 cm, weight 705 g,
    Słomska 2017.
35 *Cf.* Ulanowska 2016a; 2016b.
36 Feldtkeller 2003.
37 Grömer 2006; 2016, 100, fig. 51; Grömer this volume.
38 *Cf.* Ræder Knudsen 2002, 228–229; 2012, 259–260, fig. 11.11;
    for spool-tensioned warp in tablet weaving: Gleba 2008,
    140–141.
39 *Cf.* Grömer this volume for other uses of crescent-shaped
    weights.

Bibliography

Andersson, E. and Nosch, M.-L. 2003 With a little help from
    my friends: investigating Mycenaean textiles with help from
    Scandinavian experimental archaeology. In K. P. Foster and
    R. Laffineur (eds.), *METRON. Measuring the Aegean Bronze
    Age. Proceedings of the 9th International Aegean Conference,
    New Heaven, Yale University, 18–19 April 2002.* Aegaeum 24.
    Liège and Austin, 199–203.
Andersson Strand, E. 2010 The experimental textile archaeology.
    In E. Andersson Strand, M. Gleba, U. Mannering, C. Munkholt
    and M. Ringgaard (eds.), *North European Symposium for
    Archaeological Textiles X.* Ancient Textiles Series 5. Oxford
    and Oakville, 1–3.
Andersson Strand, E. 2012 From spindle whorls and loom
    weights to fabrics in the Bronze Age Aegean and Eastern
    Mediterranean. In M.-L. Nosch and R. Laffineur (eds.),
    *KOSMOS. Jewellery, Adornment and Textiles in the Aegean
    Bronze Age. Proceedings of the 13th International Aegean
    Conference/13e Rencontre égéenne internationale, University
    of Copenhagen, Danish National Research Foundation's
    Centre for Textile Research, 21–26 April 2010.* Aegaeum 33.
    Leuven and Liège, 207–213.
Andersson Strand, E. 2014 Sheep, wool and textile production. An
    interdisciplinary approach to the complexity of wool working.
    In C. Breniquet and C. Michel (eds.), *Wool Economy in the
    Ancient Near East and the Aegean. From the Beginnings of
    Sheep Husbandry to Institutional Textile Industry.* Ancient
    Textiles Series 17. Oxford and Philadelphia, 41–51.
Andersson Strand, E. and Nosch, M.-L. (eds.) 2015 *Tools, Textiles
    and Contexts. Investigating Textile Production in the Aegean
    and Eastern Mediterranean Bronze Age.* Ancient Textiles Series
    21. Oxford and Philadelphia.
Baioni, M., Borello, M. A., Feldkeller, A. and Schlichtherle,
    H. 2003. I pesi reniformi e le fusaiole piatti decorate della
    Cultura della Lagozza. Cronologia, distribuzione geografica e
    sperimentazioni. In M. Bazanella, A. Mayr, L. Moser and A.
    Rast-Eicher (eds.), *Textiles. Intrecci e tessuti dalla preistoria
    europea Museo Civico di Riva del Garda – La Rocca, 24 maggio
    –19 ottobre.* Trento, 99–109.
Cornaggia Castiglioni, O. 1964 I 'reniformi' della Lagozza.
    Origine e distribuzione eurasica dei pesi da telaio con fori
    apicali contrapposti. In Società archeologica comense (eds.)

Comum. Miscellanea di scritti in onore di Federico Frigerio.
    Como, 129–185.
Feldtkeller, A. 2003 Nierenförmige Webgewichte – wie
    funktionieren sie? *Archaeological Textiles Newsletter* 37,
    16–18.
Gleba, M. 2008 *Textile Production in Pre-Roman Italy.* Ancient
    Textile Series 4. Oxford.
Grömer, K. 2006 Vom Spinnen und Weben, Flechten und Zwirnen.
    Hinweise zur neolithischen Textiltechnik an österreichischen
    Fundstellen. In A. Krenn-Leeb, K. Grömer and P. Stadler (eds.),
    *Ein Lächeln für die Jungsteinzeit. Ausgewählte Beiträge zum
    Neolithikum Ostösterreichs. Festschrift für Elisabeth Ruttkay.*
    Archäologie Österreichs 17.2, 177–192.
Grömer, K. 2016 *The Art of Prehistoric Textile Making. The
    Development of Craft Traditions and Clothing in Central Europe.*
    Veröffentlichungen der Prähistorischen Abteilung 5. Wien.
Hoffmann, M. 1974 (1st edition 1964) *The Warp-Weighted Loom,
    Studies in the History and Technology of an Ancient Implement.*
    Oslo, Bergen and Tromsø.
Lassen, A. W. 2013 Technology and palace economy in Middle
    Bronze Age Anatolia: the case of the crescent shaped loom
    weight. In M.-L. Nosch, H. Koefoed and E. Andersson Strand
    (eds.), *Textile Production and Consumption in the Ancient Near
    East. Archaeology, Epigraphy, Iconography.* Ancient Textiles
    Series 12. Oxford and Oakville, 78–92.
Lassen, A. W. 2015 Weaving with crescent shaped loom weights.
    An investigation of a special kind of loom weight. In E.
    Andersson Strand and M.-L. Nosch (eds.), *Tools, Textiles and
    Contexts. Investigating Textile Production in the Aegean and
    Eastern Mediterranean Bronze Age.* Ancient Textiles Series 21.
    Oxford and Philadelphia, 127–137.
Mårtensson, L., Andersson, E., Nosch, M.-L. and Batzer, A.
    2005–2006 Technical Report. Experimental Archaeology Part 1,
    2005–2006, Tools and Textiles – Texts and Contexts Research
    Programme, The Danish National Research Foundation's
    Centre for Textile Research (CTR) University of Copenhagen
    (https://ctr.hum.ku.dk/research-programmes-and-projects/
    previous-programmes-and-projects/tools/technical_report_1_
    experimental_archaeology.pdf, accessed 25 September 2018).
Mårtensson, L., Andersson, E., Nosch, M-L. and Batzer, A.
    2006a Technical Report. Experimental Archaeology Part
    2.1 Flax, Tools and Textiles – Texts and Contexts Research
    Programme, The Danish National Research Foundation's
    Centre for Textile Research (CTR) University of Copenhagen
    (https://ctr.hum.ku.dk/research-programmes-and-projects/
    previous-programmes-and-projects/tools/technical_report_2-1_
    experimental_archaeology.pdf, accessed 25 September 2018).
Mårtensson, L., Andersson, E., Nosch, M.-L. and Batzer, A. 2006b
    Technical Report. Experimental Archaeology Part 2.2 Whorl
    or Bead?, Tools and Textiles – Texts and Contexts Research
    Programme, The Danish National Research Foundation's Centre
    for Textile Research (CTR) University of Copenhagen (https://
    ctr.hum.ku.dk/research-programmes-and-projects/previous-
    programmes-and-projects/tools/technical_report_2-2__
    experimental_arcaheology.pdf, accessed 25 September 2018).
Mårtensson, L., Andersson, E., Nosch, M.-L. and Batzer, A. 2007a
    Technical Report. Experimental Archaeology Part 3 Loom
    weights, Tools and Textiles – Texts and Contexts Research

Programme, The Danish National Research Foundation's Centre for Textile Research (CTR) University of Copenhagen (https://ctr.hum.ku.dk/research-programmes-and-projects/previous-programmes-and-projects/tools/technical_report_3__experimental_archaeology.pdf, accessed 25 September 2018).

Mårtensson, L., Andersson, E., Nosch, M.-L. and Batzer, A. 2007b Technical Report. Experimental Archaeology Part 4 Spools, Tools and Textiles – Texts and Contexts Research Programme, The Danish National Research Foundation's Centre for Textile Research (CTR) University of Copenhagen (https://ctr.hum.ku.dk/research-programmes-and-projects/previous-programmes-and-projects/tools/technical_report_4__experimental_arcaheology.pdf, accessed 25 September 2018).

Mårtensson, L., Nosch, M.-L. and Andersson Strand, E. 2009 Shape of things: understanding a loom weight. *Oxford Journal of Archaeology* 28.4, 373–398.

Miller, H. M. L. 2007 *Archaeological Approaches to Technology.* Amsterdam, Boston, Heidelberg, London, New York, Oxford, Paris, San Diego, San Francisco, Singapore, Sydney and Tokyo.

Olofsson, L., Andersson Strand, E. and Nosch, M.-L. 2015 Experimental testing of Bronze Age textile tools. In E. Andersson Strand and M.-L. Nosch (eds.), *Tools, Textiles and Contexts. Investigating Textile Production in the Aegean and Eastern Mediterranean Bronze Age.* Ancient Textile Series 21. Oxford and Philadelphia, 75–100.

Outram, A. K. 2008 Introduction to experimental archaeology. *World Archaeology* 40.1, 1–6.

Ræder Knudsen, L. 2002 La tessitura con le tavolette nella tomba 89. In P. von Eles (ed.), *Guerriero e sacerdote. Autorità e comunità nell'età del ferro a Verrucchio. La tomba del trono.* Firenze, 230–243.

Ræder Knudsen, L. 2012 Case study: the tablet woven borders of Verucchio. In M. Gleba and U. Mannering (eds.), *Textiles and Textile Production in Europe: From Prehistory to AD 400.* Ancient Textile Series 11. Oxford and Oakville, 254–263.

Rahmstorf, L., Siennicka, M., Andersson Strand, E., Nosch, M.-L. and Cutler, J. 2015 Textile tools from Tiryns. In E. Andersson Strand and M.-L. Nosch (eds.), *Tools, Textiles and Contexts, Investigating Textile Production in the Aegean and Eastern Mediterranean Bronze Age.* Ancient Textiles Series 21. Oxford and Philadelphia, 267–278.

Siennicka, M. 2012 Textile production in Early Helladic Tiryns. In M.-L. Nosch and R. Laffineur (eds.), *KOSMOS. Jewellery, Adornment and Textiles in the Aegean Bronze Age. Proceedings of the 13th International Aegean Conference/13e Rencontre égéenne internationale, University of Copenhagen, Danish National Research Foundation's Centre for Textile Research, 21–26 April 2010.* Aegaeum 33. Leuven and Liège, 65–74.

Siennicka, M. and Ulanowska, A. 2016 Contextual and experimental approach to clay 'spools' from Bronze Age Greece. In J. Ortiz, C. Alfaro, L. Turell and Ma. J. Martínez (eds.), *PURPUREAE VESTES V. Textiles and Dyes in Antiquity. Ancient Textiles, Basketry and Dyes in the Ancient Mediterranean World. Textiles, Cestería y Tintes en el mundo mediterráneo antiguo. Proceedings of the Vth International Symposium on Textiles and Dyes in the Ancient Mediterranean World (Montserrat, 19–22 March, 2014).* València, 25–36.

Słomska, J. 2017 Zeugnisse der Textilproduktion in der Siedlung Tumiany-Rybaczówka, Fundstelle 2, Kreis Olsztyn. In T. Baranowski (ed.), *Völkerwanderungszeitliche Siedlung von Tumiany (Daumen) im Kreise Allenstein. Tumiany. Woj. warmińsko-mazurskie.* Vetera et Nova VII. Warszawa/Warschau, 275–288.

Tzachili, I. 2002–2003 The clay cylinders from Akrotiri, Thera. A non literate alternative way of accounting? *MINOS. Revista de filología Egea* 37–38, 7–76.

Ulanowska, A. 2012 Odtwarzanie dawnych technik tkackich w Instytucie Archeologii Uniwersytetu Warszawskiego poprzez archeologię doświadczalną. In P. Militello and M. Camera (eds.), *Ricerche e attività del corso internazionalizzato di archeologia. Catania, Varsavia, Konya 2009–2012.* Syndesmoi 3. Palermo, 239–262.

Ulanowska, A. 2014 The economics of weaving – aspects of labour in the Bronze Age Aegean. In K. Droß-Krüpe (ed.), *Textile Trade and Distribution in Antiquity.* Philippika 73. Wiesbaden, 151–159.

Ulanowska, A. 2016a Towards methodological principles for experience textile archaeology. Experimental approach to the Aegean Bronze Age textile techniques in the Institute of Archaeology, University of Warsaw. *Prilozi Instituta za arheologiju u Zagrebu* 33, 317–339.

Ulanowska, A. 2016b Experimental approach to the ergonomics of textile production in Bronze Age Greece. Limitations and prospects. *Archaeological Textiles Review* 58, 43–56.

Ulanowska, A. 2016c Włókiennictwo Grecji epoki brązu w (akademickiej) praktyce. Nowe refleksje nad zastosowaniem archeologii doświadczalnej w nauczaniu technologii dawnego włókiennictwa. In M. Figueira and K. Żebrowska (eds.), *International Course in Archaeology. 'Papers in Mediterranean Archaeology.'* Syndesmoi 5. Catania, 215–234.

Textile tools and manufacture in the Early Bronze Age Cyclades: evidence from Amorgos and Keros

Giorgos Gavalas

Introduction

A synthesis of recently published data on textile tools from the Cycladic islands of Amorgos and Keros in the Aegean is discussed in this paper.[1] The aim is to sketch an outline of the textile manufacture history and its development during the 3rd millennium BC in the island communities of the central Aegean, where the Cycladic culture flourished.

This period and this culture are still rather obscure due to the lack of research and published accounts of important sites. In order to place this contribution in its socio-economic context, a brief introduction on the Cycladic culture of the Early Bronze Age is given below.

Introduction: the broader picture

The rigid and dry island complex of the Cyclades, in the centre of the Aegean, is particularly known as the place where the Early Cycladic (EC) culture flourished, with distinct features, in relation to cultures on both sides of the Aegean, bridging Europe and Asia. It spans the Final Neolithic to the Early Bronze Age period, the 4th and 3rd millennia BC. The Early Cycladic culture[2] is characterised by the production and consumption of prestigious stone artefacts, mainly of white marble (figurines and vessels), and of metal tools and weapons, mainly of bronze (a mixture of copper with arsenic and tin alloys), and more rarely artefacts of silver and gold.

Until recently, research has been focused on burials, isolated groups of graves and some organised cemeteries where a few indicators, such as prestige burial offerings, weapons, jewellery, marble and other stone vessels and marble figurines suggest some kind of social differentiation and hierarchical organisation. Only a few settlements have been investigated that exhibit some proto-urban characteristics. The general impression is that nuclear families were living in small and medium-size settlements, sometimes fortified and featuring architectural complexity, and were in constant communication and interaction with each other. These settlements were usually located on hills above protected bays, with visibility of the sea routes, which was important for navigation.

The material culture includes seals and sealings (indications of greater social and economic integration and related to ownership), along with other artefacts imported from distant areas. These, along with the dispersal of artefacts of Melos obsidian, suggest long-distance trade and contacts within a broader area. Agriculture, hunting, fishing and animal husbandry were the main economic resources of these societies; the exploitation of ores for metals became another notable resource during this period. High standard metal-working was practised, as bronze artefacts and metal-smelting areas indicate. For most scholars, this culture was the stage before the emergence of the more complicated socio-economical structures seen in the Aegean in the Middle and the Late Bronze Age.[3]

Although only limited evidence has been found and published so far, textile manufacture seems to have played a significant role in the social and economic life of the Early Bronze Age Cyclades,[4] as in the north-east Aegean.[5] In the main, new evidence comes from the numerous textile tools – spindle whorls – found at Markiani, a fortified settlement on Amorgos, and a few found in the central site on Dhaskalio and the special site in Dhaskalio Kavos on Keros. In relation to these, the bronze and bone tools from both sites are also discussed. Textile imprints on clay vessels and the only small piece textile found to date, mineralised on a dagger and currently under study, have allowed some comments on the raw materials used for the fibre used in textiles.

The fact that these finds come from specific areas also provides the basis of discussion on matters of craft specialisation[6] in textile production in the Cyclades during the 3rd millennium BC. The comparison of the two sites offers the opportunity to suggest that they might have operated together, creating a functional economic network.

Methodology

Several approaches have been applied in order to attempt to understand the textile production in the Cyclades during the 3rd millennium BC. First, limited iconographical analysis has been carried out on the very few depictions of cloths on preserved pieces of sculpture. For all tools, spindle whorls, pins, needles and awls, a contextual approach was used, since they all come from well stratified and absolutely dated layers. Their classification was a result of a combination of approaches, both typo-chronological and functional. Scientific analysis was limited to characterisation of the provenance of the raw materials for the tools, fabrics and wares.

No experimental spinning with replicas has yet been carried out. The intention is that this will be employed to provide a better understanding of the relationship between the raw materials, tools and range of yarns produced, as has been the case elsewhere.[7]

Iconography

The Early Cycladic iconography is limited to figurative sculptures. In the few traced petroglyphs,[8] there are only schematic representations, which do not allow comments on textiles. There are no naturalistic human representations on the pottery, where usually geometric patterns, triangles and spirals, are depicted.[9]

Figurines represent nude female figures with folded arms, and rarely male ones; there are some special standing or seated figures, such as warriors or musicians. Nudity is the main characteristic of all types, with emphasis on female genitalia. This is related to the spirit of the community, which connects the human societies with the sphere of symbolism and ideology. Painted decoration has been traced; this was used for the indication of the eyes and mouths, but also for hair, possible head covers or painted body decoration,[10] which seems to have similar symbolic function.

Textiles are rarely depicted;[11] these are limited to representations of head covers, usually conical caps, and of bands around the waist, or of postpartum bindings. Baldrics running from the right shoulder to the left side are seen on some male figures. These are presented in a schematic way and seem to suggest status, and differentiation within a hierarchical social system.

Textile tools

Textile tools, namely a small number of spindle whorls, were used as burial offerings in cemeteries: at Spedhos, Ag.

Anargyroi and Aplomata (on Naxos), Avyssos (on Paros), Chalandriani (on Syros) and Dhokathismata (on Amorgos); they were also found in settlements: in Pyrgos (on Paros), in Kastri and Chalandriani (on Syros), in Kato Akrotiri and Vigla at Katapola, and in Larnaki at Aegiali (Amorgos), in Mount Kynthos (Delos) and in Phylakopi (Melos). Some perforated clay discs were used for the same purpose.[12]

Notable new finds of textile tools have been recently revealed and studied comprehensively by the author from the recent systematic investigations carried out on two neighbouring islands, from Markiani on Amorgos[13] and Keros at its NW end, where Dhaskalio Kavos[14] and the islet of Dhaskalio[15] are located.

Markiani is a fortified settlement within the area of Notina, SW Amorgos. The density of scattered artefacts over an area of about 3000 m² defined it as a small to medium-sized rural village, situated on the top of a hill, which had visibility of the sea routes from the Dodecanese. The fortification wall surrounded the upper terraces at the north and at least three horseshoe bastions were attached to it. In the south the settlement was built in terraces and some architectural complexes incorporating natural features have been investigated: rectangular rooms, (spaces 1, 3, 5; rooms 1 and 2 in Trench 3; Trench 4), open areas (spaces 2 and 4), a drain (in spaces 6, 4, 3, 2) and a special semicircular, probably two storied, area (space 8, the 'fissure', and space 7) with three successive building phases Ma II–IV in the local chronology[16] (Fig. 16.1 b). These were absolutely dated by ¹⁴C and the pottery, and were related to the established system of Early Cycladic chronology, as follows: Ma I (Grotta-Pelos group = EC I), Ma II (Kampos group = EC I/II), Ma III (Keros-Syros group = ECII), Ma IV (early Kastri group = EC II late).[17] The occupation was less intense during phases I and II, and the site underwent expansion in phases III and IV, when it was destroyed and abandoned.

The island of Keros is situated between Amorgos and Naxos. Parts of a complex site were investigated in two areas: on Dhaskalio Kavos at the NW end of Keros and on the islet of Dhaskalio. Systematic multidisciplinary investigations have proven that the islet of Dhaskalio was originally connected to the opposite stretch of land, Dhaskalio Kavos, with an isthmus creating two ports.

On the natural cone of the Dhaskalio islet, a large settlement was found, built in terraces. On the top of the hill notable architectural complexes have been revealed; at the north end a large tripartite hall with an apsidal end and at the south a more complicated structure with many rooms connected through small passages. The stratigraphy on Dhaskalio has three successive building phases, dated absolutely by ¹⁴C: Dhaskalio phase A = Markiani III, Dhaskalio phase B = Markiani IV and Dhaskalio phase C, with pottery of the late Kastri group = EC III.[18]

At Dhaskalio Kavos, earlier finds in the northern area which had been disturbed by looting have been understood as belonging to a 'special deposit' (the 'North

Markiani Amorgos
Textile tools

phase	Space/room	Terrace 1								Trench 3		'fissure'	Trench 4
		1	2	3	4	5	6	7	8	R1	R2		
MaII (Kampos group) 2900-2700 BC	Spindle whorls							5	7				
	Shaped perforated sherds												
	Total number 12												
MaIII (Keros-Syros group) 2700-2400 BC	Spindle whorls									2	2	49	10
	Shaped perforated sherds											10	
	Total number 73												
MaIV (Kastri group) 2400-2200 BC	Spindle whorls	6	5	6	1	28	3	43					
	Shaped perforated sherds	1				5		13					3
	Total number 114												

c

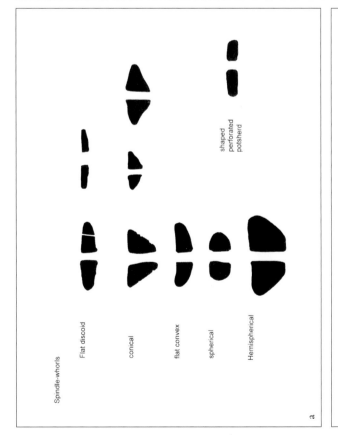

Spindle-whorls

Flat discoid

conical

flat convex

spherical

Hemispherical

shaped perforated potsherd

a

Markiani	Spindle whorls	Shaped perforated sherds
Total number	171	31
intact	81	17
fragments	90	14

b

Fig. 16.1 Markiani: a. typology of spindle whorls; b. total number of spindle whorls and perforated discs; c. table with quantities of spindle whorls in architectural spaces according to chronological phases.

Special Deposit'),[19] of broken prestigious artefacts, such as marble vessels and figurines. This became clear after the investigation of another undisturbed deposit, the 'South Special Deposit'[20] covered by a cairn of stones at the other end of this area, opposite Dhaskalio islet. These are related to symbolic, ceremonial communal activities. This place was used over a long period of time by various communities or social groups, since most of the deposited artefacts were imported from many of the Cycladic islands and elsewhere.[21]

Between the two deposits, there is an area with built structures of unknown character. In the northern area, some cist graves and kilns for metal smelting were found; to the south, a row of small caves with burials was investigated. The 'South Special Deposit' does not present clear stratigraphy; over a long period of time, artefacts were deposited in small pits, and the chronology is relative, corresponding to the Dhaskalio phases;[22] all the layers investigated in the 'North Special Deposit' were disturbed, but the pottery corresponds to the known chronology.

Markiani Amorgos

The large quantities of spindle whorls and shaped perforated sherds found in Markiani on Amorgos,[23] 203 in total, are comparable in number only with the large quantities of tools from Troy. Of these, 171 of them were recovered in successive layers inside the circular feature. Within the same deposits, 31 clay discs made from cut and perforated potsherds were found in association with the spindle whorls, as in many places on the Greek mainland and in Thermi on Lesbos,[24] and thus these are examined together (Fig. 16.1 c). They are dated from Markiani phases II to IV.

Of the 171 whorls, only six are of stone. In the case of the clay spindle whorls, the fabrics are similar to those used for pottery. Two categories that are considered local, Marble ware and Blue Schist ware, are the most frequent.

The Markiani spindle whorls were classified using typological and functional criteria:[25] shape of section, ratio of diameter to thickness and weight and diameter of perforation. The size has been determined on more accurate metrological data assimilated by recording the heights, weights and diameters of the central perforation. According to all of these criteria, the main basic types[26] are as follows (Fig. 16.1 a):

- discoidal with a few variants
- conical, low and high
- flat convex, large and small
- spherical
- hemispherical.

These were persistent for a long period of time and only a few new types emerged in the later periods. The weight and diameter of perforation ratio allowed further observations about the spindles used in Amorgos.

In Markiani phase II[27] there is a preference for wider discoidal and low conical wide types of medium and small size (Fig. 16.2 a–b); a small degree of deviation from the dominant trends may be observed. The perforation diameter reveals that there were two types of spindles, one with a stem diameter of 0.7 cm, and one of 0.8 cm (Fig. 16.2 c). With the first one, medium and lighter whorls of up to 14 g were used; with the second one, all the sizes were used, mainly with heavier whorls, up to 50 g; the light ring-like cylindrical spindle whorl was probably used in combination with another one, or for a particular type of work. These parameters reveal the second thicker spindle was more popular and that it was probably longer than the thinner one.

In Markiani phase III,[28] the basic types are seen to be the discoidal spindle whorl in a great variety of sizes, and the conical one. Most of the types continue to be wide and low, and have similar sizes with slight variation, and the biconical type is introduced (Fig. 16.3 a–b). The shaped perforated sherds are similar in size to those of stone (Fig. 16.3 d). The diameter and weight ratio (Fig. 16.3 c) shows that they were used with several more types of spindles. We are able to distinguish eight different ones, raging in diameter from 0.6 to 1.1 cm. With the thinner spindles, light whorls, weighing 7 to 10 g, were used. Lightweight spindle whorls, around 13 g, were used also with the thicker spindle that was identified, with diameter 1.0 cm. The spindles of thickness 0.7 cm were used with medium-weight whorls, from 23 to 30 g. Finally, those with a thickness of 0.8 to 1.0 cm were used with whorls weighing 37 to 39 g.

In Markiani phase IV,[29] there is a slight variation between the basic types (Fig. 16.4 a–b, d), but greater variety in size. Only the hemispherical examples are considerably heavier and larger. Discoidal whorls are small in size and low, or medium and high, while the cylindrical ones are small and low. Conical whorls have a medium to large diameter and are low and high. Biconical and the biconvex ones are of medium height and usually medium and large width. Hemispherical whorls are of medium and large height and medium and very large diameter. Spherical examples are high with medium diameters, and resemble hemispherical whorls. Finally, the disc-shaped perforated sherds are low and similar in size to the small discoidal spindle whorls, weighing 11–33 g (Fig. 16.4 d–f).

A small number of the spindle whorls bear some kind of decoration, either incised or impressed, with linear patterns known from the north-east Aegean and a unique figurative motif.[30]

We distinguish nine different spindles, ranging in thickness between 0.5–1.1 cm (Fig. 16.4 c). Spindles with thickness of 0.5, 0.6 and 0.7 cm were used with light small whorls, 7–10 g. A slightly heavier whorl, weight 13–19 g, could be used with spindles of thickness 0.5–0.9 cm. Medium-weight whorls of different types, weighing 21–36 g, could be used with all the different

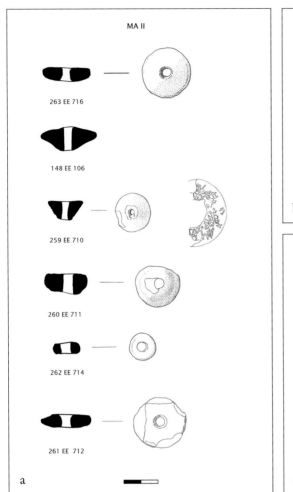

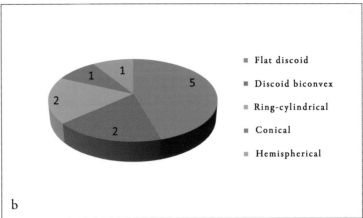

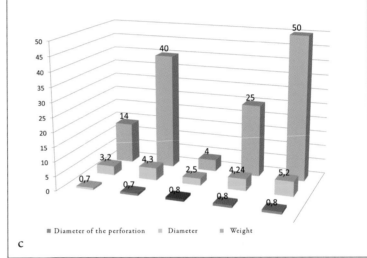

Fig. 16.2 Markiani phase II: a. typology of spindle whorls; b. quantities; c. weight-diameter ratio.

spindles. Heavier spindle whorls of 41 g were used with a spindle 0.7–0.9 cm diameter. The heavy hemispherical type, weighing 58–116 g, is seen in small quantities at Markiani; these were used exclusively with the largest spindles of 0.9 cm thickness.

Dhaskalio and Dhaskalio Kavos on Keros

At the settlement of Dhaskalio,[31] the textile tools are remarkably few in number, consisting of four clay spindle whorls and three shaped perforated sherds, found mainly in the buildings near the summit (Fig. 16.5 a). The four spindle whorls come from the building complex of Trenches XX, XXV and VII, and they are dated to Dhaskalio Phase C (EC III period = later than Ma IV). One was found in Trench II, on the east slope and has been dated to Dhaskalio Phase A (= Ma III). They are of micaceous ware and are supposed to have been imported to the site. One is flat discoidal, one conical and two biconical; they are small and low. This type, which is a combination of uneven cones, the upper flat ellipsoid, the lower truncated, is known mainly

from the north-east Aegean, from Troy and Poliochni. In general, the spindle whorls from Dhaskalio and the shaped perforated sherds, which were heavier, are rather light in weight, 11–16 g.

The range of perforation diameters of the whorls suggests that the spindles had a diameter between 0.3–0.8 cm.

To these tools should be added a unique fragment from a deep bowl[32] (Fig. 16.5 b), which seems to be a spinning bowl; this is a rim to base fragment, dimensions as follows: rim diameter 12 cm and thickness 0.45–0.50 cm, with a horizontal internal perforated lug, diameter 0.3–0.35 cm, close to the rim. It is dated to Dhaskalio phase C, and comes from the building complex at the summit, from Trench XXV, layer 24. Examples of vessels with internal lugs or handles have been found in the Aegean[33] as early as the Late Neolithic at Emporio (Chios) and from Partheni (Leros), but they are also present at Tiryns (Peloponnese) and Myrtos (Crete) during the Early Bronze Age.

At Dhaskalio Kavos on Keros, two intact and one fragmentary plain clay spindle whorl of the flat discoidal

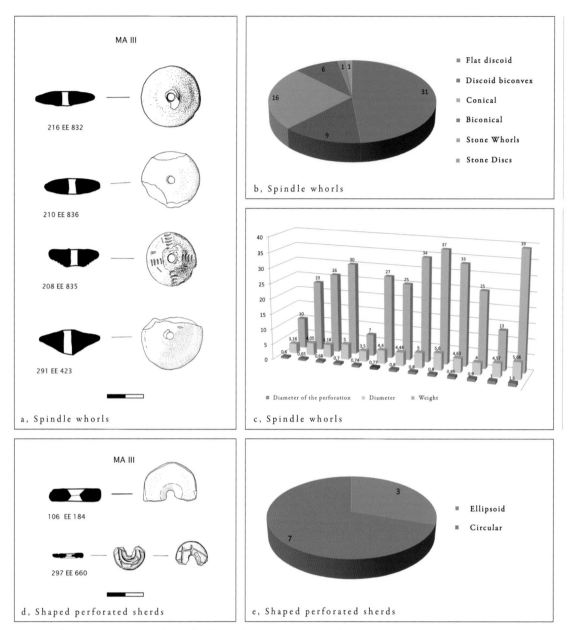

Fig. 16.3 Markiani phase III: a. typology of spindle whorls; b. quantities; c. weight-diameter ratio of spindle whorls; d. typology of shaped perforated sherds; e. quantities of shaped perforated sherds.

type (Fig. 16.5 c), and a possible shaped perforated disc, were found in the 'North Special Deposit'[34] within Trenches V and VII during the 1987 investigations. They are all assigned to a fabric category, Sandy ware, which has been supposed to have been imported to the site. The diameters of the perforation suggest at least two types of spindle, one wider (0.5 cm) and another very thin (0.2–0.3 cm), possibly for very fine yarn.

From Dhaskalio Kavos,[35] two more shaped perforated sherds (Fig. 16.5 d) were found in the 'South Special Deposit' during the 2006–2008 investigations. Their light weights, between 7 and 16 g, suggest that the threads that were produced were not very strong or of the best quality,

or suitable for proper weaving, but they could have been used for the production of rather loose rough rugs or ropes.

Other tools related to textiles and leather

Finally, in both Markiani on Amorgos and Keros, some other tools, of bronze and bone, were found related to textile manufacture and to leather processing.

The bronze pins and needles[36] from Markiani have been assigned to known types, mainly seen in the north-east Aegean. One resembles the modern bodkin or packing needle; its use was probably specialised, perhaps for sewing of rather hard materials such as leather.

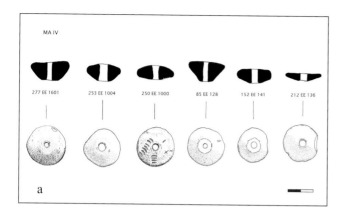

a

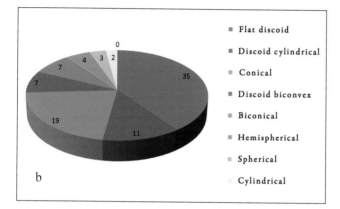

b

On Dhaskalio a few copper needles and one pin were found,[37] while at Dhaskalio Kavos, in the 'North Special Deposit', were only some bronze awls.[38]

From both Markiani[39] and Dhaskalio[40] there are some further pointed tools of bone and awls, which may have been used in the processing of leather.

Impressions of textiles and textile remains

Evidence of mat and textile impressions on potsherds was recovered from both sites. Handmade pots, air-dried to the leather hard stage, had been resting on these items. Most of the 59 mat impressions were found on pottery imported from other Cycladic islands. The mats were woven either tightly or loosely, made with the warp strands of finer material than the weft, using the twining technique, either simple twining on a parallel warp or split twining where the warp strands were alternately split or combined by the weft strands on alternate rows, and finally there was evidence of circular mats made by radial twining over a 'star-shaped' warp.

Three fragments of cloth impressions,[41] out of 72 impressions mainly of mats and leaves on pot bases, were found in Markiani. They are all small fragments, and show a simple tabby weave where the weft passes under and over alternate warp threads. K1557 is a fragment of cloth with seven rows of weft threads to 2.5 cm and is rather loosely woven with a double weft and the warp showing between

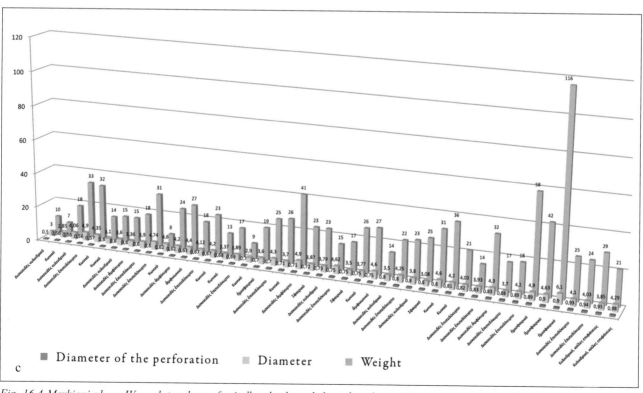

c

Fig. 16.4 Markiani phase IV: a, d. typology of spindle whorls and shaped perforated sherds; b. quantities of spindle whorls; c. weight-diameter ratio of spindle whorls; e. quantities of shaped perforated sherds; f. weight-diameter ratio of shaped perforated sherds.

each row of weft threads. K1341 shows 11 weft threads to 2.5 cm and is the finest fabric represented, while K1340 shows about 10 weft threads to 2.5 cm.

In the Dhaskalio settlement, 21 mat impressions, the same style as those from Markiani, were found, while at Dhaskalio Kavos on Keros there were only four. From the latter there was also a small cloth impression[42] (SF139) of simple tabby weave. This was a rather coarse cloth, with 10 warp threads to 1.9 cm and 5 rows of weft to 1 cm, it is quite tightly woven, so that not much of the warp is showing.

From the Dhaskalio Kavos 'South Special Deposit' there are 62 mat impressions of the techniques mentioned above.

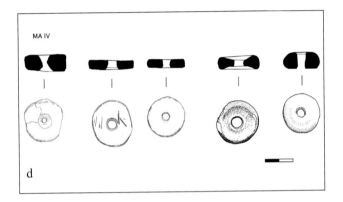

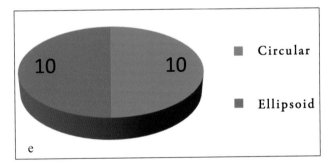

There are 20 cloth impressions,[43] comparing well with the finds from Markiani and the 'North Special Deposit' on Dhaskalio Kavos. They are all of a simple tabby weave, with the weft going over one warp and under the next, while on the next row the weft passes under the warps which in the first row it went over, and over the ones which it went under. Where the warp is visible, it seems it may consist of more than one strand, each being much thinner than the single weft. The warp and the weft were usually the same, giving the same density. Twelve examples had 40 rows per 10 cm; five had 32 rows per 10 cm and 2 had 28 rows per 10 cm; only one (KSC8) was finer, with 70 rows in 10 cm.

Only one piece of mineralised textile dated to the 3rd millennium BC has been found in the Cyclades, and this comes from Amorgos. A tabby scrap, identified as linen,[44] was found on a dagger blade from tomb 14 in Dhokathismata Amorgos by Chr. Tsountas, and is dated to EC II (Keros-Syros group). There are also threads, identified as linen, on pins.[45]

Raw materials for fibres

Further observations may be made about the raw materials exploited and used for fibres, based on the evidence of textile remains and the study of the archaeozoological material on both sites.

Evidence of the use of flax identified in the few cloth remains, and of the use of wool mainly coming from the study of animal bones, implies a rather sophisticated model of successful strategies for agriculture and animal herding, in order for necessary raw materials for fibres to be obtained.

The use of flax (*Linum usitatissimum* L.) is certain,[46] although no seeds have been found; the fibres on the mineralised cloth have been identified as such.

Wool gradually became the most commonly used raw material for textiles during the 3rd millennium BC, and it

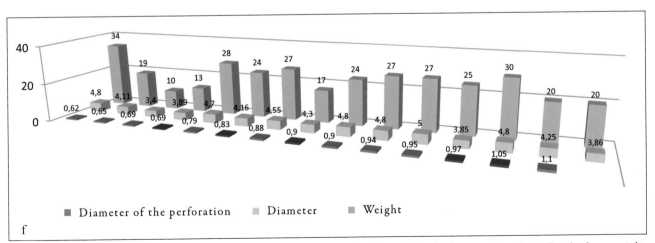

Fig. 16.4 Markiani phase IV: a, d. typology of spindle whorls and shaped perforated sherds; b. quantities of spindle whorls; c. weight-diameter ratio of spindle whorls; e. quantities of shaped perforated sherds; f. weight-diameter ratio of shaped perforated sherds.

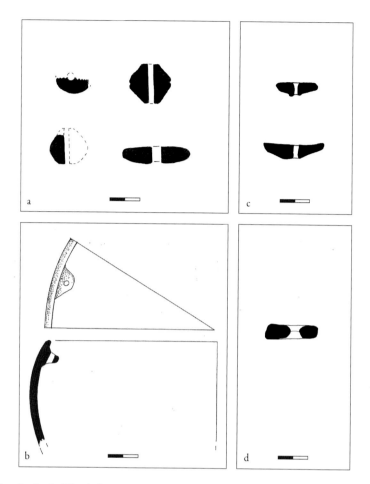

Fig. 16.5 a. Dhaskalio spindle whorls; b. Dhaskalio spinning bowl; c. Keros, Dhaskalio Kavos 'North Special Deposit', spindle whorls; d. Keros, Dhaskalio Kavos, 'South Special Deposit', shaped perforated sherd.

has been associated with the appearance of a new, larger and woolly variety of sheep.[47] In Markiani on Amorgos, it has been suggested[48] that sheep and goat were also bred for fibre. The ages of slaughtering and the estimation of wither height from sheep metapodial lengths point to this conclusion. Animal husbandry seems to have been one of the main economic activities at Markiani. This site was almost certainly also a location for leather working.

The archaeozoological material from Dhaskalio[49] suggests the animals were slaughtered at between 1 and 3 years of age. The few animal bones found there do not allow further analysis.

Discussion

Due to the large number of textile tools found at Markiani, we have abundant evidence of yarn manufacture for textiles there. The frequent presence of spindle whorls and clay discs in particular areas of the settlement provides evidence to suggest that these are possible areas where spinning and possibly other textile production took place or, at least, as

the place where textile implements were stored. A similar picture has been observed on other sites. At Asomatos on Rhodes, some small spindle whorls were found in Room D. In some areas of the building complex at Myrtos on Crete, many loom weights and some spindle whorls were found, and also perforated stone disks, as well as stone rubbers and mortars (presumably for the first processing of raw materials). In deposits in several excavated areas relating to phase V at Sitagroi in eastern Macedonia, spindle whorls, loom weights and bone tools were discovered.[50]

The range of spindle whorl types suggest an intentional variation corresponding to the production of various types of threads of different fabrics, flax or wool; they are also related to various stages of spinning. There is a preference for flat discoidal and conical spindle whorls, seen also in the rest of the Cyclades. In Asia Minor and in the islands of the east Aegean, biconical and spherical spindle whorls are more common. At the same time, on the Greek mainland, and especially on coastal sites, such as Lefkandi on Euboia and Ayios Kosmas in Attica, there is a clear preference for conical whorls, cylindrical spindle whorls of larger size, and for other varieties that are not very common in the rest of the Aegean.[51] The heavy and low hemispherical spindle whorls were thought, until recently, to have been used exclusively in the north-east Aegean, in Poliochni (on Lemnos) and Thermi (on Lesbos).[52] These were most likely used for flax spinning, while other lighter types were probably used for wool.

The exact use of perforated clay disks is more problematic. It may be that they were used in place of spindle whorls for particular specialised work;[53] their possible use reveals a variability of options for spinning, or they might have been used in the production of coarser threads, or for the first stage of spinning a loose thread, which would then be subjected to further processing.

The decoration of the spindle whorls may be another indication of their use for specialised work. The stamped pattern made with a seal on a spindle whorl from Markiani, which has a parallel to a seal from Lerna,[54] may be an indication of ownership, suggesting some social organisation of the crafters.

The small number of textile tools found in Dhaskalio suggests that textile production was very limited there. No area of the site appears to have been used specifically for making thread or producing textiles. The same pattern is also evident from the few tools found within the two 'Special Deposits' in Dhaskalio Kavos.

The biconical type of spindle whorls that is a clear import and unrelated to the Markiani spindle whorl types from this assemblage suggests the introduction of a spinning technique from another established textile tradition seen in the north-east Aegean. This is also demonstrated by the fragment of a spinning bowl, which remains unique for this period in the Cyclades; its presence suggests contacts with other areas of the Aegean and the Mediterranean, and introduction of a new innovative technique established there.

Decoration on one biconical spindle whorl from Keros, consisting of incised signs resembling potters' marks, is identical to the decoration on one of the tuyères,[55] and should be noted. This could support Völling's[56] suggestions that some artefacts identified as spindle whorls may have functioned in multiple ways, such as a means for fastening ropes,[57] with indications of ownership or workshop, and in many cases their decoration might be related to specific quantities and materials. It is notable that this biconical spindle whorl has both its weight and diameter of perforation in absolute accordance to other spindle whorls.

It is striking that no loom weights have been found from either site. As previously noted from other Cycladic sites, it seems the vertical warp loom was not in use, as *e.g.* at Troy where traces of a vertical warp loom were found, or at Thermi on Lesbos in the north-east Aegean, and at Myrtos in Crete, where discoidal loom weights were found.

The absence of loom weights from other sites in the Cyclades of this period suggest that another type of loom was in use, either the ground or a vertical type with two

beams.[58] Nevertheless, traces of either are very difficult to identify in the archaeological record.[59]

The cloth impressions on the pot bases found on all the sites are notably coarse and probably represent some sort of sacking-type cloth. The impressions show that the pieces of cloth were in worn condition, and some had holes in them, but they are not very distinct, so it is not possible to ascertain whether it was linen or woollen cloth.

The large quantity of textile-related finds is an indication of a significant activity and of craft specialisation; the coexistence of these objects in specific rooms of the site indicates special working areas for spinning and possibly weaving; the lack of evidence for the latter does not necessarily mean it was not performed.[60] The basic types of spindle whorls are standardised and continue without interruption during the entire 3rd millennium BC. The variety of the spindles shows the capability for production of different kinds of yarns.

At Markiani, there was already a strongly established tradition of spinning and producing various threads, and traditional techniques seem predominant and well maintained. The presence of other tools of bronze or bone at Markiani related to textile manufacture and to leather processing offers additional evidence for these activities.

The community at Markiani seems to have been able to produce supplies beyond their own needs, showing some organisation of production beyond a household level. Yarns and textiles, along with other commodities like barley, meat, dairy products, seem to have been commodities available for external exchange with the nearby central site of Dhaskalio and possibly with other communities. Dhaskalio was a special central site with multiple functions, where most of commodities were imported; it has been suggested that occupation there was seasonal.

This evidence at these two sites on Amorgos and Keros allows us to better understand the issues of possible organisation of production, the existence of specialised workshops and of trading networks for surplus raw materials and textiles within neighbouring areas. Evidence from other settlements in the Cyclades has not yet been published. There is still insufficient evidence to allow further theoretical remarks on the impact of textile manufacture, in terms of economic and social developments, on Amorgos or on other islands in the Cyclades during the 3rd millennium.

Notes
1 I would like to thank the organisers of the Copenhagen conference, the anonymous peer reviewers for their comments and Jenny Doole for her valuable help.
2 For an up to date overview, see Stampolidis and Sotirakopoulou 2011, 18–100.
3 For example, Renfrew 1972; Barber 1987; Broodbank 2000.
4 Spindle whorls from the EC sites of Skarkos (Ios), Kastri (Syros) and Grotta and Aplomata (Naxos) are under study

but not fully published and thus cannot be incorporated in the current paper, *cf.* Vakirtzi 2012, 227 n. 1, 229 n. 5. *Cf.* Vakirtzi this volume.

5 Balfanz 1995.

6 Renfrew 1972, 351–354.

7 Andersson Strand 2010, 14–15; Andersson Strand *et al.* 2010, 165.

8 Marangou 1990, 82, 89.

9 Stampolidis and Sotirakopoulou 2011, 42–51.

10 Getz-Preziosi 1987, 53–54, 105–107, figs. 29, 42–45; Birtacha 2017, 491–500, fig. 35.3–5.

11 Getz-Preziosi 1987, 20, figs. 11, 27.

12 Gavalas 2014, chapter 2.2.3 d, with bibliography.

13 Marangou *et al.* 2006.

14 Renfrew *et al.* 2007; Renfrew *et al.* 2013.

15 Renfrew *et al.* 2013.

16 Marangou *et al.* 2006, 87–94.

17 Marangou *et al.* 2006, 25–80.

18 Renfrew *et al.* 2013, 63–77.

19 Renfrew *et al.* 2007, 79–114.

20 Renfrew *et al.* 2015, 9–14, 209–223.

21 Renfrew *et al.* 2015, 381–390.

22 Renfrew *et al.* 2013.

23 Gavalas 2005; 2006; 2014, chapter 3.

24 Gavalas 2006, 201; 2014, chapter 3.

25 Gavalas 2006, 201, nn. 53–55.

26 Gavalas 2006, 202, fig. 8.19.

27 Gavalas 2014, chapter 3.2.6a.

28 Gavalas 2014, chapter 3.2.6a.

29 Gavalas 2014, chapter 3.2.6a.

30 Gavalas 2005, 44–45, pl. 2 a–b; 2006, 203–206, fig. 8.22, pl. 50.

31 Gavalas 2013.

32 Sotirakopoulou 2016, 195, no. C2357, fig. 4.14.

33 Sotirakopoulou 2016, 196.

34 Gavalas 2007.

35 Gavalas 2015, 310, fig. 10.12, 523.

36 Birtacha 2006, 214–215, fig. 8.24.

37 Georgakopoulou 2013, 668, fig. 32.3.

38 Georgakopoulou 2007, 380–381, fig. 11.3.

39 Trantalidou 2006, 231–232, fig. 9.1.

40 Trantalidou 2013, 439, fig. 20.6.

41 Renfrew 2006, 195–199, fig. 8.18, pl. 45.

42 Renfrew 2007, 374–376, fig. 10.16.

43 Renfrew 2015, 308–309, fig. 10.11.

44 Athens National Archaeological Museum no. 4720; Gavalas 2005, 40, n. 6.

45 Gavalas 2014, chapter 2.1.

46 Gavalas 2005, 40, n. 10.

47 Breniquet and Michel 2014.

48 Trantalidou 2006, 225–230.

49 Trantalidou 2013, 440.

50 Asomatos: Marketou 1997, 402; Myrtos: Warren 1972, 200–203; Sitagroi: Elster 1992, 36. For further references and discussion, see Gavalas 2006, 207.

51 See discussion in Gavalas 2006, 206.

52 Poliochni on Lemnos: Bernabò Brea 1976, 280; Thermi on Lesbos: Lamb 1936, 163, fig. 47, 1, 14; Gavalas 2006, 202, nn. 63 and 64.

53 Gavalas 2006, 206–207.

54 Wiencke 1969, 500, 508, pl. 129, no 191; see also some sealings from Skarkos on Ios, *cf.* Gavalas 2006, 205, n. 69, fig. 8.22.

55 Georgakopoulou 2013, 670–671, figs. 32.8, 32.9.

56 E. Völling "Spindle whorls in Troy? A critical examination of a common opinion", a paper delivered at the conference 'First Textiles. The Beginnings of Textile Manufacture in Europe and the Mediterranean,' 7–8 May 2015, Copenhagen, Denmark.

57 Gavalas 2005, 48, pl. 4; 2006, 207, nn. 92–93, fig. 8.21.

58 Gavalas 2005, 46–48; 2006, 207–208.

59 Andersson Strand this volume.

60 See discussion in Tzachili 1997, 125–128.

Bibliography

Andersson Strand, E. 2010 The basics of textile tools and textile terminology: from fibre to fabric. In C. Michel and M.-L. Nosch (eds.), *Textile Terminologies in the Ancient Near East and Mediterranean from the Third to the First Millennia BC*. Ancient Textile Series 8. Oxford and Oakville, 10–23.

Andersson Strand, E., Frei, K. M., Mannering, U., Nosch, M.-L. and Skals, I. 2010 Old textiles – new possibilities. *Journal of European Archaeology* 13, 149–173.

Balfanz, K. 1995 Bronzezeitliche Spinnwirtel aus Troia. *Studia Troica* 5, 117–144.

Barber, R. L. N. 1987 *The Cyclades in the Bronze Age*. London.

Bernabò Brea, L. 1976 *Poliochni, Citta Preistorica nell'Isola di Lemnos* 2. Roma.

Birtacha, K. 2006 The metal objects. In L. Marangou, C. Renfrew, Ch. Doumas and G. Gavalas (eds.), *Markiani on Amorgos. An Early Bronze Age Fortified Settlement. Overview of the Investigations 1987–1991*. Annual of the British School of Athens. Supplementary volume 40. London, 211–217.

Birtacha, K. 2017 Examining the paint on Cycladic figurines. In M. Marthari, C. Renfrew and M. Boyd (eds.), *Early Cycladic Sculpture in Context*. Oxford and Philadelphia, 491–502.

Breniquet, C. and Michel, C. 2014 Wool economy in the Ancient Near East and the Aegean. Introduction. In C. Breniquet and C. Michel (eds.), *Wool Economy in the Ancient Near East and the Aegean: from the Beginnings of Sheep Husbandry to Institutional Textile Industry*. Ancient Textiles Series 17. Oxford and Philadelphia, 1–11.

Elster, E. S. 1992 An archaeologist's perspective on prehistoric textile production. The case of Sitagroi. In *Η Δράμα και η περιοχή της: ιστορία και πολιτισμός. Επιστημονική συνάντηση: Δράμα 24–25 Νοεμβρίου 1989. Δράμα*, 29–46.

Gavalas, G. 2005 Νηματουργία και υφαντική στις Κυκλάδες κατά την τρίτη χιλιετία π.Χ.: προβλήματα και παρατηρήσεις. *Επετηρίς Κυκλαδικών Μελετών* 18 (2002–2003), 38–60.

Gavalas, G. 2006 The spindle whorls and related objects. In L. Marangou, C. Renfrew, Ch. Doumas and G. Gavalas (eds.), *Markiani on Amorgos. An Early Bronze Age Fortified Settlement. Overview of the Investigations 1987–1991*. Annual of the British School of Athens. Supplementary volume 40. London, 199–209.

Gavalas, G. 2007 Spindle whorls. In C. Renfrew, Ch. Doumas, L. Marangou and G. Gavalas (eds.), 2007 *Keros, Dhaskalio Kavos the Investigations of 1987–88*. Cambridge, 376.

Gavalas, G. 2013 The spindle whorls and related objects from Dhaskalio. In C. Renfrew, O. Philaniotou, N. Brodie, G. Gavalas and M. Boyd (eds.), *The Settlement at Dhaskalio, the Sanctuary on Keros and the Origins of Aegean Ritual Practice*, I. Cambridge, 649–651.

Gavalas, G. 2014 Τα σφονδύλια και τα υφαντικά βάρη από την Αμοργό. Συμβολή στην μελέτη της κλωστικής και της υφαντικής στο Αιγαίο κατά την αρχαιότητα. Unpublished PhD thesis, University of Ioannina.

Gavalas, G. 2015 The spindle whorl. In C. Renfrew, O. Philaniotou, N. Brodie, G. Gavalas and M. Boyd (eds.), *Kavos and the Special Deposits. The Sanctuary on Keros and the Origins of Aegean Ritual Practice: The Excavations of 2006–2007*, II. Cambridge, 310.

Georgakopoulou, M. 2007 The metallurgical remains. In C. Renfrew, Ch. Doumas, L. Marangou and G. Gavalas (eds.), *Keros, Dhaskalio Kavos the Investigations of 1987–88*. Cambridge, 382–403.

Georgakopoulou, M. 2013 Metal artefacts and metallurgy. In C. Renfrew, O. Philaniotou, N. Brodie, G. Gavalas and M. Boyd (eds.), *The Settlement at Dhaskalio, the Sanctuary on Keros and the Origins of Aegean Ritual Practice*, I. Cambridge, 667–692.

Getz-Preziosi, P. 1987 *Sculptors of the Cyclades, Individual and Tradition in the Third Millennium BC*. Michigan.

Lamb, W. 1936 *Excavations at Thermi, Lesbos*. Cambridge.

Marangou, L. (ed.) 1990 *Cycladic Culture. Naxos in the 3rd Millenium BC*. Exhibition Catalogue. Museum of Cycladic Art. Athens.

Marangou, L., Renfrew, C., Doumas, Ch. and Gavalas, G. (eds.) 2006 *Markiani on Amorgos. An Early Bronze Age Fortified Settlement. Overview of the Investigations 1987–1991*. Annual of the British School of Athens. Supplementary volume 40. London.

Marketou, T. 1997 Ασώματος Ρόδου. Τα μεγαρόσχημα κτήρια και οι σχέσεις τους με το Βορειοανατολικό Αιγαίο. In C. Doumas and V. La Rosa (eds.), *Η Πολιόχνη και η Πρώιμη Εποχή του Χαλκού στο Βόρειο Αιγαίο/Poliochni el'Antica Età del Bronzo nell'Egeo Setterntrionale*. Athens, 362–382.

Renfrew, C. 1972 *The Emergence of Civilization: The Cyclades and the Aegean in the Third Millennium BC*. London.

Renfrew, C., Doumas, Ch., Marangou, L. and Gavalas, G. (eds.) 2007 *Keros, Dhaskalio Kavos the Investigations of 1987–88*. Cambridge.

Renfrew, C., Philaniotou, O., Brodie, N., Gavalas, G. and Boyd, M. (eds.) 2013 *The Settlement at Dhaskalio, the Sanctuary on Keros and the Origins of Aegean Ritual Practice*, I. Cambridge.

Renfrew, C., Philaniotou, O., Brodie, N., Gavalas, G. and Boyd, M. (eds.) 2015 *Kavos and the Special Deposits. The Sanctuary on Keros and the Origins of Aegean Ritual Practice: The Excavations of 2006–2007*, II. Cambridge.

Renfrew, J. M. 2006 The leaf, mat, and cloth impressions. In L. Marangou, C. Renfrew, Ch. Doumas and G. Gavalas (eds.), *Markiani on Amorgos. An Early Bronze Age Fortified Settlement. Overview of the Investigations 1987–1991*. Annual of the British School of Athens. Supplementary volume 40. London, 195–199.

Renfrew, J. M. 2007 Leaf, mat and cloth impressions from Dhaskalio Kavos, Keros. In C. Renfrew, Ch. Doumas, L. Marangou and G. Gavalas (eds.), *Keros, Dhaskalio Kavos the Investigations of 1987–88*. Cambridge, 374–376.

Renfrew, J. M. 2015 The vine-leaf, mat and cloth impressions. In C. Renfrew, O. Philaniotou, N. Brodie, G. Gavalas and M. Boyd (eds.), *Kavos and the Special Deposits. The Sanctuary on Keros and the Origins of Aegean Ritual Practice*, II. Cambridge, 308–309.

Sotirakopoulou, P. 2016 The pottery from Dhaskalio. In C. Renfrew, O. Philaniotou, N. Brodie, G. Gavalas and M. Boyd (eds.), *The Settlement at Dhaskalio, the Sanctuary on Keros and the Origins of Aegean Ritual Practice*, IV. Cambridge.

Stampolidis, N. Ch. and Sotirakopoulou, P. 2011 Early Cycladic period: introduction; Early Cycladic architecture; Early Cycladic pottery; Early Cycladic metallurgy; Early Cycladic religion and burial habits; Early Cycladic period: trade and interconnections. In V. Sahoglu and P. Sotirakopoulou (eds.), *Across the Cyclades and Western Anatolia in the 3rd Millennium BC*. Exhibition catalogue. Sabanci Museum. Istanbul, 18–109.

Trantalidou, K. 2006 The bones and the bone tools. In L. Marangou, C. Renfrew, Ch. Doumas and G. Gavalas (eds.), *Markiani on Amorgos. An Early Bronze Age Fortified Settlement. Overview of the Investigations 1987–1991*. Annual of the British School of Athens. Supplementary volume 40. London, 223–242.

Trantalidou, K. 2013 The animal bones: the exploitation of livestock. In C. Renfrew, O. Philaniotou, N. Brodie, G. Gavalas and M. Boyd (eds.), *The Settlement at Dhaskalio, the Sanctuary on Keros and the Origins of Aegean Ritual Practice*, I. Cambridge, 429–441.

Tzachili, I. 1997 *Υφαντική και υφάντρες στο Προϊστορικό Αιγαίο*. Ηράκλειο.

Vakirtzi, S. 2012 The decorated spindle-whorls from prehistoric Akrotiri, Thera. *Talanta* 44, 227–244.

Warren, P. 1972 *Myrtos. An Early Bronze Age Settlement in Crete*. Annuals of the British School of Athens. Supplementary volume 7. Oxford.

Wiencke, M. H. 1969 Further seals and sealings from Lerna. *Hesperia* 38, 500–521.

Fibre crafts and social complexity: yarn production in the Aegean islands in the Early Bronze Age

Sophia Vakirtzi

Introduction

Yarn production is a distinct stage in the textile manufacturing process.[1] In pre-industrial contexts, it was an extremely laborious and time-consuming craft requiring technological know-how and skills.[2] The raw materials for producing yarns comprise a potentially wide range of plant and animal fibres. The production process begins with the procurement of the fibres, entangling yarn industry with other economic practices, such as wild plant gathering, agriculture and animal husbandry. After their collection, the fibres are processed in certain ways, depending on their physical properties and the targeted end products.[3] In the final stage, the processed fibres are spun into yarns either with bare hands or with the employment of the spindle, a tool that mechanises their twisting and ensures the production of a high-quality product.[4]

The study of prehistoric yarn production interlaces with a number of key archaeological research issues such as: a) the exploitation of natural resources in Palaeolithic hunter-gatherer economies;[5] b) the intensification of specific economic strategies postulated for the Neolithic and the Early Bronze Ages (EBA), also known as the 'Secondary Products Revolution';[6] c) the emergence of urbanism, craft specialisation and division of labour;[7] d) the textile-orientated political economies of early states;[8] e) gender hierarchies in past societies and economies.[9] Fibre crafts constitute, therefore, an important parameter for the study of prehistoric cultures.

This paper, stemming from my PhD research on yarn production at the Aegean islands during the Bronze Age, addresses the production of yarn by the island communities during the Early Bronze Age.[10] The chronological frame corresponds to the formative period during which complex societies emerged in the Aegean region. The geographical frame is significant since the Aegean islands, scattered between the western edge of the Asian continent and the south-eastern tip of the European continent, hosted communities which generated, received, transmitted and fused cultural influences from the mainlands around the Aegean Sea, in what has been called the 'International Spirit' of the 3rd millennium BC, *i.e.* the Early Bronze Age.[11]

The aim of this study is to present recently studied tool assemblages related to fibre crafts and to explore the impact of the yarn industry in the insular Aegean during this period of dynamic cultural, social and economic change. The paper is organised in three parts. Part I presents the analytical methodologies and the sample of the study. In Part II the results of the analyses are presented per assemblage. Part III is confined to a discussion of the results.[12]

Part I: methodology and sample

Due to their organic origin, fibres, threads and textiles do not usually survive in the archaeological record. Therefore, the prehistoric yarn industry is often studied through the tools employed in the process. The oldest and most prevalent tool for spinning fibres into yarn was the spindle, usually equipped with a spindle whorl.[13] The spindle was made of wood and does not survive in archaeological contexts either, but spindle whorls, typically made of clay, stone or bone, are usually found in large amounts, and are therefore suitable for a systematic study of prehistoric yarn production.

In this research, typological classification, metrological analysis and a study of distribution of spindle whorls are employed in order to define cultural, technological and economic aspects of the yarn industry. Whorl type can be an index of cultural diversity, while whorl size is indicative of the quality of the yarn produced on the grounds of a

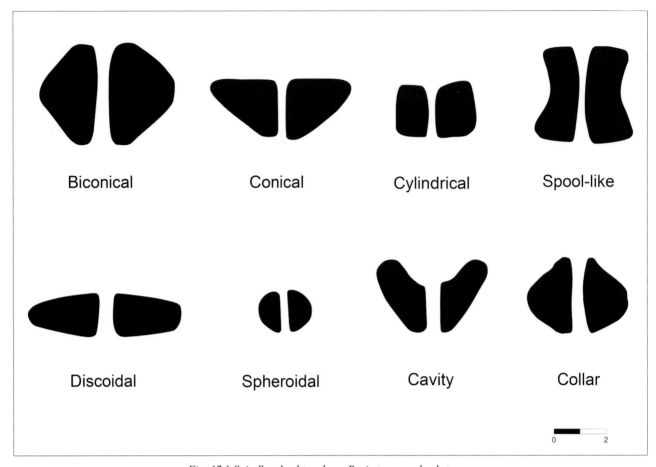

Fig. 17.1 Spindle-whorl typology. Basic types and sub-types.

relation between fibres quality (thickness/coarseness) and whorl size.[14] Tool distribution indicates the scale and the organisation of production.[15]

Typological analysis

The typological analysis is based on a typology established for this study on the basis of whorl shape (Fig. 17.1). Six basic types were distinguished in the Early Bronze Age sample: the conical, the biconical, the discoidal, the spheroidal, the cylindrical and the spool-like type. Subtypes were diagnosed based on morphological details or the diameter-height ratio. Every whorl in each assemblage was attributed to one of these basic types, except for those that were too fragmentary to diagnose.

Metrological analysis

The metrological analysis aims at the definition of the size of intact/almost intact spindle whorls by recording their diameters and weights, which are their functional parameters. The diameter reflects the degree of tightness of the yarn, and the weight reflects its thickness.[16] Each combination of diameter and weight values corresponds to a functional potential. However, the diameter and weight

values of spindle whorls in any assemblage can be extremely diverse, and a standardisation of the combinations of the diameter and weight values is necessary to allow for the classification of spindle whorls according to their functional potential.

In this study, standardisation is achieved by the creation of a functional typology on the basis of the metrological data of the functional parameters of well-preserved spindle whorls.[17] Diameter values are divided into groups of 0.5 cm intervals and weight values are divided into groups of 5 g intervals. The diameter-values groups are codified with numbers from 1 to 20 and the weight-values groups are codified with Greek letters from α to αστ'. Each combination of a diameter group with a weight group in the functional typology represents a distinct size, which in turns corresponds to a functional potential also termed 'functional type'. The functional types are laid out in the form of a grid, the horizontal axis of which consists of the diameter groups and the vertical axis denotes the weight groups. Each intact/almost intact whorl is classified into a functional type according to its recorded diameter and weight (Table 17.2). Spindle whorls of the same functional type are considered to have the same functional potential, *i.e.* they are suitable

Fig. 17.2 Site map of the Early Bronze Age assemblages examined.

for the production of similar kinds of threads. Likewise, spindle whorls of different functional types are considered effective for the production of different kinds of threads. For example, functional type 6γ represents any spindle whorl with a diameter measuring between 2.6 and 3 cm and with a weight between 10.1 and 15 g. Functional type 8η represents any spindle whorl with a diameter between 3.6 and 4 cm and a weight between 35.1 and 40 g, and so on. A spindle whorl of functional type 6γ is suitable for the production of a much finer yarn than that produced with a spindle whorl of functional type 8η.

The functional typology allows the functional comparison of spindle whorls and spindle whorl assemblages on a common basis, and facilitates the detection of the production targets in each tool assemblage. However, it should be stressed that the evaluation of the end products are expressed only in relative, qualitative terms (*i.e.* thin/thick thread, loosely spun/tightly spun thread) since so far this methodology has not been developed in order to calibrate the functional types into quantitative terms (*i.e.* thread diameter, angle of twist). Neither is it possible to determine direction of twist through the metrological analysis or the functional typology of spindle whorls.

Distribution analysis

Distribution analysis aims at distinguishing yarn production units and evaluating the scale and the organisation mode of the production. Since spindle whorls are usually found in both primary and secondary deposits, the first step is to define the nature of their context.[18] Once the context is determined, areas of primary usage of the tools are distinguished from areas of other uses (*e.g.* funerary). The spaces of primary usage are defined as production units. The number and the kind of tools assigned to each production unit define the scale and the organisation of the production.[19] This definition depends on the degree of documentation of the excavations and on the status of publications.

Sample

The Early Bronze Age sample includes 442 spindle whorls from nine archaeological sites on seven Greek islands (Fig. 17.2). These are: the settlements of Ayios Ioannis and Skala Sotiros on Thassos, and the settlement of Koukonisi on Lemnos in the north Aegean; the prehistoric settlement below the sanctuary of Hera (the Heraion) on Samos in the east Aegean; the settlements of Grotta on Naxos, Ayia

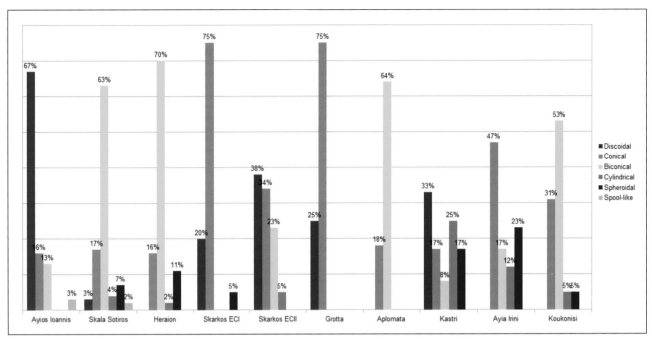

Fig. 17.3 Spindle-whorl type percentages in the studied assemblages.

Irini on Keos, Kastri on Syros and Skarkos on Ios, and the cemetery of Aplomata on Naxos in the south Aegean. The tool assemblages differ in four aspects: a) sample size: small (20 spindle whorls or less), medium (20 to 50 spindle whorls) and large assemblages (more than 50 spindle whorls) are distinguished; b) category of site (settlement/ cemetery) and type of settlement (small/large, fortified/ unfortified); c) chronology: the spindle whorl assemblages are attributed either to sub-phases within the Early Bronze Age[20] or generally within this period;[21] and d) the degree of exploration and publication of each site and consequently the artefacts found therein.

Because of the above asymmetries, the employment of the same analytical methodologies has not been equally fruitful for all nine assemblages. Nevertheless, each assemblage offers information on a significant aspect of the yarn industry, the results obtained from each assemblage are complementary to each other and allow the detection of patterns that contribute to a general narrative for yarn production in the Aegean islands during the Early Bronze Age.

Part II: presentation of results

Ayios Ioannis, Thassos

Ayios Ioannis is a small settlement on the south-eastern coast of Thassos, dated to the beginning of the Early Bronze Age.[22] An assemblage of 37 clay spindle whorls was examined, 18 of which are intact. The typology includes the discoidal type, which is dominant, the conical and the bionical types, as well as one example of the spool-like type

(Fig. 17.3). Most of the whorls have a good surface finish, but only two discoidal whorls are decorated with impressed notches (semicircles) or circles around the central hole on one surface of the tool.

The metrological analysis demonstrates a preference in large sizes. Only a few spindle whorls are medium-sized (Table 17.2). The discoidal whorls were generally manufactured in slightly larger sizes than the conical and biconical ones, suggesting that the form of the tool was relevant to the end product. Overall, the size ranges of the spindle whorls in this assemblage suggest the manufacture of thick yarns.

The spinning tools were found in the vicinity of heating structures, in an 'outdoors' area. This distribution pattern, disassociating the tools from the interiors of distinct architectural units (huts), indicates that yarn production was not organised on a strictly 'household' level. The excavation data also demonstrates that the discoidal whorls were found in more or less close proximity, unlike the other types, which were rather scattered.[23]

The zooarchaeological data suggests husbandry strategies orientated towards both primary and secondary products.[24] Therefore, it can be suggested that animal fibres were spun at the site, while plant fibres cannot be ruled out, since these do not usually leave remains in the archaeological record.

Skala Sotiros, Thassos

The settlement of Skala Sotiros on the west coast of Thassos had a fortified nucleus near the shore and an unfortified extension a little further inland. It was abandoned after the Early Bronze Age.[25] The tool assemblage includes 151

Table 17.1 Functional Typology Grid. Functional types distribution per assemblage

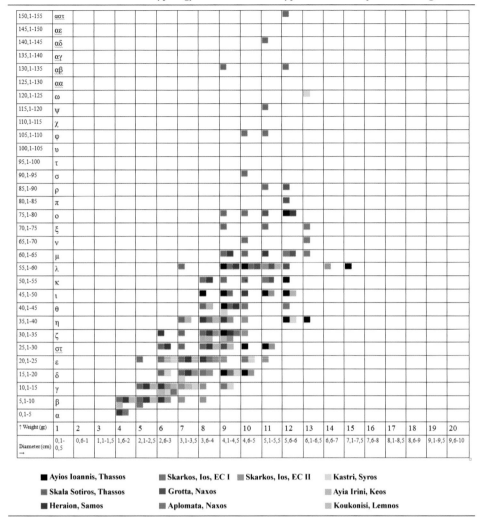

■ Ayios Ioannis, Thassos   ■ Skarkos, Ios, EC I   ■ Skarkos, Ios, EC II   ▨ Kastri, Syros

■ Skala Sotiros, Thassos   ■ Grotta, Naxos   ■ Ayia Irini, Keos

■ Heraion, Samos   ■ Aplomata, Naxos   ▨ Koukonisi, Lemnos

clay whorls. The biconical type predominates and the tall, conical type is second in preference. The rest of the types are represented in very small percentages (Fig. 17.3). Significant morphological attributes are attested in some varieties of the biconical and the conical type, such as the cavity around the hole on one end (also known as *scodelletta*)[26] and the 'collar-like' projection of the rim of the hole. Only one whorl in this large assemblage bears decoration, in the form of incised chevrons in a symmetrical syntax on the shoulder of the whorl.

In this assemblage, 58% of the spindle whorls are well preserved. Their sizes spread in a very large range. An indication of this variety is given by the minimum (5.7 g) and maximum (154.1 g) weight values recorded. In terms of functional types, the range spreads from type 4β to type 12αδ (Table 17.1). This wide size range suggests that a rich variety of yarns were produced in the settlement. However, most of the whorls cluster in functional types corresponding to small and medium sizes (functional types 6δ, 6στ, 7ε, 7ζ and 7η, Table 17.2). These sizes would have been suitable for spinning of thin to medium yarns. The much smaller and the much larger sizes are rather the exception in the assemblage, so the production of very fine and very coarse yarn must have been marginal in the settlement.

The tools were found in large numbers in deposits along the fortification walls inside the settlement, both in primary (floors) and secondary deposits. In the inland expansion of the settlement, the spindle whorls were scattered around clay structures, probably related to heating and cooking. The study of the exact organisational schemes of yarn production is in progress in view of the final publication of the site.

Heraion, Samos

The sanctuary of Hera is located in a fertile plain on the south-eastern coast of Samos. Excavations beneath the archaic temple and the surrounding area revealed a

Table 17.2 Functional types quantities per assemblage

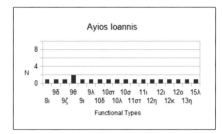
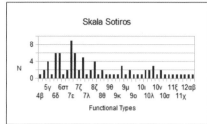
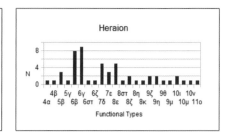
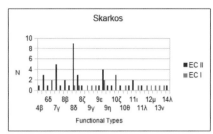
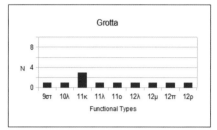
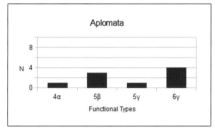
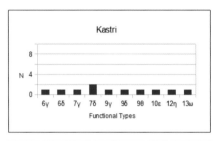
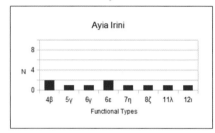
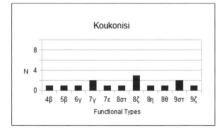

prehistoric settlement.[27] Several overlapping architectural vestiges were attributed to five chronological Early Bronze Age phases, called Heraion I–V.[28] The spindle whorls of the sample date to phases Heraion III–V.

The excavations of the prehistoric settlement yielded significant numbers of spindle whorls. In this study, 81 clay spindle whorls were examined from deposits dating to the end of the 3rd millennium BC: 10 tools derived from the excavation of two buildings attributed to Heraion III and IV,[29] while 71 were found during the excavation of buildings attributed to Heraion V.[30] The typology of this assemblage includes four types. The biconical form predominates, while the rest of the types are represented in significantly lower percentages (Fig. 17.3). The morphological attribute of the cavity around the hole is very common in this assemblage, and so is incised decoration. About 67% of the whorls in this assemblage are decorated with incised motifs (chevrons, multiple arcs and, less commonly, figurative motifs). Among these, a narrative scene including five schematic human figures is unique in the region as a decorative theme for spindle whorls.[31]

Metrological analysis was applied to 68% of the assemblage (intact/almost intact whorls). A wide range of sizes was observed, but the majority of the whorls cluster in functional types 6β, 6γ, 7δ, 7ε and 8ε (Table 17.2).

These types correspond to small and medium-sized whorls, which were suitable for the spinning of yarns of fine and medium thickness. Moreover, the high percentages of these functional types suggest a high degree of standardisation in the production as well as its intensification.

The distribution pattern is clear in the case of the 10 published specimens deriving from the Milojčić excavations. Six spindle whorls were found in a vessel in a Heraion III building designated as 'Magazine'.[32] Five of these tools were available for the current study. Three are biconical and two are conical. Their sizes fall in roughly two different ranges, a smaller and a larger range (three were attributed to the functional type 5β, one to 7δ and one to 9η). This small group of tools found in the vessel probably constitutes a spinning tool-kit for the production of thin, medium and thick yarns. Another group of five spindle whorls is published from a Heraion IV building, the 'Großes Haus'.[33] Four of them were available for study. Three of them are biconical and one is spheroidal. The intact/almost intact ones fall into the functional types 8ε, 9η and 9ζ. The production unit of the 'Großes Haus' was therefore orientated in average towards rather thicker yarns compared to those produced with the tools found in the 'Magazine'. The scales of production in the two buildings, the 'Magazine' and the 'Großes Haus', are similar; however, the targets of the production are different, defined by a mixed yarn production in the former and a more specialised in the latter.

The bulk amounts of spindle whorls examined in this study were found during the exposure of a Heraion V settlement area.[34] At this stage, a detailed distribution analysis is not feasible, since publication of the excavation is pending. It should be stressed, however, that the 71 spindle whorls derive from an area of 400 sq. m.[35] This dense concentration of spinning tools reflects an intense yarn production.

Skarkos, Ios

The settlement of Skarkos occupies a low hill in the middle of a narrow plain on the west coast of the island of Ios. Some ceramic assemblages attributable to the Early Cycladic I period (the Grotta-Pelos phase) have been identified, while the preserved architecture remains belong to a settlement of the Early Cycladic II period (the Keros-Syros phase).[36] Skarkos was destroyed by an earthquake towards the end of Early Cycladic II and remained uninhabited ever since.[37] The assemblage from Skarkos includes 102 clay spindle whorls. Twenty of them derive from Early Cycladic I deposits, and a larger group of 82 tools was found in Early Cycladic II deposits.

a) The Early Cycladic I group. The spindle whorls of this group fall basically into two types: 70% of them classify into the low conical, and 20% into the discoidal. There is one example of the spheroidal and one example of the cylindrical type (Fig. 17.3). None of these spindle whorls is decorated. In terms of their metrology, the 75% of the spindle whorls that are intact or almost intact fall into functional types that correspond to large or very large sizes (Table 17.2). The distribution pattern of this group cannot be investigated prior to the publication of the Early Cycladic I deposits.

b) The Early Cycladic II group. The 82 spindle whorls found in Early Cycladic II deposits fall into four types: the discoidal, the conical, the biconical and the cylindrical. The discoidal type predominates, while the conical type is significantly reduced in comparison to its Early Cycladic I percentage, and the biconical type enriches now the typology. Although there is a sample size difference between the Early Cycladic I and the Early Cycladic II groups, the comparison of their typologies implies a major shift in the spinning equipment at Skarkos (Fig. 17.3). Whorl decoration was practically non-existent at Skarkos during this period, given the fact that only one example is recorded in the large Early Cycladic II sub-group.[38] Morphological attributes such as the cavity around the hole, or the 'collar-like' projection of the hole rim, do not appear in the Skarkos tools.

The metrology of this assemblage points to a wide variety of sizes, ranging from relatively small (functional types 6β and 6γ) to very large (type 14λ). However, functional types corresponding to small and to very large sizes are sporadic, while the larger numbers of functional types such as 9ζ and 8δ demonstrate a preference on medium

to fairly large whorls (Table 17.2). The Early Cycladic II yarn production was thus orientated mainly towards yarns of medium thickness.

The Early Cycladic II spindle whorls were found scattered all over the settlement, both in buildings and in open spaces. The distribution pattern shows significant concentrations in three cases:

a. Building Beta. Seven spindle whorls are attributed to this building. These are further distributed by pairs in three rooms, and a single whorl was found in a fourth room. They are biconical, discoidal, conical and cylindrical. The functional types range from 6γ to 8δ. In two cases, the pairs of whorls per room are similar typologically and metrologically.

b. Building Epsilon. Five spindle whorls are attributed to this building. Three of them were found in a large room and two in a smaller space. The conical type predominates in this building. The tools here are medium to large (functional types 8β, 8ζ, 9ζ and 10ζ).

c. Building Zeta. Another set of five spindle whorls was found here, in a distribution similar to that in building Epsilon: three of them originate from a large room and two from a smaller one. The discoidal type is predominant in this building, while the sizes of these whorls are medium to large (functional types 8δ, 9ε, 9δ, 9ζ and 10δ).

The distribution pattern emerging from these three cases demonstrates similar scales of production per building, although there is a difference in the production target in each one of them. In average, yarns of finer qualities were spun in building Beta in comparison to those spun in buildings Epsilon and Zeta.

Grotta, Naxos

Grotta, on the north coast of the modern town of Naxos, is one of the type-sites of the Early Cycladic I Grotta-Pelos cultural groups of the Prehistoric Cyclades.[39] An assemblage of 12 clay spindle whorls was examined, originating from the excavation of the Early Cycladic settlement.[40] The low conical type is predominant with a percentage of 75%, followed by the discoidal type at a 25% (Fig. 17.3). None of these tools bears decoration. Most of them are very large (functional types such as 10λ, 11κ, 12π and 12ρ) and thus suitable for spinning hard fibres into very thick yarns (Table 17.2). There is only one example of a medium-sized whorl, which could have been used for spinning of thread of medium thickness. Unfortunately, no further excavation details are available. In the light of a lack of information on the exact find-spots of these tools, no estimations about the scale or the organisation of yarn production at Early Cycladic I Grotta can be made.

Aplomata, Naxos

The cemetery of Aplomata lies a little further to the north of Grotta, on a coastal hill of Naxos. Two main periods of use of the cemetery have been distinguished, an Early Cycladic and a Mycenaean one.[41] The Early Cycladic cemetery is attributed to the Keros-Syros phase of the Early Cycladic II period.[42]

Grave XX contained 11 clay spindle whorls, which were published as beads in the excavator's preliminary report.[43] They fall mainly into two types, the biconical, which predominates, and the conical (Fig. 17.3). About half of the biconical and one of the conical examples have a shallow cavity around the hole. Six of the whorls are decorated with incised motifs, such as punctuated triangles, groups of parallel arcs and other geometric patterns.

The metrological analysis of these tools demonstrates a very restricted range of small or very small sizes (functional types 4α, 5β and 6γ, Table 17.2). These whorls are funerary offerings, but typical use-wear traces on their surfaces, such as small breaks on the rim of the central hole, or slip attrition either around the hole rim or around the circumference at the maximum diameter,[44] suggest their usage as spindle whorls before being deposited in the grave.[45] Their small sizes indicate the spinning of very thin yarns.

Although the deposition of spinning tools in graves is not directly informative about the organisation or scale of yarn production, it may offer the possibility to examine other dimensions or prehistoric yarn production, and especially the symbolic and social ones. The presence of tools in tombs must be examined according to different hypotheses. Spindle whorls could have been deposited either as personal items of the deceased or they may have been offered by the relatives or the community. An array of interpretations may be considered, but they necessitate as clear contextual data as possible. In the case of the Aplomata assemblage, archaeological insights are so far hindered by the lack of adequate published data. To date, no other artefacts or skeletal remains from grave XX are mentioned in the report, therefore it is not even possible to estimate if all 11 spindle whorls correspond to a single or to multiple deposition episodes, *i.e.* if they can be considered as one spinning tool-kit or not.

Kastri, Syros

Kastri is a fortified settlement on a hill in north-eastern Syros, in the vicinity of the large Early Cycladic cemetery of Chalandriani. Kastri is the type-site of a cultural phenomenon in the Early Bronze Age Cyclades, defined by the foundation of fortified settlements and the appearance of material culture of Anatolian connotations, towards the end of the Early Cycladic II period.[46]

A small assemblage of 12 clay spindle whorls deriving from Bossert's excavations[47] was examined. They fall into five types, the discoidal type being predominant (Fig. 17.3). The conical and biconical whorls do not manifest morphological attributes such as the cavity around the hole or the 'collar-like' projection of the rim of the hole. Two spindle whorls bear decoration in the form of very thin incisions radiating from the centre of the whorl to the perimeter. A third whorl of a particularly large size bears an incised triangular motif with a small notch in one of the angles. All 12 spindle whorls are well preserved and their metrological analysis revealed a spread into several functional types corresponding to small, medium and large sizes (Table 17.2). However, the majority falls into the middle-size range, a fact that suggests a preference of yarns of medium thickness. A study of distribution was not feasible in the case of Kastri due to the lack of information on the exact find-spots of the spindle whorls.

Ayia Irini, Keos

The site of Ayia Irini lies on a small peninsula on the north-western coast of Keos and was occupied from the end of the Final Neolithic to the end of the Late Bronze Age. The Early Bronze Age levels were explored mainly in the Western Sector of the site, where an EBA building with four architectural phases was revealed.[48] The sample of the EBA spindle whorls has been attributed to phases Ayia Irini II (Early Cycladic II early) and Ayia Irini III (Early Cycladic II late–Kastri phase),[49] while a recent re-evaluation of the deposits[50] suggest a finer periodisation.

The sample includes 17 clay spindle whorls. They are attributed to four types, among which the conical dominates (Fig. 17.3). There is only one decorated example with an incised zigzag motif, attributed to period Ayia Irini II.[51] Metrological analysis was applied to 59% of the assemblage, and it resulted in a variety of functional types corresponding to small, medium and large sizes (Table 17.2). The results suggest the production of a variety of yarns.

Most of these tools were found in secondary deposits in various areas of the site.[52] Four of them, however, can be securely attributed to primary deposits.[53] These four spindle whorls are related to 'House ED', which was erected in the Western Sector in Ayia Irini III early.[54] A group of three whorls were found in Room 4.[55] Two are conical and their functional types are 4β and 8ζ, and one is cylindrical of functional type 6ε. Interestingly, the same deposit contained Anatolian-type loom weights.[56] The fourth spindle whorl of the house was found in Room 3[57] and is also a cylindrical, 6ε type. The number of whorls found in House ED indicates a rather small scale of production. The main target must have been a medium quality of yarn, produced with the medium-sized cylindrical spindle whorls, but finer and coarser qualities of yarn were also spun in smaller quantities. It is possible that the stronger yarns were used for warp while the finer yarn was used for weft in the upright warp-weighted loom that functioned in House ED. That loom was equipped with the Anatolian-type loom weights that were found in the same deposit as the three whorls from Room 4, as well as in a second deposit just above that one.[58] The Ayia Irini data suggest that the textile industry was organised at the household level, and that both spinning and weaving were taking place in the same production unit.

Koukonisi, Lemnos

Koukonisi is located on a small island in the Moudros bay in Lemnos. In prehistory it was inhabited at least from the Chalcolithic until the Mycenaean period.[59] The settlement of the Early Bronze Age was heavily disturbed due to the building activity in the Middle Bronze Age.[60]

The sample includes 19 spindle whorls from the Early Bronze Age. They are made of clay and they fall into four types (Fig. 17.3). The biconical type dominates in this assemblage, with the conical being second in preference. Both the biconical and conical types have varieties with a cavity around the hole. None of the 19 spindle whorls bears decoration.

Metrological analysis demonstrates a variety of functional types. Most of them correspond to medium sizes (functional types 8στ, 8ζ, 8η, 8θ, 8στ, 9ζ), suggesting that the primary target of yarn production at Early Bronze Age Koukonisi were strong yarns (Table 17.2).

Due to heavy disturbance of the Early Bronze Age settlement, a distribution study of the spindle whorls is particularly challenging, especially since the site is still being excavated. At this stage of research, two cases of significant distributions can be pointed out. Excavation of the Early Bronze Age level in trench 3 revealed two spaces with spinning tools.[61] Space IA contained two spindle whorls, a conical one of medium size (functional type 8η) and a fragmentary biconical one. Space IB contained one spheroidal and three biconical whorls. Two of them are small (functional types 4β and 5β) and two are medium-sized (functional types 8ζ and 8στ). A tentative suggestion prior to the final publication could be that yarn production was organised rather at the household level, with production targets varying from thin yarns to yarns of medium thickness.

Part III: discussion

Fibre crafts and yarn production constituted an important element of island economies in the Aegean throughout the Early Bronze Age. A synthesis of the data presented in Part II suggests that, although distinct local traditions related to fibre crafts were pronounced in the beginning of the period, these converged towards a common transformation of the yarn industries and their technological apparatus in the course of the 3rd millennium BC.[62]

In the Early Bronze I period, a regional distinction can be made with regard to typology. The examples of Ayios Ioannis in the north and of Skarkos and Grotta in the south suggest that, although spindle whorls were used in both regions, different types prevailed in each area: discoidal whorls were preferred in the north, while the low conical type was exclusively used in the Cyclades. Published examples from other Early Cycladic I settlements, such as Pyrgos and Avyssos at Paros, confirm the dominance of the conical type in the Cyclades.[63] Despite the differences in types, however, spindle whorls in both regions were being manufactured in large sizes, indicating that the production targets were thick yarns. This fact implies a common technological choice in both regions in this period. These communities must have had access only to, or a preference for, fibres of coarse quality. Technological, economic or other reasons could be postulated for this choice. Either the technological know-how for the acquisition or the processing of fine fibres before spinning was limited, or a certain level of division of labour, necessary for the investment of time into such processing procedures, had not yet been achieved. Alternatively, the choice could be explained by a desire or necessity to produce thick textiles in that period.

Early Bronze II–III yarn industries in the Aegean islands appear significantly different, as suggested by the data presented in Part II. Local manufacturing traditions were enriched by new tool repertoires, both in the north and in the southern Aegean, most importantly in the form of the biconical spindle whorls. Although this type was dominant at Skala Sotiros and at Koukonisi in the north, the transition is better manifested at Skarkos in the south. The low conical spindle whorls were still dominant there in the Early Cycladic II period, but they were not exclusive any more, as the number of biconical whorls increased considerably. The gradual dominance of the biconical type in the Aegean is exemplified by its overwhelming percentage at prehistoric Heraion, the only assemblage examined here that dates to the end of the 3rd millennium BC.

An important novelty of the period comes in a form of an Anatolian feature in the morphology of the spindle whorls used in the Aegean island communities, undocumented in the Early Bronze I assemblages examined here. These are spindle whorls of biconical and conical types with a cavity around the hole (*i.e. scodelletta* whorls), which may bear decoration in an 'Anatolian style' defined by particular techniques (incisions and/or impressions), motifs (linear and curvilinear geometrical patterns) and syntax (symmetrical arrangement of the motifs on the shoulder of the whorl). These types were very common in the 3rd millennium BC at key Anatolian sites such as Troy,[64] Beycesultan[65] and Aphrodisias,[66] and they first appeared in the Aegean in the Early Bronze Age.

Anatolian influence is therefore attested in the Aegean spinning equipment, but this influence is more pronounced in the eastern Aegean (*i.e.* Koukonisi,[67] Heraion). The pattern that we see in the sample is in accord with previously published data, which in some cases dates earlier than the Early Bronze II (*i.e.* at Thermi I–III on Lesbos[68] and at Emporio V on Chios[69]), and in other cases is very well established in the middle of the 3rd millennium BC (*i.e.* Poliochni Green/Red,[70] but mainly Poliochni Yellow[71] on Lemnos). This influence was infiltrated in the north Aegean and in the Cyclades, where the decorated, *scodelletta* spindle whorls appear sporadically in the archaeological record (Skala Sotiros, Aplomata, Ayia Irini II and published parallels from both the settlement of Kastri and the cemetery of Chalandriani on Syros,[72] and Dhaskalio off the coast of Keros[73]). Again, the case of Skarkos, where – despite the large size of the assemblage of Early Cycladic II spindle whorls – this Anatolian element is startlingly absent, is important in demonstrating this differential influence.[74]

Finally, a significant transformation of the yarn industries in the Aegean islands concerns the end products themselves. A major shift from large whorls in Early Bronze I assemblages, to medium-sized and small whorls in Early Bronze II assemblages is attested in the Aegean islands based on the material examined here. The very large tools of the previous period become of marginal significance, in fact they are documented exclusively at Skala Sotiros on Thassos, and in one instance at Kastri on Syros. The production of coarse yarns is significantly reduced in the Early Bronze II settlements. At the same time, a widespread availability of finer fibres is implied by the high percentages of medium and small whorls. This advance in fibre crafts could be due to technological factors such as the accumulation of technical knowledge on the processing of fibres, to socio-economic factors such as an accentuated division of labour in this period compared to Early Bronze I or to a shift in taste for finer textiles.

It should also be noted that very small whorls sizes (*e.g.* with weight below 8 g) are represented in low numbers, and it is whorls of such sizes that appear in the funerary context of Aplomata. The case of Aplomata is not unique in the Cyclades, where spindle whorls have often been found in cemeteries.[75] Both the scarcity of the tools for the production of this quality of yarns, as well as their funerary usage, imply the value of those products and the prestige of the craftspeople who could manufacture them. These phenomena indicate the emergence of specialisation in fibre crafts during this period.

The organisation of yarn production in Early Bronze II–III communities manifests similar patterns on different islands. An average concentration of five spindle whorls per building is deduced from the cases presented in Part II. The pattern of different whorl sizes per production unit underlines a tendency for self-sufficiency in terms of different yarn qualities. The data suggest that, in the Early Bronze II–III period, yarn production on the Aegean islands was circumscribed in small but self-sufficient production units probably corresponding to 'household' economy.

In conclusion, yarn production on the Aegean islands was being transformed into an intense, dynamic industry in the course of the 3rd millennium BC. Local technological traditions were negotiated at the time of the 'International Spirit'[76] when the Aegean was integrated into wider cultural spheres. This is a period when wool economy was practised intensively in Mesopotamia[77] and in Anatolia,[78] and it is likely that technological and intercultural influences related to yarn and textile production were maintained along the extended networks that linked those regions.[79] Several other practices recognised in the Aegean material culture have been related to a cognitive level of culture-sharing, expanding throughout the Near East, Anatolia, the Levant and the Aegean during this period.[80] A large possible balance weight found in an Early Cycladic context at Ayia Irini, Keos, has been linked to a weight unit for wool. According to this interpretation, this find could indicate that wool was traded in the Aegean during this period.[81]

In such a cultural and economic environment, intensification or even a first-time introduction of wool economy on some of the Aegean islands is more than likely. This development could account for the technological evolution of fibre crafts as reflected in the adaptation of the spinning equipment. The average reduction of whorl size, in particular, has been related to the intensification of wool exploitation elsewhere.[82] It is suggested that fibre crafts in general, and wool economy in particular, emerged as vital factors in the process of social complexity in the Early Bronze Aegean island communities, anticipating the importance that textile industries achieved in the Minoan and Mycenaean political economies of the 2nd millennium BC, and underlying the contribution of the insular communities in this transitional trajectory.

Notes

1   I would like to thank the organisers of the 'Textiles in Social Context' session, Dr. M. Siennicka, Dr. A. Ulanowska and Dr. L. Rahmstorf, who gave me the opportunity to present at the 2014 Istanbul EAA Conference the preliminary results of my then ongoing PhD research. Special thanks are due to the excavators Prof. C. Doumas, Prof. H. P. Isler, Dr. C. Koukouli-Chrysanthaki, Dr. S. Papadopoulos, Dr. M. Marthari and Dr. C. Boulotis, who entrusted me with the study of the spindle whorls from their excavations for the purposes of my doctoral dissertation. I would also like to thank the Ephorates of Antiquities of the Greek Ministry of Culture (Ephorates of Thassos, Lemnos, Samos and the Cyclades), for the support provided on many levels throughout this research. Thanks are also due to the Athens Archaeological Society, the American School of Classical Studies and the German Archaeological Institute at Athens for permissions to study material deriving from excavations conducted under their auspices. I am indebted to my supervisors, Professors I. Tzachili, Iph. Tournavitou and P. Militello for their guidance throughout this project. This work was supported by the project IRAKLITOS

II – University of Crete of the Operational Programme for Education and Lifelong Learning 2007–2013 (E.P.E.D.V.M.) of the National Strategic Reference Framework (2007–2013), which is co-funded by the European Union (European Social Fund) and National Resources. I would like to thank Jose Manuel Navaro for helping me with the figures and tables. Finally, I would like to thank the anonymous reviewers for their useful comments.

2   Tzachili 2007, 192; Andersson Strand 2010.
3   Barber 1991, 9–35; Andersson Strand 2014.
4   Barber 1991, 51–54.
5   Adovasio *et al.* 1996; Kvavadze *et al.* 2009.
6   Sherratt 1983; Greenfield 2010; for critique on the 'Secondary Products Revolution' model, *cf.* Halstead and Isaakidou 2011.
7   McCorriston 1997.
8   Burke 2010.
9   McCorriston 1997; Keith 1998.
10 Vakirtzi 2015.
11 Renfrew 1972, 451; Broodbank 2000; Kouka 2002.
12 Due to the limited space provided here, all parts are inevitably abridged versions of the corresponding dissertation chapters.
13 For the function of the spindle see Barber 1991, 51–54 and Andersson Strand 2015, 44–48.
14 Barber 1991, 51–54, 303; Mårtensson *et al.* 2009; Andersson Strand 2012.
15 Costin 1991.
16 Barber 1991, 52–53.
17 Vakirtzi 2015.
18 Costin 1991, 25.
19 Costin 1991, 33.
20 In the case of the unpublished sites recently excavated (Ayios Ioannis, Skala Sotiros, Skarkos and Koukonisi) the dating derives from information provided by the excavators at the current stage of study before final publication, and is tentative.
21 Especially in cases of multi-phased unpublished sites such as Koukonisi.
22 Maniatis and Papadopoulos 2011.
23 Papadopoulos *et al.* 2018.
24 Papadopoulos *et al.* 2018.
25 Koukouli-Chryssanthaki 1988; Koukouli-Chryssanthaki *et al.* forthcoming.
26 Barber 1991, 303.
27 Milojčić 1961; Isler 1973.
28 Kouka 2002.
29 Milojčić 1961; Kouka 2002.
30 Isler 1973; Kouka 2002.
31 Isler 1973.
32 Milojčić 1961, 51.
33 Milojčić 1961, 23–24.
34 Isler 1973.
35 Isler 1973.
36 Marthari 2008; 2017, 119.
37 A few later sporadic burials at the site date from the Middle and Late Bronze periods (Marthari 1997; 2008).
38 The said spindle whorl bears a few thin and shallow radial incisions, barely discernible on the distal end.
39 Hadjianastasiou 1988; Renfrew 2011, 152–157.
40 Kontoleon 1951.

41 Kontoleon 1971; 1972.
42 Rambach 2000.
43 Kontoleon 1974, 154.
44 Crewe 1998, 59–62.
45 Although the use-wear traces indicate that these objects were most probably used as spindle whorls for some time in their life-cycle, the possibility of their parallel use as beads cannot be excluded. Crewe, following Skibo, stresses the distinction between 'intended function' and 'actual function', which in the case of the whorls may be defined as spinning versus funerary offerings (Crewe 1998, 60). On the issue of multiple uses of spindle whorls, see also Vakirtzi 2012.
46 Renfrew 1972, 172–178; Angelopoulou 2008.
47 Bossert 1967.
48 Wilson 2013.
49 Wilson 1999, 162–163.
50 Wilson 2013.
51 Wilson 1999, 162, pl. 101: 342; 2013, 396, 390, table 2.
52 Wilson 1999; 2013.
53 Wilson 2013.
54 Wilson 2013, 394.
55 Wilson 1999, 163.
56 Wilson 1999, 160; Davis 1984, 162.
57 Wilson 1999, 163.
58 Wilson 1999; Wilson 2013.
59 Boulotis 1997, 246–251.
60 Boulotis 1997, 232, 236.
61 Koukonisi excavation diary 1995.
62 Some of the discussed assemblages derive from single-phase sites, while periodisation at other sites is still under study. However, the emerging synthesis conforms to the general pattern presented here, of a distinction between Early Bronze I and what follows thereafter, despite micro-regional differentiations. Whether there is a further significant transition from EB II to EB III in terms of fibre technology development in the insular Aegean region is still an issue under study.
63 Rambach 2000, I, pls. 78.4–8, 79.6.
64 Blegen 1950, part 2, fig. 222, 366.
65 Lloyd and Mellaart 1962, 274.
66 Joukowsky 1986, III, 375–376.
67 The Koukonisi EBA sample discussed here exhibits the cavity around the hole but not the incised decoration (Vakirtzi 2015).
68 Lamb 1936, 163.
69 Hood 1981, II, 639.
70 Bernabò Brea 1964, I, 2, pl. CLXVIII.5.
71 Bernabò Brea 1976, II, 1, pls. CCXXVII–CCXXXIII.
72 Tsountas 1899, 105, table 10; Rambach 2000, I, pl. 63.6.
73 Gavalas 2013, 650.
74 On the issue of the 'Anatolianising' spindle whorls in the Aegean, see Vakirtzi forthcoming.
75 Doumas 1977, 106; Rambach 2000, I, pls. 63.6, 73.3–9.
76 Renfrew 1972, 451.
77 Waetzoldt 2010; Firth 2014.
78 Biga 2014; Peyronel 2014.
79 Şahoğlu ascribed such networks to the operation of 'rich traders' distributing mainly metals originating from the reserves of the Taurus mountains over a vast area, thus coining the phrase 'Anatolian Trade Network' (ATN) (Şahoğlu 2005, 344). Note, however, that 'Anatolianising' spindle-spindle

whorls make their appearance in the West Anatolia-East Aegean region 'before' the ATN period (*cf.* Lamb 1936; Blegen *et al.* 1950; Hood 1981).

80 Rahmstorf 2006.
81 Militello 2014, 267.
82 Frangipane *et al.* 2009, 17.

Bibliography

Adovasio, J., Soffer, O. and Klima, B. 1996 Upper Palaeolithic fibre technology: interlaced woven finds from Pavlov I, Czech Republic, *c.* 26,000 years ago. *Antiquity* 70.269, 526–534.

Andersson Strand, E. 2010 The basics of textile tools and textile technology. In C. Michel and M.-L. Nosch (eds.), *Textile Terminologies in the Ancient Near East and Mediterranean from the Third to the First Millennia B. C.* Ancient Textiles Series 8. Oxford and Oakville, 10–22.

Andersson Strand, E. 2012 From spindle whorls and loom weights to fabrics. In M.-L. Nosch and R. Laffineur (eds.), *KOSMOS. Jewellery, Adornment and Textiles in the Aegean Bronze Age. Proceedings of the 13th International Aegean Conference/13e Rencontre égéenne internationale, University of Copenhagen, Danish National Research Foundation's Centre for Textile Research, 21–26 April 2010.* Aegaeum 33. Leuven and Liège, 209–213.

Andersson Strand, E. 2014 Sheep, wool and textile production. An interdisciplinary approach to the complexity of wool working. In C. Breniquet and C. Michel (eds.), *Wool Economy in the Ancient Near East and the Aegean. From the Beginnings of Sheep Husbandry to Institutional Textile Industry.* Ancient Textiles Series 17. Oxford and Philadelphia, 41–51.

Andersson Strand, E. 2015 The basics of textile tools and textile technology – from fibre to fabric. In E. Andersson Strand and M.-L. Nosch (eds.), *Tools, Textiles and Contexts. Investigating Textile Production in the Aegean and Eastern Mediterranean Bronze Age.* Ancient Textiles Series 21. Oxford and Philadelphia, 39–61.

Angelopoulou, A. 2008 The 'Kastri group': evidence from Korfari ton Amygdalion (Panormos) Naxos, Dhaskalio Keros and Akrotiri Thera. In N. J. Brodie, J. Doole, G. Gavalas and C. Renfrew (eds.), *Horizon. A Colloquium on the Prehistory of the Cyclades.* Cambridge, 149–164.

Barber, E. J. W. 1991 *Prehistoric Textiles. The Development of Cloth in the Neolithic and Bronze Ages with Special Reference to the Aegean.* Princeton.

Bernabò-Brea, L. 1964 *Poliochni. Citta preistorica nell'isola di Lemnos.* Vol. I.1–2. Roma.

Bernabò-Brea, L. 1976 *Poliochni. Citta preistorica nell'isola di Lemnos.* Vol. II.1–2. Roma.

Biga, M. G. 2014 Some aspects of the wool economy at Ebla (Syria, 24th century BC). In C. Breniquet and C. Michel (eds.), *Wool Economy in the Ancient Near East and the Aegean. From the Beginnings of Sheep Husbandry to Institutional Textile Industry.* Ancient Textiles Series 17. Oxford and Philadelphia, 139–150.

Blegen, C., Caskey, J. L., Rawson, M. and Sperling, J. 1950 *Troy. General Introduction. The First and Second Settlements.* Princeton.

Bossert, E. M. 1967 Kastri auf Syros. *Αρχαιολογικόν Δελτίον* 22 A, 53–76.

Boulotis, C. 1997 Κουκονήσι Λήμνου. Τέσσερα χρόνια ανασκαφικής έρευνας: θέσεις και υποθέσεις. In C. G. Doumas and V. La Rosa (eds.), *Poliochni el'antica eta del bronzo nell'Egeo Settentrionale.* Athens, 230–272.

Broodbank, C. 2000 *An Island Archaeology of the Early Cyclades.* Cambridge.

Burke, B. 2010 *From Minos to Midas. Ancient Cloth Production in the Aegean and in Anatolia.* Ancient Textiles Series 7. Oxford and Oakville.

Costin, C. L. 1991 Craft specialization: issues in defining, documenting, and explaining the organization of production. In M. B. Schiffer (ed.), *Archaeological Method and Theory* 3. Tuscon, 1–56.

Crewe, L. 1998 *Spindle Whorls. A Study of Form, Function and Decoration in Prehistoric Bronze Age Cyprus.* Studies in Mediterranean Archaeology pocket-book 149. Jonsered.

Davis, J. L. 1984 Cultural innovation and the Minoan thalassocracy at Ayia Irini, Keos. In R. Hägg and N. Marinatos (eds.), *The Minoan Thalassocracy. Myth and Reality. Proceedings of the Third International Symposium at the Swedish Institute in Athens, 31 May–5 June, 1982.* Acta Instituti Atheniensis Regni Sueciae 32. Stockholm, 159–165.

Doumas, C. 1977 *Early Bronze Age Burial Habits in the Cyclades.* Studies in Mediterranean Archaeology 48. Göteborg.

Firth, R. 2014 Textile texts of the Lagaš II period. In M. Harlow, C. Michel and M.-L. Nosch (eds.), *Prehistoric, Ancient Near Eastern and Aegean Textiles and Dress. An Interdisciplinary Anthology,* Ancient Textiles Series 18. Oxford and Philadelphia, 57–73.

Frangipane, M., Andersson Strand, E., Laurito, R., Möller-Wiering, S., Nosch, M.-L., Rast-Eicher, A. and Wisti-Lassen, A. 2009 Arslantepe, Malatya (Turkey): textiles, tools and imprints of fabrics from the 4th to the 2nd millennium BCE. *Paléorient* 35.1, 5–30.

Gavalas, G. 2013 Spindle whorls and related objects. In C. Renfrew, O. Philaniotou, N. Brodie, G. Gavalas and M. Boyd (eds.), *The Settlement at Dhaskalio. The Sanctuary on Keros and the Origins of Aegean Ritual Practice: The Excavations of 2006–2008* I. McDonald Institute of Monographs. Cambridge, 649–652.

Greenfield, H. J. 2010 The secondary products revolution: the past, the present and the future. *World Archaeology* 42.1, 29–54.

Hadjianastasiou, O. 1988 A Late Neolithic settlement at Grotta, Naxos. In E. B. French and K. A. Wardle (eds.), *Problems in Greek Prehistory. Papers Presented at the Centenary Conference of the British School of Archaeology at Athens, Manchester April 1986.* Bristol, 11–20.

Halstead, P. and Isaakidou, V. 2011 Revolutionary secondary products: the development and significance of milking, animal-traction and wool-gathering in Late Prehistoric Europe and the Near East. In T. Wilkinson, S. Sherratt and J. Bennet (eds.), *Interweaving Worlds: Systemic Interactions in Eurasia, 7th to 1st Millennia BC.* Oxford, 61–76.

Hood, S. 1981. *Excavations in Chios 1938–1955* II. London.

Isler, H. P. 1973 An Early Bronze Age settlement on Samos. *Archaeology* 26.3, 170–175.

Joukowsky, M. 1986 *Prehistoric Aphrodisias. An Account of the Excavations and Artifact Studies.* Louvain.

Keith, K. 1998 Spindle whorls, gender, and ethnicity at Late Chalcolithic Hacinebi Tepe. *Journal of Field Archaeology* 25.4 (Winter), 497–515.

Kontoleon, N. 1951 Ανασκαφαί εν Νάξω. *Πρακτικά της Εν Αθήναις Αρχαιολογικής Εταιρείας του Έτους 1949*, 112–122.

Kontoleon, N. 1971 Ανασκαφή Νάξου. *Πρακτικά της Εν Αθήναις Αρχαιολογικής Εταιρείας τουΈτους 1969*, 139–146.

Kontoleon, N. 1972 Ανασκαφή Νάξου. *Πρακτικά της Εν Αθήναις Αρχαιολογικής Εταιρείας του Έτους 1970*, 146–155.

Kontoleon, N. 1974 Ανασκαφαί Νάξου. *Πρακτικά της Εν Αθήναις Αρχαιολογικής Εταιρείας του Έτους 1972*, 143–155.

Kouka, O. 2002 *Siedlungsorganisation in der Nord- und Ostägäis während der Frühbronzezeit (3Jt. v. Chr.).* Internationale Archäologie 58. Rahden/Westfalen.

Koukouli-Chrysanthaki, C. 1988 Οικισμός της Πρώιμης Εποχής του Χαλκού στη Σκάλα Σωτήρος Θάσου. *Το Αρχαιολογικό Έργο στη Μακεδονία και Θράκη* 1, 389–406.

Koukouli-Chrysanthaki, C., Malamidou, D., Papadopoulos, S. and Maniatis, Y. forthcoming Οι νεότερες φάσεις της Πρώιμης Εποχής του Χαλκού στη Θάσο. Νέα δεδομένα. In C. Doumas, A. Giannikouri and O. Kouka (eds.), *The Aegean Early Bronze Age: New Evidence. Proceedings of the International Conference, Athens, April 11–14. 2008.*

Kvavadze, E., Bar-Yosef, O., Belfer-Cohen, A., Boaretto, E., Jakeli, N., Matskevich, Z. and Meshveliani, T. 2009 30,000-year-old flax fibres. *Science* 325.5946, 1359 (DOI: 10.1126/science.1175404, accessed 2 October 2018).

Lamb, W. 1936 *Excavations at Thermi in Lesbos.* Cambridge.

Lloyd, S. and Mellaart, J. 1962 *Beycesultan Vol. 1: The Chalcolithic and Early Bronze Age Levels.* London.

Maniatis, Y. and Papadopoulos, S. 2011 ¹⁴C dating of a Final Neolithic–Early Bronze Age transition period settlement at Aghios Ioannis on Thassos (north Aegean). *Radiocarbon* 53.1, 21–37.

Mårtensson, L., Nosch, M.-L. and Andersson Strand, E. 2009 Shape of things: understanding a loom weight. *Oxford Journal of Archaeology* 28.4, 373–398.

Marthari, M. 1997 *Από τον Σκάρκο στην Πολιόχνη.* In C. G. Doumas and V. La Rosa (eds.), *Poliochni e l'antica eta del bronzo nell'Egeo Settentrionale.* Athens, 362–382.

Marthari, M. 2008 Aspects of pottery circulation in the Cyclades during the early EB II period. Fine and semi-fine imported ceramic wares at Skarkos, Ios. In N. Brodie, J. Doole, G. Gavalas and C. Renfrew (eds.), *Horizon. A Colloquium on the Prehistory of the Cyclades.* McDonald Institute Monographs. Cambridge, 70–84.

Marthari, M. 2017 Cycladic figurines in settlements: the case of the major EC II settlement at Skarkos on Ios. In M. Marthari, C. Renfrew and M. Boyd (eds.), *Early Cycladic Sculpture in Context.* Oxford, 119–164.

McCorriston, J. 1997 The fibre revolution: textile extensification, alienation, and social stratification in Ancient Mesopotamia. *Current Anthropology* 38.4 (August/October), 517–535.

Militello, P. 2014 Wool economy in Minoan Crete before Linear B. A minimalist position. In C. Breniquet and C. Michel (eds.), *Wool Economy in the Ancient Near East and the Aegean. From the Beginnings of Sheep Husbandry to Institutional Textile*

Industry. Ancient Textiles Series 17. Oxford and Philadelphia, 264–282.

Milojčić, V. 1961 *Die Prähistorische Siedlung Unter dem Heraion, Grabung 1953 und 1955.* Samos I. Bonn.

Papadopoulos, S., Palli, O., Vakirtzi, S. and Psathi, E. 2018 Aghios Ioannis, Thasos: the economy of a small coastal site dated to the second half of the 4th millennium B. C. In S. Dietz, F. Mavridis, Z. Tancocic and T. Takaoglu (eds.), *Communities in Transition. The Circum-Aegean Area During the 5th and 4th Millennia BC.* Oxford, 357–366.

Peyronel, L. 2014 Form weighing wool to weaving tools. Textile manufacture at Ebla during the Early Syrian period in the light of archaeological evidence. In C. Breniquet and C. Michel (eds.), *Wool Economy in the Ancient Near East and the Aegean. From the Beginnings of Sheep Husbandry to Institutional Textile Industry.* Ancient Textiles Series 17. Oxford and Philadelphia, 124–138.

Rahmstorf, L. 2006 Zur Ausbreitung vorderasiatischer Innovationen in die frühbronzezeitliche Ägäis. *Prähistorische Zeitschrift* 81, 49–96.

Rambach, J. 2000 *Kykladen I. Die Frühe Bronzezeit Grab- und Siedlungsbefunde. Kykladen II. Die Frühe Bronzezeit Frühbronzezeitliche Beigabensittenkreise auf den Kykladen: relative Chronologie und Verbreitung.* Bonn.

Renfrew, C. 2011 (1st edition 1972) *The Emergence of Civilization. The Cyclades and the Aegean in the Third Millennium BC.* Oxford.

Şahoğlu, V. 2005 The Anatolian trade network and the Izmir Region during the Early Bronze Age. *Oxford Journal of Archaeology* 24.4, 339–361.

Sherratt, A. G. 1983 The secondary products revolution of animals in the Old World. *World Archaeology* 15, 90–104.

Tsountas, Ch. 1899 Κυκλαδικά II. *Αρχαιολογική Εφημερίς*, 73–134.

Tzachili, I. 2007 Weaving at Akrotiri, Thera. Defining cloth-making activities as a social process in a Late Bronze Age Aegean town. In C. Gillis and M.-L. Nosch (eds.), *Ancient Textiles: Production, Craft and Society. Proceedings of the First International Conference on Ancient Textiles Held at Lund, Sweden, and Copenhagen, Denmark on March 19–23, 2003.* Ancient Textiles Series 1. Oxford, 190–196.

Vakirtzi, S. 2012, Akr 8794: A miniature artifact from Akrotiri, Thera, and the 'whorl or bead' question in light of new textile evidence. In M.-L. Nosch and R. Laffineur (eds.), *KOSMOS. Jewellery, Adornment and Textiles in the Aegean Bronze Age. Proceedings of the 13th International Aegean Conference/13e Rencontre égéenne internationale, University of Copenhagen, Danish National Research Foundation's Centre for Textile Research, 21–26 April 2010.* Aegaeum 33. Leuven and Liège, 215–218.

Vakirtzi, S. 2015 Η νηματουργία στο Αιγαίο κατάτην Εποχή του Χαλκού, μέσω της παρουσίας των σφονδυλιών στις αρχαιολογικές θέσεις: μελέτη της τυπολογίας, των λειτουργικών δυνατοτήτων και της διασποράς των εξαρτημάτων του αδραχτιού που βρέθηκαν σε οικισμούς και νεκροταφεία (Yarn production in the Aegean during the Bronze Age: a study of typology, functionality and distribution of spindle whorls found in settlements and cemeteries). Unpublished PhD thesis, University of Crete.

Vakirtzi, S. forthcoming 'Ex Oriente Ars'? 'Anatolianizing' spindle whorls on the Early Bronze Age Aegean Islands and their implications for fiber crafts. In W. Schier and S. Pollock (eds.), *The Competition of Fibres. Textile Production in Western Asia and Europe (5000–2000 BC)*. Berlin Studies of the Ancient World. Berlin.

Waetzoldt, H. 2010 The colours and variety of fabrics from Mesopotamia during the Ur III period (2050 BC). In C. Michel and M.-L. Nosch (eds.), *Textile Terminologies in the Ancient Near East and Mediterranean from the Third to the First Millennium BC*. Ancient Textile Series 8. Oxford and Oakville, 201–209.

Wilson, D. E. 1999 *Ayia Irini: Periods I–III. The Neolithic and Early Bronze Age Settlements. Part 1: The Pottery and Small Finds*. KEOS IX. Mainz on Rhine.

Wilson, D. E. 2013 Ayia Irini II–III, Kea. The phasing and relative chronology of the Early Bronze Age II settlement. *Hesperia* 82, 385–434.

In search of 'invisible' textile tools and techniques of band weaving in the Bronze Age Aegean

Agata Ulanowska

Introduction

Studies on ancient textile production require combining not only several types of evidence, but also different research approaches, such as a functional and typological approach to textile tools and remains of textile workplaces, analyses of archaeological textiles and their imprints, environmental archaeology, studies of textual evidence and iconography, and comparative studies including all methods of experimental archaeology.[1] Even with this combination of various sources of textile knowledge, however, it is impossible to reconstruct the complete picture of textile production in the societies of the past.

Some of the gaps in material evidence of textile manufacture may, however, be filled in based on the general knowledge of technology of textile production. 'Invisible' textile tools constitute a category of implements substantially absent from or indiscernible in the archaeological record, yet still a prerequisite from the point of view of technological and procedural sequences of textile manufacturing.[2] This paper refers to this concept of archaeologically invisible implements and suggests that, although certain kinds of specialised looms for band weaving were known and used in Bronze Age Greece, they are not preserved in the archaeological material. It discusses a variety of possible band looms and combines technical analyses of band weaving with iconographic and textual evidence referring to bands and band making in the Aegean cultures. Special attention is paid to the loom with a rigid heddle, an efficient tool for weaving bands and starting borders of uncertain origin and date.

The ancestry of band looms and their construction

In Europe and the Mediterranean, the earliest material evidence of separately woven, plaited or twined narrow bands

and starting borders may be traced back to at least 6000 BC.[3] No traces of band looms that may have been used to make these early textiles, however, have been found. Although it has been suggested that a certain kind of tool(s) for band weaving could have preceded the invention of both horizontal and warp-weighted looms,[4] it is very difficult to find out what specific implements were employed at this early date.

Analyses of the oldest preserved fabrics make it possible to distinguish at least two technical principles according to which those textiles were made, *i.e.* weaving and twining (including 'transitional forms to plaiting with active system').[5] This in turn, may suggest what implements may have been used to make textiles, although a purely manual operation of threads, without any additional tools, cannot be ruled out, either.[6]

If textiles were made in more advanced techniques that required tools, the construction of these presumed devices may have been based on 'heddling' or 'twisting' principles. The 'heddling principle' (heddle weaving, weaving with a 'passive' warp)[7] may have been the basis for the construction of 'off loom' devices such as the paired crescent-shaped weights discussed in this volume,[8] heddle rod looms and narrow backstrap looms such as rigid heddles. Band looms constructed according to the 'heddling principle' divide warp into at least two layers and allow mechanical shed changing by drawing or lifting heddles knitted to the back layer(s) of warp threads.

The 'twisting principle' (weaving with an 'active' warp)[9] may have been used to make 'off loom' devices for twining[10] and was used in the tablet weaving technique.[11] In techniques based on the 'twisting principle', the twining of threads results from repetitive twisting of at least two active threads around at least one passive or active thread.[12] In the case of tablet weaving, sheds are changed by turning tablets, which also makes the warp threads twisted with each turn.

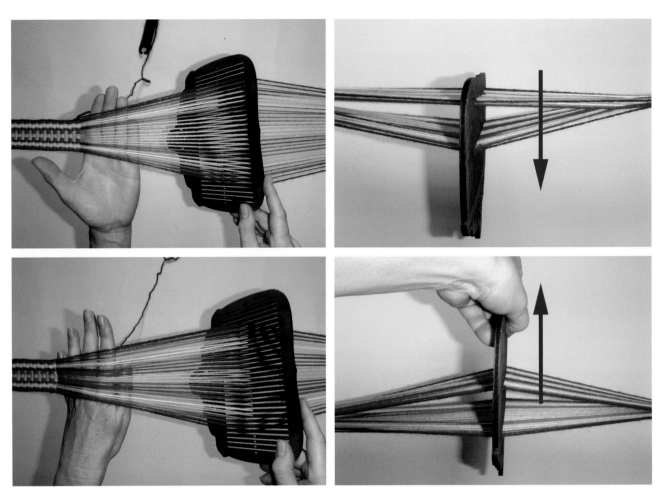

Fig. 18.1 Mechanics of weaving on the rigid heddle (photo: Agata Ulanowska).

Tablets and rigid heddles, both discussed as early types of band looms, are still well known and used today. Of these two implements, the tablets are regarded as tools of an earlier origin,[13] and the first combined evidence of tablet woven textiles and weaving tools comes from Bronze Age contexts in Central Europe[14] and Iron Age Italy.[15] The invention of the rigid heddle is more difficult to trace because the structures of Neolithic and Bronze Age warp-faced tabby or repp bands[16] and starting borders do not indicate what specific tools were used for their production.[17]

The rigid heddles are frame-like constructions, homogeneous in form, made up of a row of slats or reeds with drilled holes and narrow slots kept intentionally between them, which effectively substitutes the heddles and the shed bar. Warps threaded through the holes do not change their position in weaving – sheds are changed by lowering and raising the loom, which moves the warps threaded through the slots up and down (Fig. 18.1). Rather than any particular ancient find of a tool or textile, it was this simple but efficient construction and high expediency in warping the warp-weighted loom that has caused the rigid heddle to be considered a very ancient implement.[18] The earliest

finds of rigid heddles made of bone and bronze, all dating to the Roman period,[19] are much later than those of tablets.

Functionality of narrow bands and starting borders

While more has been said about the function of starting borders and their special technical relation to the warp-weighted loom, separate narrow bands were also important products of textile manufacturing. They may have been used as firm and decorative accessories such as belts, girdles, ties, stripes, ribbons, headbands or knee bindings, handles of bags, parts of harnesses and as reinforcing trims on the fabrics or cloths. Besides their practical function and visual attractiveness, narrow bands may also have served as a symbol of the social status of the band wearer, as has been suggested in the case of so-called Minoan 'sacral knots' and girdles, discussed in more detail in the next section of this chapter.

The starting border forms the upper selvedge of a fabric woven on the warp-weighted loom and it usually was made separately, often using a different technique than the

Fig. 18.2 Warping and weaving on the warp weighted loom with the starting border (photo: Katarzyna Żebrowska and Agata Ulanowska).

one used for the main body of the fabric. It may have the form of a woven band,[20] the length of which corresponds to the width of the main fabric, whereas its weft threads, creating long loops at one of its borders, become the future warp threads of the main piece of fabric (Fig. 18.2). The main functional advantages of the starting border may be described as follows:

- it makes it easier to space the warp threads evenly;
- it provides a stronger and attractive selvedge for the main fabric;[21]
- it makes it easier to separate two or more warp layers mechanically while warping, although in the early textiles warp threads may have been manually redistributed before the commencement of weaving on the warp-weighted loom.[22]

Band looms, such as tablets, may have also been used to weave selvedges incorporated into the main body of a fabric woven on the warp-weighted loom, whereas finishing borders may have been created by a combination of weaving, plaiting or needlework with elaborate fringes.[23]

The selvedges had the double function of a decorative finishing that, at the same time, reinforced and protected the edges of the fabrics woven on a big loom. In the Iron Age, the skill of tablet weaving and tablet-woven selvedges and bands may have also indicated a special social position of their producers and wearers.[24]

Evidence of band weaving in Bronze Age Greece

The practice of band weaving in Bronze Age Greece may be investigated directly by examining textile remains and tools that may have been used to make bands, and indirectly by examining the iconography of textiles and clothes, and textual sources that refer to band making.

Fragments of a Late Minoan band from Chania

So far, no material remains of bands or starting borders have been discovered, except tiny, carbonised fragments of the Late Minoan fine band made of goat hair (weft), linen (warp) and nettle (supplementary weft), unearthed at Ag. Aikaterini square, Kastelli Hill, in Chania.[25] The unique combination of different animal and plant fibres implies an elaborate choice of materials, *i.e.* bright-white supplementary nettle thread and the presumably dark weft threads, which resulted in a colour-contrast of this textile.

The textile has been described as a weft-faced tabby weave with a reconstructed thread count of 4–5 warp threads × 10 weft threads per cm. According to Susan Möller-Wiering, short pieces of lightly spun weft suggest that the band was plaited rather than woven.[26] The potential use of a band loom such as the heddle rod or rigid heddle would have resulted rather in a warp-faced tabby, although some difference in the average diameter of the two-plied linen warp threads (0.35 mm) and the slightly twisted goat hair weft threads (0.65 mm)[27] must have influenced the weft-faced appearance of this fabric, regardless the production technique.

Tools for band weaving

In the panoply of the Aegean Bronze Age textile implements, there are several kinds of weights and loom weights recognised as tools potentially useful for band weaving, such as crescent-shaped weights, cuboid weights, spools and heavy cylindrical weights with three perforations, and cones.[28]

The efficiency of the paired crescent-shaped weights forming an 'off loom' device for weaving narrow fabrics has been discussed in detail in this volume.[29] But the crescent-shape weights are quite uncommon finds in Bronze Age Greece and limited only to its early phase.[30] Therefore, it may be suggested that other techniques of band weaving must have prevailed.

Although no tablets have been preserved from Bronze Age Greece, Cretan cuboid weights with four perforations have been suggested as possible substitutes for normally flat tablets in a similar weaving technique.[31] The four perforations of a small diameter and use-wear marks around the holes, indicating the diagonal or horizontal positioning of these tools in weaving, may be argued to support this hypothesis, whereas the large thickness of the cubes disproves it. In order to evaluate the practical usefulness of the cuboid weights as possible substitutes for tablets, further experimenting would, therefore, be required.

The earliest examples of cuboid weights have been discovered in Middle Neolithic Knossos, but most of these tools are known from later Middle and Late Minoan contexts in eastern Crete, where they appeared in a wide range of sizes and masses. A possible continuation of the Neolithic textile tradition in eastern Crete has been suggested in relation to these particular tools, despite some differences in shape and size between the Neolithic and Bronze Age examples.[32]

A specialised use of small and light clay spools as weights in tablet weaving has been recently suggested with regard to Iron Age Italy and demonstrated experimentally.[33] The reconstruction of this particular technique of the use of small spools has been based on the wider archaeological evidence, comprising textile tools such as tablets and bone spacers with pegs, tablet-woven borders of a few Iron Age textiles and iconography of tablet weaving.

Clay spool-like objects are quite common finds at many sites in the Aegean from the Neolithic period throughout the Bronze Age. They are generally connected with textile production, but their specific use may be revealed on the basis of the size, shape and weight of the spools.[34] The smaller examples, with an average weight that clusters between *c.* 20–60 g and a height of *c.* 2–4 cm, could have been used as weights in tablet weaving. The high expediency of copies of small spools from Late Helladic Tiryns in tablet weaving has been confirmed by experience tests, undertaken by me with students of the Institute of Archaeology, University of Warsaw, and participants in experimental archaeology workshops. In these tests, we replicated the technique suggested by Lise Ræder Knudsen with regard to the Italian spools.[35] But there is no evidence of any additional equipment presumably required in this technique, such as spacers; nor are there any iconographic references to the process of band weaving in the Aegean art.

The apparent absence of spools in Middle Bronze Age Crete and in south-eastern Cyclades in contrast to mainland Greece and Anatolia[36] may suggest some differences in textile traditions and use of other, possibly more specialist tools there, although none of them, except perhaps the aforementioned cuboid weights from eastern Crete, seem to be suitable for tablet weaving.

In the experiential trials of band weaving, performed at the University of Warsaw and discussed in this volume,[37] copies of heavy weights from Early Helladic Tiryns were used for tensioning the rigid heddles set up horizontally. Both the employed implements, cylinders with three perforations and large cones, proved to be very functional weights for band weaving. But since their practical usefulness resulted predominantly from their heavy weight, more types of suspendable and heavy tools may have produced similar expediency. The observed results may generate an interesting analogy, showing the possibility of another manner of weaving on the rigid heddle, and may suggest another use of heavy weights in textile production. However, without any other evidence, they are not valid enough to suggest the actual use of the rigid heddles in Bronze Age Greece.

Iconography of bands and narrow fabrics

Aegean fashion, revealed by the rich iconography of female and male costumes, has been intensively examined and reconstructed by several scholars.[38] Among numerous types of garments variously classified according to their construction and function, the two major groups of fabrics produced with the use of band looms (that is, separate bands and narrow fabrics, as well starting borders, selvedges

a

b

Fig. 18.3 a. Separate bands and narrow widths in Aegean iconography (not to scale): 'La Parisienne', part of the Camp Stool fresco from Knossos (photo: A. Ulanowska, Archaeological Museum of Heraklion); models of 'sacral knots': ivory model from the South East House, Knossos (Evans 1921, fig. 308), faïence models from Shaft Grave IV in Mycenae (Evans 1921, fig. 309, a–b); ivory relief from Palaikastro (Evans 1921, fig. 310 d); girdles from the Temple Repositories in Knossos (Evans 1921, fig. 364); b. Dress borders in Aegean iconography and woven samples imitating their patterns: a detail of a band from the 'Saffron-gatherer' fresco, Akrotiri (modified by the author after Doumas 1992, pl. 121); a detail of a band from the 'Adorants' fresco, Akrotiri (modified by the author after Doumas 1992, pl. 102); a detail of a band from the North-west Slope Plaster Dump, Pylos (modified by the author after Peterson Murray 2016, fig. 3.48). All samples were woven by the author.

or trims integrated into larger textiles), may possibly be identified in art.

Bands belonging to the first group could be recognised in images of various belts and shawls, and in 'sacral knots' and girdles shown as parts of the Minoan and Mycenaean costumes, and as separate objects appearing in complex religious scenes, and as models of garments (possibly paired) made of ivory and faïence.[39] The second group is exclusively connected with the iconography of costumes and cloths (Fig. 18.3 a–b).

The terminology describing bands and narrow fabrics represented in art may denote the type of a garment or accessory, such as the belt, sash, strap, hip band or shawl;[40] the function of a band as a part of a textile, such as the starting border, selvedge or applied hem,[41] or its symbolic function, as in the case of the so-called 'sacral knots' and 'girdles'.

The imprecise taxonomic category of the 'sacral knots' has been recently examined by Janice Crowley, who has

distinguished two classes of knotted fabrics: the scarf and the cloak, with various appearances of particular motifs described by these two general terms.[42] Apart from the 'sacral knots', the girdles have also been regarded as symbolic, religious accessories represented as part of costumes, as well as in the form of separate models, such as the faïence girdles from the Temple Repository in Knossos.[43] The concept of the sacral or sacred garment that could be given as a votive offering to a deity or deities, or may have indicated the special priestly status of its wearer, was first suggested by Sir Arthur Evans and intensively examined since then.[44]

The construction of these narrow fabrics seems to be a less important element of the overall discussion, although the visual appearance of the represented textiles is commonly connected with real fabrics. Since the majority of the fabrics, especially the ones shown on the wall paintings from Thera, 'look readily – even easily – weavable',[45] various textile techniques have been suggested for making them.[46] With regard to the bands, two weaving techniques, based on the 'heddling' and 'twisting' principles, have been discussed. The first one has been suggested by Elizabeth Barber with reference to the 'sacral knots' and, according to her, their somehow archaic appearance, and to the decorative borders of Mycenaean tunics.[47] The 'twisting principle' has been recognised by Stella Spantidaki in the crocus pattern of the band decorating the costume of the Goddess from the 'Mistress of Animals and Saffron Gatherers' fresco from Akrotiri.[48] The pattern has been copied by her with weaving tablets in silk. Also, my own attempts at 'translating' textile motifs from the Aegean mural art into woven textiles (Fig. 18.3 b) confirm the 'weavable' character of the band patterns depicted on the frescos.

Leaving aside the floral motifs that are more difficult to connect with a specific textile technique, many of the repetitive or running geometric motifs that decorated the narrow fabrics could have been actually woven on band looms constructed according to the 'heddling' *and* 'twisting' principles. Geometric motifs based on diagonal composition, such as chevrons, diamonds or a diagonal check pattern, a horizontal check pattern, the yo-yo motif and parallel stripes may be rendered in fabrics woven on rigid heddles, *e.g.* in the warp floating (pick up) technique or with supplementary weft, as well as and in tablet weaving.[49] However, further experiments with woven reconstructions of the textile motifs represented in Aegean art may hopefully offer more conclusive arguments in favour of attributing a textile motif to a certain textile technique.

Textual evidence of specialised band makers

Among numerous professional designations of textile workers registered by the Mycenaean palatial administration in the archives of Linear B script, there is a designation of a specialist in band making. Women called *o-nu-ke-ja* and men *o-nu-ke-wi* were registered on tablets from Pylos and Thebes, and their profession was connected with band weaving,[50] whereas in Knossos the same type of fabric could have been made by *a-ke-ti-ri-ja/a-ze-ti-ri-ja* workers.[51] It is not clear whether these workers specialised in weaving separate bands or in making starting borders and warping the looms, or in elaborate finishing of the fabrics,[52] but the general correlation with band making suggests that it was a task that required specialised qualifications.

In Pylos, there was another term used to indicate headband makers – *a-pu-ko-wo-ko* – who made *a-pu-ke* bands of textile and leather.[53]

Possible depictions of band looms in Cretan Hieroglyphic signs

Recently, the presence of pictographic features in Linear B logograms and their relation with the Cretan Hieroglyphic

and Linear A, and imagery of the Aegean art has been observed with regard to the logograms designating plants and animals.[54] The relationship between textile logograms, archaeological artefacts and iconography has also been observed.[55] Specifically, the pictographic form of Cretan Hieroglyphic signs carved on seals, such as the syllabogram H *041and the logogram H *163, have been connected with textiles and weaving, and interpreted as the possible predecessors of subsequent signs in Linear A (*e.g.* AB 54) and B scripts (*e.g.* *159).[56]

Since pictographic forms, such as a spider (*e.g.* CMS I 425 – #310[57]) and a flax-like plant (H *031, H *174, *e.g.* CMS II.2 227 – #200; CMS III 227 – #242; CMS X 52 – #300), can also be recognised, the Cretan Hieroglyphic inscriptions on seals may possibly comprise some other graphic references to textiles and their production. I would like to suggest that the syllabogram H *038 ('Ladder band' motif, according to M. Anastasiadou)[58] may be seen as a pictographic designation of a loom[59] (*e.g.* CMS I 425; CMS II.2 227; CMS II.2 259 – #248; CMS III 227; CMS X 52). More signs of pictorial form possibly relating to textiles may have been engraved on one seal or in one inscription, *e.g.* the 'loom' H *038 sign could have been combined with the 'flax-like plant' H *031 and, at one time, with 'textile' H *041 (Fig. 18.4).[60]

The complexity of textile-related imagery in glyptic has been demonstrated by Catherine Breniquet in her recent study of textile manufacture in 3rd millennium BC Mesopotamia.[61] C. Breniquet has recognised several procedural sequences of textile manufacturing depicted on seals and has estimated that processing of textiles is to be found in 11–14% of representations, which suggests that textiles were quite a popular theme.[62]

Several striking similarities between the imagery of textile production in Mesopotamian glyptic of the 3rd millennium BC and Middle Minoan glyptic motifs (*c.* 2000–1700 BC) may be suggested, *e.g.* the graphic form of the syllabogram H *038 has close analogies in schematic depictions of fabrics shown together with vertical looms on several cylinders dating to the Early Dynastic period (Fig. 18.4).[63] Despite several differences in textile traditions between the two regions and cultures, on Mesopotamian seals, this type of loom has been recognised as a possible warp-weighted loom.[64] In Bronze Age Greece, the warp-weighted loom is considered the most popular, if not the only large loom used at this time, and its use is well attested by the archaeological evidence of loom weights.[65] Therefore, this cross-cultural iconographic relation may be used as an argument that lends some more validity to the overall correlation of the pictorial form of H *038 with textiles. But depictions of loom weights and the warp-weighted loom, recently recognised in the Minoan glyptic, imply different iconographic conventions adopted for rendering this tool in art.[66]

The graphic form of the Mesopotamian loom may also have had different proportions than the syllabogram H *038.

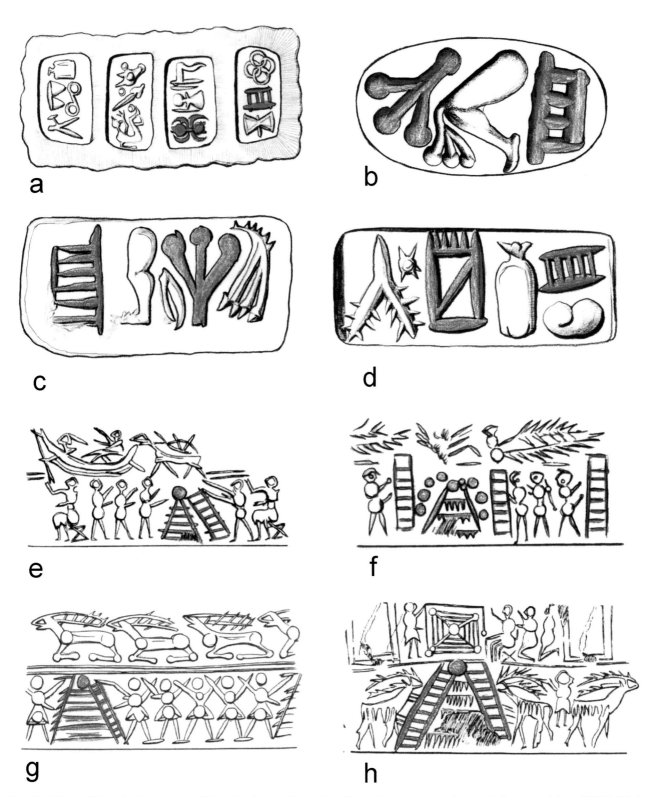

Fig. 18.4 Cretan Hieroglyphic signs possibly related to textiles and textile production engraved on seals (not to scale): a. CMS I 425; b. CMS III 227b; c. CMS X 52; d. CMS II.2 227; and representations of looms in the Early Dynastic Mesopotamian glyptic: e. Amiet 1980, no. 1446; Breniquet 2008, fig. 88.8; f. Amiet 1980, no. 1786; Breniquet 2008, fig. 88.7; g. Amiet 1980, no. 1458; Breniquet 2008, fig. 88.2; h. Amiet 1980, no. 1468; Breniquet 2008, fig. 88.4 (drawings: Agata Ulanowska).

The pictorial form of the latter varied from a rectangular to square-shaped frame with various numbers of horizontal or vertical bars,[67] but in its prevailing form it resembles the small square frame of the rigid heddle with several slots. Although it is possible to imagine that the Mesopotamian motifs representing textiles and textile tools were adapted in the Minoan glyptic (and script) to designate a familiar content, still the visual resemblance of H *038 and the rigid heddle may be purely conjectural.

Conclusions

The discussed evidence of band weaving in Bronze Age Greece implies that bands and band making were an important part of Aegean textile production. Major functional types of narrow fabrics, such as separate bands and starting borders, were produced. Moreover, specialised band weavers may have been engaged in the production, at least in the case of textile manufacture organised and controlled by the Mycenaean palaces.

The iconography of these bands shows that they constituted sophisticated and visually attractive accessories or integral parts of female and male attire. As separate garments and dress accessories, they could have had a symbolic value as sacred objects present in religious scenes, and could have operated as religious symbols and votive offerings. The 'sacral knots' and girdles, as well as the decorative borders of costumes, may also have served in the Bronze Age dress code system as indicators of the special social status of their wearers, especially as the external sign of the priesthood.

The cross-connections between the iconography and the textual evidence of band weaving and the archaeological evidence of textile tools do not give a clear answer as to what weaving techniques may have been used for band making. The complex imagery of bands in Aegean art and the textual evidence imply rather specialised and advanced textile techniques of band making, with the use of tools based on the two technical principles of heddling and twisting of warp yarns. Therefore, it also seems more likely that specialised band looms were used, rather than simple 'off loom' devices. Although the comparative evidence and the ancestry of tablet weaving seem to favour the hypothesis of the use of this technique with regard to Aegean bands, the use of other heddle looms such as the rigid heddle, although not conclusive in the light of the presented arguments, should not be disregarded.

Notes

1   I would like to express my special thanks to the authorities of the University of Warsaw and the Institute of Archaeology, Professors Alojzy Nowak, Wojciech Nowakowski and Kazimierz Lewartowski for their financial support of my

participation in the session 'Textiles in a Social Context. Textile Production in Europe and the Mediterranean in the 4th and 3rd Millennia BCE' at the 20th Annual Meeting of the European Association of Archaeologists in Istanbul. I also wish to warmly thank Andrzej Flis for improving my English. I wrote this paper during my FUGA internship grant at the Centre for Research on Ancient Technologies of the Institute of Archaeology and Ethnology, Polish Academy of Sciences, awarded by the National Science Centre in Poland (DEC-2015/16/S/HS3/00085). *Cf.* Siennicka *et al.* this volume.
2   *Cf.* Andersson Strand this volume.
3   Barber 1991, 116; Médard 2012, 370–376; Grömer 2016, 93, 96–97, 118–119.
4   Barber 1991, 254–255; 1997, 515.
5   Schlabow 1959; Burnham 1965; Barber 1991, 126–144, 254–259; Rast-Eicher 2005, 124; Desrosiers 2010, 26–27, 31–45, especially fig. 3.4; Alfaro Giner 2012; Médard 2012.
6   Desrosiers 2010, 26.
7   *Cf.* Hoffmann 1974, 108; Barber 1991, 117; Desrosiers 2010, 39.
8   *Cf.* Grömer this volume; Ulanowska this volume.
9   Desrosiers 2010, 39; Grömer 2016, 104.
10   *Cf.* Seiler-Baldinger and Médard 2014; Grömer this volume.
11   Collingwood 1982, 10–11; Grömer 2016.
12   Médard 2012, 370–371.
13   *Cf.* Hoffmann 1974, 164–165; Collingwood 1982, 11–13; Wild 1988, 39; Barber 1991, 118–122; de Diego *et al.* this volume. For the early tablet woven textiles, see Shishlina *et al.* 2003; Grömer 2013.
14   Möller-Wiering 2012, 128; Grömer 2016, 101–103.
15   Ræder Knudsen 2002; 2012; Gleba 2008, 138–153.
16   For 'repp' as one of the band weaves, see Grömer 2016, 93–94.
17   *Cf.* Médard 2012; Grömer 2013, 70; 2016, 94–96.
18   Vogt 1937; Grömer 2013, 70. *Cf.* Hoffmann 1974, 106–108 for a later invention of the rigid heddle.
19   For the evidence of rigid heddles from the Roman era, see Foulkes 2011, 44, who also observes that the limited number of slots and holes in those rigid heddles allowed weaving only narrow bands in tabby or tubular weaves.
20   For other methods of making the starting borders, see Hoffmann 1974, 141–150, 154, 175–183; Carington Smith 1975, 93–95; Barber 1991, 129; Franzén *et al.* 2012, 356; Grömer 2013, 76–77; 2016, 122.
21   Broudy 1979, 31.
22   Médard 2012; Grömer 2013.
23   Barber 1991, 135–137; Médard 2012, 371–376; Ræder Knudsen 2012; Grömer 2013, 77–79; 2016, 122–127.
24   *Cf.* Gleba 2007, 74; Banck–Burgess 2012; Ræder Knudsen 2012.
25   Möller-Wiering 2006, 1–4; Moulhérat and Spantidaki 2009; Spantidaki and Moulherat 2012, 189, fig. 7.3.
26   Möller-Wiering 2006, 3.
27   Moulhérat and Spantidaki 2009.
28   Ulanowska this volume.
29   Grömer this volume; Ulanowska this volume.
30   Siennicka 2012.
31   Carington Smith 1975, 186–187, 294; *cf.* Burke 2010, 60. For clay 'tablets' in Iron Age Italy, see Gleba 2008, 139.

32 Carington Smith 1975, 186, 293, 296; Burke 2010, 59–60. According to Jill Carington Smith, the cuboid weights in the Bronze Age were smaller and lighter, more carefully formed and fired, and perforated along their longest axis, whereas the Neolithic cubes were perforated across the shorter axis.

33 Ræder Knudsen 2002; 2012; Gleba 2007; 2008, 138–149, 152–153.

34 Rahmstorf 2005; 2008, 59–73; 2011, 320–322; Pavúk 2012, 123–128; Siennicka and Ulanowska 2016.

35 Siennicka and Ulanowska 2016.

36 *Cf.* Pavúk 2012, pl. XXXIV.

37 Ulanowska this volume.

38 *Cf.* Sapouna Sakellaraki 1971; Carington Smith 1975, 305–335, 463–487; Verlinden 1984, 98–104; Barber 1991, 314–330; Rehak 1996; 2004; Tzachili 1997, 224–250; Jones 2000; 2001; 2003; 2005; 2009; 2012; 2015; Lillethun 2003; 2012; Marcar 2004; 2005; Trnka 2007; Chapin 2008; Nosch 2008; Boloti 2009; Crowley 2012.

39 *Cf.* Schliemann 1878, 278–281, figs. 350–352; Evans 1921, 429–435, 506, figs. 308–311, 364 c–d. 'Sacral knots' have also been recognised in representations of fabrics looped around the double axes and columns, see Evans 1921, 433, fig. 310 e–d; Nilsson 1950, 210–212; Crowley 2012, 231–232.

40 *Cf.* Marcar 2005, 40–41; Verduci 2012.

41 *Cf.* Lillethun 2003; Marcar 2004, 229; 2005, 35; Jones 2009, 318–334, figs. 15, 24; 2012, 225; 2015, 67–68.

42 Crowley 2012, 232, pl. LI 1–10.

43 Evans 1921, 506; fig. 364 c–d.

44 *Cf.* Evans 1921, 429–435, 506; 1935, 397–405, 412–414; Persson 1942, 91–93; Nilsson 1950, 155–164, especially 162–164, 311; Marinatos 1993, 127–145; 2015, 154–156; Boloti 2009; 2014; 2016.

45 Barber 1991, 317.

46 *Cf.* Carington Smith 1975, 322–325; Tzachili 1990, 387–388; 1997, 224–248; Barber 1991, 317–330; Jones 2003; 2005, 711–712; 2009, 318–334; 2015, 65–66; Lillethun 2003; Trnka 2007, 128.

47 Barber 1991, 325–328; 1997, 518; *cf.* Evans 1921, 430; Carington Smith 1975, 470–472.

48 Spantidaki 2008, 45–46.

49 *Cf.* traditional Sámi band weaving, Collingwood 1982.

50 Del Freo *et al.* 2010, 345.

51 Luján 2010, 383.

52 Barber 1991, 283; Firth and Nosch 2006, 134–136; Killen 2007, 50–51; Bernabé and Luján 2008, 217; Burke 2010, 88–89.

53 Killen 2007, 50; Del Freo *et al.* 2010, 246.

54 Weilhartner 2012; 2014.

55 *Cf.* Nosch 2012.

56 Militello 2007, 41; Burke 2010, 74; Del Freo *et al.* 2010, 348–354; Nosch 2012, 304–305, fig. 1; Petrakis 2012, 78–79, pl. XXVI.1.

57 All references to the seals are given after the CMS – *Corpus der minoischen und mykenischen Siegel* – and the database Corpus of Minoan and Mycenaean Seals (http://arachne. uni-koeln.de/drupal/? q=de/node/196, accessed 6 December 2014); all references to the hieroglyphic inscriptions are after CHIC – *Corpus hieroglyphicarum inscriptionum Cretae,* Godard and Olivier 1996.

58 Anastasiadou 2011, 239, motif 139.

59 In the CHIC, H *038 belongs to group VII, classified as buildings and parts of buildings, Godard and Olivier 1996, 15.

60 Godard and Olivier 1996, 343–344.

61 Breniquet 2008.

62 Breniquet 2008, 322.

63 Amiet 1980, nos. 1342, 1446, 1447, 1450, 1458, 1468, 1786, 1787, 1790; Breniquet 2008, 297–303, especially 301, figs. 87.5, 88.

64 Breniquet 2008, 297–303, fig. 88.

65 *Cf.* Barber 1991; Tzachili 1997; Andersson Strand and Nosch 2015.

66 *Cf.* Ulanowska 2016; Ulanowska 2017.

67 Godard and Olivier 1996, 399–400.

Bibliography

Alfaro Giner, C. 2012 Textiles from the Pre-pottery Neolithic site of Tell Halula (Euphrates Valley, Syria), *Paléorient* 38.1–2. Dossier thématique/Thematic file, C. Breniquet, M. Tengberg, E. Andersson and M.-L. Nosch (eds.), Préhistoire des Textiles au Proche-Orient/Prehistory of Textiles in the Near East, 41–54.

Amiet, P. 1980 *La glyptique mésopotamienne archaïque.* Paris.

Anastasiadou, M. 2011 *The Middle Minoan Three-sided Soft Stone Prism. A Study of Style and Iconography.* CMS Beiheft 9. Mainz.

Andersson Strand, E. and Nosch, M.-L. (eds.) 2015 *Tools, Textiles and Contexts. Investigating Textile Production in the Aegean and Eastern Mediterranean Bronze Age.* Ancient Textile Series 21. Oxford and Philadelphia.

Banck-Burgess, J. 2012 Case study: the textiles from the princely burial at Eberdingen-Hochdorf, Germany. In M. Gleba and U. Mannering (eds.), *Textiles and Textile Production in Europe: From Prehistory to AD 400.* Ancient Textile Series 11. Oxford and Oakville, 139–150.

Barber, E. J. W. 1991 *Prehistoric Textiles. The Development of Cloth in the Neolithic and Bronze Ages with Special Reference to the Aegean.* Princeton.

Barber, E. J. W. 1997 Minoan women and the challenges of weaving for home, trade and shrine. In R. Laffineur and P. P. Betancourt (eds.), *TEXNH. Craftsmen, Craftswomen and Craftsmanship in the Aegean Bronze Age. Proceedings of the 6th International Aegean Conference Philadelphia, Temple University, 18–21 April 1996.* Aegaeum 16. Liège and Austin, 515–519.

Bernabé, A. and Luján, E. R. 2008 Mycenaean technology. In Y. Duhoux and A. Morpurgo Davies (eds.), *A Companion to Linear B. Mycenaean Greek Texts and their World.* Leuven, 201–233.

Boloti, T. 2009 Ritual offering of textiles and garments in the Late Bronze Age Aegean. *Archane. Occasional Publication for the History of Costume and Textiles in the Aegean and Eastern Mediterranean* 3, 52–65.

Boloti, T. 2014 *e-ri-ta*'s dress: contribution to the study of the Mycenaean priestesses' attire. In M. Harlow, C. Michel and M.-L. Nosch (eds.), *Prehistoric, Ancient Near Eastern and Aegean Textiles and Dress. An Interdisciplinary Anthology.* Ancient Textiles Series 18. Oxford and Philadelphia, 245–270.

Boloti, T. 2016 A 'knot'-bearing(?) Minoan genius from Pylos. Contribution to the cloth/clothing offering imagery of the

Aegean Late Bronze Age. In E. Alram-Stern, F. Blakolmer, S. Deger-Jalkotzy, R. Laffineur and J. Weilhartner (eds.), *METAPHYSIS. Ritual, Myth and Symbolism in the Aegean Bronze Age. Proceedings of the 15th International Aegean Conference, Vienna, Institute for Oriental and European Archaeology, Aegean and Anatolia Department, Austrian Academy of Sciences and Institute of Classical Archaeology, University of Vienna, 22–25 April 2014.* Aegaeum 39. Leuven and Liège, 505–510.

Breniquet, C. 2008 *Essai sur le tissage en Mésopotamie des premières communautés sédentaires au milieu du IIIe millénaire avant J.-C.* Travaux de la Maison René-Ginouvès 5. Paris.

Broudy, E. 1979 *The Book of Looms. A History of the Handloom from Ancient Times to the Present.* Hanover and London.

Burke, B. 2010 *From Minos to Midas, Ancient Cloth Production in the Aegean and in Anatolia.* Ancient Textiles Series 7. Oxford and Oakville.

Burnham, H. B. 1965 Çatal Hüyük – the textiles and twined fabrics. *Anatolian Studies* 15, 169–174.

Carington Smith, J. 1975 Spinning, weaving and textile manufacture in Prehistoric Greece – from the beginning of the Neolithic to the end of the Mycenaean Ages; with particular reference to the evidence found on archaeological excavations. Unpublished PhD thesis, University of Tasmania.

Chapin, C. 2008 The Lady of the Landscape: investigation of Aegean costuming and the Xeste 3 frescoes. In C. S. Colburn and M. K. Heyn (eds.), *Reading a Dynamic Canvas: Adornment in the Ancient Mediterranean.* Newcastle, 48–83.

Collingwood, P. 1982 *The Techniques of Tablet Weaving.* London.

Crowley, J. 2012 Prestige clothing in the Bronze Age Aegean. In M.-L. Nosch and R. Laffineur (eds.), *KOSMOS. Jewellery, Adornment and Textiles in the Aegean Bronze Age. Proceedings of the 13th International Aegean Conference/13e Rencontre égéenne internationale, University of Copenhagen, Danish National Research Foundation's Centre for Textile Research, 21–26 April 2010.* Aegaeum 33. Leuven and Liège, 231–238.

Del Freo, M., Nosch, M.-L. and Rougemont, F. 2010 The terminology of textiles in the Linear B tablets, including some considerations on Linear A logograms and abbreviations. In C. Michel and M.-L. Nosch (eds.), *Textile Terminologies in the Ancient Near East and the Mediterranean from the 3rd to the 1st Millennia BC.* Ancient Textiles Series 8. Oxford and Oakville, 338–373.

Desrosiers, S. 2010 Textile terminologies and classifications. In C. Michel and M.-L. Nosch (eds.), *Textile Terminologies in the Ancient Near East and the Mediterranean from the 3rd to the 1st Millennia BC.* Ancient Textiles Series 8. Oxford and Oakville, 23–67.

Doumas, Ch. 1992 *The Wall Paintings from Thera.* Athens.

Evans, A. 1921 *The Palace of Minos at Knossos* I. London.

Evans, A. 1935 *The Palace of Minos at Knossos* IV. II. London.

Firth, R. and Nosch, M.-L. B. 2006 Scribe 103 and the Mycenaean textile industry at Knossos: the Lc (1) and Od (1) sets. *Minos* 37–38 (2002–2003), 121–142.

Foulkes, S. J. 2011 Roman rigid heddles: a survey. *Archaeological Textiles Review* 52, 30–47.

Franzén, M.-L., Sundström, A., Lundwall, E. and Andersson Strand, E. 2012 Sweden. In M. Gleba and U. Mannering (eds.), *Textiles and Textile Production in Europe: From Prehistory to AD 400.* Ancient Textile Series 11. Oxford and Oakville, 349–364.

Gleba, M. 2007 Textile production in proto-historic Italy: from specialists to workshops. In C. Gillis and M.-L. B. Nosch (eds.), *Ancient Textiles, Production, Craft and Society, Proceedings of the First International Conference on Ancient Textiles, Held at Lund Sweden and Copenhagen, Denmark, on March 19–23, 2003.* Ancient Textiles Series 1. Oxford, 71–76.

Gleba, M. 2008 *Textile Production in Pre-Roman Italy.* Ancient Textile Series 4. Oxford.

Godart, J. P. and Olivier, L. 1996 *Corpus Hieroglyphicarum Inscriptionum Cretae.* Études crétoises 31. Athens.

Grömer, K. 2013 Tradition, Kreativität und Innovation – Textiltechnologische Entwicklung von der Bronzezeit zur Hallstattzeit/Tradition, creativity and innovation – The development of textile expertise from the Bronze Age to the Hallstatt Period. In K. Grömer, A. Kern, H. Reschreiter and H. Rösel-Mautendorfer (eds.), *Textiles from Hallstatt. Weaving Culture in Bronze Age and Iron Age Salt Mines. Textilien aus Hallstatt. Gewebte Kultur aus dem bronze- und eisenzeitlichen Salzbergwerk.* Archaeolingua 29. Budapest, 53–97.

Grömer, K. 2016, *The Art of Prehistoric Textile Making. The Development of Craft Traditions and Clothing in Central Europe.* Veröffentlichungen der Prähistorischen Abteilung 5. Vienna.

Hoffmann, M. 1974 (1st edition 1964) *The Warp-Weighted Loom, Studies in the History and Technology of an Ancient Implement.* Oslo, Bergen and Tromsø.

Jones, B. R. 2000 Revealing Minoan fashions. *Archaeology* 53.3, 36–42.

Jones, B. R. 2001 'The Minoan Snake Goddess': new interpretation of her costume and identity. In R. Laffineur and R. Hägg (eds.), *POTNIA. Deities and Religion in the Aegean Bronze Age. Proceedings of the 8th International Aegean Conference Göteborg, Göteborg University, 12–15 April 2000.* Aegaeum 22. Liège and Austin, 259–265.

Jones, B. R. 2003 Veils and mantles: an investigation of the construction and function of the costume and identity. In K. P. Foster and R. Laffineur (eds.), *METRON. Measuring the Aegean Bronze Age. Proceedings of the 9th International Aegean Conference, New Heaven, Yale University, 18–19 April 2002.* Aegaeum 24. Liège, 441–450.

Jones, B. R. 2005 The clothes-line: imports and exports of Aegean cloth(es) and iconography. In R. Laffineur and E. Greco (eds.), *EMPORIA. Aegeans in the Central and Eastern Mediterranean. Proceedings of the 10th International Aegean Conference: Italian School of Archaeology, Athens, 14–18 April 2004.* Aegaeum 25. Liège and Austin, 707–715.

Jones, B. R. 2009 The 'Mykenaia' and a seated woman form Mycenae. *American Journal of Archaeology* 113, 309–337.

Jones, B. R. 2012 The construction and significance of the Minoan side-pleated skirt. In M.-L. Nosch and R. Laffineur (eds.), *KOSMOS. Jewellery, Adornment and Textiles in the Aegean Bronze Age. Proceedings of the 13th International Aegean Conference/13e Rencontre égéenne internationale, University of Copenhagen, Danish National Research Foundation's Centre for Textile Research, 21–26 April 2010.* Aegaeum 33. Leuven and Liège, 221–330.

Jones, B. R. 2015 *Ariadne's Threads: The Construction and Significance of Clothes in the Aegean Bronze Age*. Aegaeum 38. Leuven and Liège.

Killen, J. T. 2007 Cloth production in Late Bronze Age Greece: the documentary evidence. In C. Gillis and M.-L. B. Nosch (eds.), *Ancient Textiles, Production, Craft and Society, Proceedings of the First International Conference on Ancient Textiles, Held at Lund Sweden and Copenhagen, Denmark, on March 19–23, 2003*. Ancient Textiles Series 1. Oxford, 50–58.

Lillethun, A. 2003 The recreation of Aegean cloth and clothing. In K. P. Foster and R. Laffineur (eds.), *METRON. Measuring the Aegean Bronze Age. Proceedings of the 9th International Aegean Conference, New Heaven, Yale University, 18–19 April 2002*. Aegaeum 24. Liège, 463–472.

Lillethun, A. 2012 Finding the flounced skirt (back apron). In M.-L. Nosch and R. Laffineur (eds.), *KOSMOS. Jewellery, Adornment and Textiles in the Aegean Bronze Age. Proceedings of the 13th International Aegean Conference/13e Rencontre égéenne internationale, University of Copenhagen, Danish National Research Foundation's Centre for Textile Research, 21–26 April 2010*. Aegaeum 33. Leuven and Liège, 251–254.

Luján, R. E. 2010 Mycenaean textile terminology at work: the KN Lc (1)-tablets and the occupational nouns of the textile industry. In C. Michel and M.-L. Nosch (eds.), *Textile Terminologies in the Ancient Near East and the Mediterranean from the 3rd to the 1st Millennia BC*. Ancient Textiles Series 8. Oxford and Oakville, 376–387.

Marcar, A. 2004 Aegean costume and the dating of the Knossian frescoes. In G. Cadogan, E. Hatzikaki and A. Vasilakis (eds.), *Knossos: Palace, City, State. Proceedings of the Conference in Herakleion Organized by the British School of Athens and the 23rd Ephoreia of Prehistoric and Classical Antiquities of Herakleion, in November 2000, for the Centenary of Sir Arthur Evans's Excavations at Knossos*. British School at Athens Studies 12. London, 225–238.

Marcar, A. 2005 Reconstructing Aegean Bronze Age fashions. In L. Cleland, M. Harlow and L. Llewellyn-Jones (eds.), *The Clothed Body in the Ancient Word*. Oxford, 30–43.

Marinatos, N. 1993 *Minoan Religion. Ritual, Image and Symbol*. Columbia.

Marinatos, N. 2015 *Akrotiri, Thera and the East Mediterranean*. Athens.

Médard, F. 2012 Switzerland: Neolithic period. In M. Gleba and U. Mannering (eds.), *Textiles and Textile Production in Europe: From Prehistory to AD 400*. Ancient Textile Series 11. Oxford and Oakville, 367–377.

Militello, P. 2007, Textile industry and Minoan palaces. In C. Gillis and M.-L. B. Nosch (eds.), *Ancient Textiles, Production, Craft and Society, Proceedings of the First International Conference on Ancient Textiles, Held at Lund Sweden and Copenhagen, Denmark, on March 19–23, 2003*. Ancient Textiles Series 1. Oxford, 36–45.

Militello, P. 2011, Immagini e realtà della produzione nella Creta minoica: i temi assenti. In F. Carinci, N. Cucuzza, P. Militello and O. Palio (eds.), *ΚΡΗΤΗΣ ΜΙΝΩΙΔΟΣ. Tradizione e identità minoica tra produzione artigianale, pratiche cerimoniali e memoria del passato. Studi offerti a Vincenzo La Rosa per il Suo 70 compleanno*. Padova, 239–258.

Möller-Wiering, S. 2006 *Tools and Textiles – Texts and Contexts. Bronze Age Textiles found in Crete* (https://ctr.hum.ku.dk/research-programmes-and-projects/previous-programmes-and-projects/tools/bronze_age_textiles_found_in_crete.pdf, accessed 25 September 2018).

Möller-Wiering, S. 2012 Germany: Bronze and Pre-Roman Ages. In M. Gleba and U. Mannering (eds.), *Textiles and Textile Production in Europe: From Prehistory to AD 400*. Ancient Textile Series 11. Oxford and Oakville, 122–138.

Moulhérat, C. and Spantidaki, Y. 2009 Cloth from Kastelli, Chania. *Archane. Occasional Publication for the History of Costume and Textiles in the Aegean and Eastern Mediterranean* 3, 8–15.

Nilsson, M. P. 1950 *The Minoan-Mycenaean Religion and its Survival in Greek Religion*. Lund.

Nosch, M.-L. B. 2008 Haute couture in the Bronze Age: a history of Minoan female costumes from Thera. In M. Gleba, C. Munkholt and M.-L. B Nosch (eds.), *Dressing the Past*. Ancient Textiles Series 3. Oxford, 1–12.

Nosch, M.-L. B. 2012 The textile logograms in the Linear B tablets: Les idéogrammes archéologiques – des textiles. In P. Carlier, C. de Lamberterie, M. Egetmeyer, N. Guilleux, F. Rougemont and J. Zurbach (eds.), *Études mycéniennes 2010. Actes du XIIIe colloque international sur les textes égéens, Sèvres, Paris, Nanterre, 20–23 septembre 2010*. Biblioteca di Pasiphae X. Pisa and Roma, 303–346.

Pavúk, P. 2012 Of spools and discoid loom-weights: Aegean-type weaving at Troy revisited. In M.-L. Nosch and R. Laffineur (eds.), *KOSMOS. Jewellery, Adornment and Textiles in the Aegean Bronze Age. Proceedings of the 13th International Aegean Conference/13e Rencontre égéenne internationale, University of Copenhagen, Danish National Research Foundation's Centre for Textile Research, 21–26 April 2010*. Aegaeum 33. Leuven and Liège, 121–130.

Persson, A. W. 1942 *The Religion of Greece in Prehistoric Times*. Berkeley and Los Angeles.

Peterson Murray, S. 2016 Patterned textiles as costume in Aegean art. In M. B. Shaw and A.P. Chapin, *Woven Threads. Patterned Textiles of the Aegean Bronze Age*. Ancient Textiles Series 22. Oxford and Philadelphia, 43–103.

Petrakis, V. P. 2012 'Minoan' to 'Mycenaean': thoughts on the emergence of the Knossian textile industry. In M.-L. Nosch and R. Laffineur (eds.), *KOSMOS. Jewellery, Adornment and Textiles in the Aegean Bronze Age. Proceedings of the 13th International Aegean Conference/13e Rencontre égéenne internationale, University of Copenhagen, Danish National Research Foundation's Centre for Textile Research, 21–26 April 2010*. Aegaeum 33. Leuven and Liège, 77–86.

Ræder Knudsen, L. 2002 La tessitura con le tavolette nella tomba 89. In P. von Eles (ed.), *Guerriero e sacerdote. Autorità e comunità nell'età del ferro a Verrucchio. La tomba del trono*. Firenze, 230–243.

Ræder Knudsen, L. 2012 Case study: the tablet woven borders of Verucchio. In M. Gleba and U. Mannering (eds.), *Textiles and Textile Production in Europe: From Prehistory to AD 400*. Ancient Textile Series 11. Oxford and Oakville, 254–263.

Rahmstorf, L. 2005 Ethnicity and changes in weaving technology in Cyprus and the eastern Mediterranean in the 12th century BC. In V. Karageorghis, H. Matthäus and S. Rogge (eds.),

Cyprus: Religion and Society. From the Late Bronze Age to the End of the Archaic Period. Proceedings of an International Symposium on Cypriote Archaeology, Erlangen, 23–24 July 2004. Möhnesee, 143–169.

Rahmstorf, L. 2008 *Kleinfunde aus Tiryns. Terrakotta, Stein, Bein und Glas/Fayence vornehmlich aus der Spätbronzezeit.* Tiryns. Forschungen und Berichte 16. Wiesbaden.

Rahmstorf, L. 2011 Handmade pots and crumbling loomweights: 'Barbarian' elements in eastern Mediterranean in the last quarter of the 2nd millennium BC. In V. Karageorghis and O. Kouka (eds.), *On Cooking Pots, Drinking Cups, Loomweights and Ethnicity in Bronze Age Cyprus and Neighbouring Regions. An International Archaeological Symposium Held in Nicosia, November 6th–7th 2010.* Nicosia, 315–330.

Rast-Eicher, A. 2005 Bast before wool: the first textiles. In P. Bichler, K. Grömer, R. Hofmann-de Keijzer, A. Kern and H. Reschreiter (eds.), *Hallstatt Textiles. Technical Analysis, Scientific Investigation and Experiment on Iron Age Textiles.* British Archaeological Reports International Series 1351, 117–132.

Rehak, P. 1996 Aegean breechcloths, kilts, and the Keftiu paintings. *American Journal of Archaeology* 100, 35–51.

Rehak, P. 2004 Crocus costumes in Aegean art. In A. P. Chapin (ed.), *CHARIS. Essays in Honor of Sara A. Immerwahr.* Hesperia Supplement 33, 85–100.

Sapouna-Sakellaraki, E. 1971 Μινωικόν ζώμα. Αθήνα.

Schlabow, K. 1959 Beiträge zur Erforschung der jungsteinzeitlichen und bronzezeitlichen Gewebetechnik Mitteldeutschlands. *Jahresschrift für Mitteldeutsche Vorgeschichte* 43, 101–120.

Schliemann, H. 1878 *Mykenae: Bericht über meine Forschungen und Entdeckungen in Mykenae und Tiryns.* Leipzig.

Seiler-Baldinger, A. and Médard, F. 2014 Les textiles cordés: armures et techniques. *Bulletin de liaison du Centre international d'etude des textiles anciens 84–85, années 2007–2008*, 21–37.

Shishlina, N. I., Orfinskaya O. V. and Golikov, V. P. 2003 Bronze Age textiles from the north Caucasus: new evidence of fourth millennium BC fibres and fabrics. *Oxford Journal of Archaeology* 22.4, 331–334.

Siennicka, M. 2012 Textile production in Early Helladic Tiryns. In M.-L. Nosch and R. Laffineur (eds.), *KOSMOS. Jewellery, Adornment and Textiles in the Aegean Bronze Age. Proceedings of the 13th International Aegean Conference/13e Rencontre égéenne internationale, University of Copenhagen, Danish National Research Foundation's Centre for Textile Research, 21–26 April 2010.* Aegaeum 33. Leuven and Liège, 65–74.

Siennicka, M. and Ulanowska A. 2016 So simple yet universal. Contextual and experimental approach to clay 'spools' from Bronze Age Greece. In J. Ortiz, C. Alfaro, L. Turell and Ma. J. Martínez (eds.), *PURPUREAE VESTES V. Textiles and Dyes in Antiquity. Ancient Textiles, Basketry and Dyes in the Ancient Mediterranean World. Textiles, Cestería y Tinten el mundo mediterráneo antiguo. Proceedings of the Vth International Symposium on Textiles and Dyes in the Ancient Mediterranean World (Montserrat, 19–22 March, 2014).* València, 25–36.

Spantidaki, S. 2008 Preliminary results of the reconstruction of Theran textiles. In C. Alfaro and L. Karalis (eds.), *PURPUREAE VESTES II. Textiles and Dyes in Antiquity. Vestidos, Textiles y Tintes. Estudios sobre la producción de bienes de consumo en la Antigüedad. Actas del II Symposium International sobre Textiles y Tintes del Mediterráneo en el mundo antiguo (Atenas, 24 al 26 de noviembre, 2005).* València, 43–47.

Spantidaki, Y. and Moulhehart, Ch. 2012 Greece. In M. Gleba and U. Mannering (eds.), *Textiles and Textile Production in Europe: From Prehistory to AD 400.* Ancient Textile Series 11. Oxford and Oakville, 185–200.

Trnka, E. 2007 Similarities and distinctions of Minoan and Mycenaean Textiles. In C. Gillis and M.-L. B. Nosch (eds.), *Ancient Textiles, Production, Craft and Society, Proceedings of the First International Conference on Ancient Textiles, Held at Lund Sweden and Copenhagen, Denmark, on March 19–23, 2003.* Ancient Textiles Series 1. Oxford, 127–129.

Tzachili, I. 1990 All important yet elusive: looking for evidence of cloth-making at Akrotiri. In D. A. Hardy, C. G. Doumas, J. A. Sakellarakis and P. M. Warren (eds.), *Thera and the Aegean World III. Proceedings of the Third International Congress, Santorini, Greece, 3–9 September 1989.* London, 380–389.

Tzachili, I. 1997 Υφαντική και υφάντρες στο Προϊστορικό Αιγαίο. Ηράκλειο and Αθήνα.

Ulanowska, A. 2016 Representations of textile tools in Aegean glyptic. Cuboid seal from the Tholos Tomb A in Aghia Triada. In P. Militello and K. Żebrowska (eds.), *Sympozjum Egejskie. Proceedings of the 2nd Students' Conference in Aegean Archaeology: Methods – Researches – Perspectives. Institute of Archaeology, University of Warsaw, Poland, April 25th, 2014.* Syndesmoi 4. Catania, 109–125.

Ulanowska, A. 2017, Textile technology and Minoan glyptic. Representations of loom weights on Middle Minoan prismatic seals. In K. Żebrowska, A. Ulanowska and K. Lewartowski (eds.), *Sympozjum Egejskie. Papers in Aegean Archaeology I.* Warsaw, 57–66.

Verduci, J. 2012 Wasp-waisted Minoans: costume, belts and body modification in the Late Bronze Age Aegean. In M.-L. Nosch and R. Laffineur (eds.), *KOSMOS. Jewellery, Adornment and Textiles in the Aegean Bronze Age. Proceedings of the 13th International Aegean Conference/13e Rencontre égéenne internationale, University of Copenhagen, Danish National Research Foundation's Centre for Textile Research, 21–26 April 2010.* Aegaeum 33. Leuven and Liège, 639–646.

Verlinden, C. 1984 *Les statuettes anthropomorphes crétoises en bronze et en plomb, du IIIe millénaire au VIIe siècle av. J.-C.* Louvain-la-Neuve.

Vogt, E. 1937 *Geflechte und Gewebe der Steinzeit.* Monographien zur Ur- und Frühgeschichte der Schweiz 1. Basel.

Weilhartner, J. 2012 Die graphische Gestaltung der Tierlogoramme auf den Linear B-Tafeln. In C. Reinholdt and W. Wohlmayr (eds.), *Akten des 13. Österreichischen Archäologientages. Klassische und Frühägäische Archäologie, Paris-Lodron-Universität Salzburg, vom 25. bis 27. Februar 2010.* Wien, 63–73.

Weilhartner, J. 2014 The influence of Aegean iconography on the design of the Linear B logograms for animals, plants and agricultural products. In G. Touchais, R. Laffineur and F. Rougemont (eds.), *PHYSIS. L'environnement naturel et la relation homme-milieu dans le monde égéen protohistorique. Actes de la 14e Rencontre égéenne internationale, Paris, Institut National d'Histoire de l'Art (INHA), 11–14 décembre 2012.* Aegaeum 37. Leuven and Liège, 297–304.

Wild, J. P. 1988 *Textiles in Archaeology.* Shire Archaeology 56. Aylesbury.

19

The Early Bronze Age textile implements from the Eskişehir region in inland north-western Anatolia

Deniz Sarı

Introduction

Based on the material evidence, it seems that new cultural and political developments emerged during the Early Bronze Age (3rd millennium BC) in western Anatolia.[1] This becomes especially apparent in the formation of new local pottery distribution areas at the very beginning of the Early Bronze Age (EBA). Those areas indicate, perhaps indirectly, the areas controlled by emerging local political powers in the region. Architectural evidence and certain find groups from the succeeding phases of the EBA support the premise that more dynamic local political powers eventually emerged and urbanism developed as a result of it. As these entities gained more and more political and economical power, the cultural and commercial relations of the region with far distant areas became more intensified. This especially led to the development of textile and metal industries.[2]

The evidence of EBA textile production in inland north-western Anatolia is gained from the excavations at Demircihöyük, Küllüoba and Keçiçayırı. The area roughly covers the Eskişehir and Upper Sakarya plains, as well as the mountainous terrain of the Phrygian Highlands (Fig. 19.1). This region reflects the characteristic features of the Phyrigian cultural region, the borders of which were mainly determined in archaeological terms by the pottery.[3] As a result of the Demircihöyük and Küllüoba excavations, an uninterrupted EBA habitation sequence has been established for the Eskişehir region and we can speak of three different EBA settlement models in the region. These are Küllüoba, which is comprised of upper and lower settlements, the small settlement of Demircihöyük and the citadel of Keçiçayırı, built in the mountainous region.

Demircihöyük settlement in the Eskişehir plain

Demircihöyük is situated on the Eskişehir plain, 25 km west of the provincial centre Eskişehir. After a brief

excavation conducted by Kurt Bittel in 1937,[4] Manfred Korfmann carried out excavations between 1975 and 1978. Based on the EBA 1 and EBA 2 settlement plan of Demircihöyük, Korfmann introduced for the first time the term of 'Anatolisches Siedlungsschema' (Fig. 19.2 a). This settlement type consisted of radially arranged, trapezoidal row-houses opening onto a central court.[5] At Demircihöyük, the houses (often with covered porch) consisted of two rooms. The back rooms had a domed oven in their rear corners and on occasion both rooms also had hearths in the centre.[6] Sometimes, there were storage pits below ground level in front of the house entrances. Several houses had sleeping platforms. At Demircihöyük, Phases D–G are dated to EBA 1; Phases H (2730 BC) and Q (2525 BC) are dated to EBA 2.[7] The finds from Demircihöyük that can be associated with textile production include loom weights, spindle whorls, brushes and pierced discs. No textile remains have been encountered at this site. Due to the lack of archaeobotanical analysis, the growing of flax is not proven. Based on the studies of animal bones,[8] it is concluded that hairy sheep and woolly sheep probably coexisted during the Early Bronze Age.[9] Therefore, the available evidence suggests that the textile production was based on wool.[10]

Spindle whorls

A total of 183 spindle whorls have been found at Demircihöyük and 96 additional spindle whorls came from the burials of Sarıket cemetery, with a wide range of forms and sizes. The forms represented in Demircihöyük are biconical-shaped, conical-shaped, globular-shaped, barrel-shaped and oval-shaped (Fig. 19.2 b). The average diameters of the spindle whorls are between 2.0 and 3.5 cm, with their heights between 1.5 and 3.0 cm. The most common forms are biconical (50%).[11] At Demircihöyük, pressure marks of wood are observed inside the holes of a few broken whorls. This is taken as proof that either the spindle whorls were

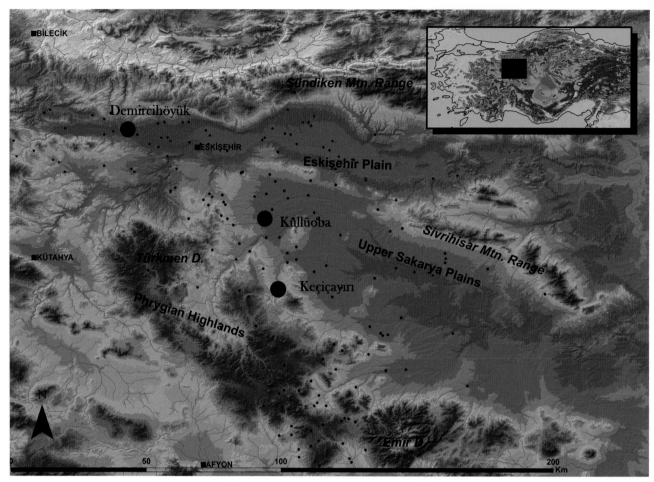

Fig. 19.1 Sites located in inland north-western Anatolia mentioned in the text.

shaped on a piece of wood, or they were attached to a sharpened piece of wood while they were still wet.[12] Some experimental studies on spinning have been carried out by Julia Obladen-Kauder. For this purpose, spindles were shaped from trees such as willow, hazelnut, ash, beech and poplar. As a result of this experiment, she argued that spinning with the whorls attached to the lower end of the spindle, as well as spinning with spindles heavier than the whorls (even though this led to rougher strings), is easier. As the spindle becomes lighter, the whorl gets heavier; as the spindle become heavier, the whorl gets lighter.[13]

Pierced discs

Pierced discs, which were shaped from broken potsherds (Fig. 19.2 c) appear across a wide timespan, from the Neolithic period up to the 2nd millennium BC, and in a wide geographical area, from the Aegean world to Mesopotamia. They are commonly associated with spinning.[14] One hundred and ninety-six pieces of pierced discs have been found at Demircihöyük.[15] The diameters of pierced discs vary between 3 and 6 cm.[16] The spatial distribution of these findings is in accordance with other findings related to textile production.

In the EBA 1 levels they are found more in the back rooms, and in the EBA 2 they are found in the front rooms.[17]

Brushes

Brushes with pierced handles have quadrilateral-like surfaces, on which there are negatives parallel to each other in four rows, which held the brush hairs (Fig. 19.5 b). The hairs were not preserved due to their being organic. These hairs must have been attached to the brush surface right after shaping of the brush and before clay was dried. The wool used in textile production was obtained by pulling from the sheep or goat or by cutting with the help of a stone/metal blade. Therefore, raw wool was most probably cleaned and combed with the help of brushes before being spun into yarn.[18]

Seven brushes have been found at Demircihöyük,[19] but not all of them are associated with textile production. For example, a brush found in Room 6 in Phase E1[20] is defined as an instrument for cleaning the ashes from hearths and ovens. Another brush was found in situ in Room 2 in Phase E1,[21] as a part of a find assemblage in a basin, consisting of miniature vessels, spindle whorl, rattle, polishing stones, polishing bone and shells with red pigment remains

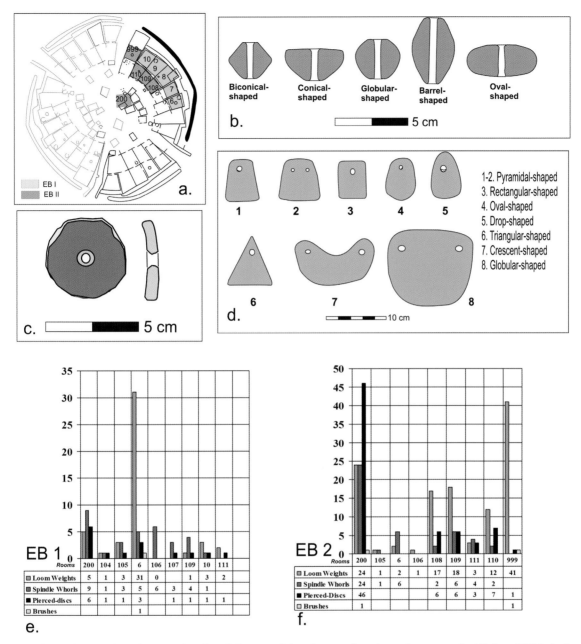

Fig. 19.2 a. The settlement plan of Demircihöyük and the spatial distribution of textile implements in the EB 1 and EB 2 (redrawn from Korfmann 1983, fig. 343); b. Spindle whorl types from Demircihöyük; c. Pierced disc; d. Loom weight types from Demircihöyük; e–f. Textile implements according to the rooms in the EB 1 and EB 2.

(Room 2). Obladen-Kauder argued that this assemblage was the make-up kit of a woman and thus this brush has been defined as an instrument of body-care.[22] However, according to C. Bachhuber, who correlated this finding group with textile production, the bathtub and the pigment remains were most probably used for dyeing spun yarn.[23]

A brush found *in situ* in Room 999 in Phase H is associated directly with textile production. It was found near a hearth. In this room some other objects, a stack of loom weights, two spindle whorls and a bone awl, have been

unearthed.[24] This room belonged to a house consisting of three rooms, different from the other two-roomed houses of the settlement. Korfmann argued that the three-roomed house might have had a special function.[25] Another brush was found in Room 80 in Phase H,[26] and again a loom weight was found near the brush in question.[27]

Loom weights

The repertory of loom weights at Demircihöyük comprises pyramidal-, rectangular-, oval-, drop-, triangular-, crescent-

and globular-shaped loom weights (Fig. 19.2 d). Pyramidal-, rectangular-, oval- and drop-shaped loom weights are known in all phases, but pyramidal-shaped with a double piercing occurred at the beginning of the EB 2 period, in Phase H. Triangular-, globular- and crescent-shaped forms are known only at the beginning of the EB 1 period. The most common forms found at Demircihöyük are pyramidal-, oval-, drop- and crescent-shaped. Double-pierced pyramidal-shaped loom weights occurred for the first time at the beginning of EBA 2 in Phase H.[28] Three different stacks of loom weights that must have fallen from looms have been recovered *in situ* at Demircihöyük.

The earliest loom weight stack at Demircihöyük was unearthed in Room 6 (Phase E, EBA 1) to the south of the domed oven.[29] Twenty-eight loom weights were found in a pit 20 cm deep.[30] Although the forms found in this pit vary a lot, based on marks of abrasion, Obladen-Kauder argued that these implements had been used at least once.[31]

The second loom weight stack was found in burnt layers of Phase H, in room 999. Thirty-three loom weights were found in a pit of approximately 20 cm depth in the north-west corner of the room.[32] They were partially lined up. The third group, consisting of seven loom weights, was found in Phase L, in room 110.[33]

While in the EBA 1 layers the spatial distribution of the loom weights is concentrated in the back rooms, in the EBA 2 period the loom weights are found more frequently in the front rooms and in the central court (Fig. 19.2 e–f). The warp-weighted looms of Demircihöyük were placed in the corners of the rooms; the loom's frame was probably leaned against the wall.[34] In that way, while the upper part of wooden frame leaned up to the wall, its lower part was placed in a pit (with a depth of about 20 cm) abutting the wall and dug into the floor and, therefore, the loom frame could have been immobilised.

Küllüoba settlement on the Yukarı Sakarya plain

The large prehistoric mound of Küllüoba, possibly considered an urban-like settlement, is situated on the western part of the Upper Sakarya Plain, 15 km north-east of the modern town of Seyitgazi and 35 km south-east of Eskişehir. The excavations under the direction of Turan Efe have been ongoing since 1996. The Küllüoba excavations have yielded an almost uninterrupted sequence starting at least as early as the middle phases of the Late Chalcolithic period (*c.* 3500 BC) continuing to the end of the EBA (*c.* 1900 BC).

In the EB 2 period (Phase IV), the settlement was comprised of upper and lower areas. Complex I, Complex II and a free-standing trapezoidal structure located within the upper settlement might have had public functions[35] (Fig. 19.3 a). Detailed studies of the small finds from Küllüoba are still in progress. The graph in Fig. 19.3 b

roughly shows the distribution of some of the finds related to textile production.

Spindle whorls

The plentiful (approximately 285 pieces) spindle whorls at Küllüoba were not always found in association with the loom weights. Most of them were found in waste and votive pits, in the room fills and inside the storage pits. The spindle whorls were made of dark-grey, grey/brown, cream/brown and red clay with fine sand, stone and mica inclusions; the surfaces were often slipped and sometimes burnished. The most common forms are globular- and biconical-shaped whorls (Fig. 19.3 d).[36]

In Küllüoba, as at Demircihöyük, pierced discs were most probably used as loom weights but, since studies of the artefacts are still in progress, it is not yet possible to give the statistical and spatial distribution of this group of finds.

Brushes

Eight brushes found here exhibit the same typology as those from Demircihöyük. There is no clear evidence to relate these brushes with textile production or weaving.

Loom weights

The loom weights at Küllüoba were often made of cream/brown, orange/brown and sometimes red clay with stone and sand inclusions. A cross motif was incised only on the top of the small pyramidal-shaped examples. The repertoire of forms comprises oval-, drop-, pyramidal- and crescent-shaped weights (Fig. 19.3 c).

In contrast to Demircihöyük, crescent-shaped loom weights at Küllüoba are found in the Late EBA 2 and continued through the EBA 3 contexts. At Demircihöyük they were only found in the EBA 1 levels. However, crescent-shaped loom weights are very common at Demircihöyük in the Middle Bronze Age.[37] Elongated examples of crescent-shaped loom weights were also found at Keçiçayırı in the Late EBA 2 period (Fig. 19.5 d).

Stacks of loom weights have been recovered at least in six burnt rooms dated to the EBA 2 period. The range of forms loom weights from Küllüoba is quite similar to those from Demircihöyük, except the absence of the triangular and globular-shaped loom weights.

A series of 19 loom weights was found in the back room of a burnt house in the Lower Settlement in the grids of U 18 in Phase IVB (Fig. 19.3 a.5). A brush, three spindle whorls, an andiron, a grindstone and various vessels were found together in the same context. The loom weights from this room are pyramidal-shaped (weighing between *c.* 80 and 100 g) and oval-shaped (*c.* 300 and 450 g). One of the oval-shaped loom weights is 868 g.

A stack of 12 pyramidal-shaped loom weights (weighing between *c.* 60 and 80 g) were found near an oven along with

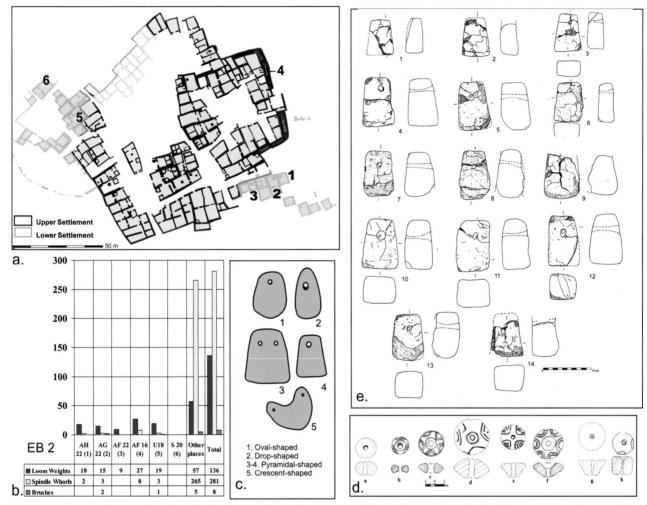

Fig. 19.3 a. The settlement plan of Küllüoba; b. Textile implements according to the rooms in the EB 2; c. Loom weight types from Küllüoba; d. Spindle whorls from Küllüoba; e. Pyramidal-shaped loom weights from AH 22 in Phase IV F.

many *in situ* vessels in a burnt room located in Complex I within the Upper Settlement in the grids of AF 16 of Phase IV E/F (Fig. 19.3 a.4). Their position suggests that weights were stored in this room rather than a loom.

Two other stacks of loom weights were found in the houses of the Lower Settlement in the grids of AH 22 and AG 22 (Phase F). Eighteen pyramidal-shaped loom weights (*c.* 150 and 450 g) and two spindle whorls were found in a small pit on the basement floor – just as in the case of Demircihöyük, Room 6 – in the corner of NW wall of the easternmost room (Figs 19.3 a.1 and 19.3 e).

On the west side, the room was severely burnt; many pots and various artefacts were found together (Fig. 19.3 a.2). Since the walls and the posts are preserved to quite a high level, the burnt deposit is very thick and the majority of the finds were found in the fill, not on the floor, there is a possibility that this building had two floors. Nine spindle whorls, three brushes, 11 loom weights, nine andirons, two figurine fragments, a stone mould and a stamp seal fragment were found together in the same context in this room. Seven

of the loom weights from this room are pyramidal-shaped (weighing between *c.* 136 and 276 g), one is pyramidal-shaped with double piercing (816 g), another one is again pyramidal-shaped with a cross motif on the top (435 g) and two other are oval-shaped (406 and 430 g). Moreover, a textile was found on the neck of a jug that contained many seeds.[38] Thus, the most important finds related to textile production at Küllüoba have been recovered from this room. The analytical work on this discovery has not yet been finished.

At Küllüoba, the pyramidal-shaped loom weights were heavier in the earlier phases of the EBA 2, and they became lighter in late phases of the EBA 2. Those of oval shape were lighter in early phases and became heavier in late phases of the EBA 2. This could be related to the changes in preferences or needs for certain types of fabrics.[39]

Keçiçayırı citadel in the Phrygian highlands

In addition to village and urban-like settlements in the plains, citadels also seem to have been built to protect and

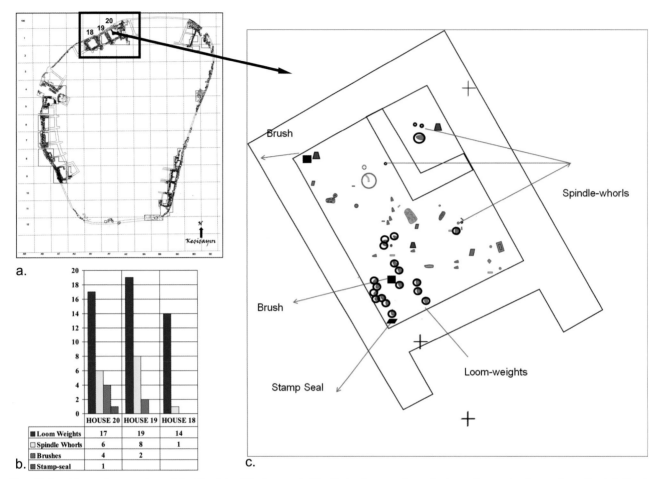

Fig. 19.4 a. The settlement plan of the Citadel of Keçiçayırı; b. Textile implements from the burnt houses in the north; c. Spatial distribution of textile implements in House 16.

exploit the natural resources in the mountainous regions, and to meet the accommodation needs of merchants and travellers.[40] The late EBA 2 citadel of Keçiçayırı, situated in the eastern part of the Phrygian highlands, around 22 km south of Seyitgazi and some 5 km south-west of the village of Bardakçı, may be an example. It reveals – to a certain extent – a different settlement layout in comparison to those of Küllüoba and Demircihöyük.

The houses are attached to the back of the fortification wall. The middle part of the settlement has been entirely destroyed. Therefore, we cannot argue that there was a central court or a centrally located structure, which might have had an administrative function in the citadel. A rich variety of objects came only from the burnt houses (Houses 14, 15 and 16) in the north (Fig. 19.4 a–b). This may suggest that this section of the citadel was reserved for the workshops. The presence of a flint quarry just to the NE of the citadel reinforces this argument.

In these houses, a lot of finds, the majority of which most probably fell from the floor above, have been recovered (Fig. 19.4 c). Among these finds, we can specify many complete and broken pottery examples, two stone moulds and

10 tuyères, indicating metallurgical activities in the citadels, as well as a marble idol, andirons and a drum-like clay object with decoration. Spindle whorls, brushes, loom weights and possibly a clay seal and a stone tool are finds related to textile production in the citadel. In total, 50 loom weights, 16 spindle whorls and five brushes have been recovered in these houses.

Spindle whorls

In total, 23 spindle whorls have been found in Keçiçayırı. The forms are mostly represented by two types: biconical-shaped forms and those with a pronounced shoulder with a broad hollow (Fig. 19.5 a). The spindle whorls in Keçiçayırı were usually made of buff, grey-brown and (rarely) red clay with stone or mica inclusions. The surfaces were commonly unslipped and were occasionally burnished. Decoration was applied only on biconical shapes.

Brushes

Five brushes in total have been unearthed in Keçiçayırı: three brushes in House 16, and two in House 15. Except for one brush, others have been found next to loom weights in Room 16 and 15 (Figs. 19.4 c and 19.5 b).

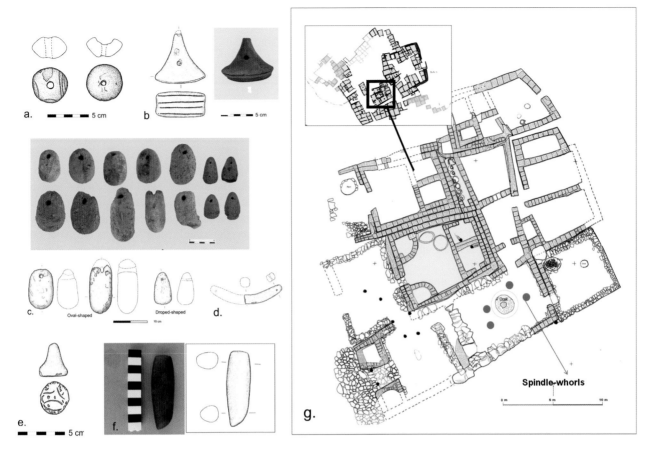

Fig. 19.5 a. Spindle whorls from Keçiçayırı; b. Brush from Keçiçayırı; c–d. Loom weights from the House 20 in Keçiçayırı; e. Stamp seal from Keçiçayırı; f. The tool to tighten the knots (?) from Keçiçayırı; g. Complex 2 from Küllüoba and the spindle whorls located around the heart in the administrative and ceremonial core of the Complex.

Loom weights

The loom weights from Keçiçayırı are made of fine clay and covered with a clay coat with small stone inclusions. Coating must have been applied after sun-drying of the loom weight. The yellowish-brown, unslipped surfaces were smoothed rather than burnished. Loom weights have been found in a row in the west corners of the entrances opening into the probable courtyard (Fig. 19.4 c). Loom weights can be classified into two form groups by comparison with those of Demircihöyük and Küllüoba: oval- and drop-shaped (Fig. 19.5 c). The two exceptional crescent-shaped examples (Fig. 19.5 d) do not come from the rooms in question. These were found in the deposit of the Period Transitional to the Middle Bronze Age excavated in the south of the citadel. It must also be noted that, even though the loom weights have been found in a row, they were not all unearthed in the basement. They may have been mixed into the upper floor's debris or the warp-weighted looms might have been located in the upper floor.

Other tools

The variety of materials from House 16 is richer than from others (Fig. 19.4 c). A stamp seal (Fig. 19.5 e) found next

to the warp-weighted loom was possibly used to produce an imprinted pattern on special types of clothing. Another stone implement can also be related with weaving. Commonly, these types of tools are interpreted as small axes. However, we can think of them as of tools to tighten the knots, since the tool uncovered at Keçiçayırı features two flat and glossy surfaces at both ends (Fig. 19.5 f). Due to its flatness on the ends, the tapered point might match with the distance between the knots to be tightened, whereas a glossy surface is favourable to prevent potential damage to fibres.

Conclusions

Demircihöyük is a small settlement with row-houses. Interior architectural features such as furnaces, ovens, ash pits and sleeping benches exist in almost all rooms. Most houses at Demircihöyük appear to have been involved in textile production. On the other hand, the contexts of finding of tools associated with yarn production (*e.g.* spindle whorls, brushes) and weaving tools are different, suggesting that processes such as carding, spinning and weaving could have been performed in different rooms of the houses or outside the houses, and thus there was not yet specialisation of production.[41]

Küllüoba is an urban-like settlement where the hierarchical structure is emphasised by differences in architectural planning, rather than the differences in the find groups.[42] The upper settlement represents a linear settlement plan with long houses adjoining the back of the irregularly running zigzag fortification wall, and large complexes (Complexes I–II), possibly administrative in function, in the centre.[43] The buildings with single rooms located beyond the fortification wall belong to lower settlement and their four sides face the opposite direction to the upper settlement houses. Since excavation of Küllüoba is still in progress, it is difficult to suggest whether textiles were produced in some of the houses belonging to lower settlement or in the service buildings of the complexes of the upper settlements, to fulfil the needs of the ruling class.

Keçiçayırı is a citadel without interior architectural features. However, the houses on the north display a different plan, as well as finds than others. Besides textile implements, the occurrence of different find groups relevant to other activities, such as metal working, gives the impression that workshops might have existed in this area. According to the current state of research, it is difficult to argue that there was any specialisation of textile production related either to the needs of the inhabitants or to a trade network. Textile production most probably took place at the household level. Even though Eskişehir region displays three different settlement layouts, the clay fabrics and forms of textile implements from the region discussed share the same characteristics.

While we can mention a variety of types of tools, especially the loom weights in Demircihöyük and Küllüoba, two types of these tools are represented in Keçiçayırı. This fact can suggest that textiles made of defined thickness of yarn were produced at that site. The loom weights were found in all three settlements, mostly in rows close to entrances, on the corners. Similarly, as in the whole western Anatolia, warp-weighted looms were used in Eskişehir, too. On the other hand, spindle whorls do not demonstrate any set spatial distribution in settlements, due to the fact that yarns could be produced in any hour of the day, and in any place.

In conclusion, I would like to emphasise that spinning is often considered as a woman's occupation. Recently, Ulf-Dietrich Schoop addressed this issue, by referring to the Demircihöyük necropolis where spindle whorls occurred in both male and female graves,[44] and also to Alaca Höyük[45] and Horoztepe[46] where spindles made of copper, silver and electrum were found in the rich graves, and stressed the possible use of spindle whorls as prestige objects beside their utilitarian function.[47]

Furthermore, some ethnographic comparanda demonstrate that, in modern nomadic cultures in Anatolia, men spin to keep their hands busy.[48] In the famous novel of Yaşar Kemal entitled *The Legend of the Thousand Bulls*, the elders of the tribe gathered in a meeting-pavilion and spun while they were discussing:

> With Old Haydar's arrival almost all the elders of the tribe were gathered now in the meeting-pavilion. The old men were silent, spinning the black goat hair and other multi-coloured wools on their spindles.[49]

Actually, if we consider this situation as the comparandum to the prehistoric periods, the find contexts of some spindle whorls would make more sense. In the case of the Complex II of Küllüoba, the central room with large hearth has been assumed to be the administrative and ceremonial core of the complex. Six spindle whorls have been recovered in total in this room, while four of them came from around the hearth (Fig. 19.5 g). We did not find any other textile implements in the same context. Maybe, just in the same way as the elders described by Kemal, people who gathered around this hearth might have spun during meetings in order to occupy their hands.

Notes

1 I would like to express my sincere thanks to Małgorzata Siennicka and Lorenz Rahmstorf for inviting me to present a paper at the 'First Textiles. The Beginnings of Textile Manufacture in Europe and the Mediterranean' conference in Copenhagen, and to Marie-Louise Bech Nosch and all people from CTR for their hospitality. Thanks also to Turan Efe for giving me the permission to publish the material from Küllüoba and Keçiçayırı.
2 For more information on the western Anatolian cultural region and pottery groups, see Efe 2003; Efe and Ay Efe 2007; Sarı 2013.
3 Bittel 1942, 160, 186; Efe 2003, 89.
4 Bittel and Otto 1939.
5 Korfmann 1983, 222, fig. 343.
6 Korfmann 1983, 243.
7 Korfmann and Kromer 1993, 139–140.
8 It is difficult to understand the difference between hairy sheep and woolly sheep. On the other hand, it is possible to determine the statistical development of hairy sheep (they are slaughtered for their meat at a young age and, therefore, they remain small in size) and woolly sheep (they are bred for their wool so they are bigger in size). Hairy sheep most probably did not become extinct right after the appearance of other species, they were most probably kept for eating, but woolly sheep were bred for their wool. Most probably the two species lived together but were not made hybrid in order to preserve the pure race; Gündem 2009, 213–214.
9 Rauh 1981, 44–45.
10 Baykal-Seeher and Obladen-Kauder 1996, 244.
11 Baykal-Seeher and Obladen-Kauder 1996, 232, figs. 158–159, pls. 91–95.
12 Baykal-Seeher and Obladen-Kauder 1996, 234.

13 Baykal-Seeher and Obladen-Kauder 1996, 233–246.
14 Blegen *et al.* 1950, 49–50; Mellink 1969, 323; Baykal-Seeher and Obladen-Kauder 1996, 224; Gibbs 2008, 90.
15 Baykal-Seeher and Obladen-Kauder 1996, 215, pls. 87–88.
16 Baykal-Seeher and Obladen-Kauder 1996, 223.
17 Baykal-Seeher and Obladen-Kauder 1996, 218.
18 Baykal-Seeher and Obladen-Kauder 1996, 253.
19 Baykal-Seeher and Obladen-Kauder 1996, 235, pls. 104.3–4, 105–106.
20 Baykal-Seeher and Obladen-Kauder 1996, pl. 104.4.
21 Baykal-Seeher and Obladen-Kauder 1996, pl. 104.3.
22 Baykal-Seeher and Obladen-Kauder 1996, 253.
23 Bachhuber 2015, 60.
24 Baykal-Seeher and Obladen-Kauder 1996, 252, pl. 105.5.
25 Korfmann 1983, 233–246.
26 Baykal-Seeher and Obladen-Kauder 1996, pl. 105.2.
27 Baykal-Seeher and Obladen-Kauder 1996, 253.
28 Baykal-Seeher and Obladen-Kauder 1996, 238–239, fig. 165.
29 Korfmann 1983, fig. 45.
30 Baykal-Seeher and Obladen-Kauder 1996, 239.
31 Baykal-Seeher and Obladen-Kauder 1996, fig. 168.
32 Korfmann 1983, fig. 188.
33 Baykal-Seeher and Obladen-Kauder 1996, 241.
34 Baykal-Seeher and Obladen-Kauder 1996, 245.
35 For detailed information on the architecture of Küllüoba, see Efe and Fidan 2008; Fidan 2012.
36 Öner 2009, 70.
37 Kull 1998, 200–205.
38 Based on a preliminary report by Özgür Çizer from Tübingen University who has studied botanical specimens from Küllüoba in the framework of her PhD thesis (Çizer 2015).
39 For detailed information on interpretations of loom weights according to their shape and weights and their relationship to the fabrics obtained, see Mårtensson *et al.* 2009.
40 Efe *et al.* 2011, 16.
41 Bachhuber 2015, 60–61.
42 Fidan 2015, 179.
43 Efe *et al.* 2018.
44 Massa 2014, 84.
45 Koşay 1951, 73, fig. 197.
46 Özgüç and Akok 1958, 51, fig. 8.1–2.
47 Schoop 2014, 438.
48 Yalman (Yalgın) 1977, 467.
49 Kemal 1976, 46.

Bibliography

Bachhuber, C. 2015 *Citadel and Cemetery in Early Bronze Age Anatolia*. Sheffield and Bristol.

Baykal-Seeher, A. and Obladen-Kauder, J. 1996 *Demircihüyük IV. Die Kleinfunde*. Mainz am Rhein.

Bittel, K. 1942 *Kleinasiatische Studien*. Istanbuler Mitteilungen Heft 5. Istanbul.

Bittel, K. and Otto, H. 1939 *Demirci-Hüyük. Eine vorgeschichtliche Siedlung an der phrygisch-bithynischen Grenze; Bericht über die Ergebnisse der Grabung von 1937*. Berlin.

Blegen, C. W., Caskey, J. L. and Rawson, M. 1950 *Troy: General Introduction, the First and Second Settlements. Excavations Conducted by the University of Cincinnati 1932–1938*. Princeton.

Çizer, Ö. 2015 Archaeobotanical investigations of plant cultivation and husbandry practices at the Early Bronze Age settlement Küllüoba in west-central Turkey: considerations on environment, climate and economy. Unpublished PhD thesis, University of Tübingen.

Efe, T. 2003 Pottery distribution within the Bronze Age of western Anatolia and its implications upon cultural, political (and ethnic?) entities. In M. Özbaşaran, O. Tanındı and A. Boratav (eds.), *Archaeological Essays in Honour of Homo Amatus: Güven Arsebük için Armağan Yazılar*. İstanbul, 87–105.

Efe, T. and Ay Efe, D.Ş. M. 2007 The Küllüoba excavations and the cultural/political development of western Anatolia before the second millennium B. C. In M. Alparslan, M. Doğan-Alparslan and H. Peker (eds.), *VITA Festschrift in Honor of Belkıs Dinçol and Ali Dinçol*. Istanbul, 251–268.

Efe, T. and Fidan, E. 2008 Complex Two in the Early Bronze Age II Upper Town of Küllüoba near Eskişehir. *Anatolica* 34, 67–102.

Efe, T., Sarı, D. and Fidan, E. 2011 The significance of the Keçiçayırı excavations in the Prehistory of inland northwestern Anatolia. In A. N. Bilgen, R. von den Hoff, S. Sandalcı and S. Silek (eds.), *Archaeological Research in Western Central Anatolia. Proceedings of the IIIrd International Symposium of Archaeology, March 2010*. Kütahya, 9–28.

Fidan, E. 2012 *Küllüoba İlk Tunç Çağı Mimarisi*. Mimarlar, Arkeologlar, Sanat Tarihçileri, Restoratörler Ortak Platformu 7, E-Dergi, 1–44.

Fidan, E. 2015 *Batı Anadolu'da Sosyal Sınıf Farklılıklarının Ortaya Çıkışı: Aşağı ve Yukarı Yerleşme Sistemi*. Tematik Arkeoloji Serisi 2. İletişim Ağları Ve Sosyal Organizasyon. İstanbul, 175–184.

Gibbs, K. T. 2008 Pierced clay disks and Late Neolithic textile production. In J. M. Córdoba, J. M. Molist, M. Pérez, M. C. Rubio, I. and S. Martínez (eds.), *Proceedings of the 5th International Congress on the Archaeology of the Ancient Near East, Madrid, April 3–8 2006*. Madrid, 89–96.

Gündem, C. Y. 2009 Animal based economy in Troia and the Troas during The Maritime Troy culture (c. 3000–2200 BC) and a general summary for west Anatolia. Unpublished PhD thesis, University of Tübingen.

Kemal, Y. 1976 *The Legend of the Thousand Bulls* (translated by T. Kemal). London.

Korfmann, M. 1983 *Demircihüyük. Die Ergebnisse Der Ausgrabungen 1975–1978. Band I. Architektur, Stratigraphie und Befunde*. Mainz am Rhein.

Korfmann, M. and Kromer, B. 1993 Demircihüyük, Besik-Tepe, Troia – Eine Zwischenbilanz zur Chronologie dreier Orte in Westanatolien. *Studia Troica* 3, 135–171.

Koşay, H. Z. 1951 *Türk Tarih Kurumu Tarafından Yapılan Alaca Höyük Kazısı: 1937–1939 daki Çalışmalara ve Keşiflere Ait İlk Raporlar/Les Fouilles d'Alaca Höyük Entreprises par la Societe d'Historie Turque: Rapport Preliminaire sur les Travaux en 1937–1939*. Ankara.

Kull, B. 1988 *Demircihüyük V, Die mittelbronzezeitliche Siedlung*. Mainz am Rhein.

Mårtensson, L., Nosch, M.-L. and Andersson Strand, E. 2009 Shape of things: understanding a loom weight. *Oxford Journal of Archaeology* 28.4, 373–398.

Massa, M. 2014 Early Bronze Age burial customs on the central Anatolian plateau: a view from Demircihöyük-Sarıket. *Anatolian Studies* 64, 73–93.

Mellink, M. J. 1969 Excavations at Karataş-Semayük in Lycia, 1968. *American Journal of Archaeology* 73.3, 319–331.

Öner, B. 2009 Küllüoba Höyüğü Geç Kalkolitik ve İlk Tunç Çağı Küçük Buluntuları (Yontma taş Aletlerve Metal Eserler Hariç). Unpublished MA thesis, University of Istanbul.

Özgüç, T. and Akok, M. 1958 *Horoztepe, Eski Tunç Devri Mezarlığı ve İskân Yeri/An Early Bronze Age Settlement and Cemetery*. Ankara.

Rauh, H. 1981 Knochenfunde von Säugetieren aus dem Demircihüyük (Nordwestanatolien). Unpublished PhD thesis, University of Münich.

Sarı, D. 2013 *Evolution culturelle et politique de l'Anatolie de l'Ouest au bronze ancien et au bronze moyen*. Lille.

Schoop, U. D. 2014 Weaving society in Late Chalcolithic Anatolia: textile production and social strategies in the 4th millennium BC. In B. Horejs and M. Mehofer (eds.), *Western Anatolia before Troy Proto-Urbanisation in the 4th Millennium BC? Proceedings of the International Symposium held at the Kunsthistorisches Museum Wien, Vienna, Austria, nov. 2012*. Vienna, 421–446.

Yalman (Yalgın), A. R. 1977 *Cenupta Türkmen Oymakları I–II*, Ankara.

Investigating continuity and change in textile making at Arslantepe (Malatya, Turkey) during the 4th and 3rd millennia BC

Romina Laurito

Introduction

The site of Arslantepe, with its long and unbroken sequence dating from the 5th millennium BC to the Byzantine period, provides a rich selection of finds that offer an excellent opportunity to study spinning and weaving activities from the Late Chalcolithic Age onwards in south-eastern Turkey.[1]

This paper will focus on the continuity and changes in elements used in Arslantepe's textile production through the analysis of textile tools and their archaeological contexts during the 4th millennium BC and the beginning of the 3rd millennium BC, and takes into account two main criteria: the morphological-technological aspects, and the archaeological contexts.

The mound of Arslantepe lies close to the right bank of the Euphrates River on the south-eastern edge of the Malatya plain (Turkey), on the western margin of the eastern Anatolian region between the Taurus mountain chain and the Anti-Taurus (Fig. 20.1).

The application of detailed stratigraphic excavation methods – the acquisition of data in the field, which are stratigraphically distinct and have been carefully analysed in respect of their functional variability and spatial distribution – together with extensive excavation strategies, also provide a unique opportunity to investigate the nature and development of textile production.

The current analysis starts from the Late Chalcolithic 3–4 (3800–3350 BC) settlement, which exhibits the earliest evidence of a hierarchical society, moves to the palace period (Arslantepe VI A, 3350–3000 BC) until the phase when the site was abandoned (Arslantepe VI B1, 3000–2900 BC), and concludes with the following period, which is characterised by a fortified village (Arslantepe VI B2, 2900–2750 BC).[2]

The Italian Archaeological Expedition at Arslantepe forms part of the European Research Programme, Tools and Textiles – Texts and Contexts, on textile tools and textile production in the entire Mediterranean Basin since 2006. It is run in collaboration with the Danish National Research Foundation's Centre for Textile Research (CTR) at the University of Copenhagen. Thus far, this fruitful collaboration has produced various articles on Arslantepe textile production[3] and more recently has undertaken an experimental programme focused on researching the technical peculiarities of the Arslantepe textile tools.[4] This paper explores textile tools from Arslantepe from a different perspective, focusing on the social contexts that have produced them. It aims to define the elements that have remained unchanged and those that have changed over two millennia in a settlement that was of key importance to the surrounding area, the Malatya plain.

Textile tools and textile production in the Late Chalcolithic and Early Bronze Age at Arslantepe

The first period that has been widely documented across the large excavated areas is period VII (Late Chalcolithic 3-4). In this phase, the settlement covered the entire mound, showing sharp functional and symbolic differences between each of the areas that were occupied. On the north-eastern edge of the site, a number of mud-brick houses with evidence of domestic activities were unearthed. An elite monumental building with columns (Fig. 20.3) was found centrally located on the top of the *tell*. A large isolated ceremonial building, Temple C, was found next to the elite residences, and a series of long rooms, probably linked to the temple, were used for craft activities.[5] All the spinning tools in Arslantepe VII were found in residential buildings (Fig. 20.2). In particular, numerous spindle whorls come from the elite residential building (Fig. 20.3 a–b). No

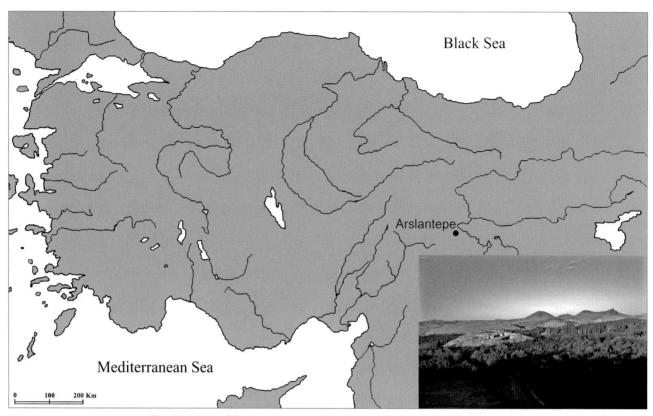

Fig. 20.1 Map of the Anatolia peninsula showing the location of Arslantepe.

loom weights were found in it. Some spindle whorls were also found in the small simple houses in the north-eastern periphery of the period VII settlement.

Some rounded and pierced sherds, possibly used for the spinning activities, may also be positively and tentatively added (Fig. 20.3 c–f). There is still some conjecture about the possible function of rounded and pierced sherds.[6] In my opinion, the small light ones might have been used to spin plant or animal fibres. However, the main doubt concerns the heavier sherds with larger diameters: they may not have related to textile production at all. No evidence of textile tools was found in the huge public ceremonial building, Temple C, and only two spindle whorls were found in the workshop areas connected to the Temple C.

Weaving activity is evidenced in a household context, and the presence of loom weights confirms the presence of warp-weighted looms. An assemblage of 23 loom weights was found *in situ* in room A923 to the west of the elite building. These hemispherical loom weights are made of unfired clay and weigh from 492 to 870 g (average 716 g), with a thickness of between 77 and 101 mm (average 90 mm).

Following the CTR principles for textile tools, as published in 2015 by Andersson Strand and Nosch,[7] spindle whorl weight and diameter are the two functional parameters that, together with the fibre quality, define the thread quality. Using these principles, the weight and thickness of the Arslantepe VII loom weights tell us that the fabric

produced would have had approximately six threads per cm in the warp.[8]

Spindle whorls are the most significant finds in period VII. The majority are made of bone and are convex or conical in shape. They constitute a predominant and homogeneous group of spindle whorls with a specific weight (*c.* 10–25 g)[9] and large diameters (over 35 mm and up to a maximum of 57 mm). A few spindle whorls were made of stone or clay.[10] It is significant that, when looking at spinning tools from contemporary sites in the Anatolian world, bone spindle whorls are not only apparently absent or very rare in western Turkey,[11] but also in more eastern areas, too,[12] and are only present in Sos Höyük.[13] Few other tools from period VII deposits are connected to the production of cloth, with the exception of bone needles (Fig. 20.4 a) and a clay spool (Fig. 20.4 b).

A smaller number of textile tools (35 in total) were discovered in contexts dating to period VI A at Arslantepe. This period is related to the Late Chalcolithic 5 and the Late Uruk culture in southern Mesopotamian terminology.[14] At the end of the 4th millennium BC, Arslantepe was characterised by a monumental complex of public and elite buildings. A series of multifunctional and interconnected buildings varying in shape and function were used for different public activities, *e.g.* ceremonial buildings, official buildings, storerooms, courtyards, open spaces, an access corridor and a monumental gate entrance. This well-

Table 20.1 Arslantepe. Chronological distribution and find contexts of textile tools. Even pierced rounded sherds are here considered, although their function as textile tools (spindle whorls or weights?) is only hypothesised. (NB: Textile tools recorded until the campaign 2008)

			VII					VI A			VI B1			VI B2		Total
			Workshop	Houses	Pits	Filling layers	Palace area	Houses	Pits	Filling layers	Houses	Pits	Filling layers	Houses	Pits	
Spindle whorls	bone	convex	2	10		6	2	2				1		3		26
		conical		4	2	4				1			1			12
		biconical		1										1		2
	clay	convex				1										1
		conical		1		1				1						3
		biconical		1								2		2	2	7
	stone	convex												1	1	2
		conical												2		2
		discoid		3	2	3	1									9
		spherical			1											1
		cylindrical						1								1
Loom weights	pottery	pierced sherd		9		3					4	4		4	3	27
	unfired clay	hemispherical		18												18
		not identifiable		5												5
	fired clay	conical						17								17
		discoid						1								1
		elliptical														
		spherical							1			2			1	4
		ovoid														
Other tools		comb						1								1
		shuttle ?						1		1						2
		tools pin beater/beater							3				1			4
		other needle		1	2					1				1		5
		spool		1			1									2
		Total	2	54	7	18	4	23	4	4	5	8	2	14	7	152

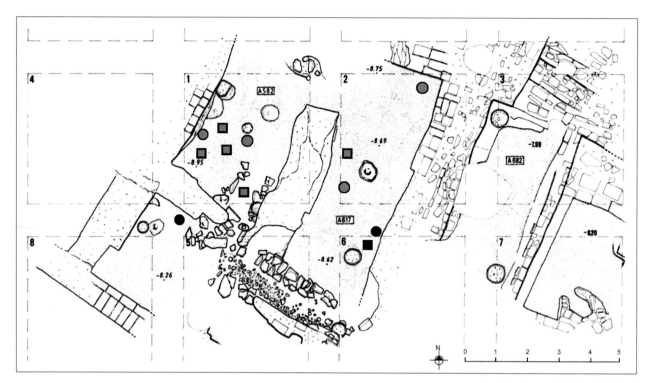

Fig. 20.2 Arslantepe, period VII. Distribution of spinning tools in the elite residential building in the south-western part of the settlement, the so-called 'column building': ● *spindle whorl found on the floor;* ◎ *spindle whorl from the filling layers;* ■ *pierced rounded sherds found on the floor;* ▣ *pierced rounded sherds from the filling layers.*

structured complex hosted a variety of different activities, which would have been public in nature.[15] However, up until now, the existence of textile activities or evidence of textile production in specific workshops has not been proved. Only three spindle whorls came from one of the side rooms in Temple A. The other numerous finds in this side room – excluding spinning tools – showed that the use of this building included various day-to-day activities.

Most of the textile tools come from the residential buildings, located to the north of the palace and probably belonging to high-status individuals. The presence of a set of loom weights attests to the presence of weaving activities as one of the daily domestic activities even in this period.[16] In one of these domestic rooms (A933), a set of 18 fired clay loom weights was found. Seventeen of these share a standardised conical shape and were grouped together, and thus were probably used in the same loom set-up. Their dimensions are concentrated in a small range (weight: 624–828 g with an average of 746 g; thickness: 77–95 mm with an average of 84 mm). CTR calculations suggest a medium-sized loom weight from Arslantepe VI A would have worked on an open fabric with a starting border width of about 75 cm and spacing of six warp threads per cm.[17] Only one loom weight, found on the floor of room A933, differed from those described above. This has a discoid-elliptical shape and is both lighter and thinner (weight: 585 g; thickness: 55 mm) than the others. In this case, the

CTR calculations demonstrate that this is more suitable for weaving a finer fabric of 6 to 11 threads per cm with thinner threads. The thousands of clay sealings/*cretulae* found in the palace enable us to compare the textile imprints on the back of the clay sealings used to close pots or sacks, with the fabric types inferred on the basis of the weaving tools found.

A plain tabby weave imprint is visible on the reverse sides of many *cretulae*. The number of threads per cm, calculated from the reverse of the sealing, varies from 8 to 12. Other *cretulae* have imprints from rather coarse textiles, and the quality of these coarse fabrics corresponds well with the quality estimated for the loom weight sets from both the VII and VI A periods, a thread count of between approximately 6 to 11 threads per cm.[18] In this way, the imprints of cloth appear to corroborate the calculations based on the CTR experience.[19] A few other tools complete the textile tool kits for the Late Chalcolithic at Arslantepe. Rare combs and brushes can be linked to the preparation of plant fibres and/or for the finishing stages of the fibre preparation.[20] Similarly, beaters and shuttles are linked to weaving (Fig. 20.4 c). Small light spools might have been used to wind yarns (Fig. 20.4 b, d).

Moreover, bone needles are found in all Late Chalcolithic areas.[21] These were not necessarily used for sewing or weaving. The hypothesis that they might have been used to create fabrics using a looping technique should be considered, since they do bear a resemblance to the

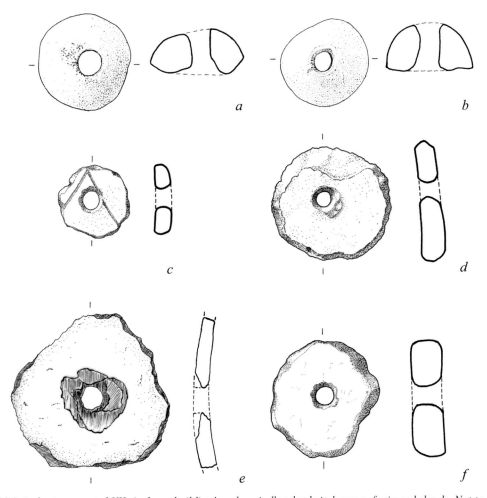

Fig. 20.3 Arslantepe, period VII, 'column building'; a–b. spindle whorls in bone; c–f. pierced sherds. Not to scale.

traditional *nålebinding* needles.[22] Again, the imprints on the reverse of the *cretulae* corroborate the existence of other stitches produced by needlework. This is a useful reminder of the advanced textile technology of this period. In general, Arslantepe does not have a large number of textile tools in its long chronological sequence. This is unusual, considering that spinning and weaving were some of the most important and intensive daily activities throughout antiquity. We should always keep in mind the possibility that many textile tools might have been made with perishable raw materials, particularly wood. This is one of the difficulties in such an investigation; looking at the 'invisible craft' of ancient textile production.[23] In my opinion, we cannot underestimate the potential impact of this absence on the analysis of textile tools and textile production. Furthermore, an intensive archaeological survey undertaken in 2003–2005[24] demonstrated that Arslantepe was the only large site occupied at the end of the 4th millennium (period VI A in Arslantepe's relative chronology) on the Malatya plain, and confirmed the presence of other small scattered settlements (perhaps the villages outlying the palace) around the tell. This corroborates what has been described to date.

Public activities were concentrated in the palace, but the site was not actually inhabited, unless by a limited group, perhaps the elite. This could explain the almost complete absence of textile tools associated with domestic level production. Spinning and weaving tools were only found in the few domestic units that have been investigated so far. This also suggests that textile production was not a centrally controlled activity. From the archaeological survey, it can be seen that there is a radical change in settlement patterns in the first half of the 3rd millennium during the Early Bronze I–II.[25] The number of sites in the Malatya area increased, but these were only temporarily occupied. This suggests that groups had greater mobility within the plain and that the population was sparsely distributed across the area. As we know, the Early Bronze Age in Arslantepe began with the sudden and violent destruction of the palace, the collapse of the centralised and early state system, and the sudden and definitive end to contacts with the Mesopotamian world. Groups of transhumant shepherds, linked to the Transcaucasian world of the Kuro-Araxes cultures, moved along the mountain range to the tell north of Arslantepe and set up camp directly on the ruins of the

a

b

c

d

Fig. 20.4 Arslantepe. Some examples of textile tools. a. needle of bone from Arslantepe VII; b. clay spool from Arslantepe VII; c. clay shuttle from Arslantepe VI A; d. clay spool from Arslantepe VI A.

palace, constructing there wattle-and-daub buildings for their seasonal activities[26] (Arslantepe VI B1, 3000–2900 BC). Immediately after this short period, textile activities were again evident for period VI B2 (around 2800 BC), which was characterised by a rural village with mud-brick houses, a massive mud-brick fortification wall and a citadel on the top of the mound.

Spinning tools were found, together with other domestic equipment, in the village,[27] suggesting that spinning was one of the daily domestic activities in period VI B2. No loom weights, which are a clear indication of the presence and use of warp-weighted looms, were found in the VI B2 village, but other kinds of looms may have existed. The use of small and portable looms or other types of loom made of completely perishable materials that leave no trace cannot be ruled out.[28] Regarding spinning tools, a significant change in the spindle whorls can be detected from period VI B2 onwards. Despite the limited number of objects, there is a significant difference between the Late Chalcolithic tools

and those of the Early Bronze Age. First of all, the raw materials used for making spindle whorls changed slightly. We observe the use of a broader range of materials during period VI B2, when an equal distribution of spindle whorls made of clay, stone and bone was recorded (Table 20.1). There is a change in terms of the spindle whorl weight and diameter: the variability in size of the whorls during period VII is larger than in period VI B2, and some spindle whorls from period VI B2 are smaller and lighter (also below 10 g).[29] Based on the CTR analysis, during period VI B2, Arslantepe's spinners were probably able to spin very thin and perhaps less tightly spun yarn in comparison to the earlier period VII. The range of the whorls indicates that, from the Early Bronze Age, it was possible to produce softer, more loosely spun yarns and perhaps a larger variety of yarns. Our experiments conducted in Rome in partnership with the Museo delle Origini, in which an expert spinner used exact replicas of the spindle whorls found at Arslantepe, confirmed the hypothesis put forward by the CTR.[30]

The archaeozoological remains offer indirect corroboration. An extraordinary increase in goat and sheep husbandry, particularly sheep, in period VI A and VI B suggests the dominance of specialised pastoralism and an increase in available woollen fibres sorted in several quality categories.[31] This increase reflects a general trend throughout Anatolia.[32]

Concluding remarks

Changes in the shape, size and weight of textile tools, as well as the apparent absence of some textile tools and the appearance of new or different tools in the archaeological record, have provided evidence of different technological levels and abilities throughout the era being examined.

In terms of spinning technology, archaeological data reveal a wide range in the weights and diameters of whorls found during period VII, with a clear tendency for their diameter to be generally large. A change in the size of spinning tools is only clearly recognisable from period VI B2, even though the very few spindle whorls from period VI A already seem to have weights concentrated in a small range.

In terms of weaving technology, the main collections of loom weights also indicate a significant change in weaving technology over time. In the Late Chalcolithic, the presence of weights indicates the use of vertical looms. They completely disappeared in period VI B, and reappeared only at the end of the Early Bronze Age.

Other tools used to work with thread and fibres are present throughout the entire estimated chronological timespan, although they are few in number, making it difficult to imagine the entire operational chain.[33]

In terms of the context of the archaeological finds relating to textile tools from Arslantepe, these are exclusively from residential settings. Another consideration is their distribution on the site: loom weights and spindle whorls were never found together in the same room or area in Arslantepe. This suggests that spinning and weaving activities were carried out in different places, alongside other domestic activities. So far, no connection has been made between textile activities and the centralised activities of the palace. Similarly, we have not found evidence of actual workshops in either the Late Chalcolithic or Early Bronze Age. Based on the current evidence, there is no reason to think that textile making was a major economic focus in either phase, nor is there any evidence of the centralised control of spinning and weaving.

A final observation is on the title of this paper: 'Investigating continuity and change in textile making at Arslantepe (Malatya, Turkey) during the 4th and 3rd millennia BC'. What is meant by the 'continuity' and 'change'? These two terms are regularly used in archaeology as being diametrically opposed, one contradicting the other. In my opinion, at least

in relation to the specific case of Arslantepe, the two concepts express alternations in textile production and consumption as a result of societal changes, where interaction with neighbouring and even distant areas played a role.

The study of fabrics and textile tools in various archaeological contexts at Arslantepe has demonstrated how changes in the demand, production and exploitation of textiles are linked to different social and cultural contexts.

Notes

1   I am deeply grateful to Marcella Frangipane for her constant confidence in me and in my work. I take this opportunity to thank Marie-Louise Nosch and Eva Andersson Strand for the chance to collaborate and work with them at the Centre for Textile Research as a Marie Curie Fellow. I also want to thank my friend and colleague Mauro Benedetti for his kind help in preparing the figures for this document. Finally, a special thank you to Małgorzata Siennicka, Lorenz Rahmstorf and Agata Ulanowska for their kind invitation to 'Textiles in a Social Context. Textile Production in Europe and the Mediterranean in the 4th and 3rd Millennia BCE', international conference (EAA, Istanbul, September 2014), where I presented this paper.

2   Frangipane and Palmieri 1983; Frangipane 2012a; 2012b.

3   Frangipane *et al.* 2002; Laurito 2010; 2012.

4   Laurito *et al.* 2014.

5   Frangipane 1993; 2000; 2012, 20–27.

6   See the technical report on Arslantepe textile tools available on https://ctr.hum.ku.dk/research-programmes-and-projects/ previous-programmes-and-projects/tools/toolsreports/ arslantepe_technical_textiles_tools_report.pdf, accessed 28 September 2018.

7   All experiments conducted on textile tools at CTR and available on https://ctr.hum.ku.dk/research-programmes-and-projects/previous-programmes-and-projects/tools/ (accessed 4 October 2018) are published in Andersson Strand and Nosch 2015.

8   Frangipane *et al.* 2009, 8–9, 12–13.

9   Actually, the weight of spindle whorls in bone might be heavier during their 'life' and usage as hypothesised in Laurito *et al.* 2014, 163–164.

10 For details on spindle whorls, see Frangipane *et al.* 2009 and Laurito *et al.* 2014.

11 Richmond 2006.

12 Keith 1988.

13 Sagona 2000; Richmond 2006, 212–214.

14 Rothman 2001.

15 Frangipane and Palmieri 1983; Frangipane 1993; 1997; 2010; 2012a.

16 Laurito *et al.* 2014, fig. 10.4.

17 Frangipane *et al.* 2009, 8–9.

18 Laurito 2007, 390–392; 2010; 2012.

19 Frangipane *et al.* 2009.

20 See https://ctr.hum.ku.dk/research-programmes-and-projects/ previous-programmes-and-projects/tools/, accessed 4 October 2018.

21 Choyke 2000.

22 Hansen 1990.
23 For the 'invisible craft' concept see: http://www.
    traditionaltextilecraft.dk/386325159 (accessed 2 October
    2018) or http://conferences.saxo.ku.dk/traditionaltextilecraft/
    (accessed 2 October 2018) and Andersson Strand this volume.
24 Di Nocera 2005; Frangipane *et al.* 2005; Frangipane and Di
    Nocera 2012.
25 Frangipane *et al.* 2005; Frangipane and Di Nocera 2012.
26 Frangipane and Palumbi 2007; Palumbi 2008.
27 Laurito *et al.* 2014, fig. 10.6.
28 In Laurito *et al.* 2014, 160–162, I suggested that some
    spherical ovoid shape objects could have been considered as
    small loom weights. Today, I am less certain. Their function is
    unclear and we should not reject the hypothesis that they may
    have been weights for the net rather than for making cloth.
29 Frangipane *et al.* 2009, 16–17, 25–26.
30 Laurito *et al.* 2014.
31 For Arslantepe data: Bökönyi 1983; Bartosiewicz 2010;
    Palumbi 2010.
32 Ryder 1983; McCorriston 1997; Huot 2000; Sudo 2010; Rast-
    Eicher and Bender Jørgensen 2013; Schoop 2014, 427–429.
33 Pollock 1999.

Bibliography

Andersson Strand, E. and Nosch, M.-L. (eds.) 2015 *Tools, Textiles
    and Contexts. Investigating Textile Production in the Aegean
    and Eastern Mediterranean Bronze Age.* Ancient Textiles Series
    21. Oxford and Philadelphia.
Barber, E. J. W. 1991 *Prehistoric Textiles. The Development of
    Cloth in the Neolithic and Bronze Ages with Special Reference
    to the Aegean.* Princeton.
Bartosiewicz, L. 2010 Herding in Period VI A. Development and
    changes from Period VII. In M. Frangipane (ed.), *Economic
    Centralisation in Formative States. The Archaeological
    Reconstruction of the Economic System in 4th Millennium
    Arslantepe.* Studi Di Preistoria Orientale 3. Roma, 119–148.
Bökönyi, S. 1983 Late Chalcolithic and Early Bronze I. Animal
    remains from Arslantepe (Malatya), Turkey: a preliminary
    report. *Origini* 12.2, 581–598.
Choyke, A. M. 2000 Bronze Age antler and bone manufacturing
    at Arslantepe (Anatolia). In M. Mashkour, A. M. Choyke and
    H. Buitenhuis (eds.), *Archaeozoology of the Near East IVA.*
    Archaeological Research and Consultancy Publication 32.
    Groningen, 170–183.
Di Nocera, G. M. 2005 Ricognizione archeologica nel territorio di
    Malatya. In A. Tangianu (ed.), *Dall'Eufrate al Mediterraneo.
    Ricerche delle Missioni Archeologiche Italiane in Turchia.*
    Ankara, 55–63.
Frangipane, M. 1993 Local components in the development
    of centralised societies in Syro-Anatolian regions. In M.
    Frangipane, H. Hauptmann, M. Liverani, P. Matthiae and M.
    Mellink (eds.), *Between the Rivers and Over the Mountains.
    Archeologica Anatolica et Mesopotamica Alba Palmieri
    Dedicata.* Roma, 133–161.
Frangipane, M. 1997 A 4th millennium Temple/Palace complex at
    Arslantepe-Malatya. North–south relations and the formation
    of early state societies in the northern regions of Greater
    Mesopotamia. *Paléorient* 23.1, 45–73.

Frangipane, M. 2000 Origini ed evoluzione del sistema centralizzato
    ad Arslantepe: dal 'Tempio' al 'Palazzo' nel IV millennio a.
    C. *ISIMU. Revista sobre Oriente Próximo y Egipto en la
    antigüedad* 3, 53–78.
Frangipane, M. 2001 The transition between two opposing forms
    of power at Arslantepe (Malatya) at the beginning of the 3rd
    millennium. *Türkiye Bilimler Akademisi Arkeoloji Dergisi* 4, 1–24.
Frangipane, M. (ed.) 2007 *Arslantepe. Cretulae. An Early Centralised
    Administrative System before Writing.* Arslantepe V. Roma.
Frangipane, M. 2010 Arslantepe. Growth and collapse of an
    early centralised system: the archaeological evidence. In M.
    Frangipane (ed.), *Economic Centralisation in Formative States.
    The Archaeological Reconstruction of the Economic System
    in 4th Millennium Arslantepe.* Studi di Preistoria Orientale 3.
    Roma, 23–42.
Frangipane, M. 2012a Fourth millennium Arslantepe: the
    development of a centralized society without urbanisation.
    Origini 34, 19–40.
Frangipane, M. 2012b The collapse of the 4th millennium
    centralised system at Arslantepe and the far-reaching changes
    in 3rd millennium societies. *Origini* 34, 237–260.
Frangipane, M., Andersson Strand, E., Laurito, R., Möller-Wiering,
    S., Nosch, M.-L., Rast-Eicher, A. and Wisti Lassen, A. 2009
    Arslantepe, Malatya (Turkey): textiles, tools and imprints of
    fabrics from the 4th to the 2nd millennium BCE. *Paléorient*
    35.1, 5–29.
Frangipane, M. and Di Nocera, G. M. 2012 Discontinuous
    developments in settlement patterns and socio-economic/
    political relations on the Malatya Plain in the 4th and 3rd
    millennia BC. In T. F. Borrell, G. M. Bouso, A. Gómez, Bach,
    C. Tornero Dacasa and O. V. Campos (eds.), *Broadening
    Horizons 3. Conference of Young Researchers Working in the
    Ancient Near East.* Bellaterra, 289–303.
Frangipane, M., Di Nocera, G. M. and Palumbi, G. 2005
    L'interazione tra due universi socio-culturali nella piana di
    Malatya (Turchia) tra IV e III millennio: dati archeologici e
    riconoscimento di identità. *Origini* 27, 123–170.
Frangipane, M. and Palmieri, A. 1983 A Protourban center of the
    Late Uruk Period. *Origini* 12.2, 287–454.
Frangipane, M. and Palumbi, G. 2007 Red-black ware, pastoralism,
    trade, and Anatolian-Transcaucasian interactions in the 4th–3rd
    millennium BC. In B. Lyonnet (ed.), *Les cultures du Caucase
    (VIe–IIIe millénaires avant notre ère). Leurs relations avec le
    Proche-Orient.* Paris, 233–255.
Hansen, E. H. 1990 Nålebinding: definition and description. In P.
    Walton and J.-P. Wild (eds.), *Textiles in Northern Archaeology.
    NESAT III: Textile Symposium in York, 6–9 May 1987.* London,
    21–27.
Huot, J.-L. 2000 Existe-t-il une 'révolution de la laine' au début de
    l'âge du Bronze oriental? In P. Matthiae, A. Enea, L. Peyronel
    and F. Pinnock (eds.), *Proceedings of the 1st International
    Congress on the Archaeology of the Ancient Near East, Rome,
    May 18th–23rd, 1998.* Rome, 640–642.
Keith, K. 1988 Spindle whorls, gender, and ethnicity at Late
    Chalcolithic in Hacinebi Tepe. *Journal of Field Archaeology*
    25, 497–515.
Laurito, R. 2007 Ropes and textiles. In M. Frangipane (ed.),
    *Arslantepe. Cretulae. An Early Centralised Administrative
    System before Writing.* Arslantepe V. Roma, 381–394.

Laurito, R. 2010 Textile tools and textile production. The archaeological evidence of weaving at Arslantepe. In M. Frangipane (ed.), *Economic Centralisation in Formative States. The Archaeological Reconstruction of the Economic System in 4th Millennium Arslantepe.* Studi Di Preistoria Orientale 3. Roma, 275–285.

Laurito, R. 2012 Changes in textile production at Arslantepe during the 4th and 3rd millennia BCE. *Origini* 34, 317–328.

Laurito, R., Lemorini, C. and Perilli, A. 2014 Making textiles at Arslantepe, Turkey, in the 4th and 3rd millennia BC. Archaeological data and experimental archaeology. In C. Breniquet and C. Michel (eds.), *Wool Economy in the Ancient Near East and the Aegean. From the Beginnings of Sheep Husbandry to Institutional Textile Industry.* Ancient Textile Series 17. Oxford and Philadelphia, 151–168.

McCorriston, J. 1997 The fiber revolution: textile extensification, alienation, and social stratification in ancient Mesopotamia. *Current Anthropology* 38.4, 517–549.

Palumbi, G. 2008 *The Red and Black. Social and Cultural Interaction between the Upper Euphrates and Southern Caucasus Communities in the Forth and Third Millennium BC.* Studi Di Preistoria Orientale 2. Roma.

Palumbi, G. 2010 Pastoral models and centralised animal husbandry. The case of Arslantepe. In M. Frangipane (ed.), *Economic Centralisation in Formative States. The Archaeological Reconstruction of the Economic System in 4th Millennium Arslantepe.* Arslantepe V. Roma, 149–163.

Pollock, S. 1999 *Ancient Mesopotamia.* Cambridge.

Rast-Eicher, A. and Bender Jørgensen, L. 2013 Sheep wool in Bronze Age and Iron Age Europe. *Journal of Archaeological Science* 40, 1224–1241.

Richmond, J. 2006 Textile production in prehistoric Anatolia: a study of three Early Bronze Age sites. *Ancient Near East Studies* 43, 203–238.

Rothman, M. S. (ed.) 2001 *Uruk Mesopotamia and its Neighbours: Cross-cultural Interactions in the Era of State Formation.* Santa Fe.

Ryder, M. 1983 *Sheep and Man.* London.

Sagona, A. G. 2000 Sos Höyük and the Erzurum region in late prehistory. In C. Marro and H. Hauptman (eds.), *Chronologies des Pays du Caucase et de l'Euphrate aux IVe–IIIe Millenaires.* Istanbul, 329–373.

Schoop, U.-D. 2014 Weaving societies in Late Chalcolithic Anatolia: textile production and social strategies in the 4th millennium BC. In B. Horejs and M. Mehofer (eds.), *Western Anatolia before Troy. Proto-Urbanisation in the 4th Millenium BC?* Oriental and European Archaeology I. Vienna, 421–446.

Sudo, H. 2010 The development of wool exploitation in Ubaid-Period settlements of North Mesopotamia. In R. Carter and G. Philip (eds.), *Beyond the Ubaid. Transformation and Integration in the Late Prehistoric Societies of the Middle East.* Studies in Ancient Oriental Civilization 63. Chicago, 169–179.